April 8–11, 2013
Philadelphia, PA, USA

**Association for
Computing Machinery**

Advancing Computing as a Science & Profession

IPSN'13

Proceedings of the 12th International Conference on
Information Processing in Sensor Networks

Sponsored by:
ACM SIGBED & IEEE

Supported by:
Microsoft Research & National Science Foundation

Part of:
CPSWeek 2013

**Association for
Computing Machinery**

Advancing Computing as a Science & Profession

ISBN: 978-1-4503-1959-1

Additional copies may be ordered prepaid from:

ACM Order Department
PO Box 30777
New York, NY 10087-0777, USA

Phone: 1-800-342-6626 (USA and Canada)
+1-212-626-0500 (Global)
Fax: +1-212-944-1318
E-mail: acmhelp@acm.org
Hours of Operation: 8:30 am – 4:30 pm ET

ACM Order No: 104135

Printed in the USA

General Chair's Welcome

It is my great pleasure to welcome you to the 12th International Symposium on Information Processing in Sensor Networks (IPSN 2013). The symposium continues its tradition of excellence with a vibrant program this year that combines the Information Processing (IP) and the Sensor Platforms (SPOTS) tracks. The goal is to bring together researchers and practitioners from industry and academia to address the gamut of challenges from theoretical foundations of information processing in sensor networks to new hardware architecture and platform prototypes. I sincerely thank the program chairs Kay Römer and Raj Rajkumar for putting together this exciting program. We owe the quality of this year's symposium to their dedicated efforts.

Being part of CPSWeek, a landmark multidisciplinary event in the area of cyber-physical systems, IPSN is co-located with four related conferences (namely, HSCC, ICCPS, HiCONS, and RTAS), and a significant number of workshops and tutorials. I sincerely thank the organizers of CPSWeek for working together with IPSN and the other conferences and workshops on ironing out all the challenging coordination details and making the coordinated event a success. CPSWeek also features three exciting keynotes: "Sensemaking for Mobile Health" by Deborah Estrin, "Aerial Robot Swarms" by Vijay Kumar, and "Challenges in Modeling Cyber-physical Systems" by Manfred Broy.

In addition to keynote and paper presentations, IPSN features a poster and demonstration session. Special thanks goes to Luca Mottola, the Demo Chair, and Tian He, the Poster Chair, for organizing it. A Ph.D. forum is also held to offer Ph.D. students a chance to present their dissertation research and to get advice on thesis directions. Thanks to Polly Huang for putting that forum together.

IPSN 2013 would not have been possible without the efforts of members of the organizing committee. In particular, I would like to thank Raghu Ganti (Publications Chair), together with Sheridan Communications, for producing the proceedings, Akos Ledeczi (Finance Chair) for keeping the event financially sound, and Aman Kansal (Workshop Chair) for his help with workshop and tutorial selection. Importantly, many thanks go to Hengchang Liu (Web Chair) for maintaining the conference webpage, as well as Li Cui, Martina Maggio, and Ying Zhang (Publicity Chairs) for their fine efforts in advertising IPSN.

I would like to acknowledge and thank ACM and IEEE for their sponsorship. In addition, significant support was received for IPSN from NSF and Microsoft Research, which also sponsored the Best Paper and Best Student Paper Awards. I would further like to thank the steering committee and its chair, Feng Zhao, for contributing useful advice and suggestions that significantly improved the event.

Last, but not least, I am deeply grateful to the authors of the papers, posters, demos, and Ph.D. forum entries. Without their contributions, IPSN 2013 would not have been possible. Also, thanks to the attendees for making this event viable. I hope you enjoy it and find it useful for academic exchange and networking.

Tarek Abdelzaher, *UIUC*
General Chair

Message from the Technical Program Chairs

We welcome you to Philadelphia, USA, and the 12th ACM/IEEE International Conference on Information Processing and Sensor Networks (IPSN).

IPSN is considered to be one of the flagship research conferences of the sensor networks community, and continues to showcase cutting-edge research into the information processing aspects of sensor networks. The conference program consists of two complementary and inter-woven tracks, one on Information Processing (the IP track) and another on Sensor Platforms, Tools and Design Methods (the SPOTS track). The conference received a total of 115 submissions (after filtering for appropriateness and completeness). The high submission count and the limited duration for presentations at the conference made paper selection a difficult task for the Technical Program Committee (TPC). Finally, after extensive deliberations at a day-long physical meeting, 24 papers were accepted for publication, 14 in the IP track and 10 in the SPOTS track. This tally yielded an acceptance rate of 20.5%. Each accepted paper had at least 3 reviews, with the majority receiving 5 reviews each, in order to ensure novelty, relevance and contributions to this established, yet growing, field. Where additional inputs were required, some papers were reviewed by appropriate experts outside the TPC. Unfortunately, many worthy papers had to be excluded solely due to the time constraints in the conference schedule. The accepted papers cover multiple dimensions of sensor networks including localization, learning from sensor data, network protocols, programming, testing, location coverage and applications.

The conference program, in addition to the traditional format of research paper presentations, will include three CPS Week Plenary presentations, a panel, a demo/poster session, a "mad-minute" session and a Ph.D. Forum.

IPSN, as an integral part of *CPS Week*, is pleased to be co-located again with its sister conferences that focus on various components of cyber-physical systems including hybrid systems, real-time systems, high-assurance networked systems and the cross-cutting aspects of cyber-physical systems. In order to stimulate the continuing growth of this global CPS community, we also encourage all conference participants to take the opportunity to attend sessions of interest at other sister CPS Week conferences, and mingle together during breaks.

This conference has been made possible due only to the contributions and efforts made by many: the CPS Week 2013 Organizing Committee, IPSN 2013 Technical Program Committee members, the many reviewers who are acknowledged at the end of these proceedings, and you the members of this flourishing community. We also express our gratitude to ACM and IEEE for co-sponsoring this conference. We especially thank the General Chair, Tarek Abdelzaher, for his tireless efforts and help.

We hope that you will enjoy the program and that you will strongly consider contributing to future versions of IPSN.

Kay Römer
University of Lübeck & ETH Zurich
Program Chair (IP)

Raj Rajkumar
Carnegie Mellon University
Program Chair (SPOTS)

Table of Contents

Session 4: SPOTS: Programming and Testing

Session 5: SPOTS: Applications

Session 6: IP: Location and Coverage

Session 7: IP: Networking

Session 8: Posters and Demo Abstracts

IPSN 2013: ACM/IEEE International Conference on Information Processing in Sensor Networks Organizers

General Chairs: Tarek Abdelzaher (*University of Illinois, Urbana-Champaign*)

Program Chair (IP track): Kay Römer (*University of Lübeck and ETH Zurich*)

Program Chair (SPOTS track): Raj Rajkumar (*Carnegie Mellon University*)

Demo Chair: Luca Mottola (*Politecnico di Milano and Swedish Institute of Computer Science*)

Poster Chair: Tian He (*University of Minnesota*)

Workshop/Tutorial Chair: Aman Kansal (*Microsoft Research*)

Publications Chair: Raghu Ganti (*IBM T J Watson Research Center*)

Finance/Sponsorship Chair: Akos Ledeczi (*Vanderbilt University*)

Web Chair: Hengchang Liu (*University of Illinois, Urbana-Champaign*)

Publicity co-chairs: Ying Zhang (*Google*)

Li Cui (*Institute of Computing Technology, Chinese Academy of Sciences*)

Martina Maggio (*Lund University*)

PhD Forum Chair: Polly Huang (*Nanyang Technological University*)

Steering Committee: Feng Zhao (*Microsoft Research Asia*) – Chair
Tarek Abdelzaher (*University of Illinois, Urbana-Champaign*)
Deborah Estrin (*Cornell Tech University*)
Leo Guibas (*Stanford University*)
William Kaiser (*University of California, Los Angeles*)
P.R. Kumar (*Texas A&M University*)
Jose Moura (*Carnegie Mellon University*)
Jack Stankovic (*University of Virginia*)
Janos Sztipanovits (*Vanderbilt University*)

IPSN 2013 Sponsors & Supporters

Sponsors:

Microsoft®
Research

Technical Supporters:

NSF

IEEE
Signal Processing Society

Sensemaking for Mobile Health

Deborah Estrin
Cornell Tech University
NYC, NY

ABSTRACT

Mobile health (mHealth) leverages the power and ubiquity of mobile and cloud technologies to support patients and clinicians in monitoring and understanding symptoms, side effects and treatment outside the clinical setting; thereby closing the feedback loops of self-care, clinical-care, and personal-evidence-creation. However, to realize this promise, we must develop new data capture, processing and modeling techniques to convert the digital exhaust emitted by mobile phone use into behavioral biomarkers. This calls for a modular layered sensemaking framework in which low level state classifications of raw data (e.g., estimated activity states such as sitting, walking, driving from continuous accelerometer and location traces), are used to derive mid-level semantic features (e.g., total number of ambulatory minutes, number of hours spent out of house), that can then be mapped to particular behavioral biomarkers for specific diseases (e.g., chronic pain, GI disfunction, MS, fatigue, depression, etc). The techniques needed to derive these markers will range from simple functions to machine learning classifiers, and will need to fuse diverse data types, but all will need to cope with noisy, erratic data sources. We are working to build an open architecture and community to speed the rate and robustness of innovation in this space, both academic and commercial (http://openmhealth.org).

Categories and Subject Descriptors

I.5.0 [Pattern Recognition]

Keywords

Mobile health

Biography

Deborah Estrin is a Professor of Computer Science at the new Cornell Tech campus in New York City and a Professor of Public Health at Weill Cornell Medical College. She is co-founder of the non-profit startup, Open mHealth. She was previously on faculty at UCLA and Founding Director  of the NSF Center for Embedded Networked Sensing (CENS). Estrin is a pioneer in networked sensing, which uses mobile and wireless systems to collect and analyze real time data about the physical world and the people who occupy it. Estrin s current focus is on mobile health (mhealth), leveraging the programmability, proximity, and pervasiveness of mobile devices and the cloud for health management. She is an elected member of the American Academy of Arts and Sciences and the National Academy of Engineering.

IPSN'13, April 8–11, 2013, Philadelphia, Pennsylvania, USA.
ACM 978-1-4503-1959-1/13/04.

Aerial Robot Swarms

Vijay Kumar
University of Pennsylvania
Philadelphia, PA
kumar@central.cis.upenn.edu

ABSTRACT

Autonomous micro aerial robots can operate in three-dimensional unstructured environments, and offer many opportunities for environmental monitoring, search and rescue, and first response. I will describe the challenges in developing small, agile robots and our recent work in addressing these challenges. I will also discuss the deployment of large numbers of aerial robots, focusing on the control and planning problems with applications to cooperative manipulation and transport, construction, and exploration and mapping.

Categories and Subject Descriptors

C.3 [Real-time and Embedded Systems]

Keywords

Aerial robots

Biography

Vijay Kumar is the UPS Foundation Professor in the School of Engineering and Applied Science at the University of Pennsylvania, and on sabbatical leave at White House Office of Science and Technology Policy where he serves as the assistant director for robotics and cyber physical  systems. He received his Ph.D. in Mechanical Engineering from The Ohio State University in 1987. He has been on the Faculty in the Department of Mechanical Engineering and Applied Mechanics with a secondary appointment in the Department of Computer and Information Science at the University of Pennsylvania since 1987. Dr. Kumar is a Fellow of the American Society of Mechanical Engineers (ASME) and the Institution of Electrical and Electronic Engineers (IEEE). He presently serves on the editorial boards of the IEEE Transactions on Automation Science and Engineering, the ASME Journal of Mechanisms and Robotics and the Springer Stracts in Advanced Robotics (STAR). He is the recipient of the National Science Foundation Presidential Young Investigator award (1991), the Lindback Award for Distinguished Teaching (1996), and best paper awards at DARS 2002, ICRA 2004, ICRA 2008, ICRA 2011, RSS 2009, DARS 2010 and RSS 2011. Most recently he was named the winner of a 2012 IEEE Robotics and Automation Society Distinguished Service Award, the 2012 ASME Mechanisms and Robotics Committee Award, and a 2012 World Technology Network Award.

Challenges in Modeling Cyber-Physical Systems

Manfred Broy
Technical University of Munich
Munich, Germany
broy@in.tum.de

ABSTRACT

Cyber-Physical Systems require more advanced modeling techniques to capture physicality including time and space, reliability in terms of probabilistic models, connectivity in terms of communication links, adaptivity, context awareness, interoperability, and autonomy. This requires a comprehensive integrated modeling framework for specification, modeling of architecture, and tracing their relationships.

Categories and Subject Descriptors

C.3 [Real-time and Embedded Systems]

Keywords

Cyber-physical systems

Biography

Manfred Broy is a full professor for Informatics at the Technische Universitat Munchen. His research interests are software and systems engineering comprising both theoretical and practical aspects. His current research interests are: System Development Processes and Tool Support, System Modelling, Requirements Engineering, Concurrent and Embedded Systems, Theoretical Foundation of Informatics, Quality, and Requirements Engineering, Systems Engineering, Cyber-Physical Systems.

IPSN'13, April 8–11, 2013, Philadelphia, Pennsylvania, USA.
ACM 978-1-4503-1959-1/13/04.

A Fresh Perspective: Learning to Sparsify for Detection in Massive Noisy Sensor Networks

Matthew Faulkner
Computer Science
Caltech
mfaulk@caltech.edu

Annie H. Liu
Computer Science
Caltech
aliu@cms.caltech.edu

Andreas Krause
Computer Science
ETH Zurich
krausea@ethz.ch

ABSTRACT

Can one trade sensor quality for quantity? While larger networks with greater sensor density promise to allow us to use noisier sensors yet measure subtler phenomena, aggregating data and designing decision rules is challenging. Motivated by dense, participatory seismic networks, we seek efficient aggregation methods for event detection. We propose to perform aggregation by *sparsification*: roughly, a sparsifying basis is a linear transformation that aggregates measurements from groups of sensors that tend to co-activate, and each event is observed by only a few groups of sensors. We show how a simple class of sparsifying bases provably improves detection with noisy binary sensors, even when only qualitative information about the network is available. We then describe how detection can be further improved by learning a better sparsifying basis from network observations or simulations. Learning can be done offline, and makes use of powerful off-the-shelf optimization packages. Our approach outperforms state of the art detectors on real measurements from seismic networks with hundreds of sensors, and on simulated epidemics in the Gnutella P2P communication network.

Categories and Subject Descriptors

C.2.1 [**Computer-Communication Networks**]: Network Architecture and Design; G.3 [**Probability and Statistics**]: Experimental Design; I.2.6 [**AI**]: Learning

General Terms

Algorithms, Experimentation, Theory

Keywords

Sparsifying transformation, basis learning, sensor networks, community sensing, event detection, ICA, SLSA

(a) CSN Participants   (b)

Figure 1: (a) CSN sensors; (b) Peak amplitude of Compton M3.4 quake measured by 4089 sensors. Note the complex spatial correlation.

1. INTRODUCTION

In recent years, millions of accelerometers have appeared across cities around the world. Most of these sensors are in privately owned, Internet-enabled devices like smartphones and laptops. Several participatory sensing projects, including the Community Seismic Network (CSN)[1], the Quake Catcher Network (QCN)[2], and iShake[3] are working to unify these numerous but noisy devices to measure and detect strong earthquakes.

Quake detection in community networks requires finding a complex spatio-temporal pattern in a large set of noisy sensor measurements. The start of a quake may only affect a small fraction of the network, so the event can easily be concealed in both single-sensor measurements and network-wide statistics. Data from recent high-density seismic studies, Fig. 1(b), show that localized variations in ground structure significantly impact the magnitude of shaking at locations only a few kilometers apart. Consequently, effective quake detection requires algorithms that can learn subtle dependencies among sensor data, and detect changes within groups of dependent sensors. In this sense, quake detection is prototypical of many challenging real-time detection problems, including detecting epidemic outbreaks [22], intrusions in networks [27], and sudden changes in traffic patterns [9].

Particularly challenging in massive networks is dealing with the flood of data. By utilizing even a small fraction of the millions of existing internet-enabled consumer sensor devices, community sensor networks can reach scales where regularly transmitting even summary statistics would

---

[1] http://csn.caltech.edu
[2] http://qcn.stanford.edu/
[3] http://ishakeberkeley.appspot.com/

be prohibitive. Instead, we adopt a decentralized approach, where sensors individually detect events and only transmit "pick" messages indicating a detection. These individual detections typically will be very noisy, including many false alarms and missed detections. This reduces the server-side problem to one of detecting event signals in a (noisy) binary activation pattern. Event detection may be the primary task, or serve as a precursor for additional data collection and processing.

Standard approaches in decentralized detection [24] assume that the sensors provide i.i.d. measurements conditioned on the occurrence or non-occurrence of an event. In this case, the fusion center would declare a detection if a sufficiently large number of sensors report picks. However, in many practical applications, the particular spatial configuration of the sensors matters, and the i.i.d. assumption is violated. Here, the natural question arises of how (qualitative) knowledge about the nature of the event can be exploited in order to improve detection performance. In this work, we propose to use *sparsification* to optimize detection. In particular, we linearly represent the network-wide noisy, binary activation patterns in a suitable basis, which is carefully chosen so that "typical" activations (associated with the events of interest) are sparsely represented in the basis. This effectively concentrates the signal energy along a small number of basis coordinates. Natural questions, addressed in this work, are thus: When can we expect sparse representations to aid detection? And, which bases are appropriate for this purpose?

As our first major contribution, we consider a wavelet basis that emerges naturally when sensors are clustered hierarchically. We prove theoretically that when the wavelet basis sparsifies the received picks, decentralized detection becomes possible in a noise regime that cannot be handled by a simple network-wide average. We derive strong bounds on the detection rate when events are drawn from a recently proposed *latent tree model* that produce strong localized dependencies and weaker long-range dependencies.

One of the strengths of the wavelet basis is that it can be constructed using as little information as a matrix of pairwise similarity between sensors. However, additional information such as event simulations or measurements of events in the network are often available. Incorporating this information should improve detection. As our second major contribution, we show how modern results from dictionary learning can be used to directly learn sparsifying bases from simulated or measured training data.

As third main contribution, we perform extensive empirical studies of detection using measurements of 1795 earthquakes following the Japanese Tohoku M9.0 quake, quake measurements from the Signal Hill dense seismic study, from the Community Seismic Network as well as simulated virus outbreaks in the Gnutella P2P network.

In summary, our main contributions are:

- New theoretical guarantees about decentralized detection of sparsifiable events,

- A framework for learning sparsifying bases from simulated or measured data, and

- Extensive experiments on real data from three seismic networks, and simulated epidemics in P2P networks.

2. PROBLEM STATEMENT

We are interested in the problem of detecting whether or not some phenomenon (say an earthquake with magnitude above some threshold, or an epidemic) is present at any locations monitored by a massive network of noisy sensors. We model the presence of the phenomenon at locations $1, \ldots, p$ as a binary vector $\mathbf{x} = [x_1, \ldots, x_p] \in \{0, 1\}^p$ that is observed by noisy sensors. The Gaussian noise model is a natural choice for sensor observations, where sensor i observes

$$y_i = x_i + \epsilon_i,$$

where $\epsilon_i \sim \mathcal{N}(0, \sigma^2)$. In our seismic detection application, the variables y_i may refer to accelerometer readings of a sensor deployed at location i. This continuous noise model captures how a subset of sensors in areas experiencing shaking observe a shift in the mean of their accelerometer measurements, while the rest of the network observes i.i.d. noise.

The decentralized setting. In many domains, collecting the raw sensor measurements of all sensors would require prohibitive bandwidth to transmit (e.g. the accelerometers in one million smartphones produce ≈ 30 Terabytes of data each day). A natural way to circumvent this bottleneck is to use decentralized detection [24] where sensors individually test their measurements and report the occurrence of a possible event. As an example, the CSN system employs a *hierarchical anomaly detection* approach [8] that allows each sensor to transmit only the results of a local anomaly detection computation (known as a *picking algorithm*) to the fusion center. We can model the resulting picks using a *binary symmetric channel* noise model, where

$$y_i = \begin{cases} x_i & \text{with prob. } 1 - \pi \\ 1 - x_i & \text{with prob. } \pi, \end{cases}$$

for some error rate $0 < \pi \leq \frac{1}{2}$. The goal of the detection problem is to distinguish the null hypothesis $\mathcal{H}_0$, $x_i = 0$ for all i (i.e., no earthquake present) from the alternate hypothesis $\mathcal{H}_1$, where $x_i = 1$ for one or more i (i.e., the earth is shaking at least at one location i).

Decentralized linear detection. While (decentralized) hypothesis testing in general has been studied extensively, here we focus on the particularly challenging, and not well understood, setting where the patterns $\mathbf{x}$ are *sparse* and have strong noise. This is exactly the case for our motivating example of community seismic networks, where we wish to detect the event as early as possible (i.e., few sensors have been reached yet), and each sensor is very noisy. Formally, we quantify the sparsity of a vector $\mathbf{x}$ as the number of non-zero elements $x_i \neq 0$, denoted by the ℓ_0-norm $||\mathbf{x}||_0$. Generally, we will be interested in quantifying the detection performance as the network grows. We say $\mathbf{x}$ is *sparse* if $||\mathbf{x}||_0$ grows as $p^{1-\alpha}$ for some $1/2 < \alpha < 1$, where a larger α means a sparser signal. Thus, as the number p of sensors grows, the ratio of sensors reached by the event $||\mathbf{x}||_0/p = p^{-\alpha}$ vanishes as $p \to \infty$.

We focus on hypothesis tests of *linear functions of the observations*, i.e. for some matrix $\mathbf{B}$ with columns $\mathbf{b}_1, \ldots, \mathbf{b}_n$, we consider hypothesis tests of the form

$$\max_i \mathbf{b}_i^T \mathbf{y} \lessgtr \tau$$

for some threshold τ. As we will show in this paper, proper choice of the basis $\mathbf{B}$ can lead to dramatically improved detection performance, i.e., with the same false positive rate much sparser signals (or much higher noise) can be tolerated.

3. DETECTING SPARSIFIABLE EVENTS

Detecting sparse signals in the decentralized setting is fundamentally challenging. Suppose the expected number of errors in the network is p^γ for some $0 < \gamma < 1$, and the per-sensor error rate $\pi = p^\gamma/p$. Could we use the observed number of picks $||\mathbf{y}||_0$ to detect a pattern with $||\mathbf{x}||_0 = p^{1-\alpha} < p^{0.5}$ non-zero entries?

Under both $\mathcal{H}_0$ and $\mathcal{H}_1$, the variance of $||\mathbf{y}||_0$ grows as p^γ. Consider the variable $||\mathbf{y}||_0/\sqrt{p^\gamma}$: it has variance converging to 1 under both $\mathcal{H}_0$ and $\mathcal{H}_1$. Under $\mathcal{H}_0$, its mean is $p^{0.5\gamma}$, and under $\mathcal{H}_1$ its mean is $p^{1-\alpha-0.5\gamma}(1-2\pi) + p^{0.5\gamma}$. For $\gamma > 2(1-\alpha)$, the distributions of $||\mathbf{y}||_0$ under $\mathcal{H}_0$ and $\mathcal{H}_1$ converge, while for $\gamma < 2(1-\alpha) < 1$ the distributions are asymptotically separable. The statistic $||\mathbf{y}||_0$ (classically used in decentralized detection) can only provide reliable detection if the *per-sensor* error rate *decreases* ($\pi = p^\gamma/p \to 0$) as the network size p grows. That is, as the network grows, the sensors must have vanishing error rate for $\mathcal{H}_0$ and $\mathcal{H}_1$ to be separable in the case of sparse signals.

Fortunately, data is rarely unstructured. Even when the network-wide activation pattern is sparse, the activation pattern *within some groups* may be dense and thus more easily detectable. Hierarchical clustering is useful for finding meaningful clusters at a range of scales, and is compatible with efficient data aggregation systems [19] for sensor networks. Recently, hierarchical clustering has been used to define wavelets bases for trees, graphs, and high-dimensional data [11, 23]. For example, a Haar wavelet basis is defined by a hierarchical clustering: whenever two clusters c_l and c_r are merged into a cluster of coarser scale, a unit vector is created,

$$\mathbf{b}_i \propto \left(\frac{1}{|c_l|}\mathbb{1}_{c_l} - \frac{1}{|c_r|}\mathbb{1}_{c_r} \right) \qquad (1)$$

where $\mathbb{1}_c$ indicates the support of cluster c. The clustering algorithm performs $p - 1$ merges; the $p - 1$ vectors $\mathbf{b}_1, \ldots, \mathbf{b}_{p-1}$ along with the constant vector $\frac{1}{\sqrt{p}}\mathbb{1}_p$ form the columns of an orthonormal matrix $\mathbf{B}$. Multiplying the network observations $\mathbf{y}$ by $\mathbf{B}$ is a projection onto a new basis, where each coordinate $\mathbf{b}_i$ corresponds to the difference between the relative number of activations in a pair of merged clusters. Fig. 3(a) illustrates the basis functions of the transformation. The transform $\mathbf{B}$ has the property that each element $\mathbf{b}_i$ corresponds to *local* averages over sets of related nodes c_l and c_r. Under the assumption that many sets usually activate (or do not activate) jointly, events may be clearly apparent as strong signal along a small number of basis elements. More formally, patterns in $\mathbf{x}$ supported on the clusters used to define $\mathbf{B}$ will tend to be concentrated in a few elements $\mathbf{b}_i$, and so $||\mathbf{B}^T\mathbf{x}||_0 \ll ||\mathbf{x}||_0$. Fig. 2 shows that sparsifiable data is inherently structured.

A basis for detection. Just as a Fourier transform maps an acoustic signal into a coordinate frame that yields insight about the frequency content of the signal, multiplying network activations $\mathbf{x}$ by the basis $\mathbf{B}$ maps the sensor data onto a new coordinate system defined by the hierarchical clustering, and can expose correlated activations. In the following, we prove that with the Haar wavelet basis, the "sparsifica-

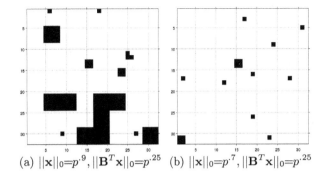

(a) $||\mathbf{x}||_0 = p^{.9}$, $||\mathbf{B}^T\mathbf{x}||_0 = p^{.25}$ (b) $||\mathbf{x}||_0 = p^{.7}$, $||\mathbf{B}^T\mathbf{x}||_0 = p^{.25}$

Figure 2: Sparsification $||\mathbf{B}^T\mathbf{x}||_0 \ll ||\mathbf{x}||_0$ exploits spatially coherent activation patterns, while small $||\mathbf{x}||_0$ produces fewer activations. The data are drawn from a quad-tree of height 5.

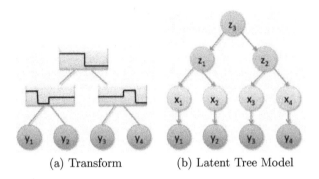

(a) Transform (b) Latent Tree Model

Figure 3: Illustration of the transform (a), constant b_0 not shown. (b) Latent Tree Model for $d = 2$ and $p = 4$. The sensors $\mathbf{y}$ measure the pattern $\mathbf{x} = [x_1, \ldots, x_4]$ up to some noise. The pattern is structured hierarchically; variables z_i represent the variables of the latent tree.

tion ratio" $\frac{||\mathbf{x}||_0}{||\mathbf{B}^T\mathbf{x}||_0}$ plays a central role in achievable error rates. In particular, the following new theorem (with proof outline in the appendix) shows the power of a sparsifying transform to concentrate the signal along at least one new coordinate without concentrating the random noise.

THEOREM 1. *Let $\mathbf{B}$ be a Haar basis that sparsifies a signal $\mathbf{x}$, i.e. $||\mathbf{B}^T\mathbf{x}||_0 = p^{1-\beta}$, $||\mathbf{x}||_0 = p^{1-\alpha}$, $0 < \alpha < \beta < 1$. Let $\mathbf{y}$ be the signal observed through a binary symmetric channel, with error rate π bounded away from $1/2$ (i.e. for some $\epsilon > 0$, $\pi < 1/2 - \epsilon$). Then applying the test $|\mathbf{b}^T\mathbf{y}| > \frac{(1-2\pi)}{2}\sqrt{\frac{||\mathbf{x}||_0}{||\mathbf{B}^T\mathbf{x}||_0}}$ to each of the $p - 1$ non-constant basis elements $\mathbf{b} \in \mathbf{B}$ gives false negative rate (FNR) and false positive rate (FPR) bounded as*

$$FNR \le 2p \exp\left(-\frac{(1-2\pi)^2}{2}\frac{||\mathbf{x}||_0}{||\mathbf{B}^T\mathbf{x}||_0} \right) \to 0 \ as \ p \to \infty,$$

$$FPR \le 2p \exp\left(-\frac{(1-2\pi)^2}{2}\frac{||\mathbf{x}||_0}{||\mathbf{B}^T\mathbf{x}||_0} \right) \to 0 \ as \ p \to \infty.$$

This theorem states that *for any constant error rate π*, as the network size p grows, the probability of a missed detection (FNR) and the probability of false alarm (FPR) are driven to 0 by the decision rule that declares "event" when $|\mathbf{b}^T\mathbf{y}|$ exceeds the specified threshold, for any of the $p-1$ non-constant basis elements $\mathbf{b}$. For comparison, recall that reliable detection using the network-wide pick count $||\mathbf{y}||_0$ (the standard statistic for decentralized detection) requires the error rate π to rapidly decay to zero as p grows.

The sparsifying basis $\mathbf{B}$ thus enables reliable detection in a broad noise regime that cannot be detected by the network-wide average. This insight shows that indeed quality of sensors can be traded against quantity. Of course, this strong result assumes that the event signal $\mathbf{x}$ is sufficiently sparsifiable by the basis $\mathbf{B}$. In this paper, we show that this assumption holds both in a natural theoretical model, as well as on real sensor data.

Modeling sparsifiable events. When is sensor data sparsifiable? Let us consider again the natural hierarchical basis $\mathbf{B}$, defined according to Eq. 1 as introduced at the beginning of this section. Singh [23] shows that for this particular basis, the assumption $||\mathbf{B}^T\mathbf{x}||_0 \ll ||\mathbf{x}||_0 \le \sqrt{p}$ is fulfilled when the pattern $\mathbf{x}$ is drawn from an intuitive class of generative models. For completeness, the model is presented here. In this model, dependencies among sensors are modeled via a *tree* of regular degree d: the leaves correspond to the event occurrence x_i at each sensor, and internal nodes correspond to the occurrence or non-occurrence of an event at a particular region and scale. Let $\ell = 0, 1, \ldots L$ denote the level in the tree, where the activations $\{x_i\}$, $i = 1, \ldots, p$ are leaves at level $L = \log_d p$, and the root is at $\ell = 0$. The internal (non-leaf) nodes in the tree capture multi-scale dependencies among the leaves. Let $\mathbf{z}$ denote all nodes in the tree. The joint distribution of $\mathbf{z}$ factorizes as

$$p(\mathbf{z}) = p(z_0) \prod_{\ell=1}^{L} \prod_{i \in V_\ell} p(z_i | z_{\text{parent}(i)}) \qquad (2)$$

where V_l denotes the vertices at layer l. The probability that a node equals its parent is specified by $\gamma_\ell = \ell\beta \log d$. This coupling is weaker near the root and stronger near the leaves, producing multi-scale dependencies. Sufficiently weak dependencies are considered negligible, and so the latent variables $z_i \in \ell_0$ at some initial level ℓ_0 are drawn independently from their parents: $p(z_i = 1 | z_{\text{parent}(i)}) = p(z_i = 1) \propto e^{\gamma_{\ell_0}}$. This approximates distant regions of the network as independent. The conditional probability of a node z_i at $\ell > \ell_o$ is

$$p(z_i | z_{\text{parent}(i)}) \propto \begin{cases} e^{\gamma_\ell} & \text{if } z_i = z_{\text{parent}(i)}, \\ 1 & \text{if } z_i \neq z_{\text{parent}(i)}. \end{cases}$$

Patterns drawn from this model are localized and multi-scale, as illustrated with a quad-tree in Fig. 2.

Bounds for finite networks. When the event $\mathbf{x}$ is drawn via Eq. (2), Singh [23] showed that as the number of sensors goes to infinity, the assumption $||\mathbf{B}^T\mathbf{x}||_0 \ll ||\mathbf{x}||_0 \le \sqrt{p}$ holds with high probability. However, these results do not clearly indicate whether the bounds are effective for large (e.g. hundreds to tens of thousands of sensors) but finite networks. Next, we provide a stronger bound on the sparsification ratio obtained by the wavelet transform, and explain how Theorem 1 can be strengthened to provide bounds on FNR and FPR for fixed network size.

THEOREM 2. *Let $\mathbf{x}$ be a pattern drawn at random from the latent tree model with uniform degree d and depth $L =$*

$\log_d p$. *Let $\ell_0 = \frac{\alpha}{\beta}$ and $\gamma_\ell = \ell\beta \log d$ for $\ell \ge \ell_0$, where $0 \le \alpha \le \beta \le 1$. Then for $0 < \epsilon < 1$,*

$$\mathbb{P}\left[\frac{||\mathbf{x}||_0}{||\mathbf{B}^T\mathbf{x}||_0} > \frac{\kappa(\epsilon)}{\log_d p} \cdot \frac{p^{1-\alpha}}{p^{1-\beta}} \right] \ge 1 - 2\exp\left(-\frac{c\epsilon^2}{2} p^{\alpha\left(\frac{1}{\beta}-1\right)} \right)$$

where $c = \left(\frac{1}{4}\right)^{\left(\frac{1}{\alpha} - \frac{1}{\beta} + 0.5\right)}$ and $\kappa(\epsilon) = \frac{(1-\epsilon)}{(1+\epsilon)} \frac{c}{d^2}$ are constant with respect to p.

This result shows that the crucial sparsification ratio $\frac{||\mathbf{x}||_0}{||\mathbf{B}^T\mathbf{x}||_0}$ in Theorem 1 grows at (within a log factor of) the desired rate $p^{1-\alpha}/p^{1-\beta}$, with probability that increases exponentially with network size p. This theorem can be used to derive bounds on FNR and FPR for a specified network size p and model parameters α, β, degree d: the bound is substituted for $\frac{||\mathbf{x}||_0}{||\mathbf{B}^T\mathbf{x}||_0}$ in Theorem 1, and the probability that the above bound does not hold can be added to the resulting FNR and FPR.

4. SPARSIFYING BASIS LEARNING

Sec. 3 shows that if an event is "sparsifiable" we can better separate $\mathcal{H}_0$ and $\mathcal{H}_1$ by projecting (multiplying by a basis $\mathbf{B}$) the observations $\mathbf{y}$ onto a different coordinate system where the signal is concentrated into fewer components (a "sparser representation" of the signal). The Haar wavelet basis is an example of a basis that improves detection of signals with certain structured (hierarchical) dependencies. In general, can we construct or learn a sparsifying basis without assuming such dependencies?

Let $\mathbf{B}$ be an orthonormal matrix and $\mathbf{x}$ a vector of uncorrupted binary activations, Theorem 1 states that the sparsification ratio $\frac{||\mathbf{x}||_0}{||\mathbf{B}^T\mathbf{x}||_0}$ directly impacts the amount of separation between $\mathcal{H}_0$ and $\mathcal{H}_1$. In fact, given that $||\mathbf{x}||_0$ is fixed, the two hypotheses are maximally separated when $||\mathbf{B}^T\mathbf{x}||_0$ is minimized. In other words, we can construct the optimal basis by solving the following optimization problem:

$$\arg\min_{\mathbf{B}} ||\mathbf{B}^T\mathbf{X}||_0, \text{ subject to } \mathbf{BB}^T = \mathbf{I} \qquad (3)$$

where $\mathbf{X}$ is a matrix that contains binary observations as its columns and $|| \cdot ||_0$ is the sum of non-zero elements in the matrix. The constraint $\mathbf{BB}^T = \mathbf{I}$ ensures that $\mathbf{B}$ remains orthonormal.

However, direct minimization of $||\mathbf{B}^T\mathbf{X}||_0$ is NP-hard in general [7]. In practice, the ℓ_0-norm is often replaced by the convex and "sparsity-promoting" ℓ_1-norm [4]. This suggests the following relaxation heuristic for (3):

$$\arg\min_{\mathbf{B}} ||\mathbf{B}^T\mathbf{X}||_1, \text{ subject to } \mathbf{BB}^T = \mathbf{I}, \qquad (4)$$

where $|| \cdot ||_1$ is the maximum absolute column sum of the matrix.

Direct approximation. For large problems, we are interested in efficiently computable heuristics for Eq. (4). *Independent Component Analysis* (ICA) is one such approximation, and solves the following optimization problem:

$$\arg\min_{\mathbf{B}} G(\mathbf{B}^T\mathbf{X}), \text{ subject to } \mathbf{BB}^T = \mathbf{I}, \qquad (5)$$

where G is a nonlinear convex smooth approximation to the ℓ_1 penalty function, e.g. $\log\cosh(x)$, $-\exp(-x^2/2)$, and x^4 [13]. Fig. 4 illustrates these functions in relation to the linear penalty function.

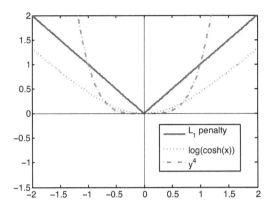

Figure 4: Smooth ℓ_1 approximation functions used in ICA with the linear ℓ_1 penalty function plotted in blue solid line.

Eq. (5) can be solved with stochastic gradient algorithm by taking the derivative of G. However this approach is often slow and requires fine tuning; this leads to the development of "FastICA", an efficient fixed-point algorithm. Implementation details of FastICA and in-depth analysis can be found in [13].

Let $g = G'$, the one unit algorithm for FastICA is given below for completeness.

$\mathbf{b} \leftarrow$ random unit vector
while $\mathbf{b}$ *not converged* **do**
    $\mathbf{b} \leftarrow \mathbb{E}\left[\mathbf{x}g(\mathbf{b}^T\mathbf{x})\right] - \mathbb{E}\left[g'(\mathbf{b}^T\mathbf{x})\right]\mathbf{x}$;
    $\mathbf{b} \leftarrow \mathbf{b}/\|\mathbf{b}\|$;

Algorithm 1: ICA one-unit solution

Noise-tolerant relaxed approximation. Ideally we want to learn from noise-free observations $\mathbf{X}$. However, training data constructed from real-world measurements will contain noise or outliers, and instead we are forced to train with $\mathbf{Y}$, which is the observation matrix $\mathbf{X}$ corrupted with noise.

Consequently, we may not be able to obtain the "best" basis by optimizing $\mathbf{B}^T\mathbf{Y}$ as in ICA. Instead, we may wish to find a basis that sparsely represents "most of" the observations. More formally, we introduce a latent matrix $\mathbf{Z}$, which can be thought of as the "cause", in the transform domain, of the noise-free signal $\mathbf{X}$. In other words $\mathbf{X} = \mathbf{BZ}$. We desire $\mathbf{Z}$ to be sparse, and $\mathbf{BZ}$ to be close to the observed signal $\mathbf{Y}$. This motivates the next optimization:

$$\arg\min_{\mathbf{B},\mathbf{Z}} \|\mathbf{Y} - \mathbf{BZ}\|_F^2 + \lambda\|\mathbf{Z}\|_1, \text{ subject to } \mathbf{BB}^T = \mathbf{I} \quad (6)$$

where $\|\cdot\|_F$ is the matrix Frobenius norm, and $\lambda > 0$ is a free parameter. Eq. (6) essentially balances the difference between $\mathbf{Y}$ and $\mathbf{X}$ with the sparsity of $\mathbf{Z}$: increasing λ more strongly penalizes choices of $\mathbf{Z}$ that are not sparse.

Although Eq. (6) is non-convex, fixing either $\mathbf{B}$ or $\mathbf{Z}$ makes the objective function with respect to the other convex. The objective can then be solved in an iterative two-step convex optimization process — *Orthogonal Procrustes* [12] and *LASSO with orthonormal design* [3]. The two-step procedure is given below.

Step 1: Orthogonal Procrustes
Fix $\mathbf{Z}$, solve $\min_{\mathbf{B}} \|\mathbf{Y} - \mathbf{BZ}\|_F^2, : \mathbf{BB}^T = \mathbf{I}$
    $M \leftarrow \mathbf{YZ}^T$;
    $M = U\Sigma V^T$;
    $\mathbf{B} \leftarrow UV$;
Step 2: LASSO with orthonormal design
Fix $\mathbf{B}$, solve $\min_{\mathbf{Z}} \|\mathbf{Y} - \mathbf{BZ}\|_F^2 + \lambda\|Z\|_1$
    $K \leftarrow \mathbf{Z}^T\mathbf{Y}$;
    $\mathbf{Z} \leftarrow \text{sign}(K) \times \max(|K| - \lambda)$;

Algorithm 2: SLSA two-step convex optimization procedure

The formulation of Eq. (6) and solution in Alg. 2 is equivalent to *Sparse Latent Semantic Analysis* (SLSA) [5], which was introduced for applications involving topic models for text data. Here we adopt the name for consistency.

We note that both Eq. (5) and Eq. (6) should be viewed as efficiently computable heuristics for Eq. (3), which is a non-convex optimization over the Stiefel manifold of all size-p orthonormal matrices. As such, they are practical expedients towards the goal of obtaining a sparsifying basis.

5. IMPLEMENTATION IN WSN

In this section, we describe practical issues necessary for using a sparsifying basis for event detection in real-world sensor networks. We highlight how the previous problem formulation can be separated into two computational steps:

- *Offline training* of basis learning and detection threshold selection;

- *Online detection* via decentralized detection or in-network data aggregation.

5.1 Offline Training

The three sparsifying bases (`haar` wavelet, `ICA`, `SLSA`) considered in this paper can be easily implemented and are available in many off-the-shelf optimization packages. Basis learning in small networks ($p < 100$) is very fast in general (within seconds) and can be done online. For larger networks ($p > 500$), offline training may be more suitable.

Basis learning. Learning a basis for p sensors requires at least p measurements of the network. If this is not available (e.g. a seismic network with 1000 sensors may not yet have observed 1000 earthquakes), then simulations provide a practical way to supplement real data. One advantage of using simulations in this way is that while simulations may be slow and compute-intensive, the learned basis produces a fast and efficient detection rule. In Sec. 6, we empirically assess the amount of data required to train a good basis and present two case studies using only data generated from simulations.

Selecting the detection threshold. An event is reported whenever $|\mathbf{b}_i^T\mathbf{y}| \geq \tau$ for any non-constant $\mathbf{b}_i \in \mathbf{B}$. The threshold τ is typically chosen as a value that satisfies constraints on the false positive rate during cross validation with historical data of event observations. This approach does not rely on positive training examples, and so a threshold τ can be learned using only the noise profile of each sensor. Suppose sensors $i = 1, 2, \ldots, p$ have binary error rates

$\pi_1, \ldots, \pi_p$, we have $\mathbb{E}\left[|\mathbf{b}^T\mathbf{y}|\right] = \sum_i^p b_i \pi_i$. Given that the basis is orthonormal, under $\mathcal{H}_0$, Hoeffding's Inequality states that

$$\mathbb{P}\left[|\mathbf{b}^T\mathbf{y}| > \tau\right] \leq \exp\left(-2\left(\tau - \mathbb{E}\left[|\mathbf{b}^T\mathbf{y}|\right]\right)^2\right).$$

By setting the right hand side to a false positive rate constraint, we can easily derive a threshold that satisfies the system requirement. In particular, in order to ensure that $|\mathbf{b}^T\mathbf{y}| \leq \tau$ for all $\mathbf{b} \in \mathbf{B}$ (i.e., no false alarm happens) with probability at least $1 - \delta$, it suffices to choose

$$\tau = \max_{\mathbf{b} \in \mathbf{B}} \mathbb{E}\left[|\mathbf{b}^T\mathbf{y}|\right] + \sqrt{\frac{1}{2}\log\frac{p}{\delta}}.$$

This approach is similar in flavor to the threshold selection method in [8].

5.2 Online Detection

At runtime, the fusion center collects information from the sensors and applies the threshold τ to the statistics $|\mathbf{B}^T\mathbf{y}|$. Depending on the network structure, this aggregation can be done in-network.

Decentralized Detection. The proposed sparsifying bases are suitable for both measurements from binary or other real-valued sensors. However, in large sensor networks such as the ones mentioned in Sec. 1, it is infeasible to constantly stream raw measurements to the fusion center. Instead, it may be desirable to offload the computation from the fusion center to each sensor locally so that only a small amount of information (e.g. a single message) is communicated infrequently when a significant signal is detected. For example, sensors in the Community Seismic Network perform *local anomaly detection* and communicate "abnormal" accelerations (using hypothesis testing) as a binary signal [8].

In-network Aggregation. If the learned basis exhibits hierarchical structure such as the `haar` wavelets inherently do, then it may be possible to adopt in-network aggregation to reduce transmission cost. This takes advantages of the resemblance of network communication topology and basis hierarchy. For example, by using the number of hops needed to communicate between a pair of nodes as a measure of the dissimilarity of two sensors, hierarchical clustering produces the transforms $\mathbf{B}$ supported over groups of communication-efficient clusters. These clusters may compute the transform $\mathbf{B}^T\mathbf{y}$ in a bottom-up fashion while simultaneously testing for detection.

For bases that lack obvious spatial hierarchy, it is possible to adaptively build a routing tree to minimize the communication distance between groups of sensors that tend to co-activate in a sparse sensor setting [10].

6. EXPERIMENTS

We empirically evaluate the detection performance of the three sparsifying bases: `SLSA`, `ICA`, and hierarchical wavelets (`haar`) trained and tested on both simulated and real measurements in different domains. The experimental setup is summarized here.

Baseline algorithms. In keeping with our focus of very large community sensor networks, we compare against base-

lines that could potentially be computed for real-time detection on tens of thousands of sensors, and that are naturally suited to the client-server communication model of internet-enabled sensors.

- `avg`: network-wide average, $1/p\sum_i^p y_i$;
- `max`: single sensor maximum, $\max_i y_i$;
- `SS-k`: scan statistics that aggregates the k-nearest neighbors for each sensor [20];
- `SS-r`: scan statistics that aggregates all sensors within a radius r for each sensor [20].

Evaluation data sets. The data sets include

- **Synthetic** data from latent tree model, 1296 nodes;
- **Gnutella P2P network**: 1769 nodes;
- **Japan seismic network**: 721 nodes;
- **CSN seismic network**: 128 nodes;
- **Long Beach** seismic network: 1,000 nodes.

Evaluation metrics and goals. We adopt two metrics in the evaluation of detection performance:

- AUC_f: measures the area-under-curve (AUC) in the Receiver Operating Characteristic (ROC) curve only for false positive rates between 0 and $f, f \leq 1$. The integral AUC_f takes values in $[0, f]$ and is normalized to 1 for simplicity. E.g. $AUC_{0.05} = 0.8$ indicates that the detection performance reaches 80% of the optimal performance under the false positive constraint of 5 false alarms every 100 tests.

- *Detection time*: the time it takes for the test statistics to exceed a threshold that is selected to satisfy a certain system false positive requirement. Rapid and reliable detection is a key requirement for many time sensitive applications. For example, in earthquake response (sub-)seconds improvement in detection time can allow utility companies to shut down large transformers that are responsible for long and costly recovering period after occurrence of a major earthquake.

6.1 Synthetic Data

We generate samples from the latent tree model for network activation as described in Sec. 3. The tree contains $p = 1296$ leaf nodes with degree $d = 6$ and depth $L = 4$. We choose the sparsifying parameters $\alpha = 0.5$ and $\beta = 0.95$ so that that the expected number of total activations $\|\mathbf{x}\|_0 < \sqrt{p}$ is sparse. Of the three bases, `haar` is constructed from the known tree model whereas `ICA` and `SLSA` are trained with 20,000 samples drawn from the model. The bases are tested on 20,000 separate samples corrupted with Gaussian or binary channel noise. For the Gaussian noise case, the range of σ is chosen to satisfy the weak signal constraint, i.e. $\sigma > \frac{1}{\sqrt{2\log p}} = 0.2641$.

Fig. 5 shows that all three bases outperform the naive baselines under both Gaussian and binary noise. Note that, perhaps surprisingly, both the learned `ICA` and `SLSA` outperform `haar` even though the latter is constructed from the known latent tree model.

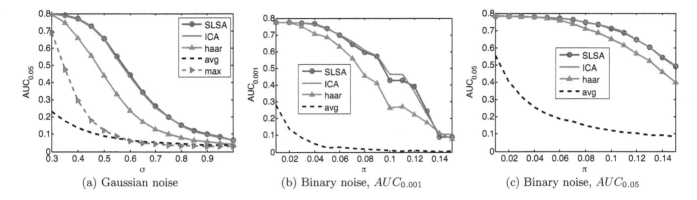

| (a) Gaussian noise | (b) Binary noise, $AUC_{0.001}$ | (c) Binary noise, $AUC_{0.05}$ |

Figure 5: Comparing the three bases — SLSA, ICA, haar to baselines — global average (and single max in (a)) on a synthetic data set generated from the latent tree model. Figures (b) and (c) evaluate two different false positive constraints. The learned bases significantly outperform the baselines under strong noise.

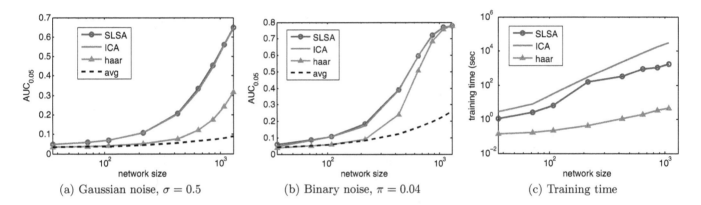

| (a) Gaussian noise, $\sigma = 0.5$ | (b) Binary noise, $\pi = 0.04$ | (c) Training time |

Figure 6: Detection performance as a function of network size $p = [36, 72, 108, 216, 432, 648, 864, 1080, 1296]$ using all 20,000 training samples. The learned bases show more than 5x performance improvement compared to the baselines in (a) and (b).

Next we study how the network size and the number of training samples affect the quality of learned basis and detection performance.

Increasing network size. We perform basis learning with subsets of the network, using $p = [36, 72, 108, 216, 432, 648, 864, 1080, 1296]$ sensors and $n = 20,000$ training samples. Fig. 6 shows that the detection performance of the learned bases grows more than 5x faster than the baseline. Note that haar is now learned from data; this accounts for the slight inferior performance compared to that in Fig. 5.

Increasing number of training samples. With the network size fixed, we evaluate bases learned from increasing numbers of training samples $n = [20, 100, 200, 1000, 2000, 4000, 10000, 15000]$. Fig. 7 shows that haar outperforms at smaller training size since it assumes a simple hierarchical structure. It also shows that it takes only 2,000 samples for ICA and SLSA to achieve the same detection performance as using all 20,000 samples.

6.2 Gnutella P2P network data

Our next set of experiments simulate virus outbreaks on a peer-to-peer network. We obtain a snapshot of the Gnutella P2P file sharing network[4] through the Stanford Network

Analysis Project (SNAP). 1,769 nodes of the highest degree of connectivity were selected from this network for the experiment. Fig. 8(a) visualizes part of this sub network. We simulate 40,000 outbreak events – "*cascades*" – that mimic virus outbreaks on this directed network. We adopt the independent cascade model, where a starting node is picked at random, and whenever a node r is infected, a connected node w is infected with decreasing probability as a function of distance to r.

Here, haar is constructed as spanning tree wavelet basis, using the known network structure [14] and Wilson's uniform spanning tree (UST) sampling method on a directed graph via random walk [26]. We also apply the subset scan baseline SS-k [20] for reference. The parameter k is "optimally" selected based on the prior knowledge that on average between 10 and 30 nodes are activated in each event in the cascade model.

Fig. 8(b) and Fig. 8(c) compare the detection performance evaluated on 40,000 testing samples. Both SLSA and ICA demonstrate superior detection performance compared to the state of the art algorithms that use additional prior knowledge of the network.

---

[4]http://snap.stanford.edu/data/p2p-Gnutella05.html

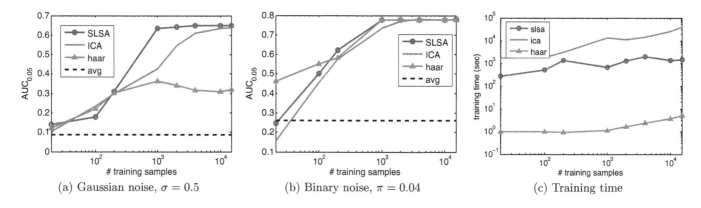

(a) Gaussian noise, $\sigma = 0.5$ (b) Binary noise, $\pi = 0.04$ (c) Training time

Figure 7: Detection performance as a function of of training data size. (a)(b) shows it only takes approximately **2,000** samples for both ICA and SLSA to achieve the same performance as using all **20,000** samples. SLSA is 10 times faster to train than ICA as shown in (c).

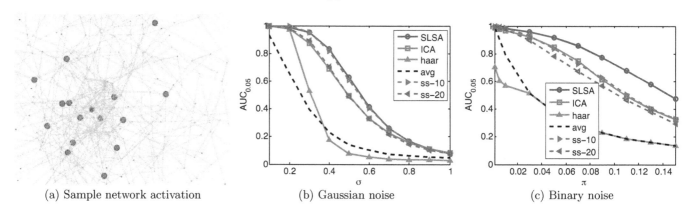

(a) Sample network activation (b) Gaussian noise (c) Binary noise

Figure 8: Experiment with Gnutella-P2P network. (a) visualizes ~ 1/10 of the total network with a sample activation pattern colored. Blue: first infected node, Red: nodes subsequently infected through the cascade. (b)(c) shows that the learned bases achieve and exceed the state of the art algorithms that use additional prior knowledge of the network.

6.3 Japan seismic network data

Next we turn to perhaps one of the most robust and long-running sensor networks in the world – the Japan seismic network. We obtain 48-hour, 150 GB of recordings from 721 *Hi-net* NIED seismometers for the dates March 18 and 19, 2011, just one week after the Tohoku M9.0 earthquake on March 11, 2011. On both days, 1,000+ events ranging from M1.0 - M6.0 were recorded in the the Japan Meteorology Agency catalog[5]. Many events triggered clustered activations as observed in Fig. 9(b).

For all 1795 events recorded on March 18, 2011, 10 snapshots of network activations at a two-second period were taken after the first detection at each event to construct the training data set of [p x n] = [721 x 17950]. The learned bases are tested on the first one-second data of the 1324 events recorded on March 19, 2011. We added binary noise of different error rate to control the problem complexity.

For the comparison with the SS-r baseline, the aggregation distance r is selected to be 20km which is roughly the distance covered by the seismic waves in a 2-second period. Fig. 9(d) presents the performance in detecting within two seconds of event arrival under a very small false positive

---

[5]http://www.hinet.bosai.go.jp/REGS/JMA/?LANG=en

constraint of 0.001. Of the three learned bases, both ICA and SLSA show significant gain in detection power, whereas haar has no improvement over the avg baseline. Perhaps surprisingly SS-r20 performs very poorly in comparison. An explanation is that most of the events during this period originated from the ocean and affects an array of stations along the coast. However, this pattern is not captured by the fixed radius subset scan construction. This explanation is supported by the plot of four prominent basis elements from ICA in Fig. 9(c). This example demonstrates the limited detection capability of subset scan for unknown patterns and the power of learning-based detection algorithms such as ICA and SLSA.

6.4 Dense and participatory seismic networks

Lastly, we return to the dense participatory sensor networks that served as a motivating example in Sec. 1. We consider two dense, real-world seismic networks in Southern California. We show that good bases can be learned without historical sensor data: instead, we simply use basic earthquake simulators to generate the binary activation patterns for training, as discussed in Sec. 5.1. In the shortage of testing data – only a small number of events have

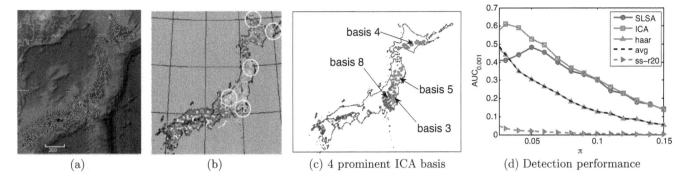

| | | (c) 4 prominent ICA basis | (d) Detection performance |
| (a) | (b) | | |

Figure 9: Japan's seismic network. The 721 Hi-net stations in (a) frequently exhibit localized activation patterns as circled in (b), which plots raw accelerations (red: large shaking, blue: no shaking). The learned bases are able to capture these nonuniform patterns with basis elements such as the ones in (c) and show 2x better detection performance compared to the baselines (d), while algorithms with hard-coded patterns such as SS-r20 fail to perform well in this scenario.

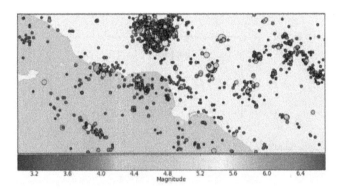

Figure 10: Southern California quakes since 1973

been recorded by these networks, not enough to reliably compute AUC scores – the detection performance is evaluated in terms of detection time with detection thresholds computed as described in Sec. 5.1. This measure of time is critical in many applications; seconds or sub-second savings may enable automated responses that prevent huge loss of capital and lives.

Generating training data. We generate training data using a basic earthquake simulator in the following two steps. First we randomly sample an earthquake from a prior distribution of seismic events in Southern California that is constructed from a list of historic earthquakes (Fig. 10) available in the USGS database[6].

Then time sequences of sensor activations are generated from an earthquake model that computes the expected wave arrival time with the encoded speed of seismic waves and distance to the hypocenter. This model is simplistic compared to many state-of-the-art earthquake simulators, yet captures qualitative spatio-temporal dependencies. An activation probability similar to that in [18] is used to simulate signal attenuation for unreliable noisy sensors.

Community Seismic Network. We simulate 1,000 network activation snapshots for 128 Community Seismic Network [6] sensors as described above. After training, each

[6]http://earthquake.usgs.gov/earthquakes/eqarchives/epic/

algorithm is then evaluated on its ability to detect four recent events using real measurements recorded by the network. Fig. 11(a) shows the spatial layout of the network and the hypocenters of the four events. Fig. 11(b) summarizes detection performance: the bases learned from simple simulations in general achieve faster detection than other algorithms, e.g. 8 seconds faster in detecting the Beverly Hills event. Note that ICA performs better than SLSA, as simulations are noise-free.

Long Beach Array. The Long Beach network consists of approximately 5,000 sensors covering an area of 5 x 7 km. The network was deployed for 6 months during the first half of 2011 to provide detailed images of the Signal Hill Oil Field in Long Beach, California. During the deployment period, a total number of 5 detectable earthquakes were recorded by the network (Fig. 12(a)). Fig. 1 is a visualization of one of the events.

We take a subset of 1,000 sensors and train the sparsifying bases with 2,000 simulated events. The results in Fig. 12(b) show that the learned bases detect on average 0.1 second faster, especially for the more difficult events that are smaller and further away. This improvement in detection time is significant considering that it only takes about one second for the quake to travel through the entire network.

7. RELATED WORK

Sparse detection. Detecting a sparse signal in the presence of strong noise is challenging without placing some assumptions on the class of signals. [23], [11], and [17] propose multi-scale bases for signals with tree structure. [14] further extends the analysis to graph structured network defined over spanning trees. The work of Singh et. al [23] is particularly relevant, as they identify the asymptotic limits of detectability for the orthonormal basis and generative models that we consider here in the centralized setting under Gaussian noise. In contrast, we focus on the decentralized case with binary channel noise, and provide theoretical guarantees that hold even in the non-asymptotic regime. [2] describes detecting sparse binary patterns with a variety of combinatoric structures under Gaussian noise. Lower bounds on minimax detection rates are given, and it is shown

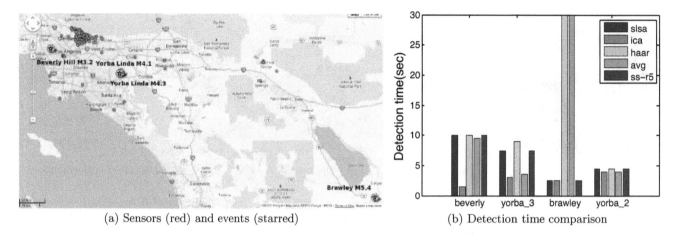

(a) Sensors (red) and events (starred)

(b) Detection time comparison

Figure 11: CSN network. (a) plots the layout of 128 sensors and epicenter of 4 recorded events. (b) The learned bases detect on average several seconds faster than the baselines under the constraint of at most one false alarm a year.

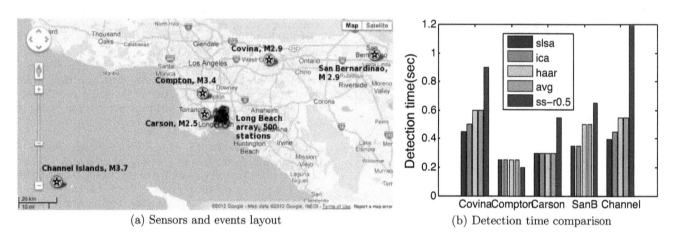

(a) Sensors and events layout

(b) Detection time comparison

Figure 12: Long Beach array. (a) shows the layout of 1,000 stations and 5 recorded events. (b) Under the constraint of at most one false alarm a year, the learned bases detect on average 0.1 seconds faster than the baselines, which is significant considering it only takes 1 second for the seismic wave to travel through the network and only 0.5 seconds for the network to be saturated with signals.

that forms of the scan statistic achieve within a log factor of these rates. However, these results are asymptotic and appear computationally intractable for large sensor networks.

Scan statistics. Spatial and space-time scan statistics were first developed to monitor health data and disease outbreaks [15]. The main idea is to evaluate all subsets of the data for possible events. Of course, enumerating all possible $O(2^n)$ subsets is infeasible for even moderately sized problems, so later refinements test only certain subsets of distinct sizes and shapes [21, 20]. This approach reduces the complexity to $O(n^2)$ (and to $O(n)$ in [20]) but may also impair the detection performance if important signals are not well captured by tested subsets.

Basis Learning. Learning a sparsifying basis is intimately related to dictionary learning and topic models. Dictionary learning [1] attempts to find an overcomplete dictionary $\mathbf{D} \in \mathbb{R}^{n,K}$, $K > n$ that can sparsely encode signals in $\mathbb{R}^n$. Similarly, topic models [25] represent text data as a linear combination of a "topics", e.g. vectors of word frequen-

cies. Topic models seek topics that sparsely approximate the documents, though the number of topics is significantly less than the number of words (i.e. the topic matrix is undercomplete).

ICA is a transformation method developed to recover nongaussian, statistically independent components $\mathbf{z}$ from their linear combination $\mathbf{x}$ [13], assuming that the linear transformation matrix $\mathbf{B}$ is orthonormal and $\mathbf{x} = \mathbf{B}\mathbf{z}$. The nongaussianity is required because the orthogonal transformation of any number of Gaussian distributions is inseparable. Strongly nongaussian data (i.e., having a very different distribution from Gaussian) is often sparse, and so nongaussianity is yet another measure of sparsity. ICA has enjoyed most success in signal separation and unsupervised feature learning. Recent work has extended it for overcomplete dictionary learning [16].

8. CONCLUSIONS

Motivated by quake detection in large community seismic networks, we proposed learning a *sparsifying basis* to enable detection of sparse event patterns in the decentralized setting. We obtain theoretical bounds on the power of sparsification using a `haar` wavelet basis and obtained strong bounds on error rates for events produced by the latent tree model that can be evaluated for any network size. These results strengthen and complement previous work on the limits of detectability of sparse patterns in Gaussian noise.

We then extended the intuition for the wavelet transform's success - its ability to concentrate signals with a small number of basis elements - and obtained a general framework to learn sparsifying bases for detection. We considered two optimizations, `ICA` and `SLSA`, for learning a basis that approximately maximizes sparsification, and explain how it can be implemented in sensor networks using real or simulated data in the absence of sufficient training data.

Finally, we thoroughly evaluate the detection performance of the sparsifying bases on several problem domains: simulated virus outbreaks on the Gnutella P2P network; detecting quakes following the Tohuku M9.0 event in the Japan seismic network with bases learned from network measurements; and detecting quakes recorded by the dense Long Beach and Community Seismic Network sensors using simulated measurements for training. In all domains, learned bases outperform previous state-of-the-art algorithms. We believe that our insights are an important step towards solving challenging detection problems using large-scale, noisy, participatory sensor networks.

Acknowledgments. The authors would like to thank their Caltech collaborators working on the Community Seismic Network project: Prof. Robert Clayton and Dr. Richard Guy of Geophysics; Prof. Thomas Heaton, Dr. Monica Kohler, and Ming-Hei Cheng from Earthquake Engineering; Prof. Mani Chandy and Michael Olson from Computer Science; Dr. Julian Bunn, Dr. Michael Aivazis, and Leif Strand from the Center for Advanced Computing Research. Special thanks to Prof. Robert Clayton and NodalSeismic Inc. for the Long Beach array data set and Prof. Masumi Yamada and NIED for the Japan data set. This research is supported in part by a grant from the Betty and Gordon Moore Foundation, by NSF award CNS0932392 and ERC StG 307036.

9. REFERENCES

[1] M. Aharon, M. Elad, and A. Bruckstein. K-svd: Design of dictionaries for sparse representation. *Proc. of SPARS*, 5:9–12, 2005.

[2] E. Arias-Castro, E. Candes, and A. Durand. Detection of an anomalous cluster in a network. *The Annals of Statistics*, 39(1):278–304, 2011.

[3] P. Bühlmann and S. van de Geer. *Statistics for High-Dimensional Data*. Methods, Theory and Applications. Springer, June 2011.

[4] S. S. Chen, D. L. Donoho, and M. A. Saunders. Atomic Decomposition by Basis Pursuit. *SIAM review*, 2001.

[5] X. Chen, Y. Qi, B. Bai, Q. Lin, and J. G. Carbonell. Sparse latent semantic analysis. *NIPS Workshop*, 2010.

[6] R. Clayton, T. Heaton, et al. Community seismic network. *Annals of Geophysics*, 54(6), 2012.

[7] G. Davis, S. Mallat, and M. Avellaneda. Adaptive greedy approximations. *Constructive Approximation*, 13(1):57–98, Mar. 1997.

[8] M. Faulkner, M. Olson, R. Chandy, J. Krause, K. M. Chandy, and A. Krause. The next big one: Detecting earthquakes and other rare events from community-based sensors. In *Information Processing in Sensor Networks (IPSN)*, 2011.

[9] R. Ganti, I. Mohomed, R. Raghavendra, and A. Ranganathan. Analysis of data from a taxi cab participatory sensor network. *Mobile and Ubiquitous Systems: Computing, Networking, and Services*, pages 197–208, 2012.

[10] J. Gao, L. Guibas, N. Milosavljevic, and J. Hershberger. Sparse data aggregation in sensor networks. In *Information Processing in Sensor Networks (IPSN)*, pages 430–439. ACM, 2007.

[11] M. Gavish, B. Nadler, and R. Coifman. Multiscale wavelets on trees, graphs and high dimensional data: Theory and applications to semi supervised learning. In *Proc. International Conf. on Machine Learning, Haifa, Israel*, 2010.

[12] J. Gower and G. Dijksterhuis. *Procrustes Problems*. Oxford Statistical Science Series. OUP Oxford, 2004.

[13] A. Hyvärinen, J. Karhunen, and E. Oja. *Independent Component Analysis*. Wiley-Interscience, June 2001.

[14] A. Krishnamurthy, J. Sharpnack, and A. Singh. Detecting Activations over Graphs using Spanning Tree Wavelet Bases. *arXiv.org*, stat.ML, June 2012.

[15] M. Kulldorff. A spatial scan statistic. *Communications in Statistics - Theory and Methods*, 26(6):1481–1496, Jan. 1997.

[16] Q. Le, A. Karpenko, and J. Ngiam. ICA with Reconstruction Cost for Efficient Overcomplete Feature Learning. *Neural Information Processing Systems*, 2011.

[17] A. Lee, B. Nadler, and L. Wasserman. Treelets—an adaptive multi-scale basis for sparse unordered data. *The Annals of Applied Statistics*, 2(2):435–471, 2008.

[18] A. Liu, M. Olson, J. Bunn, and K. M. Chandy. Towards a discipline of geospatial distributed event based systems. In *DEBS '12: Proc. of the 6th ACM International Conf. on Distributed Event-Based Systems*, July 2012.

[19] S. Madden, M. Franklin, J. Hellerstein, and W. Hong. Tinydb: An acquisitional query processing system for sensor networks. *ACM Transactions on Database Systems (TODS)*, 30(1):122–173, 2005.

[20] D. B. Neill. Fast subset scan for spatial pattern detection. *Journal of the Royal Statistical Society: Series B (Statistical Methodology)*, 74(2), 2012.

[21] D. B. Neill and A. W. Moore. Rapid detection of significant spatial clusters. In *Proc. of the tenth ACM SIGKDD . . .*, 2004.

[22] G. Shmueli and H. Burkom. Statistical challenges facing early outbreak detection in biosurveillance. *Technometrics*, 52(1):39–51, 2010.

[23] A. Singh, R. Nowak, and R. Calderbank. Detecting Weak but Hierarchically-Structured Patterns in Networks. In *The 13th International Conf. on Artificial Intelligence and Statistics (AISTATS)*, Sept. 2010.

[24] J. Tsitsiklis et al. Decentralized detection. *Advances in Statistical Signal Processing*, 2:297–344, 1993.

[25] Q. Wang, J. Xu, H. Li, and N. Craswell. Regularized latent semantic indexing. In *Proc. 34th Internat. ACM SIGIR Conf. on Research and Development in Information, SIGIR*, volume 11, pages 685–694, 2011.

[26] D. B. Wilson. Generating random spanning trees more quickly than the cover time. *Proc. of the twenty-eighth annual ACM symposium on Theory of computing*, pages 296–303, 1996.

[27] C. Zhou, C. Leckie, and S. Karunasekera. A survey of coordinated attacks and collaborative intrusion detection. *Computers & Security*, 29(1):124–140, 2010.

APPENDIX

Proof of Theorem 1. Let k be the size of clusters merged by a non-constant basis element $\mathbf{b}$. Let $\tau = \frac{(1-2\pi)}{2}\sqrt{\frac{\|\mathbf{x}\|_0}{\|\mathbf{B}^T\mathbf{x}\|_0}}$. Under $\mathcal{H}_0$, $\mathbb{E}\left[\mathbf{b}^T\mathbf{y}\right] = 0$, and is the sum of $2k$ terms (k from each cluster) taking values $\{-\frac{1}{\sqrt{2k}}, 0, \frac{1}{\sqrt{2k}}\}$. Hoeffding's inequality gives $\mathbb{P}\left[|\mathbf{b}^T\mathbf{y}| \geq \tau\right] \leq 2\exp\left(-\tau^2\right) \to 0$. Taking the union bound, FPR $\leq 2p\exp\left(-\tau^2\right) \to 0$. Under $\mathcal{H}_1$, for some $\mathbf{b}$, $\mathbb{E}\left[|\mathbf{b}^T\mathbf{y}|\right] \geq \sqrt{\frac{\|\mathbf{x}\|_0}{\|\mathbf{B}^T\mathbf{x}\|_0}}(1-2\pi)$. As under $\mathcal{H}_0$, Hoeffding's inequality bounds the probability of deviation by τ from the mean (conveniently, $\mathbb{E}\left[|\mathbf{b}^T\mathbf{y}|\right] - \tau > \tau$): $\mathbb{P}\left[|\mathbf{b}^{(k)}\mathbf{y}| \leq \tau\right] \leq 2\exp\left(\tau^2\right) \to 0$. Taking the union bound over p basis elements, FNR $\leq 2p\exp\left(-\tau^2\right) \to 0$.

Proof of Theorem 2. Let $X_T^{(i)}$ denote the leaves in the ith subtree rooted at level ℓ_0. In the latent tree model, the nodes at level ℓ_0 are independent, and so the numbers of active leaves in each subtree $\|X_T^{(i)}\|_0$, $i = 1, \ldots, d^{\ell_0}$ are i.i.d.

LEMMA 1. $\mathbb{E}\left[\|X_T^{(i)}\|\right] \geq c \cdot p^{1-\alpha}p^{-\frac{\alpha}{\beta}}$ where $c = \left(\frac{1}{4}\right)^{\left(\frac{1}{\alpha} - \frac{1}{\beta} + 0.5\right)}$ is constant with respect to p.

Let $W_T^{(i)} = \frac{\|X_T^{(i)}\|_0}{p^{1-\frac{\alpha}{\beta}}}$, and $W = \sum_i W_T^{(i)}$. There are $p^{1-\frac{\alpha}{\beta}}$ leaves in each $X_T^{(i)}$, so $W_T^{(i)} \in [0, 1]$. There are $p^{\frac{\alpha}{\beta}}$ subtrees, so by Lemma 1, $cp^{-\alpha}p^{\frac{\alpha}{\beta}} < \mathbb{E}[W]$. Hoeffding's inequality gives, for $0 < \epsilon < 1$,

$$\mathbb{P}\left[\|X\|_0 < (1-\epsilon)cp^{1-\alpha}\right] \leq \exp\left(\frac{c\epsilon^2}{2}p^{\alpha\left(\frac{1}{\beta}-1\right)}\right)$$

Next, we will say an *edge flip* occurs at level ℓ when a node at level ℓ does not equal its parent. The number of non-zero coefficients is bounded as $\|\mathbf{B}^T\mathbf{x}\|_0 \leq dL \cdot F$, where F is the number of edge flips in the tree. An edge at level ℓ flips with probability $q_\ell = 1/(1 + d^{\beta\ell}) < d^{-\beta\ell}$, so we find that

$$\mathbb{E}[F] = \frac{d^{(1-\beta)(L+1)} - d^{1-\beta}}{d^{(1-\beta)} - 1} < d \cdot d^{L(1-\beta)}$$

Let $\bar{\mu} = d \cdot d^{L(1-\beta)}$ For $0 < \epsilon < 1$, the Hoeffding inequality gives

$$\mathbb{P}\left[\left\|\mathbf{B}^T x\right\|_0 > (1+\epsilon)d^2\log_d p \cdot p^{(1-\beta)}\right] \leq \exp\left(-\frac{\epsilon^2}{3}d \cdot p^{(1-\beta)}\right).$$

$\square$

Autonomous Place Naming System using Opportunistic Crowdsensing and Knowledge from Crowdsourcing

Yohan Chon
Department of Computer
Science
Yonsei University
Seoul, Korea
yohan@cs.yonsei.ac.kr

Yunjong Kim
Department of Computer
Science
Yonsei University
Seoul, Korea
yjkim@cs.yonsei.ac.kr

Hojung Cha
Department of Computer
Science
Yonsei University
Seoul, Korea
hjcha@cs.yonsei.ac.kr

ABSTRACT

A user's location information is commonly used in diverse mobile services, yet providing the actual name or semantic meaning of a place is challenging. Previous works required manual user interventions for place naming, such as searching by additional keywords and/or selecting place in a list. We believe that applying mobile sensing techniques to this problem can greatly reduce user intervention. In this paper, we present an autonomous place naming system using opportunistic crowdsensing and knowledge from crowdsourcing. Our goal is to provide a place name from a person's perspective: that is, *functional name* (e.g., food place, shopping place), *business name* (e.g., Starbucks, Apple Store), or *personal name* (e.g., my home, my workplace). The main idea is to bridge the gap between crowdsensing data from smartphone users and location information in social network services. The proposed system automatically extracts a wide range of semantic features about the places from both crowdsensing data and social networks to model a place name. We then infer the place name by linking the crowdsensing data with knowledge in social networks. Extensive evaluations with real deployments show that the proposed system outperforms the related approaches and greatly reduces user intervention for place naming.

Categories and Subject Descriptors

C.m [**Computer Systems Organization**]: Miscellaneous-*Mobile Sensing Systems*

General Terms

Algorithms, Experimentation, Human Factors

Keywords

Location-based Services, Location Naming, Smartphone Sensing

1. INTRODUCTION

People typically carry mobile phones all the time, and a user's location can practically be tracked in everyday lives. The acquired location information is widely used in emerging mobile applications, such as location-based social networks, place recommendations, and location-based searches. However, most services have a limitation in recognizing the actual name of a place (e.g., Starbucks or Apple store) because of the noises in physical location information. For example, mobile services provide a list of nearby places based on the estimated latitude and longitude, and a user manually decides the present place. In addition, reverse geocoding, which obtains a readable address from a physical location, often generates inaccurate output due to localization error. Meanwhile, people normally refer the places by name (e.g., McDonalds), not address (e.g., Yonsei Street 100). This indicates that a gap exists between people's understanding about the place and the raw coordinates of a location. Therefore, an advanced system is necessary to provide a place name from a user's point of view, not just raw coordinates on a map.

Active studies have recently been conducted to understand and provide place naming from a user's viewpoint. Lin et al. [19] analyzed the preference of place naming: how people to refer places when interacting with others. They defined a taxonomy on place naming, such as *functional name* (e.g., shopping, food place), *business name* (e.g., Walmart, Burger King), or *personal name* (e.g., my home, my workplace). Most works in information retrieval have studied similarity functions to provide a ranked list of places. To estimate the rank, previous works have employed various features, including location [11], check-in histories at social networks [18, 27], web-based popularity [18, 24], and search histories [16]. However, previous studies still required manual user intervention, such as searching a place with additional keywords or explicitly choosing a place in a list. We believe that leveraging mobile sensing systems to solve this problem greatly improves the accuracy of place naming and reduces user intervention.

In this paper, we present an autonomous place naming system to provide a place name according to three different types, as defined in [19]: *functional, business,* and *personal name*. The proposed system uses previously untouched resources that can be collected by individual smartphones, such as user mobility, phone usage, and images captured by users. The main idea is to integrate crowdsensing data obtained from smartphone users with information in social network services (SNS) to provide the place name. Smartphones can opportunistically collect sensing data about the places in users' daily life, but manual labeling of the place name is necessary. Meanwhile, social networks have a broad set of location information manually built by business providers and users. The information typically includes physical location, place name, and place type, but location-based lookup [1] is often limited in recognizing a place, due to incorrect location estimation. Our system mines sensing data to extract semantic features of the places, which include publicness, behavior patterns of visitors, and captured pictures in places. In order to provide a place name, our system then matches extracted features with location information in SNS, which include check-in histories, posted images, and texts.

The main contributions of our paper are as follows:

- We present an autonomous system for place naming that combines opportunistic sensing data from smartphones with location information in social networks. We greatly improve the accuracy of place naming.

- We thoroughly validated the proposed system using large-scale data collected by 70 smartphone users and 31,000 social networks users in Seoul, Korea. The results show that the proposed system outperforms the related approaches and reduces manual user intervention for place naming.

- The proposed system enables us to understand human behavior patterns in city-scale by linking a place to semantic meaning. The results of automatic place naming can lead to advanced understanding of user behavior in places.

2. PRELIMINARY STUDY

We motivate our work by discussing the limitation of location-based lookup and the potential of applying a sensing system to this problem. As a preliminary study, we investigated the coverage and quality of location information in social networks. We explored the following questions:

- How many places does an SNS location information cover in real life?

- How much user intervention does location-based lookup require for place naming?

To answer these questions, we analyzed approximately 3,800 places visited by 70 smartphone users, and 130,000 locations crawled from Foursquare [11]. We deployed mobility monitoring tool [3] from November 2011 to September 2012, to collect real user traces in Seoul, Korea. We also crawled social network data from May 2012 to September 2012. The details regarding data collection are further described in Section 4.1.

2.1 Coverage of Location-based Lookup

We first investigate the coverage of location information in social networks. Intuitively, the location information in SNS would contain a subset of the places in real life, as social

---
[1]Location-based lookup is the process of finding nearby places in a location database based on a estimated location (i.e., latitude and longitude).

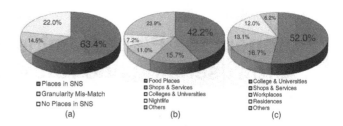

Figure 1: (a) Coverage of location information in SNS; (b) the categories of missing places and (c) granularity mismatch.

media captures a relatively small fraction of our lives by people who are active participants of SNS. To estimate the coverage, we manually matched the places visited by users in daily life to the locations in SNS. We used the labeled names and offline feedback from the participants. Figure 1(a) shows that SNS misses about 22% of the places users visited. The missing places are mostly food or shopping places with low popularity, or recently built places, as shown in Figure 1(b). Considering that our dataset is collected with 70 smartphone users, the portion of missing places would increase with more participants since the manual registration of places in SNS cannot contain all the places in real life.

Another finding is that mismatch exists in user's understanding of the actual place and the locations provided by SNS. For example, a user stays at the NexOne Inc. office, but SNS provides this place as the name of the building. A user would think that the building name could not express the place she visited, since the building has many offices, stores, and restaurants. Figure 1(a) shows that the mismatch ratio is about 14.5% of the places in our dataset. The mismatched places were mostly located in college and university regions, shopping districts, or office buildings, as shown in Figure 1(c).

In summary, our preliminary analysis indicates that crowd-sensing using smartphones has the potential to expand the coverage and improve the granularity of location information that are missed by social media.

2.2 Limitation of Location-based Lookup

We now discuss the limitation of place naming method that uses location-based lookup in SNS. Most services provide a list of nearby places since direct mapping of a user's location to a place name is challenging. We calculated the distance between the estimated location by mobile phones and the location coordinates of places in SNS. Figure 2(a) shows that only 8.6% of places are within 10 meters, and 80.4% of places are within about 100 meters. The list of nearby places should show the places within 180 meters in order to cover the actual place for 90% of the cases.

The questions to be answered, then, are *how many places does the list contain within error distance?* and *what is the rank of the actual place in the list?* If the list contains many places and the rank of the actual place is high, manual selection of a place is burdensome for some users. We statistically analyzed the location information regarding the Seoul region to answer these questions. The results show that the list contained 87.8 places within 100 meters error bound (median was 44, first percentile was 20, and third percentile was 121 places); the rank of 35% of places was higher

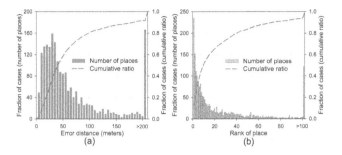

(a)　　　　　(b)

Figure 2: (a) Error distance between estimated locations in mobile phone and places in SNS and (b) the rank of actual place in the list of nearby places.

than 20, as shown in Figure 2(b). This means that manual selection of a place in the list is a serious burden for the users, due to the high density of places. A user had to enter further keywords to find his/her current place by location-based lookup. In addition, 17.9% of places were registered as more than two places, with slightly different names, in the location database. The reason for this discrepancy is that some users failed to find a place in the list and registered a new place instead, even though the place already existed in the database. Our findings indicate that to provide a place name, we need robust and efficient features beyond simple raw coordinates of location.

3. AUTONOMOUS PLACE NAMING

We propose autonomous place naming system that integrates crowdsensing data from mobile phones with location information in social networks. We first describe the usage scenario, and then present the technical details.

The proposed system automatically provides the name of places visited by users in daily life according to three types [19]: functional name (e.g., food place, nightlife, shopping place), business name (e.g., Starbucks, Apple Store), and personal name (e.g., my home, my workplace). We assume that a user does not manually provide information about the place name. When a user stays at a place for a certain period of time, the system opportunistically collects sensing data and phone usage to generate the place characteristics. The system then extracts features from sensing data collected by crowd users. The system finally matches extracted features with location information in SNS to infer the place name.

Figure 3 illustrates the overall process of the proposed system, which consists of three parts: data collector, feature extraction, and name provider. In data collector, we use GPS, WiFi, and cellular sensors to collect mobility data, along with images captured by users. On the server side, the crawler collects location and interaction data from social networks, including places, check-in histories, images, and posts in places. In feature extraction, the system applies a set of classifiers to extract the characteristics about place. We estimate the familiarity of place, residence time, and stay duration. We also analyze images to extract features about environments. Based on the extracted features, the name provider infers the place name by linking crowdsensing data with knowledge in social networks.

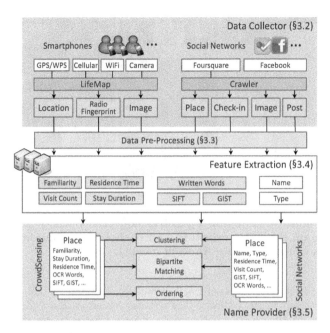

Figure 3: Overall process of the proposed system.

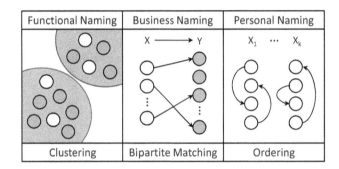

Figure 4: Conceptual description of place naming problem.

3.1 Problem Statement

We first formulate the problem of place naming. Specifically, crowdsensed data X contains a set of n places $X = \{x_1, \cdots, x_n\}$. Each node x includes four elements (L, S, R, I), in which L is a set of estimated locations, S a set of stay behaviors, R a set of radio fingerprints, and I a set of captured images. Meanwhile, location information Y in SNS includes a set of m places $Y = \{y_1, \cdots, y_m\}$. Each node y consists of six elements $(name, type, l, T, P, I)$, in which $name$ is the name of the place, $type$ the type of place, l the location information, T the set of check-in time, P the set of postings, and I the set of uploaded images.

Now, the problem is to infer the functional name, business name, and personal name of node $x \in X$. Figure 4 illustrates the conceptual descriptions of each problem. First, functional naming is defined as the inference of place type. Given X and Y, the system clusters all nodes $x \in X, y \in Y$ into different clusters $C_1, \cdots, C_k$, where k is larger than the desired number of place types. Here, the places in the same cluster are assumed to contain unique characteristics derived from the same place types. Then, the functional name of node x in C_i is a place type derived from nodes $y \in C_i$.

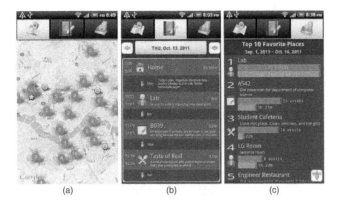

(a)   (b)   (c)

Figure 5: LifeMap visualizes collected data as (a) map, (b) daily trajectory, and (c) list form. LifeMap is available in the Android market.

Second, business naming is defined as a bipartite matching problem in graph theory. The system generates a direct edge e_{ij} from x_i to y_j. The capacity of each edge is 1, and the cost e_{ij}^c is the similarity between x_i and y_j. The goal is to find a set of edges $E \in X \times Y$ for maximizing the number of flows $|E|$ with a minimum cost $\sum_{e \in E} e^c$. In other words, the system matches nodes in crowdsensing with nodes in social networks to minimize the matching cost globally.

Last, personal naming is accomplished by ordering node $x \in X$ to choose private places. The system splits X into $X_1', \cdots, X_k'$ depending on individual users. X_i' is a set of visited places by the i-th users. We should order $x \in X_i'$ elements to find the most private place for each user.

3.2 Data Collector

We extended the mobility monitoring tool LifeMap [3, 7], for data collection in smartphones. LifeMap continuously collects a user's mobility every two minutes using WiFi, GPS, and cellular sensors. We added an image-capturing functionality to collect images captured by users. LifeMap visualizes the visited places along with collected data on map and list form, as shown in Figure 5. Users can confirm and delete collected data at each place for privacy issues.

We also developed a crawler to collect location, as well as interaction data from social networks, such as check-in histories, posted tips, pictures, and basic user information. To preserve privacy issues, we only used public data without private authorization.

3.3 Data Pre-Processing

The system first defines *a place* in a user's trajectories. We segment the stream of collected data into places with room-level accuracy and aggregate the data at identical places. Here, we describe the place segmentation technique and the node generation for pre-processing.

Place Segmentation. We used a radio fingerprint-based place learning to segment places with room-level accuracy in a user's trajectories. Let (l_t, r_t) be sensing data from data collector at time t, in which l_t is a location and r_t is a radio fingerprint. The system considers that a user stays at same place if the similarity of the received signal strengths from WiFi APs is larger than a certain threshold. We used the Tanimoto coefficient [12] to estimate the similarity of radio fingerprints, defined as:

Table 1: Summary of used features.

Features	Sources	Terms in nodes	Usage
Residence time	Stay behavior Check-in history	Discretized into 48 bins	Functional name Business name
Stay duration	Stay behavior	Discretized into 9 bins	Functional name Personal name
Words	Image Posting	Raw words	Functional name Business name
GIST	Image	Clustered ID	Functional name Business name
SIFT	Image	Clustered ID	Functional name Business name
Familiarity	Visit frequency	-	Personal name

$$\mathcal{S}(r_a, r_b) = \begin{cases} \text{stationary} & \text{,if} \frac{r_a \cdot r_b}{\|r_a\|^2 + \|r_b\|^2 - r_a \cdot r_b} \geq \varphi \\ \text{move} & \text{,else} \end{cases}$$

where φ is the similarity threshold and the output is a similarity estimated between 0 to 1. When the system continuously detects a stationary state from time t^s to time t^e (i.e., $\min_{t^s \leq t < t^e} \mathcal{S}(r_t, r_{t+1}) \geq \varphi$), we generate a stay behavior (L, R, t^s, t^e), in which L is a set of estimated locations, R a set of radio fingerprints, t^s the start time of stay, and t^e the end time of stay. Each node x then includes a set of stay behaviors. In other words, we group the collected dataset into different places based on radio fingerprints. We emprically set the threshold φ to group the places with room-level accuracy.

For social network data, place segmentation is straightforward since the location database provides the unique ID of each place.

Node Generation. The system constructs places as nodes with a bag-of-words model. One node contains all features extracted from the sensing data in an unordered manner. We denote the term as an attribute of extracted features. We discretize continuous features (e.g., the distribution of residence time or stay duration) into a series of discrete terms by certain intervals. To handle the noisy measurements in the collected dataset, the system modifies the frequency of terms within a node, based on the confidence and uniqueness. We first filter out outputs with low confidence scores, using an empirically determined threshold (see Section 4.4). The system then applies the term frequency-inverse document frequency (tf-idf) [23], which is frequently used in conventional document analysis. This technique emphasizes unique terms and reduces the weight of non-discriminative terms. For example, tf-idf decreases the frequency of common terms across all nodes, as those terms are meaningless for discrimination. The tf-idf of term w at node x in set X is defined as:

$$\text{tf-idf}(w, x, X) = \frac{f(w,x)}{\max\{f(w,x):w \in x\}} \times \log \frac{|X|}{|\{x \in X:w \in x\}|},$$

where $f(w, x)$ is a frequency of term w in node x.

3.4 Feature Extraction

We describe the features we used to model the place characteristics. Each node contains features about a user's behavior and environments, obtained from both crowdsensing and social network data. Table 1 summaries the extraced features and their usage at the name provider.

Residence Time. Residence time indicates stay behavior of users at a place tied with time-of-day (e.g., 10am or 4pm). The underlying assumption is that both the stay duration and the time-of-day imply meaningful patterns when

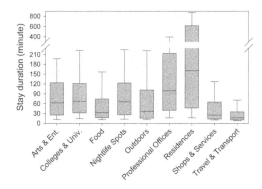

Figure 6: Distribution of stay duration according to the functional name.

people visit a certain place. Intuitive examples include people spending meal times at food places or students staying at schools from 9am to 5pm. From the stay behaviors S^x at node x, the system generates the distribution of residence time at place R^x, based on the discrete histogram of residence time set $(t_1^s, t_1^e), \cdots, (t_k^s, t_k^e)$. The probability of R^x at time t is defined as:

$$R^x(t) = p(t_i^s \leq t \text{ and } t \leq t_i^e | (t_i^a, t_i^e) \in S^x),$$

where t is a specific hour and minute of a day (e.g., 8am or 4pm). We normalize R^x as $\int_t R^x(t)\mathrm{d}t = 1$ and discretize R^x into 48 bins (i.e., 30 minutes for each bin). We use the overall distribution of residence time instead of probability at a specific time.

For social network data, we generate R^x based on check-in history T. Compared to stay behavior sensed by a smartphone, T contains a set of instant check-in time t^c, not the duration. Therefore, $R^x(t)$ is a fraction of observed check-ins at time t to overall check-in histories, defined as $p(t_i^c = t | t_i^c \in T)$.

Stay Duration. The system produces the distribution of stay duration D^x at node x in each place. This feature takes the pattern of stay behavior without time-of-day. For example, many college students visit specific classrooms with uniformly distributed patterns from 9am to 6pm, and their stay duration may show consistent patterns—i.e., the length of a class hour. D^x is a form of discrete histogram based on the set of stay duration at node x, expressed as $D^x = \{s_i = t_i^e - t_i^s | (t_i^s, t_i^e) \in S^x\}$. We discretized the stay duration into 9 bins (i.e., 15, 30, 60, 90, 120, 150, 210, 400, 400+ minutes) based on the distribution of the stay duration according to the functional name, as shown in Figure 6.

Social networks do not provide stay duration at places because the check-in operation indicates only an instant time instead of the duration. Previous work estimated stay duration approximately by using the time difference between consecutive check-ins of each user [8], but such approach requires private information (i.e., user's identification of each check-in) which is not acquired in our system. The stay duration is therefore a missing value in social network data.

Written Words. The written words found in menus, store signage, posters, or postings imply the characteristics about the place. For example, we see the brand name (e.g., Starbucks or Apple) on signs or words related to coffee (e.g., Americano or roast) in a cafe. Similarly, people post texts

about places for sharing purposes, such as recommendations of menus at restaurants or reviews of services at stores in location-based social networks.

The system mines words from the captured images in smartphones, and also from the uploaded images and texts in social networks. To mine such words in a set of captured image I, the system incorporates optical character recognition (OCR) technique [10]. From each image, the engine provides recognized words and confidence score in each result. We utilized confidence score to modify the weight of recognized words. We set the high threshold of confidence score to filter out the noisy results.

Similar to written words mined from images, the texts in social network contains meaningful words related to place characteristics. The system selects postings associated with places and parses texts into an unordered set of unigram words. To reduce the noises in extracted words, we used the dictionary to filter out non-grammatical words.

Local Features in Images. The local features describe the unique characteristics of specific objects in images. Practical examples include a brand logo on a wall or a mark on the signage. We incorporate scale-invariant feature transform (SIFT) [20] to mine local features in images. SIFT is commonly used in computer vision for object recognition or image stitching. This technique produces a set of key points in each image that describes position, scale, and orientation of each interesting pattern in images. We cluster the extracted SIFT features from all images in a dataset and generate the distribution of cluster ID at each node.

Scene Features of Images. Scene feature describes the overall scene characteristics of an image, such as major shape or visual patterns. For example, we see strong horizontal lines in supermarket shelves or round shapes of bowls in images capturing dishes in restaurants. To leverage scene features, we chose GIST feature [22], which is widely used in the literature to capture scene characteristics. We produce GIST-based feature vectors for each image. Similar to local features, we cluster GIST vectors to group images into similar sets. The system then takes the frequency of images in each cluster into the features of a place.

Familiarity. Familiarity indicates how frequently a user visits a place. We define the familiarity of node x that contains k stay behaviors, motivated by the entropy in [9], as follows:

$$\text{Familiarity}(x, S) := -\sum_{i=1}^{k-1} p(i; S) \log p(i; S),$$

where $p(i; S)$ is $\frac{t_{i+1}^s - t_i^s}{t_k^s - t_1^s}$. A place will have high familiarity if a user visits it with certain regularity (e.g., every day). Conversely, a place will have low familiarity if the distribution of stay at a place is biased or randomly observed. We use familiarity to determine the privateness of a place for each user. For example, employees at a restaurant exhibit high familiarity, as they regularly come to the restaurant for work. Conversely, customers at a restaurant show relatively lower familiarity, due to the randomness of their stay behavior.

3.5 Name Provider

We now describe the principles we applied to integrate all extracted features for inferring place names according to three types (i.e., functional, business, and personal name).

Functional Name. Functional name indicates the semantic type of place, such as food place, nightlife, or shopping place. We applied a clustering technique to infer the functional names of places. The intuition is that the functional name is a category of multiple places that exhibit the similar characteristics of sensing data. The system clusters all nodes into different groups with consistent patterns of terms. To handle no prior knowledge about the number of groups, we adopted Dirichlet process mixture (DPM) suggested by [2, 25]. DPM describes infinite Dirichlet distribution as a prior of groups, and provides a flexible scheme to estimate the number of clusters and parameters. Our system used residence time, stay duration, words from images or postings, GIST and SIFT features to compute the distance between nodes. Given a node a and b, the distance between a and b is defined as

$$u(a,b) = KL(R^a \cap D^a, R^b \cap D^b) + \alpha \frac{1}{|W^a \cap W^b|},$$

in which $KL(\cdot)$ is the symmetrized Kullbeck-Leibler (KL) measurement [15] of the residence time and the stay duration distributions, α the scaling factor, and $|W^a \cap W^b|$ the overlapped number of mined words, GIST, and SIFT features. The KL divergence measures the expected amount of information required to transform samples from a distribution into another one. The system calculates the KL divergence without stay duration if node a or b does not contain the information. We set the minimum value of $|W^a \cap W^b|$ as 1 if two nodes do not have overlapped terms. The metric indicates that the distance between two places is close if the stay behaviors at two places are similar and two places sufficiently include the same written words or features from images. For example, the residence places would be grouped in the same cluster because of shared terms in nighttime (e.g., 0am to 7am) or long stay durations (e.g., 400+ minutes). Or, the coffee places can be differentiated from the shopping places due to different observations in mined words. Given a cluster C_i, the functional name of node $x \in C_i$ is the type of node $y \in C_i$ with highest probability $\max_{type \in y} \frac{|type|}{|C_i|}$.

Business Name. Business name is the actual name of a place such as Starbucks, Apple Store, or Marche. To infer the business name, the system should generate one-on-one links between a place generated by crowdsensing and a place in SNS. We applied the bipartite matching which finds a flow between two sets with a minimum cost. The problem is to match node $x \in X$ to node $y \in Y$ with a minimum matching cost. The system generates a graph with four layers, U, X, Y, V, as illustrated in Figure 7. The system generates direct edges from U to V: $U \to X \to Y \to V$. Initially, the capacity and the flow of all edges are 1 and 0, respectively. The edges in $U \to X$ and $Y \to V$ have no cost, and the cost of edges $X \to Y$ is the similarity between two nodes, x and y, defined as:

$$\mathcal{H}(x,y) = d(x,y) \times u(x,y),$$

where $u(\cdot)$ is the similarity between two nodes and $d(\cdot)$ is the cdf form of relation between error distance and location mapping we determined empirically (see Section 2.1). In other words, we consider the difference between the distributions of terms at two nodes along with the distance between locations. $\mathcal{H}$ outputs low value if the distance between two nodes is close and the nodes shared many terms. We then employed the minimum-cost maximum-flow algorithm [1] to find an optimal flow F that derives maximum flow from U to V with minimum cost. In F, the business

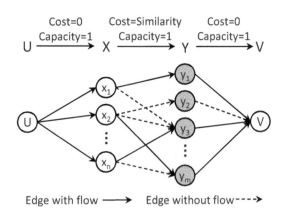

Figure 7: Conceptual description of business naming.

name of node x_i is the name of node y_j if the flow of edge e_{ij} is 1. This approach finds the match between places with a globally-minimum cost. In the list of business name, the name of node y_j is ranked at first, and the rest nodes are ordered by the similarity value.

Personal Name. Personal name is the personalized name of a place given by an individual user, such as *my home* or *my workplace*. Given set X' of a particular user, the problem is to order nodes in X' to ultimately find the most private nodes x. The system considers the places generated by mobile phones since the personal name should be provided in a personalized manner. We ordered nodes $x \in X'$ by familiarity and stay duration to infer the personal names of places. Among the places inferred as residence type, the system considers a place with the highest familiarity as *my home*. Then, excluding the residence type places, the system considers the next place with the highest familiarity as *my workplace*. We cannot directly link to *professional offices* to my workplace. For example, Starbucks should be inferred as my workplace for an employee at Starbucks, but the functional name of the place is *food place*, not *professional offices*.

4. EVALUATION

4.1 Data Collection

We deployed the data collector tool from November 2011 to September 2012 to collect data traces from 70 participants on their primary smartphones. The participants labeled the place names and categories using a user interface for ground truth. The participants also provided the place information offline at the last day of data collection. The average collection period was 94 days, and the median was 60 days. Table 2 presents the description of collected dataset. The collected traces included 3,300 images and 3,800 places over a sampling period of about 174,000 hours. Note that we are currently sharing the collected dataset in the CRAWDAD research communities [14].

We performed the crawling in Foursquare [11] for four months (from May 2012 to September 2012) and restricted spatial regions within Seoul, Korea. The dataset contains 9,200 pictures, 101,200 tips (description about places), and 1,078,100 check-ins at 130,000 locations by 31,000 unique

Table 2: Description of collected data.

| Place Type | CrowdSensing | | Social Networks | | |
	# of Place	# of Image	# of Place	# of Image	# of Posting
Arts & Entertainment	298	152	6,892	786	9,145
College & Universities	815	1,392	5,296	157	3,870
Food Place	1,337	952	46,449	4,750	58,193
Nightlife	129	84	6,212	421	4,188
Outdoors & Sports	136	86	11,909	911	7,758
Residences	183	209	1,768	38	543
Shops & Services	376	260	18,962	699	11,827
Travel & Transport	283	68	5,983	413	1,254
Professional Offices	208	117	21,117	767	10,629
Others	71	21	5,445	233	1,827

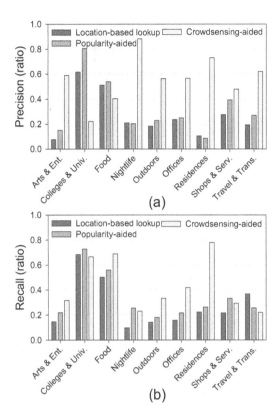

Figure 8: (a) Precision and (b) recall of related systems in functional naming.

users. We only collected the public data that are accessed without private authorization.

4.2 Implementation

We implemented the data collector client in Android SDK 2.2. The WiFi scanning intervals and window size are 2 minutes and 30 seconds, respectively. The tool monitors captured images as event-driven methods. The crawler and backend server were implemented on a Windows 7 server. The crawler collected location and interaction data using Foursquare APIs [11] every 5 minutes. For feature extraction, we set the similarity threshold of WiFi vector to 0.7 for segmenting places with room-level accuracy, as suggested in [13, 7]. We built two sets of residence-time histograms, one for the weekend and one for weekdays, as suggested in [6]. Each histogram bin represents a 30-minute period during a single day (i.e., 48 bins). The dataset derived approximately 12,000 GIST vectors and 60 million SIFT vectors from images. To discretize the large number of features from images, we applied the fast-approximate k-means clustering, provided by [21]. We followed the definition of the functional name provided by Foursquare [11]. We used 10 types of the functional name as presented in Table 2.

4.3 Macro Benchmarks

We validate the overall performance of the proposed system, compared to the related approaches below. Note that we denote the proposed system as *crowdsensing-aided*.

Location-based Lookup. This method estimates similarity between places based on physical distance. We chose the type of closest places for functional naming, and for business naming, we generated a list ordered by distance.

Popularity-aided. This method uses the quantity of interaction data in social networks [18, 24]. The basic assumption is that a user may frequently visit popular places. We used the number of check-ins and posted tips, as suggested by [18], and further utilized the number of uploaded images to determine popularity. The method chooses the most popular place among the nearby places. We considered places within 180 meters error to cover 90% of cases (see Section 2.2).

We used *precision* and *recall* metrics to evaluate the performance of functional naming. The classified type is considered correct if the ground truth is equal to the type with the highest probability. Figure 8 shows the precision and recall of the proposed systems compared with the related methods. Our system outperforms the related methods by 27% precision and 13% recall. The results indicate that user behavior

and environmental features are more effective than distance or popularity for inferring the functional name. Our system shows relatively worse precision in colleges and food places, as shown in Figure 8(a). The reason is that (1) the outputs of location-based lookup and popularity-aided method tend to be biased as food places; and (2) the distance metric works well for college and university places since those places are located densely in certain regions. This phenomenon is presented as a confusion matrix in Figure 9. Location-based lookup and popularity-aided methods infer about 34% of places as food places, due to the large number of samples of food places in social networks. Compared to the related approaches that showed 33±20% accuracy, the proposed system correctly infers the type of 56±18% places.

Regarding the performance of the proposed system in business naming, we define the accuracy of business naming as the order of places in the generated list. For example, 20% accuracy for top-5 indicates that the order of the actual place is less than five in the list for 20% of cases. The proposed system generates 29±8% higher accuracy than the related methods, as illustrated in Figure 10(a). Our system correctly inferred the business name in 38% of the cases, and 84% of places are within 10 places in the generated list. The result indicates that the semantic features from sensing data enable the precise recognition that is missed by using explicit features, such as distance or popularity. The proposed system provides less than 6.7 ranks for 80% of cases, but location-based lookup and popularity-aided output less than 22.8 and 69 ranks for 70% of cases, respectively, as shown in Figure 10(b). Considering that higher rank means greater burden on the user, the results reveal that our system

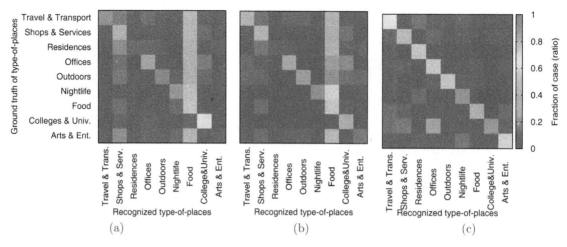

(a)　　　　　　(b)　　　　　　(c)

Figure 9: Confusion matrix of functional naming in (a) location-based lookup, (b) popularity-aided, and (c) the proposed system.

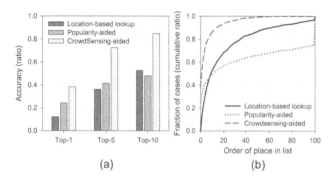

(a)　　　　　　(b)

Figure 10: (a) Accuracy of related systems in business naming and (b) the CDF form of order of all places. Left-most curve indicates better results for business naming.

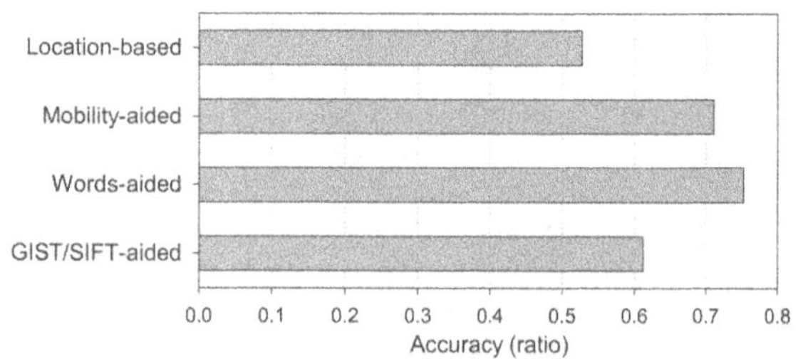

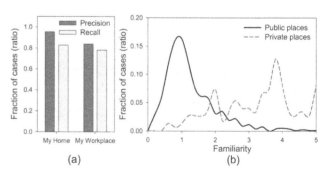

Figure 11: Accuracy of business naming in top-10 list used by different features.

greatly reduces user intervention by integrating the sensing system for place naming.

Figure 11 shows the accuracy of business naming, using different features and sources of data in isolation. Based on the use of physical location, we additionally used the features such as mobility data, words from OCR classifier and posting, and GIST/SIFT features from images. The performance gains obtained with using mobility and words are relatively larger than using GIST/SIFT features. The result indicates that the written words in the place are meaningful to differentiate the places, and people exhibit similar stay behaviors at the same place. The indoor scene classification (i.e., GIST/SIFT features) operates poorly in business naming, although the features are effective to recognize the place types [5].

For personal naming, we ignored the comparison with the related methods, as we needed private authorization to collect personal information from social networks. The proposed system correctly infers 89±8% of personal places, as shown in Figure 12(a). *My home* shows relatively higher precision and recall than *my workplace/school* because of unique stay patterns at home. The errors in recognizing my workplace/school occurred in participants with multiple places considered as workplace or school. Familiarity

Figure 12: (a) Precision and recall for personal naming and (b) distribution of familiarity in public and private places.

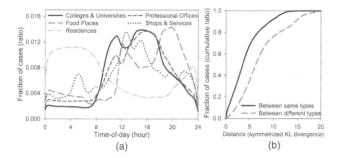

(a)

Figure 13: (a) Stay behavior pattern in several types of places and (b) similarity of patterns. The leftmost curve indicates higher similarity.

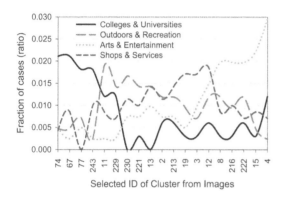

Figure 14: Distribution of terms mined from images.

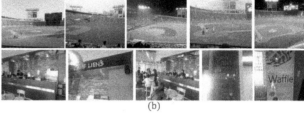

(b)

Figure 15: Example images (a) in the same cluster and (b) at the two places.

effectively measured the privateness of places, as presented in Figure 12(b). The private places show relatively higher familiarity than the public places, because of regular visit patterns on private places.

4.4 Micro Benchmarks

In exploring the discriminative power of each feature on the performance of the proposed system, we find that features regarding a user's behavior are robust for functional naming, and the environmental features mined from images or postings are effective for business naming.

Figure 13(a) presents the residence-time distribution of several place types on weekdays. We found that the stay behaviors have strong features that can differentiate some types (e.g., residences and food places), but several types (e.g., colleges and professional offices) are confused, due to similar stay patterns. We further investigated the difference of distributions between places, as shown in Figure 13(b). The figure illustrates the Kullback-Leibler divergence [15] between the residence-time distributions. The results indicate that places of the same type have higher similarities compared to places of different types.

We highlight the characteristics of the environmental features mined from images (i.e., GIST, SIFT, and OCR words). Figure 14 presents the distribution of attributes mined from images. We presented a few selected attributes since the semantic features from images were sparsely distributed over a large number of attributes. The result shows that clustered terms were observed differently on some types of places that can differentiate places. The example images in the same cluster inferred as food place are presented in Figure 15(a).

The images contains cups or bowls with round shapes that derived similar terms. Similarly, the terms mined from images at the same place show consistent patterns since those images contains similar scene or local objects, as illustrated in Figure 15(b).

In OCR words cases, the system observed a high frequency of OCR words in *food places* and most images captured at *shopping* and *travel and transport* contained written words, as illustrated in Figure 16. The words were mostly mined from images capturing store signs, menus, or a direction boards in a place. To filter out noisy results, we utilized the confidence score provided by the OCR engine. Figure 17(a) shows that false positives decrease as the threshold of confidence score increases. The result shows that even though the classifier produces noisy results, reliable results can be obtained using high threshold of confidence. The side-effect of this approach is a significant drop in true positives, but the system still extracts sufficient amount of results due to the large amounts of data collected by crowdsensing and crowdsourcing. We set the threshold of confidence as 300 to obtain high precision with small loss in recall, as illustrated in Figure 17(b). The low recall indicates that the classifier would require further investigation to obtain more classified features from noisy images. Table 3 indicates that major words on different types of places reflected the characteristics of places.

Finally, we explored the relationship between the number of samples and the performance of the proposed system. Intuitively, as shown in Figure 18, the more data leads a more accurate result. We found that a larger number of visits induced better accuracy in functional naming, and a greater number of images is effective for business naming. Places with more than 100 visits showed 80% of accuracy, while more than 20 images derived 4.3±4.9 ranks in the list. The reason is that the number of matched features of the same places increases with the number of images. The visitations would increase as time goes by in daily life, but the collection of images requires the active user participation. Considering that 9.7% of places in SNS and 34% of places in crowdsens-

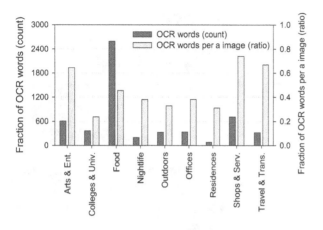

Figure 16: Distribution of recognized OCR words in several types of places.

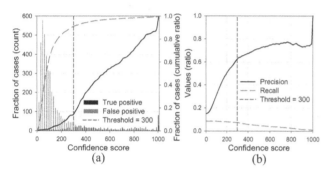

Figure 17: (a) Distribution of confidence score in OCR and (b) precision and recall according to confidence score.

ing contain image data, the reward for data collection is required to induce user participation.

5. RELATED WORK

Extensive studies have been conducted recently to extract advanced information on places, beyond simple raw coordinates. We discuss related work in three different domains: place naming, local search and recommendation, and place segmentation.

Place Naming. Lin et al. [19] analyzed people's preferences in place naming and defined the hierarchical relation of place naming taxonomy. They designed a model to predict the desired types of place names that people would use when naming in a given situation. The system, however, did not solve the problem of actual place naming. We followed their taxonomy and solved the problem of place naming in practice.

The work by Lian et al. [18] is the most relevant to our work. They designed a model to infer the current place in a given GPS point. They used check-in histories at social network websites and the quantity of interaction at location review websites, including popularity, visit frequency, and temporal information of stay. Our work improves the past works in many ways. We exploit more attributes captured by mobile phones that have not been previously covered. Our system also provides place names without user intervention.

Table 3: Top OCR words on several types of places.

Place Type	Top OCR Words
Arts & Entertainment	size, movement, sequence, lotte, mayor, world, march, admission, cctv, cinema, fantasy, films
Food Place	coffee, set, menu, café, open, lunch, free, rice, special, tea, all, close, noodles, take, chicken
Nightlife	wine, band, bar, cinnamon, glass, non, open, sparkling, available, blending, cocktail, dinner
Outdoors & Sports	forest, park, playground, cafeteria, center, children, fee, holidays, information, operation
Shops & Services	keep, new, shop, sale, thinking, fax, free, lucky, open, point, smart, women, accessory, best
Travel & Transport	airport, express, seoul, airways, america, center, departure, Incheon, seat, transfer
Professional Offices	room, public, rest, consulting, information, korea, library, service, smart, team, www

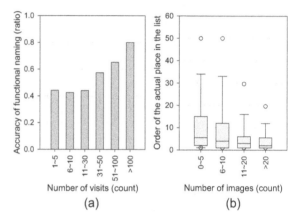

Figure 18: (a) Relation between number of stays and accuracy of functional naming and (b) box plot of relation between number of images and the order. Box indicates lower quartile, median, upper quartile and whisker indicates 10% and 90% of observation.

Recently, several works have focused on the inference of functional name of a place. Works in [4, 28, 5] used various features, such as number of radio beacons [4], phone usage [28], stay duration [4, 5], or captured images [5]. Ye et al. [27] employed check-in histories on social networks. They focused on three types of functional name (nightlife, food place, shopping place). Our previous work [5] used the topic modeling approach to infer the functional name of places. The system used image and audio data captured by mobile phone to characterize places into 7 categories. The system is, however, required to label the place name manually by smartphone users. In this paper, we utilized the feature extraction method in [5] and integrated the knowledge found in SNS to provide autonomous place naming without user intervention. Additionally, we designed the place naming method from a person's perspective (i.e., functional, business, personal name). Our system now provides autonomous naming even for business and personal name of places. This was not covered in [5].

Local Search and Recommendation. Research on local search and place recommendation produced the ranked list of relevant places based on user queries or contexts. Diverse approaches are used to estimate relevance between places. Shankar et al. [24] used public interaction data in social networks, CLR [17] employed similarity between users, and Hapori [16] used time, weather, and activity of users as given contexts. We utilized these works to estimate relevances, and we further provided the actual name of a place automatically, by combining smartphone data and SNS data.

Place Segmentation. Research on place segmentation recognized point-of-interest in user trajectories. Most studies have used the fingerprint method of surrounding radio beacons, such as Bluetooth [26] or WiFi access points [26, 7]. The basic idea is that the signal strengths of radio beacons are similar when a user stays in a certain place. We utilized radio-based place learning to segment places at room-level accuracy and generated stay duration in places.

6. DISCUSSION

We discuss the limitations of the proposed system, along with future research directions. We also highlight a number of areas that require further investigation.

Privacy. Although our data collector enables the deletion of collected data, uploading raw images into the server has privacy concerns in practice. Here, one possible solution is to process the classifiers locally in smartphones. For example, instead of uploading raw data, smartphone extracts OCR words, GIST, or SIFT features and uploads these features to server in an unordered manner. To realize this local processing technique, we need an efficient classifier with low complexity and also a job scheduler that would execute classifying/uploading operations when the device is relatively under usage (e.g., night time with battery charging). Meanwhile, one thing we counter-intuitively found in our study is that, many participants are willing to share pictures publically with others. In fact, social network users are already sharing many images, when interacting with others. Therefore, we believe that local data processing may accelerate the active and voluntary participation of end users in crowdsensing framework.

Incremental Learning. The proposed system required an non-trivial amount time of data processing in our server (several hours of processing in Intel i7 CPU 860 server with 8GB RAM). The major workload in the server is to process the learning components (i.e., feature extraction and clustering). Considering that we, in our work, used data collected in only one city and the amount of data is rapidly increasing with a widespread use of smartphones and SNS, the data processing issue is practically a big challenge in crowdsensing framework. We believe that an incremental learning scheme would be necessary to handle a large volume of data efficiently in real life.

User Participation. The proposed system requires knowledge from crowdsourcing to infer the place name. Our work expands the coverage problem on place naming by applying the SNS knowledge to information collected with the crowdsensing approach. However, the system is not able to learn additional names that are not in SNS. To solve this limitation, the system should somehow support generating new names, or at least provide a method to encourage users to put their knowledge back into SNS. Generating new names is beyond the scope of our research. We, instead, plan to investigate a reward system to induce active user participation in crowdsensing approach. Considering that SNS is missing about 22% of the places visited in daily life (see Section 2.1), an appropriate rewarding mechanism would greatly improve the coverage of place naming.

7. CONCLUSION

In this paper, we proposed an autonomous place naming system for providing place names according to three types. Our system leverages the place characteristics mined from opportunistically crowdsensed data using smartphones and crowdsourced information in social networks. By integrating sensing system and exploiting crowdsourcing to gather large volumes of data, our system is able to provide place name from a person's perspective, beyond raw location coordinates.

Our study presents the possibility of linking sensing systems to social networks, toward the advanced understanding of human life. The proposed system provides rich awareness of the places that have been annotated manually by users in previous works. Such advanced information is a building block for many context-aware applications, such as city-scale activity recognition, mobile advertising, or enhanced place recommendations. Our future work includes study on a crowdsensing framework that will explore effective incentives to encourage active participation of end users.

8. ACKNOWLEDGMENT

We sincerely thank the 70 data donators among LifeMap users in Korea. This work was supported by the National Research Foundation of Korea grant funded by the Korean government, Ministry of Education, Science and Technology (No.2011-0006464, No.2012-0005522).

9. REFERENCES

[1] R. K. Ahuja, T. L. Magnanti, and J. B. Orlin. *Network Flows: Theory, Algorithms, and Applications*. Prentice-Hall, Inc., 1993.

[2] C. Antoniak. Mixtures of dirichlet processes with applications to bayesian nonparametric problems. *The Annals of Statistics*, 2(6):1152–1174, 1974.

[3] Y. Chon and H. Cha. Lifemap: A smartphone-based context provider for location-based services. *Pervasive Computing, IEEE*, 10(2):58–67, April-June 2011.

[4] Y. Chon, Y. Kim, H. Shin, and H. Cha. Topic modeling-based semantic annotation of places using personal behavior and environmental features. In *Proceedings of Nokia Mobile Data Challenge Workshop, in Conjunction with Pervasive'12*, 2012.

[5] Y. Chon, N. D. Lane, F. Li, H. Cha, and F. Zhao. Automatically characterizing places with opportunistic crowdsensing using smartphones. In *Proceedings of the 14th International Conference on Ubiquitous Computing*, Ubicomp'12, pages 206–212. ACM, 2012.

[6] Y. Chon, H. Shin, E. Talipov, and H. Cha. Evaluating mobility models for temporal prediction with high-granularity mobility data. In *Proceedings of the 10th International Conference on Pervasive Computing and Communications*, PerCom'12, pages 206–212. IEEE, 2012.

[7] Y. Chon, E. Talipov, H. Shin, and H. Cha. Mobility prediction-based smartphone energy optimization for everyday location monitoring. In *Proceedings of the 9th ACM Conference on Embedded Networked Sensor Systems*, SenSys'11, pages 82–95. ACM, 2011.

[8] G. Colombo, M. Chorley, M. Williams, S. Allen, and R. Whitaker. You are where you eat: Foursquare

checkins as indicators of human mobility and behaviour. In *Proceedings of the 10th International Conference on Pervasive Computing and Communications Workshops*, PerMoby'12, pages 217–222. IEEE, 2012.

[9] J. Cranshaw, E. Toch, J. Hong, A. Kittur, and N. Sadeh. Bridging the gap between physical location and online social networks. In *Proceedings of the 12th ACM international conference on Ubiquitous computing*, Ubicomp '10, pages 119–128. ACM, 2010.

[10] J. Du, Q. Huo, L. Sun, and J. Sun. Snap and translate using windows phone. In *2011 International Conference on Document Analysis and Recognition*, ICDAR'11, pages 809 –813. IEEE, 2011.

[11] Foursquare Inc. Foursquare. `http://foursquare.com`.

[12] P. Jaccard. The distribution of the flora in the alpine zone. *New Phytologist*, 11(2):37–50, 1912.

[13] D. H. Kim, Y. Kim, D. Estrin, and M. B. Srivastava. Sensloc: sensing everyday places and paths using less energy. In *Proceedings of the 8th ACM Conference on Embedded Networked Sensor Systems*, SenSys '10, pages 43–56. ACM, 2010.

[14] D. Kotz and T. Henderson. Crawdad: A community resource for archiving wireless data at dartmouth. *IEEE Pervasive Computing*, 4(4):12–14, Oct.-Dec. 2005.

[15] S. Kullback and R. Leibler. On information and sufficiency. *Annals of Mathematical Statistics*, 22(1):79–86, 1951.

[16] N. D. Lane, D. Lymberopoulos, F. Zhao, and A. T. Campbell. Hapori: Context-based local search for mobile phones using community behavioral modeling and similarity. In *Proceedings of the 12th International Conference on Ubiquitous Computing*, Ubicomp'10, pages 109–118. ACM, 2010.

[17] K. W.-T. Leung, D. L. Lee, and W.-C. Lee. Clr: a collaborative location recommendation framework based on co-clustering. In *Proceedings of the 34th annual international ACM SIGIR conference on Research and development in information retrieval*, SIGIR '11, pages 305–314. ACM, 2011.

[18] D. Lian and X. Xie. Learning location naming from user check-in histories. In *Proceedings of the 19th ACM SIGSPATIAL International Conference on Advances in Geographic Information Systems*, GIS '11, pages 112–121. ACM, 2011.

[19] J. Lin, G. Xiang, J. I. Hong, and N. Sadeh. Modeling people's place naming preferences in location sharing. In *Proceedings of the 12th ACM international conference on Ubiquitous computing*, Ubicomp '10, pages 75–84. ACM, 2010.

[20] D. G. Lowe. Object recognition from local scale-invariant features. In *Proceedings of the 7th IEEE International Conference on Computer Vision*, ICCV'99, pages 1150–1157. IEEE, 1999.

[21] M. Muja and D. G. Lowe. Fast approximate nearest neighbors with automatic algorithm configuration. In *International Conference on Computer Vision Theory and Applications*, VISAPP'09, pages 331–340, 2009.

[22] A. Oliva and A. Torralba. Modeling the shape of the scene: A holistic representation of the spatial envelope. *International Journal of Computer Vision*, 42(3):145–175, 2001.

[23] G. Salton and C. Buckley. Term-weighting approaches in automatic text retrieval. *Information Processing and Management*, 24(5):513–523, 1988.

[24] P. Shankar, Y.-W. Huang, P. Castro, B. Nath, and L. Iftode. Crowds replace experts: Building better location-based services using mobile social network interactions. In *Proceedings of the 10th International Conference on Pervasive Computing and Communications*, PerCom'12, pages 20–29. IEEE, 2012.

[25] S. Tominaga, M. Shimosaka, R. Fukui, and T. Sato. A unified framework for modeling and predicting going-out behavior. In *Proceedings of the 10th International Conference on Pervasive Computing*, Pervasive'12, pages 73–90. Springer, 2012.

[26] L. Vu, Q. Do, and K. Nahrstedt. Jyotish: A novel framework for constructing predictive model of people movement from join wifi/bluetooth trace. In *Proceedings of the 9th International Conference on Pervasive Computing and Communications*, PerCom'11, pages 54–62. IEEE, 2011.

[27] M. Ye, D. Shou, W.-C. Lee, P. Yin, and K. Janowicz. On the semantic annotation of places in location-based social networks. In *Proceedings of the 17th ACM SIGKDD international conference on Knowledge discovery and data mining*, KDD '11, pages 520–528. ACM, 2011.

[28] Y. Zhu, E. Zhong, Z. Lu, and Q. Yang. Feature engineering for place category classification. In *Proceedings of Nokia Mobile Data Challenge Workshop, in Conjunction with Pervasive'12*, 2012.

Matchstick: A Room-to-Room Thermal Model for Predicting Indoor Temperature from Wireless Sensor Data

Carl Ellis
School of Computing and
Communications
Lancaster University
United Kingdom
c.ellis@comp.lancs.ac.uk

Mike Hazas
School of Computing and
Communications
Lancaster University
United Kingdom
hazas@comp.lancs.ac.uk

James Scott
Microsoft Research
Cambridge
United Kingdom
jws@microsoft.com

ABSTRACT

In this paper we present a room-to-room thermal model used to accurately predict temperatures in residential buildings. We evaluate the accuracy of this model with ground truth data from four occupied family homes (two in the UK and two in the US). The homes have differing construction and a range of heating infrastructure (wall-mounted radiators, underfloor heating, and furnace-driven forced-air). Data was gathered using a network of simple and sparse (one per room) temperature sensors, a gas meter sensor, and an outdoor temperature sensor. We show that our model can predict future indoor temperature trends with a 90th percentile aggregate error between 0.61–1.50°C, when given boiler or furnace actuation times and outdoor temperature forecasts. Two existing models were also implemented and then evaluated on our dataset alongside Matchstick. As a proof of concept, we used data from a previous control study to show that when Matchstick is used to predict temperatures (rather than assuming a preset linear heating rate) the possible gas savings increase by up to 3%.

Categories and Subject Descriptors

H.4 [**Information Systems Applications**]: Miscellaneous

General Terms

Algorithms

Keywords

Thermal Modelling; Prediction; Forced Air; Radiators; Underfloor Heating; Home Automation

1. INTRODUCTION

Home space heating systems use the largest share of energy for domestic homes in the United Kingdom. In 2009, space heating accounted for 62% of the total domestic energy consumed [1, 2]. Next to transportation, space heating is the second most energy intensive end-use in the UK. In the United States, the situation is similar with domestic space heating using 56% percent of the domestic energy share [3, 4].

Homes in the UK and US are typically equipped with a programmable thermostat, which occupants can use to specify desired temperatures ("setpoints" or "setbacks") for particular time intervals in the day. During the times when heating or cooling is required, the programmable thermostat actuates the heating, ventilation, and air conditioning (HVAC) infrastructure to bring the ambient temperature near the desired setpoint. The ambient temperature is typically that reported by a sensor contained in the programmable thermostat (often in a hallway or living room).

Prior work in the sensor network and ubiquitous computing communities has worked to improve upon such strict timer-based heating, using occupancy-reactive and arrival-predictive control [5, 6, 7]. These methods yield savings and may improve comfort during occupied times when compared to static, programmed timer schedules. However, these utilised simple heating models for their houses. Some rely upon a single measure of indoor temperature (rather than per-room) and all assume a constant, linear increase in temperature for heating periods (e.g. 0.3°C per 10 min).

Complementary to both traditional programmable thermostats and these energy approaches, a heating model could allow future temperature trends to be predicted using the current heating schedule. This allows heat controllers to verify the expected outcomes of their decisions, and adapt to different conditions. Heating controllers need to be able to answer the question "If the heat turns on now will the house be warm enough?". This might be answered by assuming a constant heating rate, but this fails to account for weather and inter-room effects.

This paper proposes that simple temperature sensors (one per room), combined with real-time algorithms can be applied to live data to enhance control solutions. The parameterised model we propose has two defining features. First, it recognises that different spaces heat and cool in different ways and at different times—not only due to insulation, but also due to the thermal masses in the heating infrastructure. Second, it automatically identifies rooms which appear to have a thermal relationship. We employ this model to provide two contributions. (1) We characterise the model's predictive performance, showing the two-hour lookahead error to be 1.50°C or better (90% confidence level) for all four houses. (2) We highlight the energy savings opportunities which would have been possible by detailing (for two houses) how the predictive model would have turned on heating later but still brought the house to setpoint by the desired time.

Compared to methodologies others have applied in buildings research [8, 9, 10, 11] our method is notable in that it uses data from deployments in occupied family homes across two countries; and it has a longer viable forecast length. We evaluate our model on a month of per-room data for four houses with different construction and heating systems, and analyse the error characteristics down to the room level.

2. RELATED WORK

There are two general types of approach for modelling a building's internal thermal interactions: process-driven and data-driven. These are also known as forward system identification and inverse system identification [12], respectively.

Process driven solutions use complex system equations based upon thermodynamic principles, and materials science. Detailed surveys provide the inputs needed for these equations, such as thermal conductance values, heat capacity, material thickness, solar incidence, and room dimensions.

Process-driven approaches have received much attention in the literature, and many tools exist to aid in their development and use. Large buildings use building information models (BIMs), which is designed at the architect's office, refined during the construction process, and then handed over to the building manager. BIMs include exact dimensions, locations, and materials of the building's components. With such detailed survey data available, process-based approaches can input a this data into a specific HVAC simulation to assess and predict the heating within the building.

There are trade industry software platforms which perform process-driven modelling, such as EnergyPlus, maintained by the US Department of Energy.[1] It should be noted that in general, EnergyPlus works over climate-sized timescales of months or years, and is designed to inform choices among HVAC technologies, layout and configuration. By contrast, data-driven solutions have the capacity to be much more fine-grained, informing real-time daily or hourly control.

Dounis et al [8] used the TRNSYS [13] simulator to model temperature whilst actuating windows to control indoor air quality. A single room was simulated with an RMS error of 0.29°C, but with residuals as high as 1.5°C.

Data driven approaches use models that are based on derived Equivalent Thermal Parameters (ETPs) [14] instead of parameters from a survey. ETPs are derived by statistical regression or neural networks [12] and used to find parameters which fit a training period of data. The parameters can be refined or updated as more data is gathered.

Coley and Penman [9] used a recursive least squares algorithm to build an inverse thermal model of a single room of a school. This model used sensor data every thirty minutes and it took ten days for the model parameters to converge. The parameter space was restricted so that the dynamic effects from input could overcome the inertia of past predictions (akin to the gain of a Kalman filter). The model had an RMS error of 1°C. It was envisioned that significant

change in model parameters against historical data would indicate deterioration of the building.

Smith et al [15] used a per-zone linear regressive model to predict a room's temperature 30 minutes into the future. The model used vent level actuation of an American home and supported zonal interactions. Environmental effects such as outdoor temperature, wind, and sunlight were captured and modelled during system off times and used in subsequent heating periods. The predictive model error was within ±2°F (±1.11°C) of ground truth.

Hybrid solutions normally begin with a detailed survey, on which an initial model is based. Live data is then fed in for refinement and to track changing values in the face of environmental and occupant-driven influences.

Mejri, Barrio, and Ghrab-Morcos [10] created a simulation system for modelling office buildings. Using sensor networks to record temperature and electrical load every hour, combined with room volumes, a whole-building thermal model was designed. This model was only applied to office buildings as the interiors and heating schedules rarely change. In simulations, the whole-building model showed an RMS error of 0.7°C.

Spindler and Norford [11] created a multi-zone (each zone had more than one room) model for mixed-mode cooling strategies. The building was surveyed to measure material values and air flow properties, combined with a week of live thermocouple data to refine the accuracy of the survey. The model accounted for thermal resistance and mass effect by using an empirically-chosen number of measurements into the past. The RMS error of most zones was 0.3–0.4°C.

Oldewurtel et al [16] discussed Stochastic Model Predictive Control (SMPC) which augments a process driven building system with a weather model that has stochastic errors. Current building measurements were fed back into the control system along with weather forecasts. The control algorithm was applied to a range of simulated buildings. It was shown that using weather predictions improved control decisions. A weather prediction horizon of one day could be used with only a 5% deviation from the ideal control schema.

Compared to the literature, we provide a model which relies on **simple and sparse (one per room) sensors**. Further, we model each room **individually** to take into account different heating elements. We also show a savings analysis when using the model with sensor data from **real occupied homes**, rather than a test cell.

3. DEPLOYMENTS

Sensors were deployed and data gathered from two homes in the United Kingdom, and two homes in the United States. A variety of sensors were used: in the UK homes custom sensors based on the .NET Gadgeteer [17] framework; and in the US homes iButton Thermochron sensors. The UK homes' data is from a previous heating control study [7], where each room's radiator could be actuated independently. All the deployments were over various winter periods in 2010–2011. The houses were designated UK1, UK2, US1, and US2. The deployment characteristics are summarised in Table 1.

In the UK deployments, a wireless sensor network was deployed which communicated its measurements using an 802.15.4 radio network to a server PC located in the house. Per-room temperature data was logged at a rate of once every five seconds; whole-house gas measurements were taken directly from the utility meters using a pulse counter sen-

---

[1]http://apps1.eere.energy.gov/buildings/energyplus/

Table 1: House Characteristics

Name	Location	Date	Floors	Rooms	Heating System
UK1	Southern UK	28th Jan – 25th Feb 2011	2	13	Underfloor/Wall-mounted
UK2	Southern UK	2nd Feb – 2nd Mar 2011	3	15	Wall-mounted
US1	Northwest US	8th Dec – 6th Jan 2012	3	12	Forced air
US2	Northwest US	8th Dec – 6th Jan 2012	2	15	Forced air

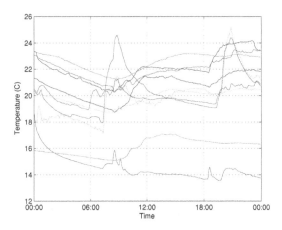

Figure 1: House with primarily underfloor heating (UK1); high thermal mass and per-room control

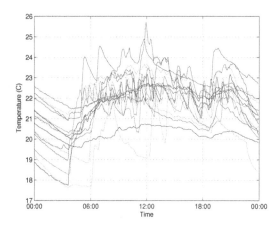

Figure 2: House with wall-mounted radiators (UK2); low thermal mass and per-room control

sor, and had a resolution dependent on the particular utility meter. Outdoor temperature was gathered from a local weather station deployed on the roof of a research building in the same city. Thermostatic radiator valves (TRVs) were actuated by using HouseHeat FHT-8Vs and controlled by the central PC. Readings were downsampled to one measurement per five minutes, for use in our experiments.

In the US deployments, twenty iButton Thermochrons were deployed, with at least one sensor in each room of the houses. For large rooms in open plan designs (e.g. a "great room"), two or three sensors were used. Furthermore, one iButton was placed outside to gather outdoor temperature, and another was placed directly on the furnace in order to sense actuation times. (The furnaces consume a near-constant amount of gas when they are on, so it was not necessary to meter the gas directly.) The sensors sampled temperature once every ten minutes, for a total of four weeks.

3.1 Building Characteristics

UK1 is a recently constructed detached two-floor building with a gas boiler, and underfloor heating on the ground floor. Rooms on the upper floor are in their own heating zone and are heated using TRV-equipped radiators. UK2 is a three-floor mid-terraced 19th century house with wall-mounted convection radiators. US1 and US2 are in the north-west of the USA and utilise forced air heating systems, powered by a furnace.

Looking at a sample of per-room temperatures for each type of heating infrastructure (Figures 1, 2 and 3), it is clear that there is a high temperature variance between rooms located within the same building (up to 5°C). And, underfloor heating in UK1 creates very different temperature

trends, compared to the convection heaters of UK2 and the US houses. Convection radiators rapidly bring rooms up to temperature while underfloor heating causes a gradual temperature change. This can be explained when looking at the properties of the different heating systems.

Radiators heat up quickly and are in direct contact with the air, causing the room to heat quickly. Similarly, forced-air systems literally pump hot air into a room. Underfloor systems are embedded in concrete floors which heat very slowly. Effects like these provide good motivation for modelling on a per-room basis, and this is especially true when the heating infrastructure has different heat transfer properties in different rooms. In Figure 1, the upper floor radiators' spiky temperature trends can be seen alongside that of the more gradual underfloor heating.

Figures 2 and 3 show temperature trends from houses with low thermal mass heating infrastructure: UK1 and US1, respectively. However, UK1 has per-room control that adapts to occupancy which means that different rooms might be heating up and cooling off simultaneously, as opposed to all rooms heating and cooling at the same time as in US1.

4. MODELLING

Having surveyed the literature, we decided to use a regression based optimisation model rather than a Kalman filter. We made this decision based on scalability, as optimisation based models can be split by room and trained separately, while existing Kalman filter–based models have been formulated such that all room parameters are trained together. This means that optimisation methods can scale pseudo-linearly while Kalman filters scale in a cubic manner, due to matrix inversions.

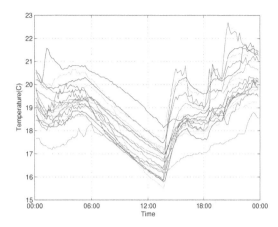

Figure 3: House with forced air convection heating (US1); low thermal mass and whole-house control

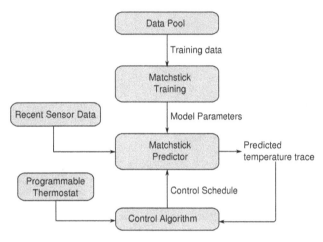

Figure 4: Flow diagram of Matchstick being used by a control algorithm

4.1 Model Overview

Our proposed model, *Matchstick*, takes into account room-to-room interactions, thermal mass delays, and outside temperature. It uses a non-linear transformation of gas use to better reflect the thermal mass present in each rooms' heating element and structure. We now discuss each of these model components and then discuss how Matchstick fits to each room in a building using logged data to periodically retrain, and how Matchstick predicts future thermal states.

Matchstick fits between the heating scheduler, such as a programmable thermostat or an occupancy predictor which dictates setpoint and setback times, and the controller of a heating system. Once it has trained on historical data, Matchstick uses current sensor measurements combined with the proposed heating schedule and then predicts what will happen. Then, using this knowledge, a heating controller can adjust the schedule until it reflects the intent of the program; saving gas and/or increasing comfort. A high-level image of how Matchstick interacts with sensor networks and control algorithms is shown in Figure 4.

An interesting feature of the domestic heating systems that we have observed is the delay between thermal energy

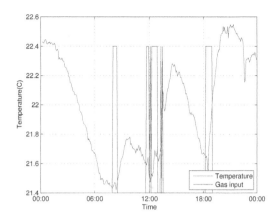

Figure 5: Temperature change and gas input for a room with underfloor heating

input, change of the heating element temperature, and ambient indoor air temperature. This is due to the thermal mass of the heat delivery system. The delay can be easily observed when looking at the plots of gas usage and room temperature, as shown in Figure 5. The room temperature continues to rise long after the boiler has stopped firing.

Air temperature is slower to rise with heating infrastructures involving large thermal masses and/or low conductivity (e.g. the underfloor system in UK1).

To account for this, we create a recursive non-linear transform function $g()$, which takes the raw gas usage for a heating system and the current valve state (in our study, either fully open or closed) for that radiator and outputs the thermal energy transfered into the air at time t:

$$\begin{aligned} g(G_t, R_{T_n}) &= \sigma(t).R_{T_n}{}^2 \\ \sigma(t) &= \sigma(t-1)(1 - R_{T_n}{}^2) + G_t \end{aligned} \quad (1)$$

These equations model the energy-storing nature of heating infrastructure, and how heat continues to be stored and radiated once the energy input (in our case, natural gas usage G_t) is off. $\sigma(t)$ represents the thermal energy stored in the room's heating element (i.e. the metal radiator or concrete floor) at time t. The amount of heat which is emitted is dependent on the thermal time constant (R_{T_n}) of the heating element, which is represented as a scalar value between 0 (no storage: energy output is immediate and equal to the gas energy input at that time), and 1 (infinite storage: all energy is stored and does not contribute to room air temperature).

R_T is empirically determined by searching the solution space $[0, 1]$ and finding the value which gives the smallest mean squared error when training the model with historic data. Figure 6 shows the energy output when compared to a sampled room's raw gas input for different values of R_T.

Other techniques to model heat dynamics use infrastructural temperatures (e.g. pipes, radiators) directly. To properly parameterise this property would have required at least one additional sensor per room, which goes beyond what one might reasonably expect in a typical home.

As shown in Section 3.1, there is a large temperature variance between different rooms in a house. As such there will be internal interactions between rooms which can be modelled as thermal flows. To model these flows, first a map of neighbouring rooms is needed. Then, these interactions

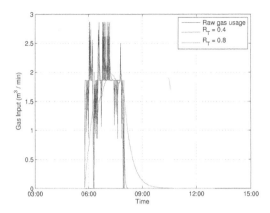

Figure 6: Equivalent gas output for different vales of R_{T_n}

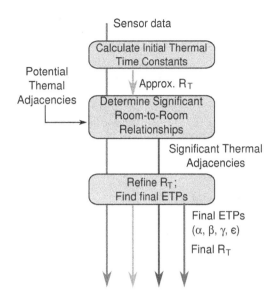

Figure 7: Flow diagram of Matchstick training, showing where variables are created and the flow through the procedure. Thermal resistance, adjacencies, and the training data are used for predictions.

must be expressed in the final system equation. However, the definition of a neighbouring room can be ambiguous. Further, depending on the building materials and heating layout, some neighbouring rooms may have little thermal flow.

To make the system model representative of reality, and to create a mapping of *significant* thermal flows between neighbours, we take an initial list of potential thermal neighbours for each room and trim them down using statistical methods.

The initial list of physically proximate neighbours is a necessary restriction to be placed upon the model training. Starting with an initial list of every room would show correlation over indirect properties such as sharing the same heating zone or having similar radiator settings. The list of neighbours does represent a small amount of survey data which must be provided to the model. However, much of this data can be obtained through sensor adjacency information, determined in an algorithmic way such as those described by Lu and Whitehouse [18]. In this way, the initial neighbour list can be generated automatically for each room, eliminating a dependence on user-supplied survey data.

To determine the thermally significant neighbours, a recursive likelihood test is performed. Initially, the model is fitted with no neighbours, and then a likelihood-ratio test is performed against a model with each possible neighbour fitted. The likelihood ratio test allows a p-value to be computed for rejection of the null hypothesis (which in this case is the reduced model). If the null hypothesis is rejected, the most likely neighbour is added to the reduced model, and the process is repeated until the null hypothesis is accepted. The neighbouring rooms added to the model are then classed as a room's significant neighbours. The p-value used to reject the null hypothesis was $p=0.2$.

4.2 Fitting the Matchstick model

Matchstick is an adaptive model which, for each day and room, determines which rooms have significant thermal connections and the thermal resistance of the heating elements. It also determines how the outdoor temperature affects each room. Model regression was performed by using MATLAB's `lsqcurvefit` function, which solves non-linear least squares problems. A high-level diagram of the Matchstick training procedure is shown in Figure 7.

Matchstick takes its training data, and initially without

setting any significant neighbours for any room, performs a search on the R_{T_n} thermal time constant for each room. Then, using the R_{T_n} values from the first stage, each room then takes its list of potential thermal neighbours and performs likelihood tests to form a list of thermally significant neighbours for each room. Finally, the R_{T_n} space is searched again, this time with thermally significant neighbours specified in the model. This allows for more accurate R_{T_n} values as heat gains from neighbouring rooms correlate with the neighbouring thermal data, rather than the gas input. The final calculated model ETPs are then used as parameters for prediction, along with the final R_{T_n} values, and the lists of thermally significant neighbours.

The mathematical form of Matchstick's system equations is as follows:

$$
\begin{aligned}
\forall n \in N, \ T_n(t+1) \ = \ & \alpha_t . T_n(t) + \alpha_g . g\Big(G(t), R_{T_n}\Big) + ... \\
& \sum_{j \in \text{neigh}(i)} \Big(\beta_{nj} . T_j(t)\Big) + ... \\
& \gamma_o . TO(t) + \epsilon,
\end{aligned}
\tag{2}
$$

where N is the set of all rooms, T_n is the temperature of room n, G is the gas used, and TO is the outside temperature. The ETPs [14] in the model represent loss of heat from the room (α_t), heat transfer from the heating system (α_g), transfer of heat from thermally significant neighbouring rooms (β_{nj}), and the heat transfer with the outside (γ_o). The system model describes how the last known temperature and thermal output affects a room, together with neighbouring room thermal flows, and environmental measurements.

Given the present temperature for each room (measured by sensors), and with forecasts for the outside temperature, this system model can then be used to predict how rooms in a house will react under different heating schedules. For example, if a room only needed to be at its set point 30 minutes before the end of a heating schedule, then the heating can be switched off earlier. A control algorithm can use

Table 2: Summary of per-room temperature prediction error

House	90th percentile range		
	0.5 hour prediction window	2 hour prediction window	6 hour prediction window
UK1	0.1°C– 1.2°C	0.3°C– 1.6°C	0.5°C– 1.8°C
UK2	0.2°C– 2.0°C	0.6°C– 2.5°C	1.2°C– 2.8°C
US1	0.1°C– 0.8°C	0.3°C– 1.2°C	0.6°C– 1.3°C
US2	0.1°C– 0.6°C	0.3°C– 1.1°C	0.5°C– 1.5°C

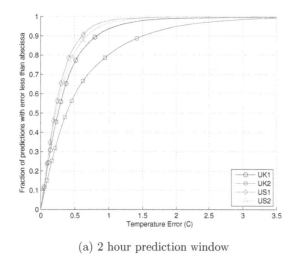

(a) 2 hour prediction window

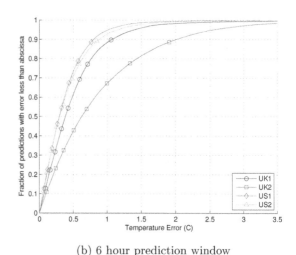

(b) 6 hour prediction window

Figure 8: Error residuals aggregates across all houses and all rooms

Equation 2 to extrapolate room temperatures given reduced heating time to determine the ideal new schedule. This can also be done in a feedback control system so long as the predictive look ahead window is large enough that control decisions will have an active effect on the house within the window.

5. EVALUATION

This section investigates the accuracy of the Matchstick model. First, we characterise the predictive accuracy of the model. Second, we analyse how the predictive accuracy changes for different rooms in different houses. Third, we investigate the effect of the model's training aspects, such as the training length and the effect of neighbouring room selection.

To evaluate the accuracy of the model, we used a total of four weeks of wintertime gas consumption and per-room temperature data for each of the four houses, and outdoor temperature data for the two cities. We give the predictive accuracy of the model across three weeks of data, using a sliding window of the prior seven days as training data. The predictor operates on the present and past per-room temperature readings, and we evaluate the success of its extrapolation for specific times in the future. In our evaluation, we supply the predictor with two types of future knowledge: the future gas inputs (which can be derived from the intended/programmed schedule of the boiler or furnace) and the future measured values of outside temperature.

While our use of outside temperature might be seen as relying upon an "oracle", it is important to note that weather forecasts in most locations are sufficiently accurate for our purposes. For example, in the UK where weather is notoriously variable, the three-hourly temperature forecasts are accurate to within $\pm 2°C$ (95% confidence).[2] Note that this level of error is similar to that which might arise from using temperature measurements taken at another site in the same locale (since not all homes/neighbourhoods have an outdoor weather station), or which arises from measurements using inexpensive, consumer-grade sensors (typically $\pm 1°C$). Regardless, we comment below on the sensitivity of prediction accuracy to errors in outside temperature forecasts.

The experimental evaluation procedure is as follows, for each day. At the beginning of the day (midnight), the model is trained (Figure 4), using the seven previous days of data. For each time step t (from 0–24 h) we take each room's current temperature and predict p hours into the future, by modelling each time step (five-minutely in the UK; ten-minutely in the US) until the time $t + p$ is reached. The predicted per-room temperatures for time $t + p$ are then stored. By modelling the future predictions starting from all time steps in the day in this way, we create a temperature trace made entirely of predictions p hours into the future. This is compared to the temperature ground truth to create temperature prediction error distributions. We varied the prediction lookahead p between one-half and six hours.

Figure 8 shows the cumulative error distribution for all the residuals from all rooms for all houses. Two lookahead windows are shown (2 and 6 h) to illustrate the difference

---

[2]http://www.metoffice.gov.uk/about-us/who/accuracy/forecasts

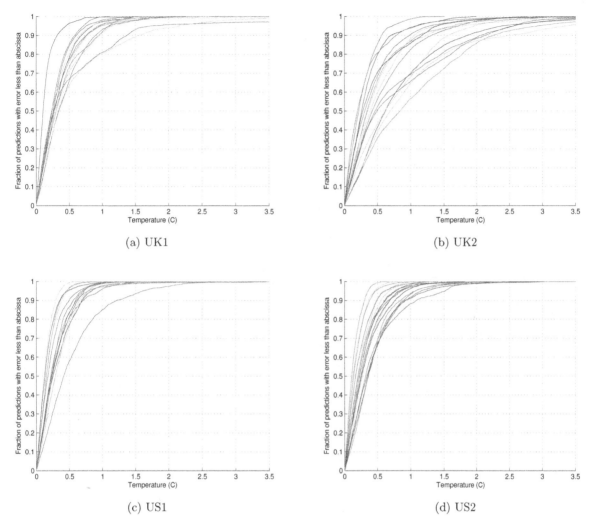

(a) UK1   (b) UK2

(c) US1   (d) US2

Figure 9: Cumulative temperature error distributions for each house; each line is a separate room in the house (Prediction length = 2 h)

in residuals. The RMS and 90th percentile error ranges for the two hour prediction window are 0.28–0.62°C and 0.61–1.50°C respectively. The RMS and 90th percentile error ranges for the six hour prediction window are 0.38–0.88°C and 0.61–1.50°C respectively.

Of interest to control system algorithm designers is prediction accuracy and how the accuracy is related to the length of the forecast. In order to address this question, we evaluated using the same method as above but set p over a range of different windows. The predictive windows we looked at were between half an hour and 6 hours lookahead. The error residuals for each prediction window p were combined across the week to get a better error distribution, and then the one-tailed 90th percentiles were plotted against p in Figure 10. As expected, shorter prediction windows have smaller error residuals, with $p = 2$ h giving 90th percentile errors of under 1.5°C for each house. However, for heating infrastructures like underfloor heating, we recommend a predictive window of at least four hours.

To investigate the effect of weather forecast error on pre-

diction error, the above experiment was repeated with a six hour prediction window, for outdoor temperature offsets of both -2°C and +2°C. The change in the 90th percentile aggregate error was no more than ±0.05°C over all the houses.

While the literature mostly deals with zonal control rather than per-room, we have errors for each room. The residuals for each room are grouped by house and plotted in Figure 9. These temperature errors are for two-hour predictions.

As the Figures show, the error results are encouraging. Per-room 90th percentile errors are summarised in Table 2 for three prediction lengths. Large prediction windows are explored as heating infrastructures, such as underfloor heating, can take more than an hour to heat a room and can still effect the air temperature hours after the system has been turned "off".

Sometimes, Matchstick trains on sensor data but gives poor predictions. We found that this was primarily due to non-measured sources of background heat gains (or losses) in the building. These sources can vary over time in a way

Table 3: Literature comparison: Using other models on our data

House	0.5 hour prediction window - 90th percentile			2 hour prediction window - 90th percentile		
	Matchstick	Smith et al. [15]	Coley and Penman [9]	Matchstick	Smith et al. [15]	Coley and Penman [9]
UK1	0.51°C	0.42°C	2.47°C	0.83°C	1.66°C	8.22°C
UK2	0.94°C	1.12°C	2.92°C	1.50°C	39.81°C	7.75°C
US1	0.36°C	0.44°C	1.19°C	0.61°C	7.80°C	3.76°C
US2	0.36°C	0.84°C	0.97°C	0.68°C	204.51°C	2.57°C

that does not correlate with the model input data. We give some specific examples below.

In UK1, there are two rooms (hall and utility) in Figure 9a which have notably larger errors than the rest of the rooms. The hall contains the front door, which will be frequently opened allowing a very fast heat exchange between the air in the hall and the outside. The utility is connected only to the hall and contains machines for doing laundry. The hall and utility were never heated during the study.

In UK2, while the errors across all rooms are typically larger than in the other houses, there is a clear higher error with certain rooms. These rooms are the utility room, kitchen, downstairs toilet, living room, and the downstairs landing. All of these rooms are on the ground floor, and the utility room and the downstairs landing both have doors to outside. The kitchen also contains cooking equipment which will give off heat using energy we do not measure.

In US1, there was only one room which had significantly larger error than the rest of the rooms: the living room. This was a great room (a large two-story space) and the dynamics of the larger body of air may have unknown effects upon temperature at the point measured by the sensor.

In US2, there was also only one room which had a particularly larger error than the rest of the rooms: the office. This room had an external wall, its door was kept closed, and it held a desktop computer which gave off heat.

These casual heat gains can lower correlation between gas use and temperature rise in neighbouring rooms, leading to poorer fits. Ways to address these issues are discussed in Section 7.

In order to evaluate our model against the literature, the modelling algorithms of Coley and Penman [9], and Smith et al. [15] were implemented and run on our dataset. Coley and Penman's algorithm was designed to run on whole house data, so we treated each room in a house as a building-like structure. The work by Smith et al. focused on zoned American homes and duct actuation, but the equivalent radiator valve data for UK homes was used instead; individual rooms were considered a zone. The US homes did not have per-room control so the vents were modelled as being always open. All the models were given one week of training data and followed the same evaluation protocol as Matchstick.

Table 3 shows the reported error for a 0.5–2 h lookahead, for each house. The model of Smith et al. has comparable error to Matchstick at the 0.5 h prediction window, but model predictions soon diverge as lookahead increases. Each room relied upon the predictions of others in their model, and this could cause predictions to diverge as increased error is introduced with each time step. Coley and Penman's model doesn't diverge at larger prediction windows, but the overall error is five to ten times that of Matchstick. This could be because the model does not capture neighbouring interactions. Without a deeper analysis we can only specu-

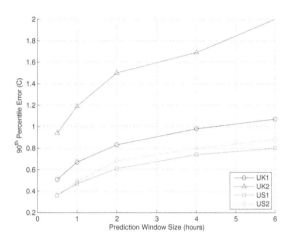

Figure 10: Prediction error as forecast length increases

late on why errors are worse than Matchstick's with larger prediction windows.

5.1 Model Tuning

There are a number of aspects which affect how Matchstick reacts to training data. In order to explore the effects of changing these, we took the second week of evaluation data and recorded the accuracy effects as we changed them. The aspects we explore are the length of training data, and how to select initial neighbouring rooms to be passed to the model.

A learning algorithm needs training data in order to understand how its inputs guide its outputs. However, the amount of training data to use is not immediately clear, with arguments for and against large and small training data windows. Small training windows better map parameters to more recent trends and allow the model to better handle drastic changes in the house environment (building work, improvements, or furniture rearrangement). Larger training windows have the advantage of being more robust to bad data (sensor failure, anomalous readings) and create a model which is tailored to a more 'typical' day of a house.

We decided to investigate how a training window that ranges from 1–7 days affects general prediction accuracy. Using the experimental framework from the main evaluation, we gathered error residuals for the week of data, but for different lengths of training window.

As Figure 11 shows, prediction accuracy gets better with more training data. UK1 and UK2 show the most improvement, with each additional day of training. By contrast, the US homes have similar accuracy statistics regardless of training window length. It is worth pointing out that the

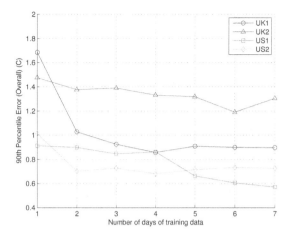

Figure 11: Prediction error as training window increases

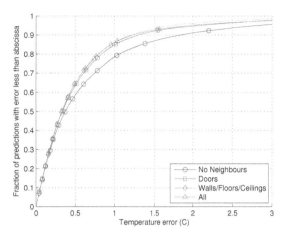

Figure 12: Prediction error when using different policies to set the initial neighbour list (5 hour prediction window)

data for the UK houses used in this experiment had per-room control. The longer training window helps account for situations where infrequent or inconsistent occupancy can result in insufficient training data. This allows for more accurate data correlation, than in shorter training windows. If the relationship between gas and temperature is not reflected in the training data, then this cannot be used by the model.

As each home showed improvement (overall) with each extra day of training, we decided to use seven days of training in the main evaluation. Using seven days also allows for the training data to contain weekend and weekday heating schedules for better correlation in the model fitting. This minimises training artefacts due to irregular heating of specific rooms (such as a utility room or guest bedroom), which again was more common in the UK houses because heating for each room was based on occupancy.

Another aspect of training is the information about potential neighbours. Neighbouring rooms (or adjacent rooms) is an ambiguous term. Is a room neighbouring another if it shares a wall, or a door? To address which policy is better suited to build the initial list of potential neighbours, we did an evaluation of model accuracy (using the same procedure as above), but using four initial lists: (1) no potential thermal neighbours; (2) potential thermal neighbours share doorways; (3) potential thermal neighbours share walls; (4) all rooms are potential thermal neighbours.

Policies 1 and 4 can be used to generate an initial list of neighbours quite trivially. However, policies 2 and 3 require either manual entry or a further supporting algorithm for automatically detecting shared walls and/or doorways [18, 19].

Figure 12 shows the changes in error residuals with the different policies. As expected, setting no neighbours leads to poorer predictions (an error of about 0.5°C worse at the 90th percentile with a six-hour prediction window). As the initial lists get more comprehensive, the accuracy increases. The error residuals for policy 3 is nearly identical, with policy 4 having a slight increase in accuracy. This means that allowing the model to select neighbours from potentially all rooms is comparable to providing a list of physically neighbouring rooms via another means (policy 2 or 3). However, using a full list (policy 4) means the algorithm will be considering possible neighbours which may have no physical relation, and will increase the time it takes to train.

6. SAVINGS ANALYSIS

In order to estimate the potential gas savings when applied to a control scenario, we took the temperature control events from a previous study [7] and used this data in combination with predictions from Matchstick to simulate and improve heating decisions. The previous study used an arrival predictor to work out: (1) when a given room is going to be occupied, and (2) when the room is going to be heated. The time difference between the two was determined by a static linear heating rate. For our savings analysis, we replaced the linear heating rate and instead used Matchstick to determine the ideal time to heat a room. The advantage of using this existing data is that the savings are directly comparable. As we can predict what the temperature will be at the expected time of arrival, Matchstick can work out the nearest time to the arrival point at which to start heating the rooms expected to be occupied. This allows us to minimise gas which took rooms above their set point using the linear heating rate.

The previous study used UK1, UK2, US1, and US2 to determine savings, but the US homes did not have per-room measurements (only a whole-house measure). As such, we perform the savings analysis on UK1 and UK2, which have per-room measurements, the predicted times of arrival for each room, and heating actuation times for each room. The previous study had two experimental conditions which were tested: scheduled heating and predictive heating. We only apply the savings analysis to the predicted days; the heating and expected times of arrival are dependent upon each other and can be leveraged for savings.

For each day of the study with a predicted condition, two events were considered for savings analysis: heat-on in the morning following the night, and heat-on in the evening when occupants come back from work. If the predicted day was a weekend and no one left the house, only the first heating period was used.

A simple control algorithm was used to determine the ex-

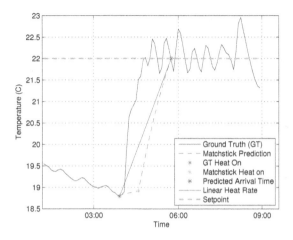

Figure 13: An example prediction trace showing how savings are calculated for a heating period

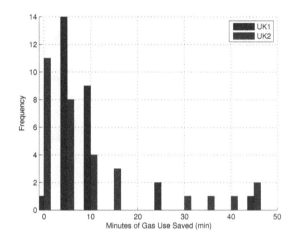

Figure 14: Distribution of gas saved in terms of minutes removed from heating periods

tra savings for heating periods using Matchstick. First, take the temperature data from when the room was originally to be heated. Then for each room, use Matchstick to predict what the room temperature will be for the time it is expected to be occupied. If the room temperature is higher than its set point, re-forecast with the heat turning on one timestep later by shifting the gas trace into the future. This effectively cut away at the gas which was being used keeping the room at a steady state, rather than the gas used to bring the room up to setpoint. This process is repeated until a room's temperature when occupied drops below its set point.

The latest possible time predicted, where all of the rooms are at their set points, is then used as the new time to turn the central heating on. Any gas used in the cut-away steady state period is saved.

6.1 Results

The above methods were used on 47 days of data from the two UK houses (27 for UK1 and 20 for UK2). Figure 13 shows an example of how the new heating times are calculated and Figure 14 shows the distribution of the minutes of gas use saved (as computed by the above method).

Overall, UK1 saved 3.3% of its total gas over the experimental period and UK2 saved 2.3%. The above experimental procedure was designed to save as much gas as possible while not impacting comfort. It's important to stress that these savings are in addition to those reported by the original study [7](8–18% across both houses) and that the savings are based on simulations using Matchstick.

7. IMPROVEMENT AND FUTURE WORK

As described in Section 5, if there are changes in the temperature which do not correlate with any heat input in the training period, or on the day Matchstick is predicting, bad prediction residuals are reported. Currently, we do not address this, but there is a scope for building **fall-back methods** for when Matchstick reports bad prediction residuals.

The parameters from a recent day with a good residual fit could be used, or a set of default model parameters, based on an average of all Matchstick's previous good fits. How-

ever, as Matchstick cannot tell if its predictions are bad until the time it has predicted has arrived, warning heuristics or methods must be developed to indicate that the model has a bad fit for the coming day. For example, when bad data is trained upon, the fitted model parameters can be significantly different from those of well-fitted models. This could be an indicator that the model has given a bad fit, but equally it could indicate that the sensors may be malfunctioning, or the local climate may have radically changed from a week ago (heat wave, cold snap).

Time-proven model parameters could be **shared** across similar houses, like in a housing estate where buildings are similar in construction. As noted by Coley and Penman [9], parameters which consistently change from what is expected can also indicate wear and tear in households, and could be used by an estate manager to aid with maintenance.

In the evaluation we have performed, we trained Matchstick at midnight of every day, used that fitted model for all predictions across the following day, and then retrained the following midnight. While certainly feasible to execute once per day, training is a non-trivial operation, and in a real scenario it would take too long to train Matchstick before every prediction, or as new sensor data arrived. We tested Matchstick's performance if retrained every six hours. This did give a marginal reduction of prediction error, but in a control scenario it would take up a lot of processing power which might be better spent elsewhere (e.g. occupancy prediction).

Currently Matchstick only supports heating infrastructure, but could very easily be extended to **support cooling** systems. However, this still needs to be tested on houses with active cooling infrastructure. Other forms of heat gains could be added to the predictive model too, so long as they are either controllable or predictable. Using a combination of non-intrusive load monitoring (NILM) [20] and occupancy tracking, it would be possible to determine likelihoods for certain electronic devices to be switched on, and their casual heat gains. Items such as computers, ovens, and TVs all have regular usage patterns and can heat a room easily. When investigating our test houses, kitchen and living room temperature rose noticeably with electricity usage.

None of the deployments used window or door sensors so we could not model (or predict) transient air filtration events such as windows opening, which may cause large thermal changes. However, our room-to-room model implicitly captures static, or near static, draughts such as doors which stay open or closed for a long time.

Ultimately, to fully verify the savings from using Matchstick and to explore the possible applications which can be built on top of it, the model **must be deployed in the wild**. Matchstick can also be used to reduce discomfort, as well as save gas. Due to the dependency on simple sensors, this could be as simple as deploying iButtons for a month (as in US1 and US2), and then using Matchstick to build an improved furnace actuation schedule. The other possibility is using a home sensor network to feed Matchstick. This could be used to provide live control decisions, as with our saving analysis.

8. CONCLUSIONS

In this paper we have introduced Matchstick, a data-driven adaptive model which relies on relatively sparse sensor deployments (one per room). For differing lookahead windows, we have evaluated how well the model predicts across three weeks of data in four houses, in two different countries. Our evaluation also characterises error distribution in a per-room fashion to give insight into which rooms of a house are more difficult to model and the reasons why.

We have shown that the model is comparable, and in many cases better, than the selected models from the literature. This accuracy was achieved despite the fact that our data was taken in real homes occupied by families, rather than using test cells. We have also shown that by using our model, rather than assuming a constant linear heat rate for warm-up periods, control systems can achieve gas savings by trimming down furnace or boiler actuation schedules.

9. ACKNOWLEDGEMENTS

We would like to thank our anonymous participants for their time and aid in deploying sensors in their homes. This work represents a primary contribution of Carl Ellis's PhD research which was funded by an EPSRC doctoral training grant, and EPSRC grant EP/I00033X/1.

10. REFERENCES

[1] L Pérez-Lombard, J Ortiz, and C Pout. A Review on Buildings Energy Consumption Information. *Energy and Buildings*, 40(3):394–398, 2008.

[2] Department of Energy and Climate. Energy Consumption in the United Kingdom. Technical report, HM Government, 2011.

[3] U.S. Energy Information Administration. Residential Energy Consumption Survey (RECS). Technical report, US Government, 2011.

[4] U.S. Energy Information Administration. Annual Energy Review. Technical report, US Government, 2011.

[5] M Gupta and S Intille. Adding GPS-control to Traditional Thermostats: An Exploration of Potential Energy Savings and Design Challenges. *In Proc. of Pervasive*, pages 95–114, 2009.

[6] G Gao and K Whitehouse. The Self-Programming Thermostat: Optimizing Setback Schedules Based on Home Occupancy Patterns. In Proc. of BuildSys, pages 67–72, 2009.

[7] J Scott, A J Brush, J Krumm, B Meyers, M Hazas, S Hodges, and N Villar. PreHeat: Controlling Home Heating Using Occupancy Prediction. In *Proc. of UbiComp*, 2011.

[8] A I Dounis, M Bruant, G Guarracino, P Michel, and M Santamouris. Indoor Air-Quality Control by a Fuzzy-Reasoning Machine in Naturally Ventilated Buildings. *Applied Energy*, 54(1):11–28, 1996.

[9] D A Coley and J M Penman. Second Order System Identification in the Thermal Response of Real Buildings. Paper II: Recursive Formulation for On-Line Building Energy Management and Control. *Building and Environment*, 27(3):269–277, July 1992.

[10] O Mejri, E Palomo Del Barrio, and N Ghrab-Morcos. Energy Performance Assessment of Occupied Buildings Using Model Identification Techniques. *Energy and Buildings*, 43(2-3):285–299, February 2011.

[11] H C Spindler and L K Norford. Naturally Ventilated and Mixed-Mode Buildings - Part I: Thermal Modeling. *Building and Environment*, 44(4):736–749, 2009.

[12] J Teeter and M Y Chow. Application of Functional Link Neural Network to HVAC Thermal Dynamic System Identification. *IEEE Trans. on Ind. Elec.*, 45(1):170–176, 1998.

[13] S A Klein. *TRNSYS: A Transient Simulation Program*. Eng. Experiment Station, 1976.

[14] R C Sonderegger. Diagnostic Tests Determining the Thermal Response of a House. *ASHRAE Journal*, 19:35–47, 1977.

[15] G Smith, T Sookoor, and K Whitehouse. Modelling Building Thermal Response to HVAC Zoning. In *Proc. of CONET*, 2012.

[16] F Oldewurtel, A Parisio, C N Jones, D Gyalistras, M Gwerder, V Stauch, B Lehmann, and M Morari. Use of Model Predictive Control and Weather Forecasts for Energy Efficient Building Climate Control. *Energy and Buildings*, 45:15 – 27, 2012.

[17] N Villar, J Scott, S Hodges, K Hammil, and C Miller. .NET Gadgeteer: A Platform for Custom Devices. In *Proc. of Pervasive*. 2012.

[18] J Lu and K Whitehouse. Smart Blueprints: Automatically Generated Maps of Homes and the Devices Within Them. In *Proc. of Pervasive*, volume 7319. 2012.

[19] Carl Ellis, James Scott, Ionut Constandache, and Mike Hazas. Creating a room connectivity graph of a building from per-room sensor units. In *Proc. of BuildSys*, pages 177–183, 2012.

[20] C Laughman, K Lee, R Cox, S Shaw, and S Leeb. Power Signature Analysis. *IEEE Power & Energy*, 1(2):56–63, 2003.

Low Power Counting via Collaborative Wireless Communications

Wenjie Zeng, Anish Arora, and Kannan Srinivasan
Computer Science and Engineering
The Ohio State University
Columbus, OH, USA
{zengw, anish, kannan}@cse.ohio-state.edu

ABSTRACT

Metrics that aggregate the state of neighboring nodes are frequently used in wireless sensor networks. In this paper, we present two primitives that exploit simultaneous communications in 802.15.4 radios to enable a polling node to calculate with low power the number (or set) of its neighbors where some state predicate of interest holds. In both primitives, the poller assigns transmission powers and response lengths to its respective neighbors for their simultaneous response to each of its poll requests. The two primitives adopt complementary schemes for power assignment such that the Received Signal Strength Indicator (RSSI) of the respective signal from each neighbor is significantly different from that of all others in one primitive and nearly equivalent to that of the others in the other. The first primitive, LinearPoll, suits sparse networks and consumes energy that is linear in the size of its neighborhood, whereas the second primitive, LogPoll, suits dense networks and consumes constant energy. Compared to the state-of-the-art solutions that use multiple sub-carriers, our primitives are simpler and more compute-efficient while provide estimation with comparable quality. Compared to single-carrier solutions, our primitives achieve comparable quality at less than half the energy cost or richer information at comparable energy cost. They are also compatible with other radio physical layers. Based on our implementation for CC2420 radios on the TelosB platform, we evaluate the primitives in different wireless environments and neighborhood topologies to study their performance, the tradeoff between their estimation accuracy and energy cost, and methods for tuning their critical parameters, and we compare them with baseline counting protocols.

Categories and Subject Descriptors

C.2.2 [**Computer-Communication Networks**]: Network Protocols

Keywords

Counting; Sensor Network; Energy Efficiency

1. INTRODUCTION

A common pattern in sensor network applications is the collection of up-to-date neighborhood metrics to perform local or distributed decision making. We may abstract this pattern in terms of a local state predicate of interest P over the sensor values or other local variables at each neighboring node. For a collector node i whose neighboring set of nodes is N_i, let P_i be the set of nodes in N_i where the predicate P holds. The pattern typically involves counting the number of nodes in P_i at i. When this count is dynamic, its efficient ongoing collection becomes material to system performance.

Examples of this pattern are found at various layers of the network. In medium access control, for instance, scheduling depends on the number of contending sensors; P in this case is whether the node has a non-empty queue. By estimating $|P_i|$, CSMA-based MAC protocols [10, 12] choose a contention window and a backoff window that optimizes efficiency and latency. Likewise, TDMA protocols [3, 15] avoid wasting time slots that are reserved for inactive neighbors. At the application layer, detection and alerting for some event of interest P is made tolerant to individual sensor false alarms by redundant collection of P_i and checking that the count of event witnesses is nontrivial. For example, in a volcano monitoring deployment [16], because the real-time seismic data of individual nodes is high in volume and low in accuracy, it is infeasible for a poling node to trust a single neighbor or to constantly download the raw data from all neighbors. Instead, a polling node only collects threshold-based events (predicates) from its neighbors based on their local processing. The bulk download of the raw data is only initiated when the number of detected events exceeds some threshold. When seismic activities are rare, the polling node spends most of its energy collecting local predicates of its neighbors rather than downloading the actual data. In such cases, employing our primitives and collect the local predicates concurrently would substantially reduce the energy consumption of the polling nodes.

In this paper, we address how neighbors collaboratively and efficiently communicate their P to a polling node i. We propose two energy efficient and complementary communication primitives that estimate P_i with different asymptotic energy costs and precisions. Rather than relying on explicit data communication, both primitives require each neighbor to immediately acknowledge a poll from i if P holds locally, using an assigned transmission power and response length.

For sparse networks, our first primitive, LinearPoll, estimates the set P_i with a cost that is linear in $|N_i|$; for dense networks, our second primitive, LogPoll, estimates $\log |P_i|$ with a constant cost. Polling nodes can choose between (or combine) the two primitives based on their neighborhood topology and application requirements. Both primitives allow users to control tradeoffs between accuracy and cost. In both, i exploits the received signal strength —as indicated by the RSSI— of the superposed signal from the responding neighbors.

Why and how we use RSSI? Although low-power radios are resource constrained, they provide access to several physical layer measures. In the latest 802.15.4 standard [1], the physical layer is required to provide three basic parameters: Energy Detection (ED), Link Quality Indicator (LQI), and Clear Channel Assessment (CCA). ED represents the RSSI detected; LQI represents the quality of a received packet, and CCA is a binary indicator based on ED. Because LQI requires successful packet reception, and hence does not work for concurrent responses, and CCA is derived from ED, we construct our primitives based on the ED metric. The actual mapping between ED and RSSI is platform specific, but nevertheless bijective [4]. For ease of exposition, we will henceforth use RSSI to represent both the signal strength (in dBm) and the integer ED values provided by the radio.

A key idea in LinearPoll is to ensure that the RSSI from each neighbor is sufficiently different from each other. It is then possible to select different response lengths for each neighbor such that measuring the drops in signal strength of the superposed responses at the poller lets it count (and in fact identify) each neighbor that responds to a poll. Conversely, a key idea in LogPoll is to ensure that both the response RSSI and the response length from each neighbor are nearly the same. As is analytically and empirically shown in this paper, the RSSI of the superposed signal (in dB) increases log-linearly with the number of responding neighbors. It is therefore possible to devise a local scheme for the poller to count the number of responding neighbors in a logarithmic scale.

As neighbors respond with the assigned power and length, the poller expects RSSI sample sequences of different structures from the two primitives: while the poller expects a cascading RSSI sequence in LinearPoll, it expects a fixed-length response of stable RSSI whose value depends on the number of responders in LogPoll. The estimation accuracy depends on how well we ensure that the measured RSSI sample sequence matches the expected sequence even in the presence of superposition of response signals, i.e., irrespective of uncertainty in the locations of the neighbors and reaction time differences in the simultaneous responses, the received signal strength of the superposed response at the poller has bounded variability with respect to its expected value.

Two factors are critical for us to ensure that the RSSI sample sequence matches what is expected: the respective response RSSI from individual neighbors and how these responses superpose. If these two factors change arbitrarily and cannot be predicted, the RSSI sequence will also become unpredictable and diverge from what is expected. In general, the RSSI of a response from a given neighbor depends on path loss, fading resulted from shadowing and multipath, and external interference. Fortunately, as we target static networks, i.e., networks consisting of static nodes in a stationary physical environment, the response RSSI can be

reliably predicted because path loss remains constant and fading changes slowly as long as the poller can effectively detect external interference and reject contaminated samples. More discussion on detecting interference is in Section 5.1; for non-static networks, mobility of both the sensor nodes and the physical environment results in unpredictable fading effects, which renders accurate estimation of response RSSI rather difficult. In such cases, our primitives may not apply. Systematic evaluation of the proposed primitives in a non-static network is beyond the scope of this paper. In the rest of the paper, we focus our discussion on static networks.

The other critical factor, i.e., the superposition of concurrent responses, is also statistically predictable. 802.15.4 uses Direct Sequence Spread Spectrum (DSSS) and maps each symbol to a pseudo-random chip sequence, which is then modulated with O-QPSK. For the superposed signals to constructively add or destructively add, these signals should be identical and be perfectly synchronized at the center (carrier) frequency. Such a high-precision synchronization is highly unlikely, even impossible, when all the nodes simply respond to a poll, albeit simultaneously. Thus, the superposition has signals with random phases and add up with a high probability to their mean, which ensures that it is unlikely for any RSSI sample to differ from its expected value by a large amount.

Last but not least, an important feature of our primitives lies in the light-weight initialization. Response power and length assignment for both primitives solely depends on the path loss between neighbors and the poller. For a given static neighborhood, since path loss is constant, both primitives need only to assign response power and length once based on a one-time measurement of the path loss.

Contributions of this paper. We present two complementary low-power counting schemes that work reliably in the presence of measurement errors, environment changes, and varying external noise and interference sources. Also, we show how and when to use these counting schemes by extensively studying their performance under varying conditions. Moreover, we discuss the general applicability of these schemes to any wireless platform (or physical layer). We identify the critical parameters for the performance of the primitives, and identify hardware induced constraints in the context of our implementation for the 802.15.4 CC2420 radio on the TelosB platform. We evaluate performance and tradeoff between cost and estimation accuracy for both primitives in two different sensor network testbeds. We show that the primitives are resilient to variation in radio sensitivity, neighborhood topology, and background environment.

The main findings are summarized as follows:

- Both primitives can be initialized either with piggyback traffic or dedicated control traffic. In the worst case where control traffic has to be sent, the control overhead is no more than 0.2%.

- When the assigned output powers ensure that response RSSI's are sufficiently differentiated, LinearPoll achieves an accuracy of at least 98% when there is sporadic interference and an accuracy of 95% even when malicious interference attacks 10% of the time.

- LogPoll achieves an accuracy of 99% (averaged over different numbers of responders) when all neighbors can adapt to a similar response RSSI and remains over

95% even when 10% of the neighbors fail to honor their power assignment.

- In LogPoll, interestingly, estimation accuracy increases with the number of responders .

Outline of the paper. Section 2 defines the system model, which in constructing the one-time measurement for predicting response RSSI used by both primitives. Based on accurate predictions of response RSSI from neighbors, Sections 3 and 4 respectively present the design, implementation, and empirical evaluation of our two primitives. Section 5 discusses their constraints and proposes extensions to relax these constraints. Section 6 recaps related work on communication primitives and protocols that exploit controlled transmission collisions. Section 7 discusses our future work and makes concluding remarks.

2. SYSTEM MODEL

Consider a node i in a static network whose neighborhood is the set of nodes N_i. Node i polls its neighborhood, and its neighbors respond immediately if and only if the predicate P holds locally. Each neighbor j responds using any one of the powers m_j from a set M, and the poller samples the RSSI of the response. Let $R(i, j, m_j)$ be the value of an RSSI sample that i obtains when a single neighbor j, $j \in N_i$, responds at power m_j.

Although $R(i, j, m_j)$ varies over time due to changes in the background noise, its variation is usually within a small bound unless interference occurs [4, 14]. This allows poller i to first construct an estimation function of $R(i, j, m_j)$, denoted as $\widehat{R}(i, j, m_j)$, based on a set of learning samples, and to later on use $\widehat{R}(i, j, m_j)$ as a prediction of the response RSSI from j at any given power $m_j \in M$. We have the following requirement over such predictions:

Requirement I (Bounded prediction error):
There exists a measurable σ_i for each poller i such that $\forall\, m_j \in M, \forall\, j \in N_i$:

$$\widehat{R}(i, j, m_j) - \sigma_i \leq R(i, j, m_j) \leq \widehat{R}(i, j, m_j) + \sigma_i . \quad (1)$$

In other words, based on the learning samples, poller i can predict the response RSSI with bounded error σ_i from any given neighbor at any power. For ease of exposition, we introduce the following symbols to represent the bounds of $R(i, j, m_j)$

$$R_l(i, j, m_j) = \widehat{R}(i, j, m_j) - \sigma_i$$
$$R_u(i, j, m_j) = \widehat{R}(i, j, m_j) + \sigma_i ,$$

and abbreviate the number of nodes in N_i as N.

When interference occurs, some samples from a response can violate Requirement I. Nevertheless, each primitive implements special mechanisms to detect interference, which we will detail in Sections 3 and 4.

Initialization for RSSI Prediction. We assume that when neighbor j responds, the RSSI obtained at node i depends linearly on power m_j:

$$R(i, j, m_j) = a_{ij} \cdot m_j + b_{ij} , \quad (2)$$

where a_{ij} and b_{ij} are coefficients that we estimate. Further, b_{ij} depends linearly on the additive background noise

ρ and the time-invariant path loss over link (i, j), denoted as $L(i, j)$, as:

$$b_{ij} = \rho - L(i, j) . \quad (3)$$

In the context of this paper, path loss $L(i, j)$ should be interpreted as the effective path loss from node j to node i that accounts for not only the free space signal attenuation, but also the shadowing and multipath effects.

For node i to predict $R(i, j, m_j)$ given m_j, it first estimates a_{ij} and b_{ij}. Poller i can acquire, and later on update, a set of learning samples (each of which is a triplet) $\{(R^k(i, j, m_j^k), m_j^k, \rho^k)\}$ by either snooping or directly receiving packets from node j, where $R^k(i, j, m_j^k)$ is the measured RSSI, m_j^k is the response power, and ρ^k is the background noise in the kth learning sample. ρ^k is computed as the mean background noise measured before and after the sample[1]. Given a number of learning samples, the estimates of a_{ij} and b_{ij}, denoted as $\widehat{a}_{ij}$ and $\widehat{b}_{ij}$, are computed using least-squares approximation. In the meanwhile, we use the average background noise as its estimate $\widehat{\rho}$. With $\widehat{a}$, $\widehat{b}$, and $\widehat{\rho}$, i can predict $R(i, j, m_j)$ and $L(i, j)$ as:

$$\widehat{R}(i, j, m_j) = \widehat{a}_{ij} \cdot m_j + \widehat{b}_{ij} \quad (4)$$
$$\widehat{L}(i, j) = \widehat{b}_{ij} - \widehat{\rho} . \quad (5)$$

Without loss of generality, we henceforth label the neighbors according to their path loss such that

$$\widehat{L}(i, j) \leq \widehat{L}(i, j + 1), \; j = 1..N - 1 .$$

It is easy to see that a neighbor with a higher node index has a higher path loss to the poller and can adapt within a lower range of response RSSI.

In the next two sections, we assume that the one-time measurement for RSSI prediction described above has been completed and that the $\{L(i, j)\}$ are amenable to the respective power assignment requirements imposed by the primitives. We will discuss techniques for combining the two primitives to deal with more general neighborhood topologies in Section 5.

3. LINEARPOLL

LinearPoll allows a poller to estimate the nodes in P_i. In this section, we will first formally analyze the preliminaries of LinearPoll and then present its detailed design, implementation and evaluation.

3.1 Preliminaries

The poller in LinearPoll estimates P_i by distinguishing different signals in the superposed response from its neighbors. The poller respectively assigns to neighbors response power and length such that the response RSSI of a neighbor is inversely related to its response length. Thus, the poller can estimate the set P_i by analyzing the drops in RSSI as it measures the superposed response signal. We formalize the inverse relationship between response RSSI and length as two requirements:

Requirement II (Sufficient difference, Δ, in RSSIs):
The power assignment $\{m_j\}$ is chosen such that for some

---

[1]Neighbor j can efficiently send its output power m to the poller by attaching to its packets a small control flag whose size depends on the number of available power levels.

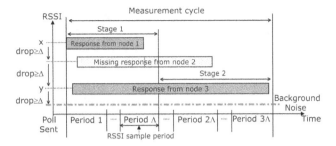

Figure 1: LinearPoll overview where 2 out of 3 neighbors have responded.

$\Delta > 2\sigma_i$ for all $j \in N_i$

$$R_l(i, j, m_j) - \rho_u \geq \Delta \ , \qquad (6)$$

$$R_l(i, j, m_j) - R_u(i, j+1, m_{j+1}) \geq \Delta \ . \qquad (7)$$

Essentially, (6) ensures that even the weakest response is above the upper bound of the noise floor. (7) ensures that lowest RSSI from the response of j is still greater than the highest RSSI from the response of $j+1$, which ensures that the poller sees a drop of at least Δ in the RSSI sequence whenever a response of higher strength terminates.

In addition to the unique response RSSI from each neighbor, for the poller to discriminate two component signals, we also let them differ in response length. Define $C(t)$ to be the number of RSSI samples the poller can obtain from a response packet of t bytes. Also define T and Λ to be the maximum packet size supported by the radio and the minimum number of RSSI samples the poller needs to identify a neighbor. We introduce the final requirement for LinearPoll:

Requirement III (Sufficient difference, Λ, in response lengths): Λ and the response length assignment $\{t_j\}$ are chosen such that for $j = 1, \ldots, N - 1$

$$C(t_{j+1}) - C(t_j) = \Lambda \qquad (8)$$

$$C(T) \geq N\Lambda \ . \qquad (9)$$

The exact values of Δ and Λ depend not only on the accuracy and efficiency requirement for LinearPoll but also on the radio platform being used. In the rest of the section, we first outline the LinearPoll protocol and then detail its individual modules. Based on our implementation of LinearPoll on the TelosB platform, we discuss the platform specific constraints on choosing Δ and Λ in Section 3.3. We conclude with an experimental evaluation of the performance of LinearPoll.

3.2 LinearPoll Design

The correctness of LinearPoll depends on Requirements I, II, and III being met. While the first two requirements depend on both the wireless environment and the radio hardware, the last one depends only on the radio.

Fig. 1 illustrates one particular round of LinearPoll in which two of the three neighbors respond to a poll. In our example, neighbor 2 has not responded and its missing response is represented by a dotted line in contrast to the two gray bars that represent the responses from neighbor 1 and 3. Here the entire duration of the superposed response constitutes a *measurement cycle*. Each measurement cycle consists of multiple *stages*, in which each stage uniquely corresponds to a responder. Each stage lasts a multiple of Λ

RSSI sample periods, in which one RSSI value is obtained at the end of each period. For each stage, one *measure* is computed based on the samples in that stage.

Each round of LinearPoll consists of a one-time step followed by two routine steps:

Step 1 (One-time-only: Assign Power and Length): To each neighbor j, i assigns a response power and length, according to Algorithm 1 to be described in Section 3.2.1. As seen in Fig. 1, the assingment pattern is that a stronger response has a shorter length. The power assignment ensures that the response RSSI from any two neighbors are at least Δ dB apart and the number of samples a response lasts is a multiple of Λ.

Step 2 (Measure RSSI): Poller i broadcasts its poll and immediately acquires RSSI samples at the highest possible rate supported by the radio.

Step 3 (Estimate P_i): Given the RSSI samples, node i groups them into stages, computes the measure of each stage, and estimates P_i according to Algorithm 2. As seen in Fig. 1, every time the response of a neighbor terminates, a drop in RSSI can be detected. In our example, given the two drops before the RSSI decreases to the noise floor, along with the timing of these drops, the poller can identify the stages that correspond to neighbor 1 and 3. Further details are discussed in Section 3.2.3. □

Once initialized, LinearPoll can skip the first two steps until Requirement I no longer holds, i.e., until the estimate of $\widehat{R}(i, j, m)$ becomes invalid viz-a-viz (1) in Requirement I. As one illustration of the rate at which the first two steps may be needed, we note that in our experiments, LinearPoll produced highly accurate estimates of P_i even if the same assignments were used for 15 minutes.

3.2.1 Response Power and Length Assignment

Algorithm 1: Power and length assignment
1 $m_N \leftarrow \operatorname{argmin}_{m \in M} (R_l(i, N, m) - \rho_u \geq \Delta)$
2 **for** $j \leftarrow N - 1$ **to** 1 **do**
3   **for** $k \leftarrow 1$ **to** $|M|$ **do**
4   **if** $R_l(i, j, M_k) - R_u(i, j+1, m_{j+1}) \geq \Delta$ **then**
5 $m_j \leftarrow M_k$
6 $t_j \leftarrow C^{-1}(\Lambda \times (N - j))$

Algorithm 1 computes the assignment $\{m_j, t_j\}$ for each neighbor j using a simple rule: the smaller the estimated path loss for j, the higher the assigned power and shorter the assigned response length.

Line 1 assigns to node N the minimum power such that $R_l(i, N, m_N)$ is at least $(\rho_u + \Delta)$, which ensures (6) for all nodes. For the remaining nodes, from node $N - 1$ down to node 1 of decreasing path loss (Line 2), it searches for the minimum power for neighbor j that is at least Δ dB above the one just assigned to neighbor $j+1$. To find such a power, it searches for the lowest power that satisfies (7) (Line 2, 3, and 4) and assigns length that satisfies (8) accordingly (Line 6). Note that C^{-1} is the inverse function of C, which returns the response length in bytes in order to obtain the given number of samples from that response. Thus, Algorithm 1 ensures that both Requirement II and III hold.

Two critical parameters need to be chosen carefully with respect to the specific wireless environment and radio platform to which LinearPoll is applied. Δ controls the minimum gap in RSSI between any two responses, while Λ controls the number of samples per stage. Below, we discuss how Δ and Λ are chosen for the testbeds where we ran our experiments.

Choosing Δ . Polling nodes measure σ_i to choose Δ accordingly. In our experiments, the weakest response is about 10 dB above the noise floor. In terms of absolute value, variation in noise will not create any visible change in the response RSSI. However, because CC2420 reports RSSI in 1 dB resolution, the slightest change in received signal strength can lead to a change of 1 dB due to rounding. For instance, we observed in our experiments that for any given neighbor j, $R(i, j, m_j)$ almost never differ by more than 1 dB from $\widehat{R}(i, j, m_j)$. It follows from (1) that σ_i is 0.5 dB and thus we thus set Δ to 2 according to Requirement II.

Choosing Λ . 802.15.4 specifies that an RSSI sample period lasts 8 symbols, which introduces a complication: the boundary of a response need not be aligned with the boundary of a sample period. A *transitional sample* is created between two stages when a sample period contains some signal from the earlier stage and some from the later stage. As a result, its RSSI is lower than that of the earlier stage but above that of the later one. As a stage can have transitional samples at both of ends, it must last at least 3 samples for its measure (the median) to reflect the actual response RSSI.

3.2.2 Interference Detection

Before P_i can be estimated, we need to verify that the RSSI samples obtained in the measurement cycle are not contaminated by interference. Just like in error detection codes, such as Cyclic Redundancy Check (CRC), where a receiver rejects a received packet if its bits leads to a incorrect CRC, LinearPoll rejects a measurement cycle if the layout of the stages does not match what can be generated from the power and length assignment.

LinearPoll utilizes two mechanisms to detect interference. First, it exploits the fact that the response length is known *a priori*. Given an assignment, RSSI drops occur only at a fixed set of samples in the measurement cycle. Although software and hardware jitters can vary the exact moments of drops, the variation is seldom more one sample. Thus, the poller can reject a measurement cycle if unexpected drops are observed. Second, measurements should be monotonically decreasing and they should be around the expected response RSSI determined by the power assignment algorithm.

A measurement cycle is rejected if it fails either of these tests. Otherwise, LinearPoll proceeds to estimate P_i based on the verified measurement cycle.

3.2.3 Algorithm for Estimating P_i

Right after the poller broadcasts a poll, it samples RSSI at the highest available rate. Let $\{r_j\}$ be the list of samples in a measurement cycle. A measurement cycle starts with the first sample that is at least Δ dB above than ρ_u and ends with the first sample that drops back below ρ_u.

To estimate P_i, the poller needs to first discover a responder and then identify that responder. The poller discovers a responder whenever it sees a drop in measure that is no less than Δ. Further, the poller identifies the responder based

on the drop's timing in $\{r_j\}$ or, equivalently, the point of termination of a stage.

Algorithm 2: P_i estimation

1 $\widehat{P}_i \leftarrow \{\}$
2 $lastTrigger \leftarrow \texttt{getMedian}(r[1:\Lambda])$
3 **for** $k \leftarrow \Lambda + 1;\ k \leq |r|;\ k \leftarrow k + \Lambda$ **do**
4     $curRss \leftarrow \texttt{getMedian}(r[k:\min(|r|, k+\Lambda-1)])$
5     $drop \leftarrow lastTrigger$ - $curRss$
6   **if** $drop \geq \Delta$ **then**
7        $responder \leftarrow \texttt{findResponder}(\{t_j\}, k)$
8        $\widehat{P}_i \leftarrow \widehat{P}_i + \{responder\}$
9        $lastTrigger \leftarrow curRss$

Algorithm 2 takes the assignment from Algorithm 1 as input and estimates P_i. $\widehat{P}_i$, the estimate of P_i, is initialized to an empty set (Line 1). *lastTrigger* represents the RSSI that triggers the last discovery and is initialized to the median of the samples[2] of the first stage (Line 2), where notation $r[a:b]$ represents the sub-array of $\{r_j\}$ from index a to b.

The number of samples that a stage lasts is a multiple of Λ, per (8). By dividing $\{r_j\}$ into sample groups of size Λ, we ensure that a stage arrives only at the boundaries of each sample group. Therefore, the **for** loop increments by Λ (Line 3). Line 4 computes the stage measure based on the samples from the current sample group. In Line 5 and 6, a new responder is discovered if the measure of the current stage is Δ lower than *lastTrigger*. After a new responder is discovered, we identify the responder via utility function $\texttt{findResponder}()$ (Line 7). Given the possible response lengths $\{t_j\}$ provided by Algorithm 1, $\texttt{findResponder}(\{t_j\}, k)$ searches for the neighbor j whose response terminates closest to the kth sample in $\{r_j\}$:

$$\texttt{findResponder}(\{t_j\}, k) = \underset{j \in N_i}{\arg\min}\{|C(t_j) - k|\} .$$

Finally, we update $\widehat{P}$ and *lastTrigger* accordingly.

3.3 Implementation Details

Here we describe our implementation of LinearPoll on the CC2420 radio-equipped TelosB platform, beginning with its response mechanism.

Since the responses are of different lengths, we cannot use the software or hardware acknowledgement features provided by CC2420. As a result, neighbors send explicit packets as response. To minimize jitter in transmission, neighbors preload the response packet before they receive the probe. Upon receiving the poll, responders send a strobe to the radio chip, which will then immediately starts the transmission.

The CC2420 radio samples signal strength at 62.5Khz and reports RSSI based on the mean value averaged over 8 symbol periods. Theoretically, we can obtain one RSSI measurement every $16\mu s$. However, given TelosB hardware limitations, we can only obtain a new RSSI reading every $113\mu s$. Given that the CC2420 radio is 250 Kbps, the number of samples $C(t)$ that we can obtain from a packet of t bytes is $C(t) \approx t/4$ samples.

---

[2]We empirically discovered that using the median of the sample group, as compared to using max, mean, and min, delivers better accuracy.

3.4 Experimental Evaluation of LinearPoll

We now describe our evaluatation of LinearPoll on the TelosB mote platform. After we describe the experiment setup, we introduce a baseline protocol for counting (identifying) and then empirically compare its performance with that of LinearPoll.

Experiment Setup. We conducted our evaluation on two 9-node arrays, one in Testbed 1 located in an office building and the other in Testbed 2 located in an industrial building shared by many occupants. LinearPoll was evaluated in both testbeds and the baseline protocol was evaluated in Testbed 2. We used channel 26 in Testbed 1 and channel 25 in Testbed 2.

While Testbed 1 is almost free-of-interference, Testbed 2 sees sporadic clusters of interference in channel 25 due to active 802.11 connections and other coexisting sensor networks. Even though the likelihood of seeing interference in a particular sample is small, the probability that a measurement cycle in LinearPoll sees interference is non-trivial as a cycle can span 40 samples. To quantify this, we collected a trace of measurements in Testbed 2 by acquiring a batch of 80 RSSI samples as fast as possible every 2 seconds before each experiment. Interference is identified whenever a sample is 3 dB above the noise floor, which accounts for 1.5% of all samples. The likelihood that there is at least one interference sample in 20, 40, and 60 consecutive samples is 3.2%, 5.3% and 7%, respectively. Therefore, the longer a measurement cycle lasts, the more likely it is affected by interference.

One node in each array is designated as the poller. In all the experiments, we set $\Delta = 2$. Each experiment proceeds in rounds and in each round the poller broadcasts a poll and estimates P_i. The poller broadcasts two polls per second and an experiment finishes when 2000 rounds are completed (16 minutes). We tested different values of Λ (2, 3, 4) and 2 experiments were run for each value. $\Lambda = 2$ was tested to verify the requirement of $\Lambda \geq 3$ as discussed in Section 3.2.1[3].

The set of responders was changed from round to round and all subsets of neighbors were evaluated.

In the beginning of every experiment, each neighbor sent to the poller 20 packets containing their power information for the poller to perform the one-time measurement for RSSI prediction as described in Section 2. *Step 1 in LinearPoll, i.e., power and length assignment, was done only once based on the measurements in the beginning of each experiment and neighbors used the same assignment until the experiment finished.* Note that the LinearPoll is expected to be initialized with regular data traffic. Also, an experiment is stopped after 16 minutes because of limited disk space to store RSSI samples rather than degraded accuracy. Even in the worst case where dedicated control traffic has to be used to re-calibrate LinearPoll every 16 minutes, the control overhead is less than 0.2% even for a neighborhood of 50 nodes as each back-to-pack control packet takes at most 2 ms to transmit on the CC2420 radio. The same remark also applies to LogPoll.

Λ		Testbed 1		Testbed 2	
		e_a	$e_r(\%)$	e_a	$e_r(\%)$
$\Lambda = 2$	$|P_i|$	0.8	34%	0.87	39%
	P_i	1.2	67%	1.65	71%
$\Lambda = 3$	$|P_i|$	0.044	4.4%	0.039	3.5%
	P_i	0.047	5%	0.043	4.5%
$\Lambda = 4$	$|P_i|$	0.011	1.1%	0.018	1.6%
	P_i	0.011	1.1%	0.018	1.6%
Baseline	$|P_i|$	N/A	N/A	0.06	3.9%
	P_i	N/A	N/A	0.065	4%

Table 1: Average error amount, e_a, and error rate e_r, for estimating P_i and $|P_i|$ with $\Delta = 2$ dB.

3.4.1 Baseline for Linear Counting

To evaluate the performance of LinearPoll, we implemented a baseline RSSI-based counting protocol according to the TDMA scheme described in [2]. In the baseline, each neighbor is assigned a unique time slot in which they respond to the poll. All neighbors respond at the highest power level to ensure detection. The poller can then identify the set of responders based on the slots that it detects energy above the noise floor[4].

3.4.2 Performance of LinearPoll

Table 1 summarizes the results. First let us define *error amount* and *error rate*. The error amount, denoted as e_a, for estimating P_i and $|P_i|$ is defined respectively as:

$$e_a = \begin{cases} |P_i \backslash \widehat{P_i}| + |\widehat{P_i} \backslash P_i| & \text{, for } P_i \\ ||P_i| - |\widehat{P_i}|| & \text{, for } |P_i| \end{cases}, \quad (10)$$

where $'\backslash'$ denotes the set complement operation; error rate, denoted as e_r, is the percentage of rounds whose e_a is greater than zero.

Let us first look at the impact of Λ. Overall, the accuracy improves as Λ increases, especially when Λ increases from 2 to 3. The high error rate for $\Lambda = 2$ is because of the difficulty in delineating RSSI stages, which verifies that *the minimum value of Λ is 3*. e_r drops substantially as Λ increases above 3 and reaches as low as 1.1% when $\Lambda = 4$.

Now we turn our attention to the cases where $\Lambda \geq 3$. The accuracy of P_i is almost identical to that of $|P_i|$, which indicates that finding the identity of an responder based on the length of its response is reliable. Moreover, we can see that e_r is almost identical to e_a, which indicates that *the number of nodes that LinearPoll overestimates or underestimates is almost never more than 1*.

Compared to the baseline, we see two advantages of using LinearPoll. Because there is no silent slot in LinearPoll, the poller can turn off its radio to save energy once the last responder finishes. In the baseline, however, the poller has to wait until the last slot. Assuming every subset of neighbors are equally likely to respond, the poller on average saves 50% of energy in LinearPoll. The second advantage of LinearPoll

---

[3]Because a stage can last as short as 2 samples for $\Lambda = 2$, we used the mean, instead of the median, as its measure of a stage.

[4]We did not rely on data communication in each slot for counting because this paper focuses on RSSI-based counting. Moreover, the small accuracy improvement of data communication incurs high energy cost due to limits on packet reception rate. The RSSI-based scheme requires a slot as short as 512 μs, whereas data communication requires a slot as long as 2ms for TelosB.

lies in its resilience to interference. While the poller in Lin-earPoll utilizes a priori knowledge about possible RSSI drops and their timings to reject interference, the baseline protocol identifies responders only by the presence of energy in their respective slots. Therefore, the baseline is more susceptible to interference. Our evaluation of the baseline protocol in Testbed 2 shows an error rate of 4%, which indicates that the baseline not only consumes more time and energy but also provides inferior accuracy as compared to the 1.6% error rate of LinearPoll.

4. LOGPOLL

LogPoll allows a poller to estimate the number of neighbors where predicate P holds on a logarithmic scale. In this section, we first analyze the basics of LogPoll and then present its detailed design, implementation and evaluation.

4.1 Preliminaries

The core idea is that the poller searches for some target RSSI Υ according to which each neighbor j adapts its power m_j such that $\widehat{R}(i, j, m_j) = \Upsilon$, i.e., the individual response RSSI from every neighbor is adjusted to be Υ. Such a power assignment, along with identical response lengths, ensures that the measure of the single stage of the superposed response from 2^u neighbors is roughly $\Upsilon + 3u$. Now, given a measure of r, the poller estimates $\log |P_i|$ by finding the $\widehat{u}$ that minimizes $|\Upsilon + 3\widehat{u} - r|$ and returns $\widehat{u}$ as the estimate of $\log |P_i|$.

To see why this sort of counting is accurate, consider how the received power of the superposed signal grows with the number of responses. For $2n$ signals that have the same frequency and the same amplitude A, their superposition has an amplitude of $2nA$ if their interference is entirely constructive, and an amplitude of 0 if their interference is entirely destructive. Because signal strength is proportional to the square of amplitude, the superposed signal from $2n$ sources is respectively 4x or 0x that of n signals in these extremal cases. The average case of the superposed signal from $2n$ sources has an expected strength that is twice, or 3 dB above, that of n sources. Hence, for 2^u responders that share the same response RSSI Υ, the superposed signal strength will be $3u$ dB above Υ.

More precisely, in addition to Requirement I, the following requirement is also needed for LogPoll to be accurate:

Requirement IV (Similar RSSIs, to Υ): *There exists a target RSSI Υ and a power assignment $\{m_j\}$ such that for $j = 1, 2, \ldots, N$:*

$$\widehat{R}(i, j, m_j) \in (\Upsilon - 1.5, \ \Upsilon + 1.5),$$

Proposition 1 implies that the RSSI of the superposed response increase by 3 dB whenever we double the number of responders. The following proposition provides the theoretical basis for the correctness of LogPoll. Let $s(u)$ be a node group of size 2^u. Let $\widehat{R}(i, s(u), \Upsilon)$ be the expected response RSSI at poller i of the superposed response from $s(u)$ whose target RSSI is Υ.

Proposition 1. *Given Requirement IV, the following holds for $u = 0, 1, 2, \ldots$ and $\forall s(u) \in N_i$:*

$$\widehat{R}(i, s(u), \Upsilon) \in (\Upsilon + 3u - 1.5, \ \Upsilon + 3u + 1.5) \quad (11)$$

Proof. We prove by nested induction. For $u = 0$, (11) follows trivially from Requirement IV. For the base case of the induction, we consider $u = 1$, i.e., for $s(1) = 2$ responders, and prove the following:

$$\widehat{R}(i, s(1), \Upsilon) \in (\Upsilon + 3 - 1.5, \ \Upsilon + 3 + 1.5)$$

Let $A(x)$ be the peak amplitude of a signal whose power is x dB. Given two signals of the same frequency that respectively have amplitudes of $A(x_1)$ and $A(x_2)$, we can compute the instantaneous power of their superposed signal, denoted as $W(t, A(x_1), A(x_2))$, at time t as:

$$W(t, A(x_1), A(x_2))$$
$$= Q \left(A(x_1) \sin(2\pi f \cdot t) + A(x_2) \sin(2\pi f \cdot t + \delta) \right)^2 ,$$

where Q is some constant, f is the frequency of the signal, and δ is phase offset between the two signals. The maximal RSSI of the superposed imposed signal is achieved when both component signals have an RSSI of $(\Upsilon + 1.5)$, the maximal increase (in dB) from one responder to two is

$$10 \cdot \log \frac{E[W(t, A(\Upsilon + 1.5), A(\Upsilon + 1.5))]}{E[W(t, A(\Upsilon + 1.5), 0)]} < 3 \text{ dB} ,$$

hence

$$\widehat{R}(i, s(1), \Upsilon) < \Upsilon + 1.5 + 3 .$$

We can likewise verify that the superposed signal reaches its minimal RSSI of $(\Upsilon + 1.5)$ when both component signals have an RSSI of $(\Upsilon - 1.5)$. Hence, we have proved (11) holds for $u = 1$.

Given that the two component signals have the same frequency f, the superposed signal will have the same frequency. If we consider the superposed signal of the two as one virtual signal whose target RSSI is $\Upsilon + 3$, Requirement IV inductively holds for the virtual signal. Now, for any $u > 1$, we can construct its proof by iterating the proof above from $u = 1$ as a superposed signal of 2^{u+1} component signals can be considered as one that consists of two virtual signals whose target RSSI is $\Upsilon + 3u$ and each of which is itself the superposed signal of 2^u component individual signals. The induction hypothesis thus holds. $\square$

Next, we overview the LogPoll protocol, and describe how Υ is chosen and how the poller can estimate $\log |P_i|$ based on Proposition 1.

4.2 Design of LogPoll

Given the one-time measurement for response RSSI prediction, LogPoll follows the same three steps as LinearPoll, except that the algorithm for response power and length assignment used in step 1 and the algorithm for estimation used in step 3 are respectively replaced with the schemes we present in Section 4.2.1 and 4.2.3.

4.2.1 Response Power and Length Assignment

All neighbors are assigned the same response length. There exists a tradeoff between the response length (and hence energy cost) and accuracy which we will study empirically in Section 4.3. As for power assignment, the poller searches for the target RSSI Υ that all neighbors can adjust to within their power ranges. According to (4), the poller can compute for each neighbor j its power to adapt $\widehat{R}(i, j, m_j)$ to Υ.

Recall that M is the set of available output powers and that nodes are labeled in the order of increasing path loss. Based on (4) we define α as the highest expected RSSI that the neighbor with the largest path loss (node N) can reach, and β as the lowest expected RSSI that the neighbor with the lowest path loss (node 1) can reach:

$$\alpha = \widehat{R}(i, N, m_N) + \widehat{a}_{iN}(M_{max} - m_N),$$
$$\beta = \widehat{R}(i, 1, m_1) - \widehat{a}_{i1}(m_1 - M_{min}).$$

Further, we define $\omega(r, j)$ as the smallest gap that node j can adjust $\widehat{R}(i, j, m_j)$ to a given value r:

$$\omega(r, j) = \min_{m \in M} \left(|\widehat{R}(i, j, m) - r| \right).$$

Obviously, Υ does not exist if $\alpha < \beta$; If $\alpha \leq \beta$, we set Υ to the value that minimizes the sum of $\omega^2(\Upsilon, j)$ over all neighbors:

$$\Upsilon = \operatorname*{argmin}_{r \in [\beta, \, \alpha]} \left(\sum_{j \in N_i} \omega^2(r, j) \right).$$

Finally, the power assignment for j is computed as:

$$m_j = \operatorname*{argmin}_{m \in M} |\widehat{R}(i, j, m) - \Upsilon|$$

4.2.2 Interference Detection

Similar to LinearPoll, we first verify that the measurement cycle is not contaminated by interference before P_i is estimated. Because all responses in LogPoll are of the same length, the number of samples that can be obtained in a round is known a priori. Also, samples in a measurement cycle should share similar RSSI. The poller can thus reject a measurement when (i) the number of samples is different from its expected value by more than some threshold.[5] or (ii) there is inconsistency in RSSI values within a measurement cycle.

4.2.3 Algorithm to Estimate P

In LogPoll, as each measurement cycle contains a single stage, which eliminates transitional samples, we use the mean of the samples, rather than the median as in Linear-Poll, as the measure of this single stage because it provides better resolution.

Now given a RSSI measure r, LogPoll estimates the number of responding neighbors with function $F_\Upsilon(r)$.

$$\log |P_i| = F_\Upsilon(r) = \operatorname*{argmin}_{u \in dom(\theta_\Upsilon)} \{|\theta_\Upsilon(u) - r|\} \qquad (12)$$

where θ_Υ is a discrete function that maps the number of responders in log scale to the expected strength of their superposed signal given a target RSSI of Υ. According to Proposition 1, we have

$$\theta_\Upsilon(u) = \Upsilon + 3u, \quad u = 0, 1, 2, \ldots \qquad (13)$$

In other words, node i uses the value u that makes $\theta_\Upsilon(u)$ closest to r as the estimate of $\log |P_i|$.

4.3 Implementation Details

Instead of detecting relative drops in RSSI in a measurement cycle as in LinearPoll, LogPoll estimates $\log |P_i|$ solely

---

[5]Empirically, we set the threshold to 1 for TelosB.

based on mean RSSI of the samples obtained. Hence, the accuracy of LogPoll depends heavily on how well the poller can measure the RSSI of the superposed response. Naturally, the more samples the poller can get from a measurement cycle, the more accurately the sample mean reflects the true RSSI of the response. We empirically observed that responses that are 32 bytes long provide almost the same accuracy as 128-byte long responses. Hence, neighbors use 32-byte responses in our implementation.

Also, we introduce a heuristic that can more accurately determine whether there is only one responder. Let us define the *peak-to-peak variability* of a measurement cycle to be the difference between the maximal sample and the minimal one. When there is only one responder, the peak-to-peak variability is seldom above 1 thanks to the absence of interference from other concurrent responses. When there are 2 or more responders with similar response RSSIs, the difference between the minimum and maximum in a measurement cycle is almost always greater than 1. Therefore, LogPoll exploits the variation in RSSI to help decide wether the number of responders is 1.

4.4 Experimental Evaluation of LogPoll

We now describe our evaluation of LogPoll on the TelosB mote platform: We begin with the experiment setup, then introduce a baseline for log scale counting, and finally empirically compare the baseline with LogPoll.

Experiment Setup. We tested LogPoll under different network conditions on three arrays in two testbeds. Two 63-node arrays, namely array A and B, are in Testbed 2 and a 43-node array, namely array C, is in Testbed 3. On each array, one node is designated as the poller. While array A represents an ideal neighborhood where all nodes satisfy Requirement IV and can choose a target RSSI above the external interference in Testbed 2, array B and array C represent different challenging network conditions. On array B, 10% of nodes do not meet Requirement IV due to the limited granularity in output power control on the TelosB platform; on array C, although the neighbors honor Requirement IV, they are far away from the poller and as a result they have to choose target RSSI lower than the external interference in Testbed 3.

Two experiment are conducted on each array and experiments on any given array share very similar results from run to run. In each experiment, we tested all groups of sizes 1, 2, 4, 8, 16, and 32 alternatively. The experiment finishes once each node group has been tested for 100 rounds.

In the beginning of every experiment, each neighbor sends to the poller 20 packets containing their power information for the poller to perform the one-time measurement for RSSI prediction as described in Section 2. *Step 1 in LogPoll, i.e., power and length assignment, is done only once based on the measurements in the beginning of each experiment and neighbors use the same assignment until an experiment finishes.*

4.4.1 Baseline for Log Scale Counting

To evaluate the performance of LogPoll, we implemented a baseline RSSI-based counting protocol based on a simplified group-testing as proposed in [2, 6]. Each round of the baseline takes multiple steps. In each step k, each responder has a probability of 2^{-k} to respond. A round finishes when no responder respond in a step. Based on the number of

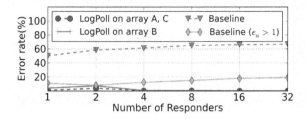

Figure 2: Comparison of error rates of LogPoll and the baseline protocol.

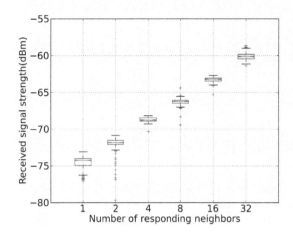

Figure 3: The distribution of RSSI measures for different numbers of responders on array A

steps n in a round, the poller can estimate the number of responder in that round to be $\min(N, 2^n)$, where again N is the number of poller's neighbors. All neighbors respond at the highest power level to ensure detection.

4.4.2 LogPoll Performance

Fig. 2 shows the LogPoll results. For a set of responders P_i and its estimation $\log |\widehat{P}_i|$, error amount e_a is defined as $e_a = |\log |P_i| - \log |\widehat{P}_i||$ and error rate is the percentage of rounds where $e_a > 0$.

When Requirement IV is honored (as on array A and C), the accuracy of LogPoll for node groups of all sizes except for 2 is close to 100% regardless of the value of Υ; the accuracy for node groups of size 2, albeit worse, is still over 96%. The reason that the accuracy of node group of size 2 suffers is because of its above-average variance in received signal strength: as we will see in section 4.4.3, the RSSI measure for node groups of size 2 varies from its expected RSSI more than node groups of other sizes.

Although the LogPoll protocol is general and can handle a broad class of topologies and densities, the radio hardware can be a constraint. To study the impact of limited range in power levels, we repeated the experiment on array B where 10% of neighbors have a response RSSI that diverges 1.5 dB to 3 dB from Υ, which fails to meet Requirement IV. We call these 10% of nodes *bad neighbors*. The accuracy is most impacted when there are no more than 2 responders because the superposed RSSI of node groups of small sizes will diverge considerable from their expected value if one or more of their members are bad neighbors. However, when there are 4 responders or more, the existence of bad neighbors is unlikely to lead to incorrect estimations because we are counting in log scale. *LogPoll becomes more resilient to coarse granularity in output power control as the number of responders increases.*

The baseline protocols suffers in terms of both accuracy and energy cost. The baseline protocol makes an error greater than 0 at least 50% of the time (as shown by the red dash line) and an error greater than 1 at least 7% of the time (as shown by the cyan line). What's worse, its accuracy decreases the number of responders increases. In terms of energy cost, each round in the baseline takes approximately $\log |P_i|$ steps and each steps takes about 4ms. On the contrary, LogPoll takes a constant time of about 4 ms.

4.4.3 Empirical Study of Proposition 1

LogPoll estimations are based on (13), whose correctness depends on Proposition 1. In this section, we empirically

verify Proposition 1 and discuss why the performance of Log-Poll is in general better as number of responders increases.

According to Proposition 1, the average RSSI of the response 32 responders should be 15 dB above that of 1 responder. Our results show that the gaps in average RSSI between 32 responders and 1 responder is 14.8, 15.2 and 14.7 results on array A, B, and C respectively, which verifies our proposition.

Fig. 3 shows the distribution of the RSSI measures for node groups of different sizes for experiment on array A. Each vertical blue box shows the distribution of RSSI measures of a given node group size. The red line is the median and the edges of the blue boxes denote the 25th and 75th percentiles. The two black whiskers cover a range of $[\mu - 2.7z, \mu + 2.7z]$, where μ and z are the mean and standard deviation of the data. For normally distributed data, the two whiskers have a coverage of 99.2%. Outliers are plotted individually using '+'. As we can see, the variance of the RSSI of the superposed signal decreases as the number of responders increases.

We observe that *the variance in response RSSI decreases decreases as the number of responders increases*. Due to the limited granularity in output power control, the mean RSSI for a single node can be 1.5 dB away from Υ and thus it can be as much as 3 dB apart from that of another neighbor. As a result, the variance for small groups is high, which explains why the accuracy for groups of size 2 or less suffers most, as shown in Fig. 2. As $|P_i|$ increases, the RSSI of the superposed response converges to $\Upsilon \cdot |P_i|$, which reduces the variance. Results on arrays B and C show similar trends of diminishing variance as the number of responders increase.

5. CONSTRAINTS AND EXTENSIONS

5.1 Handling Malicious Interference

Although non-trivial external interference was present in all of our LinearPoll and LogPoll experiments on Testbed 2, it did not noticeably degrade performance because of two reasons: (i) it is unlikely that the RSSI of the random interference resembles the RSSI of a valid responder; (ii) it is unlikely that the interference to start and end within within the polling window of 4 ms.

In this section, we introduce a malicious interferer F which attempts to make its interference resemble the response of a valid neighborin terms of timing, duration and RSSI. F not only transmits at the same time as the responders for a duration no longer than the longest valid response, it also adapts its power m_F such and $R(i, j, m_j) \approx R(i, F, m_F)$ for some $j \in N_i$.

We configured F to inject interference every 10 rounds and evaluated LinearPoll on Testbed 2 again with Λ set to 4. Although F interferes 10% of the time, the error rate increases only from 1.6% to 4.4% and error amount increases from 0.018 to 0.05.

In LogPoll, since the RSSI from I is similar to that of others and we are estimating P_i in log scale, we find that interference only leads to errors when $P_i \leq 4$. Also, F succeeds to create error only when its length is close to that of others. In a similar setting as LinearPoll above, we repeated LogPoll on array A. The error rate for two responders or less increases from 3% to 5%. Due to its very limited impact on accuracy, we skip further empirical study of the impact of smart interference on LogPoll.

5.2 Handling Topology Constraints

The limited range and granularity of the output power provided by radio hardware lead to constraints in topology. Given the RSSI measurement precision of the CC2420 radio, LinearPoll requires that the response RSSI's from any two neighbors be separated by at least 3 dB. In a topology benign to LinearPoll, neighbors have fairly different path losses and as a result the separation in response RSSI can be fulfilled even if the radio provides very limited output power levels; In the worst case where neighbors share very similar path losses, LinearPoll has to solely rely on the radio to provide the RSSI differentiation. For example, with the CC2420 radio, only 6 out of 8 output powers are at least 3 dB apart. If more than 6 neighbors share very similar path losses, LinearPoll should adopt the grouping technique that we will shortly introduce. Opposite to LinearPoll, LogPoll requires all response RSSI's to be close to some poller-dependent target RSSI Υ. In the worst case where neighbors have very different path losses, LogPoll would also have to rely on the radio to fulfill its requirement.

In general, users should take advantage of the complementary use cases of the two primitives and choose according to application needs and the radio hardware capabilities. In challenging cases where the precision of LinearPoll or the scalability of LogPoll is desired but their corresponding requirement cannot be satisfied given the specific topology, one can resort to the *vertical* or *horizontal* grouping.

In vertical grouping, we divide the neighborhood into multiple groups wherein members of each group have diverse path losses; in horizontal grouping, neighbors with similar path losses are grouped together.

Now, if the precision of LinearPoll is desired but Requirement II is not met, vertical grouping can be applied to ensure Requirement II holds in each group. If the scalability of LogPoll but Requirement IV cannot be satisfied, horizontal grouping can be applied to ensure Requirement IV holds in each group.

The information needed by either grouping scheme is already provided by the path loss estimation discussed in Section 2. Also, decomposing neighbors into groups incur minimal energy overhead on the poller, i.e., one polling message for each group, and no additional cost to the responding neighbors. We delegate evaluation of grouping to future work.

5.3 Beyond 802.15.4 Radios

For accurate counting, both primitives require that the superposition of component signals results in predicable signal strength. Were there to be highly constructive or destructive interference between component signals, the signal strength variability would increase (and the predictability would decrease). Randomness in the component signals helps avoid highly constructive or destructive superposition; this randomness could result from software jitter during response transmission but also by scripting the response to use random bits and by leveraging the physical layer properties of different radio technologies. Depending on the modulation scheme, the random bits in the packet will be modulated into random phases, amplitudes, or frequencies. As long as the poller averages RSSI samples over a period in which multiple bits are transmitted, it can still obtain a a good assessment of the mean RSSI of the superimposed signal. Thus, although we have only validated our primitives for a 802.15.4 radio, we argue that they are applicable to radios that follow other physical layers standards.

6. RELATED WORK

In-network processing approaches [9,11,17] typically focus on node-based function computation to reduce the amount of communication needed. In contrast, the processing in this paper exploits collaborative communication to reduce the overall complexity of (counter) function computation on the nodes.

In [2], the performance of three response collection methods — polling, group testing, and TDMA — is compared. As both polling and group testing require multiple rounds of communication for a single estimation, these methods are less efficient than LinearPoll and LogPoll. The TDMA approach, in which each neighbor is assigned a unique slot during which it sends back response, is closest to LinearPoll in terms of precision and energy cost. However, a poller using the TDMA approach cannot terminate its measurement cycle until the last assigned slot, whereas a poller in *LinearPoll* can terminate its measurement cycle as soon as the last responder finishes its response. On average, Linear-Poll is 2x as efficient as the TDMA approach.

In [5], Demirbas et al propose PollCast for a poller to estimate with constant cost whether $|P_i|$ is 0, 1, or greater than 1 based on Channel Clear Assessment (CCA). The poller detects no channel activity if $|P_i| = 0$, receives a response packet if $|P_i| = 1$, and detects collisions if $|P_i| \geq 1$. In comparison, LinearPoll not only counts but also identifies in a single round of communication.

In [6], *tcast* extends PollCast and estimates whether $|P_i|$ is greater than some threshold t at a cost of $O(2t \cdot (\log \frac{N_i}{2t}))$ in the worst case. In comparison, LogPoll estimates $\log |P_i|$ at a constant cost.

Dutta et al have proposed a simultaneous transmission scheme [7] that provides the same counting capability as LinearPoll. Their scheme identifies the set of responders, albeit it exploits the properties in Orthogonal Frequency Division Multiplexing (OFDM) modulation that is more suited for technologies with higher power radios such as IEEE 802.11 WLAN and WiMax. Although their scheme needs only a few symbols of response, it is computationally more expensive than LinearPoll as it requires Fourier transformations. Cross platform performance is difficult to compare, that said, its reported accuracy numbers appear to be similar to those of LinearPoll. While SMACK was only evaluated on a 3-node array, our primitives has been evaluated at scale in different testbeds. Also, their proposed scheme is limited by the number of available subcarriers as each neighbor require a unique subcarrier. One can relax such limitation by extending SMACK to utilize our primitives to detect the existence of multiple responders in each sub-carrier.

Our primitives can be readily integrated into existing MAC protocol designs. A-MAC [8] is a receiver-initiated MAC protocol that allows the receiver to quickly determine whether there is any neighboring node with pending traffic. It exploits the constructive interference of identical hardware-generated acknowledgement packets, which allows the receiver to successfully receive a superimposed acknowledgement with high probability. In StrawMAN [13], senders contend for the medium by simultaneously responding to the receiver's probe with request packets of random lengths and the sender with the longest request packet wins the medium. In both MAC protocols, either LinearPoll or LogPoll can be integrated for the receiver to gain more information about its neighborhood at no extra energy cost.

The RSSI reading on sensor motes is not always accurate and sometimes require calibration. Chen et al showed that the RSSI reading on TelosB motes have a constant offset compared to a reference curve [4]. Although this is important for protocols whose correctness depends on RSSI values reported from different nodes, the RSSI readings in our work are measured and used locally by the poller. As a result, our primitives are robust with respect to the RSSI offset.

7. CONCLUSIONS AND FUTURE WORK

In this paper, we investigated the problem of estimating neighborhood counts via collaborative communications. We showed that by carefully choosing the response packet length and output powers for neighbors, it is possible to encode information in their simultaneous responses to poll requests. We designed LinearPoll and LogPoll that allow the poller to collect the neighborhood metric at different precisions and asymptotic costs.

LinearPoll allows the poller to estimate P_i in a single round of communication whose duration is linear to the neighborhood size. We identified two parameters, namely the difference in response RSSI between neighbors and minimum duration of a response, that are critical for the performance of LinearPoll. We studied the constraints on choosing these parameters analytically and evaluated our implementation on the TelosB platform. Results show that LinearPoll achieves an accuracy of at least 98% for a neighborhood of 8 nodes in environments with sporadic interference and an accuracy of 95% even when malicious interference attacks 10% of the time.

LogPoll allows the poller to estimate $\log |P_i|$ at a constant cost. The accuracy of LogPoll the reliability of Proposition 1 which states signal strength from concurrent responses add up linearly. We analytically proved Proposition 1 and showed that it matches results on 3 different large node arrays in two testbeds. With our implementation of LogPoll on the TelosB motes, we showed that the accuracy of Log-Poll is 99% (averaged over different numbers of responders)

when all neighbors can adapt to a similar response RSSI and remains over 95% even when 10% of the neighbors fail to honor their power assignment.

In future work, it would be desirable to generalize our primitives for counting for P that are multivalued (instead of binary) predicates. A line of exploration would extend LogPoll as follows: since responders in LogPoll use fixed-length responses, it is feasible to encode more information using a variable response length. Let $v \in [V_{min}, V_{max}]$ be some variable of interest, which each neighbor j maintains locally as v_j. By dividing $[V_{min}, V_{max}]$ into bins, we can extend LogPoll by assigning to neighbor j a response length of $kC^{-1}(\Lambda)$ if v_j is in the kth bin. The poller can then aggregate the distribution of v in the neighborhood by counting in log scale the number of neighbors in each bin.

8. REFERENCES

[1] IEEE Computer Society Standard for local and metropolitan area networks–part 15.4: Low-Rate Wireless Personal Area Networks (LR-WPANs). IEEE, 2011.

[2] M. Ammar and G. Rouskas. On the performance of protocols for collecting responses over a multiple-access channel. In *Proceedings of the Tenth Annual Joint Conference of the IEEE Computer and Communications Societies. Networking in the 90s., IEEE*, pages 1490–1499, 1991.

[3] N. Burri, P. Von Rickenbach, and R. Wattenhofer. Dozer: Ultra-low power data gathering in sensor networks. In *2007 6th International Symposium on Information Processing in Sensor Networks*, pages 450–459, 2007.

[4] Y. Chen and A. Terzis. On the mechanisms and effects of calibrating RSSI measurements for 802.15. 4 radios. *Wireless Sensor Networks*, pages 256–271, 2010.

[5] M. Demirbas, O. Soysal, and M. Hussain. A singlehop collaborative feedback primitive for wireless sensor networks. In *IEEE INFOCOM The 27th Conference on Computer Communications*, pages 2047–2055, 2008.

[6] M. Demirbas, S. Tasci, H. Gunes, and A. Rudra. Singlehop collaborative feedback primitives for threshold querying in wireless sensor networks. In *Parallel and Distributed Processing Symposium*, pages 322–333, 2011.

[7] A. Dutta, D. Saha, D. Grunwald, and D. Sicker. Smack: a smart acknowledgment scheme for broadcast messages in wireless networks. In *ACM SIGCOMM Computer Communication Rev.*, volume 39, pages 15–26, 2009.

[8] P. Dutta, S. Dawson-Haggerty, Y. Chen, C.-J. M. Liang, and A. Terzis. Design and evaluation of a versatile and efficient receiver-initiated link layer for low-power wireless. In *Proceedings of the 8th ACM Conference on Embedded Networked Sensor Systems*, pages 1–14, 2010.

[9] C. Intanagonwiwat, R. Govindan, D. Estrin, J. Heidemann, and F. Silva. Directed diffusion for wireless sensor networking. *Networking, IEEE/ACM Trans. on*, 11(1):2–16, 2003.

[10] K. Jamieson, H. Balakrishnan, and Y. Tay. Sift: A MAC protocol for event-driven wireless sensor

networks. In *Wireless Sensor Networks*, pages 260–275. Springer, 2006.

[11] S. R. Madden, M. J. Franklin, J. M. Hellerstein, and W. Hong. TinyDB: an acquisitional query processing system for sensor networks. *ACM Trans. Database Syst.*, 30(1):122–173, 2005.

[12] V. Namboodiri and A. Keshavarzian. Alert: An adaptive low-latency event-driven mac protocol for wireless sensor networks. In *2008 International Conference on Information Processing in Sensor Networks*, pages 159–170, 2008.

[13] F. Österlind, N. Wirström, N. Tsiftes, N. Finne, T. Voigt, and A. Dunkels. Strawman: Making sudden traffic surges graceful in low-power wireless networks. In *Workshop on Hot Topics in Embedded Networked Sensors*, 2010.

[14] K. Srinivasan and P. Levis. RSSI is under appreciated. In *Proceedings of the Third Workshop on Embedded Networked Sensors*, 2006.

[15] T. Van Dam and K. Langendoen. An adaptive energy-efficient mac protocol for wireless sensor networks. In *Proceedings of the 1st International Conference on Embedded Networked Sensor Systems*, page 171, 2003.

[16] G. Werner-Allen, K. Lorincz, J. Johnson, J. Lees, and M. Welsh. Fidelity and yield in a volcano monitoring sensor network. In *OSDI '06: Proceedings of the 7th symposium on Operating systems design and implementation*, pages 381–396, Berkeley, CA, USA, 2006. USENIX Association.

[17] Y. Yao and J. Gehrke. The cougar approach to in-network query processing in sensor networks. In *SIGMOD Rec.*, volume 31, pages 9–18, 2002.

SoNIC: Classifying Interference in 802.15.4 Sensor Networks

Frederik Hermans
Uppsala University, Sweden
frederik.hermans@it.uu.se

Olof Rensfelt
Uppsala University, Sweden
olof.rensfelt@it.uu.se

Thiemo Voigt
SICS and Uppsala University
thiemo@sics.se

Edith Ngai
Uppsala University, Sweden
edith.ngai@it.uu.se

Lars-Åke Nordén
Uppsala University, Sweden
lln@it.uu.se

Per Gunningberg
Uppsala University, Sweden
per.gunningberg@it.uu.se

ABSTRACT

Sensor networks that operate in the unlicensed 2.4 GHz frequency band suffer cross-technology radio interference from a variety of devices, e.g., Bluetooth headsets, laptops using WiFi, or microwave ovens. Such interference has been shown to significantly degrade network performance. We present SoNIC, a system that enables resource-limited sensor nodes to detect the type of interference they are exposed to and select an appropriate mitigation strategy. The key insight underlying SoNIC is that different interferers disrupt individual 802.15.4 packets in characteristic ways that can be detected by sensor nodes. In contrast to existing approaches to interference detection, SoNIC does not rely on active spectrum sampling or additional hardware, making it lightweight and energy-efficient.

In an office environment with multiple interferers, a sensor node running SoNIC correctly detects the predominant interferer 87% of the time. To show how sensor networks can benefit from SoNIC, we add it to a mobile sink application to improve the application's packet reception ratio under interference.

Categories and Subject Descriptors

B.8.1 [**Performance and Reliability**]: Reliability, Testing, and Fault-Tolerance.

Keywords

Interference Classification, Wireless Sensor Networks, SoNIC, Decision Tree, Mobile Sink

1. INTRODUCTION

Due to a rapid increase in the number of technologies and devices operating in the license-free 2.4 GHz band, radio interference becomes an increasing problem for low-power wireless sensor networks. It has been shown that interference from other devices reduces sensor network performance, as it causes packet loss, reduces throughput, increases delay, and drains the sensor nodes' limited energy reserves [3, 24, 25].

The problem is exacerbated by the diversity of technologies that share access to the 2.4 GHz band. At any given time, a sensor network may have to compete with WiFi devices, Bluetooth peripherials, microwave ovens, baby monitors, or car alarms. All these technologies differ widely in when they access the spectrum, what frequencies they use, and for how long they use them [2]. It has been shown that when the interference source is known, using a specialized mitigation approach can improve performance [4, 15]. For example, the BuzzBuzz protocol [15] improves the delivery rate in sensor networks exposed to WiFi interference.

We address the problem of detecting and classifying interference within a 802.15.4 sensor network, so that the network can select a suitable mitigation strategy. Existing approaches to interference detection rely on sampling the spectrum continuously and over long durations for patterns in signal strength that are characteristic of certain interferers [1, 4, 14, 26]. Such active sampling is often prohibitively costly for battery-powered sensor nodes, where a radio in receive mode is commonly the most energy-hungry component. Some of the approaches require nodes to tune into different 802.15.4 channels to gauge the spectral footprint of an interferer [1]. This channel hopping makes it complicated for the sensor network to continue operation during interference detection. Furthermore, some approaches depend on additional hardware such as software-defined radios [14] or PC-class computers for processing [1, 26].

We present the S̲ensor N̲etwork I̲nterference C̲lassification (SoNIC) system, which takes a novel path to interference detection. Rather than actively sampling the spectrum, a node using SoNIC detects interferers by considering individual corrupted 802.15.4 packets, i.e., packets that the node has received, but for which the received payload did not match the packet's checksum. Through extensive measurements, we establish that different interferers corrupt individual 802.15.4 packets in distinct patterns, thereby leaving a "fingerprint" on the packet. The interferer's fingerprint becomes visible in *(i)* how the signal strength varies during packet reception, *(ii)* in the link quality indication (LQI) associated with the packet, and *(iii)* which bytes of the payload are corrupted. SoNIC exploits retransmissions to identify the corrupted parts of a packet. By solely relying on corrupted packets from regular sensor network traffic, SoNIC does not incur additional communication costs.

To demonstrate the feasibility of our approach, we have implemented SoNIC for the TelosB platform. We define a set of simple features that characterize the different fingerprints, and use a supervised learning approach to create a classifier that classifies corrupted packets. We assess the performance of SoNIC in both a controlled radio environment and an uncontrolled environment. Our results show that SoNIC reaches a mean accuracy of 72% when classifying individual corrupted packets. In a challenging office environment with multiple interferers and under mobility, SoNIC correctly detects the predominant interference source 87% of the time by considering a set of corrupted packets. We also show how a mobile sink application can be augmented with SoNIC and two mitigation techniques to increase the application's network performance under interference.

In summary, our three key contributions are:

- We establish that different interferers corrupt individual 802.15.4 packets in unique patterns, and show that these patterns prevail in different radio environments. We show that by using these patterns, a classifier can attribute corrupted packets to an interference type.

- We demonstrate that the classification is feasible on resource-constrained sensor nodes at moderate computational overhead, while maintaining a high classification accuracy. We show that SoNIC correctly detects the predominant interferer in a challenging radio environment with multiple interferers.

- We show how sensor networks can benefit from SoNIC by augmenting a mobile sink application with the system. With SoNIC, the application's packet reception rate under heavy interference is improved from 45% to 61%.

The rest of the paper is organized as follows. We develop the approach of classifying corrupted packets in Sec. 2. In Sec. 3, we describe how the approach can be implemented in a system for resource-constrained sensor nodes. The system's overhead and its performance in a controlled environment are considered in Sec. 4. We evaluate SoNIC in an uncontrolled radio environment in Sec. 5, and show how a mobile sink application benefits from SoNIC, using straightforward WiFi and microwave mitigations strategies in Sec. 6. Related work is described in Sec. 7. After a brief discussion on new and multiple interferers, we conclude the paper in Sec. 9.

2. CLASSIFYING CORRUPTED PACKETS

In this section, we develop the underlying idea of our approach: classifying corrupted 802.15.4 packets according to the source of interference. We begin by describing a set of measurements in which we systematically expose a sensor network to different interferers.

2.1 Characterizing Interference

To study the effect of interference on individual 802.15.4 packets, we set up thirteen TelosB sensor nodes alongside

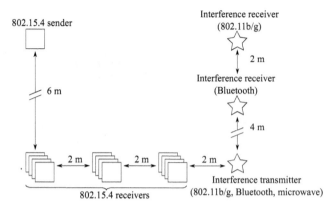

Figure 1: Experimental setup in the anechoic chamber

different interferers in an anechoic chamber (Fig. 1). The TelosB nodes are referred to as 802.15.4 sender and receivers in the figure, respectively. In each experiment, the 802.15.4 sender periodically broadcasts packets while one of the interferers is active. Three groups of four receivers are placed at varying distances from the sender and interferer. The anechoic chamber is shielded from outside radio emissions, so we are confident that corruption in 802.15.4 packets is caused by emissions from the active interferer. We focus on three sources of interference that are prevalent in indoor environments.

WiFi. We use two 802.11b/g routers to create WiFi interference. One of the routers acts as an access point streaming constant bitrate UDP traffic to the other router, which acts as a client. The resulting traffic resembles a video streaming session. We repeat the experiments for all 802.11b/g bitrates and modulations.

Microwave ovens. We heat a bowl of water in a residential-type microwave oven to create interference typical of these devices.

Bluetooth. To create Bluetooth interference, a Bluetooth dongle sends back-to-back packets to another dongle. Since Bluetooth uses adaptive frequency hopping, we reset the dongles before each experiment.

Non-interfered weak links. We also perform an experiment without interference. We set the sender's transmission power so that the signal strength at the receivers is close to the sensitivity threshold, causing corruption and packet loss. These experiments serve as a reference case for packet loss not caused by interference.

All experiments are repeated with hardware from different vendors, i.e., different models of WiFi routers, Bluetooth dongles, and microwave ovens. We also use a range of 802.15.4 channels to vary the frequency offset between interferer and sensor network. The packet length is varied from 16 to 124 bytes.

2.2 Features of Corrupted Packets

The receiving nodes logged about 900,000 *corrupted packets* during our experiments. These are packets that were received, but for which the received payload did not match the packet's checksum. Note that we distinguish corrupted packets from *lost packets*, for which the receiver failed to detect the packet preamble and hence was unaware of the transmission attempt.

For each corrupted packet, the receiver logs the signal

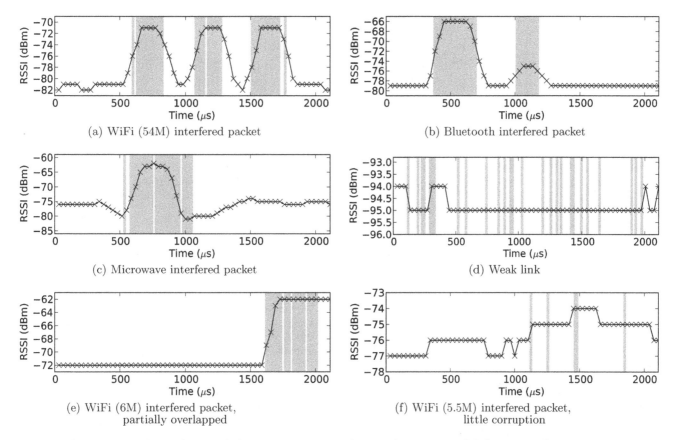

(a) WiFi (54M) interfered packet

(b) Bluetooth interfered packet

(c) Microwave interfered packet

(d) Weak link

(e) WiFi (6M) interfered packet,
partially overlapped

(f) WiFi (5.5M) interfered packet,
little corruption

Figure 2: Corruption and signal strength for some 802.15.4 packets in the presence of different interferers. SoNIC classifies corrupted packet based on the variations in signal strength and payload corruption.

strength during packet reception, the LQI associated with the packet, and the received (corrupt) payload. LQI is a measure of link quality that an 802.15.4-compatible transceiver provides for each received packet. In case of the CC2420 that is used on TelosB and many other sensor node platforms, LQI can be understood as the inverse of the chip error rate of the packet's preamble. To obtain the signal strength during packet reception, we modify the radio driver in Contiki. Our modified driver starts sampling RSSI whenever an interrupt signals an incoming packet, and it keeps sampling at a rate of one sample/byte until the last byte of the packet is received. Finally, since we know the correct packet payload from our log data, we determine which symbols of the received payload suffered transmission errors[1].

Fig. 2 shows examples of corrupted 802.15.4 packets that were received in the presence of different interferers. Each subfigure represents one 64-byte long 802.15.4 packet. The shaded areas indicate incorrectly decoded symbols in the packet payload, whereas the non-shaded area indicate correctly received symbols. The line shows the signal strength at the receiver during packet reception. A valid packet would have a mostly straight RSSI line with occasional quantization noise. The top three subfigures each represent one packet that was corrupted by WiFi, Bluetooth, and mi-

crowave interference respectively. The corruption coincides with distinct peaks in signal strength, caused by emissions from the interferer. Note that the packets are quite distinct in the amount and location of corruption and in the shape of the RSSI series. We exploit these kinds of regularities to classify corrupted packets. For comparison, Fig. 2d shows a packet that was not interfered, but that was received over a weak link with a signal strength close to the sensitivity threshold. Note the low RSSI compared to the other figures. This packet was also corrupted, but the corrupted symbols are spread much more evenly over the whole packet, and the low variation in signal strength is an effect of the transceiver's quantization of RSSI values rather than external emissions.

We attempt to capture the regularities that are exemplified in the packets shown in Fig. 2a–2d to create a classifier. However, we do not want and cannot aim to achieve perfect classification accuracy. For example, the packet in Fig. 2e was partially overlapped by a WiFi transmission at 6 MBit/s. Due to the short overlap, little information is available for classifying such packets. Similarly, the packet in Fig. 2f has only very few corrupted symbols and shows little variation in signal strength. Thus, we aim to achieve a reasonable classification accuracy per packet, so that we can infer the presence of an interferer from a set of corrupted packets.

We now describe a set of simple features that can be calculated for each corrupted packet. Based on these features, we train a classification algorithm to distinguish packets that

---

[1]In 802.15.4, one byte is represented by two four-bit symbols, which are transmitted as 32-bit chip sequences [11]. Decoding of an incoming chip sequence to a symbol is commonly performed in hardware. Thus, the finest granularity at which we can detect transmission errors is one symbol.

Feature	Purpose
LQI > 90	Detect sudden changes in channel conditions caused by interferers
range(RSSI)>2 dB	Distinguish interference from weak links
Mean error burst spacing	Capture temporal behavior of interferers, esp. for Bluetooth, WiFi
Error burst spanning	
Mean normalized RSSI	Characterize RSSI series, esp. for microwave
1 - mode(RSSI$_{normed}$)	

Table 1: SoNIC uses six features that in combination enable classification of corrupted packets.

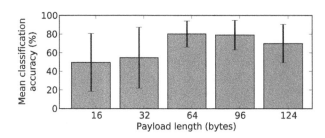

Figure 3: A mean classification accuracy larger than 70% is reached for packets of 64 bytes and more, whereas short packets are not classified accurately mostly due to insufficient overlap with the interferer's emissions.

have been corrupted by WiFi, Bluetooth, microwave ovens or weak links. The features are summarized in Tab. 1.

LQI threshold. If a packet has a high LQI but is corrupted, this is an indication that channel conditions were good when reception started, but then deteriorated. We observe such sudden changes in channel conditions when an interferer starts emitting during packet reception. In contrast, packets that are corrupted due to a weak link usually have a low LQI because channel conditions are equally poor over the whole packet reception time. To help distinguish interference from weak links, we define a binary feature that indicates whether the LQI of a corrupted packet is greater than 90. This threshold value is chosen empirically.

Error bursts. We define an error burst in a packet to be a sequence of corrupted symbols that may contain subsequences of at most four consecutive correct symbols. For example, we consider the packet in Fig. 2a to contain three error bursts.

MAC and PHY layers commonly impose strict timing constraints on transmissions. For example, Bluetooth devices stay on one frequency for a duration of 625 μs, and WiFi mandates strict inter-frame spacings. These constraints become visible in the error bursts. Rather than trying to detect specific timings, we define two general features to characterize the temporal behavior of different interferers. One is the mean number of symbols between error bursts in a packet, which depends on the interferer's inter-frame spacings; the other feature is the number of symbols between the first burst's start and the last burst's end, which depends on the interferer's transmission duration and frame spacing.

RSSI-based features. We define another binary feature to indicate whether the range of RSSI values associated with a packet is greater than 2 dB. Packets that are corrupted due to interference often show distinct peaks in RSSI, whereas packets received on a weak link contain little variation in signal strength. Before considering further features, note that RSSI depends on transmission power and the distances between receiver, sender, and interferer. To avoid these dependencies while preserving the series' shape, we normalize each series. We also reduce quantization noise by smoothing the series with a moving average filter.

We define the arithmetic mean of the normalized RSSI series to be a feature. We observe distinct distributions for the mean for packets corrupted by different interferers. This is because the RSSI series for packets corrupted by a given interferer often have similar, distinct shapes, and the mean is one way to characterize the shape, albeit a very coarse one. Next, we define a feature to capture a pattern that we commonly observe in packets interfered by microwave ovens: the signal strength slightly drops, then peaks, and drops

again (Fig. 2c). We attribute this pattern to the operation of the CC2420's gain control, as observed earlier [2]. We define the feature as $1 - mode$, where $mode$ is the most common value of the normalized series. A series which exhibits the pattern has a low value for the feature.

We have selected the above described feature set from the features we considered during our research, because the set is small, and the features are simple to compute and give a reasonable classification accuracy, as we will show next.

2.3 Feasibility of Classification

We use a supervised learning approach to create and evaluate a classifier. The classifier assigns a corrupted packet to one of four classes: interfered by WiFi, microwave oven, Bluetooth, or corrupted due to a weak link. We create a training and a testing set from the packets collected in the experiments. To ensure that the classifier is not biased to specific nodes, the testing set contains packets corrupted by one set of nodes, and the training set contains packets corrupted by another set from different vendors. We also balance the testing set with respect to the classes and the experiment parameters (e.g., frequency offset, packet sizes, WiFi rates). The testing set contains packets of 16, 32, 64, 96 and 124 bytes. We restrict the training set to packet sizes of 64 and 96 bytes, so we can test whether the classifier can classify packets of length that it has not been trained for.

Based on our datasets, we create a support vector machine (SVM) classifier on a PC using libsvm[2]. SVMs are considered to be the best "out-of-the-box" classifiers [17], and thus provide a good benchmark for testing the usefulness of our features for interference classification.

Fig. 3 shows the mean classification accuracy averaged over all classes for different packet sizes, with the error bars indicating variance between classes. While packets of 64, 96, and 124 bytes are correctly classified with an accuracy of 80%, 79% and 70% respectively, short packets have much lower classification accuracy. This is because short packets overlap only partially with the interferer's emission, and thus often do not carry enough information for meaningful classification. The accuracy does not significantly improve when we include short packets in the training set. We conclude that our classification approach requires packets of 64 bytes or more.

The classification accuracy for packets of 64 bytes and more is shown in Tab. 2. The row labels denote the (true) interferer, whereas the column labels denote the classification

---
[2]www.csie.ntu.edu.tw/~cjlin/libsvm/

		Classification result			
		Bluetooth	microwave	weak link	WiFi
Interferer	Bluetooth	**87.8%**	11.5%	0.4%	0.3%
	microwave	29.5%	**60.2%**	0.8%	9.5%
	weak link	0.1%	3.2%	**96.1%**	0.7%
	WiFi	16.4%	20.9%	1.2%	**61.5%**

Table 2: Classification results for 64 bytes and longer packets. The diagonal shows the classification accuracy.

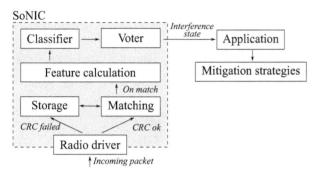

Figure 4: Overview of the SoNIC system

result. The diagonal indicates the percentage of correctly classified packets. Our approach performs best for Bluetooth interference and weak links. At around 60%, accuracy is slightly lower for WiFi- and microwave-interfered packets, but it is still vastly in excess of random chance (25%). Misclassifications occur for packets similar to those shown in Fig. 2e, 2f. We verified that accuracy is similar over all sets of parameter combinations, e.g., WiFi rates and channel offsets. No parameter combination stands out as being extremely hard to classify. The above results demonstrate that our features can effectively characterize the source of interference for a corrupted packet.

3. THE SONIC SYSTEM

We implement the classification approach that we laid out in the previous section in SoNIC, a system that enables a resource-limited sensor node to detect interference sources. Our implementation is based on Contiki [6]. An overview of SoNIC is shown in Fig. 4. The system is comprised of a modified *radio driver* that samples RSSI during packet reception and then hands off the received packet to the *storage module* (if the packet is corrupt) or to the *matching module* (if the packet is valid). The matching module identifies corrupted symbols in the stored packets, and then feeds them to the *feature calculation* module. This module calculates the features described in the previous section and inputs them to the *classifier*. Classification results are collected by the *voter*, which infers an interference state that it indicates to the application. We briefly consider the respective modules of SoNIC.

3.1 Radio Driver

We modify the CC2420 radio driver in Contiki to sample RSSI during packet reception. Sampling starts when an interrupt indicates an incoming packet and ends when the last byte of the packet has been received. No specific functionality is needed to obtain corrupted packets. The radio chip merely indicates that a packet is corrupted (i.e., failed

the CRC), rather than discarding it, and thus the corrupted packet is readily available to the node. If a corrupted packet is received, its payload, the sampled RSSI values, and LQI are saved in the storage module. A correct packet is passed up the stack and then handed over to the matching module.

3.2 Storing and Matching Packets

To identify corrupted symbols, SoNIC exploits retransmissions, which are used in many sensor network protocols such as the Collection Tree Protocol [7]. SoNIC stores corrupted packets in a FIFO buffer. When a valid packet is received, the matching module compares the payload of the valid packet against all payloads stored in the buffer. Each corrupted packet that is sufficiently similar to the received, valid packet is passed to the feature calculation module.

Note that if a corrupted packet is accidentally matched to the wrong packet, i.e., a valid packet that is not a retransmission of the corrupted packet, error bursts cannot be correctly identified. To minimize accidental matching, we use a matching algorithm that requires two payloads to share large contiguous regions to be considered a match.

3.3 Feature Calculation

The feature calculation takes as input a valid and a corrupted payload of a packet, and the RSSI values and LQI of the corrupted packet. It uses these inputs to calculate the features summarized in Tab. 1. Testing whether the LQI exceeds 90 and whether the range of RSSI values exceeds 2 dB is straight-forward. Error bursts are identified by a symbol-wise comparison of the valid to the corrupt payload. After the comparison, the mean burst spacing and the spanning of the bursts can be easily calculated. To avoid costly floating-point operations, we use fixed-point arithmetics to normalize the RSSI values and calculate their mean. By using fixed-point arithmetics, the normalization and mean calculation is reduced to a series of computationally cheap integer operations. To determine the most common RSSI value (referred to as the mode in Tab. 1), we sort the RSSI values and count element occurrences.

3.4 Classification

The features are fed into a classification algorithm. The SVM classifier that we have used to asses the feasibility of our features makes extensive use of floating-point operations. We therefore deem it unsuitable for implementing SoNIC on a severely limited platform. Instead, we use a decision tree classifier [5]. Classifying with a decision tree requires traversing the tree and comparing feature values against values stored at the tree's nodes. Thus, classification consists of a series of computationally cheap tests for inequality. We use the C4.5 algorithm [5] on a PC to create a decision tree from the training set collected in the anechoic chamber. The resulting tree consists of 365 inner nodes and 366 leaves.

3.5 Voting

From our investigation of feasibility in Sec. 2.3, we expect the classifier to occasionally misclassify a packet. To tolerate such errors, we use a voting mechanism. The voter considers recently received, corrupted packets taken from a configurable time window. The most common class of packets in the window is indicated as the interference state to the application. In our experiments, we use a window length of

30 s, which we found to give a good trade-off between fast interference detection and high confidence in the voting result.

During our initial experiments in an uncontrolled environment, it emerged that packets with very few corrupted symbols that were classified as active interference (as opposed to a weak link) negatively affected voting performance. We believe this to be an effect of overtraining in the anechoic chamber for packets with little corruption. Indeed, if only very few symbols are corrupted, there is little basis for an informed classification. Therefore, the voter discards packets with less than eight corrupted symbols that are classified as interfered. In the case of the testing set, 13.8% of the packets would be discarded after classification.

3.6 Using and Extending SoNIC

SoNIC reports the interference state to the application. It intentionally does not mandate what mitigation strategy to use, or when to activate and deactivate it. The reason is that the cost of interference, as well as the cost of mitigation, can only be estimated with the requirements of the specific application in mind.

SoNIC's classifier distinguishes between WiFi, Bluetooth and microwave oven interference, and packets that are corrupted due to low TX power. To add detection capabilities for a new interference type, suitable features must be defined and the classifier needs to be retrained.

4. MICROBENCHMARKS

We begin our evaluation by considering the feasibility of classification on resource-constrained sensor nodes. To this end, we first assess the cost of feature calculation and classification, and then evaluate the classification accuracy of the decision tree classifier.

4.1 Memory and Computational Overhead

SoNIC's memory requirements are dominated by the need to store the decision tree in the sensor node's RAM, which requires 1.8 KB. If an application has very tight memory requirements, the C4.5 algorithm can be configured to produce a smaller tree at the cost of classification accuracy. In its default configuration, SoNIC uses 1 KB to store corrupted packets in the FIFO buffer for later matching. This buffer can be adjusted if an application uses large packets. Furthermore, another static buffer of 128 bytes is used to store valid packets, so they can be matched after they have been processed by the network stack. In summary, SoNIC's static memory consumption amounts to ca. 3 KB. We consider this an acceptable memory overhead, and thus have not tried to further optimize memory consumption.

The computational overhead of SoNIC is comprised of feature calculation and classification. We select 1000 packets at random from the testing set and measure the time it takes to calculate features and classify them on a TelosB node. The mean feature calculation time of 26.5 ms ($\sigma = 7.0$ ms) is dominated by normalizing the RSSI values, which accounts for about 60% of the total calculation time, because it requires repeated 32-bit integer divisions. The variance is due to differences in packet length. One classification takes 1.2 ms on average ($\sigma = 0.5$ ms). Note that newer sensor nodes feature a faster CPU that executes typical operations more than 10 times faster than a TelosB, even when the CPU does not run at full speed [13]. On a modern Cortex-M3-

		Classification result			
		Bluetooth	microwave	weak link	WiFi
Interferer	Bluetooth	**68.1%**	23.9%	0.3%	7.6%
	microwave	25.3%	**63.9%**	0.7%	10.1%
	weak link	0.1%	0.8%	**98.5%**	0.6%
	WiFi	14.3%	24.1%	1.1%	**60.4%**

Table 3: The decision tree achieves a mean classification accuracy of 72.8%, almost on par with more powerful support vector machines (76.4%).

based platform, the time required for feature calculation and classification would hence be lower than the transmission time of a medium-sized 802.15.4 packet. Together with the energy needed to keep the MCU on during packet reception to sample the RSSI, the feature calculation is the only additional energy cost for interference classification with SoNIC.

4.2 Accuracy of Decision Tree Classifier

SoNIC uses a decision tree on the sensor nodes due to its low computational complexity. In contrast to SVMs, a decision tree does not perform feature space transformation and separates classes linearly[3]. To test whether the decision tree significantly degrades classification accuracy, we evaluate it on a TelosB sensor node using the data set from the anechoic chamber. The results are summarized in Tab. 3. The mean classification accuracy is 72.8%, which is close to the accuracy of the SVM (76.4%). The decision tree performs slightly better for packets corrupted by microwave, WiFi, or weak links, but performs worse for packets corrupted by Bluetooth (87.8% vs. 68.1%). Most of the misclassified Bluetooth-interfered packets are attributed to microwave. We assume that while the SVM finds a good non-linear separation for the classes Bluetooth and microwave, the C4.5 algorithm that we use to create the decision tree avoids this separation because it aims to build a tree with few nodes. Although a better classification accuracy may be achieved by configuring C4.5 to create a larger tree, we will show that the accuracy we observe in Tab. 3 is sufficient to detect Bluetooth interference.

We conclude that classifying corrupted packets according to their source of interference is feasible even on resource-constrained sensor nodes when using a lightweight classification approach.

5. EVALUATION

So far we considered interference in an anechoic chamber, an idealized environment that is shielded from external radio emissions and that minimizes multipath propagation. We now address classifying interference in a more representative environment: an office corridor with heavy multipath effects and multiple interferers.

5.1 Experimental Settings

The layout of our testbed is shown in Fig. 5. There are six stationary sensor nodes and one mobile sensor node, all TelosB. We use a testbed infrastructure that includes robots for sensor mobility and provides repeatable movement patterns [21]. The mobile node's path follows the corridor and

---

[3]Strictly speaking, an SVM also only uses linear hyperplanes for separation of classes, but using a transformation allows for non-linear separations in feature space.

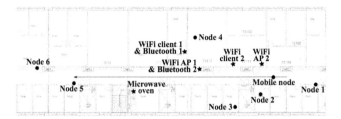

Figure 5: Experiment layout in the office corridor. We omit the location of interferers that we do not control, such as Bluetooth keyboards and university WiFi.

is 32 m long. By using a mobile sensor node, we test SoNIC over a variety of distances between interferers, senders and receivers. Thereby we can evaluate whether our approach is coupled to the specific setup in the anechoic chamber.

The testbed includes two WiFi access points and clients, as well as two Bluetooth dongles, and a microwave oven (stars in Fig. 5). We use these devices to create interference during our experiments. However, there are a number of radio devices in the corridor that we cannot control. The university's WiFi is present on all 802.11g channels. Bluetooth mice and keyboards, which periodically beacon their presence even when not actively used, can be found in many offices. Furthermore, we confirmed with a spectrum analyzer that emissions from microwave ovens located on adjacent floors reach our floor. Thus, the sensor nodes are exposed to varying and uncontrolled interferers during all experiments. We deliberately do not aim to control these interferers because we want to understand how robust our approach is in the presence of such background interference.

5.2 Link Conditions under Interference

We first consider the effect of interference in the corridor. Our aim is to quantify the performance impact and to demonstrate that a considerable fraction of packets is received as corrupted packets.

Methodology. We focus on the link from node 1 to the mobile node. Node 1 sends 64-byte long packets with a period of 125 ms to the mobile node, which travels away from the sender at a speed of 0.12 $\frac{m}{s}$ along the arrow shown in Fig. 5. That means that one packet is sent every 1.5 cm. We first perform two experiments without controlled interference, in which the sender's TX power is set to 0 dBm (maximum), and -7 dBm respectively (weak link case). We then perform three experiments under interference from WiFi AP 1 and client 1, the Bluetooth devices, and the microwave oven respectively. The sender uses maximum TX power in these experiments. Our metrics are packet error ratio (PER = 1−PRR) and packet corruption ratio (PCR), which we define as the ratio of received corrupted packets to sent packets. This means that PER includes both lost and corrupted packets, whereas PCR only includes corrupted packets. Results are averaged over ten runs for each experiment.

Results. When none of our interferers is active and the sender uses maximum TX power, PER is stable and varies between 0% and 15%, as we expect for an indoor environment. PER and PCR for the weak link (low TX power) are shown in Fig. 6a as a function of location of the receiving mobile node. The gray shaded areas denote one standard deviation calculated over the experiment repetitions. We attribute the variance primarily to background RF activity.

There is a strong increase in PER at 10–24 m, which we attribute to multipath effects in that area (which features many reflective obstacles) causing a notable drop in signal-to-noise ratio (SNR). After 24 m, SNR recovers and PER drops, probably due to the corridor acting as a wave guide.

PER and PCR under interference from different sources are shown in Figs. 6b–6d. The peaks in packet loss roughly correspond to the interferers' locations, which is an effect of the near-far problem [20]. The interferers incur different amount of packet loss due their different channel utilization. WiFi causes the highest packet loss, since its traffic saturates the channel. By principle of operation, the microwave has a "channel utilization" of 50% [2], which corresponds closely to the peak PER observed in Fig. 6c. The microwave has the strongest signal, and hence affects packets at the start and end of the track. Bluetooth interference incurs the least packet loss, because it only briefly overlaps with the sensor network channel due its frequency hopping.

SoNIC requires corrupted packets for classification. Thus, an important observation from Figs. 6a–6d is that regardless of the cause of packet loss, the ratio of corrupted packets is between 10%-20% when the link suffers significant packet loss, i.e., when PER is above 20%.

5.3 Classification Results

Next, we consider the classification results from the measurements we just described. Our aim is to evaluate how well the classifier, which has been trained on data from the anechoic chamber, can classify corrupted packets in a realistic radio environment with background RF activity. Note that because the experiments were performed in a live radio environment that we cannot fully control, we do not have the ground truth on whether a given corrupted packet was indeed corrupted by the interferer that we have activated during the experiment. Therefore, we estimate the classification accuracy by statistical means instead. We consider all classifications done during the last 30 s, i.e., all classifications in the voting window. This decision is based on the insight that the dominant interferer causes a significant amount of packet corruption and that a sliding window approach will reduce overreaction to sporadic misclassifications, but that it will on the other hand slow down the reaction time.

Results. We consider the distribution of classes in the voting window at each location of the receiver, i.e., we determine the fraction of packets in the window that are classified to each of the four classes. For example, if the window contains six Bluetooth-, one WiFi-, one microwave-, and two weak-link-classifications, the fractions are 0.6, 0.1, 0.1, and 0.2, respectively.

Fig. 7 shows the distribution of classes at each receiver location, averaged over ten runs. Areas of heavy packet loss (PER > 20%) are marked in gray. Each subfigure shows results for experiments under one type of interference. Each line represents the fraction of packets that have been classified to a given interferer. The most important observation from these figures is that under packet loss, most packets are classified to the interferer that was activated during the experiment. That is, on average SoNIC correctly attributes most of the packets to the dominant interference source.

In the case of low TX power and no controlled interference (see Fig. 7a), most packets are attributed to a weak link during heavy packet loss (11 m–25 m, 28 m–30 m). The accuracy is slightly poorer than the one in the anechoic

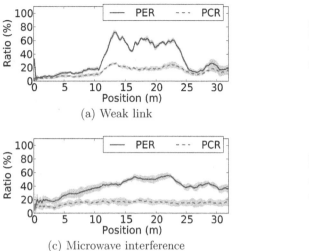

(a) Weak link

(b) WiFi interference

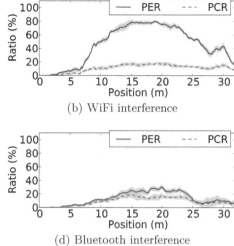

(c) Microwave interference

(d) Bluetooth interference

Figure 6: Packet error ratio and ratio of corrupted packets in the office corridor. A substantial fraction of packets is corrupted, which is necessary for classification.

chamber, which we attribute to uncontrolled radio devices. Most corrupted packets between 0 m and 11 m are attributed to WiFi and Bluetooth interference. This is expected, because the corridor contains a number of WiFi and Bluetooth devices that we do not control.

Fig. 7b shows results for experiments under WiFi interference. As the mobile receiver gets closer to the interferers, the number of packets classified as WiFi increases, until it peaks at the interferers' location at around 15 m. This dependency on distance can be explained as follows. We observed that the amount of corrupted symbols per packet strongly depends on distance in the case of WiFi interference. As the receiver gets closer, it can detect the error bursts in the packets more clearly, and thus the error-burst features take values closer to the values observed in the anechoic chamber. Furthermore, note that a number of packets at the edge of the area of heavy packet loss are attributed to a weak link. This is an effect of the voter discarding packets with very little corruption, as described in Sec. 3.5. Nonetheless, most packets are correctly classified as WiFi when packet loss exceeds 20%.

The classification results under microwave oven interference are shown in Fig. 7c. In contrast to the anechoic chamber, a considerable number of corrupted packets are classified as WiFi interference. When inspecting individual experiment runs, we found that in four consecutive runs out of the ten runs under microwave interference, a large number of packets was classified as WiFi interference. These four runs strongly affect the average results shown in the figure. The 802.15.4 channel we used in these experiments overlapped with 802.11g channel 11, on which we observed most WiFi traffic from the university WiFi. Thus, it is conceivable that runs were indeed exposed to WiFi interference. However, we do not remove the runs from the data, since we ultimately cannot gauge the impact of the university's WiFi on these four runs. We also point out that a certain number of misclassifications are expected from the accuracy observed in the anechoic chamber. Nonetheless, most of the packets are classified as being interfered by a microwave oven.

Finally, Fig. 7d shows the average distribution of classifi-

cation results in the presence of Bluetooth interference. The majority of corrupted packets is classified as interfered by Bluetooth. A number of instances is classified as corrupted by microwave, which is in line with the anechoic chamber classification.

The above results show that the classifier, which has been trained on data from the anechoic chamber, is able to classify the dominant interference source in our experiments. We conclude that our features characterize interferers not only in the anechoic chamber, but also in the uncontrolled radio environment under background RF activity.

5.4 Detection Results

The results from the previous section are averaged over multiple runs. The averaging hides variations in performance between runs. Therefore, we now consider the amount of time that the voter indicated each interference state, while under heavy packet loss. This metric exposes the performance during each run.

The results are shown in Tab. 4, normalized by the total time under heavy packet loss. The table's rows show the true interferer, and the columns show the detected interference state. SoNIC returns the state *unknown* in case there is an insufficient number (< 5) of classified packets for voting. SoNIC correctly detects that the receiver is experiencing interference almost all of the time, and rarely returns the state *unknown*. Furthermore, the time that each interference state is detected corresponds to the results from the previous section. Both weak links and Bluetooth interference are detected with high accuracy. WiFi interference is correctly declared 82% of the time, but 16.2% of the time, SoNIC attributes the packet loss to a weak link. This is in agreement with Fig. 7b, which shows that at the edges of the interference zone, WiFi interference is misclassified as a weak link. Note that if we defined heavy packet loss as PER above 50% (instead of 20%), SoNIC correctly detects WiFi interference 95% of the time. Finally, microwave interference is correctly declared 74.1%. As mentioned before, four consecutive runs of the microwave experiments contained a large number of WiFi classifications, so there may indeed have been uncontrolled WiFi activity during these runs. In

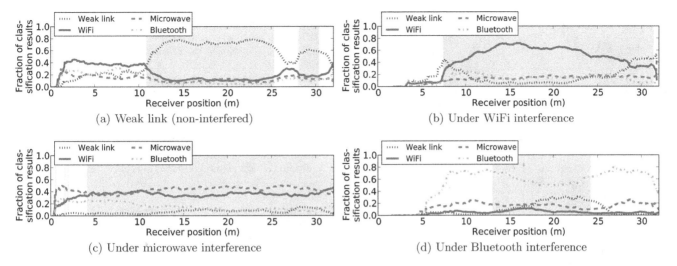

Figure 7: Average distributions of classification results in the voting window. Under heavy packet loss (gray areas, PER > 20%), SoNIC correctly attributes most corrupted packets to the dominant interferer.

		Percentage of time per detected interference state				
		unknown	weak link	WiFi	microwave	Bluetooth
Interferer	weak link	0.3%	**97.6%**	0.5%	0.3%	0.6%
	WiFi	0.1%	16.2%	**82.0%**	0.5%	1.1%
	microwave	0.6% (0.7%)	0% (0%)	23.2% (17.4%)	**74.1% (79.5%)**	2.0% (2.3%)
	Bluetooth	0%	3.7%	0%	0%	**96.3%**

Table 4: The duration that SoNIC detects an interference state is shown in columns, the dominant interferer is shown in rows. Overall, the correct interferer is detected 87.5% of the time.

parentheses, we state the amount of time per interference state when discarding these four runs, which increases detection to 79.5%.

We conclude that when experiencing packet error ratios of 20% and more, SoNIC correctly detects the interference state 87.5% of the time on average.

6. AUGMENTING A MOBILE SINK WITH SONIC

To show how a sensor network can benefit from SoNIC, we add it to a mobile sink application to detect and mitigate interference. The mobile sink polls its stationary one-hop neighbors for data in a round-robin fashion. When a stationary node receives a request, it responds with a stream of 20 packets of 64 bytes. Retransmissions are used to handle packet loss. We set the number of retransmissions to 30, the same value used in the Collection Tree Protocol [7] implementation in TinyOS.

Mitigation. The mobile sink implements two exemplary mitigation strategies. When WiFi interference is detected, the mobile sink switches communication to another 802.15.4 channel, separated 30 MHz from the interfered channel. In this way, it avoids a frequency overlap with the WiFi channel. To mitigate microwave interference, the nodes time their transmission so they do not coincide with the microwave emissions. Microwave emissions are very regular in time, following a 10 ms on, 10 ms off pattern [2]. When the mobile sink detects microwave oven interference, it requests its peers to schedule transmissions 20 ms apart. If a peer does not receive an ACK for a transmission, it randomizes

PRR under interference, without SoNIC	45.3% ($\sigma = 0.94\%$)
PRR under interference, with SoNIC	61.7% ($\sigma = 6.16\%$)
PRR without interference	70.0% ($\sigma = 0.00\%$)
Mean time to detect WiFi interference	18.14 s ($\sigma = 23.9$ s)
Mean time to detect microwave interference	2.57 s ($\sigma = 1.41$ s)

Table 5: Summary of the results for mobile sink experiments. The PRR is improved by choosing a suitable mitigation strategy.

its transmission time to avoid synchronization with the microwave oven. We selected these two mitigation approaches due to their simplicity. Note that SoNIC can readily be used with other approaches as well, e.g. [4, 15].

Mitigation decisions. The mobile sink uses the following approach to making a mitigation decision. If the average PER of the links to its neighbors exceeds 40%, the mobile sink enters a back-off phase of ten seconds. If PER still exceeds 40% after the back-off phase and either WiFi or microwave interference is detected, the sink activates the respective mitigation strategy. Using a back-off ensures that after the network conditions have changed (as indicated by the increase in PER), a sufficient amount of time is spent in the new conditions to collect corrupted packets.

Scenario. The mobile sink travels along the path denoted by the arrow in Fig. 5 and polls data from the stationary sensor nodes 1–6. For the duration of the whole experiment, the WiFi AP 2 (located near the beginning of the track)

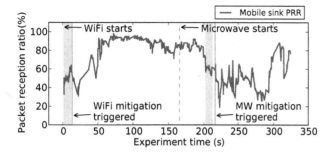

Figure 8: Annotated run of the mobile sink experiment. After PRR has dropped, SoNIC quickly indicates the detected interferer to the application

streams constant bitrate UDP traffic on channel 6, which overlaps with the 802.15.4 channel that the sensor nodes are using for communication. When the mobile sink has traveled half of the path, the microwave is activated for the rest of the run's duration. We repeat the experiment six times.

Results. The key results are summarized in Tab. 5. Using SoNIC significantly improves the number of correctly received packets under interference. In all runs, the mobile sink correctly detected and mitigated WiFi interference at the beginning of the track. It correctly detected and mitigated the microwave interference in five of the six runs. In the remaining run, the mobile sink erroneously detected WiFi interference instead. This performance matches our observations from the previous sections.

Fig. 8 demonstrates the operation of the mobile sink using SoNIC during one run. The figure shows the sink's PRR, and the annotations indicate when the respective interferers have been activated and when the sink has detected them and made a mitigation decision. The gray areas show when the mobile sink backs off after a drop in PRR, before making a mitigation decision. In the beginning of the experiment, the mobile sink experiences poor performance due to WiFi interference. It correctly detects WiFi interference after the 10 s back-off period and activates the appropriate mitigation, i.e., it changes to channel 23, a channel that is heavily affected by microwave interference [2]. PRR gradually increases as the sink informs the other nodes of the new channel. At 165 s, the microwave is activated. The sink's PRR does not drop instantaneously, because it happens to be communicating to a nearby node (and hence is not as strongly affected by the interference), and because the PRR estimation introduces a slight lag. However, once the drop in PRR is registered, the mobile sink backs off and then correctly detects microwave interference and activates the mitigation strategy. PRR does not recover to non-interference levels; this is partly because the microwave mitigation is not as effective as the channel switching, but also caused by the fact that most sensor nodes are located near the beginning of the track, and hence the mobile sink experiences poor connectivity to those nodes regardless of interference.

On average, it takes the mobile sink 18.1 s after the back-off period to trigger a mitigation decision in the case of WiFi interference. This average is inflated by two runs, in which it took 59.0 s and 43.8 s respectively before the mitigation decision was made. There were two reasons: (i) the mobile sink was communicating with nearby nodes with strong links, and thus the PER did not exceed 40% after the back-off had elapsed. (ii) when querying nodes on links that were strongly affected by the interference, it took a while to collect enough corrupted packets for classification. Taking a decision to mitigate microwave interference took 2.5 s on average after the back-off time. Since microwave ovens are usually operated for short durations in the order of a few minutes, such quick detection is especially desirable.

7. RELATED WORK

The problem of interference in wireless sensor networks is well-known. For example, Sikora and Groza have studied the impact of microwave ovens, Bluetooth and WiFi on packet loss in sensor networks [25]. Petrova et al. have quantified the impact of 802.11 devices on sensor networks [19]. Sha et al. have studied the spectrum usage in home area networks and realized that wireless conditions in homes and hence interference are more complex than in office environments [23]. Also in the context of body area networks, interference is recognized as a problem [8, 10, 12]. Various techniques have been proposed to classify the source of interference for wireless sensor networks. Zacharias et al. have monitored a single IEEE 802.15.4 channel to classify the source of inference using RSSI readings [26]. However, the main part of their data analysis was done offline in Matlab, which is different from the real-time analysis performed by individual sensors in our SoNIC system. Similarly, Bloessl et al. have presented an interferer classification framework, which measures RSSI in a predefined spectrum and displays the signal strengths and their corresponding frequencies in real-time [1]. Different from the above work, SoNIC provides a comprehensive approach to explore a wide range of features for interference classification, including LQI, RSSI and error bursts.

Many authors have proposed solutions for mitigating interference. Some of the solutions are agnostic to the source of interference. For example, Boano et al.'s approach to make MAC protocols robust against interference does not consider the interference source [3]. There are further multi-channel protocols that avoid interference by switching channels [22, 27]. Noda et al. have devised a channel metric to quantify interference that is per design agnostic to the interference source [18]. In contrast to these solutions, we explicitly classify the source of interference and adapt our mitigation strategy to the source of interference.

Alternatively, there are solutions to mitigate interference by observing pattern of specific interference sources [2]. For example, Hauer et al. have suggested how to mitigate the effects of RF interference through RSSI-based error recovery [9]. Liang et al. have specifically targeted WiFi interference and applied forward error detection to combat the impact of this interference source [15]. Chowdhury and Akyildiz have presented an approach that based on the spectral characteristics distinguishes between WiFi and microwave interference [4]. In contrast to us they use a distributed approach that has been evaluated in simulation only. While we aim at classifying the source of interference, Musaloiu-E. and Terzis's goal has been to detect WiFi interference by means of periodic RSSI samples [16]. Both Chowdhury and Musaloiu-E.'s approaches are based on active channel sampling which requires sensor nodes to turn on the radio and hence contributes to higher power consumption by idle listening. On the contrary, SoNIC does not rely on active spectrum sampling over long timespans or additional hardware, which makes it lightweight and well-suited for low-power sensor nodes.

8. DISCUSSION

SoNIC's classifier distinguishes between WiFi, Bluetooth and microwave oven interference, and packets that are corrupted due to low TX power. To add detection capabilities for a new interference type, suitable features must be defined and the classifier needs to be retrained.

In the experiments in Sec. 5 and Sec. 6 there are a number of interfering devices that we cannot control, in particular the university's WiFi. We have, however, not performed any explicit experiments with multiple interferers. SoNIC is currently designed to identify the main interferer. As described in Sec. 3.5, the voter chooses the most common class of packets in the window as the interfering state and passes this state to the application. To address multiple interferers of different kinds, we would change the voting algorithm to, for example, estimate the likelihood of the presence of a specific interferer.

An open question is if we need to provide additional features or change the features to classify corrupted packets in the presence of multiple interferers. Communication protocols usually have mechanisms to avoid simultaneous transmissions from two or more devices and hence packets are seldomly corrupted by concurrent transmissions. Therefore, packets are not corrupted differently in the presence of multiple interferers of the same type which suggests that our current features are sufficient to handle this case.

Unfortunately, protocols are usually not designed with coexistence in mind and obviously microwave ovens do not consider communication protocols. Hence, there is a higher chance that packets form different interferers are transmitted simultaneously and corrupt packets in ways different from what our features are designed for. We leave the investigation of this problem for future work.

9. CONCLUSION

Sensor networks that use 802.15.4 at 2.4 GHz face cross-technology interference from many other technologies operating in the same frequency band. Previous research has shown that interference mitigation in sensor networks can be more effective if the type of interference is known. This paper addressed the problem of classifying and detecting interference in a sensor network. We introduced a novel approach to interference classification that considers individual, corrupted 802.15.4 packets, rather than using costly continuous spectrum sampling. The evaluation has shown that our implementation of the approach is sufficiently lightweight for use on resource-constrained sensor nodes, and that it correctly detects the predominant interferer in an uncontrolled office environment.

10. ACKNOWLEDGEMENTS

This work has been funded by the VINNOVA through the Uppsala VINN Excellence Center for Wireless Sensor Networks (WISENET). It has been partially supported by the European Commission with contract INFSO-ICT-317826 (RE-LYonIT). Thanks to our shepherd Chenyang Lu and the reviewers for their comments.

11. REFERENCES

[1] B. Bloessl, S. Joerer, F. Mauroner, and F. Dressler. Low-Cost Interferer Detection and Classification using TelosB Sensor Motes. In *Poster Session, MobiCom 2012*, Istanbul, Turkey, August 2012.

[2] C. A. Boano, T. Voigt, C. Noda, K. Römer, and M. Zúñiga. JamLab: Augmenting Sensornet Testbeds with Realistic and Controlled Interference Generation. In *International symposium on Information processing in sensor networks (IPSN)*, Chicago, IL, USA, Apr. 2011.

[3] C. A. Boano, T. Voigt, N. Tsiftes, L. Mottola, K. Römer, and M. Zuniga. Making Sensornet MAC Protocols Robust Against Interference. In *European Conference on Wireless Sensor Networks (EWSN)*, Coimbra, Portugal, Feb. 2010.

[4] K. Chowdhury and I. Akyildiz. Interferer Classification, Channel Selection and Transmission Adaptation for Wireless Sensor Networks. In *International Conference on Communication (ICC)*, June 2009.

[5] R. O. Duda, P. E. Hart, and D. G. Stork. *Pattern Classification (2nd Edition)*. Wiley-Interscience, 2 edition, Nov. 2001.

[6] A. Dunkels, Björn Grönvall, and T. Voigt. Contiki - a Lightweight and Flexible Operating System for Tiny Networked Sensors. In *1st Workshop on Embedded Networked Sensors (EmNetS)*, Tampa, Florida, USA, Nov. 2004.

[7] O. Gnawali, R. Fonseca, K. Jamieson, D. Moss, and P. Levis. Collection Tree Protocol. In *International Conference on Embedded Networked Sensor Systems (SenSys)*, Nov. 2009.

[8] J.-H. Hauer, V. Handziski, and A. Wolisz. Experimental Study of the Impact of WLAN Interference on IEEE 802.15.4 Body Area Networks. In *European Conference on Wireless Sensor Networks (EWSN)*, Cork, Ireland, Feb. 2009.

[9] J.-H. Hauer, A. Willig, and A. Wolisz. Mitigating the Effects of RF Interference through RSSI-Based Error Recovery. In *European Conference on Wireless Sensor Networks (EWSN)*, Coimbra, Portugal, Feb. 2010.

[10] J. Hou, B. Chang, D. Cho, and M. Gerla. Minimizing 802.11 Interference on ZigBee Medical Sensors. In *International Conference on Body Area Networks (BodyNets)*, Apr. 2009.

[11] IEEE Computer Society. *802.15.4: Wireless Medium Access Control (MAC) and Physical Layer (PHY) Specifications for Low-Rate Wireless Personal Area Networks (WPANs)*, 2006.

[12] J. Ko, T. Gao, and A. Terzis. Empirical Study of a Medical Sensor Application in an Urban Emergency Department. In *International Conference on Body Area Networks (BodyNets)*, Apr. 2009.

[13] J. Ko, K. Klues, C. Richer, W. Hofer, B. Kusy, M. Bruenig, T. Schmid, Q. Wang, P. Dutta, and A. Terzis. Low Power or High Performance? A Tradeoff Whose Time Has Come (and Nearly Gone). In *European Conference on Wireless Sensor Networks (EWSN)*, Trento, Italy, Feb. 2012.

[14] K. Lakshminarayanan, S. Sapra, S. Seshan, and P. Steenkiste. RFDump: An Architecture for

Monitoring the Wireless Ether. In *ACM CoNEXT 2009*, Dec. 2009.

[15] C.-J. M. Liang, N. B. Priyantha, J. Liu, and A. Terzis. Surviving Wi-Fi Interference in Low Power ZigBee Networks. In *International Conference on Embedded Networked Sensor Systems (SenSys)*, Zürich, Switzerland, Nov. 2010.

[16] R. Musaloiu-E. and A. Terzis. Minimising the Effect of WiFi Interference in 802.15.4 Wireless Sensor Networks. *Int. Journal of Sensor Networks*, 3:43–54, 2008.

[17] A. Ng. Support Vector Machines – CS229 Lecture Notes, 2011.

[18] C. Noda, S. Prabh, M. Alves, T. Voigt, and C. Boano. Quantifying the Channel Quality for Interference-aware Wireless Sensor Networks. *ACM SIGBED Review*, 8(4):43–48, 2011.

[19] M. Petrova, L. Wu, P. Mahonen, and J. Riihijarvi. Interference Measurements on Performance Degradation between Colocated IEEE 802.11g/n and IEEE 802.15.4 Networks. In *International Conference on Networking (ICN), 2007*, Sainte-Luce, Martinique, Apr. 2007.

[20] T. Rappaport. *Wireless Communications: Principles and Practice*. Prentice Hall PTR, Upper Saddle River, NJ, USA, 2nd edition, 2001.

[21] O. Rensfelt, F. Hermans, P. Gunningberg, L. Larzon, and E. Björnemo. Repeatable Experiments with Mobile Nodes in a Relocatable WSN Testbed. *The Computer Journal*, 54(12):1973–1986, 2011.

[22] M. Sha, G. Hackmann, and C. Lu. Arch: Practical Channel Hopping for Reliable Home-area Sensor Networks. In *17th IEEE Real-Time and Embedded Technology and Applications Symposium (RTAS)*, Chicago, IL, USA, Apr. 2011.

[23] M. Sha, G. Hackmann, and C. Lu. Multi-channel Reliability and Spectrum Usage in Real Homes: Empirical Studies for Home-area Sensor Networks. In *IEEE 19th International Workshop on Quality of Service (IWQoS)*, San Jose, CA, USA, June 2011.

[24] S. Y. Shin, H. S. Park, and W. H. Kwon. Mutual interference analysis of IEEE 802.15.4 and IEEE 802.11b. *Computer Networks*, 51(12):3338 – 3353, 2007.

[25] A. Sikora and V. Groza. Coexistence of IEEE 802.15.4 with other Systems in the 2.4 GHz-ISM-Band. In *IEEE Instrumentation and Measurement Technology Conference (IMTC)*, 2005.

[26] S. Zacharias, T. Newe, S. O'Keeffe, and E. Lewis. Identifying Sources of Interference in RSSI Traces of a Single IEEE 802.15.4 Channel. In *International Conference on Wireless and Mobile Communications*, Venice, Italy, June 2012.

[27] G. Zhou, Y. Wu, T. Yan, T. He, C. Huang, J. Stankovic, and T. Abdelzaher. A Multifrequency MAC Specially Designed for Wireless Sensor Network Applications. *ACM Transactions on Embedded Computing Systems (TECS)*, 9(4):39, 2010.

Camazotz: Multimodal Activity-Based GPS Sampling

Raja Jurdak[1], Philipp Sommer[1], Branislav Kusy[1], Navinda Kottege[1],
Christopher Crossman[1], Adam McKeown[2], David Westcott[2]

[1]Autonomous Systems Lab, CSIRO ICT Centre, Brisbane, QLD, Australia
[2]CSIRO Ecosystem Sciences, Cairns, QLD, Australia
firstname.lastname@csiro.au

ABSTRACT

Long-term outdoor localisation with battery-powered devices remains an unsolved challenge, mainly due to the high energy consumption of GPS modules. The use of inertial sensors and short-range radio can reduce reliance on GPS to prolong the operational lifetime of tracking devices, but they only provide coarse-grained control over GPS activity. In this paper, we introduce our feature-rich lightweight Camazotz platform as an enabler of Multimodal Activity-based Localisation (MAL), which detects activities of interest by combining multiple sensor streams for fine-grained control of GPS sampling times. Using the case study of long-term flying fox tracking, we characterise the tracking, connectivity, energy, and activity recognition performance of our module under both static and 3-D mobile scenarios. We use Camazotz to collect empirical flying fox data and illustrate the utility of individual and composite sensor modalities in classifying activity. We evaluate MAL for flying foxes through simulations based on retrospective empirical data. The results show that multimodal activity-based localisation reduces the power consumption over periodic GPS and single sensor-triggered GPS by up to 77% and 14% respectively, and provides a richer event type dissociation for fine-grained control of GPS sampling.

Categories and Subject Descriptors

C.2.1 [**Computer-Communication Networks**]: Wireless Communication

Keywords

Wireless Sensor Networks, Tracking

1. INTRODUCTION

Embedded systems technology has been developing at remarkably fast rates, which has led to heightened expectations for a wide range of applications. End-users now expect platforms to continuously follow intuitive trends, such as shrinking in size and weight while having longer battery lives. In order to deliver on all those expectations concurrently, system developers typically reduce the number of sensing modalities on monitoring platforms and the sensor sampling frequencies. For many mobile sensing applications, including bird tracking at continental scales, the requirement for multiple sensing modalities and durable lightweight platforms are continuously in tension.

Recent work [1] has aimed for lightweight long-distance and long-term tracking of the endangered Whooping Crane in North America, using custom-designed platforms that include GPS, cellular, and weigh just above 100 g. While this work has provided a proof-of-concept of large scale and lightweight wildlife tracking, this technology cannot be used for tracking smaller flying animals, as the sheer weight of the devices would prevent the animals from flying freely. This paper is motivated by the need to track one such species of particular interest, namely flying foxes. Flying foxes, also known as fruit bats, are megabats that spread virulent and deadly diseases such as Ebola, Hendra, and the recently discovered SARS-like Coronavirus [26], at a global scale.

Tracking flying foxes requires platforms and algorithms that can deliver position and activity information from highly mobile individual animals over long-durations. While position monitoring can use GPS as the main sensor modality, behaviour and activity classification require additional sensor modalities, such as inertial, acoustic, and air pressure sensors. For instance, audio signals can be used for detecting previously unknown congregation areas, or roosting camps, for flying fox populations. The introduction of new sensing modalities places a burden on the limited node energy, processing, and memory resources, as well as an indirect cost of more complex system management. The uncontrolled 3-D mobility associated with bird tracking can also have unpredictable effects on the performance of node components, particularly transceivers and solar panels. All of the above challenges highlight the need for holistic design of feature-rich mobile sensing platforms with early prototyping to incorporate these subtle dependencies among system components.

This paper introduces Camazotz[1], a lightweight and feature-rich mobile sensing platform, which aims at long-term wildlife tracking. Camazotz uses a CC430 system on chip (SoC) with a low power GPS, inertial, acoustic, air pressure and temperature sensors, two solar panels, 300 mAh Li-Ion battery, with a total weight just under 30 g targeted at tracking smaller wildlife such as flying foxes. We describe our holistic design

---

[1]Camazotz was a bat god in Mayan mythology.

process for the platform that relies on early prototyping and empirical evaluation of three key aspects: (1) the impact of 3-D mobility on radio performance using an unmanned aerial vehicle for controlled mobility experiments; (2) the performance of low power GPS as a function of shutoff time and its implications on node lifetime; and (3) the ability to perform in situ activity recognition using audio and inertial sensors through basic signal processing on Camazotz. Based on the evaluation results, we show how Camazotz can enable Multimodal Activity-based Localisation (MAL) that detects activities of interest by combining multiple sensor streams for fine-grained control of GPS sampling times.

Our evaluation shows that 3-D mobility has limited effect on Camazotz's radio connectivity to a ground base station. We mainly find signal degradation for high angles of alignment between Camazotz and the base. Our GPS evaluations confirm a weak dependence of the time to first fix on GPS off time, and our on-bat experiments show that the GPS design of Camaztoz achieves consistent position accuracies below 10 m. Solar experiments from nodes on bats yield an estimate of 3 mA average solar current during the day, which we use to set duty cycles that deliver energy-neutral operation to Camaztoz. Our activity recognition results from flying fox experiments with Camazotz demonstrate the detection of interaction and waste removal events with audio and inertial sensors respectively, and confirm that air pressure sensors can provide a much more precise estimate of altitude than GPS. Finally, we use these results to demonstrate MAL by considering how simple fusion of audio and inertial sensor events through logical OR and AND operations can dissociate event types, deliver fine-grained activity-based control of GPS samples, and by doing so, save power consumption.

The remainder of the paper is organised as follows. Section 2 motivates the design of Camaztoz. Section 3 presents our empirical validation experiments to evaluate the platform's performance. Section 4 shows how Camazotz can enable multimodal activity-based localisation to accurately detect events and extend node lifetime. Section 5 discusses related work, and Section 6 concludes the paper.

2. CAMAZOTZ PLATFORM

2.1 Motivating Application

Surprisingly little is known about flying-fox ecology behaviour due to difficulties associated with studying animals that are nocturnally active and which roost in large aggregations (often 40-50000 animals at a single site [23]). Recent research shows that the source of our difficulties in studying these animals lies in the extra-ordinary mobility exhibited by individuals and by flying-fox populations. Studies show that individual animals are highly mobile, travelling on average 20 km to their first feeding site in a night and over 100 km during nightly foraging [25]. Over weeks and months individuals can move hundreds or thousands of kilometres [4]. This mobility is also observable at the scale of the population with flying-fox populations moving in and out of regions, often over periods of just days [23].

Flying-foxes are of great interest to wildlife managers in Australia. On the one hand these animals are listed as threatened species, and at the same time, they are recognised as agricultural pests, causing as much as $20 million of damage to fruit crops per year [24]. Most importantly, flying-foxes are effective vectors of a number of viru-

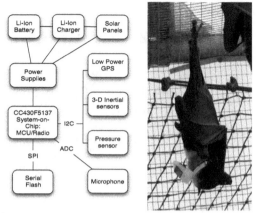

(a) Functional components of Camazotz   (b) Flying fox with Camazotz attached

Figure 1: The Camazotz platform couples a SoC with GPS, inertial, acoustic, air pressure and temperature sensors, two solar panels, 300 mAh Li-Ion battery, with a combined weight < 30 g.

lent emerging infectious diseases that threaten both humans and livestock. Developing effective management responses to these flying-fox impacts requires that assumptions are made about their mobility.

Our application requirements are to obtain day roost locations for comparison with surveyed camp locations. Where these locations do not match with known camps, we need to know whether the animal is roosting alone or in a small group, or, whether it is at an unknown camp. This requires visiting each such location – an impossible task given that such events could happen multiple times each day across the range of the species (i.e. 2800 km) and will often be in inaccessible locations. Since flying-foxes in camps are highly vocal animals [19] an alternative would be to use collar node-based microphones to make recordings of flying-fox noise to provide an index of the number of animals at a roost.

Most flying-fox risks, such as crop damage and transmission of disease, are incurred away from camps at the locations where flying-foxes are feeding. Predictive models of how these risks will be distributed within a landscape require an understanding of how flying-foxes respond, in terms of their movement and choice of foraging locations, to the structure of landscapes and the distribution of resources within them, and how this varies across landscapes, seasons and individuals. Developing such an understanding requires high temporal and spatial resolution data on movement during nighttime foraging sessions, with sample frequencies as high as 1 Hz potentially under some circumstances.

The devices that can achieve the goals outlined above must be capable of: (1) collecting regular daytime fixes (with an accuracy of 10 m) at camps to identify new camps; (2) collecting high-frequency nighttime fixes to monitor movement patterns and landscape use, and doing this with an accuracy of 10 m or less using inertial sensors during fine-scale movements; (3) making daytime audio recordings to allow estimation of camp size; (4) operate over long periods, i.e. 12 months, and preferably longer; and (5) provide data download capability.

Such simultaneous goals are clearly at odds with current technology but can be approached through smart power, sensor and data management algorithms and flexible duty-cycling. Available technologies, such as Platform Terminal Transmitter (PTT) and GPS tags [18], cannot hope to achieve these goals because their power demands conspire to make the tags useful for only single aspects of the study described above. That is, they can either collect a handful of daytime fixes at regular intervals over long-periods, or they can collect high-frequency movement data over short periods. No tags are currently capable of collecting audio data. This paper addresses this gap for accurate, flexible and energy-efficient position tracking of flying-foxes. This work is part of a large national project that aims to deploy hundreds of tracking nodes (up to 1000) on individual flying foxes.

2.2 Design Challenges

bioacoustic signals alongside inertial and altitude information for real-time activity classification.

To achieve the above goals, we need to address specific design challenges relating to dimension constraints of tracking nodes and to the mobility dynamics of migratory birds. According to animal ethics regulations in Australia, the *weight* of any objects placed on flying foxes must not exceed 5 % of their body weight, corresponding to target cumulative weights of 30 to 50 g for all the electronics and enclosures for tracking. The range of target weights stems from the weight differences of individual animals between adolescents and larger males. This weight restriction obviously constrains the size and capacity of batteries on the devices.

Size is another issue, where tracking devices cannot exceed a few centimetres in height or length and 2 cm in depth to ensure that the devices do not hinder or affect the animal's ability to fly freely. In addition to placing further constraints on the battery and electronics, this size restriction is likely to affect the size of the recommended GPS antenna which may in turn impact location accuracy.

The *mobility dynamics* of flying foxes represent yet another major challenge. Flying foxes are able to fly up to 100 km in a single night and they are known to visit truly remote areas at continental and transcontinental scale. Because they are likely to spend significant portions of time either in remote areas or across country borders, cellular coverage may not be available. Additionally, cellular modules would add significant weight, size, and energy cost to the overall platform. We choose to transfer position data by installing base stations at known roosting camps and using short-range radio communication opportunistically when the animals are in these camps. However, only a small proportion of the camps where these animals congregate to roost is known, and there is no deterministic mapping of an individual animal to one or more known roosting camps. These dynamics suggest that the design of tracking devices has to account for a high degree of delay tolerance in both hardware, providing enough memory to store position and activity data for periods of disconnectivity, and software, to compress stored data and opportunistically deliver it once connectivity returns.

2.3 Hardware

Given such tight constraints on the size and weight of the platform, we select a system on chip (SoC) for the microcontroller and radio transceiver. In particular, we compare the size, RAM, and Flash capacity of existing SoC options, as shown in Table 1. Based on this comparison, we use the Texas Instruments CC430F5137 which includes an MSP430 core and a CC1101 radio. Apart from its favourable physical size/capacity advantage, the MSP430 core supports low power operation and offers high compatibility with popular sensor network operating systems. The CC1101 equivalent radio transceiver provides a GFSK communication in the 915 MHz band.

Figure 1(a) illustrates the functional components of Camazotz. Key to its success in the field is to maximise location accuracy for the available size, weight, and energy resources. We adopt the u-blox MAX-6 GPS module, which optimises for size and power consumption and provides the high performance of the u-blox 6 series positioning engine.

The localisation hardware also includes the GPS antenna, which involves a design choice between antenna size/type on one hand, and the GPS signal directionality and strength on the other. Table 2 shows two considered GPS antenna options: a Taoglas GPS patch antenna with integrated amplifier, which while providing strong signal reception will also have high directionality and take up a reasonable amount of space and weight; and a Fractus small planar monopole GPS antenna [9], which is lighter, less directional, yet provides weaker signal reception. The smaller antenna's omni-directional radiation pattern maintains consistent GPS reception in any orientation, which is particularly favourable for the 3-D mobility of flying foxes. We therefore select the Fractus antenna and augment it with a 20 dB low noise amplifier (LNA) to boost its signal to comparable levels as the patch antenna, whilst consuming less power.

One disadvantage with our antenna choice is that it requires an adjacent ground plane that is nearly 12 times its size to work efficiently. We opportunistically match the size of the ground plane to the overall Camazotz board footprint, so that the same Camazotz board that includes all the functional components has a dual role as the ground plane for the GPS module. This design choice keeps the overall node's weight and size within their respective targets.

Figure 2 shows the top and bottom views of the Camaztoz platform, while Figure 1(b) shows the node within its enclosure on a bat during one of our field trials. Note the dual solar panels in Figure 1(b) on opposite sides of the enclosure, in order to maximise the chances of energy harvesting when foxes are roosting in a camp (typically in the upside down position, where the node slightly flops down), or flying at the beginning or end of the day, which exposes the top-side panel to the sun.

The energy charging architecture of Camaztoz is yet another design consideration. Since nodes on flying foxes will

Device	Size (mm)	RAM (Bytes)	Flash (KB)
TI CC430F5137	7×7	4096	32
Freescale MC12311	8×8	2048	32
Nordic nRF9E5	5×5	256	4
Atmel ATA8743	5×5	256	4

Table 1: Comparison of 900 Mhz SoC devices.

Type	Size(mm)	Gain (dB)	Power@1.8 V
Taoglas AP.10F	10×10×4	-10 + 20	9
Fractus Geofind + LNA	10×10×0.9	1.5 + 20	5.61

Table 2: Comparison of small GPS antennas.

Figure 2: Top (left) and bottom (right) view of Camazotz prototype device without battery and solar panel. Dimensions are 54×30×14 mm.

have unpredictable and intermittent access to solar energy, we need a flexible energy architecture that opportunistically exploits available solar energy. In particular, there will be situations when node batteries are either fully charged or fully flat. In both these cases, it is beneficial to power the node directly through the solar panel to make the most of the node's sun exposure. We therefore incorporate a solar bypass circuit to enable Camazotz to consume energy directly from the solar panels during extreme battery states. The flat battery state occurs when the battery is completely flat and is only trickle charging at a very low current. In this case, the bypass allows the device to power up cleanly, rather than relying on the flat battery to power up, which would risk oscillation around a minimum voltage threshold leading to data loss. During the fully charged state, the bypass circuit on Camazotz can use any excess solar energy (that would otherwise be wasted) for increased sampling or computation.

The design of Camazotz also adopts a low power approach in its selection of sensors and in the integration of these sensors into the board. We select low power sensors for Camazotz to suit its restricted energy budget, with an eye towards Multimodal Activity-based Localisation for fine-tuned GPS sampling control. In particular, we select the Bosch BMP085 pressure sensor, the STMicroelectronics LSM303 3-axis accelerometer/magnetometer and a Knowles microphone. The BMP085 pressure sensor draws only $12\,\mu\text{A}$, and when combined with a static node's pressure reading, can provide us with a more accurate height measurement (see Figure 11(a)). The LSM303 accelerometer consumes $830\,\mu\text{A}$ of current and allows for detection of different behaviours (see Figure 10). The final sensor is the Knowles microphone, which is connected to the 12-bit ADC on the microcontroller, and consumes less than $1\,\text{mA}$ in operation. The microphone can be used in conjunction with other sensors for more robust activity detection.

Integrating these sensors into Camazotz requires a design decision in itself. Having access to a limited energy supply and a goal of long term operation dictates that we duty-cycle the node components. This is a particular focus to ensure that we could minimise the energy consumption in the sleep state. Rather than putting all the peripheral components into their standby modes, which are in the order of $40\,\mu\text{A}$ total, we create a single digital line that can cut power to all peripherals surrounding the SoC prior to entering sleep state for the lowest possible energy consumption of $12\,\mu\text{A}$ on average.

2.4 Software

The Camazotz platform runs the Contiki operating system, which provides a threaded programming environment using the C programming language. We add two key features on top of the Contiki core: remote procedure calls, and a logging abstraction.

As the Camazotz device will be deployed on wild animals, retrieval the node for reconfiguration is not an option. To address this issue we implement remote procedure calls (RPC), allowing us to send a radio command to the device to perform certain actions (e.g. reading memory blocks or status information) or to adjust configuration parameters such as the GPS duty-cycle. Every RPC command is sent as a unicast or broadcast packet containing a unique command identifier and a list of arguments. Our implementation of RPC commands serves as a basic building block to support additional functionality for future use cases. For example, a base station located at a roosting camp can query status information of a mobile node to request sensor data stored in the flash memory to be sent over the radio.

Logging on the Camazotz device is critical to its success, due to the delay-tolerant nature of the flying fox application. Communication outage times may range from hours, days, weeks or even months before there is an opportunity to offload data. Initially, data will be logged at a high sample rate to a Secure Digital (SD) flash card, for board and code verification, and then switch to external flash for final testing. To address this requirement for interchangeable storage, we introduce a data logging abstraction, which provides a consistent application programming interface (API), regardless of the underlying storage mechanism. The advantage of the logging abstraction approach is that we can log high sample rate sensor data to the SD card while in the development and testing phases, then for the final version we reduce the sampling rate, required by our energy budget, and with minimal code changes, switch to use the external flash for logging. Current mechanisms supported by the logging abstraction include the radio, external flash and SD card.

3. EVALUATION

This section empirically evaluates the Camazotz platform's communication, energy, and sensing features.

3.1 Mobility

Flying foxes are active animals that can cover distances of up to 100 km at cruising speeds of 7-8 ms^{-1}. They participate in complex social behaviour while at roosting camps that frequently result in their location change. Our deployment setup includes a base station with 3G connectivity that is deployed within the roosting camp close to the ground. The Camazotz platform needs to be able to communicate with the base station from the surrounding trees, within a distance of 200 m, as well as enable bats-to-bat communication outside of roosting camps. In this section, we study the impact of the height and mobility of the Camazotz transceiver on the received radio signal quality. We study three antenna types to maximise packet reception rates at the base station.

3.1.1 Experimental Platform

We use AscTec Pelican UAV platform [22], which is a flexible quad-copter platform designed for easy integration with a variety of payloads, up to a maximum of 650 g. The

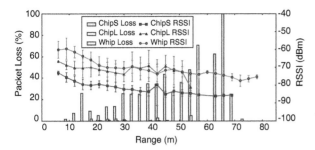

Figure 3: Comparison of mobile to base RSSI and packet loss for two chip antennas (large and small) and a whip antenna.

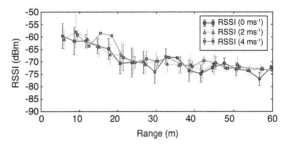

Figure 4: Correlation of mobile to base RSSI signal, conditional on the relative speed of the UAV and the base station.

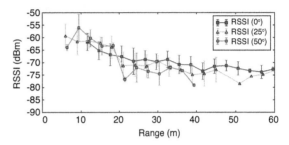

Figure 5: Correlation of mobile to base RSSI signal over their distance, conditional on the altitude angle between the UAV and the base station.

platform is equipped with inertial and GPS chips and an autopilot that enables non-experts to pilot the platform out of the box after a few minutes of training. Our payload consists of the Camazotz prototype with radio and GPS chips, high-capacity Li-Ion battery to power the prototype, and a mount for different test antennas. The maximum flight time with our payload is about 30 mins. Altogether, our experiments include more than 10 hours of flight data covering a distance of more than 20 km without any major incident, a testament to the robustness and reliability of today's UAV technology.

The Camazotz node on the UAV broadcasts packets with a payload of 32 bytes and a frequency of 8 packets per second. The base station node is installed at approximately 1.5 m above the ground and is equipped with a ground plate with a diameter of approximately 20 cm. We record the radio signal strength indicator (RSSI) for each received packet. The packet reception rate (PRR) is estimated using sequence numbers included in the broadcasted packets and each packet is timestamped by the PC time at the reception.

The Pelican platform provides a software development kit that enabled us to log GPS and inertial data from the Pelican autopilot. This data is useful in evaluating GPS accuracy, as well as correlating Camazotz radio performance to the relative speed, height, or distance between Camazotz and the base station. We use an XBee connected to a laptop to communicate with the UAV and recorded the autopilot data at 4 Hz. We use the UAV's GPS for latitude, longitude, and heading and UAV's inertial sensors for altitude and speed estimates to compensate for GPS errors. We have also written a Python interface to Google Earth that shows the location of the UAV in real time and can replay the recorded experiments.

3.1.2 Antenna Selection

We consider two basic antenna types for our platform: an EZConnect 868 MHz chip antenna manufactured by Fractus [9] and a quarter-wavelength whip antenna. We test two versions of the chip antenna as the ground-plane in the development kit was significantly larger than the footprint of our platform. The smaller configuration was designed to match the footprint of Camazotz.

We run experiments for each antenna flying the UAV along random trajectories, covering a number of different heights, speeds, and distances. The overall length of the recorded data for each antenna is approximately the same. The distance between the flying node and the base station is estimated from the UAV GPS data and the known location of the base station.

We plot our results in Fig. 3. The chip antenna with a small ground-plane (ChipS) is clearly performing the worst and experiences significant packet losses at distances of 20-30 m. Somewhat surprisingly, the simple whip antenna outperforms the unmodified chip antenna (ChipL) at most distances and experiences almost no packet loss at all tested points. In addition, its performance is much more dependable as shown by the smaller variance of the RSSI signal. Our conclusion is to use the quarter-wavelength whip antenna as it provides superior performance at a lower cost.

3.1.3 Impact of Speed

We next study the impact of the relative speed of the Camazotz radios on the packet reception rates. We have flown our UAV platform in a series of experiments designed to resemble flying fox flight patterns at up to half of their cruising speeds. Figure 4 does not show any significant correlation between the speed and the received signal quality, so the radio scheduling algorithm thus does not need to constrain packet transmissions based on the speed.

3.1.4 Impact of Angle

Finally, we study the impact of the node orientation on the radio reception. Due to the constraints on the payload of our UAV test platform, we did not study the impact of the node heading as simulating a bat would require attaching a one litre bottle of water to Camazotz. We thus focus our study on the altitude angle between the node and the base station. As the transmission pattern of antennas is not a perfect sphere, radio performance is expected to decrease at higher angles (when nodes are directly above base station).

Figure 5 confirms our expectations, albeit showing only a minor degradation of the signal quality at higher angles. We attribute this to the ground plate used at the base station that helps to reflect some of the energy from the antenna null areas. However, even with the ground plate, the radio communication is sensitive to the altitude angle which should be considered during the deployment phase. In particular, we need to refrain from installing the base station directly under the trees populated by flying foxes.

3.2 GPS

We conduct two different experiments to evaluate the performance of Camazotz's GPS module. The first experiment uses a Camazotz board in a static outdoor setup, while in the second experiment the Camazotz board has been attached to a captive live flying fox in a large outdoor cage.

For the first experiment, we attach the Camazotz board to a tree on our campus to have similar conditions as in a camp. The GPS receiver has a partly unobstructed view of the sky. We configure the Contiki application running on the Camazotz to switch off the u-blox MAX-6 GPS receiver 60 s after a position fix has been acquired. During the off phase, only the backup voltage of the GPS module is active which powers its real-time clock and the RAM. Therefore, the GPS receivers can still keep the ephemeris information in RAM and is able to do a warm start. We select the off time interval uniformly at random between 10 s and 60 min and measure how long it takes to acquire the first fix after power to the module has been enabled again. The measurement results for the time to first fix are shown in Figure 6(a). Our results indicate that the time to first fix (TTFF) is correlated with the time interval the GPS receiver was switched off, confirming results from older GPS modules [6].

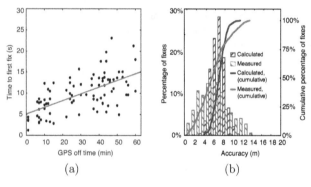

(a)   (b)

Figure 6: GPS performance of Camazotz; (a) time to first position fix for various off-time intervals, (b) comparison of reported accuracy estimate and a measure of true accuracy.

During the experiment on the living flying fox, the Camazotz logged 1 Hz GPS data to its SD card, and continuously sent status update messages via radio to a base station nearby. We assess the true accuracy of the GPS against the accuracy reports from the GPS module. We set the true accuracy as the distance of the GPS locations from the known location of the animal for a period of time when it was roosting in a single location. We choose a one hour period of the day when we observed that the animal was in the one location, hanging from a roosting location and occasionally grooming and fanning itself. During this period the GPS was in tracking mode where it was collecting fixes continually at 1 Hz, collecting 3600 fixes. We took the average location of all of these fixes over the time period and use it as the true location of the animal. Geo-referenced high

Component	Power 100% (mW)	Duty Cycle %	Power DC (mW)
GPS	74	3	2.2
Radio	99	2	2
Cpu	13.2	5	0.7
Flash	40	1	0.4
Acc/Mag	2.6	10	0.3
Pressure/Temp	0.1	100	0.1
Mic	3.3	1	0.03
Totals	232.2		5.7

Table 3: Power consumption at 100% and target duty cycles of Camaztoz components.

resolution imagery [11] with a spatial accuracy of 1 m was then used to confirm the coordinates for this location, which was considered the true location. To measure the accuracy we calculate the distance from each fix to this true roosting location, and for each fix compare this figure to the accuracy estimate calculated by the GPS unit.

Figure 6(b) summarises our results. The measured accuracy (M=5.9, SD=3.0) is significantly lower than the reported accuracy ((M=7.2 , SD=1.3); t(7206)=24.2 , p<0.01) from the GPS module, with a minimum accuracy value reported by the GPS of 3.9 m, while the measured accuracy data indicates that 3% of the fixes were within 1 m accuracy. The calculated accuracy values are much more clustered than the measured values, with 87% of the calculated values being between 5 and 9 m. These results indicate that the GPS unit generally provides conservative estimates of its accuracy in our experiment, as the true positions are more accurate than the reported accuracy measurements suggest.

We note that the GPS results in our experiments are only indicative of the module's performance in our specific testing scenario. Both the TTFF and the reported accuracy may vary as flying foxes move to different environments. While this paper introduces GPS sampling based on multimodal sensor inputs, an interesting future direction for this work is to adapt GPS sampling schedules to observed variations in GPS module performance in addition to observed context.

3.3 Long-term Operation

3.3.1 Solar on collars

The Camazotz platform makes use of solar panels to help ensure long term operation. Figure 7 shows the result of an experiment logging solar charge current at 1 Hz that includes two Camaztoz platforms, one on a live bat and another nearby on the ground in full sun exposure. The large dips shown in the static node's solar charge current are caused by shadows from the structure of the bat enclosure that the device was deployed in. The measured solar charge current of the bat node is significantly lower than the the reference static node, as one would expect given the non optimal orientation of the bat node and also the bat's insistence on resting in a shady location for the majority of this experiment. The small peaks over 5 mA shown in the bat node's solar charge current occurred when small glimpses of sunlight were caught by the solar panel, and are more representative of what would be achieved depoyed on bats in the wild that tend to spend long periods in the sun while roosting.

3.3.2 Lifetime Implications

Building on these solar current experiments, we now ex-

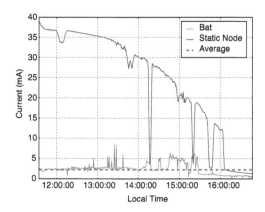

Figure 7: Solar current captured from static node versus bat node.

plore the lifetime implications for our nodes. Camazotz will have a 300 mAh Li-Ion battery with an average voltage of 3.8 V (range of about 3.3 - 4.3 V depending on charge state). The on-bat solar experiments indicate that we can obtain an average of at least 3 mA for 12 hrs from the solar panels, which equates to about 5.7 mW average power input for a full day.

We aim to keep the battery close to full charge to avoid trickle charging, so we design for energy neutral operation considering the energy consumption and harvesting. Table 3 shows the power consumption of the Camazotz components in full operation mode and in operation at our selected duty cycles. The average power consumption with these settings is just below 5.7 mW (recalling that 5.7 mW is a conservative estimate for harvestable energy), which meets the energy neutral target and promotes long-term operation subject to the lifetime of the physical components and the recharge cycles of the battery.

Note that within the allowable 3% duty cycle of the GPS module, setting a sampling schedule for the module remains an issue for further investigation. Our forthcoming paper [13] provides a detailed empirical analysis on the GPS tradeoffs involving the off time, target position accuracy and its corresponding energy consumption. We aim to characterise the performance of the newer u-blox MAX-6 GPS module on Camazotz and use a similar analysis to determine the most appropriate GPS schedules.

3.4 Activity Recognition

In addition to tracking where flying foxes go, we are interested in what they are doing. The key activities of interest are shown in Table 4. Flying is a key activity that requires position estimates at high sampling frequencies (ideally in the order of seconds) and should be trackable through the GPS, air pressure (for height), and potentially inertial sensors for wing beat frequency. Frequent daily interactions at roosting camps among multiple animals fighting for territory or in mating advances can be captured through a combination of distinctive sequential sounds and increased movement. Urinating and defecating are important to detect and localise for determining where and how flying foxes spread seeds from fruits they have eaten. For that reason, GPS fixes are desirable when these events occur. Detection is possible using the accelerometer to capture the instance that an animal switches from its normal upside down stance to a right side up stance. Grooming animals are typically in the

upside down position yet moving their head/neck to groom themselves, which may be detectable through the inertial sensors, and using their claws to scratch their bodies, which creates a scratching sound. Resting is the default state for most animals in a roosting camp, which typically does not require the position lock and can be used as a baseline low activity state for differentiating from other states. The lack of a hardware motion trigger on the accelerometer indicates this state, and pressure sensors can be used to estimate the height at which animals are roosting for establishing hierarchies within a camp.

It is clear that detecting the above activities requires multiple sensory modalities, and in some cases the detection of an activity should trigger a position lock through the GPS. The remainder of this section empirically evaluates to what extent the sensory modalities on our platform can capture these activities of interest.

3.4.1 Audio

While acoustics associated with echolocating micro-bats has been well covered in the literature [10], not much attention has been given to using flying fox vocalisations as an automated means of monitoring them. Some very early work by Nelson [19] and relatively recent work by Parijs et al. [21] presents some characterisation of the different calls made by flying fox species. Adult and juvenile flying foxes emit calls within the human audible frequencies mostly during interaction events [17].

The in-built microphone on the Camazotz node is used to capture audio at a sampling rate of 22.4 kHz. This is sufficient to cover the full spectrum of sounds emitted by flying foxes based on our initial studies using high quality audio sampled at 96 kHz. These recordings at known roosting camp sites show the most energetic part of the signal to be within the 2 - 4 kHz range and the upper harmonics to start fading away around 8 kHz. The audio data used in this paper is first down sampled to 16 kHz and high-pass filtered with $f_c = 1$ kHz. We then process the audio stream via an energy based detector as described in [2] to extract acoustic events. These include vocalisations from the collared individual as well as other bats within range. The events include other background 'noise' such as bird calls and anthropogenic sounds depending on the geographical location of the roosting camp. In our dataset, we also have loud scratching sounds when the bat is scratching the collar node along with human voices, construction site sounds as well as motor vehicle sounds.

Amongst the bat vocalisations, we identify multiple different call patterns. We focus on the sustained repetitive call associated with aggressive interaction events [19]. We use a set of three simple features to detect these particular calls which are associated with interaction events: (1) mean sound level, (2) call duration and (3) mean normalised frequency. An example of a repetitive call associated with an interaction event along with these features are shown in Figure 8. To facilitate implementation on the Camazotz node, the features are based on calculating the mean signal energy and counting the number of zero crossings of a 1024 sample sliding window with an overlap of 50 %. This gives us a convenient and non-resource intensive method for extracting acoustic features with reasonable accuracy by heuristically setting the threshold levels. Figure 9 illustrates the process of selecting a suitable threshold for acoustic activ-

Activity	Sensors				Timing		
	Audio	Inertial	Air Pressure	Solar	Event Duration	Event Frequency	GPS Sampling Period
Flying		X	X		hours	daily	high
Interacting	X	X			seconds	frequent	on event
Urinating/Defecating		X			seconds	frequent	on event
Grooming	X	X			seconds	very frequent	none
Resting		X	X	X	hours	daily	infrequent

Table 4: Key activities of flying foxes, their timing profile, and the sensors we use to detect them.

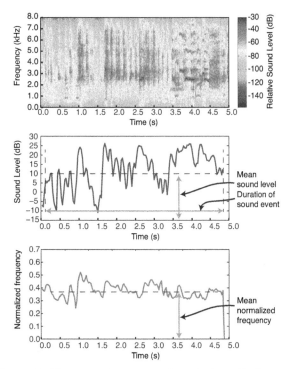

Figure 8: Top: spectrogram of typical audio interaction event. Middle: corresponding sound level and zero crossings. Bottom: normalised frequency. Arrows show derived acoustic features.

ity classification. Figure 9 plots accuracy, precision and the performance metric [15] as the threshold is increased from 0. The performance metric is the product of accuracy, precision, sensitivity and specificity and serves as an indicator for selecting a threshold which gives the highest accuracy while maintaining a high level of precision. Figure 9 also shows the receiver operator characteristic (ROC) curve which plots the true positive rate vs. the false positive rate as the threshold is varied. The indicated operating point corresponds to the selected threshold of 0.002. Two-fold cross validation was done over 1000 iterations to evaluate the performance of the classification by splitting the dataset in half. This resulted in a mean accuracy of 77.5 % and a mean precision of 70.5 % relative to manually marked ground truth obtained via video footage and external audio recordings.

3.4.2 Inertial

The inertial sensors on our platform enable the detection of activities such as interaction among multiple animals, urinating/defecating, and grooming behaviour, either individually or in combination with other sensors. For instance, accelerometers can be combined with acoustic sensor data to

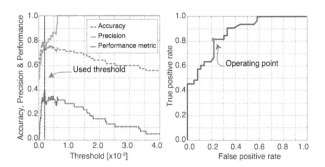

Figure 9: Plot of accuracy, precision and performance metric vs. classification threshold (left), and receiver operator characteristic (ROC) curve for acoustic activity classification (right) showing the operating point corresponding to the used threshold of 0.002.

detect interactions among multiple animals. Alternatively, accelerometers can independently detect the full reversal of orientation that occurs when flying foxes engage in waste removal from their bodies.

We examine accelerometer signals collected from a flying fox collar at 128 Hz during the captive bat experiments. Video footage and visual inspection serve as the ground truth for this experiment. In order to visually distinguish the angular inversion that occurs during urination activities, we compute the mean three-dimensional vector during a 7 min portion of the experiment. The reason for choosing the mean vector is that the flying fox remains in a down facing position for most of the experiment, which indicates that the mean vector should provide a decent estimate of the constant gravitational force and serve as a reference for orientation reversal. Figure 10 (top) shows the XYZ components of the accelerometer signal projected on the mean vector. There are clear sign inversions in all the accelerometer dimensions in two instances in the trace. However, using sign inversions to detect orientational flips is susceptible to corner cases where one of the accelerometer dimensions is orthogonal to the gravity vector.

We detect inversion events instead by computing the angle θ between the current 3-D acceleration vector $\vec{c}$ and the inferred gravity vector $\vec{g}$, using the following equation:

$$tan(\theta) = norm(\vec{g} \times \vec{c}, \vec{g} \cdot \vec{c}) \qquad (1)$$

where θ is in degrees, and $norm$ is the vector norm function. The rationale for using angular shifts is that any 180° inversion in orientation will result in a significant shift in θ that is greater than 90° for a sustained period, which can only correspond to waste removal events in flying foxes.

Figure 10 (bottom) shows the resulting angles. The rectangular boxes indicate two detected instances of inversion events, while the left and right images show the correspond-

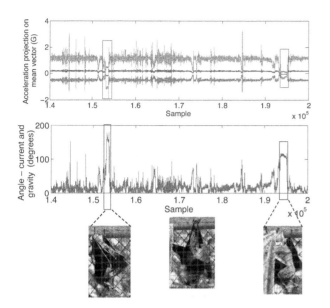

Figure 10: Top: Projected 3-D axis acceleration values over the duration of the experiment; Bottom: Angle between the inferred gravity vector and current acceleration vector. Two events with a sustained angle shift are detected.

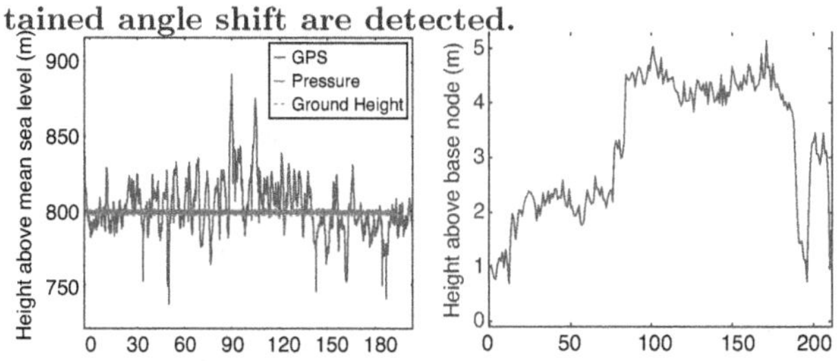

(a) GPS verses air pressure height above mean sea level

(b) Flying fox altitude relative to base node.

Figure 11: Air pressure for estimating altitude.

ing video frames. The central image shows the typical flying fox orientation during the remainder of the experiment. Examining the signals corresponding to the two detected events, we can see a sustained angular shift of above 90° in (θ) for the two detected events.

In order to verify our ability to automatically classify inversion events on the Camazotz inertial signals, we manually marked the ground truth inversion events for 3 hrs of recorded on-bat accelerometer data during the afternoon, using the video footage for ground truth. The ground truth showed 11 true inversion events during this time period, with an average duration of 5.91 s for each event. We then ran a classifier on the entire dataset to detect angle-shift events by identifying contiguous samples of at least 4 s where the angle was shifted by at least 90°. Our classifier detects all 11 true events, yielding 100% accuracy and precision.

3.4.3 Air Pressure

The altitude at which flying foxes fly or roost is of high significance to ecologists, in order to characterise individual and social behaviour. GPS is notoriously poor at providing altitude information, where the vertical error is estimated as twice the horizontal error on average. While a typical

GPS fix will have a horizontal error within 10 m, the vertical error of 20 m does not provide sufficiently granular data for understanding fine-grained flying fox interactions, such as positional hierarchies in a roosting camp. We rely instead on air pressure sensors for altitude estimation. Air pressure itself can provide inaccurate estimates altitude because of variations in atmospheric conditions. However, air pressure measurements can use a ground-based reference measurement in order to provide fairly accurate estimates of the mobile nodes ground elevation. In the flying fox application, known roosting camps will have base station nodes, so it is easy to include an air pressure sensor at these nodes to serve as ground reference.

When flying foxes are near roosting camps, they can use the latest air pressure measurement from the nearest base station. When they are far away from roosting camps, we can revert to a nominal air pressure at sea level as a reference. An interesting direction for future work would be to try to fuse air pressure and GPS altitude data to determine if there is a performance gain for estimating altitude.

We conduct experiments with a collar-based mobile node that measures air pressure on a flying fox at a bat hospital. The flying fox is free to move within a large cage with a variable height of up to 5 m, and a base station on the ground measures air pressure for reference. Both the mobile node and the base station measure air pressure in Pa, which does not map linearly to altitude. We use the following equation to convert the sensor readings from each of the two nodes into the estimated height above mean sea level:

$$H = 44330 * (1 - (P/1013.25)^{\frac{1}{5.255}}) \qquad (2)$$

where P is the measured air pressure in hPa. In order to estimate the ground height of the mobile node, we simply take the difference between the H values from the mobile node and the base node.

Figure 11(a) compares the altitude estimation of GPS and air pressure on a Camazotz node on a bat collar. The air pressure estimate is based on the ground reference at the base station, which is located at 797 m above sea level. The figure clearly shows the stability and consistency of the altitude estimate based on air pressure compared to the extremely noisy GPS altitude estimate.

Figure 11(b) illustrates the estimated ground height (the difference between the bat and ground node altitudes from Figure 11(a)) of the flying fox during a field trial of nearly 6 hrs. The data has been averaged over 1 min time windows. During the first 20 min, the fox is being fitted with the collar in a 1 m high cage before being released into the larger cage for the remainder of the experiment. The dip at around 200 min into the experiment happens at feeding time when the bats descend. The height estimates were verified to be representative of the animal's movements through visual inspections and video recordings. Fluctuations in consecutive samples appear to be within 0 to 50 cm, which establishes an uncertainty bound for height estimates.

4. MULTIMODAL ACTIVITY BASED LOCALISATION

The tight weight, size, and energy constraints of long-term localisation mean that the GPS module has to be aggressively duty cycled. Because we require position fixes when flying foxes engage in activities of interest, we use the diverse

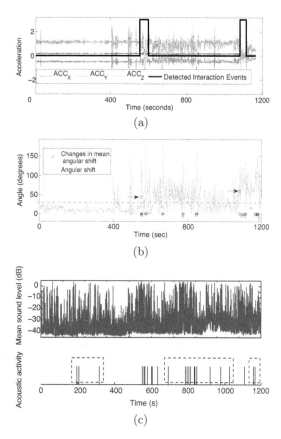

(a)

(b)

(c)

Figure 12: Activity detection; (a) accelerometer signal - thick black line indicating detected interaction events, (b) angular shift between gravity and current acceleration vector. The changes in mean angular shift clearly identify the start of the two true events, (c) mean sound level - dashed lines show detected acoustic interaction activity that involve nearby animals but not the collared animal.

sensor modalities on Camazotz to detect these activities. While some of these activities, such as urination/defecation, can typically be detected with a single sensor, others, such as interactions of multiple animals, require the fusion of multiple sensor outputs in order to determine that the activity is taking place and whether the collared animal is engaged in it.

We focus on detecting and locating interaction events that involve the collared animal interacting with nearby animals or the nearby animals interacting among themselves, as this aids in mapping the social dynamics within a roosting camp. We are particularly focused on longer interaction events that may last from 25 s up to 1 min rather than spurious interactions in the order of a few seconds, especially since localising this activity may require a multi-second start-up time from the GPS module. During these interactions, the animals tend to repeatedly bend their body from their upside-down stance, and on many occasions this movement is associated with multiple sequential vocalisations. Both the accelerometer and microphone can detect interactions involving the collared animal, but only the microphone also can detect interactions among nearby animals. We investigate further, using 20 min accelerometer and audio data traces from our

captive bat experiments, and using video footage as ground truth.

For the accelerometer trace, we observe that interaction events exhibit much shorter term inversions than urination / defecation events in the accelerometer traces, sometimes for just above 10 ms, before reverting back to normal stances. What distinguishes this activity is the repetitiveness of the inversions within a window of several seconds. We can therefore distinguish interaction events through the average angular shift between gravity and the current orientation over a window in time corresponding to typical interaction event durations. In particular, interaction events involving the collared animals begin with an initial jerk where the animal is agitated and nearly changes orientation before engaging in repetitive short-term angular shifts.

We identify only two such events in our 3-hour data trace (with durations of 25 and 54 seconds) using video footage as ground truth. We use these two events to empirically define thresholds for interaction event detection through accelerometers to demonstrate the MAL concept, and we leave the validation of threshold for when more data becomes available. The accelerometer trace and true events are shown in Figure 12(a), while the angles are shown in Figure 12(b). It is clear that true events correspond to repeated short-term inversions of 120° or more in the angle trace, while some false events also exhibit sporadic angular shifts above 120°. We differentiate these shifts by averaging angular shifts. For every sample with at least 120° angular shift, we compute the average angular shift in the subsequent 54 second window, and take the derivative of the resulting average angular shift. The starting times of the two true events in our data trace correspond to the highest differentials in average angular shifts of 43.8° and 60° (indicated by arrows in Figure 12(b)), which capture initial jerks by a flying fox when engaging another fox in aggressive interactions. The next highest peak corresponding to a non-interaction event is at 18°. We therefore adopt 30° as our empirical threshold for the differential in mean angular shift to distinguish interaction events of the collared animal.

The mean sound level and detected interaction events are shown in Figure 12(c). Each vertical line in the acoustic activity plot represents an instance of sustained repetitive vocalisation lasting for approximately 5 s. As seen from this plot, acoustic activity of other bats within range is also captured by the in-built microphone of the Camazotz node and detected by the acoustic activity detection mechanism described in Section 3.4.1.

Table 5 summarises how MAL contributes to better characterisation of activities. While the accelerometer can capture the main interaction events of the collared animal, it does not provide any information on interactions among neighbouring animals, thereby missing two of the four events of interest. The audio sensor is capable of detecting all four events, but it is not able to distinguish which events involve the collared animal. It is only through the combination of these two sensor modalities that we can dissociate these two types of events.

MAL can achieve the event type dissociations with minimal increases to energy consumption over single-sensor triggered approaches. We analyse the proportion of detected events and the node power consumption that arises from each strategy. We use the component power consumption data from Table 3 and GPS lock time data from Figure 6(a)

Localisation Approach	Animal interactions		
	Collared	All	Dissociated
Duty cycled GPS	X		
Accelerometer-triggered	X		
Audio-triggered		X	
Accel. AND Audio	X		
Accel. OR Audio		X	X

Table 5: MAL can detect all events and dissociate interaction event involving collared animal or nearby animals.

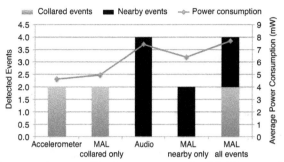

Figure 13: Performance of MAL against accelerometer- and audio-triggered GPS. MAL can be tuned to capture either interaction events of the collared animal, or nearby interaction events only. MAL can also detect and dissociate both types of interaction events with comparable power consumption to audio.

in our simulations. We compare a baseline approach of a duty cycled GPS with a period of 20 s with triggered GPS sampling approaches based on the accelerometer only, audio only, or on the combination of audio and accelerometer sensors. We group all detected ground truth interactions into events that meet the 25 s to 1 min duration constraint. A successful detection in our simulation is when the algorithm obtains at least one GPS sample during the event.

During the given time window, the duty cycled GPS module remains active for a total of 451 s (including lock times) and successfully obtains GPS samples during each of the four events of interest, yielding an overall node power consumption of around 33 mW. Figure 13 summarises the results of sensor-triggered GPS sampling. The accelerometer-triggered GPS manages to detect only two events (only the events from the collared bat) with a cumulative GPS active time of 21 s and power saving of 86 % over the GPS duty cycled approach. In comparison, the audio-triggered GPS can detect all four interaction events of interest while keeping the GPS active for a total of 64 s, corresponding to a node power consumption of 7.42 mW. However, the audio-triggered approach can only determine that interaction events are occurring nearby, but not whether the collared animal is involved.

MAL can be tuned to capture only interaction events involving the collared animal, with comparable detection to accelerometer and slightly higher power consumption for powering the audio sensor. Alternatively, MAL can be tuned to capture only nearby interaction events, yielding a 14% reduction in power consumption over audio and correct detection of the two interaction events involving only nearby animals. Triggering the GPS on the basis of both the accelerometer and audio activity detectors yields comparable energy consumption to audio and correctly dissociates the two types of detected events.

The main benefit of MAL is that it provides users with the flexibility to tune performance to their current activities of interest. If users are interested in collared bat interactions only, they can simply use accelerometer triggers for obtaining GPS samples and save energy in the process. If they are interested in the cumulative set of interaction events regardless of individual animal association with activities, then audio is sufficient. If, on the other hand, users are interested in pinpointing individual animals associated with each activity, multimodal triggering of the GPS can provide the data granularity for dissociating these event types.

5. RELATED WORK

The Networked Cow project [8] used PDAs with GPS and adhoc-mode WiFi to route position information to a base station. The work in [6] extends this cattle tracking application to use short-range radio for relative localisation

alongside GPS. The ZebraNet project [5] reports individual position records for zebras every few minutes. In order to make the energy problem more tractable ZebraNet collars include a solar panel, which assume that the panels are resilient to normal animal activities. Positioning is done by GPS only, and the nodes propagate their information by flooding in order to facilitate data acquisition by the mobile sink. Dyo e al. [3] use a heterogeneous sensor network consisting of RFID-based tags and base stations to track European Badgers over a prolonged period of time and highlight the importance of interaction with domain scientists and early prototyping, which are also central to our methodology in design Camazotz. Our work shares the long-term monitoring goals and network topology with [3], but Camazotz includes GPS modules on the wildlife tags and aims to push the size, weight, and lifetime of the nodes to new limits through aggressive duty cycling based on MAL.

Anthony et al. [1] developed the CraneTracker system for long-range long-duration tracking of the endangered whooping Crane. Their platform, weighing about 100 g, includes GPS and inertial sensors as well as cellular and an Atmel RF230 radio for short-range communication. Their design aims at two GPS fixes/day and a communication latency of less than 24 hours. While our work also targets long-range and long-duration tracking of small birds, our target application tracking flying foxes has much stricter design goals. For instance, the device can not weigh more than 30 to 50 g or 5% of the bodyweight of the animals. Additionally, we aim for position logs at the frequency of at least once every half hour which results in a much higher utilisation of the GPS module. The combined smaller footprint and higher GPS sampling frequency for our application motivates our design of the Camazotz platform. The use of accelerometers has also been proposed as a low power indicator of movement to supplement GPS duty cycling [20] [14]. Guo et al. [12] also consider the use of directional and angular speed for cattle behaviour classification. The work in [7] addresses the tradeoff between localisation accuracy and energy efficiency. A key difference with our work is that we use multiple sensor modalities to trigger GPS duty cycling for more fine-grained activity detection.

Recently, Liu et al. [16] proposed a sample-and-process approach to dramatically reduce the active time for GPS position sampling by up to three orders of magnitude. While this approach is promising for reducing power consumption, it requires post-facto offline processing to recover positions and involves storing and transferring large amounts of data per fix. An interesting direction for future work is to explore the energy-implications of this sample-and-process approach for long-term flying fox tracking.

6. CONCLUSION

This paper has introduced the feature-rich lightweight Camazotz platform for long-term tracking of flying foxes. We have provided a comprehensive empirical evaluation of Camaztoz in both laboratory and on-animal experiments. Our results reveal a moderate radio communication dependency on communication angle in 3-D mobile environments, and confirm that whip antennas perform best. We have characterised the time-to-first-fix of our GPS design as a function of off-time on the ground. This was followed by on-bat experiments that showed most of the GPS positions that the GPS module accuracy estimate was generally conservative. We also evaluate the expected solar charge for our design, and plan the scheduling of our node components accordingly.

We have shown how multiple sensor modalities on Camazotz can individually or collectively detect flying fox activities. Based on these findings, we have proposed and evaluated the utility of Multimodal Activity-based Localisation, where multiple sensors can jointly trigger the GPS for localising interaction events. Our results demonstrate that combining sensor event detections can dissociate on-collar and surrounding interactions for fine-grained control of GPS sampling.

7. ACKNOWLEDGMENTS

This work was supported by the Batmon Project in CSIRO's Sensor and Sensor Networks Transformation Capability Platform. The authors thank the paper shepherd Jakob Eriksson and the anonymous reviewers for their valuable comments that improved the paper quality.

8. REFERENCES

[1] D. Anthony et al. Sensing through the continent: towards monitoring migratory birds using cellular sensor networks. In *Proc. IPSN*, pages 329–340, 2012.

[2] B. Croker and N. Kottege. Using feature vectors to detect frog calls in wireless sensor networks. *The Journal of the Acoustical Society of America*, 131(5):EL400–EL405, 2012.

[3] V. Dyo et al. Evolution and sustainability of a wildlife monitoring sensor network. In *Proc. Sensys*, pages 127–140, 2010.

[4] P. Eby. Seasonal movements of grey-headed flying-foxes. *Wildlife Research*, 18:547–559, 1991.

[5] P. Zhang et al. *Habitat Monitoring with ZebraNet: Design and Experiences*, chapter Wireless Sensor Networks: A Systems Perspective. Artech House, 2005.

[6] R. Jurdak et al. Adaptive gps duty cycling and radio ranging for energy-efficient localization. In *Proc. Sensys*, pages 57–70, 2010.

[7] S. Tilak et al. Dynamic localization control for mobile sensor networks. In *IPCCC*, pages 587–592, 2005.

[8] Z. Butler et al. Virtual fences for controlling cows. In *Proc. ICRA*, pages 4429–4436, 2004.

[9] Fractus. Dipole antenna. `http://www.fractus.com/index.php/fractus/srw_868/`.

[10] M.A. Gadziola, J. M. S. Grimsley, P. A. Faure, and J. J. Wenstrup. Social vocalizations of big brown bats vary with behavioral context. *PLoS ONE*, 7(9):e44550, 2012.

[11] Queensland Government. North queensland 50cm digital ortho-rectified aerial photography. Technical report, Queensland Government, 2011.

[12] Y. Guo and G. Poulton et al. Using accelerometer, high sample rate gps and magnetometer data to develop a cattle movement and behaviour model. *Ecological Modelling*, 220(17):2068 – 2075, 2009.

[13] Raja Jurdak, Peter Corke, Alban Cotillon, Dhinesh Dharman, Chris Crossman, and Guillaume Salagnac. Energy-efficient localisation: Gps duty cycling with radio ranging. *Transactions on Sensor Networks*, 9(3), 2013. in press.

[14] M. B. Kjaergaard et al. Entracked: energy-efficient robust position tracking for mobile devices. In *Proc. MobiSys*, pages 221–234, 2009.

[15] Navinda Kottege, Frederieke Kroon, Raja Jurdak, and Dean Jones. Classification of underwater broadband bio-acoustics using spectro-temporal features. In *Proceedings of the Seventh International Conference on Underwater Networks and Systems*, 2012.

[16] Jie Liu, Bodhi Priyantha, Ted Hart, Heitor Ramos, Antonio A.F. Loureiro, and Qiang Wang. Energy efficient gps sensing with cloud offloading. In *Proc. SenSys*, November 2012.

[17] J. Marko. "Pteropus scapulatus" (On-line), 2005. http://animaldiversity.ummz.umich.edu/site /accounts/information/Pteropus_scapulatus.html.

[18] A. McKeown and D.A. Westcott. Assessing the accuracy of small satellite transmitters on free-living flying-foxes. *Australian Ecology*, 37:295–301, 2012.

[19] J. E. Nelson. Vocal communication in australian flying foxes (pteropodidae; megachiroptera). *Zeitschrift für Tierpsychologie*, 21(7):857–870, 1964.

[20] J. Paek et al. Energy-efficient rate-adaptive gps-based positioning for smartphones. In *MobiSys*, pages 299–314, 2010.

[21] S. M. Van Parijs and P. J. Corkeron. Ontogeny of Vocalisations in Infant Black Flying Foxes, Pteropus alecto. *Behaviour*, 139(9):1111–1124, 2002.

[22] `http://www.asctec.de/uav-applications/research/products/asctec-pelican/`.

[23] L. A. Shilton et al. Landscape-scale redistribution of a highly mobile threatened species. *Austral Ecology*, 33(4):549–561, 2008.

[24] C.R. Tidemann and M.J. Vardon. Pests, pestilence, pollen and protein: the need for community-based management of flying-foxes in australia. *Australian Biologist*, 10:77–83, 1997.

[25] DA Westcott et al. The spectacled flying-fox, pteropus conspicillatus. Technical report, June 2001.

[26] A.M. Zaki, S. van Boheemen, T.M. Bestebroer, A.D.M.E. Osterhaus, and R.A.M. Fouchier. Isolation of a novel coronavirus from a man with pneumonia in saudi arabia. *New England Journal of Medicine*, 2012.

SCPL: Indoor Device-Free Multi-Subject Counting and Localization Using Radio Signal Strength

Chenren Xu[†], Bernhard Firner[†], Robert S. Moore[*], Yanyong Zhang[†]

Wade Trappe[†], Richard Howard[†], Feixiong Zhang[†], Ning An[§]

[†]WINLAB, Rutgers University, North Brunswick, NJ, USA
[*]Computer Science Dept, Rutgers University, Piscataway, NJ, USA
[§]Gerontechnology Lab, Hefei University of Technology, Hefei, Anhui, China

ABSTRACT

Radio frequency based device-free passive (DfP) localization techniques have shown great potentials in localizing individual human subjects, without requiring them to carry any radio devices. In this study, we extend the DfP technique to count and localize multiple subjects in indoor environments. To address the impact of multipath on indoor radio signals, we adopt a fingerprinting based approach to infer subject locations from observed signal strengths through profiling the environment. When multiple subjects are present, our objective is to use the profiling data collected by *a single* subject to count and localize *multiple* subjects without any extra effort. In order to address the non-linearity of the impact of multiple subjects, we propose a successive cancellation based algorithm to iteratively determine the number of subjects. We model indoor human trajectories as a state transition process, exploit indoor human mobility constraints and integrate all information into a conditional random field (CRF) to simultaneously localize multiple subjects. As a result, we call the proposed algorithm *SCPL* – sequential counting, parallel localizing.

We test SCPL with two different indoor settings, one with size 150 m^2 and the other 400 m^2. In each setting, we have four different subjects, walking around in the deployed areas, sometimes with overlapping trajectories. Through extensive experimental results, we show that SCPL can count the present subjects with 86% counting percentage when their trajectories are not completely overlapping. Our localization algorithms are also highly accurate, with an average localization error distance of 1.3 m.

Categories and Subject Descriptors

C.3 [**Special-Purpose and Application-Based Systems**]: Real-time and embedded systems

General Terms

Algorithm, Experimentation, Measurement

Keywords

Device-free Localization, Counting, Tracking, Trajectory, Multiple Subjects, Fingerprint, Nonlinear Fading

1. INTRODUCTION

Ambient Intelligence (AmI) envisions that future smart environments will be sensitive and responsive to the presence of people, thereby enhancing everyday life. Potential applications include eldercare, rescue operations, security enforcement, building occupancy statistics, etc. The key to enable these ubiquitous applications is the ability to localize various subjects and objects in the environment of interest. Device-free passive (DfP) localization has been proposed as a way of detecting and tracking subjects without the need to carry any tags or devices. It has the additional advantage of being unobtrusive while offering good privacy protection. Over the past decades, researchers have studied ways of tracking device-free human subjects using different techniques such as camera [10], capacitance [21], pressure [16], infrared [4] and ultrasonic [7]. However, they all suffer from serious limitations such as occlusion [10, 4], high deployment cost [16, 21] or short range [7].

Radio frequency (RF)-based techniques have the advantages of long-range, low-cost, and the ability to work through non-conducting walls and obstacles Several RF-based DfP localization techniques have been proposed in [29, 31, 17, 12, 23, 3, 24, 27, 8], and these approaches observe how people disturb the pattern of radio waves in an indoor space and derive their positions accordingly. To do so, they collect training data to profile the deployed area, and form mathematical models to relate observed signal strength values to locations. DfP algorithms can be broadly categorized into two groups: *location-based*, and *link-based*. Location-based DfP schemes collect a radio map with the subject present in various predetermined locations, and then map the test location to one of these trained locations based upon observed radio signals, which is also known as fingerprinting, as studied in [29, 27]. Link-based DfP schemes, however, capture the statistical relationship between the received signal strength (RSS) of a radio link and whether the subject is on the Line-of-Sight (LoS) of the radio link, and consequently determine the subject's location using geometric approaches [31, 17, 3, 8].

Recognizing that merely tracking an individual might not be sufficient for typical indoor scenarios, researchers have been pushing a great amount of effort towards scaling to multiple device-free subjects, such as in [32, 30, 14, 24, 27, 15]. They observe the change of RSS mean or variance and propose different tracking algorithms.

The common thing missing is that the number of subjects is known, which is a strong assumption. In addition, in cluttered indoor environments, subjects can cause collective nonlinear fading effects, which might significantly degrade the tracking performance and is not explicitly treated in the work above. On the other hand, location-based schemes can be straightforward but prohibitive due to the exponential increase in the training overhead if we need to profile the system with different combinations of these subjects.

In this study, we propose and evaluate an efficient DfP scheme for tracking multiple subjects using the training data collected by a single subject to avoid expensive training overhead.

Our algorithm consists of two phases. In the first phase, we *count* how many subjects are present using successive cancellation in an iterative fashion. In each iteration, we detect whether the room is empty. If it is not empty, we identify the location for one subject, and then subtract her impact on the RSS values from the collective impact measured in the experiment. Care must be taken when subtracting a subject's impact as the change in the RSS values caused by multiple subjects at the same time is smaller than the sum of RSS changes from each individual subject. In order to compensate for this, we need to multiply a coefficient to a subject's impact and then perform subtraction. The coefficient is specific to the subject's location as well as the link under consideration.

In the second phase, we localize the subjects after their number is known. We partition the deployment area into cells and represent a subject's location using its cell number. We formulate the localization problem as a conditional random field (CRF) by modeling indoor human trajectories as a state transition process and considering mobility constraints such as walls. We then identify the cells occupied by these subjects simultaneously. Since our counting process is sequential and our localization process is parallel, we call our algorithm *SCPL*.

We have tested SCPL in two indoor settings. The first setting is an office environment consisting of cubicles and narrow aisles, which is partitioned into 37 cells. We used the 13 transmitters and 9 receivers that were deployed for some earlier projects. The second setting is an open floor indoor environment, which is partitioned into 56 cells and deployed with 12 transmitters and 8 receivers. In the training phase, we measured the RSS values using a single subject. In the testing phase, we had four subjects with different heights, weights and gender, and designed four different real life office scenarios. These scenarios all had periods of time when multiple subjects walked side by side and thus had overlapping trajectories. We can count the number of subjects accurately, with a 88% counting percentage when the subjects were not walking side by side, and a 80% counting percentage when they were.

Our localization results have good accuracies, with a average error distance of 1.3 m considering all the scenarios. We find that it is beneficial to consider indoor human movement constraints according to the floor map when localizing moving subjects and demonstrate 24% improvement on average compared with no floor map information provided.

Our technique, SCPL, is unique in at least four contributions: (i) to our knowledge, it is the first work to systematically perform simultaneous counting and localization for up to four device-free subjects (moving or stationary) in large-scale deployments only using RF-based techniques; (ii) we designed a set of algorithms to count and localize multiple subjects relying on the calibration data collected by only a single individual; (iii) We also use plausible trajectory constraints (e.g. not walking through walls) based on floor map information, and integrate this information into the radio calibration data to further improve the tracking accuracies; and (iv) we recognize the nonlinear fading effects caused by multiple sub-

jects in cluttered indoor environments, and design the algorithms to mitigate the resulting error.

The rest of the paper is organized as follows. In Section 2, we discuss the applications that benefit from passive localization as well as our solution framework. Our solution consists of two phases, counting the number of subjects (in Section 3) and localizing the subjects (in Section 4). Then we describe our experimental setup in Section 5 and our detailed results in Section 6. We discuss the limitation and future direction of our work in Section 7 and review the related work in Section 8. Finally, we provide the concluding remarks in Section 9.

2. BACKGROUND

Before presenting our SCPL algorithm, we first discuss potential applications and the formulation of the problem.

2.1 Applications that Can Benefit from Passive Localization

Passive localization can find application in many important domains. Below we give a few examples:

Elderly/Health Care: Elder people may fall down in their houses for various reasons, such as tripping, momentary dizziness or overexertion. Without prompt emergency care, this could lead to life-threatening scenarios. Using trajectory based localization information, DfP can perform fall detection quickly because the monitored subject will remain in an unusual location for a long period of time.

Indoor Traffic Flow Statistics: Understanding patterns of human indoor movement can be valuable in identifying hot spots and corridors that help energy management and commercial site selection. DfP provides a non-intrusive and private solution to capturing indoor locations.

Home Security: DfP based home security is a major improvement over camera-based intrusion detection because it can not only detect the intrusion, but also track the intruders.

2.2 Problem Formulation

To solve the passive multi-subject localization problem, we adopt a cell-based fingerprinting approach, similar to the one discussed in [27].

Before we address the multi-subject problem, let us first look at how we localize a single subject. We first partition the deployed area into K cells. In the training phase, we first measure the ambient RSS values for L links when the room is empty. Then a single subject appears in each cell, walks randomly within that cell and takes N RSS measurements from all L radio links. By subtracting the ambient RSS vector from the collected data, we have a profiling dataset $\mathcal{D}$. $\mathcal{D}$, a $K \times N \times L$ matrix, quantifies how much a single subject impacts the radio RSS values from each cell. Having this profiling dataset $\mathcal{D}$, *we model the subject's presence in cell i as state S_i* and thus $\mathcal{D} = \{\mathcal{D}_{S_1}, \mathcal{D}_{S_2}, ..., \mathcal{D}_{S_K}\}$. In the testing phase, we first measure the ambient RSS values when the room is empty. Then a subject appears in a random location, and measures the RSS values for all L links while making random moves in that particular cell. Then we subtract the ambient RSS vector from this measured data, and form an RSS vector, O, which shows how much this subject impacts the radio links from this unknown cell. Based on $\mathcal{D}$ and O, we can run classification algorithms to classify the cell number of the unknown cell, thus localizing the subject.

Next we discuss how we extend the same framework to formulate the multi-subject localization problem. In the training phase,

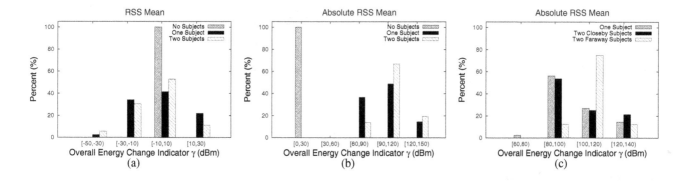

Figure 1: In terms of overall energy change indicator γ, (a) "RSS Mean", for zero, one, and two subjects. (b) "Absolute RSS Mean" for the same measurement shows better discrimination between zero and more than zero subjects. (c) Two subjects separated by more than 4 meters are clearly distinguishable from one subject.

our objective is to still *use a single subject's training data* to keep the training overhead low. Taking the training data for different number of subjects will lead to prohibitive overheads, which we will avoid. In the testing phase, multiple subjects appear in random cells, sometimes in the same cell, and we measure the RSS values for all the radio links. We calculate O in the same way as in the single-subject case.

To calculate the locations for these subjects, we need to go through two phases. In the first phase, we identify the number of subjects that are present simultaneously, C, which we call the *counting* phase. In the second phase, we identify in which cells are these C subjects, which we call the *localizing* phase. Please note that subjects are not stationary, but they move around within the deployed area.

3. COUNTING THE NUMBER OF SUBJECTS

In this section, we first provide empirical data to help the readers understand the impact of having multiple subjects on the radio signals, especially nonlinear fading effect, and then describe our sequential counting algorithm.

3.1 Understanding the Impact of Multiple Subjects on RSS Values

Let us first understand the relationship between a single subject's impact on the room RSS level and multiple subjects' impact. In particular, we would like to find out whether the relationship is linear.

As shown in previous studies such as [29, 31, 22, 3, 27], the RSS level of a radio link changes when a subject is near its Line-of-Sight (LoS). Based on this observation, we make a simple hypothesis: *more subjects will not only affect a larger number of spatially distributed radio links, but they will also lead to a higher level of RSS change on these links*. If this is true, we can infer the number of subjects that are present from the magnitude of the RSS change that we observe in the deployed area. We use the sum of the individual link RSS change to capture the *total energy change* in the environment as

$$\gamma = \sum_{l=1}^{L} O^l,$$

where O^l is the RSS change on link l.

Next we look at how to capture the RSS change of link l. A straightforward metric is to subtract the mean ambient RSS value

for link l (when the room is empty) from the measured mean RSS value for link l, the result of which is referred to as *RSS mean difference*. RSS mean difference is a popular metric that has been used in several studies, e.g., as seen in [29, 22, 3, 27]. However, upon deliberation, we find that RSS mean difference is not suitable for our purpose, mainly because the value is not always positive. Due to the multi-path effect, the presence of a subject does not always weaken a link, but sometimes, it may actually strengthen a link! As a result, the RSS mean difference can be negative. In this case, summing up each link's RSS mean difference does not lead to the correct total energy change in the environment because their values may cancel out each other. To address this issue, we thus propose to use *absolute RSS mean difference* which has a more compact data space than RSS mean when a cell is occupied.

Our experimental results confirm that the absolute RSS mean difference is a more suitable metric. In this set of experiments, we collect the RSS values when there are 0, 1 and 2 subjects who make random movements (with pauses) in the deployed area. We compute the corresponding γ value by using both RSS mean difference and absolute RSS mean difference, and plot their histograms in Figures 1(a)-(b) respectively. In Figure 1(a), when the room is empty, we observe γ values $\in [-10, 10)$ which means the overall energy level is rather stable. However, with 40% to 50% of chances, we still observe $\gamma \in [-10, 10)$ when subjects are present. This is because individual RSS mean differences can cancel out each other, and thus their sum is not a good indicator of the total energy change caused by having multiple subjects.

Absolute RSS mean difference is a better metric, as shown in Figure 1(b). The γ value when there are two subjects is statistically greater than the γ value when there is only one subject. As a result, in the rest of this paper, unless explicitly noted, we use absolute RSS mean difference as the metric to capture the RSS change in the environment. Finally, we note that the γ value alone is inadequate to distinguish between one or two subjects.

By looking at the two-subject data more carefully, we can further separate them into two groups based on the distance between the subjects. If the distance is more than 4 meters (we choose this threshold from the data sets), we call the two subjects *faraway*, and call the subjects *nearby* if the distance is less. We then plot the histograms of these groups in Figure 1(c). When subjects are close to each other, more links will be affected by both subjects, and fewer links are affected by only one of the subjects. Consequently, the γ value in this case will be smaller than the γ value when the two subjects are farther apart. Furthermore, we point out that the

γ value when we have C subjects at the same time is smaller than the sum of the individual γ value from each subject. As a result, it is hard to distinguish having two subjects close to each other from having only one subject.

In summary, we have two main observations from these experiments. First, the absolute RSS mean difference is a suitable metric to capture the impact caused by the appearance of a subject. Second, the total energy change, γ, reflects the level of impact subjects have in the room, but we cannot rely on the value of γ alone to infer how many subjects are present because γ is not linearly proportional to the number of subjects.

3.2 Counting Subjects Using Successive Cancellation

We use successive cancellation to count the number of subjects. When multiple subjects coexist, it often so happens that one subject has a stronger influence on the radio signal than the rest. Thus, our counting algorithm goes through several rounds. In each round, we estimate the strongest subject's cell number in this round assuming there is only a single subject, i, and then subtract her share of RSS change from the remaining RSS vector O to obtain the new remaining RSS vector that will be used in the next round.

If this problem were linear, we could simply subtract the mean vector μ_i associated with cell i in the profiling data $\mathcal{D}$ from the observed RSS vector O. However, as shown in the previous subsection, the total impact from multiple subjects is not linear to the number of subjects – the impact observed when C subjects appear at the same time is smaller than the sum of each subject's impact if they appear one at at time. To be more precise, O is an underestimation of the linear combination of the mean values of the associated cells that we collected in $\mathcal{D}$. To address this issue, instead of subtracting μ_i directly from O, we multiply a coefficient that is less than 1 to μ_i and subtract this normalized term from O. This coefficient, however, is not uniform across all the cell and link combinations; instead, it is specific to each cell and link pair because different cells have different impacts on a link. We will then calculate the location-link coefficient matrix, $\mathcal{B} = (\beta_{i,l})$ where $\beta_{i,l}$ is the coefficient for cell i and link l.

Our algorithm to calculate the coefficient matrix $\mathcal{B}$ is detailed in Algorithm 1. The basic idea is that, for each link l, we compute the correlation between a cell pair, (i, j) with respect to link l. The two cells that both are close to a link are highly correlated with respect to this link. We use h_{ij}^l to denote this correlation[1]. Note that all the RSS values in profiling data are non-negative, and thus we have $h_{ij}^l \geq 0$. For each cell i, we pivot that cell and compute the β_{il} as

$$\beta_{il} = \frac{h_{ii}^l}{\sqrt{\sum_{j=1}^{K} {h_{ij}^l}^2}}.$$

Basically, when two subjects occupy cells i and j respectively, and only one of them affects link l, they have low correlation and the value of h_{ij}^l is close to 0. On the other hand, when they both affect link l, the value of h_{ij}^l will reflect their positive correlation.

Once we determine the location-link coefficient matrix $\mathcal{B}$, we describe our successive cancellation based counting algorithm (shown in Algorithm 2), which can identify the subject count C from the observation RSS vector O using the profiling RSS matrix $\mathcal{D}$ collected by a single subject. We first compute γ^0's and γ^1's from the

[1]Notice that we use correlation h_{ij}^l instead of correlation coefficient ρ_{ij}^l because ρ_{ii}^l will always be 1 and thus guarantee its dominance among the all the cells on all the links when the cell i is detected first, which is not true.

Algorithm 1: Location-Link Correlation Algorithm

input : $\mathcal{D}$- The training data collected from L links among K states/cells
output: $\mathcal{B}$ - The location-link coefficient matrix

1 **for** $l = 1 \rightarrow L$ **do**
2     $h \leftarrow$ zero matrix of $K \times K$
3   **for** $i = 1 \rightarrow K$ **do**
4   **for** $j = 1 \rightarrow K$ **do**
5           $I \leftarrow$ training data indices associated with state S_i
6           $J \leftarrow$ training data indices associated with state S_j
7   // Compute the link correlation
8           $h_{ij} \leftarrow E[\mathcal{D}_{Il}\mathcal{D}_{Jl}]$
9   **for** $i = 1 \rightarrow K$ **do**
10        $normfactor \leftarrow \sqrt{\sum_{j=1}^{K} {h_{ij}}^2}$
11   // Compute the location-link coefficient for cell i and link l
12        $\beta_{il} \leftarrow \frac{h_{ii}}{normfactor}$

---

ambient RSS vector and the profiling RSS matrix $\mathcal{D}$ respectively. Then, we construct a 95% confidence interval for the distribution of γ^0's and γ^1's and refer to the associated lower and upper bounds as $c_L^0, c_U^0, c_L^1, c_U^1$. From the observation RSS vector, O, we first compute its γ value and then perform a presence detection: if $\gamma < c_U^0$, we claim the room is empty. Otherwise, we will claim there is at least one subject present and start to iteratively count the number of subjects using successive cancellation to finally determine the value of C.

In each successive cancellation iteration, we do the following:

- *Presence Detection.* We first perform a presence detection by checking if $\gamma \geq c_U^1$ to find out whether there is any more subject in the room. Please note that this condition is stronger than $\gamma \geq c_U^0$, and we will take care of the last iteration separately. If the presence detection returns a 'yes', we increment the detected subject count C, and go to the next step. Otherwise, we end the algorithm.

- *Cell Identification.* If there is a subject in this iteration, we estimate the occupied cell q by

$$q = \underset{i \in \mathcal{S}}{\operatorname{argmax}} P(O|S_i),$$

where $\mathcal{S}$ is the set of remaining unoccupied cells.

- *Contribution Subtraction.* Next, we cancel the impact of this subject from cell q by subtracting $\mu_{ql} \cdot \beta_{ql}$ from O^l for each link l.

In the last round, we simply check if $\gamma < c_U^1$, which actually relax the lower bound of γ^1, which means we consider the possibility that when the last subject is detected in our algorithm, the corresponding γ is lower than the c_L^1. This further compensates for the over-subtraction in our earlier iterations.

4. LOCALIZING MULTIPLE MOVING SUBJECTS WHEN THE SUBJECT COUNT IS KNOWN

In this section, we discuss how we localize multiple moving subjects when the subject count is known. In SCPL, we track multiple subjects in parallel, unlike in the counting phase where we count the number of subjects sequentially. Radio interference is very complex and unpredictable, especially when multiple subjects are present and a link is affected by multiple people. In this case, it is hard to quantify the exact impact of a subject. Even after considering the cell link coefficient matrix $\mathcal{B}$, we may still overestimate (or, underestimate) a subject's impact on a link. These errors, while insignificant enough not to hurt the counting process, will lead to inferior localization results. On the other hand, parallel tracking keeps all the raw RSS values and can provide better results.

4.1 Understanding the Challenge of Localizing Multiple Subjects

Before presenting our localization algorithm, we first take a closer look at how multiple subjects collectively affect the RSS values and thus complicate the localization problem through empirical data. The complexity of this problem mainly stems from the multi-path effect [18], a typical error source in RF-based indoor localization. In this problem, multi-path can cause nonlinear interference in a radio space when multiple subjects are present. More precisely, when multiple subjects coexist in different locations, the resulting RSS value will not be simply the summation of the individual RSS values from a single subject independently in those locations. The

gap between these two is larger when these subjects are close to each other. To validate this conjecture, we randomly select a few positions with certain distances apart. We first have one subject, A, collect the RSS measurements by standing stationary in these locations. Then, we involve another subject, B with similar height and weight as A, and have them stand in two different positions, say i and j. We use O_i and O_j to denote the measured RSS vector when A is standing in positions i and j independently, and O_{ij} the measured RSS vector when A and B are standing in positions i and j simultaneously. In a linear space, vector O_{ij} would be simply the summation of O_i and O_j. However, as mentioned before, this problem is nonlinear, especially when subjects are close to each other. To quantify the degree of nonlinearity, we define the *RSS Error Residual* as

$$\Delta O^l = O_{ij}^l - O_i^l - O_j^l,$$

for link l. A larger ΔO^l value indicates a higher non-linear degree. To articulate the nonlinearity nature, we remove link l if its O_{ij}^l, O_i^l, O_j^l values are all less than 1 because these links are actually not affected by the subjects in any case. We plot the histograms of the remaining O^l values in Figure 2.

From Figure 2, we have three main observations. Firstly, when the two subjects stand side by side (i.e., the distance between them is 0 m), there are only about 30% and 50% chances that we see $|\Delta O^l| < 2$ for RSS mean and absolute RSS mean respectively, which validates our problem is indeed nonlinear. As the distance becomes longer than 2 m, the probability of having $|\Delta O^l| < 2$ rises to more than 70% for both RSS mean difference and absolute RSS mean difference. Secondly, the error residual can be negative under RSS mean difference, but is positive under absolute RSS mean difference in most cases, suggesting O_{ij} is consistently an underestimation of $O_i + O_j$. This property is desirable because it ensures Monotonicity.

Finally, we define the *total RSS Error Residual* as:

$$\varepsilon = \sum_{l=1}^{L} |\Delta O^l|,$$

which measures the deviation between the profiling data and the RSS measurement in a multi-subject problem. We plot the histogram in Figure 3 and observe that the absolute RSS mean has a smaller ε value, and thus more appropriate for our purposes.

4.2 Conditional Random Field Formulation

Tracking moving subjects actually introduces new optimization opportunities - we can improve our localization results by considering the fact that human locations from adjacent time intervals should form a continuous trajectory, which can be further modeled as a state transition process under conditional random field (CRF) [11]. CRFs are a type of discriminative undirected probabilistic graphical model. We use them to decode the sequential RSS observations into continuous mobility trajectories.

The first step towards formulating a conditional random field is to form the sensor model and transition model respectively. In our problem, we have K states: $\mathcal{S} = \{S_1, S_2, ..., S_K\}$. In a single-subject problem, state S_i means the subject is located in cell i. The sensor model essentially infers the current state based on the observation RSS vector O, which is to generate a cell likelihood map based upon O. For a single subject case, we would like to maximize the likelihood $P(q = S_i|O, \mathcal{D})$ when cell i is occupied. In other words, when the subject is located in cell i in the testing phase, we would like to maximize the probability that the estimated state/cell q matches the actually occupied cell i. We assume the

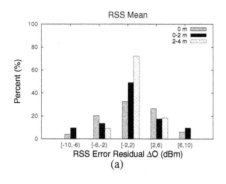 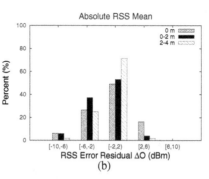 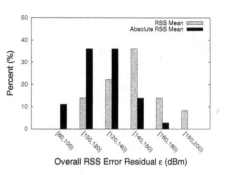

Figure 2: The RSS residual error forms a double-sided distribution when using RSS mean, while it is approximately single-sided distributed using absolute RSS mean.

Figure 3: Absolute RSS mean has a smaller overall RSS error residual distribution.

observed RSS vectors in each state follow a multivariate Gaussian with shared covariance, as in [27], and denote

$$\delta_i(O) = P(O|S_i),$$

where

$$P(O|S_i) \sim \mathcal{N}(\mu_i, \Sigma).$$

However, the sensor model is imperfect because of the deep fading effect that can cause estimation error through only a few links[2]. Therefore, the cell associated with the maximum probability might be far from the ground truth.

Next, we look at the transition model. In each clock tick $t = 1, 2, ..., T$, the system makes a transition to state q_t. This process models the movement of a subject – the subject moves to a new cell in each tick. We choose a first order CRF, which means the next cell number depends on the current cell number, rather than any earlier history because we do not want to assume any specific human movement trajectories. In our model, subjects can either walk along a straight line, take turns or wander back and forth.

The subject's trajectory can thus be characterized as a parametric Markov random process with the *transition model* defined as the probability of a transition from state i at time $t-1$ to state j at time t in form of

$$T = P(q_t|q_{t-1}),$$

where

$$T_{ij} = P(q_t = S_j|q_{t-1} = S_i).$$

The intuition here is that people cannot walk through walls or cross rooms in a single tick. We believe these mobility constraints can be used to fix most of the errors in the sensor model caused by deep fades.

In our cell-based approach, we define the following:

Cell neighbors are a list of adjacent cells which can be entered from the current cell without violating mobility constraints.

Order of neighbor is defined as the number of cells a person must pass through to reach a specific cell from the current cell without violating mobility constraints. We assume the subject moves to a new cell every clock tick. For example, as far as cell i is concerned, the 1-order neighbors include its immediate adjacent cells, and its 2-order neighbors include the immediate adjacent cells of its 1-order neighbors (excluding i and i's first order neighbors).

---

[2]Because of deep fading from multipath, adjacent points can have dramatically different RSS values, leading to large estimation errors.

Trajectory ring with radius r is defined as the area consisting of cell i, i's 1-order neighbors, 2-order neighbors, ..., up to its r-order neighbors. Particularly, 0-order trajectory ring consists of all the cells.

Let $\Omega_r(i)$ be the cells included in i's r-trajectory ring and let $N_r(i)$ be the size of $\Omega_r(i)$. Our transition model thus becomes:

$$T_{ij} = \begin{cases} \frac{1}{N_r(i)} & \text{for} \quad j \in \Omega_r(i) \\ 0 & \text{for} \quad j \notin \Omega_r(i) \end{cases}$$

4.3 Localization Algorithm

Having constructed the sensor model and transition model, we can translate the problem of subject tracking to the problem of finding the most likely sequence of state transitions in a continuous time stream. The *Viterbi algorithm* [6] defines $V_j(t)$, the highest probability of a single path of length t which accounts for the first t observations and ends in state S_j:

$$V_j(t) = \operatorname*{argmax}_{q_1, q_2, ..., q_{t-1}} P(q_1 q_2 ... q_t = j, O_1 O_2 ... O_t | T, \delta).$$

By induction

$$V_j(1) = \delta_j(O_1),$$

$$V_j(t+1) = \operatorname*{argmax}_i V_i(t) T_{ij} \delta_j(O_{t+1}),$$

which is similar as discussed in [26].

Generalizing to the multi-subject case, we denote $\delta_{1:K}(O) = \{\delta_1(O), \delta_2(O), ..., \delta_K(O)\}$ from the sensor model to represent the likelihood of each state. We denote $Q = \{q^1, ..., q^C\}$, where C is the total number of present subjects. For the current state Q_t, we have $\binom{K}{C}$ possible permutations of subject locations. For each permutation j, we denote $Q_j = \{q^1, ..., q^C\}$ and compute the Viterbi score

$$F_j = \sum_{i=1}^C \delta_{q_t^i}(O_t) T_{q_{t-1}^i q_t^i}.$$

We then pick the j value that is associated with the maximum Viterbi score as the current state.

We describe our device-free multi-subject localization algorithm in Algorithm 3. We believe we can achieve best localization results when we consider 1 or 2-order trajectory ring, which is better than the 0-order case used in our earlier work [27], and is also confirmed by our experimental results presented in Section 6.

Algorithm 3: Trajectory-Based Device-free Multi-subject Localization Algorithm

input : $\mathcal{D}$- The training data collected from L links among K cells
T- The transition model
$O_{1:t}$- The testing data collected from L links when subjects are in unknown locations
C- The estimated number of present subjects in the deployed area
Q_1- The initial state(s) of the present subjects
output: $Q_{1:t}$- The most like sequence of the trajectories of the present subjects

1 **for** $i = 2 \to t$ **do**
2     $\delta_{1:K}(O_i) \leftarrow P(O_i|\mathcal{D})$
3     $\Pi \leftarrow$ is the set of all the possible permutations of $\binom{K}{C}$
4     $Q_i \leftarrow \text{argmax}_{j \in \Pi} \text{ViterbiScore}(Q_{i-1}, Q_j, \delta_{1:K}(O_i), T)$

5. EXPERIMENTAL SETUP

In this section, we briefly describe the experimental setup, the data collection process and the metric we use for performance evaluation.

5.1 System Description

The radio devices used in our experiments contain a Chipcon CC1100 radio transceiver and a 16-bit Silicon Laboratories C8051-F321 microprocessor powered by a 20 mm diameter lithium coin cell battery, the CR2032. The receivers have a USB connector for loss-free data collection but are otherwise identical to the transmitters. In our experiments, the radio operates in the unlicensed bands at 909.1 MHz. Transmitters use MSK modulation, a 250 Kbps data rate, and a programmed output power of 0 dBm. Each transmitter periodically broadcasts a 10-byte packet (8 bytes of sync and preamble and 2 bytes of payload consisting of transmitter's id and sequence number) every 100 millisecond. When the receiver receives a packet, it measures the RSS values and wraps the transmitter id, receiver id, RSS, timestamp (on the receiver side) into a "data packet". The packets are forwarded to a centralized system where the data can be analyzed by independent "solvers" that perform various data processing functions. These include packet loss calculations [5], mobility detection [9], counting, localization, and data interpolation. More detail of the system can be found on the Owl Platform website [1].

5.2 Data Collection

In our experiments, the RSS data is collected as a mean value over a 1 second window for each link. We choose a 1 second window because a normal person can at most walk across one cell during a second. In the training phase, a single subject made random walk for 30 seconds in each cell and collected 30 RSS vectors as the profiling data. In this testing phase, we designed four scenarios for each environment, and in each scenario the subject(s) individually form a continuous mobility trajectory for about 30 seconds. The subjects are walking at a speed of about 0.5 m per second. The training phase was performed in the early morning while the testing phase happened the afternoon of the same day.

5.3 Deployment Cost

In this study, we deployed our system in two different indoor settings which we will shown in Section 6. Our "solver" is running on a laptop (Intel i7-640LM 2.13GHz, 8GB RAM). For the 150 m^2 setting, it took 15 minutes to collect the training data, 0.003 seconds for the solver to fit the model parameters, and 3.4 seconds to compute the location-link correlation coefficients. The second

area was 2.7 times larger (400 m^2), but data collection only took 30 minutes, the solver was actually faster (0.002 seconds), and the time to compute the correlation coefficients only increased by a factor of about 1.5 (5.3 seconds).

5.4 Performance Metrics

We use the following performance metrics to measure our counting and localizing algorithms.

Counting Percentage is given by:

$$1 - \frac{|\hat{C} - C|}{C},$$

where $\hat{C}$ is the estimated subject count and C is the actual subject count.

Error Distance is defined as:

$$d(Q, \hat{Q}) = \frac{1}{C} \min_{\pi \in \Pi} \sum_{i=1}^{C} d(q^i, \hat{q}^{\pi(i)}),$$

where Π includes all the possible permutations of $\{1, 2, ..., C\}$, $d(q, \hat{q})$ is the Euclidean distance between the ground truth q and the estimated position $\hat{q}$. $Q = \{q^1, q^2, ..., q^C\}$ and $\hat{Q} = \{\hat{q}^1, \hat{q}^2, ..., \hat{q}^C\}$ are within the pre-profiled finite states $\mathcal{S} = \{S_1, S_2, ..., S_K\}$. In this study, q is the subject's actual location and $\hat{q}$ is her estimated location (i.e., center of the estimated cell).

6. EXPERIMENTAL RESULTS

In this section, we summarize the results we have obtained from two indoor settings. In each setting, we had multiple subjects each walking along a trajectory.

6.1 Results from Office Setting

Our first setting is a typical office environment, consisting of cubicles and aisles with a total area of 150 m^2. The environment is quite cluttered as shown in Figure 4(a). The area is broken down to 37 cells such as cubicles and aisle segments, as shown in Figure 4(b). We utilized 13 radio transmitters and 9 radio receivers, whose locations and corresponding link LoS's are shown in Figure 4(c). Here, we need to point out that these devices were installed for some earlier projects, not specifically for this one, and therefore, the link density per cell is non-uniform. This, however, represents a more realistic setting, through which we can show that SCPL can achieve good results without dedicated sensor deployment.

We had four subjects (A, B, C and D) in this series of experiments. We went through several example scenarios and illustrate them in Figure 5:

- *One Subject Scenario:* A left her boss's office, and walked along the aisle to her cubicle.

- *Two Subject Scenario:* When B entered the room, A was walking on the aisle towards him. B waited until they met and walked together for some time, and then separated to go back to their own seats.

- *Three Subject Scenario:* While A and B followed the movement patterns in the above two subject scenario, C walked on the other aisle from one cubicle to another.

- *Four Subject Scenario:* While A, B, and C followed the movement patterns in the above three subject scenario, D was sitting on her seat.

(a) Test Field

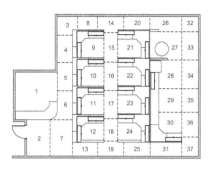
(b) Cell Locations

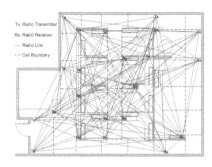
(c) Radio Link Distribution

Figure 4: In (a), we show the office in which we deployed our system. In (b), we show that the office deployment region is partitioned into 37 cubicle-sized cells of interest. In (c), we show the locations of the pre-installed 13 radio transmitters, 9 radio receivers and the corresponding Line-of-Sight links.

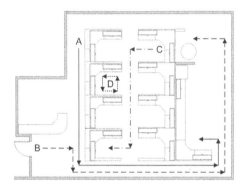

Figure 5: We show the experimental trajectories of subjects A, B, C and D in the office setting. Note the the trajectories of A and B are partially overlapped at the same time.

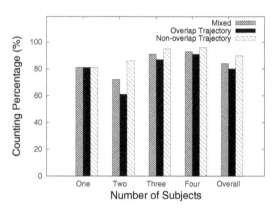

Figure 6: In a multi-subject case, our counting algorithm has a better performance when their trajectories are not overlapped than overlapped.

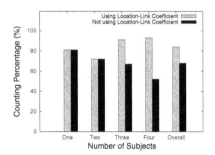

Figure 7: Counting percentage improvement when the RSS change is normalized by location-link coefficients in the office setting.

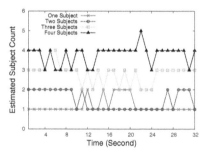

Figure 8: Estimated subject count over time using our successive cancellation-based counting algorithm in the office setting.

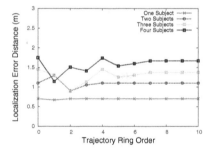

Figure 9: We achieve best localization accuracy averaging all the test cases when we adopt 1 or 2-order trajectory rings in the office setting.

6.1.1 Counting Results

The difficulty of subject counting increases when multiple subjects walk together (in the same cell). Thus, we present our counting results in the following three ways: (a) all the experimental data (referred to as *mixed*), (b) the experimental data for when multiple subjects walked together and thus had overlapping trajectories (referred to as *overlap trajectory*), and (c) the experimental data for

when multiple subject trajectories did not overlap (referred to as *non-overlap trajectory*). Figure 6 shows the counting percentages in all three cases.

We observe that when we have multiple subjects, the counting percentage is higher in the non-overlap trajectory case. The average counting percentage across all cases is 84%, the average counting percentage for non-overlap cases is 90%, and the average counting percentage for overlap cases is 80%.

Next, we show the performance improvement of subtracting a normalized RSS contribution by location-link coefficients compared to directly subtracting a cell's mean RSS change. We show the counting percentage results in these two cases in Figure 7. When we have one or two subjects, the non-linearity is not very obvious, and these two methods have very similar results. When we have more than two subjects, the non-linearity of the signal change becomes very pronounced, and using a normalized RSS contribution can yield better counting results. Specifically, we observe a 36% improvement with three subjects, and a 24% improvement with four subjects.

Finally, we show our subject counting results in Figure 8, in which all the four tests last 32 seconds. In the single-subject case, we see two individuals, between time tick 12 and 20. This is likely because there is an overestimate of γ near cells 13, 19, and 25, because of a denser than average link space or proximity to the receiver. In the two-subject case, we under-estimate the subject count by one between time tick 10 and 26 because the two subjects merged their trajectories in those time periods. The errors caused by temporally overlapping trajectories can also be easily addressed as follows. We continuously run the counting algorithm, and once we notice the estimated subject count suddenly drops, we check their locations before the sudden drop. If no subject's location was close to the exit, then we can conclude that two or more (depending upon the change in the count) were in close proximity. Of course, this information should be validated from the subject location information. For the three subjects case, we see the same problem when subjects A and B merge their trajectories. For the four subject case, this error is reduced a bit because subject D is always in cell 10, where has a relatively high density of radio links.

6.1.2 Localization Results

We show the mean of localization error distances in Figure 9 with different ring order parameters. In our setting, we choose 10 as the upper bound of the ring order because all cells are within 10 hops of each other.

Our first observation is that the use of the trajectory information can improve the localization performance by 13.6% – the overall mean localization error distance drops from $1.25m$ (with 0-order trajectory ring) [27] to about $1.08m$ (with 1-order trajectory ring). We note that the error distance for a single subject does not benefit from using trajectory information because the profiling data is good enough for this case [29, 27]. Multiple subjects, especially when they are close to each other, will cause non-linear radio interference, and thus the data collected from the mutually affected links alone cannot give very accurate localization results. Therefore, the sensor model alone is insufficient for high accuracies. Secondly, we observe that the localization results are less accurate in those cells with lower radio link densities, such as in cell 34-37, because subjects may cause negligible changes to the RSS space at a few points in those cells. Thirdly, trajectory information helps prevent the error distance increases dramatically as the increasing number of subjects. Finally, our environment is an office space consisting of cubicles and aisles, and the possible paths a subject can take are rather limited. As a result, we achieve the best localization accuracies with 1 or 2 order trajectory ring. Due to the movement constraints, a higher order trajectory ring has the same result as not considering any neighbors at all (i.e., 0 ring order). We hypothesize that this may not be true in a more open indoor environment such as (large) homes, malls and museums.

6.2 Results from Open Floor Space

The second test setting is a more open floor of total 400 m^2,

as shown in Figure 10(a). We used this setting to model an open hall with a few posters on exhibition, and SCPL can be used to detect traffic flow and infer the most popular poster. We deployed 12 transmitters and 8 receivers in such a way that the link density has a relatively even distribution across the cells, as shown in Figure 10(b). We would like to point out that we used fewer devices in this setting than in the previous one, though this one had a larger area. Also, this environment is even more challenging in that half of the radio devices are deployed on a wall which also has dozens of computers and other metal parts, significantly degrading radio propagation.

The space was partitioned into a uniform grid of 56 cells, and we involved four different subjects in this test and show their trajectories in Figure 10(c). We repeated the same four scenarios as in the previous setting. We plot our counting results in Figure 11. We achieve a 100% counting percentage when there was only a single subject, which is better than the previous setting because the link density is more even in this case. We achieve a counting percentage of 83%, 80%, and 82% for two, three and four subjects respectively, resulting in a 86% counting percentage in total. We have achieved better results when we normalize a subject's impact from a certain cell on the RSS with the location-link coefficients. We observe similar trends as in the previous setting: the results are the same for one or two subjects, and improved from 67% to 80%, and from 75% to 86% when we have three and four subjects, respectively. The estimated subject is shown in Figure 12.

We present the localization results in Figure 13. In the localization part, we observe similar patterns as in the previous setting: we achieve better localization accuracy using trajectory information. We achieve the best localization accuracy when we adopt the 2 order trajectory ring, which is 1.49 m, a 35% improved compared to the 0-order trajectory ring case [27].

7. LIMITATIONS AND FUTURE WORK

In this section, we discuss the limitation of SCPL.

7.1 Algorithms

Recognizing human mobility constraints in indoor environments leads to different trajectory-based tracking optimizations. Under our framework of discretized physical space, our localization algorithm relies on a greedy search for the optimal solution to find the most likely trajectories followed by the individuals. Unfortunately, this has factorial computation complexity because it involves C-permutations of K^3 and potentially introduces prohibitive overhead to meet real-time requirements, especially when K grows rapidly in a large-scale environment. However, as we observed from the experimental results from the two different settings, we have achieved the best localization accuracies using only the 1 or 2-order trajectory ring, which means we can not only achieve good accuracy, but also significantly reduce the computational complexity by reducing the permutation space from $\binom{K}{C}$ to $\binom{K'}{C}$, where K' is the cell union of each individual's 1 or 2-order trajectory rings. Under 1-order trajectory ring, it took 0.87 seconds and 0.88 seconds to count and localize four subjects in our two different settings respectively. We would expect that it will take more than 1 second to track at least five subjects, which fails to afford real-time tracking requirement with this hardware. Another family of trajectory based tracking incorporates a particle filter [2], such as the one used in [24, 14]. However, the primary weakness of particle filters is the computational complexity required to run the algorithm for the large number of particles needed to achieve accurate re-

---

^3C is the subject count and K is the total number of cells.

(a) Test Field

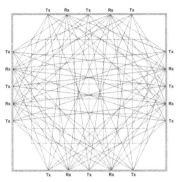

(b) Radio Link Distribution

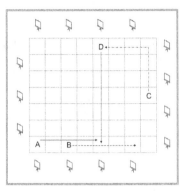

(c) Test Trajectories

Figure 10: In (a), we show the open floor space used for poster exhibition in which we deployed our system. In (b), we show the locations of the 12 radio transmitters, 8 radio receivers and the corresponding Line-of-Sight links. In (c), we show the experimental trajectories of subjects A, B, C and D in the open floor space which is partitioned into a uniform grid of 56 cells.

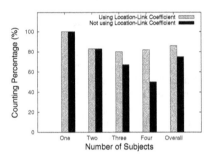

Figure 11: Counting percentage improvement when the RSS change is normalized by location-link coefficients in the open floor space.

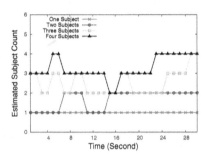

Figure 12: Estimated subject count over time using our successive cancellation-based counting algorithm in the open floor space.

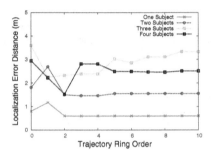

Figure 13: We consistently achieve best localization accuracy when we adopt 1 or 2-order trajectory rings in the open floor space

sults. For example, 500 particles were needed for tracking each individual and it took 7.6 seconds for four subjects in each time step, as reported in [14]. Overall, there is plenty space to optimize the trade-off between accuracy and computational cost in tracking multiple subjects for future work.

7.2 Long-term Test

In a long-run test, any RF-based localization schemes suffer not only from temporal fading, but also from environmental changes. A small piece of metal can change the tuning of the antenna shift the radiation pattern or even the radio frequency of the nearby transmitter or receiver. Either or both of these effects can change the underlying propagation pattern and, hence, the RSS values on the links. To avoid frequent manual recalibration, we present two schemes in our earlier work [27, 28] to maintain the localization accuracy over a long-term test. In [27], we simply remove the radio links experiencing deep fading by watching RSS values over time, which is able to maintain a cell estimation accuracy of 90% over one month. In [28], we present a camera-assisted auto recalibration – when the camera occasionally turns on, it localizes the subject and calibrates the RF data automatically. Both schemes have limitations: the performance of the first scheme will degrade when the number of remaining links is too small, while the second one needs extra hardware. Realizing these limitations, we will investigate sophisticated auto-calibration methods as part of the future work.

8. RELATED WORK

In this section, we briefly review the related literature in RF-based counting and localizing device-free human subjects.

8.1 Device-Free Counting

Nakatsuka et al. [13] first demonstrated the feasibility of using radio signal strength to estimate the crowd density. The authors setup two radio nodes and observe that RSS decreases as the number of subjects increases when they are all sitting between the nodes. We, however, point out that SCPL is the first work that systematically counts device-free subjects in large scale deployment, to our best knowledge.

8.2 Device-Free Localization

In 2006, Woyach et al. [25] first experimentally demonstrated the feasibility of localizing device-free subjects by observing a difference in RSS changes by a subject moving between (resulting signal shadowing effect) and in the vicinity (causing small-scale fading) of a pair of transmitter and receiver. From then on, several DfP approaches have been proposed in the literature, which can be broadly categorized into two groups as follows.

Location-based schemes: This approach is also known as "fingerprinting", a popular approach for RF-based localization. It was first studied in [29] in the context of passive localization. The authors first collect a radio map with the subject present in a few prede-

	Grid Array [30]	RTI [8]	NUZZER [19]	SCPL
Meausred physical quantity	RSS variance	RSS attenuation	RSS change	RSS change
Non-LoS localization	No	Yes	Yes	Yes
Nodes density	High	High	Low	Median
Prior knowledge of node locations	Yes	Yes	No	No
Tracking static subjects	No	Yes	Yes	Yes
Deployment scale	Median	Small	Large	Large
Training overhead	Low	Low	High	Median

Table 1: Comparison of different RF-based passive localization systems.

termined locations, and then map the test location to one of these trained locations based upon observed radio signals. This method explicitly measures the multipath effect on RSS in each different position, and thus avoids modeling errors. In addition, it does not require a node deployment as dense as in link-based schemes because when the subject is in the position has no intersection with any radio LoS links, the RSS ground truth still can provide a distinguishable record from other positions. This work is extended to a much larger deployment in Nuzzer [19]. In [27], Xu et al. propose to formulate this localization problem into a probabilistic classification problem and use a cell-based calibration with random walk method profiling the system in order to mitigate the error caused by the multipath effect in cluttered indoor environments, improve the localization accuracy and meanwhile reduce the profiling overhead. However, the downside of fingerprinting is also evident: the calibration procedure is relatively tedious.

Link-based schemes: These techniques look for those radio links close to the target subjects and further determine the locations of the targets based on the RSS dynamics. Zhang et al. [31] set up a sensor grid array on the ceiling to track subjects on the ground. An "influential" link is one whose RSS variance exceeds a empirical threshold. The authors determine a subject's location based upon the observation that these influential links tend to cluster around the subject. This technique forms a consistent link-based model to relate the subject's location relative to the radio link locations. In [32]. the authors extend their algorithms to track up to subjects separated by at least 5 m. In [30], the monitored area is partitioned into different triangle sections, and the nodes in neighbor section are working at different communication channels to reduce the interference among nodes. The authors applied support vector regression model to track up to two subjects. The fundamental limitations of this series of work is that (i) not all the monitored places have the facilities to mount nodes on the ceiling; (ii) this work uses RSS variance as the data primitive, which is essentially the amplitude and phase shift of the ground reflection multipath caused by the of human subjects only in motion. In other words, the system might fail to work if the subjects stop walking. Another sets of work following Link-based DfP is radio tomographic imaging (RTI). Wilson et al. [22] use tomographic reconstruction to estimate an image of human presence in the deployment area of the network. RSS attenuation is used as data primitive in [22], which effectively works in outdoor or uncluttered indoor space without rich multipath. Recognizing the nature of multipath fading, Wilson et al. defined the concept of fade-level [24], which captures the ambient RSS characteristics of each link and categorize the links into deep fade (the RSS will increase on average when the LoS is blocked) and anti-fade (the RSS decreases when the LoS is obstructed) through fitting the calibration data to a skewed Laplace distribution. The authors demonstrate this technique's effectiveness through testing in same setting over time and a totally different setting without the effort of

re-estimating the model parameters. Kaltiokallio et al. [8] further exploit channel diversities to enhance the tracking accuracy. Taking the framework of RTI, another sets of work is done based on sequential Monte Carlo sampling techniques. Chen et al. [3] propose to use auxiliary particle filtering method to simultaneously localize the nodes and a single subject in an outdoor setting. In [20], the author introduce a measurement model which assumes the attenuation in RSS due to the simultaneous presence of multiple subjects on the LoS is approximately equal to the sum of the attenuations caused by the individuals. This model is then applied in [14, 15] for tracking up to four subjects in outdoor and indoor settings. In general, link-based schemes have two advantages: (i) the algorithms are robust to the environmental change because the subject's location is directly estimated based on its relative distance to each individual radio link LoS; (ii) it requires less calibration effort - only sensor locations and ambient RSS for each link is needed. However, it requires a dense nodes deployment to provide enough radio LoS links to cover all the physical space.

Finally, we summarize the differences between our system and the recent DfP RF-based localization systems in Table 1.

9. CONCLUSION

In this paper, we present SCPL, an accurate counting and localization system for device-free subjects. We demonstrate the feasibility of using the profiling data collected with only a single subject present to count and localize multiple subjects in the same environment with no extra hardware or data collection. Through extensive experimental results, we show that SCPL works well in two different typical indoor environments of 150 m^2 (office cubicles) and 400 m^2 (open floor plan) deployed using an infrastructure of only 20 to 22 devices. In both spaces, we can achieve about an 86% average counting percentage and 1.3 m average localization error distance for up to 4 subjects. Finally, we shows that though a complex environment like the office cubicles is expected to have worse radio propagation, we can leverage the increased mobility constraints that go with a complex environment to maintain or even improve accuracy in these situations.

Finally, we point out that if we rely on a single subject's training data, the number of subjects that can be accurately counted and localized is rather limited. We had success with up to 4 subjects, but were not very successful with more subjects. In our future work, we will look at how we can accurately localize a larger number of subjects with reasonable overheads.

Acknowledgments

We sincerely thank the anonymous reviewers for their valuable feedback on this paper. We also thank Neal Patwari for shepherding the final version of this paper. We finally thank Jinwei Wu, Zhuo Chen, Kai Su and Sugang Li for their extensive effort involved in the experiments.

10. REFERENCES

[1] Owl platform: The great owl watches all things. http://www.owlplatform.com/.

[2] *Beyond the Kalman Filter: Particle Filters for Tracking Applications (Artech House Radar Library)*. Artech Print on Demand, Jan. 2004.

[3] X. Chen, A. Edelstein, Y. Li, M. Coates, M. Rabbat, and A. Men. Sequential monte carlo for simultaneous passive device-free tracking and sensor localization using received signal strength measurements. In *Proceedings of the 10th international conference on Information Processing in Sensor Networks*, IPSN '11, pages 342 –353, 2011.

[4] D. De, W.-Z. Song, M. Xu, C.-L. Wang, D. Cook, and X. Huo. Findinghumo: Real-time tracking of motion trajectories from anonymous binary sensing in smart environments. In *Proceedings of the 32nd IEEE International Conference on Distributed Computing Systems*, ICDCS '12, pages 163–172, 2012.

[5] B. Firner, C. Xu, R. Howard, and Y. Zhang. Multiple receiver strategies for minimizing packet loss in dense sensor networks. In *Proceedings of the eleventh ACM international symposium on Mobile ad hoc networking and computing*, MobiHoc '10, pages 211–220, 2010.

[6] J. Forney, G.D. The viterbi algorithm. *Proceedings of the IEEE*, 61(3):268 – 278, March 1973.

[7] T. W. Hnat, E. Griffiths, R. Dawson, and K. Whitehouse. Doorjamb: unobtrusive room-level tracking of people in homes using doorway sensors. In *Proceedings of the 10th ACM Conference on Embedded Network Sensor Systems*, SenSys '12, pages 309–322, 2012.

[8] O. Kaltiokallio, M. Bocca, and N. Patwari. Enhancing the accuracy of radio tomographic imaging using channel diversity. In *Proceedings of the 9th IEEE International Conference on Mobile Ad hoc and Sensor Systems*, MASS '12, pages 254–262, 2012.

[9] K. Kleisouris, B. Firner, R. Howard, Y. Zhang, and R. P. Martin. Detecting intra-room mobility with signal strength descriptors. In *Proceedings of the eleventh ACM international symposium on Mobile ad hoc networking and computing*, MobiHoc '10, pages 71–80, 2010.

[10] J. Krumm, S. Harris, B. Meyers, B. Brumitt, M. Hale, and S. Shafer. Multi-camera multi-person tracking for easyliving. In *Proceedings of Third IEEE International Workshop on Visual Surveillance*, IWVS '00, pages 3 –10, 2000.

[11] J. D. Lafferty, A. McCallum, and F. C. N. Pereira. Conditional random fields: Probabilistic models for segmenting and labeling sequence data. In *Proceedings of the Eighteenth International Conference on Machine Learning*, ICML '01, pages 282–289, 2001.

[12] R. S. Moore, R. Howard, P. Kuksa, and R. P. Martin. A geometric approach to device-free motion localization using signal strength. Technical Report DCS-TR-674, Rutgers University, Sept. 2010.

[13] M. Nakatsuka, H. Iwatani, and J. Katto. A study on passive crowd density estimation using wireless sensors. In *Proceedings of the 4th international conference on Mobile Computing and Ubiquitous Networking*, ICMU '08, 2008.

[14] S. Nannuru, Y. Li, M. Coates, and B. Yang. Multi-target device-free tracking using radio frequency tomography. In *Proceedings of the Seventh International Conference on Intelligent Sensors, Sensor Networks and Information Processing*, ISSNIP '11, pages 508 –513, 2011.

[15] S. Nannuru, Y. Li, Y. Zeng, M. Coates, and B. Yang. Radio frequency tomography for passive indoor multi-target tracking. *IEEE Transactions on Mobile Computing*, PP(99):1, 2012.

[16] R. J. Orr and G. D. Abowd. The smart floor: a mechanism for natural user identification and tracking. In *CHI '00 extended abstracts on Human factors in computing systems*, CHI EA '00, pages 275–276, 2000.

[17] N. Patwari and J. Wilson. Rf sensor networks for device-free localization: Measurements, models, and algorithms. *Proceedings of the IEEE*, 98(11):1961 –1973, Nov. 2010.

[18] T. Rappaport. *Wireless Communications: Principles and Practice*. Prentice Hall PTR, Upper Saddle River, NJ, USA, 2nd edition, 2001.

[19] M. Seifeldin and M. Youssef. A deterministic large-scale device-free passive localization system for wireless environments. In *Proceedings of the 3rd International Conference on PErvasive Technologies Related to Assistive Environments*, PETRA '10, pages 51:1–51:8, 2010.

[20] F. Thouin, S. Nannuru, and M. Coates. Multi-target tracking for measurement models with additive contributions. In *Proceedings of the 14th International Conference on Information Fusion*, FUSION '11, pages 1 –8, July 2011.

[21] M. Valtonen, J. Maentausta, and J. Vanhala. Tiletrack: Capacitive human tracking using floor tiles. In *IEEE International Conference on Pervasive Computing and Communications*, PerCom '09, pages 1 –10, 2009.

[22] J. Wilson and N. Patwari. Radio tomographic imaging with wireless networks. *IEEE Transactions on Mobile Computing*, 9(5):621–632, May 2010.

[23] J. Wilson and N. Patwari. See-through walls: Motion tracking using variance-based radio tomography networks. *IEEE Transactions on Mobile Computing*, 10(5):612 –621, May 2011.

[24] J. Wilson and N. Patwari. A fade level skew-laplace signal strength model for device-free localization with wireless networks. *IEEE Transactions on Mobile Computing*, 11(6):947–958, June 2012.

[25] K. Woyach, D. Puccinelli, and M. Haenggi. Sensorless sensing in wireless networks: Implementation and measurements. In *Proceedings of the 4th International Symposium on Modeling and Optimization in Mobile, Ad Hoc and Wireless Networks*, pages 1 – 8, 2006.

[26] C. Xu, B. Firner, Y. Zhang, R. Howard, and J. Li. Trajectory-based indoor device-free passive tracking. In *Proceedings of 2nd International Workshop on Mobile Sensing*, IWMS '12, 2012.

[27] C. Xu, B. Firner, Y. Zhang, R. Howard, J. Li, and X. Lin. Improving rf-based device-free passive localization in cluttered indoor environments through probabilistic classification methods. In *Proceedings of the 11th international conference on Information Processing in Sensor Networks*, IPSN '12, pages 209–220, 2012.

[28] C. Xu, M. Gao, B. Firner, Y. Zhang, R. Howard, and J. Li. Towards robust device-free passive localization through automatic camera-assisted recalibration. In *Proceedings of the 10th ACM Conference on Embedded Network Sensor Systems*, SenSys '12, pages 339–340, 2012.

[29] M. Youssef, M. Mah, and A. Agrawala. Challenges: device-free passive localization for wireless environments. In *Proceedings of the 13th annual ACM international conference on Mobile computing and networking*, MobiCom '07, pages 222–229, 2007.

[30] D. Zhang, Y. Liu, and L. Ni. Rass: A real-time, accurate and scalable system for tracking transceiver-free objects. In *Proceedings of the 9th IEEE International Conference on Pervasive Computing and Communications*, PerCom '11, pages 197 –204, 2011.

[31] D. Zhang, J. Ma, Q. Chen, and L. M. Ni. An rf-based system for tracking transceiver-free objects. In *Proceedings of the 5th IEEE International Conference on Pervasive Computing and Communications*, PerCom '07, pages 135 –144, 2007.

[32] D. Zhang and L. M. Ni. Dynamic clustering for tracking multiple transceiver-free objects. In *Proceedings of the 7th IEEE International Conference on Pervasive Computing and Communications*, PerCom '09, pages 1–8, 2009.

Volcanic Earthquake Timing Using Wireless Sensor Networks

Guojin Liu[1,2], Rui Tan[2,3] *, Ruogu Zhou[2], Guoliang Xing[2], Wen-Zhan Song[4], Jonathan M. Lees[5]

[1]College of Communication Engineering, Chongqing University, P.R. China
[2]Department of Computer Science and Engineering, Michigan State University, USA
[3]Advanced Digital Sciences Center, Illinois at Singapore
[4]Department of Computer Science, Georgia State University, USA
[5]Department of Geological Sciences, University of North Carolina at Chapel Hill, USA

ABSTRACT

Recent years have witnessed pilot deployments of inexpensive wireless sensor networks (WSNs) for active volcano monitoring. This paper studies the problem of picking arrival times of primary waves (i.e., P-phases) received by seismic sensors, one of the most critical tasks in volcano monitoring. Two fundamental challenges must be addressed. First, it is virtually impossible to download the real-time high-frequency seismic data to a central station for P-phase picking due to limited wireless network bandwidth. Second, accurate P-phase picking is inherently computation-intensive, and is thus prohibitive for many low-power sensor platforms. To address these challenges, we propose a new P-phase picking approach for hierarchical volcano monitoring WSNs where a large number of inexpensive sensors are used to collect fine-grained, real-time seismic signals while a small number of powerful coordinator nodes process collected data and pick accurate P-phases. We develop a suite of new in-network signal processing algorithms for accurate P-phase picking, including lightweight signal pre-processing at sensors, sensor selection at coordinators as well as signal compression and reconstruction algorithms. Testbed experiments and extensive simulations based on real data collected from a volcano show that our approach achieves accurate P-phase picking while only 16% of the sensor data are transmitted.

Categories and Subject Descriptors

C.3 [**Special-purpose and Application-based Systems**]: Signal processing systems; C.4 [**Performance of Systems**]: Measurement techniques; J.2 [**Physical Sciences and Engineering**]: Earth and atmospheric sciences

---

*The first two authors are listed in alphabetic order.
Part of this work was completed while Guojin Liu and Rui Tan were with Michigan State University as visiting scholar and postdoctoral Research Associate, respectively.

Keywords

Volcano monitoring, P-phase picking, hypocenter estimation, compressive sampling, wireless sensor network

1. INTRODUCTION

Volcanic eruptions have become a major hazard due to ever growing human population and urbanization around volcanoes. It is estimated that about 500 million people today live close to active volcanoes [1]. Existing volcano monitoring systems often employ broadband seismometers that collect high-fidelity seismic signals, but are expensive, bulky, and difficult to install. As a result, many of the most threatening volcanoes are monitored by fewer than 20 stations. Such poor spatial granularity limits scientists' ability to study the volcano dynamics and predict eruptions.

Recent years have witnessed pilot deployments of inexpensive wireless sensor networks (WSNs) for active volcano monitoring [30, 31, 27]. These deployments demonstrated the potential of long-term, large-area, and fine-grained volcano coverage by deploying large numbers of low-cost sensors. Significant research has been focused on improving system robustness, time synchronization, network efficiency, and communication performance issues. In previous small-scale deployments [30, 31, 27], detection and analysis of volcano activity were accomplished by transmitting raw data to a base station for centralized processing. However, as the sensor signals are sampled at high frequencies (e.g., 50 to 200 Hz), it is virtually impossible to continually collect raw, real-time data from a large-scale and dense WSN. This is due primarily to severe limitations of energy and bandwidth of current WSN platforms.

The goal of this paper is to design algorithms that can accurately determine the arrival times of primary waves (i.e., P-waves) received by seismic sensors *inside* the network, without transmitting raw measurements to the base station for centralized processing. Earthquake signal timing is a fundamental task in seismology. P-wave arrival times (i.e., P-phases) are essential information for advanced volcano monitoring tasks such as earthquake hypocenter estimation and seismic tomography [20]. Hypocenter estimation uses the P-phases of distributed sensors and a model of the P-wave propagation speed at different depths (a.k.a. velocity model) to estimate the earthquake source location. Seismic tomography updates the velocity model based on the sensors' P-phases and the associated hypocenters of earthquakes. The estimated dynamic velocity model is important for understanding the physical processes inside the volcano conduit systems and issuing early warnings. In volcano observatories, P-phase picking is often done by visual inspection of experienced seismologists. When the volume and rate of data capture is large, however, this process is extremely labor-intensive, time-consuming, and subject to inconsistency across different examiners. In the last two decades, automated P-phase picking algorithms have been developed in seismology community for earthquake timing [14, 32, 26]. However, these algorithms are designed for powerful nodes with substantial computation, storage and power resources. It remains an open question if it is possible to implement automated *in-situ* volcanic earthquake timing in resource-constrained WSNs without transmitting a large volume of raw sensor data.

The key contribution of this paper is the development of new in-network signal processing algorithms for P-phase picking. To balance the system lifetime and network coverage, we adopt a hierarchical network architecture that consists of low-end nodes (referred to as *sensor*s) and high-end nodes (referred to as *coordinator*s). A large quantity of inexpensive, mote-class sensors can provide fine-grained monitoring with long lifetime, while a small number of coordinators (e.g., Imote2 and embedded PCs like Gumstix [2]) enable advanced in-network seismological signal processing. Based on this network architecture, we develop a suite of in-network P-phase picking algorithms. (1) Lightweight algorithms are designed for sensors to coarsely pick the P-phases and estimate the signal sparsity. The coarse P-phase is an important hint of the amount of new information that the sensor can contribute. The signal sparsity determines the volume of data transmission if the sensor sends its signal to a coordinator for accurate P-phase picking. (2) A sensor selection algorithm uses signal sparsities and coarse P-phases to choose a subset of the most informative sensors to transmit compressed data subject to a given upper bound on communication overhead. The bound can be set by the network designer to meet various practical system constraints, such as bandwidth limitation, energy budget, and real-time requirement. (3) A signal compression algorithm for sensors and a reconstruction algorithm for coordinators are developed based on wavelet transform and compressive sampling theory [12]. The above algorithms work collaboratively to achieve energy-efficient and accurate in-network earthquake timing. The approach presented in this paper can be extended and then applied in various monitoring applications that need accurate signal arrival times. Moreover, it has important implications to a broader class of applications that need to accurately extract features from real-time, high-frequency signals gathered by resource-constrained WSNs.

We implement and evaluate the proposed algorithms on a testbed of TelosB motes that are loaded with real seismic data collected on Mount St. Helens. The results demonstrate the feasibility of deploying our algorithms on volcano monitoring WSNs. We also conduct extensive simulations based on real data traces that contain 30 earthquakes. The results show that our algorithms can achieve accurate earthquake timing while only 16% of the sensor data are transmitted.

The rest of this paper is organized as follows. Section 2 reviews related work. Section 3 states the problem and approach overview. Section 4 studies the sparsity of earthquake signal and presents the signal pre-processing algorithms at sensors. Section 5 formulates the sensor selection problem. Section 6 discusses the compression/reconstruction algorithms. Section 7 discusses how to apply our approach to other applications. Section 8 presents the evaluation results. Section 9 concludes this paper.

2. RELATED WORK

The first field application of WSN for monitoring volcano was in 2004 [30], where four MICA2 nodes were deployed on Volcán Tungurahua, Ecuador. The system successfully collected three days of acoustic data. In 2005, the same research group deployed sixteen Tmote nodes equipped with seismic and acoustic sensors on Volcán Reventador, Ecuador, for three weeks [31]. In 2007, they deployed eight Tmote nodes on Volcán Tungurahua again and applied the Lance framework [29] to select a subset of sensors such that the total value of the raw data collected from the selected sensors is maximized subject to the network lifetime constraint. However, Lance adopts a heuristic metric to guide the sensor selection and does not apply signal compression before transmission. In the Optimized Autonomous Space In-situ Sensorweb (OASIS) project [27], twelve Imote2 nodes were deployed on Mount St. Helens in 2008. It demonstrated a long-term sustainable WSN in a challenging environment, and delivered a long-period (up to half a year), high-fidelity sensor dataset. The design of the above volcano monitoring WSNs [30, 31, 29, 27] mainly focused on the basic network services such as node sustainability, network connectivity, time synchronization and data collection. As raw sensor data were continually collected, these systems either had short lifetimes [30, 31] or had to employ heavy batteries [27]. We previously proposed a volcanic earthquake detection approach based on in-network signal processing [28]. The TelosB-based testbed experiments show that the in-network signal processing scheme reduces the node energy consumption to one sixth of the raw data collection approach. In contrast to [28], whose target was to detect the occurrence of earthquakes, this work builds on previous results by adding in the task of accurately picking P-phases after an earthquake is detected.

The seismology community previously developed several algorithms for P-phase picking. They are typically based on the identification of changes in signal characteristics such as energy, frequency and characteristics of autoregressive models [32]. The widely adopted STA/LTA approaches [14] continuously compute the ratio of short-term average (STA) to long-term average (LTA) over a signal characteristic and raise a detection once the ratio exceeds a specified threshold. Although STA/LTA approaches are suitable for sensors with limited resources, associated accuracies are much lower than minimal requirements of volcanic earthquake timing [32]. Moreover, the heuristic STA/LTA approaches often require empirical tuning of numerous parameters, making these methods difficult to adapt to different regions or temporally changing environments. Another important category of picking algorithms is based on autoregressive (AR) models [26]. These methods pick the time instance to maximize the dissimilarity of two AR models for signals before and after the picked time instance. AR-based algorithms need few user settings and are the most accurate and robust P-phase picking algorithms to date. However, since both AR models must be constructed for each time instance, they incur high computational complexity and memory usage.

Various in-network signal processing approaches have been proposed for different applications in data-intensive WSNs.

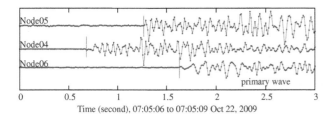

Figure 1: The seismic signals received by three sensors when an earthquake happens on Mount St. Helens. The vertical lines represent the P-phases.

For instance, in [18], the structural damage localization task is decentralized by pushing the feature extraction algorithms to distributed vibration sensors. VanGo [17] can calibrate the parameters of the software filters running on low-end sensors, such that uninterested high-frequency sensor data are not transmitted. However, the simple filters included in VanGo, e.g., gating, cannot meet the stringent accuracy requirements of earthquake timing.

3. PROBLEM STATEMENT AND APPROACH OVERVIEW

3.1 Design Objectives

The P-phase is the first arrival time of a P-wave of a seismic signal. Fig. 1 shows the seismic signals received by three sensors deployed on Mount St. Helens [27] along with the manually picked P-phases. It can be seen that the sensors receive different P-phases due to different signal propagation delays. P-phase variations provide critical information for volcano monitoring applications such as earthquake hypocenter estimation and seismic tomography [20]. The task of picking the P-phases of spatially distributed sensors is referred to as *volcanic earthquake timing*. When the network is dense and P-wave velocities are high, the differences between sensors' P-phases can be small, e.g., at most one second in Fig. 1. This imposes stringent accuracy requirements on volcanic earthquake timing. In this paper, we aim to develop a holistic and energy-efficient approach to accurate volcanic earthquake timing in resource-constrained WSNs. Our approach is designed to meet the following two key objectives. First, picked P-phases must achieve satisfactory precision and maximize the accuracy of earthquake hypocenter estimation that takes P-phases as inputs. Second, to achieve expected network lifetime, the volume of seismic data transmission in each timing process must meet a specified energy budget.

3.2 System Model

Hierarchical network architecture. We adopt a hierarchical network architecture that consists of *sensors* with limited resources and *coordinators* with more processing capability and higher battery capacity. Each sensor continuously samples and buffers the signal in its memory, which is consistent with the design of previous volcano monitoring WSNs [27, 31]. A considerable number of inexpensive sensors can be deployed over the volcano to provide a high level of coverage, and work with a small number of coordinators to achieve accurate P-phase picking. The adoption of this architecture is motivated by the fact that P-phase picking

Table 1: Specification of WSN platforms [3]

Node	MCU frequency (MHz)	RAM capacity (KB)	Active power (mA)	Sleep power (μA)
MSP430-based	8-18	2-16	1.12-3.98	0.5-1.8
ATmega-based	6-16	1-8	3.12-11.0	4.2-40
Imote2	13-416	32000	$\geq$31	390
BTnode	8	180	12	3000
Preon32	8-72	64	3.7-28.3	1300
SunSPOT	180	512	24	520

[a] Only MCU's power is considered. The active powers of MSP430-/ATmega-based nodes are under the condition of 8MHz and $V_{cc} = 3$V.
[b] 73% WSN platforms are based on MSP430 and ATmega MCUs [3]. As MSP430 is more energy-efficient, we adopt TelosB as *sensor* in this paper.
[c] As Imote2 has the highest processing capability and lowest sleep power among the high-end platforms, we adopt Imote2 as *coordinator*. Sleep power is an important parameter because the nodes sleep most of the time in the absence of earthquake (cf. Section 8.3.1).

algorithms are computation-intensive and hence cannot be executed by mote-class sensors. According to Table 1, the autoregressive Akaike Information Criterion (AR-AIC) picking algorithm [26], which needs at least 52 KB RAM, can be executed on only a few powerful WSN platforms such as Imote series, BTnode, Preon32, and SunSPOT. However, the power consumption of these nodes can be up to dozens of times higher than that of mote-class platforms based on MSP430 and ATmega processors. According to our numerical study in Section 8.3.1, the hierarchical network architecture can reduce the per-node energy consumption by 68%, compared with a network composed of only powerful nodes. The hierarchical architecture thus not only allows us to increase the coverage over a volcano, but also extends the network lifetime. Such a hierarchical architecture has also been adopted in other WSN systems [15]. In this paper, we adopt TelosB as the sensor and Imote2 as the coordinator.

Sensor clustering. The network is organized into one or multiple clusters. Each cluster consists of a number of sensors and a coordinator as the *cluster head*. Our approach can be integrated with various existing clustering algorithms [8]. In Section 8.3.2, we will discuss two clustering schemes and the setting of cluster size through simulations. The rest of this paper is focused on the design of the in-network signal processing algorithms in a single cluster. As data transmissions only happen between cluster head and associated member sensors, exhaustive data collection from the whole network can be avoided.

Synchronization and earthquake onset time. All sensors are time-synchronized by on-node GPS modules [27] or an in-network synchronization service [31]. We assume that the network can detect the occurrence and onset time of earthquake. The *earthquake onset time* is a coarsely estimated time instance, typically to second precision, at which the earthquake process starts. The STA/LTA [14, 31] or Bayesian [28] methods can be used to detect the earthquake onset time. In particular, the Bayesian earthquake detection approach [28] developed in our previous work is based on in-network signal processing and decision fusion, in which local decisions of sensors are fused and onset time is estimated at the coordinator, and sent back to each sensor. Using the

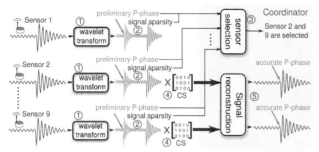

Figure 2: Illustration of in-network earthquake timing.

earthquake onset time, sensors can largely narrow the range of searching for the P-phases.

3.3 Approach Overview

We propose a suite of algorithms running at the coordinator and associated sensors, which will work together to achieve the objectives discussed in Section 3.1. The operation flow of these algorithms is illustrated in Fig. 2. (1) When an earthquake is detected, each sensor chooses a segment of seismic signal around the detected earthquake onset time and applies a wavelet transform to the signal. The wavelet transform sparsifies the signal representation, reducing the volume of data transmission. (2) Based on the transformed signal, each sensor estimates the signal sparsity and executes a lightweight picking algorithm to find a preliminary P-phase. Each sensor then sends the estimated signal sparsity and the preliminary P-phase to the coordinator. (3) The coordinator selects a subset of sensors such that the expected error of earthquake hypocenter estimation, computed from the preliminary P-phases, is minimized subject to a given upper bound on communication overhead. The communication overhead can be exactly predicted from the signal sparsities of the selected sensors. (4) The selected sensors then employ compressive sampling (CS) [12] to compress the seismic signals and transmit to the coordinator. (5) Finally, the coordinator reconstructs the seismic signals and executes high-accuracy P-phase picking algorithms and possibly other advanced seismic signal analyses. In our implementation, the coordinator adopts the AR-AIC picking algorithm [26], which is widely used in seismology, although other algorithms might be used instead.

The key novelty of this paper is the efficient integration of various algorithms into a holistic approach to achieve accurate volcanic earthquake timing in resource-constrained WSNs. Our approach has the following three advantages. First, by sensor selection, the earthquake timing process has upper-bounded communication overhead. The system designer can set this bound to meet various practical system constraints such as bandwidth limitation, energy budget, and real-time requirement. Second, our approach significantly reduces the computation and communication overhead of the sensors. By employing CS algorithms based on a binary random matrix, the signal compression at sensors only involves the computation of sums. Moreover, the coordinator can determine the volume of compressed signal prior to compression, enabling efficient sensor selection and data transmission scheduling before sensors compress signals. As a result, the unselected sensors can avoid compression computation. Third, our approach allows the coordinator to

integrate a variety of centralized seismic signal analysis algorithms on the reconstructed signals, such as Fourier and polarization analyses. The coordinator can send estimated P-phases to the base station for advanced, joint hypocenter estimation across all clusters. Moreover, it can transmit the reconstructed signals to the base station for offline analysis.

4. SEISMIC PRE-PROCESSING AT SENSORS

In this section, we first study the sparsity of seismic signals received by sensors. We then present a lightweight preliminary P-phase picking algorithm that is executed at sensors.

4.1 Sparsity of Volcanic Seismic Signal

In this paper, we adopt the common definition of sparsity in signal processing [12]. Let n denote signal length. Suppose Ψ is an orthonormal basis $\Psi = [\psi_1 \psi_2 \cdots \psi_n] \in \mathbb{R}^{n \times n}$ where ψ_i is the ith column of Ψ. A signal $\mathbf{s} \in \mathbb{R}^{n \times 1}$ in the time domain is expanded with basis Ψ as $\mathbf{s} = \Psi \mathbf{x}$, where $\mathbf{x} \in \mathbb{R}^{n \times 1}$ is the coefficient sequence of $\mathbf{s}$. The signal $\mathbf{s}$ is k-sparse if the number of non-zeros in $\mathbf{x}$ is less than or equal to k. The sparsity of signal $\mathbf{s}$, denoted by ρ, is defined as $\rho = k/n$. In practice, $\mathbf{x}$ typically contains small values rather than zeros. Considering $\mathbf{x}_{(k)}$ obtained by keeping only the k largest coefficients of $\mathbf{x}$ and setting others to zero, the corresponding signal $\mathbf{s}_{(k)}$ is $\mathbf{s}_{(k)} = \Psi \mathbf{x}_{(k)}$. The signal $\mathbf{s}$ is k-sparse if the relative error $\frac{\|\mathbf{s} - \mathbf{s}_{(k)}\|_{\ell_2}}{\|\mathbf{s}\|_{\ell_2}}$ is smaller than a threshold, where $\| \cdot \|_{\ell_2}$ represents the ℓ_2-norm. In this paper, the threshold is set to be 5% unless otherwise specified.

For each sensor, we choose a signal segment for 16 seconds, where 10 seconds before and 6 seconds after the earthquake onset time. Hence, $n = 16 \cdot f_s$, where f_s represents the seismic sampling rate. This setting of signal length is the minimum requirement of the AR-AIC picker [26] running at the coordinator. As the difference between the P-phases received by sensors is typically shorter than two seconds [31], this setting also ensures that all sensors' P-phases are included. The first columns of Figs. 3 and 4 show the chosen signals at Node01 and Node10 deployed on Mount St. Helens in the OASIS project [27], where f_s is 100 Hz. Vertical dashed lines represent the earthquake onset time detected by a Bayesian approach [28] and vertical red lines represent the P-phases picked by the AR-AIC picker [26]. It is clear that the P-phases are covered by the chosen signals.

4.1.1 Sparsity in Wavelet Domain

The time-domain seismic signal is often not sparse. For instance, for the signal shown in Fig. 4(d), the sparsity is 0.57. In this paper, we adopt discrete wavelet transform (DWT) with Daubechies basis to reduce signal sparsity, which produces reduced wireless data transmission. As DWT preserves time-domain characteristics, it is preferable for P-phase analysis. Moreover, the downsampling scheme of DWT allows us to develop an efficient preliminary P-phase picking algorithm in Section 4.2. The second columns of Figs. 3 and 4 show the 4-level DWT coefficients of Node01 and Node10 for two earthquakes. The vertical dotted lines represent edges between two adjacent frequency subbands in the wavelet domain. Setting the level of the DWT will be discussed in Section 4.2. Our analysis shows that the sparsity in the wavelet domain is significantly lower than that in the time domain. For instance, for the four data traces

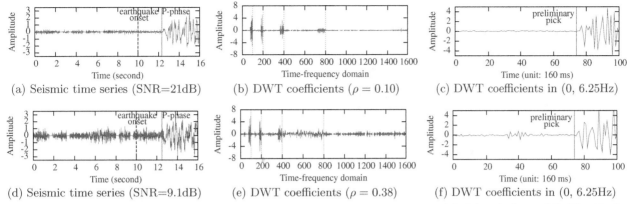

(a) Seismic time series (SNR=21dB) (b) DWT coefficients ($\rho = 0.10$) (c) DWT coefficients in (0, 6.25Hz)

(d) Seismic time series (SNR=9.1dB) (e) DWT coefficients ($\rho = 0.38$) (f) DWT coefficients in (0, 6.25Hz)

Figure 3: Earthquake01 during 12:39:23 to 12:39:39 on November 4, 2009. (a)-(c): Node01; (d)-(f): Node10.

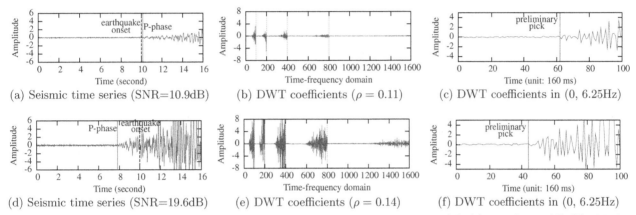

(a) Seismic time series (SNR=10.9dB) (b) DWT coefficients ($\rho = 0.11$) (c) DWT coefficients in (0, 6.25Hz)

(d) Seismic time series (SNR=19.6dB) (e) DWT coefficients ($\rho = 0.14$) (f) DWT coefficients in (0, 6.25Hz)

Figure 4: Earthquake02 during 00:23:58 to 00:24:14 on November 3, 2009. (a)-(c): Node01; (d)-(f): Node10.

shown in Figs. 3 and 4, the sparsity can be reduced by up to 75% using the wavelet domain.

4.1.2 Diverse Sparsity

We make the following important observations from the case study shown in Figs. 3 and 4. First, for the same earthquake, sensors receive data with different signal-to-noise ratios (SNRs), leading to different significance of P-phases. For instance, in Earthquake01 shown in Fig. 3, Node01 has a higher SNR and a more significant P-phase than Node10. As the seismic signal attenuates with propagation distance, sensors far away from the earthquake source receive weak signals, lower SNRs, and less pronounced P-phases. Second, due to highly variable event magnitude and source location, the SNR and significance of P-phase are dynamic and unpredictable. For instance, as opposed to Earthquake01, in Earthquake02 (Fig. 4), Node10 receives a much higher SNR than Node01. Third, the sparsity depends on SNR and the position of P-phase. For instance, since Node01 receives a higher SNR than Node10 in Earthquake01, the sparsity of Node01 is lower than Node10. However, although Node10 receives very high SNR in Earthquake02, its sparsity is comparable to that of Node01. This is because Node10 receives P-phase much earlier than Node01, resulting in more nonzeros in the wavelet domain. We evaluated extensively the sparsity of transformed signals based on the data traces received by 12 nodes for 30 earthquakes in the OASIS project [27]. Fig. 5 shows sparsity versus the threshold of relative error $\frac{\|\mathbf{s}-\mathbf{s}_{(k)}\|_{\ell_2}}{\|\mathbf{s}\|_{\ell_2}}$ for determining sparsity. This result vali-

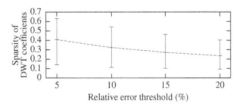

Figure 5: The sparsity (with 90% confidence interval) of 360 seismic data traces received by 12 sensors.

dates our hypothesis of diverse sparsity. For instance, if the threshold is set to 5%, the sparsity ranges from 0.16 to 0.63.

The above observations of dynamic, unpredictable and diverse sparsity provide important guidelines for designing volcanic earthquake timing algorithms for resource-constrained WSNs. First, due to the diversity of signal sparsity, it is desirable to collect only the most sparse seismic signals to meet a specified node energy budget keeping with the real-time requirement of data transmission. Second, as the sparsity is dynamic and unpredictable, sensors need to compute sparsity on demand when an earthquake is detected. The sparsity can then be used to predict the volume of data transmission if the coordinator requests the signal.

4.2 Preliminary P-Phase Picking at Sensors

In this section, we present a lightweight and efficient preliminary P-phase picking algorithm that runs on the sensors. Due to the downsampling scheme, the lowest frequency subband in the wavelet domain is a zoomed-out version of the low-pass filtered signal. Hereafter, this subband is referred to as the *thumbnail* of the original signal in the time domain. The last columns of Figs. 3 and 4 show the thumbnails of the corresponding original signal in the first column. The thumbnails apparently preserve the shapes of the arriving P-waves. If the seismic sampling rate is f_s and the level of DWT is l, the lowest frequency subband of the wavelet domain is $[0\,\text{Hz}, \frac{f_s}{2^{l+1}}\,\text{Hz}]$. By setting l such that $\frac{f_s}{2^{l+1}} \geq 5\,\text{Hz}$, the thumbnail can preserve the shape of the P-wave, which typically has a frequency lower than 5 Hz [28]. In our approach, the preliminary P-phase is picked from the thumbnail to reduce the computational complexity. However, as the time resolution of the thumbnail reduces to $(1000 \cdot 2^l)/f_s$ milliseconds, the P-phase picking error caused by the downsampling will be $(500 \cdot 2^l)/f_s$ milliseconds. For the cases shown in Figs. 3 and 4, the number of data points that a sensor needs to process is reduced from 1600 to 100, and the error caused by downsampling is 80 milliseconds. This resolution is satisfactory for the preliminary P-phase picking.

Our lightweight preliminary P-phase picking algorithm is as follows. For a candidate P-phase $\hat{p}$, the sensor computes the signal energies (i.e., the sample variances) of the thumbnail signals with length of two seconds before and after $\hat{p}$. The preliminary P-phase, denoted by p, is given by

$$p = 2^l \times \arg\max_{\hat{p} \in \text{thumbnail}} \frac{\text{signal energy after } \hat{p}}{\text{signal energy before } \hat{p}}. \tag{1}$$

Note that the scaling factor 2^l maps the pick in the thumbnail to the original time domain. The complexity of the above algorithm is $\mathcal{O}(n/2^l)$. In contrast, existing advanced picking algorithms have significantly higher complexity, e.g., $\mathcal{O}(n^3)$ for AR-AIC picker [26]. By maximizing the signal energy ratio in Eq. (1), the preliminary P-phase divides the thumbnail signal into two segments with significantly different signal energies. In the last columns of Figs. 3 and 4, the vertical red lines represent the preliminary P-phases. We can see that the preliminary P-phase picker accurately extracts the P-phases from the thumbnails. In Section 8, we will conduct extensive evaluation of the accuracy of the preliminary picker.

5. SENSOR SELECTION FOR EARTHQUAKE TIMING

In this section, we present the sensor selection algorithm that aims to maximize the accuracy of earthquake hypocenter estimation subject to a given upper bound on communication overhead. Earthquake hypocenter estimation, which takes sensors' P-phases as inputs, is the base of many advanced volcano monitoring applications such as seismic tomography [20]. The sensor selection best directs the limited network resources, e.g., bandwidth and energy, to acquire the sensor data for accurate earthquake timing.

5.1 Impact of Timing on Hypocenter Estimation

As the propagation speed of P-wave varies with the depth in earth, the earthquake hypocenter estimation is a nonlinear inversion problem involving residual reduction coupled with seismic ray tracing [20]. Suppose a set of sensors, denoted by S, belongs to the cluster under consideration. Let $\mathbf{z}_i$ and $\mathbf{z}_o$ denote the 3-dimensional Cartesian coordinates of sensor i and the earthquake source, p_i and p_o de-

note the P-phase picked by sensor i and the earthquake time origin of the source, and $\mathbf{v}$ denote a list of P-wave speeds at different depths. We assume that $\{\mathbf{z}_i | i \in S\}$ and $\mathbf{v}$ are known, which can be obtained by inquiring the GPS module on sensors [27] and from existing tomographic studies [20], respectively. The $\mathbf{z}_o$ and p_o are the unknowns to be estimated from the P-phases $\{p_i | i \in S\}$. We have

$$p_i - p_o = \tau(\mathbf{z}_i, \mathbf{z}_o | \mathbf{v}) + \epsilon_i, \quad \forall i \in S \tag{2}$$

where $\tau(\mathbf{z}_i, \mathbf{z}_o | \mathbf{v})$ is the P-wave travel time from the source to sensor i given the velocity model $\mathbf{v}$, and ϵ_i is the random error experienced by sensor i. We employ the ray tracing algorithm in the RSEIS R package [21] to calculate $\tau(\mathbf{z}_i, \mathbf{z}_o | \mathbf{v})$. We assume that ϵ_i follows zero-mean normal distribution with variance ς^2. The variance ς^2 captures the error of the P-phase picked from the seismic signal with respect to the true P-phase. As will be shown later, the hypocenter estimation algorithm and its accuracy analysis are independent of ς^2. Hence, the variance ς^2 can be unknown to the network. The unknown p_o can be canceled out by subtracting Eq. (2) with $i = r$ from the same equation with $i \in S \setminus \{r\}$, yielding $p_i' = \tau(\mathbf{z}_i, \mathbf{z}_o | \mathbf{v}) - \tau(\mathbf{z}_r, \mathbf{z}_o | \mathbf{v}) + \epsilon_i'$, where sensor r is the *reference node*, $i \in S \setminus \{r\}$, $p_i' = p_i - p_r$, $\epsilon_i' = \epsilon_i - \epsilon_r$. Note that ϵ_i' follows zero-mean normal distribution with variance $2\varsigma^2$. We adopt maximum-likelihood (ML) approach to estimate $\mathbf{z}_o$. The ML estimate of $\mathbf{z}_o$, denoted by $\widetilde{\mathbf{z}}_o$, is given by:

$$\widetilde{\mathbf{z}}_o = \arg\min_{\mathbf{z}_o} \sum_{i \in S \setminus \{r\}} \left(p_i' - \tau(\mathbf{z}_i, \mathbf{z}_o | \mathbf{v}) + \tau(\mathbf{z}_r, \mathbf{z}_o | \mathbf{v}) \right)^2. \tag{3}$$

We now analyze the accuracy of $\widetilde{\mathbf{z}}_o$. As there is no closed-form formula for $\tau(\mathbf{z}_i, \mathbf{z}_o | \mathbf{v})$, to make the analysis tractable, we let $\tau(\mathbf{z}_i, \mathbf{z}_o | \mathbf{v}) = \|\mathbf{z}_i - \mathbf{z}_o\|_{\ell_2}/v$, where v represents the average P-wave speed. Define $\mathbf{g}_i = \frac{\mathbf{z}_r - \mathbf{z}_o}{\|\mathbf{z}_r - \mathbf{z}_o\|_{\ell_2}} - \frac{\mathbf{z}_i - \mathbf{z}_o}{\|\mathbf{z}_i - \mathbf{z}_o\|_{\ell_2}}$ and let $\mathbf{G}$ denote the matrix composed of $\{\mathbf{g}_i | \forall i \in S \setminus \{r\}\}$ as columns. By extending the result in [13], the Fisher information matrix, denoted by $\mathbf{J}$, is given by $\mathbf{J} = \frac{1}{2v^2\varsigma^2}\mathbf{G}\mathbf{G}^{\mathrm{T}} \in \mathbb{R}^{3\times 3}$, where the diagonal elements of $\mathbf{J}^{-1}$ are the theoretical lower bounds for the variances of the coordinates in $\widetilde{\mathbf{z}}_o$. A widely adopted error metric is $\text{tr}(\mathbf{J}^{-1}) = 2v^2\varsigma^2\text{tr}\left((\mathbf{G}\mathbf{G}^{\mathrm{T}})^{-1} \right)$. As $2v^2\varsigma^2$ is a scaling factor in $\text{tr}(\mathbf{J}^{-1})$, we define the error metric as

$$\mathcal{E} = \text{tr}\left((\mathbf{G}\mathbf{G}^{\mathrm{T}})^{-1} \right). \tag{4}$$

Note that $\mathcal{E}$ depends on the true but unknown source location $\mathbf{z}_o$. In our approach, we replace $\mathbf{z}_o$ in Eq. (4) with its ML estimate $\widetilde{\mathbf{z}}_o$ to calculate the error metric.

The theoretical error metric given by Eq. (4) is the same for different P-phase pickers that yield zero-mean errors with respect to the true P-phase. As will be shown in Section 8, the preliminary P-phase picker has zero-mean error with respect to the AR-AIC picker that has near zero-mean error (100 ms with respect to the manual picks [26]). Hence, the error metric calculated from the preliminary P-phases is a good estimate of the error metric calculated from the P-phases picked by AR-AIC at the coordinator.

5.2 Dynamic Sensor Selection Problem

Our study in Section 4 shows that sensors have diverse signal sparsity. As a result, the volume of data transmission varies significantly across different sensors. The coordinator requests the compressed signals from a subset of sensors to minimize hypocenter estimation error subject to a given upper bound on communication cost. We make the following assumptions. First, the volume of compressed signal is given by $m(\rho_i)$, where ρ_i is the sparsity of sensor i. The expression of $m(\rho_i)$ will be given in Section 6. Second, the communication cost of a data unit from sensor i to the coordinator is c_i, which is referred to as *unit communication cost*. The sensor selection problem is formulated as follows:

Sensor Selection Problem. *When an earthquake is detected, given the sparsity of all sensors $\{\rho_i|\forall i\}$ and the unit communication costs $\{c_i|\forall i\}$, find a subset of sensors S such that the error metric $\mathcal{E}$ given by Eq. (4) is minimized, subject to $\sum_{i \in S} c_i \cdot m(\rho_i) \leq C$.*

In the above problem, C is the upper bound on the total communication cost in each earthquake timing process. By properly setting the unit communication costs, the upper bound C can represent different costs, e.g., the number of transmitted packets, the energy consumed in an earthquake timing process, or the latency of the data collection. Moreover, c_i can incorporate the residual battery energy such that the solution can balance sensors' energy consumption for multiple rounds of earthquake timing. For instance, by defining c_i as the reciprocal of sensor i's residual energy, the most informative sensors with more residual energies and less transmission volume will be selected.

In our approach, the coordinator first solves Eq. (3) using the Nelder-Mead algorithm [23]. For any candidate sensor subset, we consistently use $\widetilde{\mathbf{z}}_o$ to compute $\mathcal{E}$. As $\mathcal{E}$ is a nonlinear and non-convex function, it is difficult to solve the sensor selection problem in polynomial complexity. In our implementation (cf. Section 8.1.1), the execution time of the Nelder-Mead algorithm on Imote2 is around 4 seconds. A brute-force search takes 0.08 and 8.2 seconds when the cluster size is 10 and 16, respectively. Note that our numerical study in Section 8.3.2 shows that the gain of hypocenter estimation performance rapidly diminishes after the cluster size is greater than 15. Therefore, the computation overhead of the brute-force search is acceptable without sacrificing too much hypocenter estimation accuracy due to the setting of cluster size. In Section 5.3, we propose an approximate sensor selection algorithm that can scale with the cluster size but will sacrifice hypocenter estimation accuracy.

If the coordinator is equipped with a seismometer to sample the seismic signal, it can be always selected to improve the hypocenter estimation accuracy. Moreover, the P-phase picked from the coordinator's signal can be used as a reference to identify wrong preliminary P-phases sent from the sensors as well as wrong P-phases picked from the reconstructed signals at the coordinator.

5.3 Approximate Sensor Selection Algorithm

In this section, we propose a new heuristic metric that allows us to develop an efficient sensor selection algorithm. The metric is defined as

$$\mathcal{V} = \sum_{i \in S} \frac{1}{(p_i - \widetilde{p}_o - \tau(\mathbf{z}_i, \widetilde{\mathbf{z}}_o | \mathbf{v}))^2}, \qquad (5)$$

where S is the subset of selected sensors and $\widetilde{p}_o$ is the ML estimate of p_o. Specifically, $\widetilde{p}_o = \frac{\sum_{\forall i} p_i - \tau(\mathbf{z}_i, \widetilde{\mathbf{z}}_o | \mathbf{v})}{N}$, where N is the number of sensors in the cluster. The denominator in Eq. (5) is the squared error in P-phase. The sensor selection problem is to select a subset of sensors S to maximiz $\mathcal{V}$ sub-

ject to the constraint $\sum_{i \in S} c_i \cdot m(\rho_i) \leq C$. This problem is a 0-1 knapsack problem, which can be solved optimally in pseudo-polynomial time. Eq. (5) is a specialization of the heuristic metric adopted in Lance [29] that defines the total value of selected sensors as the sum of the values of individual sensors. A key difference is that Lance does not consider signal compression. The evaluation results in Section 8.2.2 show that the solution given by this approximate algorithm approaches to the optimal solution described in Section 5.2 when the constraint C becomes larger.

6. COMPRESSIVE SAMPLING FOR EARTHQUAKE TIMING

This section presents our approach of compressing and collecting the seismic signals from the selected sensors based on compressive sampling (CS) [12]. We first briefly review the CS theory. Let $\mathbf{y} \in \mathbb{R}^{n \times 1}$ denote the compressed signal and $\mathbf{A} \in \mathbb{R}^{m \times n}$ denote the random projection matrix, where $m < n$. The compression is expressed as $\mathbf{y} = \mathbf{A}\mathbf{x}$, where $\mathbf{x}$ is a vector of wavelet coefficients of the original signal. Note that the typical use of CS is to apply the combined transform and random projection (i.e., $\mathbf{A}\Psi^{-1}$) to the time-domain signal $\mathbf{s}$. However, in our approach, these two steps are separated to efficiently estimate the preliminary P-phase in the lowest subband of $\mathbf{x}$ and the sparsity. These two numbers are important inputs to the sensor selection algorithms. If $\mathbf{x}$ is k-sparse and $\mathbf{A}$ complies with the *restricted isometry property* (RIP) of order k, the original signal $\mathbf{s}$ can be exactly reconstructed from $\mathbf{y}$ [12]. The wavelet transform of the reconstructed signal, denoted by $\widetilde{\mathbf{x}}$, is given by $\widetilde{\mathbf{x}} = \arg\min_{\mathbf{x}} \|\mathbf{x}\|_{\ell_1}$ subject to $\mathbf{y} = \mathbf{A}\mathbf{x}$. The above optimization can be solved by various algorithms such as the iterative hard thresholding method [11]. With $\widetilde{\mathbf{x}}$, the reconstructed seismic signal is given by $\Psi\widetilde{\mathbf{x}}$.

We now discuss the design of CS for earthquake timing. We adopt the binary random projection matrix [9] that is promising for the implementation on resource-constrained sensors. Specifically, only the positions of '1's need to be stored and the multiplication $\mathbf{A}\mathbf{x}$ is simply the sum of the elements of $\mathbf{x}$ at these positions. The binary random matrix complies with RIP of order k if $m \geq h \cdot k \cdot \log(n/k)$, where h is an unknown constant [9]. From the results shown in Fig. 5, the sparsity ρ of volcanic seismic signal typically ranges from 0.1 to 0.6. Hence, $\log(n/k) = \log(1/\rho)$ ranges from $\log(1.67)$ to $\log(10)$. We define $\eta = \log(10) \cdot h$. If $m \geq \eta \cdot \rho \cdot n$, the RIP condition must be satisfied. Therefore, we let

$$m(\rho) = \eta \cdot \rho \cdot n. \qquad (6)$$

Many studies have reported that $\eta = 4$ is a safe setting that ensures satisfactory reconstruction [12]. However, as the sparsity ρ estimated in Section 4.1 does not follow the strict definition of sparsity (i.e., the ratio of non-zeros), the setting of $\eta = 4$ might be overly conservative for earthquake timing, which may result in excessive data transmission. In Section 8, we evaluate in detail the impact of η on the quality of seismic signal reconstruction as well as the P-phase picking. The results show that the setting of $\eta = 1.5$ can lead to a good trade-off between the volume of data transmission and the P-phase picking error introduced by reconstruction. In practice, the setting of η can also be determined based on the seismic data obtained in offline earthquake shaking table experiments. We note that the CS-compressed signal can be further compressed by other data compression algorithms if more computation resource is available.

7. DISCUSSION

The approach presented in this paper can be applied to a broader class of sensor network applications where sensors sample the physical phenomena at high frequencies and extract signal features from the samples. Many signal feature extraction algorithms are not affordable for resource-constrained sensors because of either the large volume of data or high complexity of the algorithms. Therefore, it is desirable to select a subset of most contributory sensors to transmit their compressed data to a more powerful node for feature extraction.

To apply our approach, a lightweight algorithm should be available to compute a coarse estimate of the feature, and a closed-form expression or heuristic metric is then used to predict the quality of upper-layer application based on the coarsely estimated features. In particular, our approach can be applied to structural damage localization [18] and most applications based on time difference of arrival (TDOA). As the P-phase picking addressed in this paper is a critical component in a class of TDOA-based applications such as acoustic event localization, our approach can be easily applied to these applications. We now briefly discuss how to extend our approach to the structural damage localization based on the natural frequencies received by distributed vibration sensors [18]. The natural frequency identification algorithm involves high-order curve fitting, and hence can be computationally prohibitive for low-end sensors due to the lack of floating point arithmetic support. To apply our approach, low-end sensors can use simple peak detectors [10] to coarsely estimate the natural frequencies, and the coordinator can use the Damage Localization Assurance Criterion [18] to guide the sensor selection.

8. PERFORMANCE EVALUATION

In this section, we conduct testbed experiments and extensive simulations based on real data traces collected by 12 nodes on Mount St. Helens in the OASIS project [27]. Our system implementation and testbed experiments verify the feasibility of the proposed signal processing algorithms on low-end sensor platforms. The trace-driven simulations extensively evaluate the performance of our approach. We finally conduct two numerical studies to evaluate the energy efficiency of the hierarchical network architecture and the impact of sensor clustering on earthquake timing.

8.1 Testbed Experiments

8.1.1 System Implementation

Sensors: Our system implementation is based on TelosB motes. Similar mote-class sensor platforms were also used in previous volcano monitoring systems [30, 31, 29, 28]. We implement all the four seismic processing algorithms, i.e., DWT, sparsity estimation, preliminary P-phase picker and CS in TinyOS 2.1. We conducted extensive code optimization on all the signal processing algorithms. First, we adopt fixed point arithmetic, which can speed up the decimal computation up to 10 fold on TelosB with respect to default floating point arithmetic. Second, we maintain a single input/output data buffer for the four pipelined algorithms and wire the output of each algorithm back to the

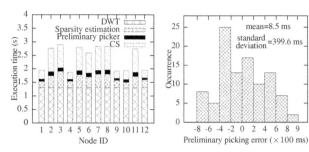

Figure 6: Sensors' workloads in an earthquake.

Figure 7: Distribution of preliminary picking error.

buffer. This pipeline implementation significantly reduces RAM usage. Our current implementation of CS uses predefined binary random matrices for sensors, which avoids the overhead of online matrix generation each timing process. In future work, we will explore efficient methods to generate the same binary random matrix on sensor and coordinator without incurring high communication costs. A possible solution is to use a common seed to generate the same projection matrix on both the sensor and coordinator. To improve the realism of the experiments, we reserve 320 KB on the mote's flash and load it with real seismic data trace collected by the OASIS system [27]. A mote acquires 100 seismic samples from flash every second, which is consistent with the sampling rate in OASIS. Our implementation uses 21 KB ROM and 8 KB RAM.

Coordinator: We use a laptop computer to simulate the coordinator and implement all its algorithms in ANSI C. The ANSI C implementation can be easily ported to embedded computing platforms such as Imote2. To evaluate the computational overhead of these algorithms, we cross-compile the programs and run them in the SimIt-ARM 3.0 [5], which simulates the XScale processor on Imote2.

8.1.2 Experiment Results

We evaluate the computation and storage overhead of the algorithms running on sensors in a testbed of 12 TelosB motes, loaded with the real data traces sampled by 12 nodes of the OASIS system [27] in an earthquake. Fig. 6 shows the execution times of various signal processing algorithms at different sensors during an earthquake event. It is clear that the end-to-end execution time does not exceed 3 seconds, which introduces moderate workload and energy consumption to the sensors. Moreover, our implementation of CS is very efficient and most computation overhead is due to the DWT. The variation of execution time is mainly caused by sparsity estimation and CS. In the sparsity estimation algorithm, the wavelet coefficients are sorted using quick sort, which has a variable execution time. As seismic signals at sensors have different sparsities, sensors have different numbers of rows in the project matrix $\mathbf{A}$, leading to a variable execution time of CS. Nonetheless, as the variation is less than one second, the computation overhead is relatively evenly distributed among the sensors.

8.2 Trace-Driven Simulations

Our simulations use a data set collected by 12 Imote2-based nodes on Mount St. Helens in the OASIS project [27], which spans 5.5 months and comprises 30 significant earthquakes. In this section, we simulate a cluster of 12

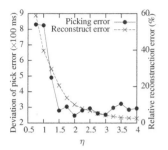
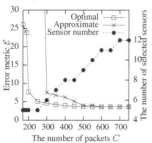

Figure 8: P-phase picking error and relative reconstruction error vs. the coefficient η.

Figure 9: The error metric and the number of selected sensors vs. the allowed number of packets.

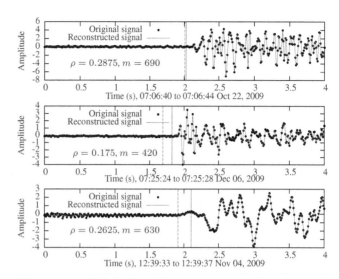

Figure 10: Original and reconstructed signals with picks. Vertical dashed/solid lines represent the picks by AR-AIC algorithm on the original/reconstructed signals.

sensors, which exactly correspond to the 12 nodes in the OASIS project [27]. Note that the cluster size of 12 is a reasonable setting that will be evaluated in Section 8.3.2. For each earthquake, we use a Bayesian approach [28] to detect the onset time based on 10 minutes of data traces. In our simulations, we also use the locations of OASIS nodes and a velocity model $\mathbf{v}$ (cf. Section 5.1) obtained in a tomographic study of Mount St. Helens [20].

8.2.1 Accuracy of P-phase Picking

We first evaluate the accuracy of the preliminary P-phase picker described in Section 4.2. The error is defined as the absolute difference between the preliminary P-phase and the P-phase picked by the AR-AIC picker [26] on the original seismic signal. Fig. 7 shows the distribution of preliminary picking error based on 100 sensor data traces. The mean error is 8.5 milliseconds. Therefore, the preliminary P-phase picker can be approximated as a zero-mean error picker with respect to the AR-AIC picker. The standard deviation is about 400 milliseconds. To evaluate the effectiveness of the preliminary picker, we also calculate the error of the earthquake onset time with respect to the P-phase picked by the AR-AIC picker. The mean and standard deviation of the error of earthquake onset time are 280 and 1310 milliseconds, respectively. Therefore, compared with the earthquake onset time, the results of the preliminary picker are more concentrated on the true P-phases.

The coefficient η in Eq. (6) is an important coefficient for CS. We now evaluate the impact of η on the quality of seismic signal reconstruction as well as the P-phase picking at the coordinator. The relative reconstruction error is calculated as $\|\widetilde{\mathbf{s}} - \mathbf{s}\|_{\ell_2}/\|\mathbf{s}\|_{\ell_2}$ where $\mathbf{s}$ and $\widetilde{\mathbf{s}}$ are the original and reconstructed signals. The picking error is calculated as the difference between the P-phases picked by the AR-AIC picker on $\mathbf{s}$ and $\widetilde{\mathbf{s}}$. Fig. 8 shows the standard deviation of picking error as well as the relative reconstruction error versus the coefficient η based on 100 data traces. We can see that the standard deviation of picking error dramatically drops when η increases from 0.75 to 1.5 and becomes flat after 1.5. Therefore, $\eta = 1.5$ is a proper setting to achieve the satisfactory gain of P-phase picking accuracy to the data transmission volume. When $\eta \geq 1.5$, the mean picking error is within $[-15\,\mathrm{ms}, 15\,\mathrm{ms}]$. Therefore, it is shorter than 1.5 sampling periods given that the sampling rate is 100 Hz. This time error can be translated to an error distance of 75 to 120 meters based on the P-wave speed (5 to 8 km/s). As the precision for distance in volcano models (e.g., $\mathbf{v}$ in

Section 5.1) is typically in the order of kilometers [20], the error of 15 ms is small and can be safely approximated as zero-mean error. With $\eta = 1.5$, Fig. 10 shows the original and reconstructed signals received by a sensor for three earthquakes. It is apparent that the signals are accurately reconstructed and P-phases are well preserved.

8.2.2 Effectiveness of Sensor Selection

In our simulations, each sensor directly communicates with the coordinator. Each packet carries total ten 4-byte data points. Therefore, by setting the unit communication cost $c_i = 1/10$, the upper bound of communication cost C characterizes the number of packet transmissions that are allowed in an earthquake timing process. Fig. 9 plots the error metric $\mathcal{E}$ (given by Eq. (4)) of the optimal (cf. Section 5.2) and approximate (cf. Section 5.3) sensor selections versus C in an earthquake. The figure also illustrates the number of selected sensors in the optimal solution. Note that the number of selected sensors in the approximate solution is at most one more than that of the optimal solution. From the figure, we can see that if more packet transmissions are allowed, the coordinator will select more sensors to collect data from them. Consistent with intuition, the error metric decreases with the number of packet transmissions. When $C \in [170, 250]$, a total of four sensors are selected. However, the selected four sensors can be different. When more packets are allowed, sensors with higher ρ's, though more contributory to hypocenter estimation, will be selected. We can see that the error metric for the optimal solution becomes flat when more packets are allowed. This result can be exploited to reduce the communication cost without sacrificing too much hypocenter estimation accuracy. When C is lower than 300, the approximate solution has much worse performance than the optimal solution. However, the approximate solution approaches the optimal solution when C is greater than 500.

8.2.3 Impact of Random Packet Loss

As volcano monitoring WSNs are deployed in harsh environments, sensors are subject to unreliable communication

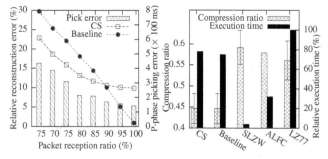

Figure 11: Impact of packet loss on the reconstruction and P-phase picking.

Figure 12: Compression ratios and relative execution times of various schemes in 30 earthquakes.

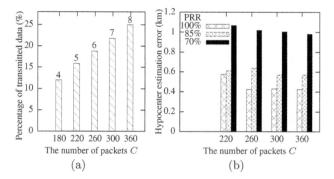

Figure 13: Hypocenter estimation results for an earthquake at 16:56:47 Nov 03 2009: (a) The percentage of transmitted data versus the allowed number of packets C; (b) Hypocenter estimation error versus C under various PRRs.

links [27]. We evaluate the impact of random packet loss on our earthquake timing approach. In the simulations, we assume that each link from sensor to coordinator has the same packet reception ratio (PRR). The coordinator can detect lost packets from the sequence numbers in the received packets. When the coordinator reconstructs the signal, it only uses the rows in the projection matrix **A** that correspond to the received data points. Therefore, the effect of packet loss is similar to choosing a smaller m in CS. We compare our CS-based approach with a baseline that implements a lossy compression scheme. The baseline transmits the largest coefficients together with their indexes in the wavelet domain. The number of transmitted coefficients is chosen to make sure that the baseline produces the same number of packets as our approach. The curves in Fig. 11 plot the relative reconstruction errors of our CS-based approach and the baseline versus PRR. When no packet loss happens, the baseline outperforms our approach. This result is consistent with previous studies on CS [16]. When the PRR is lower than 90%, our approach outperforms the baseline. It has been observed in previous deployments [30, 27] that the PRR varies with time due to changing environment and can be lower than 90%. Therefore, we can switch between the baseline and CS according to recent PRRs (e.g., measured in the per-second earthquake onset time detection [28]). The histograms in Fig. 11 plot the average P-phase picking error of our CS-based approach. We can see that the reconstruction is resilient to packet loss when the PRR is no lower than 80%. Error correction mechanisms such as Forward Error Correction can be integrated with the baseline to improve its resilience to packet loss. However, they can increase both computation and communication overhead. A comprehensive comparison that accounts for error correction mechanisms is left for our future work.

8.2.4 Compression Efficiency

We now compare our CS-based approach with several baselines in terms of compression ratio and execution time. In addition to the lossy baseline approach used in Section 8.2.3, we adopt the following three lossless baseline algorithms: (1) SLZW [25], a lossless compression algorithm designed for WSNs; (2) ALFC [19], a real-time predictive lossless compression algorithm developed for OASIS [27]; (3) Lempel-Ziv coding (LZ77), a widely employed scheme used in traditional data-collection-based volcano monitoring systems. Compression ratio is defined as the ratio of compressed size

to the original size. Fig. 12 plots the compression ratios and relative execution times of various approaches. The relative execution time is calculated with respect to LZ77. Our approach and the lossy baseline approach have comparable compression efficiency. Our approach saves more than 10% data transmission volume compared with the lossless baselines. It is faster than LZ77 but slower than SLZW and ALFC. However, none of the lossless baseline algorithms can predict the exact volume of compressed signal prior to compression. Therefore, they do not allow effective scheduling of data transmission.

8.2.5 Earthquake Hypocenter Estimation

As the data transmission scheduling is guided by the accuracy of hypocenter estimation, the final set of simulations evaluate the impact of our timing approach on the hypocenter estimation. We first use the P-phases picked by AR-AIC on the original signals of all 12 sensors to localize the earthquake source. This source location is regarded here to be the groundtruth location. We then localize the earthquake source based on the P-phases obtained in our timing approach. The hypocenter estimation error is the Euclidean distance from the groundtruth location. Fig. 13(a) plots the percentage of transmitted data in our timing approach with respect to the total volume of raw data at sensors. The number over each bar is the number of selected sensors. We observe that when C ranges from 180 to 360, only 12% to 25% of the sensor data are transmitted. Fig. 13(b) plots the corresponding hypocenter estimation errors under different PRRs. Note that when $C = 180$, the hypocenter estimation error is around 9 km (not shown in Fig. 13(b)). Consistent with intuition, the hypocenter estimation error decreases with C and PRR. From the two figures, by setting $C = 220$, the hypocenter estimation error is below 1 km, a common result in volcano seismology [20], at the expense of only 16% data transmission.

8.3 Impact of Network Architecture and Clustering

In order to choose the right hardware platform and network organization, a sensor network designer must carefully consider the trade-offs between many factors, including hardware availability, energy consumption, sensing coverage, system delay, and etc. In this work, we adopt a hierarchical network architecture where mote-class sensors sample fine-grained signals and powerful coordinators run computation-intensive seismological algorithms. However, one may argue that a network composed of only powerful nodes such as Imote2 is more desirable in data-intensive applications like volcano monitoring. In contrast to mote-class nodes, these nodes can collect and directly process the seismic signals for various advanced monitoring tasks, reducing the energy cost of communication with the cluster heads. In this section, we quantitatively study the impact of network architecture and sensor clustering on the energy efficiency and performance of earthquake timing under realistic settings.

8.3.1 *Energy Efficiency under Different Network Architectures*

This numerical study compares the per-node energy consumption under the *hierarchical* and *non-hierarchical* network architectures discussed in Section 3.1. In the non-hierarchical network, a cluster is composed of only high-end sensors and each sensor runs the AR-AIC algorithm. In the hierarchical network, we consider our CS-based approach proposed and a centralized approach. To simplify the analysis, we assume a 1-hop star topology centered at the coordinator. For our approach, we assume all sensors are always selected. For the centralized approach, each sensor transmits a segment of raw seismic signal (cf. Section 4.1) to the coordinator. Since earthquakes are usually rare events, the network must perform earthquake detection most of the time in order to capture these events. We should thus also model the energy consumed in earthquake detection. Assume each sensor detects earthquake every second using some detection algorithm. The sensors send detection results to the cluster head, which then fuses the results to make the final detection decision, subsequently sends the earthquake onset time back to the sensors in case of positive decision. This is a common detection approach adopted in previous volcano monitoring systems [31, 28]. Due to space limitation, the details of the energy consumption modeling are omitted here and can be found in [22]. We compare the energies consumed in computation and communication by a sensor per day under the two network architectures. Fig. 14 shows the map and contours of the ratio of energies under the hierarchical (CS-based approach) and non-hierarchical networks. Note that the execution time of the detection algorithm on TelosB (i.e., X-axis of Fig. 14) varies, depending on the detection algorithm. For instance, the STA/LTA-based and Bayesian detection algorithms require around 10 ms and 100 ms on TelosB [28], respectively. The execution time on Imote2 is scaled accordingly. From Fig. 14, we observe that the hierarchical network consumes much less energy in computation and communication than the non-hierarchical network under a range of settings. This is true because, primarily, when the sensors sleep most of the time in the absence of earthquake, the sleep power of Imote2 is at least 18 times of that of TelosB [6, 4].[1] After the current draw of the sensor circuit is taken into consideration [27], the sensor's projected lifetimes over two D-cell batteries are about 6 and 2 months, re-

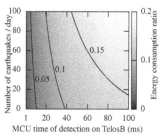
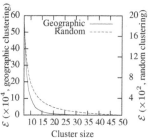

Figure 14: Ratio of energy consumed by a sensor in the hierarchical (CS-based) and non-hierarchical networks.

Figure 15: Hypocenter estimation error metric $\mathcal{E}$ versus cluster size under two clustering schemes.

spectively, under the hierarchical (CS-based approach) and non-hierarchical architectures, if a STA/LTA-based earthquake detection algorithm is adopted and 100 positive detection decisions are made by the detection algorithm per day. Moreover, our CS-based approach can increase lifetime by 7% and 12% compared with the centralized approach if 100 and 200 positive detection decisions are made per day, respectively. Note that the network will make more than 200 positive detection decisions per day if its false alarm rate is no lower than 3%, which is common for earthquake detection algorithms [28].

8.3.2 *Impact of Sensor Clustering*

This numerical study evaluates the impact of sensor clustering on earthquake timing. A hundred sensors are randomly deployed over a $6 \times 6\,\text{km}^2$ square region. We assume that the earthquake occurs at 10 km beneath the center of the region. We consider the following two clustering schemes. (1) *Geographic clustering*: A cluster head is randomly selected from the network and the sensors that are geographically closest to it are its members. This approach is similar to a class of sensor clustering algorithms based on sensor locations [8]. (2) *Random clustering*: Sensors are randomly selected from the network to form a cluster. Although this scheme is not practical, it gives the upper bound on the hypocenter estimation accuracy because sensors are most scattered. Fig. 15 shows the hypocenter estimation error metric (given by Eq. (4)) of a cluster averaged over many runs versus the cluster size under the two schemes. We observe that, for both schemes, the hypocenter estimation error has a sharp drop initially and then becomes flat when the cluster size increases. This result implies that adding a sensor becomes less beneficial for a larger cluster. From the figure, a setting of around 15 for cluster size is preferable. Although this numerical study is based on simplified assumptions, it provides insights into the impact of sensor clustering on earthquake hypocenter estimation. In practice, similar numerical studies, which integrate available geographical information such as the volcano surface altitude data, can be conducted to guide the sensor clustering as well as the setting of cluster size.

9. CONCLUSION AND FUTURE WORK

This paper presents a holistic and energy-efficient approach to accurate volcanic earthquake timing in WSNs. We develop a suite of in-network seismic signal processing algo-

---

[1]We assume that the sensors can sleep with the help of Direct Memory Access controller in signal sampling [24]. The results become more favorable to the hierarchical architecture if the sensors stay in idle state instead of sleep, because the energy ratio increases from 18 to at least 20 [6, 4].

rithms that collaboratively pick the arrival times of seismic primary waves received by sensors. A dynamic sensor selection problem is formulated to maximize the performance of earthquake hypocenter estimation subject to a given upper bound on communication overhead. We further develop the signal compression and reconstruction algorithms based on compressive sampling theory. Testbed experiments and extensive simulations based on real data traces collected on an active volcano demonstrate the effectiveness of our approach.

In this paper, we use an XScale processor simulator on a laptop to simulate the coordinator (cf. Section 8.1.1). In our future work, we plan to use Imote2 to extensively evaluate the computation and communication overhead of coordinator's algorithms, which allows us to accurately study the trade-off between energy consumption of coordinator and lifetime extension of sensors. The results can guide the choices of batteries for both coordinator and sensors. Moreover, we plan to deploy and further evaluate our approach in a real volcano monitoring WSN system [7].

10. ACKNOWLEDGMENTS

The authors thank our shepherd Dr. John Stankovic and the anonymous reviewers for providing valuable feedbacks to this work. This work was supported in part by U.S. National Science Foundation under grants OIA-1125163, CNS-0954039 (CAREER), CNS-1218475, OIA-1125165, CNS-1066391, in part by National Natural Science Foundation of China under grant 61171089, and in part by the Fundamental Research Funds for the Central Universities under grant CD-JZR10160005.

11. REFERENCES

[1] AlertNet. http://bit.ly/f9JhLc.
[2] Gumstix. http://www.gumstix.com.
[3] List of wireless sensor nodes. http://bit.ly/TfLEom.
[4] Power modes and energy consumption for the imote2 sensor node. http://bit.ly/THlmRz.
[5] SimIt-ARM. http://bit.ly/T44mj1.
[6] TelosB datasheet. http://bit.ly/Psjj2S.
[7] VolcanoSRI project. http://sensornet.cse.msu.edu.
[8] A. Abbasi and M. Younis. A survey on clustering algorithms for wireless sensor networks. *Computer communications*, 30(14):2826–2841, 2007.
[9] R. Berinde, A. Gilbert, P. Indyk, H. Karloff, and M. Strauss. Combining geometry and combinatorics: A unified approach to sparse signal recovery. In *Annu. Allerton Conf. Commun., Control, and Comput.*, 2008.
[10] F. Blais and M. Rioux. Real-time numerical peak detector. *Signal Processing*, 11(2):145–155, 1986.
[11] T. Blumensath and M. Davies. Iterative hard thresholding for compressed sensing. *Applied and Computational Harmonic Analysis*, 27(3), 2009.
[12] E. Candès and M. Wakin. An introduction to compressive sampling. *IEEE Signal Process. Mag.*, 25(2), 2008.
[13] Y. Chan and K. Ho. A simple and efficient estimator for hyperbolic location. *IEEE Trans. Signal Process.*, 42(8), 1994.
[14] E. Endo and T. Murray. Real-time seismic amplitude measurement (RSAM): a volcano monitoring and prediction tool. *Bulletin of Volcanology*, 53(7), 1991.

[15] O. Gnawali, B. Greenstein, K.-Y. Jang, A. Joki, J. Paek, M. Vieira, D. Estrin, R. Govindan, and E. Kohler. The TENET Architecture for Tiered Sensor Networks. In *SenSys*, 2006.
[16] V. Goyal, A. Fletcher, and S. Rangan. Compressive sampling and lossy compression. *IEEE Signal Process. Mag.*, 25(2), 2008.
[17] B. Greenstein, C. Mar, A. Pesterev, S. Farshchi, E. Kohler, J. Judy, and D. Estrin. Capturing high-frequency phenomena using a bandwidth-limited sensor network. In *SenSys*, 2006.
[18] G. Hackmann, F. Sun, N. Castaneda, C. Lu, and S. Dyke. A holistic approach to decentralized structural damage localization using wireless sensor networks. In *RTSS*, 2008.
[19] A. Kiely, M. Xu, W. Song, R. Huang, and B. Shirazi. Adaptive linear filtering compression on realtime sensor networks. In *PerCom*, 2009.
[20] J. Lees and R. Crosson. Tomographic inversion for three-dimensional velocity structure at mount st. helens using earthquake data. *J. Geophysical Research*, 94(B5), 1989.
[21] J. M. Lees. RSEIS: Seismic time series analysis tools. http://bit.ly/Qcj60K.
[22] G. Liu, R. Tan, R. Zhou, G. Xing, W.-Z. Song, and J. M. Lees. Volcanic earthquake timing in wireless sensor networks. Technical Report MSU-CSE-12-8, CSE Dept, Michigan State University, 2012.
[23] J. Nelder and R. Mead. A simplex method for function minimization. *The computer journal*, 7(4), 1965.
[24] J. Polastre, R. Szewczyk, and D. Culler. Telos: enabling ultra-low power wireless research. In *IPSN*, 2005.
[25] C. Sadler and M. Martonosi. Data compression algorithms for energy-constrained devices in delay tolerant networks. In *SenSys*, 2006.
[26] R. Sleeman and T. van Eck. Robust automatic p-phase picking: an on-line implementation in the analysis of broadband seismogram recordings. *Physics of the earth and planetary interiors*, 113, 1999.
[27] W. Song, R. Huang, M. Xu, A. Ma, B. Shirazi, and R. LaHusen. Air-dropped sensor network for real-time high-fidelity volcano monitoring. In *MobiSys*, 2009.
[28] R. Tan, G. Xing, J. Chen, W. Song, and R. Huang. Quality-driven volcanic earthquake detection using wireless sensor networks. In *RTSS*, 2010.
[29] G. Werner-Allen, S. Dawson-Haggerty, and M. Welsh. Lance: optimizing high-resolution signal collection in wireless sensor networks. In *SenSys*, 2008.
[30] G. Werner-Allen, J. Johnson, M. Ruiz, J. Lees, and M. Welsh. Monitoring volcanic eruptions with a wireless sensor network. In *EWSN*, 2005.
[31] G. Werner-Allen, K. Lorincz, J. Johnson, J. Lees, and M. Welsh. Fidelity and yield in a volcano monitoring sensor network. In *OSDI*, 2006.
[32] M. Withers, R. Aster, C. Young, J. Beiriger, M. Harris, S. Moore, and J. Trujillo. A comparison of select trigger algorithms for automated global seismic phase and event detection. *Bulletin of the Seismological Society of America*, 88(1), 1998.

In-Pavement Wireless Weigh-In-Motion

Ravneet Bajwa, Ram Rajagopal, Erdem Coleri, Pravin Varaiya and Christopher Flores

Sensys Networks, Inc
1608 4th St, Suite 200
Berkeley CA 94710
{rbajwa, rrajagopal, pvaraiya, cflores } @sensysnetworks.com, ecoleri@ucdavis.edu

ABSTRACT

Truck weight data is used in many areas of transportation such as weight enforcement and pavement condition assessment. This paper describes a wireless sensor network (WSN) that estimates the weight of moving vehicles from pavement vibrations caused by vehicular motion. The WSN consists of: acceleration sensors that report pavement vibration; vehicle detection sensors that report a vehicle's arrival and departure times; and an access point (AP) that synchronizes all the sensors and records the sensor data. The paper also describes a novel algorithm that estimates a vehicle's weight from pavement vibration and vehicle detection data, and calculates pavement deflection in the process. A prototype of the system has been deployed near a conventional Weigh-In-Motion (WIM) system on I-80 W in Pinole, CA. Weights of 52 trucks at different speeds and loads were estimated by the system under different pavement temperatures and varying environmental conditions, adding to the challenges the system must overcome. The error in load estimates was less than 10% for gross weight and 15% for individual axle weights. Different states have different requirements for WIM but the system described here outperformed the nearby conventional WIM, and meets commonly used standards in United States. The system also opens up exciting new opportunities for WSNs in pavement engineering and intelligent transportation.

Categories and Subject Descriptors

C.3 [**Special-Purpose and Application-Based Systems**]: Realtime and Embedded Systems, Signal Processing Systems; I.5.4 [**Applications**]: Signal Processing, Waveform Analysis

General Terms

Design, Measurement, Experimentation, Algorithms

Keywords

Weigh-In-Motion (WIM), traffic monitoring, pavement vibrations, pavement deflection, real-time pavement monitoring, structural health monitoring, pavement-vehicle interaction model, accelerometers

1. INTRODUCTION

Transportation agencies such as Caltrans use weigh stations to enforce weight limits, collect fees, and record truck weight data. For assessment of pavement life and pavement quality, it is critical to know the loads being applied to the pavement. The weight data is, therefore, used to make important decisions concerning road maintenance, pavement design, and transportation policy at both the state and national levels [10]. Federal Highway Administration (FHWA) recognizes the importance of weight data and recommends an increase in the number of stations collecting such data. However, traditional static weight stations are very expensive to install and operate, and also require that the trucks are stopped and weighed individually. An alternative to traditional weigh station is a weigh-in-motion (WIM) system that is installed on an existing highway lane and can estimate the weight of vehicles at highway speeds without disrupting the traffic flow. However, since the typical cost of a WIM system is around $0.5M, they are very expensive for widespread deployment. The main reasons for such high cost are: use of expensive force sensors; construction work required to embed the *wired* sensors in the road; and the prolonged road closures during installation and maintenance. In this paper we describe an alternative system comprising an embedded *wireless* sensor network that measures pavement vibration, temperature and vehicle speed to infer the individual axle loads of moving vehicles. Unlike current WIM systems, the wireless WIM uses relatively inexpensive sensors and a much easier installation procedure to reduce the overall cost. We believe this is the first wireless sensor network capable of weigh-in-motion in individual lanes at highway speeds.

Current WIM technologies. The most widely used WIM technologies consist of a pair of wired magnetic loops and a force sensor, as shown in Figure 1. The magnetic loops detect vehicles and estimate their speed. The force sensors (piezoelectric plates, load cells or bending plate sensors) measure the instantaneous force (or load) applied by the tires of a vehicle. A major drawback of these technologies is that they require smooth concrete pavement to be built around the force sensors to achieve the desired accuracy.

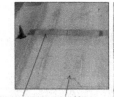

Force sensor Wired loop

Load cells Control cabinet

Figure 1: WIM station consisting of two wired magnetic loops and piezoelectric plates in the middle for measuring force (*left*). Installation procedure for a WIM station (*right*). The load cells are installed first and smooth concrete pavement is built around them to reduce the effect of vehicle's suspension system on measured load [2].

Pavement roughness excites the vehicle's suspension system causing the instantaneous axle load to be different from the static load. The difference between the instantaneous and static load, known as the *dynamic component* of applied load, is reduced by having a smooth pavement. However, this construction increases the system cost and the installation time, typically requiring several days or even weeks of lane closure. As an alternative to this approach, the use of *multiple force sensors* on existing pavement has been suggested to improve the estimate of static load [5], but current technologies are too costly to make this approach feasible. The WSN described here uses a different sensing principle, and makes this multi-sensor approach much more cost effective.

Contributions. Enabling wireless WIM requires overcoming significant challenges in sensing, pavement modeling, signal processing and estimation. The main contributions of this paper to enable this concept are:

- An easy to install embedded wireless vibration sensor capable of measuring pavement acceleration in a very noisy environment (Section 3).

- Design and verification of the wireless WIM system comprising vibration, speed and temperature sensors, and an access point that can be used to compute loads in real-time (Section 3, 7).

- A simplified and novel model relating individual axle load to pavement acceleration (or displacement), temperature and speed of the vehicle (Section 5).

- A new algorithm to estimate pavement displacement from ground acceleration and to isolate individual axle responses from the combined response (Section 5).

- A novel load estimation procedure that calibrates for temperature, vehicle speed, and local pavement conditions (Section 5).

- Experimental testing of the system on a real highway, under different weather conditions, and a variety of axle load distributions (Section 6).

The paper is organized as follows. Section 2 describes the problem of weigh-in-motion, related work, proposed solution and its challenges. Section 3 describes the wireless WIM and associated components. Section 4 describes the experimental setup used to collect data for calibration and system evaluation. Section 5 proposes a simplified pavement-vehicle interaction model and describes the load estimation algorithm. Section 6 reports experimental results and Section 7 concludes the paper.

2. WEIGH-IN-MOTION

In this section, we state the problem of weigh-in-motion and propose a wireless solution. We list the challenges the system must overcome and conclude with a discussion of related work done in the field.

2.1 Problem statement

A vehicle with K axles moves in a traffic lane at v miles per hour. Axle i weighs f_i and the total vehicle weight is f pounds. The goal of a WIM system is to detect the presence of a vehicle, measure its speed v, count the number of axles K and measure inter-axle spacing, and provide estimates of f_i and f with a required statistical accuracy. The system can be calibrated once a year, utilizing a few pre-weighed vehicles.

There are some important additional requirements that any solution to this problem must meet. The system should weigh vehicles in individual lanes and should be accurate independent of time and weather conditions. It should also be able to account for vehicle wander, i.e., vehicles moving slightly off-center in a given lane. Finally, installation and maintenance costs should be kept at a minimum to enable widespread deployment. A significant portion of the cost is due to traffic disruption from lane closures during installation and maintenance. These costs are easily five to ten times more than the cost of measurement system.

2.2 Proposed solution: Wireless WIM

Reducing cost of the WIM system requires rethinking the most critical component of the system: the force sensor. The force sensor works by replacing part of the pavement with a platform that bears the full load of each axle, and providing signals to estimate it. In order to avoid replacing the pavement, we propose utilizing the existing *pavement itself as the transducer* and estimating individual axle loads from the measured vibration response of the roadway. Small vibration and vehicle detection sensors are embedded in the pavement utilizing a convenient and low cost procedure. The vehicle detection sensors [13] report the arrival and departure times of a vehicle which are used to calculate its speed and length. The vibration sensors report the pavement's vertical acceleration and its temperature. Multiple arrays of vibration sensors are used to average out the dynamic component of load. The acceleration data is processed to extract the pavement's response due to each individual axle. This, along with speed and temperature data are then used to estimate axle loads. The axle loads are simply added to get gross vehicle weight. Vehicle length, number of axles and axle spacing are estimated using the Axle Detection (ADET) algorithm described in [2].

2.3 Challenges

The system needs to overcome several challenges:

Measurement: The road pavement is designed to experience very small vibrations from vehicle movement [5]. The vibration sensor must measure these small vibrations while being immune to the high environment noise arising from vehicle sound and traffic in neighboring lanes.

Modeling: The relationship between applied axle load and pavement vibrations is not well-understood. Most pavement models relate pavement deflection to applied load, but estimating pavement *deflection* from acceleration is a challenging problem in itself. Moreover, the response is highly dependent on pavement temperature and speed of the vehicle, and these variables must be properly accounted for. Another challenge is to estimate static load from dynamic load, as discussed before.

Signal processing: The pavement response at any given time and location is an accumulated response due to all vehicles in the vicinity, therefore response due to other vehicles needs to be filtered out. An even harder challenge is to extract the pavement response due to each axle because at any given time, all the axles of a vehicle are affecting sensor measurements. Additionally, the signal processing algorithms have to be simple enough for real-time execution and efficient enough to conserve energy for a longer lifetime.

Design: The sensors should be well coupled to the pavement and robust enough to withstand the tire forces. The system should also be insensitive to vehicle wander. It should be cost-effective and convenient to install and maintain, and have a lifetime of at least 4 years [4].

2.4 Related work

We identify four areas related to this work: applications of wireless sensor networks (WSN) in transportation, applications of sensor networks in infrastructure monitoring, weigh-in-motion sensor technologies, and algorithms that estimate pavement displacement from acceleration.

Applications of WSNs in transportation have been growing. WSNs have been used for vehicle detection using magnetic sensors [7, 15, 23], classification of vehicles in different categories [2], and increasing road safety by intervehicular information sharing [22]. Much less has been done in terms of monitoring the response of road infrastructure itself.

Monitoring large infrastructures using accelerometer sensor networks has been studied for structural monitoring of bridges [14], buildings [6] and underground structures such as caves [16]. Wired embedded sensors in concrete structures have been investigated [19] but usually require complex installation procedures and have limited lifetime if used in roads.

WIM technologies have not advanced much in the last decade and focus has shifted on using multiple WIM sensors to improve system accuracy, as opposed to requiring special-material pavement near the sensors [10, 3]. A novel WIM sensor based on perturbation theory of microwave resonant cavities is presented in [17], and a special fiber optic sensor based on measuring light loss under mechanical stress is discussed in [18]. However, both sensors were tested in a controlled laboratory setting, and challenges regarding road installation and sensor durability under heavy loads were not addressed.

Estimating pavement deflection (or displacement) from acceleration is a challenging problem in itself. Simple double integration amplifies the low frequency noise leading to a large unpredictable drift [6]. Popular techniques for drift correction include fitting some polynomial during the silent periods to estimate drift, and subtracting it from the calculated displacement to correct it [12, 1]. However, corrected signals are highly sensitive to the choice of the drift polynomial, and these techniques do not perform as well for low SNR measurements.

3. WIRELESS WIM SYSTEM

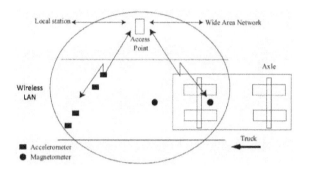

Figure 2: Wireless WIM system: The accelerometer and magnetometer sensors report data to the access point. The data is stored locally on hard drives and can be transferred remotely via a cellular modem [2].

Figure 2 shows the schematic of the proposed system. There are four components: vibration sensors, vehicle detection sensors, access point (AP), and a pan-tilt-zoom (PTZ) camera (not shown) connected to the AP. The vibration and vehicle detection sensors are installed in the pavement as shown whereas the rest of the equipment is mounted on a 15ft pole on the side of the road. The vibration and vehicle detection sensors follow a TDMA schedule to transmit their data to the AP. The camera captures images of vehicles to validate that the sensor data corresponds to the correct vehicles. For accurate time stamps on the data, the sensors, the AP, and the camera are periodically synchronized to a common Network Time Protocol (NTP) server. Data from the site can be collected 24x7 and the AP saves all this data locally. The data can be retrieved through a local WiFi connection to the AP or remotely via a cellular connection. In fact, the entire system can be monitored and controlled this way. We now describe the network components and their communication protocol.

3.1 Sensor network components

Wireless vibration sensor. Figure 3 shows the block diagram for the sensor. Vibrations from the pavement are converted to analog voltage by a MEMS accelerometer on board [8]. The voltage signal is then passed through a filter stage. The output of the filter stage is sampled at 512 Hz by a 12-bit ADC included in MSP430 microprocessor. The collected samples are then transmitted via the radio transceiver using a TDMA based, low power consuming protocol. Along with each packet of acceleration data, the vibration sensor also sends out a temperature reading using the on-board analog temperature sensor. The average current consumption of the vibration sensor is 1.96 mA in active mode and 35 μA in idle mode. Using a 7200 mAhr battery, the respective lifetimes are around 5 months and 23 years respectively. For data collection purposes, lifetime is sufficient and techniques such as in-sensor processing (Section 7) can extend this for other applications.

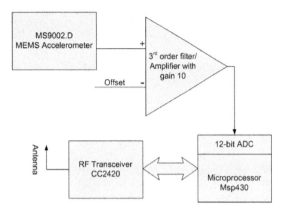

Figure 3: Block Diagram of the vibration sensor [2].

Simulations reported in [21] revealed that the sensor must have a resolution of 500 μg at a bandwidth of 50 Hz. The highway environment is extremely noisy, and noise from sound alone is a few mg if the sensor is not properly isolated. Another problem is that vehicles in the neighboring lanes cause pavement vibrations and corrupt our measurements. In order to estimate the load of a given vehicle, we need the pavement vibrations corresponding to that vehicle alone. Any measured vibrations due to another vehicle will contribute to error in our load estimates.

Filtering signals above 50Hz with a steep filter can eliminate sound noise significantly. It was shown in [2] that a low pass filter with frequency response $H(j\omega) = \frac{1}{(1+\frac{j\omega}{50})^2(1+\frac{j\omega}{500})}$ successfully isolates the sensor from most of the sound. Moreover, the sensor case shown in Figure 5 attenuates sound before it reaches the accelerometer, providing more isolation.

To provide isolation from traffic in neighboring lanes, the sensors are placed towards the middle of the lane. Pavement vibrations are maximum at the location of applied load and magnitude decreases exponentially away from that location [11]. Center placement maximizes the distance of neighboring-lane vehicles from the sensors, thus minimizing lane-to-lane interference.

Vehicle detection sensor. A wireless magnetic sensor is used to infer the presence of a vehicle by measuring changes in the local magnetic field. The sensor transmits the arrival time t_a and departure time t_d of a vehicle as it arrives at the sensor and traverses it. Multiple sensors are combined to estimate speed. These sensors have a lifetime of over 10 years [13].

Pan-tilt-zoom (PTZ) camera. The PTZ camera takes vehicle images from the side of the road and transmits them to the AP using a wired connection. The power to the camera and AP is provided through Caltrans controller box on the side of the road.

Access point (AP). Figure 4 shows the schematic of the access point. This equipment provides remote control and observation of the WSN. The AP contains: (i) A processor with attached radio and 2TB hard drive storage; (ii) a power controller that controls power to each connected device; (iii) an ethernet hub through which a local area network (LAN) is setup for devices to communicate with each other; (iv) a 3G modem that acts as a gateway to the wide area network (WAN) and enables remote access to the system; and (v) a Wi-Fi bridge and an ethernet data port for local access to the system. Once a remote computer is connected to the AP, it can communicate to any of the connected devices through the LAN. It can, for instance, use the power controller to turn on/off individual components in the box, send commands to the sensors via the radio, change the settings of the PTZ camera, and start collecting video and sensor data remotely.

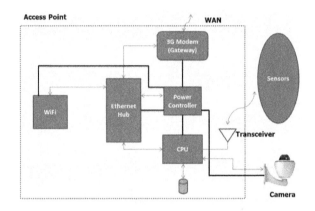

Figure 4: Schematic of the access point.

3.2 Communication protocol

We focus on the communication protocol followed by the wireless sensor nodes and the AP. Other components follow widely used standard protocols and are not discussed here. The sensors follow a TDMA protocol that uses headers very similar to IEEE 802.15.4 MAC layer. Time is divided into multiple frames with each frame about 125 ms long. Each frame is further divided into 64 time slots, numbered 0 to 63, most of which can be used by the sensor nodes to transmit data. Timeslot 0 is used by the AP to send clock synchronization information and other commands to the sensors. The AP assigns every node unique time slots and a network address (or node ID) to communicate with it. This schedule enables individual nodes to stay awake for the minimum amount of time and prevents packet collisions. There are three major applications of this protocol: synchronization, sensor management, and firmware update.

Synchronization. This application ensures clock synchronization of all nodes within 60 μs. Sync packets are sent by the AP on a periodic basis with very low jitter. Nodes must first synchronize their clocks before transmitting. When a sensor node first starts, it listens to sync packets every 125 ms. It learns the difference between its clock and the AP's clock, and over time improves its estimate of the AP's clock. As the estimate improves, the node converges to a steady state in which it listens for a sync packet only once in 30

s. If a node loses sync, it repeats the above process to get synchronized again. In addition to sending clock information, the sync application is also used to send commands to individual sensors like *change mode, set RF channel, reset sensor* .

Sensor management. This is the most important application for both sensors. For the vibration sensor, the application controls when to turn on the accelerometer and related circuitry, when to sample, and when to wake up the radio to transmit the data collected. There are two main modes in this application: *idle* mode and *raw data* mode. In *idle* mode, the accelerometer and related conditioning circuitry are turned off by disabling the voltage regulator that powers this part of the circuit. Even the microcontroller and the radio transceiver are put in a low power consuming state most of the time. Once every 30 seconds, the microcontroller and the transceiver wake up and acquire the sync packet. In *raw data* mode, the accelerometer and related circuitry are turned on. The microcontroller wakes up every 1/512 seconds and samples the analog output from the accelerometer unit, as shown in Figure 3. In addition to waking up for the sync packet, the transceiver wakes up right before its allotted timeslots to send the sampled data. Due to challenging environment of highways, sensors frequently suffer from packet loses. To fix this problem, we transmit every packet twice after a slight delay.

For the detection sensor, the application is similar. The key difference is that instead of the raw data mode there is a *vehicle detect* mode. The magnetometer is constantly sampled at 128 Hz, followed by in-sensor processing to determine if the vehicle is present or not. Only in case of a detection is any data transmitted, as opposed to the vibration sensor which continuously transmits raw data. Since the data throughput from detection sensors is very small, each packet is retransmitted until an acknowledgement is received from the AP.

The AP receives data from each sensor, appends useful information such as the timestamp, Received Signal Strength Indicator (RSSI), the Link Quality Indicator (LQI), and records it into a file that can be processed offline.

Firmware update. This application allows reprogramming the entire flash memory of a sensor node over the air, via the AP. Using this mode, any future upgrades in the sensor firmware can be made remotely and since no lane closures are needed, it considerably reduces maintenance costs.

3.3 System design

In order to overcome the measurement challenges described in Section 2.3, sensor casing, system layout, and installation procedure need to be selected carefully.

Sensor casing. In order to withstand large forces in a harsh environment, the sensors must be packaged for durability before installation. The circuit board and the battery are placed in a hard plastic casing as shown in Figure 5. The casing is then filled with fused silica and sealed air tight. This protects the electronics from rain water, oil spills etc on the road and further attenuates interference from sound.

System layout. Figure 6 shows the selected layout. The vehicle detection sensors are set in the standard recommended configuration. There are four arrays of vibration sensors in-

Figure 5: Packaging of the sensors in a sealed case [2].

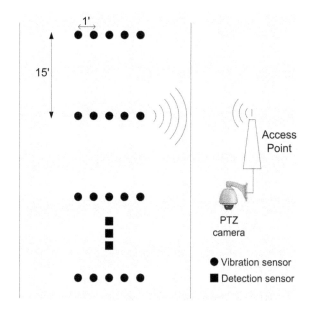

Figure 6: System layout: detection sensors report vehicle detection time and multiple array of vibration sensors report pavement acceleration for load estimation [2].

stalled 15 ft apart, with five sensors in each array. The sensor layout is designed to minimize lane-to-lane interference and maximize the in-lane signal-to-noise ratio. The pavement response at the sensor location reduces exponentially with the distance between the sensor and applied force [11]. Thus we minimize the interference from neighboring lane vehicles by placing the sensors in the middle of each lane as this maximizes the distance between the sensors and neighboring lane vehicles. An additional important benefit is that this placement *minimizes the effect of vehicle wander*. The left and right wheels of a vehicle contribute additively to sensor measurements. Vehicles moving off-centered in the lane will have one wheel closer to the sensors than the other. Therefore, reduction in measurements from one wheel are compensated by the other to ensure that their sum remains almost constant.

Installation procedure. In order to minimize the system cost, the installation procedure must be quick and simple.

To install a sensor in the pavement, we drill a 4-inch diameter hole, approximately $2\frac{1}{4}$ inches deep at the desired location. The sensor is placed in the hole, properly leveled with the earth's surface, and the hole is sealed with fast-drying epoxy [23], as shown in Figure 7. Each sensor can be installed in the road in less than 10 mins. The AP and the PTZ camera are mounted on a 15ft high pole on the side of the road, and don't require any lane closures.

4. EXPERIMENTAL SETUP

Figure 7: Installation procedure for embedding the sensors in the pavement [2].

This section describes deployment challenges and data collection procedure used to test our system.

Deployment challenges. A test system was installed on I-80 W in Pinole, CA, about 300 ft away from an existing WIM station. This WIM station, operated by Caltrans, measures and records weights for every passing truck which we planned to use as ground truth for training and testing our system. However, the data provided by this station turned out to be inaccurate (Figure 18). Renting individual trucks for testing, on the other hand, is extremely expensive. Fortunately, we were able to collect ground truth data from a static weigh station in Cordelia, CA but it required extensive coordination with local and state agencies, and posed additional challenges. Each truck had to be stopped and weighed individually, and required the presence of a California Highway Patrol (CHP) officer. Moreover, the station is located about 25 miles upstream from the wireless WIM in Pinole, and some of the trucks take alternative routes and never arrive at our site. Identification of trucks that reach our site is also very challenging, given the volume of trucks that go over the wireless WIM every day. The trucks also cannot be directed to drive in our installation lane and often traveled in neighboring lanes. All these factors limited the size of our final dataset.

Data collection. Randomly selected class 9 trucks were weighed individually at the static weigh station. These trucks have 3 axles, 1 single axle and 2 tandem axles. Class 9 trucks were chosen because these are the most common trucks on highways and other truck classes are made up of different combinations of these two axle types. For truck identification, pictures of each truck were taken at the station and matched with images collected by the road-side PTZ camera of the wireless WIM. Timestamps provided by the PTZ camera are then used to extract data reported by the sensors:

- *Speed data.* Timestamps from the camera images are matched with the detection sensor timestamps to get the data corresponding to the truck. Each vehicle detection sensor reports both the time of arrival and time of departure of the truck. A pair of sensors (i, j) installed at a fixed known distance (d_{ij}) apart from

each other are used to estimate speed. Given the arrival times t_{ai} and t_{aj} at the two sensors i and j, the speed v is given by $v = \frac{d_{ij}}{|t_{aj}-t_{ai}|}$. The speed can then be used to estimate the length (L) of the vehicle as $L = v(t_{dj} - t_{aj})$, where t_{dj} is the departure time reported by sensor j. These measurements have been shown to be accurate in practice [13].

- *Acceleration data.* The arrival and departure times reported by detection sensors are used to estimate the time window during which the truck passed each array of vibration sensors. This time window is then used to extract the corresponding acceleration reported by each sensor.

- *Temperature data.* Temperature readings reported by vibration sensors around the time of vehicle's arrival are averaged to get a single estimate of pavement temperature around that time.

The collected ground truth data is a very good representation of the distribution of loads, speeds, and pavement temperatures for this site. Axle weights range from 10,000 to 35,000 lbs, speeds vary from 15 to 65 mph, and pavement temperature from 15 to 40°C. In fact, most common WIM standards use only a couple of pre-weighed vehicles at different speeds to verify WIM performance [10, 9]. In order to test the system under different environmental conditions, we collected data on three different days over a span of six months. Most WIM standards finish their testing on a single day. In addition to the ground truth from static weigh station, we also obtained loads reported by the nearby WIM station. This data provides a useful one-on-one comparison between our system and an operational WIM system currently used by the government.

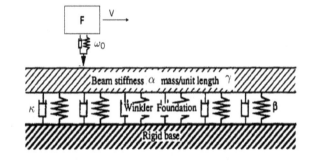

Figure 8: Euler beam model for vehicle-pavement interaction [5].

5. LOAD ESTIMATION

In this section, we propose a model for vehicle-pavement interaction that directly relates pavement acceleration, vehicle speed, and pavement temperature to applied axle load. We then describe the procedure used to extract pavement response due to individual axles from the measured response. We end the section by describing how the model is calibrated for load estimation.

5.1 Pavement-vehicle interaction model

We start by describing the model for pavement acceleration (and displacement) at a constant temperature, and then explain how measurements can be properly compensated for temperature variation. The simplest vehicle-pavement interaction model is a composite one dimensional Euler beam resting on an elastic Winkler foundation as shown in Figure 8 [5, 21]. The vehicle is modeled as a moving force modulated by its suspension system. A typical pavement response due to a moving load is shown in Figure 9. As an axle approaches the pavement is pushed down, but it returns to its original location after the axle has passed. The response of the pavement at any fixed location can be approximated as $y(t) = F\Phi(vt)$ [21], where $y(t)$ is the vertical displacement or deflection of the pavement, and the function $\Phi(\cdot)$ mainly depends on the structural and material properties of the pavement. The model is linear in F, and vehicle speed v just scales the function $\Phi(\cdot)$ in time. This is a simplifying assumption, and in general $\Phi(\cdot)$ has some dependency on v and unknown suspension frequencies of the vehicle [21].

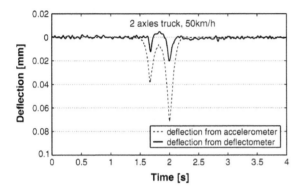

Figure 9: **Example of pavement deflection due to two-axle truck moving at 50 km/h. Image taken from [1].**

Based on typical measured responses (Figure 9) and theory developed in [5, 21], we assume that the shape of pavement response due to a single axle load is closely approximated by a Gaussian function. $\Phi(vt)$, in our model, can be interpreted as the pavement response due to a unit force moving at speed v. Let η be the amplitude of pavement response for a unit force, then $\Phi(t)$ and $y(t)$ can be written as:

$$\Phi(t) = \eta e^{\frac{-t^2}{2\sigma_0^2}},$$
$$y(t) = F\Phi(vt),$$
$$= F\eta e^{\frac{-v^2 t^2}{2\sigma_0^2}},$$
$$y(t) = F\eta e^{\frac{-t^2}{2\sigma^2}}. \tag{1}$$

The last step is obtained by assuming $\sigma = \frac{\sigma_0}{v}$, where σ_0 is the width of pavement response due to a unit force, which depends on pavement properties. Since we measure acceleration and not displacement, we can convert the model into a more appropriate form,

$$a(t) = \ddot{y}(t) = F\ddot{\Phi}(vt),$$
$$= -F\eta\frac{v^2}{\sigma_0^2}\left(1 - \frac{t^2}{\sigma^2}\right)e^{\frac{-t^2}{2\sigma^2}}.$$

Now, let $\Psi(t,\sigma) = -\left(1 - \frac{t^2}{\sigma^2}\right)e^{\frac{-t^2}{2\sigma^2}}$ and $\alpha = \frac{F\eta v^2}{\sigma_0^2}$, and we have the following relation for pavement acceleration due to a single axle load:

$$a(t) = \alpha\Psi(t,\sigma).$$

From the definition of α, we see that

$$F = \frac{\sigma_0^2}{\eta}\frac{\alpha}{v^2} = \beta\frac{\alpha}{v^2}, \tag{2}$$
$$y(t) = \alpha\frac{\sigma_0^2}{v^2}e^{\frac{-t^2}{2\sigma^2}} = \alpha\sigma^2 e^{\frac{-t^2}{2\sigma^2}}.$$

The last step is obtained by combining Equations (2) and (1). The unknowns α and σ can be estimated from the measured acceleration (Section 5.2), but β depends on axle type (single or tandem) and pavement properties, and needs to be calibrated using trucks of known weights (Section 5.3). For a K axle truck, with the ith axle arriving at the sensor at time μ_i and applying a force f_i, the response can be written as the superposition of individual axle responses $(a_i(t))$i.e.

$$a_i(t) = \alpha_i\Psi(t - \mu_i, \sigma_i), \tag{3}$$

$$\boxed{a(t) = \sum_{i=1}^{K}\alpha_i\Psi(t - \mu_i, \sigma_i).} \tag{4}$$

Using a non-linear curve fitting procedure, described in Section 5.2, we estimate α_i, μ_i, and σ_i for each axle. Once these have been estimated, each axle can be treated separately to estimate quantities like individual axle loads (F_i) and pavement displacement $(y_i(t))$ due to each axle,

$$F_i = \beta_i\frac{\alpha_i}{v^2},$$

$$\boxed{y_i(t) = \alpha_i\sigma_i^2 e^{\frac{-(t-\mu_i)^2}{2\sigma_i^2}}.} \tag{5}$$

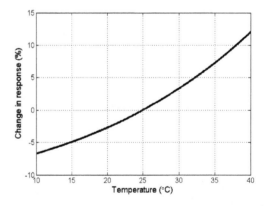

Figure 10: **Percentage change in pavement response with temperature. For the same applied load, pavement acceleration (or displacement) increases with increasing temperature.**

Temperature compensation. The above model is valid for a constant temperature but pavement response for asphalt-concrete layer is highly dependent on temperature. Using the thickness of different layers and material parameters for the pavement at this site, we developed a layered elastic theory (LET) model to simulate the effect of temperature on the pavement response [20]. Figure 10 shows how the pavement acceleration changes with temperature according to the LET model. The plot shows that pavement response can change over 15% with changes in temperature alone and proper temperature compensation is needed for accurate load estimation.

Let $\tau(T)$ be the ratio of the modeled response at 25°C and at temperature T. To compensate for temperature, we normalize all our measurements to the reference temperature of 25°C as $a(t, T = 25°C) = a(t, T)\tau(T)$, where $\tau(T)$ is calculated using the LET model. It can be seen from Equation (4) that $\alpha_i(T = 25) = \alpha_i(T)\tau(T)$, and accordingly

$$F_i = \beta_i \frac{\alpha_i}{v^2}\tau(T). \tag{6}$$

5.2 Extracting individual axle response

In order to extract individual axle response, we follow a two stage process. In the first stage, measurements from multiple sensors are combined to get an average pavement response for the whole vehicle. In the second stage, we fit this response to the model described by Equation (4) and estimate α_i, μ_i, and σ_i for each axle.

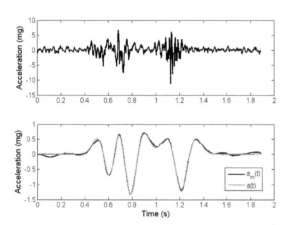

Figure 11: Top plot shows the raw acceleration signal measured by the reference sensor. Bottom plot shows the average pavement response $a_m(t)$ and the fitted response $a(t)$. There are 3 mexican-hat functions in $a(t)$ (at 0.6, 0.8, and 1.2 s resp.), each corresponding to an axle. The response due to last axle is well isolated from the others but the response for the first two axles is not isolated.

Average pavement response. The average pavement response requires aligning the measurements from each sensor. Each signal is first passed through a low pass filter to filter out high frequency noise. The highest amplitude signal is then designated as the reference signal, and signals from all other sensors are time-shifted to align with the reference signal. Let $a_m^k(t)$ be the time-shifted signal for the kth sensor, and I the number of available sensors. Then the average

pavement acceleration $a_m(t)$ can be estimated as:

$$a_m(t) = \frac{1}{I}\sum_{k=1}^{I} a_m^k(t).$$

Figure 11 shows an example of the raw acceleration data from a sensor, and the average pavement response $a_m(t)$. The improvement from filtering and combining signals can be easily seen in the plot. Figure 11 also highlights another important challenge in estimating individual axle loads. Response due to each axle needs to be decoupled and extracted from $a_m(t)$. Because of high speeds and relatively short axle spacings, the trailing axles of a truck arrive at the sensor before the pavement has relaxed from the first axle's load. To extract each $a_i(t)$ from $a_m(t)$, we use the following algorithm.

Curve fitting algorithm. Let $a(t)$ be the modeled response of a K axle truck, given by Equation (4). Let $\epsilon(t)$ be the error between the measured and modeled response for the truck at time t i.e. $\epsilon(t) = (a_m(t) - a(t))$. We can now write the measured response as:

$$a_m(t) = \sum_{i=1}^{K} \alpha_i \Psi(t - \mu_i, \sigma_i) + \epsilon(t). \tag{7}$$

We estimate the unknown parameters $\{\alpha_i\}_{i=1}^{K}$, $\{\sigma_i\}_{i=1}^{K}$ and $\{\mu_i\}_{i=1}^{K}$ by minimizing the mean square error i.e.

$$(\alpha_i^*, \sigma_i^*, \mu_i^*) = \arg\min_{\alpha_i, \sigma_i, \mu_i} \int_{-\infty}^{\infty} (a_m(t) - a(t))^2 dt,$$

$$(\alpha_i^*, \sigma_i^*, \mu_i^*) = \arg\min_{\alpha_i, \sigma_i, \mu_i} \int_{-\infty}^{\infty} \left(a_m(t) - \sum_{i=1}^{K} \alpha_i \Psi(t - \mu_i, \sigma_i)\right)^2 dt.$$

$$\tag{8}$$

This is a non-linear least-squares problem that can be solved using standard techniques. Once the fit is performed, acceleration and displacement corresponding to each axle can be calculated using Equations (3) and (5). Figure 11 shows an example of how good the modeled response fits the measurements.

5.3 Model calibration

Before individual axle loads can be estimated using Equation (6), the parameter β_i needs to be calibrated. In general, β_i is site specific and can depend on axle type but a set of pre-weighed trucks can be used to estimate it. Let N be the number of trucks used in the training data, $\hat{f}_i^n$ be the load estimate for the ith axle of nth truck, f_i^n be the true weight, v_n be the speed, α_i^n be the corresponding fitted parameter α_i^*, and e_i^n be the percentage error associated with the load estimates. The optimal β_i can be calculated by minimizing the mean-square percentage errors for the load estimates,

$$\hat{f}_i^n = \beta_i \frac{\alpha_i^n}{v_n^2} \tau(T), \tag{9}$$

$$e_i^n = \frac{\beta_i \frac{\alpha_i^n}{v_n^2} \tau(T) - f_i^n}{f_i^n} \times 100,$$

$$= (\beta_i \frac{\alpha_i^n}{f_i^n v_n^2} \tau(T) - 1) \times 100,$$

$$\beta_i^* = \arg\min_{\beta} \frac{1}{N} \sum_{i=1}^{N} (e_i^n)^2,$$

$$\boxed{\beta_i^* = \arg\min_{\beta} \sum_{i=1}^{N} (\beta \frac{\alpha_i^n}{f_i^n v_n^2} \tau(T) - 1)^2.} \tag{10}$$

Equation (10) is a standard linear least squares problem and can be solved for β_i^*. Once β_i^* is known, individual axle loads can be estimated using Equation (9).

6. RESULTS AND DISCUSSION

The results discussed in this section serve three goals: verify that the proposed model fits the data well, evaluate the accuracy of wireless WIM, and understand the effect of dynamic component of load on system accuracy.

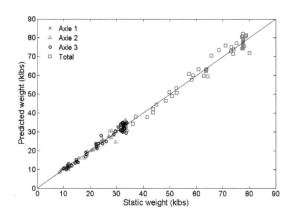

Figure 12: Plot shows the estimated weights against the ground truth static weights.

Model verification. We calibrate the model using the entire set of trucks and examine how closely it explains the data. Figure 12 compares the axle weights estimated by our system with their true weights. The estimated loads track the true loads very closely ($R^2 = 0.99$) but there is one interesting observation. The error in $klbs$[1] increases as the true weight increases. This is, however, by design as percentage errors (e_i^n) are more important for WIM systems, and we calibrate the system to minimize the percentage errors. If error in $klbs$ is minimized, the lighter axles will tend to have much higher percentage errors. Figure 13 shows the estimated probability distribution function of errors for each axle. The means and standard deviations associated with these bell-shaped curves are summarized in Table 1.

[1] klb, also known as kip, is a non-SI unit of force and equals 1000 pounds-force.

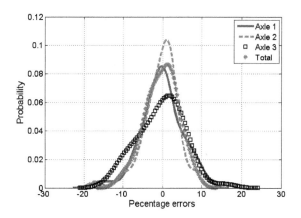

Figure 13: Plot shows the probability distribution of percentage errors in load estimates for each axle and the entire vehicle.

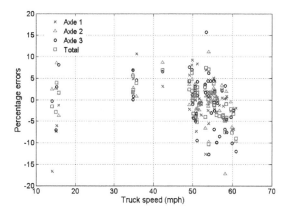

Figure 14: Plot shows the percentage error in load estimates against truck speeds. Errors are statistically uncorrelated to speed.

Figure 14 shows the percentage errors in load estimates at different truck speeds. The errors are uncorrelated to speed, implying that the $\frac{1}{v^2}$ term in the model captures the speed dependence of the pavement response pretty well.

Figure 15 shows the percentage errors of load estimates at different pavement temperatures. The errors are uncorrelated to temperature and compensation $\tau(T)$ captures the effect of pavement temperature well. Figure 16 shows that the errors are much higher when no temperature compensation is used (i.e. $\tau(T) = 1 \ \forall T$). Consistent with pavement models [20], without temperature compensation loads are overestimated at higher temperatures and underestimated estimated at lower temperatures. This is because pavement response for any load is higher at higher temperatures. Quantitatively, the errors for both scenarios are provided in Table 1. Clearly, temperature compensation is a very crucial step in our load estimation algorithm.

Wireless WIM accuracy. For the results above, we use the entire dataset for training our system. For a more realistic evaluation of the system accuracy, we now run 1000

Table 1: Effect of pavement temperature on load estimation. Errors in total weight estimates are below 8.2% at a confidence level of 95% when temperature compensation is applied. When no temperature compensation is used, the 95% error bound on total weight estimate increases to 11.3%.

	Temperature compensation		No compensation	
	Mean Error (%)	Std of errors (%)	Mean Error (%)	Std of errors (%)
Axle 1	-0.27	5.25	-0.44	6.66
Axle 2	-0.22	4.75	-0.39	6.27
Axle 3	-0.33	5.81	-0.43	6.63
Total	-0.19	4.09	-0.33	5.61

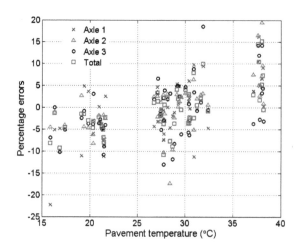

Figure 16: Plot shows the percentage error in load estimates against pavement temperature when temperature compensation is not applied. Errors increase with increase in temperature.

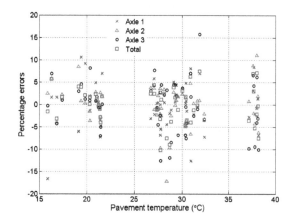

Figure 15: Plot shows the percentage error in load estimates against pavement temperature when measurements are compensated for temperature variation.

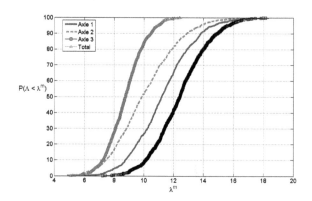

Figure 17: Plot shows cumulative distribution for the LTPP errors from the 1000 trials. Majority of trials pass the LTPP specification for allowed errors.

different training and testing trials. In each trial, we randomly select 26 out of 52 trucks for estimating β_i^* and use it for estimating loads of trucks in the testing set. To judge each trial, we now define a widely used performance measure for WIM systems, called the LTPP error. The Long-Term Pavement Performance (LTPP) specification defines the WIM system error as the 95% confidence bound on error, assuming a normal distribution of errors. Let μ_e^m and σ_e^m be the mean and standard deviation of test set errors for the mth trial. The LTPP error (λ_m) for the mth trial can be calculated as

$$\lambda_m = \max\{|\mu_e^m - 1.96\sigma_e^m|, |\mu_e^m + 1.96\sigma_e^m|\}.$$

Table 2 contains the mean LTPP error ($\bar{\lambda}$) from the 1000 trials and the maximum allowed errors by the LTPP standard. The mean LTPP error in each case is less than the allowed error. Figure 17 shows the cumulative distribution of λ^m. The LTPP error is less than the maximum allowed error for majority of the trials.

We now provide a one-on-one comparison of wireless WIM with the nearby WIM station. Figure 18 shows the percentage errors in loads reported by the Caltrans station. Due to technical difficulties, weights from this station were not available for one of our testing days, thus reducing the dataset for comparison to 31 trucks. Table 2 compares the

accuracy of both systems. The wireless WIM clearly outperforms the conventional WIM in every category. The conventional WIM meets the required LTPP accuracy levels for only axle 1, and fails in all other cases. It is worth noticing in Figure 19 that even a single lane of wireless WIM outperforms the conventional WIM (except for Axle 1).

Effect of dynamic component. Road roughness and the vehicle suspension system cause the applied load F to be different from the static load F_s that we are interested in estimating. In general, the instantaneous applied load can be written as $F = F_s + F_d \sum_i cos(\omega_i t)$, where ω_i depends on the suspension system and F_d is usually within 30% of F_s [5]. To reduce the error ($F - F_s$) or the dynamic component, we average measurements from multiple arrays. Figure 19 shows how the LTPP error decreases when the number of arrays increase. Each array essentially measures the static load with some uncertainty, and by averaging multiple measurements we reduce the amount of uncertainty in our load

Table 2: Comparison of mean LTPP errors between our system and the nearby conventional WIM. The errors for the conventional WIM are much higher than the errors allowed by the LTPP standard.

	Wireless WIM error	Conventional WIM error	Maximum allowed error
Axle 1	11.29	18.67	20
Axle 2	10.07	26.49	15
Axle 3	12.44	37.35	15
Total	8.76	23.23	10

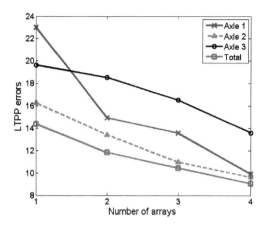

Figure 19: Plot shows that errors in static loads decrease as the number of arrays increase. The more the number of arrays, the better we filter out the dynamic component.

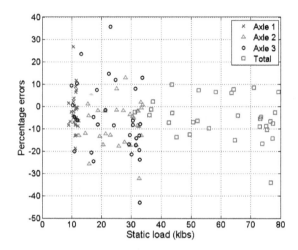

Figure 18: Plot shows errors in load estimates for the nearby WIM system. These are much higher than expected and fail to meet the LTPP standard.

estimate. Adding more arrays to the system could improve the system accuracy, but the system achieves the required LTPP accuracy with 4 arrays.

7. CONCLUSIONS AND FUTURE WORK

Conclusions. A wireless WIM system that uses pavement vibrations to estimate axle loads was built and tested in this study. The wireless vibration sensor designed for this system is capable of measuring very small pavement vibrations in an extremely noisy environment. A new pavement-vehicle interaction model that relates applied load to pavement vibrations, temperature, and speed of the vehicle was also developed and evaluated. The system was tested on a real highway and passed the WIM accuracy standards. The system achieved the required accuracy of 15% for individual axle loads and 10% for total load, and outperformed a nearby conventional WIM system. As part of load estimation, the system also estimates the pavement deflection, and therefore can be used for long-term pavement monitoring.

Future work. Even though we have provided a proof-of-concept for the wireless WIM, more work needs to be done before the system can be widely used. The following are some avenues for future work.

- **In-sensor processing.** As mentioned in Section 3.1, the lifetime of the vibration sensors is only 5 months

because they continuously transmit all the raw data. One efficient way to reduce the current consumption of the sensor is to only send out processed data. This can be done by implementing a version of the fitting algorithm inside the sensor and only sending the fitted coefficients. This should immediately increase the lifetime of the sensor to a few years. The challenge, however, is to preserve the accuracy of the system while reducing the current consumption. To learn about the trade-off between current consumption and system accuracy, we simulated the in-sensor processing of data. Instead of combining the raw data from all sensors and then using the fitting algorithm, we apply the fitting algorithm to individual sensor data and average the fitted coefficients to get the average pavement response. The load estimates based on this procedure are shown in Figure 20. The LTPP errors were 10.33, 12.09, 12.36, and 9.45 percent respectively for axle 1, 2, 3, and the total weight. These are very similar to our previous results and still pass the accuracy levels defined by the LTPP specification. The in-sensor fitting algorithm needs to be implemented and tested.

- **Testing on different pavements.** Pavement response is highly dependent on pavement's structural and material properties. More tests need to be done using different kinds of pavements to understand the effect of pavement properties on the load estimation procedure.

- **Pavement monitoring.** We plan on working with pavement engineers to use this system as a pavement monitoring tool. Long-term pavement monitoring systems are practically non-existent currently but many interesting problems can be studied using such systems.

8. ACKNOWLEDGEMENTS

We would like to thank the California Department of Transportation for letting us install the system near their oper-

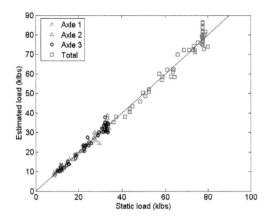

Figure 20: Expected results of load estimation after in-sensor processing. The results are very similar to Figure 12

ational WIM, and California Highway Patrol at Cordelia for helping us collect ground truth data for trucks. Special thanks to Ben Wild for his contributions to the load estimation algorithm. This project was funded by the National Science Foundation under Award Number IIP-0945919.

9. REFERENCES

[1] M. Arraigada, M. Partl, S. Angelone, and F. Martinez. Evaluation of accelerometers to determine pavement deflections under traffic loads. *Materials and Structures*, 42:779–790, 2009.

[2] R. Bajwa, R. Rajagopal, P. Varaiya, and R. Kavaler. In-pavement wireless sensor network for vehicle classification. In *Information Processing in Sensor Networks (IPSN), 2011 10th International Conference on*, pages 85 –96, april 2011.

[3] P. Burnos, J. Gajda, P. Piwowar, R. Sroka, M. Stencel, and T. Żegleń. Accurate weighing of moving vehicles. *Metrology and Measurement Systems*, 14(4):507–516, 2007.

[4] R. Bushman and A. Pratt. Weigh in motion technology–economics and performance. In *Presentation on the North American Travel Monitoring Exhibition and Conference (NATMEC). Charlotte, North Carolina*, 1998.

[5] D. Cebon. *Handbook of Vehicle-Road Interaction*. Swets and Zeitlinger Publishers, 1999.

[6] M. Ceriotti, L. Mottola, G. Picco, A. Murphy, S. Guna, M. Corra, M. Pozzi, D. Zonta, and P. Zanon. Monitoring heritage buildings with wireless sensor networks: The Torre Aquila deployment. In *Information Processing in Sensor Networks, 2009. IPSN 2009. International Conference on*, pages 277–288. IEEE, 2009.

[7] S. Y. Cheung, S. Coleri, B. Dundar, S. Ganesh, C.-W. Tan, and P. Varaiya. Traffic measurement and vehicle classification with single magnetic sensor. *Transportation Research Record: Journal of the Transportation Research Board*, 1917:173–181, 2006.

[8] Colibrys, Inc, accelero.us@colibrys.com. *MEMS Capacitive Accelerometers Datasheet MS9000.D.*

[9] A. Designation. E 1318-94, standard specifications for highway weigh-in-motion (wim) systems with user requirements and test methods. American Society for Testing and Materials, 1994.

[10] Federal Highway Administration, U.S. Department of Transportation. *Traffic Monitoring Guide*, May 2001.

[11] M. C. Fehler. *Seismic Wave Propagation and Scattering in the Heterogenous Earth*. Springer, 2009.

[12] M. Gindy, H. H. Nassif, and J. Velde. Bridge displacement estimates from measured acceleration records. *Transportation Research Record: Journal of the Transportation Research Board*, 2028(-1):136–145, 2007.

[13] A. Haoui, R. Kavaler, and P. Varaiya. Wireless magnetic sensors for traffic surveillance. *Transportation Research C*, 16(3):294–306, 2008.

[14] S. Kim, S. Pakzad, D. Culler, J. Demmel, G. Fenves, S. Glaser, and M. Turon. Health monitoring of civil infrastructures using wireless sensor networks. In *IPSN '07: Proceedings of the 6th international conference on Information processing in sensor networks*, pages 254–263, New York, NY, USA, 2007. ACM.

[15] A. N. Knaian. A wireless sensor network for smart roadbeds and intelligent transportation systems. Master's thesis, Massachusetts Institute of Technology, 2000.

[16] M. Li and Y. Liu. Underground structure monitoring with wireless sensor networks. In *Proceedings of the 6th international conference on Information processing in sensor networks*, pages 69–78. ACM, 2007.

[17] C. Liu, L. Guo, J. Li, and X. Chen. Weigh-in-motion (wim) sensor based on em resonant measurements. In *Antennas and Propagation Society International Symposium, 2007 IEEE*, pages 561–564. IEEE, 2007.

[18] R. B. Malla, A. Sen, and N. W. Garrick. A special fiber optic sensor for measuring wheel loads of vehicles on highways. *Sensors*, 8(4):2551–2568, 2008.

[19] C. Merzbacher, A. Kersey, and E. Friebele. Fiber optic sensors in concrete structures: a review. *Smart materials and structures*, 5:196, 1996.

[20] D. Parl, N. Buch, and K. Chatti. Effective layer temperature prediction model and temperature correction via falling weight deflectometer deflections. *Transportation Research Record: Journal of the Transportation Research Board*, 1764:97–111, 2001.

[21] R. Rajagopal. *Large Monitoring Systems: Data Analysis, Deployment and Design*. PhD thesis, University of California, Berkeley, 2009.

[22] H. Sawant, J. Tan, and Q. Yang. A sensor networked approach for intelligent transportation systems. In *Intelligent Robots and Systems, 2004. (IROS 2004). Proceedings. 2004 IEEE/RSJ International Conference on*, volume 2, pages 1796 – 1801 vol.2, 2004.

[23] Sensys Networks, Inc, 2650 9th Street, Berkeley CA 94710. *The Sensys Wireless_{TM} Vehicle Detection System*, 1.1 edition.

FixtureFinder: Discovering the Existence of Electrical and Water Fixtures

Vijay Srinivasan[*]
Samsung Research America
75 W. Plumeria Dr
San Jose, CA, USA
v.srinivasan@sisa.samsung.com

John Stankovic and Kamin Whitehouse
Dept of Computer Science
University of Virginia
Charlottesville, VA, USA
{stankovic, whitehouse}@cs.virginia.edu

ABSTRACT

The monitoring of electrical and water fixtures in the home is being applied for a variety of "smart home" applications, such as recognizing activities of daily living (ADLs) or conserving energy or water usage. Fixture monitoring techniques generally fall into two categories: fixture recognition and fixture disaggregation. However, existing techniques require users to explicitly identify each individual fixture, either by placing a sensor on it or by manually creating training data for it. In this paper, we present a new *fixture discovery* system that automatically infers the existence of electrical and water fixtures in the home. We call the system *FixtureFinder*. The basic idea is to use *data fusion* between the smart meters and other sensors or infrastructure already in the home, such as the home security or automation system, and to find repeating patterns in the fused data stream. To evaluate FixtureFinder, we deployed the system into 4 different homes for 7-10 days of data collection. Our results show that FixtureFinder is able to identify and differentiate major light and water fixtures in less than 10 days, including multiple copies of light bulbs and sinks that have identical power/water profiles.

Categories and Subject Descriptors

C.3 [**Special-Purpose and Application-Based Systems**]: Real-time and Embedded Systems

Keywords

Fixture Discovery, Smart Homes, Data Fusion, Smart Meters, Disaggregation

1. INTRODUCTION

Over the past several decades, several new technologies have emerged to monitor the use of electrical and water fixtures in the home. This information is being applied for a

---

[*]This work was performed while the author was at the University of Virginia.

variety of "smart home" applications, such as recognizing activities of daily living (ADLs) or conserving energy or water usage.

Fixture monitoring techniques generally fall into two categories. The first category includes *fixture recognition* techniques, that identify when a particular fixture is turned on or off. For example, the ElectriSense [10] and HydroSense [7] systems attach a sensor to a wall socket or hose bib to monitor high frequency noise in the voltage and water pressure, respectively. The user trains the system by manually turning fixtures on or off so that the system can learn each fixture's noise profile. Then, the system automatically recognizes those fixtures each time they are used in the future. The second category includes *fixture disaggregation* techniques, that identify how much energy or water is used by each individual fixture. For example, the Viridiscope [17] and NAWMS [16] systems attach a sensor to each electrical or water fixture to recognize when they are used, and also use a smart meter on the electrical or water mains to monitor aggregate energy/water usage in the entire house. Based on the assumption that the total energy/water usage of the home is equal to the sum of energy/water usage of individual fixtures, these systems learn the quantity of energy or water used by the individual fixtures. However, all of these techniques have one key limitation: they require an initialization phase where the user must first identify the individual fixtures, either by manually creating training data for each fixture, or by placing a sensor on each fixture.

We present a new *fixture discovery* system that automatically infers the existence of electrical and water fixtures in the home. Many major appliances are distinctive enough to be discovered through the smart meter data alone, due to their periodicity (e.g. refrigerators and space heaters [3]) or a predictable progression through multiple modes of operation (e.g. dishwashers and washing machines [22]). However, small, simple fixtures tend to be much less distinctive and can easily be buried in the noise of other, simultaneous fixtures. Furthermore, power/water meter data alone cannot distinguish between multiple, identical fixtures in a home such as 60W light bulbs or bathroom sinks. To address this problem, we use *data fusion* between the smart meters and other sensors or infrastructure already in the home, such as the home security or home automation system. Then, we search for repeating patterns in this fused data stream to uncover the existence of small fixtures, and to differentiate between multiple, identical fixtures. For example, sink activity may be highly correlated with motion sensor data from the bathroom and the home water meter data; light fixture activity in the living room may be correlated with the home power meter data and light sensor data from the living room. The basic insight behind our approach is that every fixture has a distinctive profile in the home, even if it is not distinctive in the smart meter or ambient sensor data alone. By fusing multiple data streams, we are able to uncover *multi-modal fixture profiles* that are not apparent in the smart meter or ambient sensor data alone.

In this paper, we present *FixtureFinder*, a prototype of a complete fixture discovery system. Our current prototype focuses on light fixtures, sinks, and toilets. These fixtures are among the most difficult to discover because of their non-distinctive power/water profiles, and because numerous copies of each are likely to be found in most homes. Thus, our demonstration on these fixtures provides a proof-of-concept for the basic principles presented in this paper. Our prototype performs data fusion of smart meters with typical security and home automation sensors, since such sensors are already deployed in over 32 million homes in the US [21]. By combining commercial home sensors with the smart power and water meters that are already widely deployed by utility companies [1], FixtureFinder can enable fixture recognition and disaggregation across millions of homes, without requiring an initialization phase where a person manually identifies the individual fixtures.

FixtureFinder uses two aspects of the motion sensors typically found in home security and automation systems: the detection of infrared activity and the detection of ambient light levels (many motion detectors contain sensors in the visible light spectrum for calibration purposes). Using this data, FixtureFinder performs four steps to recognize light and water fixtures: (1) it detects all rising edges and falling edges in the four data streams: power, water, motion, and light; (2) it fuses the data streams by identifying pairs of co-temporal edges in different data streams; (3) it uses clustering algorithms to recognize repeating patterns of multi-modal pairs, and uses Bayesian matching to select only those rising/falling edges that have a matching falling/rising edge with the same multi-modal profile; (4) it clusters all discovered ON-OFF events based on their multi-modal profile to discover the unique fixtures in a home. Unlike fixture recognition, the goal of fixture discovery is not to recognize every ON/OFF event but rather to select only those events that are very likely not to be caused by spurious noise. Once a set of such events is recognized, it can be used to create a training set for existing fixture recognition or disaggregation systems such as ElectriSense and Viridiscope. In this paper, we show how the principles and algorithms behind Fixture-Finder can also be applied for fixture recognition and disaggregation. To our knowledge, this is the first system that can automatically discover the presence of small, simple fixtures; that can perform fixture recognition; and that can disaggregate power and water usage, all in a completely unsupervised fashion.

To evaluate FixtureFinder, we deployed between 25-40 sensors in 4 different homes for 7-10 days of data collection. The sensors included a whole-house power meter and water meter, a motion and light sensor in every room, and ground-truth sensors on light and water fixtures in the home. Using this data, we demonstrate that FixtureFinder is able to discover all water fixtures and 37 out of 41 light fixtures monitored in less than 10 days, including multiple copies of light bulbs and sinks that have identical power/water

profiles. The 4 light fixtures that were not detected were specialized task lighting such as under-cabinet lights that were not heavily used. FixtureFinder was able to recognize fixture usage events and disaggregate water and electrical usage with about 90% accuracy.

2. RELATED WORK

Fixture monitoring generally falls into two categories: fixture recognition and fixture disaggregation. Some existing systems in these two categories are built upon principles that could in theory also be used for fixture discovery, but to date this potential has not been fully explored for any existing system. Below, we describe examples of both types of systems, touching on their potential to discover fixtures where appropriate.

2.1 Fixture Recognition

Fixture recognition systems identify when a particular fixture is turned on or off. Perhaps the most well-known approach for fixture recognition is *non-intrusive appliance load monitoring (NIALM)* [11], which can be used to recognize the usage of electrical fixtures in the home based on their power signatures. These signatures can be extracted using only a single power meter, which is already available in many homes today [1]. Some appliances have a unique profile of real and reactive power, while other appliances such as washing machines and dishwashers exhibit characteristic electrical patterns over time. When a home contains multiple similar appliances, however, NIALM techniques cannot identify *which* appliance is being used. Furthermore, due to low power state transitions from complex appliances such as the television or the HVAC system, NIALM techniques are not effective for small fixtures such as electric lights that exhibit constant, low power values [11]. In theory, NIALM signatures can be used to automatically discover major appliances [22]. However, this approach would require a large database with the electrical signatures of every appliance ever manufactured. Despite over two decades of discussion, no such database has been created and, despite some recent home energy data sets [2, 18], to our knowledge there is no current effort to create one. Furthermore, the number of manufactured appliances is enormous, and comparing a noisy electrical signal against a large space of electrical signatures is likely to produce spurious detections of appliances that do not exist. Further investigation into the potential of this approach is needed.

Approaches similar to NIALM have also been developed to recognize water fixtures. For example, one system uses flow signatures, such as flow rate, flow duration and, in the case of washing machines and dishwashers, patterns of flow to identify types of fixtures and appliances [20]. Another system uses patterns in the presence or absence of flow in both water pipes and drain pipes [6], as detected by microphones installed in the basement. These systems achieve high accuracy in recognizing high consumption appliances, but low accuracy in differentiating between different instances of the same fixture category such as different instances of identical sinks, toilets, or showers in the same home.

Recently, new solutions have been developed to recognize fixtures based on noise profiles in the power or water lines. For example, two systems use an easy-to-install, plug-in sensor that leverages unique high frequency EMI(Electromagnetic Interference) signals on the power line to recognize electrical fixtures. The first system called Flick-of-a-switch [24] can recognize mechanically switched appliances while the second system called ElectriSense [10] can detect fixtures that use switched-mode power supplies (SMPS) such as low-voltage electronics or CFL bulbs. Similarly, HydroSense [8] samples a water pressure sensor at 500Hz from anywhere in the piping system, such as a hose bib outside the home. The system recognizes water fixtures based on the "water hammer" signature caused when a fixture is turned on or off. These three approaches can differentiate between multiple, identical fixtures such as light bulbs, sinks, and toilets. However, they all require users to manually train the system by labeling ON and OFF events for every single fixture. If fixtures are added or moved throughout the house, training must be performed again. The ElectriSense signatures may be persistent across houses, and the authors suggest that a large database of such signatures would be sufficient for fixture discovery. However, this assertion must still be fully explored, and is subject to many of the same challenges as the NIALM approach discussed above.

2.2 Fixture Disaggregation

Fixture disaggregation systems identify how much energy or water is used by each individual fixture. The simplest approach to measure power and water usage at individual fixtures is to place a sensor on each one [13]. This approach is sometimes called *direct sensing*, and requires sensors that can directly be integrated into pipes or electrical wiring, which can be expensive to install in terms of both hardware and installation time. Alternatively, *indirect sensing* approaches fuse data from smart meters with sensors placed on or near each appliance. For example, Viridiscope [17] uses one specialized sensor node per appliance to measure light, acoustic, and/or magnetic field changes, and tries to correlate the intensity of the indirect measurement with the amount of power used by the appliance. This is performed through a global calibration process based on the assumption that all fixtures are instrumented, and that the whole house power demand is equal to the sum of the individual fixtures. Viridiscope makes a firm assumption that each fixture being monitored is paired with a different sensor: if any sensor's magnetic field, acoustic, or light values are strongly influenced by more than one fixture, the system would treat them as a single fixture and would produce an incorrect calibration function. FixtureFinder provides the mathematical machinery (in the form of Bayesian clustering and matching algorithms) to help Viridiscope dissociate two or more fixtures detected by the same sensor, and to combine a single fixture that is being detected by multiple sensors.

The principles underlying Viridiscope have also been demonstrated for water systems, where accelerometers were used on the pipes to measure vibration and a centralized water meter was used on the water mains [16]. Several other, similar techniques have been proposed for power or water disaggregation [9, 14, 26]. However, these techniques all require a single sensor per fixture, and sometimes even additional sensors internal to the power and water infrastructure. The goal of FixtureFinder is to automatically discover fixtures based on sensors and infrastructure that is already present in the home, such as security systems or home automation sensors, that were not deployed with the explicit purpose of fixture disaggregation.

FixtureFinder builds on earlier results in water disaggregation by the authors, that were published at a workshop [27]. This paper focuses on the fixture discovery aspects of that work, and generalizes the solution to include both electrical and water fixtures.

In theory, fixture recognition and fixture disaggregation techniques could be used in combination. For example, the user could install an ElectriSense sensor to measure noise on the electrical lines. After a manual training process, the ElectriSense system could recognize when each appliance is used, and the Viridiscope system could use that information to disaggregate their individual energy usage levels. FixtureFinder is also expected to work in cooperation with systems like these, in order to avoid the need to explicitly add sensors or manually create training data for each fixture.

3. APPROACH OVERVIEW

The goal of the FixtureFinder algorithm is to combine smart meters with in-home sensors to form a fused data stream, and to discover frequently repeating patterns within that stream. For example, it will detect when a 5 liter/minute water flow repeatedly co-occurs with activity in a particular motion sensor. We call these patterns multi-modal fixture profiles, because they represent the signature of a fixture's usage as viewed by multiple sensor types simultaneously. FixtureFinder's mathematical machinery is based on two underlying insights: 1) the usage of a fixture often has a repeating signature in multiple different sensor streams simultaneously, and 2) the ON and OFF events of a fixture come in pairs. Additional states other than ON and OFF could be incorporated into Step III without loss of generality, but FixtureFinder does not yet address multi-state fixtures. The FixtureFinder algorithm has four Steps. In Step I, it uses edge detection to compute a sequence of timestamped *rising and falling edges* in each data stream. In Step II, data streams are fused by finding events in multiple streams that frequently co-occur in time, and combining them to creating *edge pairs*. This fusion step eliminates spurious edges that exist in only one stream, but are not observed in the other data streams as expected. In Step III, the edge pairs are matched in rising/falling sequences called *usage events*, and all edge pairs that do not successfully match are discarded. This matching process eliminates additional spurious edges that do not correspond to a fixture ON or OFF event. In Step IV, the usage events are clustered into groups that have similar multi-modal profiles. These clusters represent the fixtures that have been discovered.

Algorithm 1 shows the mathematical formalism behind the four main steps of the FixtureFinder algorithm. The variables shown in bold indicate the output of each step. The final output of Step IV is thus the **Fixture Set**. The inputs to the algorithm are two sensor streams S^i, S^j from sources i and j respectively; however, Steps II, III, and IV could be extended in the future to handle more than two sensor streams. We expand on algorithm 1 below and explain the intuition behind each step in detail.

Step I: Event Detection: For every sensor i in the system that produces a time series $S^i = s_1^i, s_2^i, s_3^i, ..., s_t^i$, the first step performed by FixtureFinder is to apply an edge detection algorithm on S^i to produce a set of **Edges** E^i. Lines 1:2 in algorithm 1 show Step I. Each edge $e^i = (m^i, t^i) \in E^i$ is an ordered pair, where m^i is the magnitude of the edge and t^i is the timestamp of the edge. If $m^i > 0$ then e^i is

---

Algorithm 1 Steps in the FixtureFinder algorithm

Inputs: Sensor streams S^i, S^j

Event Detection:
1: **Edges** $E^i = [M^i \ T^i] \leftarrow \text{EdgeDetect}(S^i)$
2: **Edges** $E^j = [M^j \ T^j] \leftarrow \text{EdgeDetect}(S^j)$

Data Fusion:
3: **Edge Pairs** $P^{i,j} = \{\}$
4: **for all** edge pairs (e^i, e^j), where $(e^i = (m^i, t^i) \in E^i) \wedge (e^j = (m^j, t^j) \in E^j)$ **do**
5:     **if** $(|t^i - t^j| < T \wedge (m^i * m^j) > 0)$ **then**
6:         Add (e^i, e^j) to $P^{i,j}$
7:     **end if**
8: **end for**

Matching:
9: Edge Cluster $C^i \leftarrow \text{Cluster}(M^i)$
10: Edge Cluster $C^j \leftarrow \text{Cluster}(M^j)$
11: **for all** edge pairs $p = (e^i, e^j) \in P^{i,j}$ **do**
12:     Edge pair probability $P(p) = \sum\limits_{c^i \in C^i} \sum\limits_{c^j \in C^j} P(e^i|c^i) * P(e^j|c^j) * P(c^i|c^j) * P(c^j)$
13: **end for**
14: **for all** (p_x, p_y), where $(p_x = (e_x^i, e_x^j) \in P^{i,j}) \wedge (p_y = (e_y^i, e_y^j) \in P^{i,j})$ **do**
15:     Pair match probability $P(p_x, p_y) = (\sum\limits_{c^i \in C^i} P(e_x^i|c^i) * P(-e_y^i|c^i)) * (\sum\limits_{c^j \in C^j} P(e_x^j|c^j) * P(-e_y^j|c^j))$
16:     Pair match weight $W(p_x, p_y) = -log(P(p_x) * P(p_y) * P(p_x, p_y))$
17: **end for**
18: **Usage Events** $F^{i,j} = [E_{on}^i \ E_{off}^i \ E_{on}^j \ E_{off}^j] \leftarrow \text{Min Cost Bipartite Matching}(W)$

Fixture Discovery:
19: **Fixture set** $\leftarrow \text{Cluster}([M_{on}^i \ M_{on}^j])$
20: **return Fixture Set**

---

a *rising edge*, otherwise it is a *falling edge*. Every type of sensor will produce a stream with a different structure, and will therefore require a different type of edge detection algorithm with parameters set appropriately by the user. In sections 3.1 and 3.2, we discuss the particular edge detection approaches used for each sensor type.

Step II: Data Fusion: FixtureFinder creates a set of **Edge Pairs** $P^{i,j}$ by combining every pair of edges that are generated by the two sensor modalities, that are both rising or falling edges, and that co-occur in time. Lines 3:8 in algorithm 1 show Step II of the FixtureFinder algorithm. More specifically, for every pair of edges $e^i = (m^i, t^i)$ and $e^j = (m^j, t^j)$ from the two streams S^i and S^j respectively, FixtureFinder creates a new *edge pair* $p = (e^i, e^j)$ if m^i and m^j have the same sign (i.e. both rising or both falling) and $|t^i - t^j| < T$, where T is a time windowing parameter that defines how close a pair of edges must be. Any edge that does not co-occur with an edge from another data stream is not used to create an edge pair, and is therefore not considered further.

The value of T depends on the sampling rate of the sensors, and possibly on any time synchronization errors between the sensors. Due to a noisy data stream S^j or simultaneous human activity in the home, we frequently pair a single edge e^i from one stream S^i to multiple noisy edges e^j from S^j that occur within time window T; in Step III, we eliminate noisy edge pairs by only retaining frequently oc-

curring edge pairs that can be successfully matched to edge pairs of the opposite polarity.

Step III: Matching: Once all edge pairs are created, FixtureFinder matches rising edge pairs p_x with falling edge pairs p_y in order to create multi-modal fixture **Usage Events** $F^{i,j}$. Lines 9:18 in algorithm 1 show Step III of the Fixture-Finder algorithm. First (in lines 9:17), we compute a weight function $W(p_x, p_y)$ between any two edge pairs p_x and p_y from set $P^{i,j}$; the weight function is designed to be very low if the two edge pairs are highly likely to be from a single fixture's ON-OFF event. A min-cost, bipartite matching algorithm [19] is then used to match edge pairs based on W, and each edge pair can only be matched once; any unmatched edge pairs are thus eliminated as noise.

We compute the weight function $W(p_x, p_y)$ (line 16) for the matching algorithm based on two probability functions: (i) the probabilities $P(p_x)$ and $P(p_y)$ that the individual edge pairs p_x and p_y are created as a result of frequent fixture usage and not as a result of noise, and (ii) the probability $P(p_x, p_y)$ that both edge pairs are from the same fixture's ON-OFF event. To compute the edge pair probabilities (i) and (ii), we first cluster the edges E^i from each sensor i based only on their magnitudes M^i to a set of clusters C^i, as seen in lines 9:10. We use a soft clustering algorithm to obtain the probabilities $P(e^i|c^i)$ that any edge $e^i \in E^i$ belongs to any cluster $c^i \in C^i$. The intuition is that each fixture generates a unique edge cluster combination (c^i, c^j) in two data streams.

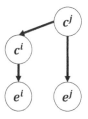

Figure 1: Bayesian network used to compute $P(e^i, e^j)$ for edges e^i and e^j from sensors i and j respectively.

Probability (i) is then computed using the equation in line 13, which follows from our simple Bayesian network formulation shown in figure 1. Observed edges e^i and e^j are dependent on hidden clusters c^i and c^j respectively; clusters c^i and c^j co-occur whenever the underlying fixture generating these two clusters of events is triggered. In line 13, $P(c^j)$ is the fraction of events in cluster c^j relative to other clusters, and $P(c^i|c^j)$ is the fraction of events in c^j that are paired with events in c^i. In line 15, we compute probability (ii) as the probability that both edge pairs are from the same edge cluster creating the rising edge pair.

Before the matching algorithm is executed in line 18, certain matches are eliminated by setting their weight to zero, including

- any match where the rising edge occurs after the falling edge.
- any match where, before the falling edge occurs, the total power or water usage drops below the magnitude of the rising edge.

This last condition is designed to avoid matches where, for example, it appears that a sink is turned on and off 2 minutes apart, but during that interval, the total water flow actually dropped to zero. After the matching process is complete, any unmatched edge pair is not included in a usage event and is therefore no longer considered. The set of matched fixture usage events $F^{i,j}$ thus consists of multi-modal rising (E_{on}^i, E_{on}^j) and falling edges (E_{off}^i, E_{off}^j) from both sensor streams S^i and S^j.

Step IV: Fixture Discovery: Once all usage events $F^{i,j}$ are created, FixtureFinder clusters them based on the multi-modal profile, i.e. the magnitudes of rising edge values from the two fused data streams ($[M_{on}^i \ M_{on}^j]$). Step 19 shows the fixture discovery step; every cluster produced represents a discovered fixture, and the usage events associated with that cluster represent instances when that fixture was used. It is important to note that the fixtures discovered in Step IV represent only those fixtures with a multi-modal profile in sensor streams S^i and S^j, such as the whole house power meter and the light sensor in the living room; to discover fixtures in other rooms such as the kitchen, we run the fixture finder algorithm on other pairs of sensor streams, such as the whole house power meter and a light sensor from the kitchen.

3.1 Case Study: Light Fixture Discovery

In the first case study, FixtureFinder combines the whole-house smart power meter with ambient light sensors to discover light fixtures, infer their nominal wattage values and usage times. We considered other sensor pairings such as the smart power meter and ambient motion sensors, but found that the false positive rate in this pairing was too high to accurately identify light fixture events; in the future, we plan to include more than two sensor streams including motion and other sensors to improve accuracy.

We assume that each room or area in the home has one light sensor. When we observe light edges in multiple light sensors simultaneously with the same polarity, we only retain the light edge with maximum intensity, since that edge is most likely from the sensor in the same room as the light fixture. Finally, we independently apply the FixtureFinder algorithm 1 on each light sensor paired with the whole-house power meter to discover the individual light fixtures in each room.

Figure 2 shows an example of this process using real data traces from a whole house power meter and a bedroom light sensor, on typical day from 6AM to 4PM. The top box shows the two true light fixture ON-OFF events observed during the time period shown. The power meter data (right side) and bedroom light sensor data (left side) are both used to generate edges. On the left side, we show the light edges created by a simple window-based edge detection algorithm and also the effect of applying additional filters (explained in detail below) to eliminate spurious edges caused due to human movement or natural light changes. In both the light sensor and power meter data, a large number of spurious edges are difficult to differentiate from the true fixture usage events shown on top. By fusing the two data streams and looking for matched ON/OFF events, two true light usage events are discovered (top).

To perform Step I, we choose edge detection algorithms based on the characteristics of the power and light data. Certain major appliances such as HVAC are very salient in the power trace (right side of figure), but small fixtures such as light bulbs are buried in the noise. Furthermore, many low power noisy events occur within 2-3 seconds of each other while a few light fixtures take more than a second for a full edge transition. These two cases can be difficult to differentiate due to the 1Hz sampling frequency of the TED power meter. For this reason, we must use a very aggressive edge detection algorithm that finds all edges besides very low intensity edges (noise), or edges that rise too slowly (most likely because they are aggregates of smaller edges). Specifically, we apply a custom sliding window technique that detects all power edges with at least a minimum intensity dP and a maximum time window bound $maxwinP$ set to 5 seconds.

We use the same sliding window technique to find edges in the ambient light data. Most changes due to natural lighting result in gradual changes, and are eliminated using our window-based edge detection algorithm which only looks for high intensity edges within a short time window. As seen on the left side of the figure, the window-based edge detection still produces a very large amount of false edges due to shadows and partial cloudiness. We use two key insights to differentiate artificial lighting from the noise natural lighting:

- Lights are not turned on and off very quickly.
- Lights are not turned on and off repeatedly for long periods of time.

Thus, any highly frequent or very rapid or very gradual edges are filtered.

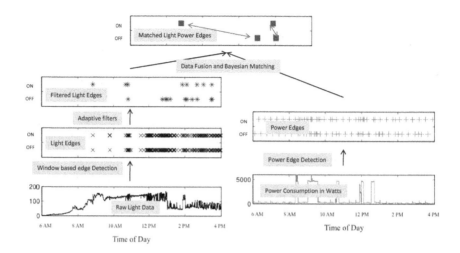

Figure 2: These data traces are from a bedroom light sensor and whole house power meter from 6AM to 4PM in House 2. FixtureFinder eliminates false positive light and power edges by performing data fusion and matching.

In Step II, we chose a parameter value $T = 12 seconds$ for the data fusion to account for time synchronization errors and delays in observing the power edges in the off-the-shelf power meter (caused due to transmission delays on the noisy power line infrastructure).

In Step III we chose Quality Threshold Clustering [12] as our clustering algorithm to generate the edge clusters from each sensor stream. The advantage of Quality threshold clustering is that it allows us to control the *maximum difference* between any two edges in a given edge cluster; this allows us to use prior knowledge about the typical error distribution of light fixture edges in a home. Based on empirical experiments, instead of using a fixed maximum difference, we modified the quality threshold algorithm to use a maximum *relative difference* (difference between two edges as a proportion of the smaller of the two edges); we used a maximum relative difference of 0.25 in our deployments. Because Quality Threshold clustering is a hard clustering approach, we estimate cluster membership probabilities of edges $p(e^i|c^i)$ by fitting a normal distribution to each edge cluster as an approximation. In Step IV, we again use the Quality Threshold Clustering algorithm with a maximum relative difference of 0.25 to generate our final set of fixtures from the multi-modal fixture usage events.

3.2 Case Study: Water Fixture Discovery

In the second case study, FixtureFinder combines the smart water meter with motion sensors to discover water fixtures, and to infer their water flow and usage times. We did not consider other pairings such as the water meter with the light sensor, since in some homes, light fixtures may only be used a small fraction of the time that water fixtures are used; in the future, we plan to include these additional sensor streams to improve accuracy.

Figure 3(a) shows two examples of simultaneous flush events in different bathrooms of house 1 and 2, respectively, plotted together with the motion sensor data from the both bathrooms and the kitchen in each home. House 1 has two identical toilets, but FixtureFinder is able to use the motion sensor

signatures to differentiate the two flow events as originating from different bathrooms. House 2 has different models of toilet, each with different flow rates of approximately 0.3 kl/hour and 0.6kl/hour. Thus, even when they occur at essentially the same time, as shown in the figure, it can also differentiate them based on the difference in their flow rates. Notice that FixtureFinder must still use the motion sensor signatures to differentiate these flow events from, for example, a dishwasher fill cycle. This is particularly true because the flow rates change when the events co-occur, due to limited water flow. In the case of simultaneous flush events in House 1 where the flow rates are identical, FixtureFinder would not necessarily be able to associate the events with the correct fixture.

We assume a single motion sensor in each room containing a water fixture. Our off-the-shelf X10 motion sensors represent a challenge since the sensors already filter and aggregate the passive infrared data and send binary event messages whenever motion is detected. In contrast to light fixture discovery, we consider all the ambient motion sensors as a single multi-dimensional sensor stream to be paired with the water meter data stream using the FixtureFinder algorithm 1; the reason is that water fixture events may generate motion signatures spanning multiple binary motion sensors.

In Step I, for the water meter, we use the Canny edge detection algorithm [4]. To perform Step I on the motion sensor stream, we simply generate a multi-dimensional distance vector D corresponding to each water edge, that contains temporal distances between each water edge and the closest binary motion event from each motion sensor considered. In Steps III and IV we use the Quality Threshold Clustering [12] algorithm with a maximum relative difference of 0.25 to generate edge clusters from the water flow data. For the motion sensor data, we simply define a fixed set of clusters R corresponding the rooms in which the motion sensors are deployed. Given a room $r \in R$ with a motion sensor, and a water edge cluster c, we can evaluate the Bayesian network shown in Figure 1 after we compute $P(D|r)$ and $P(r|c)$; we do not discuss these probability computations here due to

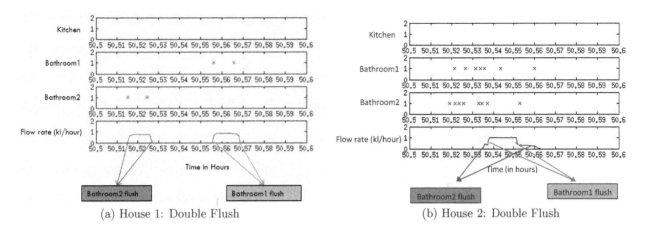

| (a) House 1: Double Flush | (b) House 2: Double Flush |

Figure 3: These data traces show aggregate water flow and motion sensor data for two simultaneous flush events, in different homes. FixtureFinder can use both the motion sensor data and the flow rates to distinguish between two otherwise similar fixtures, even when they are used simultaneously.

space constraints, but more details on this Bayesian network evaluation can be found in our earlier work [27]. Thus, each fixture computed in Step IV represent a fixture with a unique water flow signature and a unique room assignment; given that the various fixtures in a single room typically have unique water flow signatures, our FixtureFinder approach is likely to find the set of all water fixtures in the home.

Additionally, we use simple heuristics to label low flow matched events (less than 0.3 kl/hour) as sinks and higher flow matched events as toilet flushes. As we increase the number of types of fixtures, more sophisticated classification schemes for fixture type will be necessary, and we expect to leverage established work in this area [22].

4. EXPERIMENTAL SETUP

To evaluate the FixtureFinder system, we deploy sensors in four multi-resident homes for 10 days each. All four homes had multiple residents, multiple bathrooms, and a wide array of light and water fixtures. Details of the deployments are summarized in Table 1. In contrast to many existing fixture studies that use bench top testing or controlled testing in homes, we performed our evaluation *in-situ*: the data traces were collected over the course of multiple days while people lived normal lives in the home. Naturally, other fixtures and appliances aside from those being measured were also used during the experiment period. This in-situ evaluation setup ensures that FixtureFinder is able to operate even in the presence of real-world noise and signals commonly present in households. For example, the homes operated complex appliances such as dishwashers and washing machines, as well as central HVAC, space heaters, microwaves, and in some cases plasma televisions. Plasma televisions present a particularly challenging noise problem because, unlike LCD screens, the power usage of a plasma television changes with the brightness of the scene, creating high-magnitude and rapidly-changing noise patterns on the electrical lines. Most of the rooms in the homes had windows, which introduced a light variability in the light readings that typically far exceeded any changes in light value caused by artificial lights. This reveals one major difference with the Viridiscope system, which intentionally put the light sensors very close to the light and used a simple threshold value to

detect whether the lights were turned on or off. In contrast, FixtureFinder is opportunistically using light sensors that were deployed to detect ambient light levels, which includes natural lighting and can include multiple light fixtures. Our in-situ study also captured the natural simultaneous usage of water fixtures, one artifact of which is a change in flow rate: when the toilet is flushed and the sink is turned on, the aggregate water flow is typically lower than the sum of the two fixtures individually. This effect is often more extreme in homes with older piping infrastructure that has limited water flow, and is commonly known to cause burning hot showers whenever a toilet is flushed. Finally, our in-situ deployments also encountered a diverse range of light fixtures including incandescent bulbs, CFLs, and halogen lights, and both dimmable and non-dimmable switches with different light intensities and wattages, as seen in figure 6. Due to all of these complex and natural sources of noise, variety, and interference, *in-situ* testing is an important part of our empirical validation. To our knowledge, this is the first study to perform in-situ evaluation of a fixture monitoring system across a range of multiple, diverse homes. This testing was enabled by the specific sensing and ground truth system that we developed, as described below, which can be considered one of the contributions of this paper.

Sensors: To execute FixtureFinder in these homes, we deployed a single water flow sensor on the water mains and a single power meter on the power mains. To measure aggregate water flow, we used the Shenitech Ultrasonic water flow meter that clamps on to the outside of the water mains pipe. It uses the Doppler effect to measure the velocity and resulting flow of water through the pipeline. The flow meter reports instantaneous water flow (in cubic meters per hour) at a frequency of 2Hz using the home's Wi-Fi connection to transmit data. We expect that utility water flow meters being deployed in a large scale in homes will have a similar setup. To measure aggregate power usage, we used the The Energy Detective (TED) 5000 power meter, which uses a clamp-on ammeter that measures total current drawn by the home appliances. The power meter reports instantaneous power (both real and reactive) at a rate of approximately 1Hz. Figure 4.a shows the installation of the smart power

Home#	Type	#Residents	#Rooms	#Lights	#Sinks	#Toilets
1	3 Story house	3	8	12	-	-
2	3 Bedroom student housing	3	6	6	-	-
3	1 Bedroom condo	2	8	9	3	2
4	2 Story house	4	9	14	3	2

Table 1: Our deployments involved four homes with multiple residents, and a variety of lights and water fixtures. Due to cost limitations, smart water meters were only installed in two of the four homes.

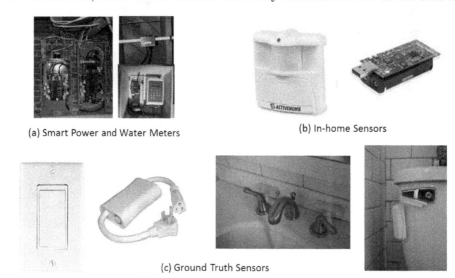

(a) Smart Power and Water Meters   (b) In-home Sensors

(c) Ground Truth Sensors

Figure 4: Our deployments included 25-40 sensors per home, including (a) a smart power and water meter (b) a motion and light sensor in every room. For experimental ground truth, we also deployed (c) Z-wave light switches, Z-wave plug load meters, and Z-wave contact switches on the water fixtures.

and water meter in one of our home deployments. Because the Shenitech water meters are much more expensive than the TED power meters ($2000 vs. $200 each), we deployed a water meter in only two of the homes, and water meter data was collected for only 7 days in each home. An example of a home deployment is illustrated in Figure 5.

In addition to the smart meters, FixtureFinder requires data from other sensors or infrastructure in the home, such as a security or home automation system. Off-the-shelf motion sensors for security and automation typically measure both motion and light. Since our test homes did not have a pre-existing home automation system, we deployed one motion sensor and light sensor per room to emulate a typical home automation system. Although one sensor per room may be redundant for some home security systems, we believe that smart homes of the future will contain at least one occupancy sensor per room to support diverse applications such as medical activity monitoring or home energy.

In our deployments, we used off the shelf X10 motion sensors inside rooms to detect occupancy, as shown in Figure 4.a. These sensors are inexpensive ($5 each) and can be installed with double-sided tape. The X10 motion sensors send a binary ON message whenever motion is seen with a minimal damping interval of 7 seconds between ON messages. In general, we installed one motion sensor per room in a prominent location with good visibility over the entire room, if possible. In Home 2, one of the motion sensors in a bathroom malfunctioned during our week long deployment, so we used a motion sensor in an adjacent bedroom with

a partial view of the bathroom in our analysis. Because of the challenges of accessing ambient light sensors in existing motion sensors, we instead used the cheap Hamamatsu photo diode connected to a telosb mote [25], as shown in Figure 4.a, sampling at approximately 2Hz; in the future, we expect more open, commercial sensors that allow users to access the raw light sensor data similar to our deployments. Our light sensors were installed near the locations where a motion sensor would be installed. Across our four homes, we used one sensor per room in all but 3 rooms, where two sensors were required to achieve coverage of the user's living space.

Ground Truth: To measure ground truth, we instrumented all of the light and water fixtures in each house. To instrument the light switches, we replaced all existing switches in each home with wireless ZWave smart switches, that transmit a wireless message whenever the light switch is turned on or off. For plug-in lamps, we installed a wireless ZWave smart plug load meter that measures the power consumption of the appliance plugged into it. We assume that any non-zero power consumption indicates that the lamp is switched on. For sinks and toilets, we installed Z-Wave door/window sensors (i.e. magnetic reed switches) on the faucet and flush handles. Figure 4.c shows examples of each of the 4 different types of Z-Wave installations used for ground truth. Due to cost and deployment constraints, the ground truth sensors were not installed on all fixtures and appliances that were used during our in-situ study; in particular, showers, and faucets connected to dishwashers

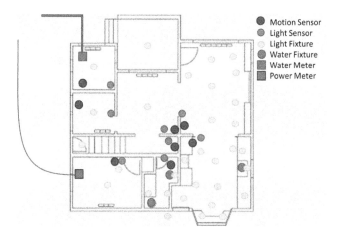

Legend:
- Motion Sensor
- Light Sensor
- Light Fixture
- Water Fixture
- Water Meter
- Power Meter

Figure 5: This diagram illustrates one home, including the locations of the meters, sensors, and fixtures. Many of the light fixtures are not used during the deployment period, and are not considered for our analysis of FixtureFinder.

and washing machines, were not instrumented. Our evaluation on water fixtures is thus limited to sinks and toilets. In total, we observed 41 light fixtures being used across the 4 homes over 10 days. We obtained a total of 775 ON-OFF pairs from all the light fixtures; the number of usage events attributed to each light fixture is shown in figure 6. We observed 10 water fixtures across 2 of our test homes over the 7 day deployment period. The 10 water fixtures were used for a total of 424 times; the distribution of usage events across the 10 fixtures is shown in figure 11.

5. RESULTS

For each house, we executed the FixtureFinder system on the data traces from the power meter, water meter, motion sensors and light sensors. The current version of FixtureFinder extracts correlations between the power meter and the light sensors, and between the water meter and the motion sensors. We plan to extend the system to also extract light-water and motion-power correlations, which is only expected to improve performance. The main result of this system is generated by Step IV in the FixtureFinder system, which produces a list of clusters, each with a multi-modal fixture profile. FixtureFinder discovered the top 90% of energy consuming light fixtures in each home, reporting the nominal wattage of each light fixture within $\pm 5W$. The multi-modal profile of each fixture is shown in Figure 6, and includes the nominal wattage as measured by the power meter, the lighting intensity as measured by the light sensors, the name of the light sensor that detected it (typically, a room name), and the number of usage events (ON-OFF pairs) originating from each fixture. FixtureFinder also discovered the sinks and toilets in each house. The multi-modal profile of the water fixtures were generally the same for all sinks and toilets, and are not shown due to lack of space. We observed several anecdotal instances of water fixtures such as the shower or the sprinkler system being discovered by FixtureFinder, but we currently limit our evaluation to only those fixtures monitored by our ground truth sensors. In the future, we intend to expand our evaluation to a larger set of fixtures and appliances.

From the the number of ON-OFF event pairs for each light fixture shown in Figure 6, we observe that the FixtureFinder system is able to discover light fixtures with a wide range of usage counts, ranging from as few as 5-10 events to as high as 50-100 events; this variability in usage counts suggests that FixtureFinder takes very few usage events to stabilize and identify individual fixtures, and stability is not significantly affected as more usage events occur over time. Of the 41 light fixtures that we instrumented, FixtureFinder was not able to discover 4 light fixtures that consumed very little energy, either because they were rarely used or because they had a very low wattage, e.g. LED bulbs. These fixtures include two in House #1 and three in House #4. All four of the undiscovered lights were *task lighting* fixtures, including under-cabinet lighting, coffee-bar lighting, and exit/entrance door lighting; all four fixtures were located in the kitchen, where task lighting is most common in homes. The fixtures were rarely used (1-3 times), had very low wattage, and were not easily detected by ambient light sensors because of their task-oriented nature.

5.1 Bootstrapping a Training Set

In addition to discovering the fixtures, FixtureFinder simultaneously produces a set of usage events that it associates with each fixture, where each event includes ON/OFF times and power or water flow measurements. These events can be used as an automatically created training set for supervised learning systems such as ElectriSense or HydroSense. For example, if FixtureFinder provides 100 usage events that are associated with the bathroom sink, HydroSense can use the ON/OFF times associated with those usage events to learn features of the pressure waves caused by that sink, so that it can recognize it again in the future. Thus, FixtureFinder can serve to bootstrap a training set, effectively converting HydroSense from a supervised learning system into an unsupervised system.

Usage events are associated with each fixture during Step IV of the FixtureFinder algorithm, when they are clustered together based on their multi-modal profile to initially provide support for a fixture's existence. However, not all of these usage events are necessarily caused by the same fixture; some may have been caused by other fixtures or spurious noise, and accidentally had the same multi-modal profile. The degree to which these clusters correctly separate usage events from different fixtures dictates the degree to which FixtureFinder will be useful as an unsupervised bootstrapping technique. We measure this clustering accuracy in terms of two metrics:

Precision: the number of events correctly associated with a fixture, divided by the total number of events associated with that fixture.

Recall is the number of events correctly associated with a fixture, divided by the total number of events generated by that fixture.

For the purposes of bootstrapping a training set, we care more about precision: we do not want spurious events incorrectly associated with a fixture, because they will cause errors in the training set. Recall is not as important: we don't need all usage events of a fixture, only enough to have a sufficiently large training set.

We analyze the trade off between precision and recall by

House 1				
ID	# of times used	Room	Power (W)	Light value
1	10	MasterBed	135	23
2	4	Livingroom	35	193
3	13	Livingroom	40	29
4	9	Kitchen	90	20
5	13	MasterBath	20	36
6	6	MidBathroom	10	62
7	8	BottomBath	40	41
8	7	MasterBath	42	0
9	2	BottomBath	40	27
10	2	Kitchen	5	-
11	3	TopRoom	80	923
12	1	Kitchen	95	-

House 2				
ID	# of times used	Room	Power (W)	Light value
1	13	Livingroom	185	366
2	20	Bedroom1	90	55
3	15	Kitchen	120	71
4	25	Bedroom2	35	50
5	4	Bedroom3	50	414
6	123	Bathroom	50	260

House 3				
ID	# of times used	Room	Power (W)	Light value
1	9	Livingroom	95	155
2	29	Livingroom	115	59
3	71	Bathroom1	220	1187
4	91	Bedroom	95	70
5	53	Kitchen	110	181
6	30	Officeroom	90	55
7	29	Bathroom2	305	1157
8	6	Diningroom	200	182
9	12	Livingroom	55	239
10	-	Diningroom	100	19

House 4				
ID	# of times used	Room	Power (W)	Light value
1	11	Frontroom	55	311
2	10	Basement	325	353
3	4	Kitchen	250	60
4	53	Bathroom	395	1028
5	12	Kitchen	280	125
6	12	Livingroom	80	50
7	10	Dining Room	200	110
8	32	Bedroom	95	69
9	4	Bathroom1	95	649
10	6	Nursery	55	129
11	6	Bedroom	60	32
12	2	Kitchen	70	-
13	3	Kitchen	30	-
14	2	Kitchen	110	-

Figure 6: FixtureFinder discovered 37 of the 41 light fixtures that we instrumented, and produces a multi-model profile for each (wattage + light intensity). Four low-power, infrequently used, and specialized task lighting fixtures (shown in gray) in the kitchen were not discovered. There was one false alarm fixture, namely fixture #10 in House 3 (shown in black). The light fixture numbers here match the light fixture numbers in figure 10.

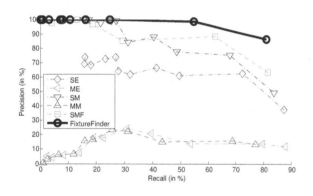

Figure 7: FixtureFinder is able to achieve 98% precision, with recall values of 55%, in order to bootstrap training data sets. Variants of the system illustrate the limited value of edge detection, matching, or fusion alone.

varying the threshold used for edge detection in the Step I of the algorithm: higher thresholds result in fewer event detections (and thus higher precision), while lower thresholds result in more event detections (and thus higher recall). For the sake of brevity, we only present the results for light fixture discovery here, but water fixture discovery presents a similar underlying trade off. The dark, black line in Figure 7 corresponding to FixtureFinder shows the recall/precision that is achieved when varying the edge detection thresholds. In this figure, we show the recall/precision over all light fixtures in the four homes considered. This figure shows that precision at or near 98% can be achieved, for recall values close to 55%. Thus, we conclude that FixtureFinder can produce training data sets with few if any errors. Recall levels of 55% merely indicate that the system will take longer to produce that training set.

5.2 Analysis

In this section, we explore each of the components of the FixtureFinder algorithm in order to explain the degree to which they contribute to its overall performance. Specifically, we examine (i) edge detection, (ii) matching, and (iii) fusion by creating five variants of FixtureFinder that infer the existence of individual light fixture events based on the following criteria:

- **SE** – Sensor Edge Only: distinct changes in sensor readings only, using our edge detection algorithms
- **ME** – Meter Edge Only: distinct changes in smart meter readings only, using our edge detection algorithms
- **SM** – Sensor Matching: distinct changes in sensor readings that have corresponding ON/OFF matches, using our edge detection and matching algorithms
- **MM** – Meter Matching: distinct changes in power meter readings that have corresponding ON/OFF matches, using our edge detection and matching algorithms
- **SMF** – Sensor/Meter Fusion: changes in sensor/meter readings that occur co-temporally, by applying Steps I and II of the FixtureFinder algorithm

Figure 7 shows the recall/precision across four homes that is achieved by each of these algorithms when varying the edge detection thresholds; we show the results only for light fixtures for the sake of brevity. The results show that smart meter data alone (ME) are not sufficient to identify fixtures with anything greater than 25% precision. This is consistent with previous studies of power meter data [11], due to the power of light fixtures being small compared to noise from other, simultaneous fixtures. Similarly, sensor data alone (SE) is not sufficient because, e.g. artificial lights have low light output compared to natural variations in sunlight and the effects of person movement and other shadows.

When ON/OFF matching is used, many spurious edges are eliminated which allows higher precision for a given recall value. Because of the very large number of edges in

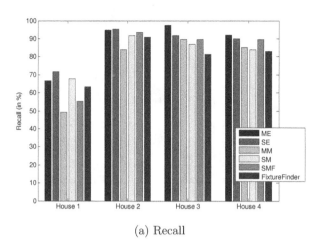

(a) Recall

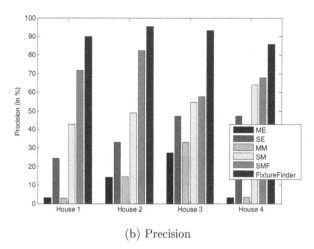

(b) Precision

Figure 8: FixtureFinder achieves consistently higher precision than variants of the system in all 4 houses. Each house shows variability in the performance of the variant schemes depending on the particular electrical and ambient light noise present in that house.

smart meter data, matching produces little benefit (MM). Matching improves the discovery precision using sensor data (SM) to be above 99%, but only up to recall values of less than 28%. Fusion of the sensor and smart meter data further eliminates edges in either data stream that do not have a co-occurring event in the other data stream (SMF), but because of the very large number of edges in the smart meter data stream, this approach does not perform as well as FixtureFinder. When we combine the fusion, matching, and Bayesian clustering algorithms that eliminate all but frequently occurring sensor/meter pairs, we create the FixtureFinder algorithm that is able maintain precision at 98% for recall values up to 55%.

Figure 8 shows a snapshot of the recall and precision of the five component schemes and FixtureFinder in our four test homes; the snapshot is shown at the same parameter settings used to achieve greater than 80% recall and precision for FixtureFinder in Figure 7. We observe from Figure 8 that the FixtureFinder approach trades off a small reduction in recall for a significant increase in precision. In all four homes, by applying data fusion, matching, and Bayesian clustering, FixtureFinder achieves a precision ranging from 80-90% with only a negligible reduction recall. We observe in general that there is variability in the precision achieved by the 5 component schemes implemented. House 1 had the most noisy light environment due to wall-sized windows on most floors; thus, we observe the worst performance among all four homes from schemes SE and SM that use the light sensor data. Interestingly, House 2, which had the least electrical noise, achieves close to 80% precision only through data fusion with ambient light sensor data (SMF). Houses 3 and 4 had significant noise from both light sensors and the power meter, and thus require the aggressive FixtureFinder algorithm to remove false positive fixture events.

In general, we observed no difference in light intensity changes, power meter changes, water flow changes, light-power correlation, and motion-water correlations between day and night. For other pairings, such as light-water, we might expect significant differences in correlation between day and night, as some bathroom or kitchen lights may be

used only at night; thus, in the future, time of day may need to be incorporated into the multi-modal sensor clusters that we produce, to improve accuracy. Also, we observed that 15.8% of the light fixture events occur within 10 seconds of each other, and 32.3% of all light fixture events occur within 20 seconds of each other. These co-occurrences make the data fusion and matching steps more challenging, by introducing numerous candidate choices for fusion and matching (in addition to noisy edges inherent in the system); in spite of these co-occurrences, FixtureFinder is able to accurately identify individual fixture events in the home with high accuracy, by combining the matching, data fusion, and Bayesian clustering steps.

6. RECOGNITION AND DISAGGREGATION

In this section, we demonstrate that FixtureFinder can also be used to perform fixture recognition and disaggregation, allowing smart power and water meter data to be used to infer activities and/or disaggregated energy usage merely by piggybacking on other sensors and infrastructure already in the home.

To perform fixture discovery, FixtureFinder must be configured to achieve high precision, possibly sacrificing recall (98% and 55% respectively, according to our results in Section 5). To perform fixture recognition, it must be configured to achieve more balanced precision and recall values. Figure 7 shows that the system can also achieve an operating point with about 86% precision and 81% recall. In other words, about 14% of the usage events associated with a fixture are actually caused by another fixture, while 19% of the events actually caused by the fixture are not associated with it.

To perform fixture disaggregation, FixtureFinder leverages the multi-modal profile of each fixture event that was created during fixture recognition, which includes the power or water consumption levels of that event. FixtureFinder estimates the total power/water usage for each event by summing the usage levels of all events assigned to each fixture. Figures 9 and 10 illustrate both the actual and the estimated energy/water usage for each of the water and light fixtures in

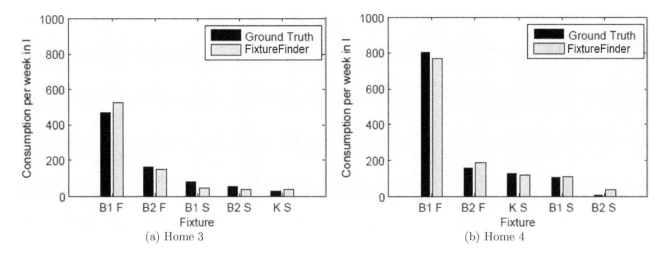

(a) Home 3   (b) Home 4

Figure 9: The water consumption estimated by FixtureFinder for each water fixture in the two homes with water meters closely matches the ground truth values for the most high flow fixtures, generally achieving 85-90% accuracy (B stands for bathroom, K for kitchen, S for sink, and F for flush).

the four test homes. Results show that FixtureFinder computes the water usage with 80-90% average accuracy across all water fixtures, and the energy usage with 91% average accuracy for the light fixtures consuming 90% of the home's lighting energy.

FixtureFinder's disaggregation results are surprisingly high given its recognition accuracy. The reason is that fixture recognition is most likely to make assignment errors on events with low power/water usage, and is most likely to assign the event to another fixture with similar average power/water usage. The errors often cancel out and do not significantly affect the overall energy/water estimates. For example, Figure 11 shows the confusion matrices for water fixture classification in the two homes that contained a smart water meter (element [x,y] in the confusion matrix indicates the number of times an event from fixture x was associated with fixture y). Most misclassifications that did occur were due to simultaneous occupancy in multiple rooms from fixtures with similar flow signatures, such as high confusion between sink usage in the kitchen and bathroom2 in Home 3. In Home 4, there is about 7% confusion between the two flush fixtures. These misclassifications cause limited degradation in water consumption accuracy because they are infrequent, typically between fixtures with similar flow rates, and are roughly symmetric across the diagonal. Therefore, the recognition errors often cancel each other out in the disaggregation results.

7. LIMITATIONS

This paper presents a proof-of-concept of the FixtureFinder principles: that fixtures can be discovered and differentiated based on multi-modal profiles, even if a home contains multiple identical fixtures, and even if the fixtures are too simple and basic to be discovered based on smart power or water meter data alone. The results presented in this paper are not intended to represent a complete exploration of this concept, and the current version only explores a small subset of sensors and fixtures. In future work, we plan to study a more complete set of fixtures, including both major appliances and smaller appliances. We expect

to use NIALM-like approaches to discover major appliance, but that FixtureFinder will be needed to narrow the set of appliance candidates and perhaps by identifying the number of appliances in the home. We expect that ElectriSense-like approaches can be used to discover very small, low-power and battery powered devices, such as cell phone chargers, electric toothbrushes, and music players. The current results do not yet demonstrate how this approach will scale to large numbers of low-power and battery powered devices.

The results presented in this paper indicate that FixtureFinder was unable to detect 4 of the 41 light fixtures due to their task-specific lighting capabilities that were not detected by ambient light sensors. Also, we require at least one sensor per room in our current deployments and evaluation. In future work, we expect to address this problem by exploring the use of a broader range of sensors and data streams. Previous work has shown the feasibility and usefulness of harvesting information from home infrastructure such as the home router, air pressure, and gas lines [5,15,23], and we will build on that work to also perform fixture discovery. As the variety of home sensors and automation devices proliferate, and as devices in the home increasingly become wireless and connected, the number of devices that must be automatically discovered will continue to grow, and the amount of information available to discover them will also grow.

The current implementation of FixtureFinder is limited to simple fixtures with ON/OFF events, but Step III could be extended to appliances with a wider variety of states without loss of generality. In the future, we expect FixtureFinder to leverage established work in this area to address a broader range of fixtures [9]. Also, due to sensor sampling rate limitations, if a set of light fixtures is switched on and off simultaneously (within 1 second of each other) within a single room in a consistent manner, the system will treat them as a single fixture; the use of additional data sources from the home may allow FixtureFinder to disambiguate these multi-fixture scenarios. Finally, in the current FixtureFinder implementation, we use fixed time thresholds for data fusion under the assumption that fixture usage simultaneously affects different sensor streams; an interesting direction for

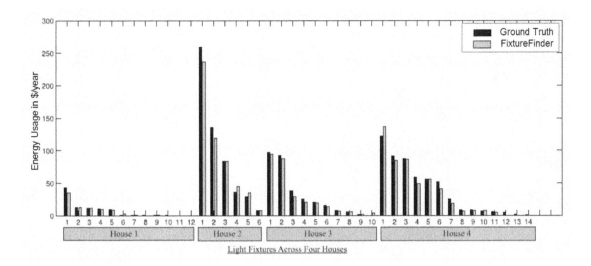

Figure 10: FixtureFinder accurately reports the energy usage of the top energy-consuming light fixtures in each home (as measured in dollars), achieving 90% accuracy for the 90% of appliances consuming the most energy. Importantly, the ordering of the light fixtures based on estimated energy usage is correct. This is a promising next step for FixtureFinder.

Fixtures	# of usage events	K S	B1 S	B1 F	B2 S	B2 F
K S	17	8	0	0	8	1
B1 S	22	1	19	0	2	0
B1 F	50	0	1	49	0	0
B2 S	22	3	1	0	16	2
B2 F	15	0	0	0	1	14

(a) Home 3

Fixtures	# of usage events	K S	B1 S	B1 F	B2 S	B2 F
K S	94	81	10	0	3	0
B1 S	90	7	78	0	5	0
B1 F	91	1	0	85	0	5
B2 S	7	0	1	0	6	0
B2 F	16	0	0	2	1	13

(b) Home 4

Figure 11: FixtureFinder accurately classifies water flow events for most of the monitored water fixtures across the two homes as seen in the fixture level confusion matrices (B stands for bathroom, K for kitchen, S for sink, and F for flush). Confusion between fixtures of the same type occurs due to simultaneous occupancy of different rooms, but has limited effect on water flow estimates. Confusion between fixtures of different types of fixtures is less common because the flow rates are distinctive.

future work is to automatically learn these temporal correlations between sensor streams over different time-scales.

8. CONCLUSIONS

In this paper, we present the FixtureFinder system that automatically infers the existence of electrical and water fixtures in the home. It uses data fusion between the smart meters and other sensors or infrastructure already in the home, such as the home security system, and searches for repeating patterns in the fused data stream. Unlike fixture recognition systems, Fixture Find does not try to recognize every ON/OFF event. Instead, it tries to select only those events that are very likely not to be caused by spurious noise. Once a set of such events is recognized, it can be used to create a training set for existing fixture recognition or disaggregation systems such as ElectriSense and Viridiscope. To our knowledge, this is the first system that can automatically discover the presence of small, simple fixtures.

We evaluated FixtureFinder by deploying between 25-40 sensors into 4 different homes for 7-10 days of data collection. Our results indicate that FixtureFinder is able to identify and differentiate major light and water fixtures in less than 10 days, including multiple copies of light bulbs and sinks that have identical power/water profiles. It can also produce clean training data sets to be used by other algorithms that require supervised training. In effect, FixtureFinder can be used to bootstrap other fixture recognition and disaggregation techniques at low cost by piggybacking on data from other sensors and infrastructure, such as home security or automation systems. In the future, the techniques described in this paper can be made more general and more effective by combining with other sensors and infrastructure, such as cell phones, home routers, gas meters, and the millions of home automation devices being sold today.

Acknowledgment

This work was supported, in part, by NSF grants CNS-1017363 and EFRI-1038271.

9. REFERENCES

[1] Pike research smart grid deployment tracker. http://www.pikeresearch.com/research/smart-grid-deployment-tracker-3q10.

[2] S. Barker, A. Mishra, D. Irwin, E. Cecchet, P. Shenoy, and J. Albrecht. Smart*: An open data set and tools for enabling research in sustainable homes. *The 1st KDD Workshop on Data Mining Applications in Sustainability (SustKDD)*, 2011.

[3] C. Beckel, W. Kleiminger, T. Staake, and S. Santini. Improving device-level electricity consumption breakdowns in private households using on/off events. *SIGBED Rev.*, 9(3), 2012.

[4] J. Canny. A computational approach to edge detection. *Pattern Analysis and Machine Intelligence, IEEE Transactions on*, (6):679–698, 1986.

[5] G. Cohn, S. Gupta, J. Froehlich, E. Larson, and S. N. Patel. Gassense: appliance-level, single-point sensing of gas activity in the home. In *Proceedings of the 8th international conference on Pervasive Computing*, Pervasive'10, 2010.

[6] J. Fogarty, C. Au, and S. Hudson. Sensing from the basement: a feasibility study of unobtrusive and low-cost home activity recognition. In *Proceedings of the 19th annual ACM symposium on User interface software and technology*, pages 91–100. ACM, 2006.

[7] J. Froehlich, E. Larson, T. Campbell, C. Haggerty, J. Fogarty, and S. Patel. HydroSense: infrastructure-mediated single-point sensing of whole-home water activity. In *Proceedings of the 11th international conference on Ubiquitous computing*, pages 235–244. ACM, 2009.

[8] J. Froehlich, E. Larson, T. Campbell, C. Haggerty, J. Fogarty, and S. Patel. Hydrosense: infrastructure-mediated single-point sensing of whole-home water activity. In *Proc. UbiComp*, volume 9, pages 235–244. Citeseer, 2009.

[9] H. Goncalves, A. Ocneanu, and M. Berges. Unsupervised disaggregation of appliances using aggregated consumption data. *The 1st KDD Workshop on Data Mining Applications in Sustainability (SustKDD)*, 2011.

[10] S. Gupta, M. Reynolds, and S. Patel. Electrisense: Single-point sensing using emi for electrical event detection and classification in the home. In *Proceedings of Ubicomp*, 2010.

[11] G. Hart. Nonintrusive appliance load monitoring. *Proceedings of the IEEE*, 80(12):1870–1891, 1992.

[12] L. Heyer, S. Kruglyak, and S. Yooseph. Exploring expression data: identification and analysis of coexpressed genes. *Genome research*, 9(11):1106, 1999.

[13] X. Jiang, S. Dawson-Haggerty, P. Dutta, and D. Culler. Design and implementation of a high-fidelity ac metering network. In *Proceedings of IPSN*, 2009.

[14] D. Jung and A. Savvides. Estimating building consumption breakdowns using on/off state sensing and incremental sub-meter deployment. In *SenSys*, pages 225–238, 2010.

[15] Y. Kim, R. Balani, H. Zhao, and M. B. Srivastava. Granger causality analysis on ip traffic and circuit-level energy monitoring. In *Proceedings of the 2nd ACM Workshop on Embedded Sensing Systems for Energy-Efficiency in Building*, BuildSys '10, pages 43–48, 2010.

[16] Y. Kim, T. Schmid, Z. Charbiwala, J. Friedman, and M. Srivastava. Nawms: nonintrusive autonomous water monitoring system. In *Proceedings of the 6th ACM conference on Embedded network sensor systems*, pages 309–322. ACM, 2008.

[17] Y. Kim, T. Schmid, Z. Charbiwala, and M. Srivastava. Viridiscope: design and implementation of a fine grained power monitoring system for homes. In *Proceedings of Ubicomp*, 2009.

[18] J. Z. Kolter and M. J. Johnson. Redd: A public data set for energy disaggregation research. *The 1st KDD Workshop on Data Mining Applications in Sustainability (SustKDD)*, 2011.

[19] H. Kuhn. The hungarian method for the assignment problem. *Naval research logistics quarterly*, 2(1-2):83–97, 1955.

[20] P. Mayer and W. DeOreo. *Residential end uses of water*. American Water Works Association, 1999.

[21] Parks Associates Research and Analysis for Digital Living. Home security system forecasts: 2005 and beyond, November 2005.

[22] O. Parson, S. Ghosh, M. Weal, and A. Rogers. Non-intrusive load monitoring using prior models of general appliance types. *AAAi*, 2012.

[23] S. Patel, M. Reynolds, and G. Abowd. Detecting human movement by differential air pressure sensing in hvac system ductwork: An exploration in infrastructure mediated sensing. In *Pervasive Computing*, Lecture Notes in Computer Science, 2008.

[24] S. Patel, T. Robertson, J. Kientz, M. Reynolds, and G. Abowd. At the flick of a switch: Detecting and classifying unique electrical events on the residential power line. *Lecture Notes in Computer Science*, 4717:271, 2007.

[25] J. Polastre, R. Szewczyk, and D. Culler. Telos: enabling ultra-low power wireless research. In *Proceedings of IPSN*, 2005.

[26] A. Rowe, M. Berges, and R. Rajkumar. Contactless sensing of appliance state transitions through variations in electromagnetic fields. In *Proceedings of Buildsys*, 2010.

[27] V. Srinivasan, J. Stankovic, and K. Whitehouse. Watersense: Water flow disaggregation using motion sensors. In *The 3rd ACM Workshop On Embedded Sensing Systems For Energy-Efficiency In Buildings (BuildSys), in conjunction with ACM SenSys*, 2011.

Strip, Bind, and Search: A Method for Identifying Abnormal Energy Consumption in Buildings

Romain Fontugne[1,5], Jorge Ortiz[2], Nicolas Tremblay[3], Pierre Borgnat[3]
Patrick Flandrin[3], Kensuke Fukuda[4], David Culler[2] and Hiroshi Esaki[1]

[1]The University of Tokyo   [2]University of California, Berkeley
[3]CNRS, Ecole Normale Supérieure de Lyon   [4]National Institute of Informatics
[5]Japanese-French Laboratory for Informatics

ABSTRACT

A typical large building contains thousands of sensors, monitoring the HVAC system, lighting, and other operational sub-systems. With the increased push for operational efficiency, operators are relying more on historical data processing to uncover opportunities for energy-savings. However, they are overwhelmed with the deluge of data and seek more efficient ways to identify potential problems. In this paper, we present a new approach called the Strip, Bind and Search (SBS); a method for uncovering abnormal equipment behavior and in-concert usage patterns. SBS uncovers relationships between devices and constructs a model for their usage pattern relative to other devices. It then flags deviations from the model. We run SBS on a set of building sensor traces; each containing hundred sensors reporting data flows over 18 weeks from two separate buildings with fundamentally different infrastructures. We demonstrate that, in many cases, SBS uncovers misbehavior corresponding to inefficient device usage that leads to energy waste. The average waste uncovered is as high as 2500 kWh per device.

Categories and Subject Descriptors

H.4 [**Information Systems Applications**]: Miscellaneous

Keywords

Building; Energy Consumption; Anomaly Detection

1. INTRODUCTION

Buildings are one of the prime targets to reduce energy consumption around the world. In the United States, the second largest energy consumer in the world, buildings account for 41% of the country's total energy consumption [26]. The first measure towards reducing the building's energy consumption is to prevent electricity waste due to the improper use of the buildings equipment.

Large building infrastructure is usually monitored by numerous sensors. Some of these sensors enable building administrators to view device power-draw in real time. This allows administrators to determine proper device behavior and system-wide inefficiencies. Detecting misbehaving devices is crucial, as many are sources of energy waste. However, identifying these saving opportunities is impractical for administrators because large buildings usually contain hundreds of monitored devices producing thousands of streams and it requires continuous monitoring. As such, the goal of this work is to establish a method that automatically reports abnormal device-usage patterns to the administrator by closely examining all of the continuous power streams.

The intuition behind the proposed approach is that each service provided by the building requires a minimum subset of devices. The devices within a subset are used at the same time when the corresponding service is needed and a savings opportunity is characterized by the partial activation of the devices. For example, office comfort is attained through sufficient lighting, ventilation, and air conditioning. These are controlled by the lighting and HVAC (Heating, Ventilation, and Air Conditioning) system. Thus, when the room is occupied both the air conditioner (heater on a cold day) and lights are used together and should be turned off when the room is empty. In principal, if a person leaves the room and turns off *only* the lights then the air conditioner (or heater) is a source of electricity waste.

Following this basic idea we propose *Strip, Bind and Search* (SBS), an unsupervised methodology that systematically detects electricity waste. Our proposal consists of two key components:

Strip and Bind The first part of the proposed method mines the raw sensor data, identifying inter-device usage patterns. We first *strip* the underlying traces of occupancy-induced trends. Then we *bind* devices whose underlying behavior is highly correlated. This allows us to differentiate between devices that are used together (high correlation), used independently (no correlation), and used mutually exclusively (negative correlation).

Search The second part of the method monitors devices relationships over time and reports deviations from the norm. It learns the normal inter-device usage using a robust, longitudinal analysis of the building data and detect anomalous usages. Such abnormalities usually present an opportunity to reduce electricity waste or events that deserve careful attention (e.g. faulty device).

SBS overcomes several challenges. First, noisy sensor traces that all share a similar trend, making direct correlation analysis non-trivial. Device energy consumption is mainly driven by occupancy and weather, all the devices display a similar daily pattern, in roughly overlapping time intervals and phases. Therefore, one of the main contributions of this work is uncovering the intrinsic device relationships by filtering out the dominant trend. For this task we use Empirical Mode Decomposition [14], a known method for de-trending time-varying signals.

Another key contribution of this work is in using SBS to practically monitor building energy consumption. Moreover, the proposed method is easy to use and functions in any building, as it does not require prior knowledge of the building nor extra sensors. It is also tuned through a single intuitive parameter.

We validate the effectiveness of our approach using 10 weeks of data from a modern Japanese building containing 135 sensors and 8 weeks of data from an older American building containing 70 sensors. These experiments highlight the effectiveness of SBS to uncover device relationships in a large deployment of 135 sensors. Furthermore, we inspect the SBS results and show that the reported alarms correspond to significant opportunities to save energy. The major anomaly reported in the American building lasts 18 days and accounts for a waste of 2500 kWh. SBS also reports numerous small anomalies, hidden deep within the building's overall consumption data. Such errors are very difficult to find without SBS.

In the rest of this paper, we detail the mechanisms of SBS (Section 3) before evaluating it with real data (Section 5) then we discuss different outcomes of the proposed methodology (Section 7) and conclude.

2. PROBLEM DESCRIPTION

The primary objective of SBS is to determine *how* device usage patterns are correlated across all pairs of sensors and discover when these relationships change. The naive approach is to run correlation analysis on pairs of sensor traces, recording their correlation coefficients over time and examining when there is a statistically-significant deviation from the norm. However, this approach does not yield any useful information when applied to *raw data traces*. For example, the two raw signals shown in Figure 3 are from two independent HVAC systems, serving different rooms on different floors. Since each space is independently controlled, we expect their power-draw signals to be uncorrelated (or at least distinguishable from other signal pairs). However, their correlation coefficient (0.57), is not particularly informative – it is statistically similar to the correlation between itself and other signals in the trace.

Using a larger set of devices, Figure 1 shows a correlation matrix with 135 distinct lighting and HVAC systems serving numerous rooms in a building (described later on in Section 4.1). The indices are selected such that their index-difference is indicative of their relative spatial proximity. For example, a device in location 1 is closer in the building to a device in location 2 than it is to a device in location 135. The color of the cell is the average pairwise correlation coefficient for devices in the row-column index. The higher the value,

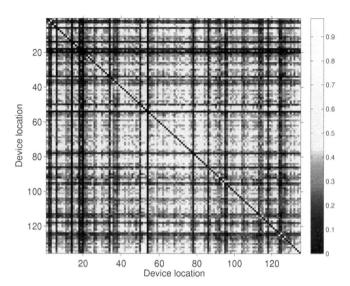

Figure 1: Correlation coefficients of the raw traces from the Building 1 dataset (Section 4.1). The matrix is ordered such as the devices serving same/adjacent rooms are nearby in the matrix.

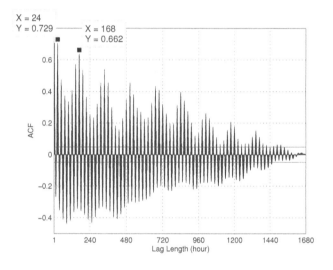

Figure 2: Auto-correlation of a usual signal from the Building 1 dataset. The signal features daily and weekly patterns (resp. $x = 24$ and $x = 168$).

the lighter the color. Devices serving the same room are along the diagonal. Because these devices are used simultaneously, we expect high average correlation scores, lighter shades, along the diagonal figure. However, we observe no such pattern. Most of the signals are correlated with all the others and we see no discernible structure.

An explanation for this is that the daily occupant usage patterns drive these results. Figure 3 demonstrates this more clearly. It shows two 1-week raw signals traces which feature the same diurnal pattern. This trend is present in almost every sensor trace, and, it hides the smaller fluctuations providing more specific patterns driven by local occupant activity. Upon deeper inspection, we uncovered several dominant patterns, common among energy-consuming devices in buildings [27]. Figure 2 depicts the auto-correlation of a usual electric power signal for a device. The two highest values in the figure correspond to a lag of 24 hours and 168 hours (one week). Therefore, the signal has some periodicity and similar (though not equal) values are seen at daily and weekly time scales. The daily pattern is due to daily office hours and the weekly pattern corresponds to weekdays and weekends. Correlation analysis on *raw* signals cannot be used to determine meaningful inter-device relationships because periodic components act as non-stationary trends for high-frequency phenomenon, making the correlation function irrelevant. Such trends must be removed in order to make meaningful progress towards our aforementioned goals.

In the next section we describe SBS. We discuss *strip and bind* in section 3.1, which addresses de-trending and relationship-discovery. Then, we describe how we *search* for changes in usage patterns, in section 3.2, to identify potential savings opportunities.

3. METHODOLOGY

3.1 Strip and Bind

Discovering devices that are used in concert is non-trivial. SBS decomposes each signal into an additive set of components, called Intrinsic Mode Functions (IMF), that reveals the signal patterns at different frequency bands. IMFs are obtained using Empirical Mode Decomposition (see Figure 3 and Section 3.1.1). We only consider IMFs with time scales shorter than a day, since we are interested in capturing short-scale usage patterns. Consequently, SBS aggregates the IMFs that fall into this specific time scale (see *IMF agg.* in Figure 3). The resulting partial signals of different device power traces are compared, pairwise, to identify the devices that show un/correlated usage patterns (see *Corr. Coeff.* in Figure 3).

3.1.1 Empirical Mode Decomposition

Empirical Mode Decomposition (EMD) [14] is a technique that decomposes a signal and reveals intrinsic patterns, trends, and noise. This technique has been widely applied to a variety of datasets, including climate variables [20], medical data [4], speech signals [12, 11], and image processing [21]. EMD's effectiveness relies on its empirical, adaptive and intuitive approach. In fact, this technique is designed to efficiently decompose both non-stationary and non-linear signals without requiring any a priori basis functions or tuning.

EMD decomposes a signal into a set of oscillatory components called intrinsic mode functions (IMFs). An IMF satisfies two conditions: (1) it contains the same number of extrema and zero crossings (or differ at most by one); (2) the two IMF envelopes defined by its local maxima and local minima are symmetric with respect to zero. Consequently, IMFs are functions that directly convey the amplitude and frequency modulations.

EMD is an iterative algorithm that extracts IMFs step by step by using the so-called sifting process [14]; each step seeks for the IMF with the highest frequency by sifting, then the computed IMF is removed from the data and the residual data are used as input for the next step. The process stops when the residual data becomes a monotonic function from which no more IMF can be extracted.

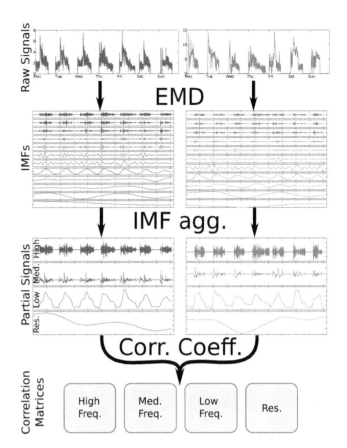

Figure 3: *Strip and Bind* **using two raw signals standing for one week of data from two different HVACs. (1) Decomposition of the signals in IMFs using EMD (top to bottom:** c_1 **to** c_n**); (2) aggregation of the IMFs based on their time scale; (3) comparison of the partial signals (aggregated IMFs) using correlation coefficient.**

We formally describe the EMD algorithm as follows:

1. Sifting process: For a current signal $h_0 = X$, let m_0 be the mean of its upper and lower envelopes as determined from a cubic-spline interpolation of local maxima and minima.

2. The estimated local mean m_0 is removed from the signal, giving a first component: $h_1 = h_0 - m_0$

3. The sifting process is iterated, h_1 taking the place of h_0. Using its upper and lower envelopes, a new local mean m_1 is computed and $h_2 = h_1 - m_1$.

4. The procedure is repeated k times until $h_k = h_{k-1} - m_{k-1}$ is an IMF according to the two conditions above.

5. This first IMF is designated as $c_1 = h_k$, and contains the component with shortest periods. We extract it from the signal to produce a residual: $r_1 = X - c_1$. Steps 1 to 4 are repeated on the residual signal r_1, providing IMFs c_j and residuals $r_j = r_{j-1} - c_j$, for j from 1 to n.

6. The process stops when residual r_n contains no more than 3 extrema.

The result of EMD is a set of IMFs c_i and the final residue r_n, such as:

$$X = \sum_{i=1}^{n} c_i + r_n$$

where the size of the resulting set of IMFs (n) depends on the original signal X and r_n represents the trend of the data (see *IMFs* in Figure 3).

For this work we implemented a variant of EMD called Complete Ensemble EMD [25]. This algorithm computes EMD several times with additional noise, it allows us to efficiently analyze signals that have flat sections (i.e. consuming no electricity in our case).

3.1.2 IMF aggregation

By applying EMD to energy consumption signals we obtain a set of IMFs that precisely describe the devices consumption patterns at different frequency bands. Therefore, we can focus our analysis on the smaller time scales, ignoring the dominant patterns that prevent us from effectively analyzing raw signals.

However, comparing the IMFs obtained from different signals is also not trivial, because EMD is empirically uncovering IMFs from the data there is no guarantee that the two IMFs c_i^1 and c_i^2 obtained from two distinct signals S^1 and S^2 represent data at the same frequency domain. Directly comparing c_i^1 and c_i^2 is meaningless unless we confirm that they belong to the same frequency domain.

There are numerous techniques to retrieve IMF frequencies [15]. In this work we take advantage of the Generalized Zero Crossing (GZC) [13] because it is a simple and robust estimator of the instantaneous IMF frequency [15]. GZC is a direct estimation of IMF instantaneous frequency using critical points defined as the zero crossings and local extrema (round dots in Figure 4). Formally, given a data point p, GZC measures the quarter (T_4), the two halves (T_2^x), and the four full periods (T_1^y), p belong to (see Figure 4) and the instantaneous period is computed as:

$$T = \frac{1}{7}\{4T_4 + (2T_2^1 + 2T_2^2) + (T_1^1 + T_1^2 + T_1^3 + T_1^4)\}$$

Since all points p between two critical points have the same instantaneous period GZC is local down to a quarter period. Hereafter, we refer to the time scale of an IMF as the average of the instantaneous periods along the whole IMF. Because the time scale of each IMF depends on the original signal, we propose the following to efficiently compare IMFs from different signals. We cluster IMFs with respect to their time scales and partially reconstruct each signal by aggregating its IMFs from the same cluster. Then, we directly compare the partial signals of different devices.

The IMFs are clustered using four time scale ranges:

- The *high frequencies* are all the IMFs with a time scale lower than 20 minutes. These IMFs capture the noise.

- The *medium frequencies* are all the IMFs with a time scale between 20 minutes and 6 hours. These IMFs convey the detailed devices usage.

- The *low frequencies* are all the IMFs with a time scale between 6 hours and 6 days. These IMFs represent daily device patterns.

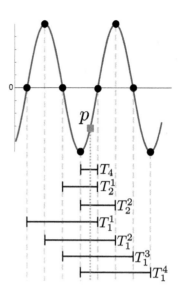

Figure 4: Generalized Zero Crossing: the local mean period at the point p is computed from one quarter period T_4, two half periods T_2^x and four full periods T_1^y (where $x = 1, 2$, and, $y = 1, 2, 3, 4$).

- The *residual data* is all data with a time scale higher than 6 days. This is mainly residual data obtained after applying EMD. Also, it highlights the main device trend.

These time scale ranges are chosen based on our experiments and goal. The 20-minute boundary relies on the sampling period of our dataset (5 minutes) and permits us to capture IMFs with really short periods. The 6-hour boundary allows us to analyze all patterns that have a period shorter than the usual office hours. The 6-day boundary allows us to capture daily patterns and weekday patterns.

Aggregating IMFs, within each time scale range, results in 4 partial signals representing different characteristics of the device's energy consumption (see *Partial Signals* in Figure 3). We do a pairwise device trace comparison, calculating the correlation coefficient of their partial signals. In the example shown in Figure 3, the correlation coefficient of the raw signals suggests that they are highly correlated (0.57). However, the comparison of the corresponding *partial signals* provides new insights; the two devices are poorly correlated at high and medium frequencies (respectively -0.01 and -0.04) but highly correlated at low frequencies (0.79) meaning that these devices are not "intrinsically" correlated. They only share a similar daily pattern.

All the devices are compared pairwise at the four different time scale ranges. Consequently, we obtain four correlation matrices that convey device similarities at different time scales. Each line of these matrices (or column, since the matrices are symmetric) reveals the behavior of a device – its relationships with the other devices at a particular time scale. The matrices form the basis for tracking the behavior of devices and to search for misbehavior.

3.2 Search

Search aims at identifying misbehaving devices in an unsupervised manner. Device behavior is monitored via the correlation matrices presented in the previous section. Using numerous observations SBS computes a specific reference that exhibits the normal inter-device usage pattern. Then, SBS compares the computed reference with the current data and reports devices that deviate from their usual behavior.

3.2.1 Reference

We define four reference matrices, which capture normal device behavior at the four time scale ranges defined in Section 3.1.2. The references are computed as follows: (1) we retrieve the correlation matrices for n consecutive time bins. (2) For each pair of devices we compute the median correlation over the n time bins and obtain a matrix of the median device correlations.

Formally, for each time scale range the computed reference matrix for d devices and n time bins is:

$$R_{i,j} = \text{median}(C_{i,j}^1, ..., C_{i,j}^n)$$

where i and j ranges in $[1, d]$.

Because anomalies are rare by definition, we assume the data used to construct the reference matrix is an accurate sample of the population; it is unbiased and accurately captures the range of normal behavior. Abnormal correlation values, that could appear during model construction, are ignored by the median operator thanks to its robustness to outlier (50% breakdown point). However, if that assumption does not hold (more than 50% of the data is anomalous), our model will flag the opposite – labeling abnormal as normal and vice-versa. From close inspection of our data, we believe our primary assumption is sound.

3.2.2 Behavior change

We compare each device behavior, for all time bins, to the one provided by the reference matrix. Consider the correlation matrix C^t obtained from the data for time bin t ($1 \le t \le n$). Vector $C_{i,*}^t$ is the behavior of the ith device for this time bin. Its normal behavior is given by the corresponding vector in the reference matrix $R_{i,*}$. We measure the device behavior change at the time bin t with the following Minkowski weighted distance:

$$l_i^t = \left(\sum_{j=1}^d w_{ij} \left(C_{i,j}^t - R_{i,j} \right)^p \right)^{1/p}$$

where d is the number of devices and w_{ij} is:

$$w_{ij} = \frac{R_{i,j}}{\sum_{k=1}^d R_{i,k}}.$$

The weight w enables us to highlight the relationship changes between the device i and those highly correlated to it in the reference matrix. In other words, our definition of behavior change is mainly driven by the relationship among devices that are usually used in concert. We also set $p = 4$ in order to inhibit small differences between $C_{i,j}^t$ and $R_{i,j}$ but emphasize the important ones.

By monitoring this quantity over several time bins the abnormal device behaviors are easily identified as the outlier values. In order to identify these outlier values we implement a robust detector based on median absolute deviation (MAD), a dispersion measure commonly used in anomaly detection [16, 7]. It is a measure that robustly estimates the variability of the data by computing the median of the absolute deviations from the median of the data. Let

$l_i = [l_i^1, ..., l_i^n]$ be a vector representing the behavior changes of device i over n time bins, then its MAD value is defined as:

$$\text{MAD}_i = b \, \text{median}(|l_i - \text{median}(l_i)|)$$

where the constant b is usually set to 1.4826 for consistency with the usual parameter σ for Gaussian distributions. Consequently, we define anomalous behavior, for device i at time t, such that the following equation is satisfied:

$$l_i^t > \text{median}(l_i) + \tau \, \text{MAD}_i$$

Note, τ is a parameter that permits to make SBS more or less sensitive.

The final output of SBS is a list of alarms in the form (t, i) meaning that the device i has abnormal behavior at the time bin t. The priority of the alarms in this list is selected by the building administrator by tuning the parameter τ.

4. DATA SETS

We evaluate SBS using data collected from buildings in two different geographic locations. One is a new building on main campus of the University of Tokyo and the other is an older building at the University of California, Berkeley.

4.1 Engineering Building 2 - Todai

Engineering building 2, at the University of Tokyo (Todai), is a 12-story building completed in 2005 and is now hosting classrooms, laboratories, offices and server rooms. The electricity consumption of the lighting and HVAC systems of 231 rooms is monitored by 135 sensors. Rather than a centralized HVAC system, small, local HVAC systems are set up throughout the buidling. The HVAC systems are classified into two categories, EHP (Electrical Heat Pump) and GHP (Gas Heat Pump). The GHPs are the only devices that serve numerous rooms and multiple floors. The 5 GHPs in the dataset serve 154 rooms. The EHP and lighting systems serve only pairs of rooms and which are directly controlled by the occupants. In addition, the sensor metadata provides device-type and location information (room number), therefore, the electricity consumption of each pair of rooms is separately monitored.

The dataset contains 10 weeks of data starting from June 27, 2011 and ending on September 5, 2011. This period of time is particularly interesting for two reasons: 1) in this region, the summer is the most energy-demanding season and 2) the building manager actively works to curtail energy usage as much as possible due to the Tohoku earthquake and Fukushima nuclear accident.

Furthermore, this dataset is a valuable ground truth to evaluate the Strip and Bind portions of SBS. Since the light and HVAC of the rooms are directly controlled by the room's occupants, we expect SBS to uncover verifiable devices relationships.

4.2 Cory Hall - UC Berkeley

Cory Hall, at UC Berkeley, is a 5-story building hosting mainly classrooms, meeting rooms, laboratories and a datacenter. This building was completed in 1950, thus its infrastructure is significantly different from the Japanese one. The HVAC system in the building is centralized and serves several floors per unit. There is a separate unit for an internal fabricated laboratory, inside the building.

This dataset consists of 8 weeks of energy consumption traces measured by 70 sensors starting on April 5th, 2011. In contrast to the other dataset, a variety of devices are monitored, including, electric receptacles on certain floors, most of the HVAC components, power panels and whole-building consumption.

These two building infrastructures are fundamentally different. This enables us to evaluate the practical efficacy of the proposed, unsupervised method in two very different environments.

4.3 Data pre-processing

Data pre-processing is not generally required for the proposed approach. Nevertheless, we observe in a few exceptional cases that sensors reporting excessively high values (i.e. values higher than the device actual capacity) that greatly alter the performance of SBS by inducing a large bias in the computation of the correlation coefficient. Therefore, we remove values that are higher than the maximum capacity of the devices, from the raw data.

5. EXPERIMENTAL RESULTS

In this section we evaluate SBS on our building traces. We demonstrate the benefits of striping the data by monitoring patterns captured at different time scales. Then, we thoroughly investigate the alarms reported by SBS.

5.1 Shortcomings

Because our analysis is done on historical data, some of the faults found by SBS could not be fully corroborated. In order to fully examine the effectiveness of our approach, we must run it in real time and physically check that the problem is actually occurring. When a problem is detected in the historical trace, months after it has occurred, the current state of the building may no longer reflect what is in the traces. Some of the anomalies discussed in this section uncover interpretable patterns that are difficult to find in practice. For example, simultaneous heating and cooling is a known, recurring problem in buildings, but it is very hard to identify when it is occurring. Some of the anomalies we could not interpret might be interpretable by a building manager, however, we did not consult either building manager for this study. Therefore, the results of this study do not examine the true/false positive rate exhaustively.

The true/false negative rate is impractical to assess. It may be examined through synthetic stimulation of the building via the control system. However, getting cooperation from a building manager to hand over control of the building for experimentation in non-trivial. Therefore, we forgo a full true/false negative analysis in our evaluation.

Because of these challenges, the evaluation of SBS focuses on comparing the output with known fault signatures. We examine anomalies, in either building, where the anomaly is easily interpretable but difficult to find by the building manager. We forego a comparison of SBS with competing algorithms because related algorithms require detailed knowledge of the building, *a priori*. The advantage of SBS is that it requires no such information to provide immediate value.

5.2 Device behavior at different time scales

The Strip and Bind part of SBS is evaluated using the data from Eng. Bldg 2. This dataset is appropriate to measure SBS's performance, since lighting and HVAC systems serving the same room are usually used simultaneously. Consequently, we analyze this data using SBS and verify that the higher correlations at medium frequencies correspond to devices located in the same room.

The dataset is split into 10, one-week bins and each bin is processed by SBS. Using the 10 correlation matrices at each time scale range, SBS uncovers the four reference matrices depicted in Figure 5.

High frequencies.

In this work the high frequencies correspond to the signals *noise*, therefore, we do not expect any useful information from the corresponding matrix (Figure 5a). Indeed, the corresponding reference matrix does not provide any help to determine a device's relative location. Thus, we emphasize that high frequency data should be ignored for uncovering device relationships (in contrast to [10]). Interestingly, we find that the sensors monitoring the lights generate consistent noise.

Medium frequencies.

Our main focus is on the medium frequencies as it is designed to capture the intrinsic device relationships. Figure 5b shows the correlation matrix at medium frequencies. It is significantly different from the one obtained with the raw signals (Figure 1): high correlation coefficients are concentrated along the matrix diagonal. Since devices serving the same or adjacent rooms are placed nearby in the matrix it validates our hypothesis: *high correlation scores within the medium frequency band shows strong inter-device relationships.*

Considering this reference matrix as an adjacency matrix of a graph, in which the nodes are the devices, we identify the clusters of correlated devices using a community mining algorithm [5]. As expected we obtain mainly clusters of only two devices (light and HVAC serving the same room), but we also find clusters that are composed of more devices. For example a cluster contains 3 HVAC systems serving the three server rooms. Although these server rooms are located on different floors, SBS shows a strong correlation between these devices. Coincidentally, they are managed similarly. Interestingly, we also observe a couple of clusters that consist of independent devices serving adjacent rooms belonging to the same lab. The bigger cluster contains 33 devices that are 2 GHP devices and the corresponding lights. This correlation matrix and the corresponding clusters highlight the ability for SBS to identify such hidden inter-device usage relationships.

Low frequencies.

Low frequencies capture daily patterns, embedded in all the device traces. Figure 5c depicts the corresponding reference matrix which is similar to the one of raw signal traces (Figure 1) and it shows no particular structure.These partial signals are discarded as they do not help us in identifying inter-device usage patterns.

Residual data.

The residual data shows the weekly trend, which gives us no information about device relationships. But, surprisingly, by reordering the correlation matrix based on the type

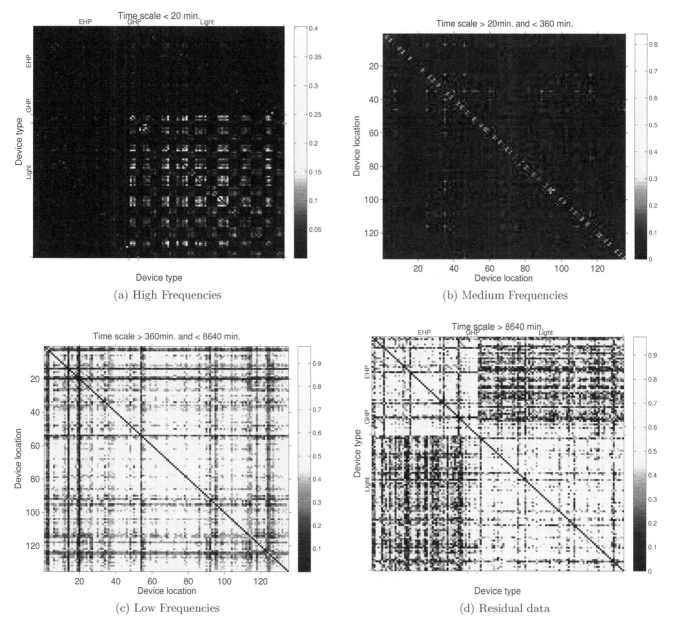

(a) High Frequencies

(b) Medium Frequencies

(c) Low Frequencies

(d) Residual data

Figure 5: Reference matrices for the four time scale ranges (the diagonal $x = y$ is colored in black for better reading). The medium frequencies highlight devices that are located next to each other thus intrinsically related. The low frequencies contains the common daily pattern of the data. The residual data permits to visually identify devices of the similar type.

of the devices (Figure 5d) we can visually identify two major clusters. The first cluster consists of HVAC devices (see EHP and GHP in Figure 5d) and the second one contains only lights. An in-depth examination of the data reveals that long-term trends are inherent to the device types. For example, as the consumption of both the EHP and GHP devices is driven by the building occupancy and the outside temperature, these two types of devices follow the same trend. However, the use of light is independent from the outside temperature thus the lighting systems follow a common trend different from the EHP and GHP one.

We conduct the same experiments by splitting the dataset in 70 bins of 1 day long and observe analogous results at high and medium frequencies but not at lower frequencies. This is because the bins are too short to exhibit daily oscillations and the residual data captures only the daily trend.

5.3 Anomalies

We evaluate the *search* performance of SBS using the traces from the Eng. Bldg 2 and Cory Hall. Due to the lack of historical data, such as room schedule or reports of energy waste, the evaluation is non-trivial. Furthermore, getting ground truth data from a manual inspection of the hundreds traces of our data sets is impractical. The lack of ground truth data prevents us from producing a systematic

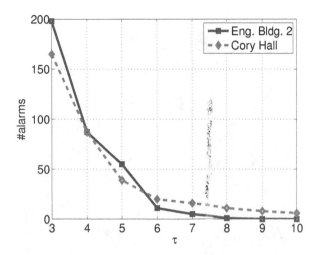

Figure 6: Number of reported alarms for various threshold value ($\tau = [3, 10]$).

	High	Low	Punc.	Missing	Other
Eng. Bldg 2	9 (5)	6 (5)	1 (1)	36 (1)	3 (3)
Cory Hall	25 (7)	7 (3)	4 (4)	0 (0)	3 (3)

Table 1: Classification of the alarms reported by SBS for both dataset (and the number of corresponding anomalies).

analysis of the anomalies missed by SBS (i.e. false negatives rate). Nevertheless, we exhibit the relevance of the anomalies uncovered by SBS (i.e. high true positive rate and low false positive rate) by manually checking the output of SBS.

Anomaly classification.

To validate SBS results we manually inspect the anomalies detected by the algorithm. For each reported alarm (t, i) we investigate the device trace i and the devices correlated to it to determine the reason for the alarm. Specifically, we retrieve the major relationship change that causes the alarm (i.e. $\max(|w_j(C_{i,j}^t - R_{i,j})|)$, see Section 3.2) and examine the metadata associated to the corresponding device. This investigation allows us to classify the alarms into five groups:

- *High power usage*: alarms corresponding to electricity waste.

- *Low power usage*: alarms representing the abnormally low electricity consumption of a device.

- *Punctual abnormal usage*: alarms standing for short term (less than 2.5 hours) raise or drop of the electricity consumption.

- *Missing data*: alarms raised due to a sensor failure.

- *Other*: alarms whose root cause is unclear.

Experimental setup.

For each experiment, the data is split in time bins of one day, starting from 09:00 a.m. – which is approximately the

office's opening time. We avoid having bins start at midnight since numerous anomalies appear at night and they are better highlighted if they are not spanning two time bins. Only the data at medium frequencies are analyzed, the other frequency bands are ignored, and the reference matrix is computed from all time bins.

The threshold τ tunes the sensitivity of SBS, hence, the number of reported alarms. Furthermore, by plotting the number of alarms against the value of τ for both datasets (Figure 6) we observe an elbow in the graph around $\tau = 5$. With thresholds lower than this pivot value ($\tau < 5$), the number of alarms significantly increases, causing less important anomalies to be reported. For higher values ($\tau > 5$), the number of alarms is slowly decreasing, providing more conservative results that consist of the most important anomalies. This pivot value provides a good trade off for either data set.

Table 1 classifies the alarms reported by SBS on both datasets. Anomalies spanning several time bins (or involving several devices) may raise several alarms. We display these in Table 1 as numbers in brackets – the number of anomalies corresponding to the reported alarms.

5.3.1 Engineering Building 2

SBS reported 55 alarms over the 10 weeks of the Eng. Bldg 2 dataset. However, 36 alarms are set aside because of sensor errors; one GHP has missing data for the first 18 days. Since this device is highly correlated to the GHP in the reference matrix, their relationship is broken for the 18 first bins and for each bin one alarm per device is raised.

In spite of the post-Fukushima measures to reduce Eng. Bldg 2's energy consumption, SBS reported 9 alarms corresponding to high power usage (Table 1). Figure 7a depicts the electricity consumption of the light and EHP in the same room where two alarms are raised. Because the EHP was not used during daytime (but is turned on at night, when the light is turned off) the relationship between the two devices is "broken" and an alarm is raised for each device. Figure 7b shows another example of energy waste. The light is on at night and the EHP is off. The top-priority anomaly reported by SBS is caused by the 10 days long constant use of an EHP (Figure 7d) and this waste of electricity accounts for 165 kWh. SBS partially reports this anomaly but lower values of τ permits us to identify most of it.

We observed 6 alarms corresponding to abnormally low power use. Upon further inspection we notice that it corresponds to energy saving initiatives from the occupants – likely due to electricity concerns in Japan. This behavior is displayed in Figure 7c. The room is occupied at the usual office hours (indicated by light usage) but the EHP is not on in order to save electricity.

5.3.2 Cory Hall

SBS reported 39 alarms for the Cory Hall dataset (Table 1). 7 are classified as low power usage, however, our inspection revealed that the root causes are different than for the Eng. Bldg 2 dataset. We observe that the low power usage usually corresponds to device failures or misconfiguration. For example, Figure 8a depicts the electricity consumption of the 2nd floor chiller and a power riser that comprises the consumption of multiple systems, including the chiller. As the chiller suddenly stops working, the correlation between

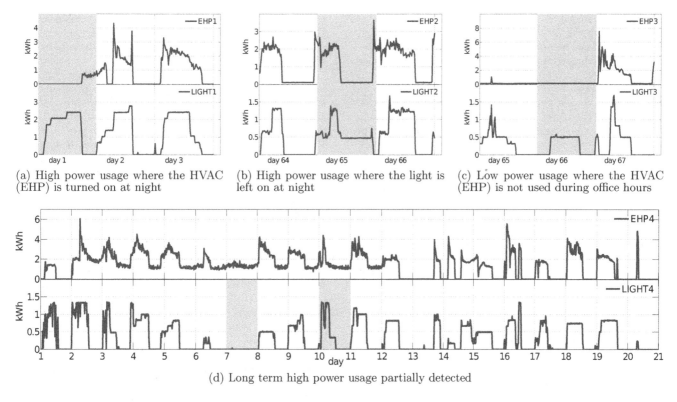

(a) High power usage where the HVAC (EHP) is turned on at night

(b) High power usage where the light is left on at night

(c) Low power usage where the HVAC (EHP) is not used during office hours

(d) Long term high power usage partially detected

Figure 7: Example of alarms (red rectangles) reported by SBS on the Eng. Bldg 2 dataset

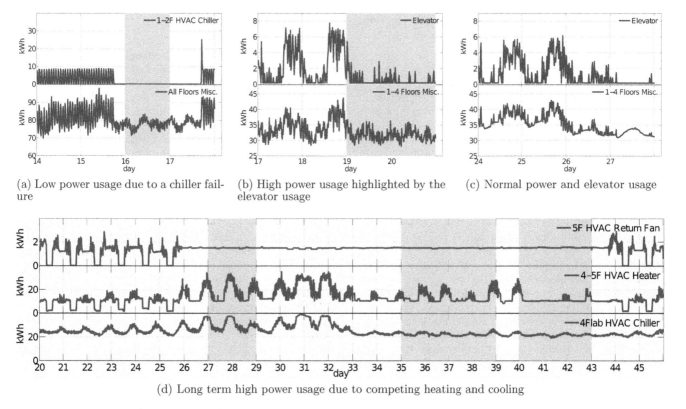

(a) Low power usage due to a chiller failure

(b) High power usage highlighted by the elevator usage

(c) Normal power and elevator usage

(d) Long term high power usage due to competing heating and cooling

Figure 8: Example of alarms (red rectangles) reported by SBS on the Cory Hall dataset

both measurements is significantly altered and an alarm for each device is raised.

SBS also reports 25 alarms corresponding to high power usage. One of the identified anomalies is particularly interesting. We indirectly observe abnormal usage of a device from the power consumption of the elevator and a power panel for equipment from the 1st to the 4th floor. Figure 8b and 8c show the electricity consumption for both devices. SBS uncovers the correlation between the these two signals, as the amount of electricity going through the panel fluctuates along with the elevator power consumption (Figure 8c). In fact, the elevator is a good indicator of the building's occupancy. Anomalous energy-consumption is identified during a weekend as the consumption measured at the panel is independently fluctuating from the elevator usage. These fluctuations are caused by a device that is not directly monitored. Therefore, we could not identify the root cause more precisely. Nevertheless, the alarm is worthwhile for building operators to start investigating.

The most important anomaly identified in Cory Hall is shown in Figure 8d. This anomaly corresponds to the malfunctioning of the HVAC heater serving the 4th and 5th floors. The heater is constantly working for 18 consecutive days, regardless of the underlying occupant activity. Moreover, in order to maintain appropriate temperature this also results in an increase of the 4th floor HVAC chiller power consumption and several fans, such as the one depicted in Figure 8d. This situation is indicative of simultaneous heating and cooling – whereby heating and cooling systems are competing – and it is a well-know problem in building management that leads to significant energy waste. For this example, the electricity waste is estimated around 2500 kWh for the heater. Nevertheless, as the anomaly spans over 18 days, it is hidden in the building's overall consumption, thus, it is difficult to detect by building administrators without SBS.

6. RELATED WORK

The research community has addressed the detection of abnormal energy-consumption in buildings in numerous ways [17, 18].

The rule-based techniques rely on a priori knowledge, they assert the sustainability of a system by identifying a set of undesired behaviors. Using a hierarchical set of rules, Schein et al. propose a method to diagnose HVAC systems [23]. In comparison, state machine models take advantage of historical training data and domain knowledge to learn the states and transitions of a system. The transitions are based on measured stimuli identified through a domain expertise. State machines can model the operation of HVAC systems [22] and permit to predict or detect the abnormal behavior of HVAC's components [3]. However, the deployment of these methods require expert knowledge and are mostly applied to HVAC systems.

In [24], the authors propose a simple unsupervised approach to monitor the average and peak daily consumption of a building and uncover outlier, nevertheless, the misbehaving devices are left unidentified.

Using regression analysis and weather variables the devices energy-consumption is predicted and abnormal usage is highlighted. The authors of [6] use kernel regression to forecast device consumption and devices that behave differently from the predictions are reported as anomalous. Re-

gression models are also used with performances indices to monitor the HVAC's components and identify inefficiencies [28]. The implementation of these approaches in real situations is difficult, since it requires a training dataset and non-trivial parameter tuning.

Similar to our approach, previous studies identify abnormal energy-consumption using frequency analysis and unsupervised anomaly detection methods. The device's consumption is decomposed using Fourier transform and outlier values are detected using clustering techniques [2, 27, 8]. However, these methods assume a constant periodicity in the data and this causes many false positives in alarm reporting. We do not make any assumption about the device usage schedule. We only observe and model device relationships. We take advantage of a recent frequency analysis technique that enables us uncover the inter-device relationships [10]. The identified anomalies correspond to devices that deviate from their normal relationship to other devices.

Reducing a building's energy consumption has also received a lot of attention from the research community. The most promising techniques are based on occupancy model predictions as they ensure that empty rooms are not over conditioned needlessly. Room occupancy is usually monitored through sensor networks [1, 9] or the computer network traffic [19]. These approaches are highly effective for buildings that have rarely-occupied rooms (e.g. conference room) and studies show that such approaches can achieve up to 42% annual energy saving. SBS is fundamentally different from these approaches. SBS identifies the abnormal usage of any devices rather than optimizing the normal usage of specific devices. Nevertheless, the two approaches are complementary and energy-efficient buildings should take advantage of the synergy between them.

7. DISCUSSION

SBS is a practical method for mining device traces, uncovering hidden relationships and abnormal behavior. In this paper, we validate the efficacy of SBS using the sensor metadata (i.e. device types and location), however, these tags are not needed by SBS to uncover devices relationships. Furthermore, SBS requires no prior knowledge about the building and deploying our tool to other buildings requires no human intervention – neither extra sensors nor a training dataset is needed.

SBS is a best effort approach that takes advantage of all the existing building sensors. For example, our experiments revealed that SBS indirectly uncovers building occupancy through device use (e.g. the elevator in the Building 2). The proposed method would benefit from existing sensors that monitor room occupancy as well (e.g. those deployed in [1, 9]). Savings opportunities are also observable with a minimum of 2 monitored devices and building energy consumption can be better understood after using SBS.

SBS constructs a model for normal inter-device behavior by looking at the usage patterns over time, thus, we run the risk that a device that constantly misbehaves is labeled as normal. Nevertheless, building operators are able to quickly identify such perpetual anomalies by validating the clusters of correlated devices uncovered by SBS. The inspection of these clusters is effortless compare to the investigation of the numerous raw traces. Although this kind of scenario is possible it was not observed in our experiments.

In this paper, we analyze only the data at medium frequencies, however, we observe that data at the high frequencies and residual data (Figure 5) also permits us to determine the device type. This information is valuable to automatically retrieve and validate device labels – a major challenge in building metadata management.

This paper aims to establish a methodology to identify abnormalities in device power traces and inter-device usage patterns. In addition, we are planning to apply this method to online detection using, for example, a sliding window to compute an adaptive reference matrix that evolve in time. However, designing such system raises new challenges that are left for future work.

8. CONCLUSIONS

The goal of this article is to assist building administrators in identifying misbehaving devices in large building sensor deployments. We proposed an unsupervised method to systematically detect abnormal energy consumption in buildings: the Strip, Bind, and Search (SBS) method. SBS uncovers inter-device usage patterns by striping dominant trends off the devices energy-consumption trace. Then, it monitors device usage and reports devices that deviate from the norm. Our main contribution is to develop an unsupervised technique to uncover the true inter-device relationships that are hidden by noise and dominant trends inherent to the sensor data. SBS is used on two sets of traces captured from two buildings with fundamentally different infrastructures. The abnormal consumption identified in these two buildings are mainly energy waste. The most important one is an instance of a competing heater and cooler that caused the heater to waste around 2500 kWh.

Acknowledgments

The authors thank Hideya Ochiai for providing the data from the University of Tokyo. This research was partially supported by the JSPS fellowship program and the CNRS/JSPS Joint Research Project. This work is also supported in part by the National Science Foundation under grants CPS-0932209 and CPS-0931843.

9. REFERENCES

[1] Y. Agarwal, B. Balaji, S. Dutta, R. K. Gupta, and T. Weng. Duty-cycling buildings aggressively: The next frontier in hvac control. In *IPSN'11*, pages 246–257, Chicago, IL, USA, 2011.

[2] G. Bellala, M. Marwah, M. Arlitt, G. Lyon, and C. E. Bash. Towards an understanding of campus-scale power consumption. Buildsys'11, page 6, Seattle, WA, Nov. 1, 2011.

[3] G. Bellala, M. Marwah, A. Shah, M. Arlitt, and C. Bash. A finite state machine-based characterization of building entities for monitoring and control. pages 153–160, 2012.

[4] M. Blanco-Velasco, B. Weng, and K. E. Barner. Ecg signal denoising and baseline wander correction based on the empirical mode decomposition. *Computers in biology and medicine*, 38(1):1–13, jan. 2008.

[5] V. D. Blondel, J.-L. Guillaume, R. Lambiotte, and E. Lefebvre. Fast unfolding of communities in large networks. *J.STAT.MECH.*, 2008.

[6] M. Brown, C. Barrington-Leigh, and Z. Brown. Kernel regression for real-time building energy analysis. *Journal of Building Performance Simulation*, 5(4):263–276, 2012.

[7] P. Chan, M. Mahoney, and M. Arshad. Learning rules and clusters for anomaly detection in network traffic. In *Managing Cyber Threats*, volume 5 of *Massive Computing*, pages 81–99. Springer US, 2005.

[8] C. Chen and D. J. Cook. Energy outlier detection in smart environments. In *Artificial Intelligence and Smarter Living*, volume WS-11-07 of *AAAI Workshops*. AAAI, 2011.

[9] V. L. Erickson, M. Á. Carreira-Perpiñán, and A. Cerpa. Observe: Occupancy-based system for efficient reduction of hvac energy. In *IPSN'11*, pages 258–269, Chicago, IL, USA, 2011.

[10] R. Fontugne, J. Ortiz, D. Culler, and H. Esaki. Empirical mode decomposition for intrinsic-relationship extraction in large sensor deployments. In *IoT-App'12, Workshop on Internet of Things Applications*, Beijing, China, 2012.

[11] T. Hasan and M. Hasan. Suppression of residual noise from speech signals using empirical mode decomposition. *Signal Processing Letters, IEEE*, 16(1):2 –5, jan. 2009.

[12] H. Huang and J. Pan. Speech pitch determination based on hilbert-huang transform. *Signal Processing*, 86(4):792 – 803, 2006.

[13] N. E. Huang. Computing frequency by using generalized zero-crossing applied to intrinsic mode functions. *U.S. Patent 6,990,436 B1*, 2006.

[14] N. E. Huang, Z. Shen, S. R. Long, M. C. Wu, H. H. Shih, Q. Zheng, N.-C. Yen, C. C. Tung, and H. H. Liu. The empirical mode decomposition and the hilbert spectrum for nonlinear and non-stationary time series analysis. *Proceedings of the Royal Society of London. Series A*, 454(1971):903–995, 1998.

[15] N. E. Huang, Z. Wu, S. R. Long, K. C. Arnold, X. Chen, and K. Blank. On instantaneous frequency. *Advances in Adaptive Data Analysis*, pages 177–229, 2009.

[16] P. Huber and E. Ronchetti. *Robust Statistics*. Wiley Series in Probability and Statistics. Wiley, 2009.

[17] S. Katipamula and M. Brambley. Review article: Methods for fault detection, diagnostics, and prognostics for building systemsâĂŤa review, part i. *HVAC&R Research*, 11(1):3–25, 2005.

[18] S. Katipamula and M. Brambley. Review article: Methods for fault detection, diagnostics, and prognostics for building systemsâĂŤa review, part ii. *HVAC&R Research*, 11(2):169–187, 2005.

[19] Y. Kim, R. Balani, H. Zhao, and M. B. Srivastava. Granger causality analysis on ip traffic and circuit-level energy monitoring. BuildSys'10, pages 43–48, Zurich, Switzerland, Nov. 2, 2010.

[20] T. Lee and T. B. M. J. Ouarda. Prediction of climate nonstationary oscillation processes with empirical mode decomposition. *Journal of Geophysical Research*, 116, 2011.

[21] J. C. Nunes, S. Guyot, and E. Delechelle. Texture analysis based on local analysis of the bidimensional

empirical mode decomposition. *Machine Vision and Applications*, 16:177–188, 2005.

[22] D. Patnaik, M. Marwah, R. Sharma, and N. Ramakrishnan. Temporal data mining approaches for sustainable chiller management in data centers. *ACM Transactions on Intelligent Systems and Technology*, 2(4), 2011.

[23] J. Schein and S. Bushby. A hierarchical rule-based fault detection and diagnostic method for hvac systems. *HVAC&R Research*, 12(1):111–125, 2006.

[24] J. E. Seem. Using intelligent data analysis to detect abnormal energy consumption in buildings. *Energy and Buildings*, 39(1):52 – 58, 2007.

[25] M. Torres, M. Colominas, G. Schlotthauer, and P. Flandrin. A complete ensemble empirical mode decomposition with adaptive noise. In *IEEE International Conference on Acoustics, Speech and Signal Processing (ICASSP)*, pages 4144 –4147, May 2011.

[26] U.S. Energy Information Administration. Annual Energy Review 2011, 2012.

[27] M. Wrinch, T. H. EL-Fouly, and S. Wong. Anomaly detection of building systems using energy demand frequency domain anlaysis. In *IEEE Power & Energy Society General Meeting*, San-Diego, CA, USA, 2012.

[28] Q. Zhou, S. Wang, and Z. Ma. A model-based fault detection and diagnosis strategy for hvac systems. *International Journal of Energy Research*, 33(10):903–918, 2009.

Nemo: A High-fidelity Noninvasive Power Meter System for Wireless Sensor Networks

Ruogu Zhou, Guoliang Xing
Department of Computer Science and Engineering, Michigan State University, USA
{zhouruog,glxing}@cse.msu.edu

ABSTRACT

In this paper, we present the design and implementation of *Nemo* – a practical *in situ* power metering system for wireless sensor networks. Nemo features a new circuit design called *shunt resistor switch* that can dynamically adjust the resistance of shunt resistors based on the current load. This allows Nemo to achieve a wide dynamic current range and high measurement accuracy. Nemo transmits real-time power measurements to the host node solely through the power line, by modulating the current load and the supply voltage. This feature leads to a noninvasive, plug & play design that allows Nemo to be easily installed on existing mote platforms without physical wiring or soldering. We have implemented a prototype of Nemo and conducted extensive experimental evaluation. Our results show that Nemo can transmit high-throughput measurement data to the host through voltage/current load modulation. Moreover, it has satisfactory measurement fidelity over a wide range of operating conditions. In particular, Nemo yields a dynamic measurement range of 250,000:1, which is 2.5X and 7X that of two state-of-the-art sensor network power meter systems, while only incurring an average measurement error of 1.34%. We also use a case study to demonstrate that Nemo is able to track the highly dynamic sleep current consumption of TelosB motes, which has important implications for the design of low duty-cycle sensor networks that operate in dynamic environments.

Categories and Subject Descriptors

C.2.3 [**Computer-communication Networks**]: Network Operations—*Network monitoring, Network management*; C.4 [**Performance of Systems**]: Measurement techniques

Keywords

Wireless Sensor Networks, Power Monitoring, Power-line Communication

1. INTRODUCTION

Energy-efficiency is one of the most important design objectives of wireless sensor networks due to limited energy resources. Despite the significant research efforts in energy-aware approaches at various network layers (MAC/routing/application), it remains challenging to actually validate the energy-efficiency claims of existing solutions, largely due to the lack of ability to track the real-time power consumption of a sensor network at runtime. In addition, real-time power usage data is vital for senor nodes to modify their behavior and adapt to variable network conditions and dynamic physical environments. For example, in the four-month habitat monitoring sensor network deployment on Great Duck Island, many nodes experienced unknown energy issues and died prematurely [19]. If low-power *in-situ* meters were employed to continuously monitor the power consumption of nodes, node failures may be diagnosed or even avoided through runtime adaptation.

The aforementioned requirements have motivated the development of *in-situ* power metering systems [5] [12] [17] [11] [8] [13] [18] that can measure the power consumption of sensor nodes in real-time. A practical power meter system must meet several key requirements due to the unique characteristics of wireless sensor networks. First, it must achieve high measurement fidelity, including wide dynamic range, high sampling rate, high measurement resolution and accuracy. The current consumption of a sensor node is highly dynamic and has a wide range of at least 5 orders of magnitude, from about a few uA in sleep state to about several hundreds mA in active state. The high resolution measurement of low current consumption (<10 uA) is particularly important because most sensor networks operate under low duty-cycles and their lifetime is largely determined by the sleep current consumption.

Second, a power meter should be minimally *invasive* to the host node in terms of both installation and operation. Most existing sensor network platforms do not have any built-in power metering capability. To be practically useful, a power meter should be easy to install on existing sensor hardware, with little or no physical wiring/soldering. Moreover, it should operate in a stand alone manner, without relying on host resources like memory and CPU. This ensures that the performance of the host nodes is not compromised in the presence of power metering, improving the fidelity of measurement.

Third, a power meter must be able to communicate with the host node in real time. This will not only allow the host node to dynamically configure the meter, but also enable real-time feedback of power measurement to the host node for run-time adaptation. Unfortunately, the requirement of real-time host-meter communication often leads to an invasive hardware design. For instance, although I/O ports of MCU can implement high-speed data transfer, they require physical wiring or soldering between power meter and the host node.

In this paper, we present *Nemo* – a Noninvasive high-fidElity power-Meter for sensOrnets. As a key advantage, Nemo connects to the host node using only the power/ground lines, requiring no dedicated data communication wires. At the same time, Nemo implements real-time, high-speed bi-directional communication with the host node based on current/voltage modulation, in which the current load and the supply voltage of power line are modulated to carry information. The power line communication based on current/voltage modulation allows Nemo to retrofit existing sensor network platforms with power metering capability via a wire-free, plug & play installation. Nemo also employs a circuit design called *shunt resistor switch* that can dynamically adjust the resistance of shunt resistors based on the current load. This allows Nemo to achieve a wide dynamic current range without resorting to expensive and power-hungry components like high-resolution analog-to-digital converters (ADCs).

We have implemented a prototype of Nemo (as shown in Fig. 2) and conducted extensive experimental evaluation. Our results show that Nemo has satisfactory measurement fidelity under a range of operating conditions. In particular, Nemo yields a dynamic measurement range from 0.8 uA to 200 mA, a sampling rate of 8 KHz, and a minimum resolution of 0.013 uA, while only incurring an average measurement error of 1.34%. We also present a case study where Nemo is used to track the current consumption of TelosB motes. Our results reveal that the sleep current consumption varies significantly (as much as five times) with environmental temperature and also across different motes. This finding has important implications for the design of low duty-cycle sensor networks that operate in dynamic environments, demonstrating the benefits of high-fidelity *in-situ* power measurement using Nemo.

2. RELATED WORK

A common practice in sensor network design is to infer the power consumption of a node based on the expected active time of the components and their power consumption models measured offline [16]. A representative example of such approach is PowerTOSSIM [16]. However, the power models measured in laboratory settings cannot reflect the variations of hardware components and environmental factors. Due to this drawback, most software based power estimation approaches suffer large estimation errors. It is shown in [20] that the simulation error of PowerTOSSIM [16] can be as high as 30%.

In-situ power meters can provide run-time power consumption of a hardware device. Commercial power monitoring ICs such as DS2438, BQ2019 and ADE7753 are widely used in portable devices like cellphones for real-time battery monitoring. However, to the best of our knowledge, none of these ICs can meet the requirements of power metering in sensor networks, including wide dynamic range ($10^5 : 1$) and high sampling rate (> 5 KHz). For example, DS2438

only provides a maximum dynamic range of 1024:1 and a sampling rate up to 40 Hz [2].

Targeted low-power sensor networks, SPOT [11] provides a dynamic range of 45,000:1 and a resolution of lower than 1 uA. However, since SPOT needs an external +5.5V power supply, it cannot be directly powered by the onboard batteries. Although SPOT is designed to be integrated with current sensor platforms, it still requires wiring and soldering to the I/O pins of the sensor board. Moreover, SPOT measures energy consumption over a time period, rather than real-time fine-grained power consumption.

iCount [5] is another example of *in-situ* power meters for sensor networks. iCount measures power consumption by differentiating the measured energy, which is inferred from the frequency of the pulses appeared on the inductor pin of the switching regulator. Due to the low oscillating frequency of switching regulators, the sampling rate and resolution of iCount are significantly limited (only 80Hz sampling rate when resolution is 100 uA). Moreover, due to the nonlinear frequency-current relationship of the switching regulator, iCount suffers high measurement errors (up to 20%) [5]. Finally, iCount cannot work in a stand alone manner and must rely on onboard resources (CPU, RAM and timer). Therefore, it often incurs considerable computational overhead (a minimum of 13% host CPU time when sampling at 8 KHz) and cannot conduct measurement when the host falls asleep.

The current/voltage modulation schemes adopted by Nemo are inspired by the power-line networking technology [21]. However, the power-line networking literature adopts sophisticated techniques, such as OFDM, to modulate the AC voltage of power grid infrastructures for LAN communication, which is significantly different from the voltage/current modulation scheme we propose for low-power mote-class platforms. Several technologies, such as I2C, can realize low-power bi-directional communication over single data wire. However, they are not applicable to Nemo, which utilizes a single power wire, instead of a dedicated data wire, for bi-directional communication.

3. SYSTEM OVERVIEW

3.1 Design Objectives and Challenges

High measurement fidelity. In this work, the fidelity requirement includes wide dynamic range, high sampling rate, high measurement resolution and accuracy. In the design of Nemo, we mainly focus on the first two metrics as high resolution and accuracy are relatively easy to achieve as shown in our experiments in Sec. 7.

The current draw of a sensor node in active state ranges from 2 mA to 200 mA [1] [3] [22]. The sleep current consumption ranges from 2 uA [11] to several hundred uA. Although the sleep current consumption seems to be negligible, it largely determines the system lifetime of low duty-cycle networks. For example, for a TelosB mote with a 0.1% duty cycle, a mere 10 uA increase of sleep current will shorten the mote lifetime by 26%. Moreover, the sleep currents of even the same type of sensor nodes may differ significantly due to environmental factors (see Section 7.5), on-board components that sleep independently of CPU [9], and misconfigurations due to software bugs [23]. To accurately measure the current draw of both active and sleep

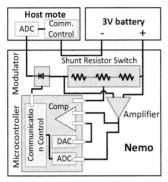
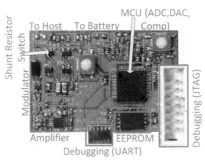
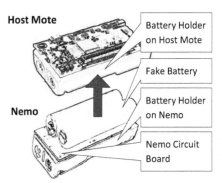

Figure 1: Nemo system architecture. Figure 2: A prototype implementation of Nemo.

Figure 3: A possible Nemo packaging for easy installation on TelosB motes.

states, Nemo must achieve a dynamic range of 100,000:1 (from 2 uA to 200 mA). The switching between different power states of the electrical components can lead to sudden current consumption spikes [11]. Our experiment shows that such spikes typically occur within a short duration ranging from 200 us to 400 us on TelosB motes. Nemo must capture such dynamic transitions because they provide important temporal variation of node power consumption, which can be used, for example, for system debugging and fault diagnosis. As a result, the minimum sampling rate needs to be at least 5 KHz.

Noninvasiveness. Nemo is designed to be noninvasive to the host sensor node in two aspects. First, hardware wiring or soldering should be minimized or completely avoided when connecting Nemo to the host node. Nemo is a plug & play component that can be easily installed on a variety of different existing sensor network platforms. This is particularly important for aftermarket sensor platforms without accessible I/O ports, e.g., sealed sensor nodes [10] or customized nodes without I/O expansion ports [7]. Second, Nemo must be a stand alone device that does not rely on on-board resources including RAM and CPU during run time. This ensures that the performance of the host nodes is not compromised in the presence of power metering, improving the fidelity of power measurement.

Real-time host-meter communication. A key advantage offered by *in-situ* power meters is that the measurement results can be fed back to the host node for real-time power monitoring and analysis, which enables run-time adaptation of a sensor network system. For example, when an energy-aware routing protocol is adopted, real-time power consumption data is crucial for making network-wide routing decisions. Furthermore, the host-meter communication also allows the host node to dynamically configure Nemo, e.g., shutting it down for energy conservation when real-time power monitoring is not needed.

Low power consumption. Low power consumption is another critical requirement for a power meter due to the limited energy resource of sensor nodes. In particular, many system issues are difficult to diagnose without long term power monitoring at a high sampling rate. However, achieving low power consumption and high measurement fidelity at the same time is challenging.

3.2 System Architecture

Fig. 1 illustrates the system architecture of Nemo, which consists of a microcontroller (MCU), a current measurement

circuit, and a voltage modulator. A prototype implementation of Nemo is shown in Fig. 2. The measurement circuit measures the current draw of the host node, and sends the measurement to the MCU. The voltage modulator, which is directly connected to an I/O pin of the MCU, modulates the voltage on the power line to transmit data to the host node. A battery pack is connected to the meter through which the host sensor node is powered. The power and ground wires are the only physical connection between the meter and the host node.

The MCU inside the meter processes measurement data, and stores the data into an EEPROM on the meter. The MCU also runs the host-meter communication protocol. The current that passes through the measurement circuit creates a small voltage over the shunt resistor, which is proportional to the current intensity. The voltage is then amplified by a differential amplifier. After amplification, the voltage signal is first digitalized by the on-chip low power 12-bit ADC in the MCU, and then converted to the current intensity.

The key difference between Nemo's current measurement circuit and traditional designs [15] is the shunt resistor. Typical current sensing design uses a single shunt resistor and a low resolution ADC, which cannot achieve wide dynamic current range and high sampling rate at the same time. In contrast, Nemo adopts a series of shunt resistors called *shunt resistor switch* whose resistance can be dynamically adjusted according to the required dynamic range. This design provides wide dynamic range without requiring expensive and power-hungry high-resolution ADCs.

During sleep state, the current draw of the sensor node is small and does not change drastically. In our design, Nemo can automatically enter sleep state when the host node falls asleep. A comparator on Nemo acts as a host wake-up detector which notifies the MCU of Nemo when the host wakes up. This design offers good energy saving without compromising measurement fidelity.

A key feature of Nemo is that the meter can communicate with the host node without dedicated data wires[1]. This is achieved by a novel technique called current/voltage modulation, in which the current load and the supply voltage are modulated to carry information. Specifically, when the host node transmits data to Nemo, it modulates its own current draw to encode data bits. On the reversed link where the data is transmitted from Nemo to the host node, the supply voltage of the host is modulated by Nemo to

---

[1]Nemo also supports conventional I/O or bus communications.

encode data bits. Our design achieves high link throughput while incurring low computational overhead. As shown in Section 7, although this technique introduces minor supply voltage fluctuation, it has no impact on the performance of host nodes.

The power line modulation techniques remove the need for any data wires between Nemo and the host node. As a result, with proper packaging, Nemo can be easily installed on almost any existing mote platforms without hard wiring or soldering. Fig. 3 illustrates a possible Nemo packaging[2] for easy installation on existing mote platforms with a battery pack.

4. HIGH FIDELITY CURRENT MEASUREMENT

The core of Nemo measurement subsystem is the current sensing circuit. A typical current sensing circuit consists of a shunt resistor, preamplifiers and a digital convertor. Two popular design choices that can achieve wide dynamic range are adjusting the amplification rate or using high resolution digital converters. However, the former requires sophisticated, power-hungry noise reduction circuits to achieve the desirable dynamic range while the latter incurs expensive, high power consumption convertors. As a result, limited by the low power consumption budget, neither of these two approaches can achieve favorable dynamic range.

4.1 Shunt Resistor Switch

Nemo adopts a technique used in auto-ranging digital multimeters to satisfy the fidelity requirement without incurring high power consumption. It features a series of shunt resistors which we refer to as *shunt resistor switch*. As illustrated in Fig. 4, the shunt resistor switch is composed of a series of resistors and electrically controlled switches. The resistance of the shunt resistor switch can be adjusted by shorting one or more resistors via switches. According to the ADC readings, a large (small) resistance is chosen when measuring small (large) current. With this design, both low and high currents can be accurately amplified to a proper voltage level for digitalization. As a result, a fixed pre-amplifier and a low resolution ADC can be adopted in the following subsequent stages of Nemo without compromising the measurement fidelity.

When the resistance of shunt resistor switch is high (i.e., measuring small current), a sudden current surge, which typically happens within tens of microseconds when host node switches its working mode, may cause a large voltage drop on the shunt resistor switch. This in turn leads to a significant supply voltage drop to the host node and even the malfunction of onboard components. If MCU only monitors the ADC readings, it cannot react to the sudden current surge promptly by adjusting the shunt resistor switch due to the long ADC sampling interval (>100 us). This issue is particularly critical when the host node wakes up from deep sleep, resulting in a sharp current increase up to four orders of magnitudes in several microseconds. We address this issue by using a comparator to generate an interrupt to MCU upon the sudden current increase. A comparator

compares the voltage on its two inputs, i.e. non-inverting input and inverting input, and outputs a high or low voltage indicating which input has larger voltage. In our design, the non-inverting input is tethered to the output of the pre-amplifier. The inverting input is connected to the output of a DAC which provides a reference voltage. The DAC output is set according to the maximum allowable voltage drop on the shunt resistor switch. For example, if the maximum allowable voltage drop is 30 mV and the amplification rate is 50X, then a reference voltage of 1.5V is output by the DAC. A voltage higher than 1.5V triggers the comparator to generate an interrupt to the MCU, which immediately adjusts the resistance of the shunt resistor switch. We note that the delay before the actual resistance adjustment, typically shorter than 2us in our measurements, results in a short transient high voltage drop. However, due to the decoupling capacitors and inductors on the power loop of the host, the voltage drop on the shunt resistor switch is slowly built up, resulting in no significant impact on the supply voltage.

The voltage after pre-amplification is digitalized by a 12-bit ADC on the MCU, and then converted to the current intensity. The adjustment of shunt resistor switch creates a sudden voltage change at the inputs of the differential amplifier and ADC. Nemo pauses the ADC sampling for 5us after switching, which allows these components to settle and avoids generating erroneous measurement results. The ADC measurement results are stored in an EEPROM on Nemo. Since the ADC generates measurement results at a high rate, the EEPROM can be filled up quickly. Nemo uses a simple compression algorithm to reduce the volume of data. The MCU stores a new measurement result only if it differs significantly from the previously stored one. Our experiments show that when a difference threshold of 1.6% is chosen, Nemo can achieve a compressing ratio up to 0.6% on TelosB motes running a typical sense-and-send application. We carefully optimized the code of compression and were able to process the measurement sampled at 8 KHz on the 8MHz MSP430 MCU. When Nemo is connected to a PC to upload measurements, a sampling rate of 100 KHz can be achieved by disabling the compressing algorithm.

4.2 Sleep Management

Even though Nemo employs a low power design, it still consumes considerable amount of power in the active state. Sensor network applications often employ duty cycles to conserve energy. When the host node is asleep, its current consumption is almost constant in a short time window. Our experiment shows that the variance of sleep current consumption of TelosB motes is less than 0.5 uA in 5 s time windows. This constant current draw clearly offers an opportunity for Nemo to save energy via sleep scheduling.

In our design, Nemo automatically falls asleep when the host node enters sleep state, and periodically wakes up to conduct measurements. Since the current draw fluctuation of the host node in sleep is rather small, the reduced sampling rate does not cause degradation of measurement fidelity. Wake-up of host components usually causes significant surge of the current draw, which must be captured to ensure high measurement fidelity. To detect such events, Nemo utilizes a comparator which raises an interrupt and immediately wakes up Nemo to resume high frequency sampling when the current draw of the node exceeds a certain thresh-

---

[2]The dimension of the current prototype of Nemo is 3" by 4". The PCB board can be made smaller in future by removing debugging components, including JTAG ports, LEDs, and buttons, and easily fit into a 2-AA battery pack.

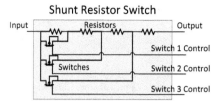

Figure 4: The resistance of the shunt resistor switch is adjusted by shorting one or more resistors.

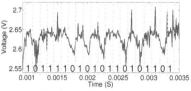

Figure 5: A voltage signal modulated at 8 Kbps carrying the data 0x0BD5AD.

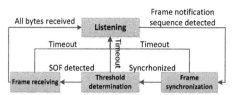

Figure 6: The receiving procedure state machine.

old. The threshold can be determined offline or measured in system initialization phase. During sleep, the MCU, ADC, and internal voltage reference are turned off to conserve energy. The amplifier, comparator, and DAC remains powered to detect the wake-up of the host node. The total current consumption of Nemo in sleep state is 150 uA.

5. HOST-METER COMMUNICATION

A key advantage of Nemo is that it enables a wire-free, plug & play installation on aftermarket sensor systems. However, this design choice rules out the possibility of using any dedicated on-board data wires of the host node. To implement the communication between host and meter, Nemo modulates voltage/current load of the power line, without using any dedicated communication wire. Specifically, the host node transmits data to the meter by modulating its own current draw. On the reversed link, the meter modulates the supply voltage of the host node to carry data. The two links work in half-duplex, sharing the same single power line.

5.1 Supply Voltage Modulation

Our basic idea of enabling the communication link from meter to host node is to encode information by modulating the amplitude of supply voltage while the host node decodes the information by measuring the voltage change. As a result, the measurement data can be transmitted from Nemo via a single power line. This approach is motivated by the fact that today's sensor network platforms can readily measure the supply voltage with on-MCU ADCs. In our design, a diode paralleled with an electrically controlled switch is used as the voltage modulator. As the diode causes a constant voltage drop, switching it on and off will generate a pulse signal over the amplitude of supply voltage. By controlling the switch of diode, the supply voltage of the host can be precisely modulated to carry information bits. However, a potential concern of this approach is that the fluctuation of the supply voltage caused by modulation may lead to malfunctioning of the host node. To address this issue, a low forward voltage drop Schottky diode is employed to create only a 100 mV voltage drop during modulation. In Section. 7.4, we show that such a small fluctuation has little impact on the performance of the host node. On the host node, the modulated signal is sampled by the ADC. The voltage samples are then decoded by a simple demodulating routine, as discussed in Section. 5.3.

5.2 Current Load Modulation

The idea of supply voltage modulation is not applicable to the communication link from host node to meter because the host node usually cannot vary the supply voltage. To realize the communication on the power line, the host n-

ode modulates its current draw, and the modulated current signal is then measured and decoded by the meter.

Controlled by the MCU, various electrical components on the host node can be turned on/off to create variation of the current draw. These components form simple but effective current modulators. Information can be encoded into the current draw patterns, which are measured by the ADC on the meter for receiving information. To achieve high communication bandwidth, the modulator must be toggled at a high frequency and generate sufficient current change. Commonly available on most sensor networks platforms, LEDs make perfect current modulators. They are usually directly connected to I/O pins of the MCU and thus can be switched at a high frequency. The current draw of a typical LED is several milliamp, which can generate sufficient current change during modulation while incurring low extra power consumption.

Other onboard components can also cause variations of current draw, leading to interference to data transmissions. To address this issue, the communication can be initialed at the end of active period in a duty cycle, when most onboard components fall asleep. The resulting low bandwidth is not a concern because the host node usually only sends short poll messages while most of the data is originated from the meter. On the receiving side, the meter measures the current consumption of the host and decodes the current modulated signal. As the meter samples the current consumption at a high frequency, it ensures a sufficient modulation rate on the link.

We note that on nodes equipped with energy harvesting devices such as solar panels, the supply voltage may not be constant. This does not affect the current/voltage-modulated communication performance because each transmission only lasts for a very short time period (several hundred ms), during which the output voltages of most energy harvesting devices remain largely constant.

5.3 The Communication Protocol

We now discuss the host-meter communication protocol in detail. The protocol implements half-duplex communication between host node and Nemo. The half-duplex mode is sufficient because most traffic occurs in the direction from the Nemo to the host when Nemo responds to the host's queries and sends back the power consumption data. The main design objective of the protocol is to achieve high throughput, which ensures system energy efficiency even when the host needs to frequently query Nemo.

The communication frame consists of a header, the payload and a checksum byte, as shown in Tab. 1. The Start of Frame (SOF) field which is always 0x5a is used to notify the receiver of the frame beginning. The one-byte command (CMD) field indicates the purpose of this frame. The two-

SOF	CMD	LEN	Timestamp	Payload	Checksum
1 byte	1 byte	2 bytes	4 bytes	N bytes	1 byte

Table 1: Structure of the frame

byte frame length field (LEN) indicates the total length of the frame in bytes. The timestamp field is filled upon the actual transmission of the frame. It can be used for time synchronization between the host node and the meter. The checksum field allows the receiver to check the correctness of the received frame.

The frame is modulated using binary ASK which is similar to the Universal Asynchronous Receiving/ Transmitting (UART) protocol. We choose binary ASK mainly because it can be easily implemented and incurs little computational overhead on the host node. The modulation rate can be set to 2Kbps, 4Kbps, 8Kbps or 16Kbps, according to the link quality. A preamble consisting of a series of alternating symbols is always sent before each frame. The preamble has two parts that are sent sequentially: the frame notification sequence and the receiver training sequence. The former is always modulated at 4 Kbps to notify the receiver of the incoming of a frame. The latter, which is modulated at the same rate as the frame, provides information for the receiver to learn the receiving parameters. Fig. 5 depicts the waveform of a voltage modulated signal captured by an oscilloscope. The current modulated signal has a similar shape and thus is not shown here.

On the receiver, a state machine controls the receiving procedure. The state machine has four states: listening, frame synchronization, threshold determination, and frame receiving. The receiver stays in listening state after powering up, seeking for the frame notification sequence in the preamble. After seeing a frame notification sequence, the receiver synchronizes to the modulated signal, which is important for achieving high SNR. Frame synchronization is performed by measuring the modulation rate and the optimal sampling timing from the receiver training sequence. The modulation rate is calculated by the receiver from the measured symbol period. After frame synchronization, the receiver determines decision threshold by measuring and averaging the signal amplitudes of 10 consecutive symbols. After the decision threshold is measured, the type of the symbol can be determined by comparing the signal amplitude against the decision threshold. After all the bytes are received, the receiver goes back to listening state, searching for a new preamble. Fig. 6 depicts the whole receiving process. Three types of frames are used in communication: configuration, data request, and response. We omit the details of the frame format here due to the space limitation.

5.4 Discussion

The power-line modulation techniques described in this section enable the bidirectional communication between the host node and Nemo. To avoid high overhead on the host node, Nemo adopts a poll-response communication scheme in which the communication is always initiated by the host. Moreover, to achieve satisfactory link quality, the communication is only initiated when the host node is in a stable power state (e.g., at the end of active period in a duty cycle when most of the host components enter sleep state). Because of these requirements, Nemo and the host cannot

```
interface host_meter_comm {
  // Interface control
  command error_t enable_rx_comm();
  command error_t disable_rx_comm();

  // Transmission and receiving
  command error_t transmit(NemoCom * frame, uint16_t len);
  async event void receive(NemoCom * frame, uint16_t len);
}
```

Figure 7: TinyOS API for host-meter communication.

maintain a "always-on" communication link. However, this limitation does not lead to performance degradation of power metering because the data transmitted between host and Nemo is not delay-sensitive. First, Nemo can be configured by the host at any time without degrading the measurement performance. Second, power measurement results are time-stamped and buffered on Nemo, which can be queried by the host later. The power measurement results of the current duty-cycle can be queried at the end of the duty-cycle, which incurs little delay. The delay between the host issues a query and the communication may occur is typically small, e.g., in the order of a duty cycle. Such short delay does not affect the host's capability of real-time adaption (e.g., adjusting its duty cycle) based on the feedback from Nemo.

6. IMPLEMENTATION

We have implemented a prototype of Nemo. The dimension of the implementation is 3" by 4". The size of the PCB board can be further reduced in future generations (e.g., by removing debugging components including JTAG ports, LEDs, and buttons) and easily fit into a 2-AA battery pack, as shown in Fig. 3. This would allow a wire-free installation of Nemo on any sensor platforms that have a 2-AA battery pack. A TI MSP430F2618 ultra-low power MCU is adopted on Nemo, which has 96KB Flash ROM, 8KB RAM, and on-chip peripherals such as ADC, DAC and comparator. The abundant on-chip resources enable us to use a single chip to implement various tasks, eliminating the need of dedicated ICs such as ADC. This design reduces the cost and power consumption of the system. The MCU has a maximum clock rate of 16 MHz, which is deliberately downclocked to 8 MHz to conserve energy. The shunt resistor switch is composed of 5 resistors (0.1 Ohm, 1 Ohm, 10 Ohm, 100 Ohm and 470 Ohm) and 4 MOSFETs as switches. Additional resistors and switches can be added to further extend the dynamic range. We choose TI OPA2333 as the pre-amplifier, which offers sufficient bandwidth, low offset error, and low quiescent current consumption (17 uA). A Winbond 8 MByte high-speed SPI Flash chip is adopted to store measurement results.

The firmware of Nemo is mainly implemented in C. Some performance critical code such as ADC sampling and data compressing is written in assembly. The implementation of measurement control, compression, and host-meter communication protocol has a footprint of 8KB and uses 5 K-B memory. We define an interface in TinyOS to support the host-meter communication on host nodes, as shown in Fig. 7. Our implementation of the host-side protocol has a footprint of 1 KB and uses 250 Bytes RAM. We calibrated Nemo with an Aglient 34410A benchtop digital multimeter (DMM). The calibration data is loaded into MCU.

7. PERFORMANCE EVALUATION

Section 7.1 – Section 7.4 evaluate the performance of Nemo. Section 7.5 presents a case study of using Nemo to track dynamic sleep power consumption of motes under different temperatures. Lastly, we compare the performance of Nemo with two state-of-the-art power meters in Section 7.6.

7.1 Measurement Fidelity

We evaluate the measurement fidelity including dynamic range, resolution, and measurement accuracy in this section. To measure dynamic range, resolution and static accuracy, potentiometers are used to generate current load ranging from 0.1 uA to 200mA. In the experiment of dynamic measurement accuracy, a TelosB mote is used instead. An Aglient 34410A benchtop digital multi-meter is connected in series with the potentiometer or TelosB mote to measure the ground-truth current. The current measurement of the digital multi-meter is transmitted to a desktop PC via Ethernet at 10 KHz rate. Nemo transmits its raw ADC readings and the shunt resistor setting to the same PC via the UART debugging port. During the experiment, we slowly vary the current from 0.1 uA to 200 mA by changing the resistance of the potentiometer. The measurements from both the meter and the digital multi-meter are recorded by the PC for data analysis.

7.1.1 Dynamic Range and Resolution

Dynamic range and resolution are important performance measures of a power meter. They give the maximum range and the minimum quanta of the current that the meter can accurately measure. Fig. 9(a) depicts the relationship between input current and output raw ADC readings. It can be seen that the ADC reading first linearly increases with the input current and then suddenly drops to a lower level. This pattern is repeated throughout the whole input current range. The sudden drop is caused by the resistance adjustment of the shunt resistor switch, when the voltage drop on the shunt resistor switch is larger than 20 mV. The dynamic range of Nemo is the linear region of the input-output curve, which ranges from 0.8 uA to 202 mA, corresponding to a dynamic range of over 250,000:1.

The resolution of Nemo is the difference between input current of two adjacent ADC readings, which can be also interpreted as the slope of the input-output curve of Nemo. Fig. 9(b) shows the resolution computed from the slope of the curve in Fig. 9(a). We notice that the resolution is not constant and increases each time when a resistance adjustment occurs. The minimum and maximum resolutions are 0.013 uA and 48 uA, respectively. This variable resolution is resulted from the dynamic input current ranges of each shunt resistor switch setting. Since the digitalization resolution of Nemo is always 12 bits, the measurement resolution increases when a higher measurement range is chosen.

The results in this section show that Nemo has satisfactory dynamic range and measurement resolution. As shown in Section 7.6, Nemo significantly outperforms state-of-the-art sensor network power meters in both metrics. These features make Nemo ideal for measuring the power consumption of sensor networks under a wide range of applications and operating conditions. In particular, as many sensor networks operate under low duty cycles and stay in sleep state (with just a few uA current consumption) most of the time, the fine measurement resolution ($\sim$0.01uA) of Nemo enables accurate assessment of the system lifetime.

7.1.2 Measurement Accuracy

In this set of experiments, we measure the accuracy of Nemo. Fig. 10(a) shows the measurement errors across the whole dynamic range. A CDF of the errors is given in Fig. 10(b). The error is computed as the ratio of the absolute measurement error to the ground-truth data. It can be seen from Fig. 10(a) that, the error has multiple peaks across the dynamic range. They are mainly resulted from the quantization error of the ADC after shunt resistor switch is adjusted. The maximum error, 8.3%, occurs at the lowest end of the dynamic range. When the input current is larger than 10 uA, most of the errors fall below 2%. As can be seen from the CDF in Fig. 10(b), 90% of the errors are below 3%, and the mean error is only 1.34%.

We also examine the measurement error of Nemo in real deployment scenarios when a TelosB mote is attached. The TelosB mote runs a typical sense-and-send application in this experiment. Due to the significant current variation of mote, the measurements of Nemo and digital multi-meter need to be synchronized in order to compare the accuracy. At the beginning of this experiment, a pulse signal is output to an I/O pin of the host mote, which triggers Nemo and multi-meter to begin their measurements. Fig. 11(a) shows the current measurement containing a wake-up event of the mote. It can be seen that the current profile generated by the mote is highly dynamic, containing sharp current increases and decreases over 2 orders of magnitude. However, even with such significant dynamics, Nemo can track the change of the current closely. Fig. 11(b) shows the CDF of the measurement errors. Over 90% of the errors fall below 5%. The mean error is only 2.09%.

7.2 Host-Meter Communication

We first evaluate the BER of the host-meter link in both directions under different modulation rates and frame lengths. A TelosB mote is used as the host mote. We modified the sense-and-send application used in previous experiments, so that the mote transmits a frame to the meter when a button is pressed. The meter transmits back the same frame. The payload contains 3000 bytes of random numbers. The modulation rates tested in this experiment are 2Kbps, 4Kbps, 8Kbps, and 16Kbps. For each modulation rate, 100 runs of the experiments are conducted.

We measure the BER of each modulation rate with different frame sizes. Fig. 12 shows the BER of both links. Note that we did not observe any bit error on the host to meter link at 2 Kbps rate and thus omit the result here. We can see that, on both links, the frame length has a substantial impact on the BER of the link. For smaller frame sizes (<400 Bytes), no bit error occurred. However, when the frame size increases to a certain level, BER starts to grow rapidly. This critical frame length varies with different modulation rates, but is generally larger when a lower modulation rate is adopted. The reason for this phenomenon is that the synchronization between frame and the receiver gradually deteriorates after the initial frame synchronization, due to the different clock rates of transmitter and receiver. As a result, the SNR of the receiver gradually decreases and bit errors appear after the SNR drops below a certain threshold. We note that the bit errors resulted from large frame size can

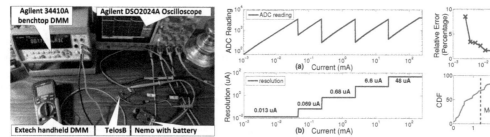

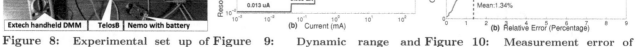

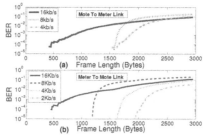
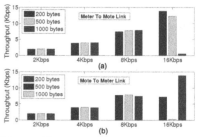

Figure 8: Experimental set up of performance evaluation.

Figure 9: Dynamic range and resolution of Nemo.

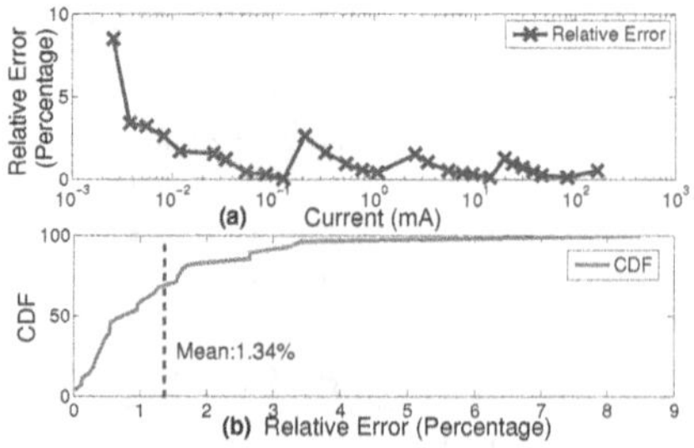

Figure 10: Measurement error of Nemo.

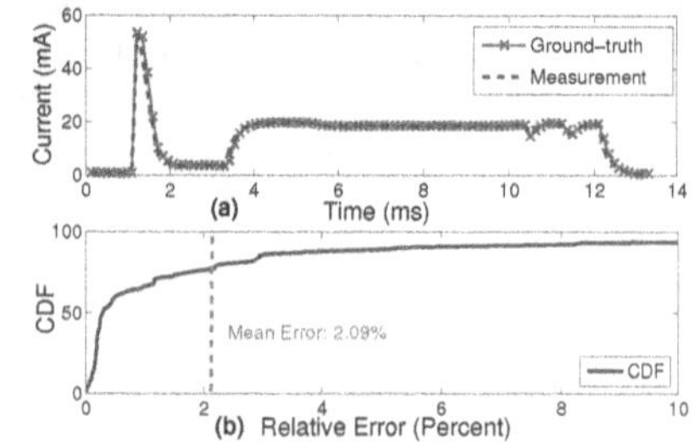

Figure 11: Dynamic accuracy of Nemo.

Figure 12: BER vs datarate vs. frame length.

Figure 13: Host-meter throughput vs. data rate vs. frame length.

be mitigated by maintaining clock synchronization between host mote and meter. However, this is left for future work.

In the second experiment, we examine the throughput of the host-meter communication. The mote continuously transmits 100 frames to the meter, who replies by transmitting the same frames back to the host mote. The frames with incorrect checksums are discarded. We test three frame size settings: 200, 500, and 1000 bytes. For each modulation rate and frame size combination, 10 rounds of experiments are conducted.

Fig. 13 shows the resulted throughput. We can see that, for the 2Kbps, 4Kbps and 8Kbps modulation rates, the throughputs are very close to the corresponding modulation rates, although shorter frames lead to slightly lower throughput due to the higher link overhead. For the 16Kbps modulation rate, the throughput under different frame size settings shows large variations. For example, on the meter to host link, the three frame settings can achieve a throughput of 13.87 Kbps, 7.76 Kbps and 0.25 Kbps, respectively. This observation suggests that frame segmentation is needed for transmitting data chunks larger than 400 bytes using 16Kbps.

In summary, the results in this section show that the Nemo and host can achieve robust communication performance. The high communication throughput allows Nemo to continuously track the system power consumption and feed back to the host in real-time. It also leads to low overhead to the host, as we show in next subsection.

7.3 Power Consumption and Overhead

In this section, we evaluate Nemo's power consumption and the overhead of host-meter communication. Nemo is connected to a host mote running a sense-and-send application. We use the Aglient 34410A benchtop to measure the total current consumption, and use Nemo to measure the current consumption of the host mote. The difference is the current consumption of Nemo. Figure. 16 shows the dynamic current consumption of Nemo when host mote varies its working states. The host mote wakes up around

0.8 ms, right before the appearance of the high current spike. Nemo wakes up immediately after the host mote and its current consumption increases sharply from the sleep level (150 uA) to the active level (4.6 mA). During the active state, Nemo maintains a stable current consumption. The minor spikes of Nemo's current consumption are mainly resulted from measurement errors. As discussed in Section 4, to conserve energy, Nemo can automatically enter the sleep state after the host falls asleep. As shown in Fig. 16, after the host mote goes back to sleep, Nemo remains active for another 1 ms. This is due to the fact that the sleep state of host mote is confirmed by Nemo only when the current draw is constantly below a threshold longer than 1 ms. We note that, when the host does not need to monitor its sleep current, it can command Nemo to completely shut down before falling asleep, which will further reduce the current consumption by 150 uA.

As shown in Section 7.2, due to the low SNR of power line, the host-meter communication can only achieve a maximum throughput of 14 Kbps, which is slower than using I/O pins or onboard buses. This incurs additional energy overhead since data transmissions will take longer to finish. We now evaluate this overhead in a typical sense-and-send application. The mote wakes up every 10 s and remains active for 10 ms, resulting in a 0.1% duty-cycle. When the host is active, Nemo continuously measures its power consumption at 8KHz sampling rate. When the host is asleep, Nemo takes a measurement once every 2 seconds because the sleep power consumption remains constant within a short period of time. During the experiment, Nemo maintains a data buffer of 4K bytes and transmits the buffered data to the host once the buffer is full. We are interested in the ratio of the time it takes Nemo transmit the 4K data to the host and the time it takes to collect the measurement. As both the host and Nemo must remain active for transferring the measurement data, this ratio quantifies the overhead of host-meter communication. We conduct the experiment for 10 runs, and on average, it takes Nemo 389 s to fill the 4K buffer and 2.32 s to transmit the data to host mote using 16 Kbps

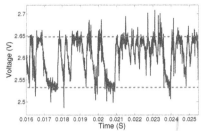

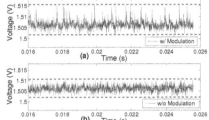

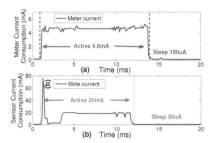

Figure 14: Supply voltage fluctuation caused by modulation.

Figure 15: Variation of the reference voltage on ADC w/ and w/o modulation.

Figure 16: Dynamic current consumption of Nemo and host mote running a sense-and-send application.

modulation rate, resulting in a 0.6% overhead. We note that this overhead is likely even lower in practice because the host may not need all the power measurement data.

7.4 Impact on Host Mote

Nemo communicates with the host by modulating the supply voltage. A potential concern is that the resulted fluctuation of the supply voltage may cause some components on the host to malfunction. In this experiment, we study the impact of the supply voltage modulation on the operation of the host mote.

We first measure the voltage fluctuation experienced by the host under the voltage modulation. We use an oscilloscope to measure the supply voltage during the host-meter communication. Fig. 14 depicts the waveform on the power line during supply voltage modulation. The modulation causes a maximum fluctuation of 130 mV. For digital components that are powered by switching regulators, a 130 mV fluctuation is common during their normal operations. Due to the switching nature, these regulators often cause supply voltage fluctuations called ripples. Typical ripples of boost regulators with 3.3 V output are 100 mV [14]. For example, the boost regulator MAX1724 used in iCount [5] has a ripple of at least 75mv when attached to the sensor node. As a result, the 130 mV supply voltage fluctuation introduced by the modulation will not cause problems to the normal operation of most digital components.

Analog components like sensors are usually sensitive to power supply noise. In particular, the voltage fluctuations may have impact on the conversion accuracy of ADC[3] even when there is small variation of the reference voltage. The MCU of TelosB mote exposes the internal reference voltage on an I/O pin, whose stability directly reflects the ADC performance. We measure the reference voltage using oscilloscope during a meter to host transmission. For comparison, the voltage without ongoing voltage modulation is also measured. Fig. 15 shows the results. We can see that the modulation causes a 4 mV peak-to-peak increase of the reference voltage, which is mainly resulted from the occasional minor voltage spikes. This variation will lead to a maximum ADC conversion error of mere 0.27% (4 mV/ 1.5 V). The impact of such a small ADC error on sensor readings is negligible.

---

[3]All sensors are connected to the ADC for digitalizing the sensor measurements.

7.5 Case Study

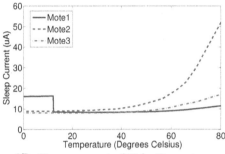

Figure 17: Sleep current of TelosB vs. temperature

With the high measurement fidelity and robust host-meter communication performance, Nemo can enable a wide range of sensor network applications to track their power consumption in real-time. This section presents a case study to demonstrate the benefits of power metering with Nemo. In the case study, we use Nemo to track the sleep current consumption of TelosB motes across different temperatures. It is well known that heat can lead to leakage power of electronic components [6]. However, to our best knowledge, the scale of such heat-induced power consumption dynamics and how it affects sensor network lifetime has not been systematically studied.

We install the *NULL* application from the TinyOS distribution on three TelosB motes. The *NULL* application simply enters the sleep mode after booting, which results in a very low power consumption. We attach Nemo to the three motes and also use a thermal probe to measure the surface temperature of their circuit boards. The probe is connected to a digital multi-meter through which the temperature readings can be logged. The motes are initially placed on top of an electric heater. When their temperature reaches 80 °C, they are moved outdoor where the temperature is about 0 °C. We log the temperature of the motes as they cool down. Fig. 17 shows the sleep current measurement of three motes.

We can see from Fig. 17 that the three motes have very different current consumption profiles. Their current consumption generally increases with the temperature. This is expected as the current leakage of most electric components increases with temperature. However, the slopes of current growth are significantly different. The three motes have similar sleep current consumption at room temperature (8, 8, and 9 uA). However, when they are heated to 80 °C, they consume 11.5, 52, and 17 uA, respectively, resulting in up to 6 times of difference. For a TelosB mote operating at 0.1% duty cycle, an increase of sleep current consumption

	Nemo	iCount	SPOT
Dynamic range	250,000:1 (0.8 uA - 202 mA)	100,000:1	45,000:1 (1 uA - 45 mA)
Resolution	0.013 uA (<50 uA), 0.068 uA (50 uA-250 uA), 0.68 uA (250 uA-2.5 mA), 6.6 uA (2.5 mA -25 mA), 48 uA (>25 mA))	varies w/ sampling rate 10 uA (8 Hz), 100 uA (80 Hz), 1mA (800 Hz)	varies w/ sampling rate 10 uA(220 Hz), 100 uA (2200 Hz), 1 mA (22 KHz)
Sampling rate	8 KHz (w/ compression), 100 KHz (w/o compression)	66 KHz max 80 Hz @ 100 uA resolution	N/A
Measurement error	average 1.34%, max 8%	max ±20%	average 3%
Sleep power measurement	Yes	No	Yes
Power consumption	154 uA (0.1% duty-cycle) 195 uA (1% duty-cycle)	1% of host current plus energy loss on regulator (>10%)	1.7 mA
Host CPU overhead	0.6% w/ comm., otherwise none	13% at 8KHz sampling rate	N/A
Host resource usage	none	Timer, one I/O pin	I2C bus, multiple I/O pins
Ease of installation	very easy, wire-free plug n' play	soldering of wire to host mote	soldering of board onto host; extra 5.5V power supply

Table 2: Comparison between Nemo, iCount and SPOT.

from 8 uA to 52 uA will shorten the mote lifetime by 61.1%. Another interesting observation is that the current of Mote 1 suddenly increases by 100% when cooled to 12 °C. The same experiment was repeated for a number of times, and the same phenomenon was always observed. We suspect that this has to do with the circuit design and thermal characteristics of some components on this mote. However, a detailed investigation is left for future work.

In summary, our results show that the sleep current of motes varies significantly with environmental temperature. We believe this finding has important implications for the design and deployment of sensor network applications. As many sensor networks operate under extremely low duty-cycles, their lifetime is often determined by the sleep power consumption. Existing work often assumes that low-power motes consume constant power during sleep. While this assumption may hold in static environments, when deployed in the field, motes may yield significant variations and dynamics in their sleep power, largely due to environmental factors like temperature. Nemo can track the resulted power consumption dynamics and energy imbalance in real-time, and enable the host mote to make informed decisions on runtime adaptation for prolonging network lifetime.

We also note that, the power consumption of Nemo is affected by the temperature, which potentially introduces uncertainty in the power measurement. We have carefully designed the component layout and ensured sufficient shielding in the circuit board of Nemo, which are known effective to mitigate temperate-induced dynamics. Moreover, in several critical circuit sections, we choose components (e.g., industry-grade components) that can tolerate wider temperature range. These measures prove effective, as no significant change of the power consumption of Nemo is observed when it experienced severe temperature variations.

7.6 Comparison with iCount and SPOT

In this section, we compare Nemo with two state-of-the-art sensor network power meter systems iCount [5] and SPOT [11]. Since we do not have access to the iCount and SPOT hardware, the performance data of the two systems are obtained from two papers [5] [11]. Tab. 2 summarizes the comparison of the three power metering systems. Note we focus on the performance of power measurement instead of energy measurement.

As shown in Tab. 2, Nemo outperforms both iCount and

SPOT in terms of dynamic range and resolution. In particular, Nemo's dynamic measurement range is 2.5X and 7X the range of iCount and SPOT, respectively. It's important to note that there exists a fundamental tradeoff between the resolution and sampling rate of iCount and SPOT. Both of them convert current to frequency for achieving wide dynamic ranges. A high resolution requires a long sampling time to collect sufficient number of pulses, which inevitably leads to a low sampling rate. This is particularly serious for iCount whose highest counting frequency is only around 100 KHz. We now use an example to illustrate the issue. The Max1724 regulator adopted by iCount has a 800 Hz oscillating frequency when the output current is 1 mA [5]. Assume that the regulator has a linear frequency-current relationship and zero offset. If a resolution of 100 uA is needed, the counter must gather at least 10 pulses (1 mA/ 100 uA) during a sampling interval to ensure a 100 uA resolution. However, since the oscillating frequency is only 800 Hz, this would lead to a sampling rate of only 80 Hz (800/ 10). As a result, such approaches cannot achieve high resolution and sampling rate at the same time.

Both Nemo and SPOT can achieve high measurement accuracy while the error of iCount is as high as 20%. Moreover, iCount uses host CPU for frequency counting and hence cannot measure the sleep power consumption of the host. As shown in Section 7.5, real-time measurement of sleep power consumption is critical for estimating the system lifetime for sensor networks deployed in dynamic environments. The power consumption of Nemo can be adjusted based on sleep duty-cycles while iCount and SPOT consumes fixed and much higher power. Compared with iCount and SPOT, Nemo poses negligible CPU overhead for the host node and consumes no host resources. Lastly, installation of both iCount and SPOT normally requires soldering between the meter and host. In contrast, Nemo is specially designed for easy, noninvasive installation on existing sensor network platforms, with the power line being the only physical connection between the host and Nemo.

8. DISCUSSION

Nemo is particularly suitable for *in-situ* power monitoring of sensor network systems that must operate for long periods of time in dynamic environments. Representative examples include habitat monitoring [19], civil structure health monitoring [4], etc. These sensor network systems often need real-time feedback on power consumption to adapt their working modes and duty cycles in response to environmental dynamics.

Nemo has a non-negligible power consumption (about 150 uA) which is an inevitable overhead for its high fidelity and low cost. On the other hand, many applications do not always need to be monitored at the highest fidelity. Nemo can be configured to work in a standby mode most of the time in which Nemo consumes very little power (a few uW). Nemo can also be duty-cycled and dynamically configured by the host node at run time to adapt to the different accuracy and power requirements. In the current design, many components (e.g., ADC, DAC and comparator) are integrated in MCU, which achieves a good balance among power consumption, cost, system complexity, and design flexibility. By adopting ultra-low power components (DAC, comparator, etc.), the sleep power consumption of Nemo could be further reduced to around 50 uA , although this will likely increase the cost of Nemo (by $20 - $50) and introduce extra complexity to the implementation.

9. CONCLUSION AND FUTURE WORK

This paper presents *Nemo* – a practical *in-situ* power metering system for wireless sensor networks. Nemo is based on a noninvasive, plug & play design that allows it to be easily installed on existing sensor platforms without physical wiring or soldering. Using only the power line, Nemo implements real-time, high-speed communication with the host node by modulating the current load and the supply voltage to transmit information. Nemo achieves a wide dynamic current range and high measurement accuracy based on a new circuit design called *shunt resistor switch* that can dynamically adjust the resistance of shunt resistors based on the current load. Nemo has a dynamic measurement range of 250,000:1 while only incurring an average measurement error of 1.34%. We also present a case study to demonstrate the benefits of high-fidelity *in-situ* power measurement using Nemo. We show that Nemo is able to track the highly dynamic sleep current consumption of motes.

In the future, we will integrate Nemo with Quanto [8], which is a component-level energy tracking algorithm for sensor networks. The high-fidelity power measurement of Nemo will enable Quanto to profile energy consumption of system components and programmer-defined activities in fine granularity. We believe that the power line modulation techniques adopted by Nemo can be applied to a more general class of embedded and mobile devices. For instance, there is a growing need for real-time energy usage profiling on smartphone systems. However, the battery meter of current smartphones only provides low-frequency (about 1 Hz) energy readings to the OS. Leveraging the power line modulation techniques of Nemo, a specially packaged power meter may be attached to the original phone battery to provide high-frequency energy sensing. The measurement results can be transmitted back to the system via voltage modulation.

10. ACKNOWLEDGEMENT

The authors thank the shepherd Dr. Adam Wolisz and anonymous reviewers for providing valuable feedbacks to this paper. This work was supported in part by U.S. National Science Foundation under grants OIA-1125163 and CNS-0954039 (CAREER).

11. REFERENCES

[1] Corssbow telosb production web page. http://bullseye.xbow.com: 81/Products/productdetails.aspx?sid=252.

[2] Ds2438 production web page. http://www.maxim-ic.com/datasheet/index.mvp/id/2919.

[3] Imote2 documents website. http://wsn.cse.wustl.edu/index.php?title=Imote2_Documents.

[4] E. Clayton, B.-H. Koh, G. Xing, C.-L. Fok, S. Dyke, and C. Lu. Damage detection and correlation-based localization using wireless mote sensors. In *Intelligent Control, 2005. Proceedings of the 2005 IEEE International Symposium on, Mediterrean Conference on Control and Automation*, pages 304 –309, june 2005.

[5] P. Dutta, M. Feldmeier, J. Paradiso, and D. Culler. Energy metering for free: Augmenting switching regulators for real-time monitoring. In *Proceedings of the 7th international conference on Information processing in sensor networks*, IPSN '08, pages 283–294, Washington, DC, USA, 2008. IEEE Computer Society.

[6] F. Fallah and M. Pedram. Standby and active leakage current control and minimization in cmos vlsi circuits. *IEICE Transactions*, 88-C(4):509–519, 2005.

[7] C. Fay, S. Anastasova, C. Slater, S. Buda, R. Shepherd, B. Corcoran, N. O'Connor, G. Wallace, A. Radu, and D. Diamond. Wireless ion-selective electrode autonomous sensing system. *Sensors Journal, IEEE*, 11(10):2374 –2382, oct. 2011.

[8] R. Fonseca, P. Dutta, P. Levis, and I. Stoica. Quanto: tracking energy in networked embedded systems. In *Proceedings of the 8th USENIX conference on Operating systems design and implementation*, OSDI'08, pages 323–338, Berkeley, CA, USA, 2008. USENIX Association.

[9] R. N. Handcock, D. L. Swain, G. J. Bishop-Hurley, K. P. Patison, T. Wark, P. Valencia, P. Corke, and C. J. OạfNeill. Monitoring animal behaviour and environmental interactions using wireless sensor networks, gps collars and satellite remote sensing. *Sensors*, 9(5):3586–3603, 2009.

[10] J. Hayes, S. Beirne, K.-T. Lau, and D. Diamond. Evaluation of a low cost wireless chemical sensor network for environmental monitoring. In *Sensors, 2008 IEEE*, pages 530 –533, oct. 2008.

[11] X. Jiang, P. Dutta, D. Culler, and I. Stoica. Micro power meter for energy monitoring of wireless sensor networks at scale. In *Proceedings of the 6th international conference on Information processing in sensor networks*, IPSN '07, pages 186–195, New York, NY, USA, 2007. ACM.

[12] X. Jiang, J. Taneja, J. Ortiz, A. Tavakoli, P. Dutta, J. Jeong, D. Culler, P. Levis, and S. Shenker. An architecture for energy management in wireless sensor networks. *SIGBED Rev.*, 4(3):31–36, July 2007.

[13] G. Lu, D. De, M. Xu, W.-Z. Song, and J. Cao. Telosw: Enabling ultra-low power wake-on sensor network. In *INSS*, 2010.

[14] M. S. Mike Wens. *Design and Implementation of Fully-Integrated Inductive DC-DC Converters in Standard CMOS*. Springer, 2011.

[15] A. Rice and S. Hay. Decomposing power measurements for mobile devices. In *Pervasive Computing and Communications (PerCom), 2010 IEEE International Conference on*, pages 70 –78, 29 2010-april 2 2010.

[16] V. Shnayder, M. Hempstead, B.-r. Chen, G. W. Allen, and M. Welsh. Simulating the power consumption of large-scale sensor network applications. In *Proceedings of the 2nd international conference on Embedded networked sensor systems*, SenSys '04, pages 188–200, New York, NY, USA, 2004. ACM.

[17] T. Stathopoulos, D. McIntire, and W. J. Kaiser. The energy endoscope: Real-time detailed energy accounting for

wireless sensor nodes. In *Proceedings of the 7th international conference on Information processing in sensor networks*, IPSN '08, pages 383–394, Washington, DC, USA, 2008. IEEE Computer Society.

[18] B. S.-H. C. Sukwon Choi, Hayun Hwang. Hardware-assisted energy monitoring architecture for micro sensor nodes. *Journal of System Architecture, Elsevier*, 58:73–85, 2012.

[19] R. Szewczyk, A. Mainwaring, J. Polastre, J. Anderson, and D. Culler. An analysis of a large scale habitat monitoring application. In *Proceedings of the 2nd international conference on Embedded networked sensor systems*, SenSys '04, pages 214–226, New York, NY, USA, 2004. ACM.

[20] M. J. Thomas Trathnigg and R. Weiss. A low-cost energy measurement setup and improving the accuracy of energy simulators for wireless sensor networks. In *REALWSN*, 2008.

[21] Y.-M. Wang. Towards dependable home networking: an experience report. In *DSN*, 2000.

[22] Z. Zheng Peng; Zhong Zhou ; Jun-Hong Cui ; Shi. Aqua-net: An underwater sensor network architecture: Design, implementation, and initial testing. In *OCEANS*, 2009.

[23] Y. Zhou, X. Chen, M. Lyu, and J. Liu. Sentomist: Unveiling transient sensor network bugs via symptom mining. In *Distributed Computing Systems (ICDCS), 2010 IEEE 30th International Conference on*, pages 784 –794, june 2010.

FlockLab: A Testbed for Distributed, Synchronized Tracing and Profiling of Wireless Embedded Systems

Roman Lim   Federico Ferrari   Marco Zimmerling   Christoph Walser
Philipp Sommer*   Jan Beutel
Computer Engineering and Networks Laboratory, ETH Zurich, Switzerland
*Autonomous Systems Lab, CSIRO ICT Centre, Australia
lim@tik.ee.ethz.ch   http://www.flocklab.ethz.ch/

ABSTRACT

Testbeds are indispensable for debugging and evaluating wireless embedded systems. While existing testbeds provide ample opportunities for realistic, large-scale experiments, they are limited in their ability to closely observe and control the distributed operation of resource-constrained nodes—access to the nodes is restricted to the serial port. This paper presents FLOCKLAB, a testbed that overcomes this limitation by allowing multiple services to run *simultaneously* and *synchronously* against all nodes under test in addition to the traditional serial port service: tracing of GPIO pins to record logical events occurring on a node, actuation of GPIO pins to trigger actions on a node, and high-resolution power profiling. FLOCKLAB's accurate timing information in the low microsecond range enables logical events to be correlated with power samples, thus providing a previously unattained level of visibility into the distributed behavior of wireless embedded systems. In this paper, we describe FLOCKLAB's design, benchmark its performance, and demonstrate its capabilities through several real-world test cases.

Categories and Subject Descriptors

C.4 [**Computer Systems Organization**]: Performance of Systems—*measurement techniques*; D.2.5 [**Software Engineering**]: Testing and Debugging—*distributed debugging, tracing*; C.3 [**Computer Systems Organization**]: Special-Purpose and Application-Based System—*real-time and embedded systems*; C.2.1 [**Computer-Communication Networks**]: Network Architecture and Design—*wireless communication*

General Terms

Design, Experimentation, Measurement, Performance

Keywords

Testbed, GPIO tracing, GPIO actuation, power profiling, adjustable power supply, wireless sensor network

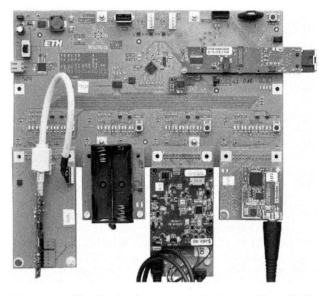

Figure 1: FlockLab observer with Tmote Sky, IRIS, Opal, and Tinynode connected via interface boards.

1. INTRODUCTION

Testbeds play a key role in developing real-world wireless embedded systems by providing the facilities to debug and evaluate protocols and applications in a controlled, yet realistic distributed environment. A review of the spectrum of existing testbeds yields a long list: relocatable testbeds to study applications in the intended target environment [29], testbeds with robots for controlled mobility experiments [18], testbeds performing distributed power measurements [15], homogeneous testbeds with hundreds of devices [9], and emulation platforms [12] and heterogeneous testbed federations [4] to assess large-scale services on thousands of nodes.

Despite this broad spectrum, the current practice of testbed-assisted development revolves around LED and `printf` debugging: developers use the nodes' on-board LEDs to observe conditions in the running program and `printf` statements to log diagnostic messages, performance counters, or program state over the serial port. However, it is well known that `printf`s alter the timing behavior and are therefore unsuitable for analyzing timing sensitive code such as radio drivers and MAC protocols. Perhaps one reason for the unchallenged popularity of these techniques is their ease of use [31]. Another reason is that current testbeds allow access to the devices under test only through the serial port. As a result, developers are left with no other option than to use `printfs`, a means suitable for a number of long-term profiling tasks but cumbersome, highly intrusive, and unsuitable for detailed investigation of interactions among multiple devices, especially real-time issues.

The current solution for debugging low-level software and hardware interactions is a logic analyzer and a mixed-signal oscilloscope allowing to capture and trigger events of interest (*e.g.*, changes in program state or packet transmissions) at high timing resolution. Different from `printfs`, setting digital GPIO pins on a node introduces a known delay of just a few clock cycles, which makes GPIO tracing a powerful tool for debugging timing sensitive code. The required equipment, however, limits the setup to a few nodes on a table, bearing little resemblance to a real multi-hop setting.

The main contribution of this paper is FLOCKLAB, a testbed with services providing a previously unattained level of visibility into wireless embedded systems. FLOCKLAB's novelty stems from the combined capability of tracing and actuating logical state changes at high level of detail, accurate timing information in the low microsecond range, and the possibility to profile and control power over the whole testbed. By coupling a powerful, stateful *observer* platform directly with every device under test, the *target*, FLOCKLAB overcomes the bottleneck at the single sink of centralized data collection systems. FLOCKLAB leverages distributed target-observer pairs with deep local storage that are capable of capturing event and power traces of all targets locally, simultaneously, synchronously, and at high rates without sacrificing on timing accuracy or incurring data rate limitations of traditional backchannel-based testbeds [14, 37].

As such, FLOCKLAB combines the capability of a logic analyzer, power analyzer, serial data logger, and programmable power supply with network synchronization and deep local storage adjacent to each target—distributed across the entire testbed. FLOCKLAB also supports multiple target platforms, allowing for comparative analysis of applications and protocols on the same physical topology. It performs distributed power measurements at higher rate, resolution, and synchronization accuracy than prior testbeds. Users may apply power profiling and GPIO tracing against all targets to correlate power samples and logical events, or dynamically adjust the target supply voltage to emulate battery depletion effects. Sec. 2 details the services available in FLOCKLAB.

Sec. 3 presents the design of FLOCKLAB to meet the challenges that arise when providing these services. Based on our current FLOCKLAB deployment at ETH Zurich, which consists of 30 observers in a mixed indoor/outdoor setting that host Opal, IRIS, Tinynode 184, and Tmote Sky targets as shown in Fig. 1, we benchmark FLOCKLAB's performance in Sec. 4. We find, for instance, that FLOCKLAB can capture GPIO events reliably up to a rate of 10 kHz; it can timestamp distributed events and power samples with an average pairwise error below $40\,\mu s$; and it measures power draw with an average error smaller than $0.4\,\%$ over six orders of magnitude, while providing a highly stable and programmable supply voltage. We further demonstrate in Sec. 5 the utility of FLOCKLAB through various real-world test cases, including an experiment in which we take a detailed look into packet propagation and power draw during a Glossy network flood [10]. Gaining similar multi-modal insights at this level of detail would hardly be feasible with any prior testbed. We review related work in Sec. 6 and conclude in Sec. 7.

Platform	Microcontroller	Speed	Cycles	Time
Tmote Sky	MSP430 F1611	4 MHz	5	1,250 ns
Tinynode 184	MSP430 F2417	12 MHz	5	417 ns
Opal	ARM Cortex-M3	96 MHz	5	52 ns
IRIS	ATMega1281	8 MHz	2	250 ns

Table 1: Clock cycles and time needed to set a GPIO pin on the current FlockLab targets. *The known, minimal delay of GPIO tracing allows for virtually non-intrusive debugging of timing sensitive code.*

2. FLOCKLAB SERVICES

FLOCKLAB delivers new insights into wireless embedded systems by providing the following key services.

GPIO tracing. An observer can trace level changes of five target GPIO pins at a rate of up to 10 kHz. Setting a GPIO pin takes only 2–5 clock cycles on current target platforms, as listed in Table 1. Thus, using simple code instrumentation, this service allows for virtually non-intrusive tracing of events of interest; for example, a trace of packet exchanges may help debug a MAC or routing protocol. Like a mixed-signal oscilloscope that can trigger on digital signals and capture on analog signals, it is also possible to couple GPIO tracing with GPIO actuation and power profiling using a callback mechanism: upon detecting a defined pin edge, an observer can set another GPIO pin or start measuring power.

GPIO actuation. An observer can set, clear, and toggle up to three target GPIO pins, one of which is the target's reset pin, either periodically or at predefined times. This is useful, for example, to create controlled experiments by triggering some action on all targets at the same time, such as starting or stopping the nodes, turning on the radio, transmitting a packet, or freezing and logging a state variable.

Power profiling. An observer can sample the current draw of the target at a maximum frequency of 28 kHz when operating the ADC in high-resolution mode and up to 56 kHz when operating it in high-speed mode. FLOCKLAB defaults to the high-resolution mode since it provides a higher SNR than the high-speed mode, as further described in Sec. 3.4. Users specify time windows during which this service should be running. The resulting power traces can aid in developing energy-efficient applications and have also been used for conformance testing [38] and failure diagnosis [20].

Adjustable supply voltage. An observer can dynamically adjust the target supply voltage between 1.8 V and 3.3 V in steps of 100 mV. To introduce repeatable voltage changes, users can select from a range of predefined charge/discharge curves or define their own voltage-time profiles. This can be used, for example, to study discharge-dependent behavior.

Serial I/O. Finally, an observer can read or inject data over the target's serial port, which is a standard service available on almost any testbed. FLOCKLAB currently supports ASCII data, TOS messages, and SLIP datagrams, making it compliant with the serial communication available in state-of-the-art operating systems like TinyOS and Contiki.

FLOCKLAB allows a user to run any combination of the above services *simultaneously* and *synchronously* on any subset of observers. FLOCKLAB *accurately timestamps* data acquired during a test *across all services and observers*, thus providing previously unattained insights into local and distributed system behavior both in detail and at scale. To the best of our knowledge, this makes FLOCKLAB unique in the spectrum of testbeds for wireless embedded systems.

3. FLOCKLAB ARCHITECTURE

Providing the above services presents several challenges to the design of FLOCKLAB. This section highlights these challenges and describes FLOCKLAB's hardware and software architecture designed to solve them.

3.1 Challenges

- **Minimum disruption:** FLOCKLAB must not perturb the behavior of the system under test beyond the minimum necessary to obtain the desired measurements.
- **High accuracy and resolution:** FLOCKLAB needs to provide highly accurate power samples over a dynamic range that spans six orders of magnitude in current draw, from sleep currents of just $2\,\mu$A on a Tinynode up to active currents on the order of $100\,$mA. The resolution of power measurements and event traces must approach or exceed $10\,$kHz to capture ephemeral radio events, such as clear channel assessments, which last only 100–$200\,\mu$s.
- **Time synchronization:** FLOCKLAB must tightly time-synchronize the observers against a stable global clock, so as to precisely correlate events and power samples of one observer as well as across multiple observers. With sampling rates of at least $10\,$kHz, events and power samples must thus be timestamped with $50\,\mu$s accuracy or better.
- **Large data volume:** FLOCKLAB needs to cope with large data volumes that arise particularly during high-resolution power profiling. Samples should not be lost and be quickly processed to achieve high testbed utilization.
- **Platform support:** FLOCKLAB's hardware and software architecture must be designed in such a way that new platforms can be supported with little effort and cost.

3.2 Overview

FLOCKLAB consists of several distributed target-observer pairs and a set of servers. *Observers* are powerful platforms that can host up to four devices under test, the *targets*, connected through relatively simple *interface boards*. Observers implement all services available in FLOCKLAB in hardware or software. They connect to several backend servers responsible for coordinating their distributed and synchronized operation, for processing and storing collected results, and interacting with FLOCKLAB users.

3.3 Observer Hardware

Observers are based on a custom-designed PCB assembly as depicted in Fig. 2. Its heart forms a Gumstix XL6P COM embedded computer, which is driven by a $624\,$MHz Marvell XScale PXA270 microprocessor and equipped with $128\,$MB SDRAM and $32\,$MB flash memory. We add an $8\,$GB SD card to cache test configurations, program images, and test results. Observers connect to FLOCKLAB servers preferably through the Ethernet expansion of the Gumstix; USB Wi-Fi adapters can be used if Ethernet proximity is lacking.

A switching regulator converts a 5–$56\,$V DC input voltage to the $5\,$V on-board voltage required by the Gumstix. A linear regulator with low output noise further down-converts to the $3.3\,$V on-board voltage required by other components. The ADS1271, a 24-bit delta-sigma ADC, is used for power profiling as detailed in Sec. 3.4. Additionally, there are three USB connectors and a humidity/temperature sensor. In our current deployment, described in Sec. 3.8, we use the readings of the latter to control a USB-powered fan on four outdoor observers to prevent humidity and overheating issues.

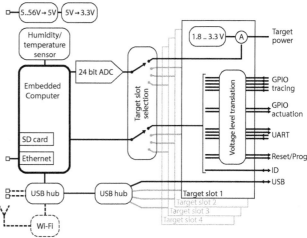

Figure 2: High-level schematic of the FlockLab observer hardware.

An observer provides four pin header connectors to attach targets through interface boards, and replicates the following main components for each connector: an LM3370 switching regulator to adjust the target supply voltage in the range of 1.8–$3.3\,$V with $100\,$mV resolution; a MAX9923H current-sense amplifier for power measurements; five incoming and two outgoing GPIO lines to trace and actuate GPIO pins of the target; UART lines to read and inject data over the target's serial port; lines to reset and program the target; an ID line to identify the interface board as further discussed in Sec. 3.6; and a USB port for USB-enabled targets and interface boards. Two 8-bit signal translators match the variable voltage of the target with the $3.3\,$V on-board voltage of the observer. Finally, an observer provides nine LEDs controlled by the GPIO and UART data lines for visual inspection.

Because of the limited number of GPIO pins on the Gumstix, we need to multiplex the available signal lines between the four targets. We achieve this by letting the Gumstix enable the two voltage level translators and the current-sense amplifier of the desired target and disable them for all other slots. The Gumstix can thus control one target at a time.

The cost of the complete observer PCB assembly amounts to a rough total of 1000 USD including manufacturing costs.

3.4 Measuring Power

To measure power, we put a small shunt resistor between the switching regulator and the target. The voltage across the resistor is proportional to the current draw of the target. We use a MAX9923H high-side current-sense amplifier to amplify the sense voltage by a gain of 100. The MAX9923H has low offset voltage and high gain accuracy, providing precise measurements also at low sense voltages. The output of the amplifier is then fed into an ADS1271 ADC, whose samples are fetched by the Gumstix over an SPI bus. Conversion into current is done in the FLOCKLAB backend based on the shunt resistance, the gain of the amplifier, the reference voltage of the ADC, and the supply voltage of the target. We assess the stability of the latter in Sec. 4.2, showing that the voltage drops only by a few mV at typical current draws.

The choice of the shunt resistor presents a tradeoff. Using a small resistor reduces the influence on the measurements, whereas using a large resistor gives a better SNR. Another important factor is the wide dynamic range of current draw. For instance, a Tinynode draws only $2\,\mu$A in sleep mode,

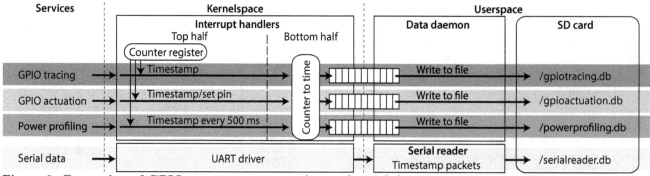

Figure 3: Processing of GPIO events, power samples, and serial data on an observer. *Timestamping occurs in the bottom half of an interrupt handler using a tick count taken in the top half, which increases precision and throughput.*

whereas an Opal draws as much as 49 mA when both radios are turned on. To prepare FLOCKLAB for even higher current draws of future platforms, we want to support up to 160 mA. Based on these considerations, we decided to use a relatively small 150 mΩ shunt resistor, which still enables the high-gain amplifier to accurately measure low signal levels.

The ADC has a resolution of 24 bits, which gives a theoretical resolution of 10 nA in current draw based on the specifications of shunt resistor, amplifier, and ADC. The ADC features two modes of operation that are interesting for FLOCKLAB, selectable by a jumper: high-speed and high-resolution. Using a 14.3 MHz clock source, the ADC samples at 56 kHz in high-speed mode and at 28 kHz in high-resolution mode. FLOCKLAB defaults to the latter as it has a higher SNR of 109 dB, while still providing a sufficiently high sampling rate to capture short-lived radio events.

3.5 Observer Software

Observers run OpenEmbedded Linux and use Chrony as an NTP [25] client to synchronize every 1–2 min with the FLOCKLAB NTP server (see Sec. 3.7). This provides the basis for accurately timestamping GPIO events, power samples, and serial messages. Observers cache the timestamped data locally before uploading them to the FLOCKLAB database server, and have a collection of Python scripts that are used by the FLOCKLAB test management server to trigger scheduled actions such as starting and stopping a test, reprogramming a target, and setting the target supply voltage.

Data acquisition and timestamping. To gain access to hardware connected to the Gumstix—in our case the GPIO lines and the SPI bus which interfaces with the ADC—we implement data acquisition and timestamping as kernel modules. Kernel processes run with highest priority, which helps reduce processing delays and thus increase throughput.

As shown in Fig. 3, data acquisition for GPIO tracing, GPIO actuation, and power profiling starts in interrupt handlers. Triggered by a hardware or timer interrupt, the top half of a handler serves the interrupt, reads a register to obtain the current tick count, and requests that the bottom half of the handler be executed at some future time. The bottom half uses then the tick count to compute a precise timestamp. This approach increases throughput and timestamp precision, because it minimizes the execution time of the top halves, enabling interrupt requests to be served at high rate and low jitter.

As for GPIO tracing and GPIO actuation, an observer timestamps single events. This is however different for power profiling. To reduce system load and memory consumption, we generate a timestamp only every 500 ms. Using the constant sampling rate of the ADC, the FLOCKLAB backend later interpolates the timestamps of single power samples.

Timestamping of serial messages is less critical since these are already affected by non-deterministic UART transfer delays [5] and therefore should not be used to log data that require highly accurate timestamps. For this reason, we process and timestamp serial messages in userspace.

Data caching. When using FLOCKLAB's power profiling service, the observers have to deal with enormous amounts of data, so efficient data handling is key. Motivated by this, we use a custom-built binary log file mechanism rather than a full-blown database system. As shown in Fig. 3, kernel FIFO queues are used for transferring acquired data from kernel to userspace, where a daemon receives the data and writes them into separate files on the SD card. Upon request from the FLOCKLAB test management server, an observer uploads accumulated data to the database server.

3.6 Supporting Diverse Target Platforms

FLOCKLAB possesses the flexibility to support diverse target platforms with little effort in terms of hardware and software. Every observer can host four targets of possibly different form factors, connectors, features, and tools required for installing program images. Key to this flexibility is the use of interface boards: simple PCB assemblies that interconnect the components on an observer (see Fig. 2 and Sec. 3.3) with the corresponding components on the target.

Every platform requires its own custom-designed interface board, since there is no standardized connector or pin layout for wireless embedded devices. An interface board may also need to make provisions for different logic levels.

Additionally, FLOCKLAB imposes a few constraints on the design of an interface board. First, it needs to fit certain maximum dimensions and have an appropriate header connector. Second, the components on an interface board must work with one of the available power supplies: 3.3 V, 5.0 V, or the 1.8–3.3 V DC adjustable voltage. Third, an interface board must feature a serial ID chip that is compliant with the widely used DS2401, which is needed to automatically identify the mapping of target slots to interface boards.

Besides interface boards for Tmote Sky, Tinynode, and Opal designed by us, external collaborators from IBM designed an interface board for IRIS, which also supports Mica2 and MicaZ due to pin-compatibility. We leverage these interface boards in our current FLOCKLAB deployment at ETH Zurich to attach four different platforms to each observer, as shown in Fig. 1.

On the software side, it is sufficient to port the reprogramming tool to the Gumstix to support a new platform. As for serial I/O, FLOCKLAB observers already support ASCII data, TOS messages, and SLIP datagrams. The target software requires no special measures, since embedded operating systems already provide functions for serial I/O and accessing GPIO pins, and power is measured by the observer.

3.7 Backend Infrastructure

Observers connect via Ethernet or Wi-Fi to a set of servers that provide all what it takes to make FLOCKLAB a testbed.

Time synchronization server. FLOCKLAB operates its own NTP server that synchronizes against another server on campus and a high-accuracy pulse per second (PPS) signal output by a GPS receiver, which provides a precise time reference. All observers synchronize against this NTP server.

Web server. Users interact with this server to schedule and configure their tests. Every user is allowed to reserve FLOCKLAB for a certain maximum duration and number of tests at a time. A test configuration consists of a single XML file to setup the services and one or more compiled binaries. A user can run a test as soon as possible or during some specified time slot, abort a running test, and fetch the results of successfully completed tests. If requested, a user receives email notifications about started and completed tests.

Test management server. This server is responsible for operations related to starting, running, and finalizing scheduled tests. If a test is about to start, it parses the configuration, prepares flashable images from the supplied binaries, and dispatches these data to the observers. While a test is running, it periodically queries the observers for results and stores them in a database. When a test has finished, it processes the raw data (*e.g.*, interpolate timestamps, convert to current) and stores them in a compressed archive.

Database server. This server hosts a MySQL database, which stores test configurations, test results, and user-specific data such as quotas and login information.

Monitoring server. Finally, we use Zabbix and Cacti to constantly monitor all server instances, networking components, and observers. In case of an abnormal situation, FLOCKLAB admins are automatically informed via e-mail and/or SMS to ensure maximum uptime of the testbed.

3.8 Deployment

The current FLOCKLAB deployment at ETH Zurich consists of 30 observers, each hosting a Tmote Sky, IRIS, Opal, and Tinynode 184. As illustrated in Fig. 4, 26 observers are deployed indoors across one floor in an office building, distributed in offices, hallways, and storerooms. Four observers are deployed outside, sitting on the roof of an adjacent building a few meters beneath the floor with the indoor observers.

All indoor observers connect via Ethernet, and have a light acrylic glass cover to protect against dust. To help the accuracy of NTP by reducing communication latency and jitter, they are all in the same LAN segment. The outdoor observers use Wi-Fi due to lack of Ethernet on the roof, and are housed in robust polycarbonate boxes with controlled ventilation to avert humidity and overheating problems.

During testbed idle times, the test management server runs an RSSI scanner on all target platforms, determining the noise level on all channels and frequency bands, and a test where targets broadcast 500 30-byte packets each and then report the number of packets they received from any

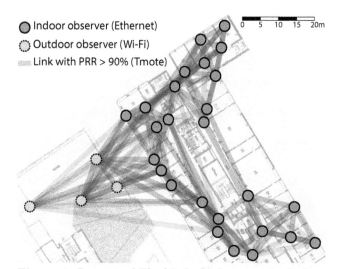

Indoor observer (Ethernet)
Outdoor observer (Wi-Fi)
Link with PRR > 90% (Tmote)

Figure 4: Layout of FlockLab deployment including information about link qualities and noise.

other target, which gives an estimate of the link qualities in the testbed. This information is stored in the database and displayed on the FLOCKLAB website as an overlay on the deployment map as shown in Fig. 4, giving users an idea as to what extent their tests may be affected by external interference (*e.g.*, from co-located Wi-Fi) or limited connectivity.

4. BENCHMARKING FLOCKLAB

Using our current deployment, we benchmark in this section the accuracy and the limits of key FLOCKLAB services. We start by evaluating FLOCKLAB's timing accuracy, which is fundamental to exploit the full potential of the GPIO and power profiling services, check the stability of the power supply and the accuracy of the power measurements, and finally determine the maximum rate for capturing GPIO events.

4.1 Timing Accuracy

4.1.1 GPIO Tracing and Actuation

Setup. We randomly select 7 Ethernet-connected observers, and put one Wi-Fi-connected observer indoors on a table. We evaluate GPIO tracing and actuation in two separate 1 h tests. In the first test, we use a signal cable to connect a GPS clock to one GPIO pin of each observer. The GPS clock generates a PPS signal, and the observers timestamp the corresponding GPIO events. In the second test, we connect one GPIO pin of each observer to a Tektronix MSO4054B mixed-signal oscilloscope. All observers simultaneously toggle the pins every second, and the oscilloscope measures the actual timing of these events.

Pairwise timing error. We first measure the pairwise timing error between simultaneous GPIO events at different observers. This evaluates the alignment of GPIO traces collected by different observers and, for GPIO actuation, the precision with which simultaneous actions can be triggered.

Table 2 shows that the average pairwise error is smaller than $40\,\mu s$ when using the 7 Ethernet-connected observers. If we add the Wi-Fi-connected observer, the error increases significantly due to higher and more variable delays in the exchange of NTP packets over Wi-Fi. The error is similar for GPIO tracing and actuation, as an observer executes similar operations when timestamping an event or setting a pin.

GPIO	7 Ethernet			7 Ethernet, 1 Wi-Fi		
service	avg	85th	max	avg	85th	max
Tracing	$36\,\mu s$	$69\,\mu s$	$255\,\mu s$	$166\,\mu s$	$527\,\mu s$	$1{,}161\,\mu s$
Actuation	$30\,\mu s$	$54\,\mu s$	$394\,\mu s$	$138\,\mu s$	$334\,\mu s$	$1{,}170\,\mu s$

Table 2: Pairwise timing error of GPIO services. *The average error is smaller than $40\,\mu s$ with Ethernet observers.*

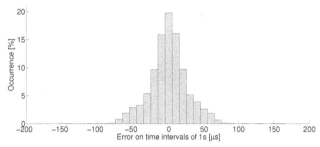

Figure 5: Distribution of the error on time intervals between GPIO events. *The average error is -0.011 μs.*

These results show that FLOCKLAB allows users to align GPIO traces and to set GPIO pins with an error as small as a few tens of microseconds when using the indoor observers. This high accuracy is more than sufficient to trace packet transmissions among targets, as we demonstrate in Sec. 5.5. The results also show that because of the higher NTP synchronization error over Wi-Fi, the outdoor observers are less suited for tests that require sub-millisecond timing accuracy.

Error on time intervals. Using data from the previous experiment, we also assess the error on time intervals. We compute for each observer the difference between timestamps of consecutive GPIO events and compare it to the PPS signal. In this way, we evaluate the precision with which an observer measures the interval between GPIO events.

Fig. 5 shows the distribution of the error on time intervals, as measured by all 8 observers used in the experiment. We see that it approaches a normal distribution with a sample mean of -0.011 μs and a sample standard deviation of 27 μs. The average error is small because each timestamp is similarly affected by variable interrupt delays on an observer. We show in Sec. 5 that this precision allows to profile the radio activity or to measure the clock drift of a target.

4.1.2 Power Profiling

Setup. To evaluate the timing accuracy of the power profiling service, we run a 2 min test on 6 Tmote Sky targets attached to Ethernet-connected observers. One *transmitter* generates a 30-byte packet every 62.5 ms. The other 5 *receivers*, located in the transmission range of the transmitter, have their radios turned on and receive the packets. The corresponding observers enable GPIO tracing and power profiling, measuring current[1] draws at 28 kHz.

When a start frame delimiter (SFD) interrupt signals the start of a packet reception, a receiver toggles a GPIO pin and turns on its three on-board LEDs. As shown in Fig. 6(a), these operations generate a GPIO event and an increase in current draw from 22 mA to 34 mA. When the next SFD interrupt signals the end of a reception, each receiver turns off its LEDs and the current decreases accordingly. We consider

---

[1]We use power and current interchangeably in Secs. 4 and 5, because FLOCKLAB supplies a known, stable voltage (see Sec. 4.2) and thus power is directly proportional to current.

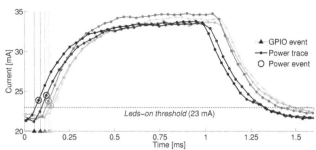

(a) Simultaneous GPIO and power events on 5 observers.

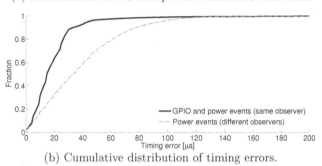

(b) Cumulative distribution of timing errors.

Figure 6: Timing errors of power profiling. *Observers timestamp simultaneous power events with an average pairwise timing error of $39\,\mu s$.*

these events as occurring at the same time, as we measure with an oscilloscope that the lag due to different time of flight and interrupt delays is smaller than 1 μs. To compare power timestamps, we define that a *power event* occurs when the current rises above a *leds-on threshold* of 23 mA.

Timing error between GPIO and power events. We measure the timing error between GPIO and power events on the *same* observer by computing the interval between the GPIO and the respective power timestamp (*i.e.*, between a vertical line and the corresponding circle in Fig. 6(a)).

The solid line in Fig. 6(b) shows the cumulative distribution of the timing error, which is 20 μs on average and smaller than 29 μs in 85 % of the cases. We see that the average error is close to half the power sampling period (17 μs): power profiling has a lower resolution than GPIO tracing and most of the timing error comes from the random delay between a GPIO event and the following power sample.

Pairwise timing error. We now look at the pairwise timing error between simultaneous power events on *different* observers (*i.e.*, between two circles in Fig. 6(a)).

The dashed line in Fig. 6(b) shows the cumulative distribution of this pairwise timing error, averaging around 39 μs with an 85th percentile below 68 μs. The error is comparable to that of simultaneous GPIO events in Sec. 4.1.1, since the sources of time inaccuracies are similar. Fig. 6(a) and the test case in Sec. 5.5 confirm that the precise alignment of power traces in FLOCKLAB allows to match the power draw of a target to packets exchanged with other targets.

4.2 Power Accuracy

We use ad-hoc experiments to check whether an observer accurately measures the current draw of the target with only minimal impact on the stability of the target supply voltage.

Setup. We connect the target slot of an observer to a high-precision Agilent N6705A power analyzer, which acts as a target that draws predefined currents. The current draws

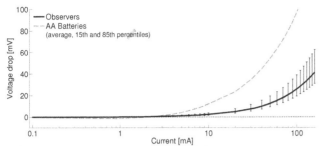

(a) The average voltage drop is small for typical target currents and less than 42 mV even when a target draws 160 mA.

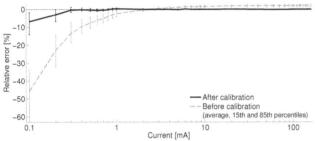

(b) Calibration using linear regression reduces the average relative error on current draw to -0.39 %.

Figure 7: Stability of the power supply and accuracy of the power measurements in FlockLab.

Number of GPIO pins	Power profiling	Captured GPIO events 99 %	100 %
1	no	$80\,\mu s$	$290\,\mu s$
	yes	$90\,\mu s$	$280\,\mu s$
5 interleaved	no	$20\,\mu s$	$80\,\mu s$
	yes	$30\,\mu s$	$90\,\mu s$

Table 3: Minimum required interval between consecutive GPIO events to capture 99% and 100% of generated events. *An observer captures 99 % of events on one GPIO pin if they are at least $90\,\mu s$ apart.*

The dashed line in Fig. 7(b) shows that FLOCKLAB underestimates at currents below 2 mA and slightly overestimates at higher currents. The relative error is particularly significant for low currents: static offset errors of the current-sense amplifier, manufacturing errors of the shunt resistor, and inaccuracies of the amplifier gain introduce a constant offset and a constant multiplication factor into the measurements. Motivated by this observation, we use linear regression to estimate these constants by comparing the measurements from the observers with those from the power analyzer, effectively calibrating FLOCKLAB's power profiling service.

For each observer and target slot, we repeat the experiment and correct the measured current draw by applying our calibration based on the constants computed from the previous experiment. The solid line in Fig. 7(b) shows that the calibration reduces the relative error on current draw significantly, especially for currents below 1 mA. For currents between 0.1 mA and 160 mA, the accuracy of the power measurements increases by a factor of 6 after calibration.

Based on calibration parameters we computed for all target slots on all 30 observers, the FLOCKLAB test management server corrects the power measurements before delivering them to the user. We show in Sec. 5.3 that this results in accurate power measurements allowing to precisely measure the energy consumed by a target throughout a test.

4.3 Limits in Capturing GPIO Events

The sampling rate of the ADC defines the interval between power samples. This is different for tracing GPIO events on an observer: the minimum required interval to reliably capture consecutive events depends on the interrupt delay and the execution time of the top half of the interrupt handler. We run experiments to determine this minimum interval.

Setup. We use all 30 Tmote Skys and let them toggle GPIO pins with an increasing interval. Starting from $10\,\mu s$, targets increase the interval in steps of $10\,\mu s$ up to 1 ms, and generate at each setting 100 GPIO events. We run four tests, each repeated ten times: two where they toggle a single pin and two where they toggle five pins interleaved. In both cases, we run one test with and one test without power profiling.

Minimum interval between GPIO events. For each interval, we compare the number of captured events with the number of generated events. Table 3 lists the minimum required interval to capture 99 % and 100 % of events. First, we see that FLOCKLAB captures more frequent events when they are interleaved on 5 GPIO pins. This is because every GPIO pin is mapped to a specific interrupt flag, and no new events can be captured until the respective flag is cleared.

We further observe that the minimum required interval to capture GPIO events increases by $10\,\mu s$ when the power profiling service is enabled. This service increases the load on an observer, leading to higher interrupt delays and thus

cover the full dynamic range and proceed in a step-wise fashion as follows: from 0 mA to 1 mA in steps of 0.1 mA, from 1 mA to 10 mA in steps of 1 mA, and from 10 mA to 160 mA in steps of 10 mA; each of the 35 steps lasts 3 s. During the experiment, the observer supplies a nominal voltage of 3.3 V and records the current drawn by the power analyzer with a resolution of 14 kHz, while the power analyzer records the voltage supplied by the observer with a resolution of 24 kHz. We repeat the experiment 32 times, using the four target slots of eight randomly chosen observers.

Stability of power supply. We first look at the stability of the supply voltage. To this end, we measure the voltage drop as the difference between the zero-load voltage (*i.e.*, when no current is drawn by the power analyzer) and the voltage supplied at a certain current draw. The solid line in Fig. 7(a) shows that the average voltage drop is at most a few mV for typical current draws of our targets; for example, an Opal draws 49 mA when fully active, yielding an average voltage drop of 13 mV. The voltage drop of the other target platforms is even smaller, because they draw less current.

To put these numbers into perspective, we measure the voltage drop of two AA alkaline batteries, a typical power supply in real deployments. The dashed line in Fig. 7(a) shows that their average voltage drop is higher than that of an observer, and is above 23 mV already at a current draw of 20 mA. We compute a linear fit between voltages and currents and find that a target sees an average resistance of $259\,m\Omega$ when connected to an observer, which is almost four times smaller than what a target would see with AA batteries ($947\,m\Omega$). The results show that power profiling with FLOCKLAB minimally affects the target supply voltage.

Accuracy of power measurements. Next, we evaluate the accuracy of power measurements by computing the relative error between the current draw measured by the observers and the current drawn by the power analyzer.

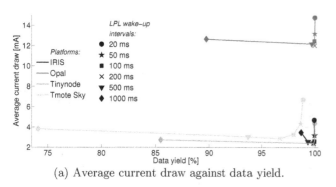

(a) Average current draw against data yield.

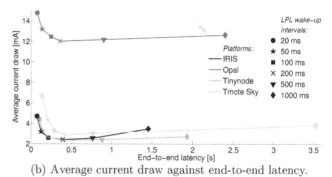

(b) Average current draw against end-to-end latency.

Figure 8: FlockLab enables comparative performance analyses of the same application on multiple platforms. *The plots show performance results from CTP running atop LPL for different LPL wake-up intervals and platforms, including IRIS (2.4 GHz, 3 dBm), Opal (868 MHz, 6 dBm), Tinynode (868 MHz, 12.5 dBm), and Tmote Sky (2.4 GHz, 0 dBm).*

to a lower probability that events are successfully captured. Finally, we note the significant difference between the minimum required intervals for capturing 99 % or 100 % of events, since sporadic activity on the observers (*e.g.*, exchanging and processing NTP packets or storing measurement data into a file) may sometimes increase the interrupt delay, too.

The following section shows that FLOCKLAB's GPIO tracing service allows to accurately record MCU and radio activity, measure end-to-end packet delays, monitor the exchange of packets, and measure the clock drift of a target.

5. FLOCKLAB IN ACTION

After presenting the architecture of FLOCKLAB and evaluating its performance, we now demonstrate the utility of FLOCKLAB for testing, debugging, and evaluating wireless embedded systems through several real-world test cases.

5.1 Comparative Multi-Platform Analysis

One feature that sets FLOCKLAB apart from other testbeds is the possibility to test multiple platforms on the same physical topology. Comparative analyses of this type can provide valuable feedback, for example, to developers of communication protocols, because the characteristics of the underlying platform may affect the performance of these protocols considerably and in non-trivial ways.

In this test case we perform a comparative multi-platform analysis of the standard TinyOS data collection application. The application uses CTP [13] on top of the LPL [27] link layer to collect data from a set of nodes at a single sink. We use all 30 observers and all four targets available in FLOCK-LAB: Opal, Tinynode, Tmote Sky, and IRIS. The radios of these platforms differ in terms of frequency band, maximum transmit power, modulation scheme, and data rate. For each individual platform we let the nodes transmit at the highest power setting, and all nodes but the sink generate a packet every 5 s for a duration of 35 min.

We are interested in how each platform affects the trade-offs between energy consumption, data yield, and end-to-end latency. Since these key performance metrics are known to be influenced by the operational parameters of the link-layer protocol [40], we further test for each platform six different LPL wake-up intervals: 20, 50, 100, 200, 500, and 1,000 ms. We thus expect to gain insights into the platform-dependent sensitivity of the system performance to changes in the LPL wake-up interval, too.

Without FlockLab. Despite the lack of multiple platforms on other testbeds, it is not trivial to obtain reliable and unobtrusive measurements of the performance metrics we are interested in. Data yield can be measured quite straightforwardly based on the sequence numbers of received packets, but measuring energy and latency is more difficult.

On testbeds that do not support power profiling, energy consumption must be estimated in software. For example, Energest [6] provides accurate energy estimations in Contiki but is also intrusive (see Sec. 5.3). Other operating systems like TinyOS lack a standard energy estimator. This increases the overhead to obtain energy estimates in the first place, may lead to incomparable results from different custom-built estimators, and generally encourages the use of radio duty cycle as a proxy for energy consumption, which may not be meaningful toward the total node energy budget.

One approach to measure the end-to-end latency is to log a message over the serial port when generating a packet at the source and another message when receiving a packet at the sink. However, serial logging alters the timing behavior of the application, and the resulting timestamps are inaccurate due to non-deterministic UART delays [5]. Another approach is to run a dedicated time synchronization protocol such as FTSP [23] concurrently to the protocol under test and to timestamp packets at the source. But, as shown in [3], running multiple network protocols concurrently entails the risk of unanticipated interactions between protocols that can lead to performance losses or even failures. Furthermore, for some combinations of platforms and operating systems there may not be a synchronization protocol readily available.

With FlockLab. The power profiling service in FLOCKLAB provides non-intrusive current measurements for computing the energy consumption. The GPIO tracing service can be used to measure the end-to-end latency: the application toggles a GPIO pin when a source generates a packet and another GPIO pin when the sink receives a packet. Taking the interval between both events of the same packet, we obtain non-intrusive measurements of the end-to-end latency of received packets. The effort is limited to inserting two GPIO tracing statements in the application code and configuring the FLOCKLAB services in an XML file.

Fig. 8(a) shows data yield and Fig. 8(b) shows end-to-end latency against average current draw[2], for all platforms and

---

[2]The high current draw with Opal is due to a software issue that prevents the nodes from entering a low-power mode.

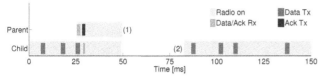

Figure 9: GPIO trace showing a misconfiguration of CTP and LPL on Tinynodes. *After receiving a packet, the parent turns off the radio (1) before the child sends the next packet (2), causing packet loss due to queue overflows.*

LPL wake-up intervals. As expected, higher data yield and lower end-to-end latency can generally be achieved at the expense of higher average current draw. While this holds for all platforms, data yield and end-to-end latency are better with IRIS, Opal, and Tinynode than with Tmote Sky, since the higher transmit power of the former platforms leads to shorter routing paths with CTP. Interestingly, IRIS is least sensitive to changes in the LPL wake-up interval, and all four platforms draw minimum current at 200 ms LPL wake-up interval, which is thus the most energy-efficient parameter setting for this particular topology and traffic load.

5.2 Finding and Fixing Bugs

GPIO tracing is also a very powerful debugging tool. We already found and fixed several bugs this way, and as a concrete example we describe next how we found and fixed a protocol misconfiguration that caused a poor performance during initial experiments of the previous test case.

Finding the bug. With LPL wake-up intervals of 500 ms and 1 s, the initial results from Tinynode and Opal nodes were significantly worse than expected in terms of data yield and end-to-end latency. All sources were seemingly affected, and we could not pinpoint specific nodes to debug with a logic analyzer. We thus instrumented the radio stacks to set different GPIO pins according to the current radio state (*i.e.*, sleeping, active, receiving, or transmitting) and repeated the experiments with GPIO tracing enabled. Using `printfs` instead of GPIO, we would have run the risk of breaking the timing-sensitive operation of the radio driver and LPL.

After aligning the GPIO traces of all nodes, we noticed that nodes located farther away from the sink could communicate properly. The bug indeed affected mostly nodes close to the sink, which delivered only a small fraction of the many packets they had to forward. We decided to focus on these nodes and, by looking deeper into the transfers between a child and its parent, we found that children were transmitting at most one packet during an LPL wake-up interval, although they had multiple packets ready to be sent.

Fixing the bug. With the help of GPIO traces, we were also able to find and fix the cause of this bug. Fig. 9 shows an example of the problem, based on GPIO traces collected from two Tinynodes. After a successful packet reception, the parent kept the radio on for a short time but went to sleep (1) before the child could transmit the next packet (2). As a result, children had to wait until the next regular wake-up of their parents before they could send the next packet, which caused severe data loss at long wake-up intervals.

This prompted us to check the configurations of CTP and LPL. Based on our settings, a Tinynode or Opal node kept the radio on for 20 ms after a reception, but its children transmitted additional packets only after 32 ms (the default CTP setting for generic platforms). We fixed this misconfig-

uration by changing the value of these parameters based on the radios' data rate and experimental results. For example, on Tinynodes a parent keeps the radio on for 36 ms after a reception, and a child transmits the next packet after 10 ms.

5.3 Controlling and Profiling Applications

When evaluating applications like data collection it is often desirable not only to precisely measure performance figures but also to control nodes during an experiment, for example, to specify which nodes generate packets and when [40], or to emulate failures by turning some nodes off during a certain interval [13]. We now show that FLOCKLAB greatly helps control and profile typical data collection applications.

In this test case, we run the default data collection application of Contiki on Tmote Sky targets, that is, Collect on top of ContikiMAC. The wake-up interval of the latter is 128 ms. We want one node to generate a packet every 2 s for 260 s, from $t = 30$ s to $t = 290$ s. We also want to measure the energy consumed by that node during these 260 s.

Controlling without FlockLab. A common approach to control an experiment is to add some logic that, for example, starts and stops the generation of packets depending on the current time and the identifier of the node. This approach requires to recompile the application program for tests that need different parameterization, which is time-consuming. Most importantly, some form of in-band time synchronization is also needed if several nodes are to simultaneously start and stop generating packets, which can, however, degrade the performance of the application under test [3].

Controlling with FlockLab. With GPIO actuation we can control the targets without employing an additional time synchronization within the application. In our test case, the observer connected to the node of interest sets a GPIO pin at $t = 30$ s and clears it at $t = 290$ s: the target starts and stops generating packets accordingly. Because the observers are time-synchronized, it is also possible to let multiple targets start and stop generating packets simultaneously. Moreover, we can test different generation patterns by simply modifying the GPIO actuation timings in the test configuration.

Profiling without FlockLab. On testbeds without power profiling, the energy consumption of a node can be estimated in software. For example, Energest measures the time spent by the node in different states [6], which can be combined with the current draws in each state to estimate energy. This method is however intrusive, since it requires nodes to start and stop counters whenever they change state, and requires changes to existing code to be used on a different platform.

Profiling with FlockLab. Power profiling allows to measure the energy consumption of any supported target in a completely non-intrusive fashion. GPIO tracing allows also to profile a target's operation and measure state timings by setting GPIO pins according to the MCU and radio states.

In our test case, we enable power profiling between $t = 30$ s and $t = 290$ s. Fig. 10(a) shows the energy consumption measured by FLOCKLAB, averaged over eight test repetitions, and compares it with measurements from a power analyzer attached to the target and with software-based estimations using Energest. The non-intrusive FLOCKLAB measurements are slightly more accurate than the estimations provided by Energest: the former measures an average energy consumption that is 3.6 % higher than the one measured with the power analyzer, while the latter underestimates it by 4.6 %. We also see from Fig. 10(b) that the state timings

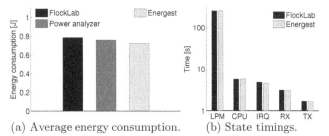

(a) Average energy consumption.   (b) State timings.

Figure 10: FlockLab can be leveraged to obtain non-intrusive and highly accurate energy measurements.

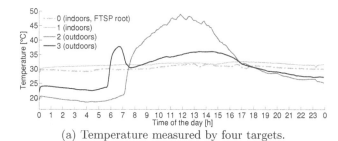

(a) Temperature measured by four targets.

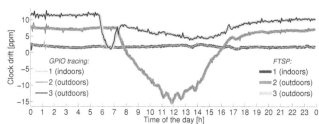

(b) Clock drift of three targets compared to the FTSP root, measured with GPIO tracing and by FTSP.

Figure 11: With FlockLab it is possible to accurately measure clock drift on multiple targets during an experiment with minimal intrusiveness.

measured with GPIO tracing correspond on average within 2.7 % to those reported by Energest. FLOCKLAB is however less intrusive than Energest; for example, we measure on a Tmote Sky that Energest requires 11 and 21 MCU cycles to start and stop a counter, whereas only 5 cycles are required to set the level of a GPIO pin on a Tmote Sky.

5.4 Measuring Clock Drift

When evaluating communication and time synchronization protocols, it is often desirable to measure how much the clock of a target drifts from the nominal frequency during a test. We now demonstrate that FLOCKLAB allows to run tests where targets experience different clock drifts (*e.g.*, by using targets located outdoors) and to measure the actual drift during a test accurately and minimally intrusive.

In this test case, we want to measure the clock drift of 30 Tmote Sky targets during a 24 h experiment. In particular, we are interested in comparing the drift of indoor and outdoor targets, and in relating the drift to the temperature measured by the targets' on-board sensors during the test.

Without FlockLab. A possible method to measure the clock drift is to employ FTSP, the default time synchronization protocol in TinyOS, as it periodically estimates how much the clock of a node drifts compared to the clock of a root [23]. As previously discussed, time synchronization protocols are however intrusive and may affect the behavior and the performance of the application under test.

With FlockLab. With GPIO tracing we can measure the clock drift of a target in a simpler and less intrusive way, without the need of running a synchronization protocol on the target. In our test case, we instrument the application to toggle a GPIO pin every 0.5 s, and measure the clock drift by comparing the difference between consecutive GPIO timestamps with the nominal value of 0.5 s. We then average these drift values over intervals of 5 min to limit the GPIO timing errors discussed in Sec. 4.1.1. To evaluate the accuracy of our measurements, we enable FTSP with a resynchronization interval of 3 s and use an indoor target as the root.

Fig. 11(a) shows the temperature measured during the 24 h by the FTSP root and three other targets, one located indoors and two outdoors. We notice that during daytime the outdoor targets experience significant (but different) temperature variations, while the indoor targets measure fairly constant temperatures. Fig. 11(b) shows how the clocks of the three targets drift compared to the clock of the FTSP root, measured with GPIO tracing and by FTSP. As expected, we see that variations in temperature translate into variations in the targets' clock speed and thus into varying drift. We also notice that the drift measured with GPIO tracing corresponds to that estimated by FTSP: their

difference is hardly noticeable in Fig. 11(b) and averages 0.003 ppm. An observer performs such accurate drift measurements despite temperature variations affect also its clock speed, because it resynchronizes at least every 2 min with the FLOCKLAB NTP server.

5.5 Multi-Modal Monitoring at Network Scale

The possibility of monitoring the activity of multiple targets while simultaneously measuring their current draws is invaluable for developers of low-power wireless applications. This allows, for example, to trace the exchange of packets among targets, to analyze in which states targets consume most energy, or to detect possible misbehaviors that may cause targets to reach undesired states or to draw more current than expected. Unlike any existing testbed, FLOCKLAB offers this possibility, and with a minimal effort from a user.

As a test case we use the Glossy flooding protocol, which lets an initiator flood a packet to all receivers within a few milliseconds [10]. We set the transmit power of 26 Tmote Sky targets to -10 dBm and let Glossy flood a 30-byte packet every 24 ms, using different initiators in consecutive floods.

Without FlockLab. With current testbeds, the only possibility to monitor state transitions or packet exchanges is to instrument an application to store timestamps (*e.g.*, into external flash memory) whenever an event of interest occurs. Nodes print these timestamps at the end of a test, and the testbed collects them from the serial ports. As mentioned before, this approach is very intrusive and provides meaningful results only if the nodes employ some form of in-band time synchronization. Alternatively, network simulators like Cooja [26] can be used to visualize the exchange of packets, but their channel and hardware models may not accurately reproduce what happens during an experiment on real devices. With either approach, however, no information about the instantaneous current draws of the nodes is available.

With FlockLab. GPIO tracing allows to monitor the radio states of the targets and the exchange of packets among them with minimal intrusiveness. In our test case, we simply

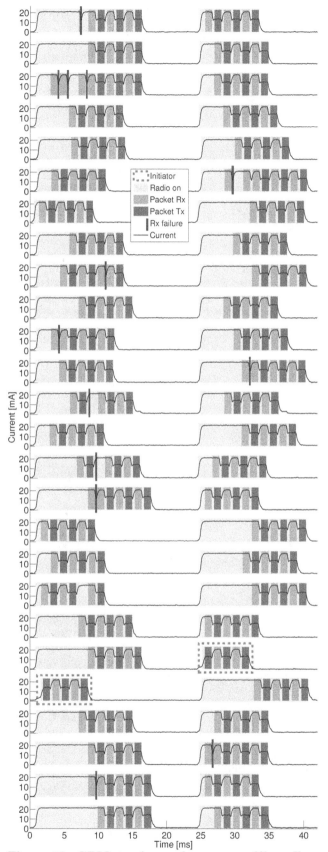

Figure 12: GPIO tracing and power profiling allow for monitoring the activity of multiple targets while simultaneously measuring their current draw.

instrument Glossy to toggle four GPIO pins whenever the radio state changes: when it is turned on or off, when it starts or stops receiving or transmitting a packet, and when a packet reception fails (*e.g.*, because of packet corruption). Together with GPIO tracing, we enable also power profiling to measure the current draw of the 26 targets.

Fig. 12 shows a graphical representation of the radio states and the current draws of the 26 targets during two consecutive floods with different initiators, based on a short excerpt of the GPIO and power traces collected with FLOCKLAB. The timing accuracy of FLOCKLAB allows to precisely monitor how packets propagate in the network based on the reported radio states. For example, it is clearly visible that multiple targets transmit packets simultaneously, which is a peculiarity of Glossy. It is also possible to analyze the sets of targets transmitting or receiving at a certain time instant, and study how they are related to the network topology.

This type of visualization resembles that of the Cooja simulator, but with FLOCKLAB it is based on information collected during experiments on real devices and over real wireless links. FLOCKLAB provides also the current draws of the targets during the experiment. It is thus possible to correlate logical states and power samples and, for example, to measure the energy cost of different states. As expected, Fig. 12 shows that targets draw most current when the radio is turned on, and in particular when they are receiving or waiting for a packet; transmissions are indeed cheaper due to the low transmit power used in the experiment.

To the best of our knowledge, FLOCKLAB is the first testbed that, among other features, provides the functionality of multiple logic analyzers and power analyzers—distributed and synchronized across the entire testbed. We maintain that developers of distributed applications and low-power wireless protocols can significantly benefit from such augmented debugging and testing capabilities.

6. RELATED WORK

Sensor network testbeds. Departing from most of the early installations [9, 37], emerging testbeds are increasingly diverse and specialized: relocatable testbeds to evaluate applications in the intended target environment [29], testbeds with robots for controlled mobility experiments [18], and testbed federations to assess large-scale services [4]. FLOCKLAB, instead, aims to provide visibility into the distributed behavior of protocols and applications, to detect bugs and inefficiencies early in the development cycle. As such, to the best of our knowledge, FLOCKLAB is the first testbed with verified support for distributed, synchronized GPIO tracing and actuation coupled with high-resolution power profiling.

Closest to FLOCKLAB are PowerBench [15], SANDbed [16], and w-iLab.t [2]. As shown in Table 4, these testbeds also provide distributed power measurements at comparable or lower rates and resolutions. FLOCKLAB also achieves a better synchronization, allowing for a better alignment of power traces recorded at different nodes. Furthermore, FLOCKLAB supports four different platforms and future platforms can be added with little effort, whereas the other testbeds support only one platform. We note that w-iLab.t also seems to support GPIO-based services, but there exists no public information on the performance of these services in w-iLab.t.

DSN provides coarse network-wide power sensing by sampling the nodes' current draw every few minutes [8]. In addition, like MoteLab [37], DSN instruments one node with

Testbed	#Nodes	Supported Platforms	Sampling Rate	Resolution	Synchronization Error
PowerBench	28	TNOde	5 kHz	12 bit	$\sim 1,000 \, \mu s$
SANDbed	28	MicaZ	40 kHz	16 bit	$\sim 10,000 \, \mu s$
w-iLab.t	200	Tmote Sky	10 kHz	12 bit	unknown
FLOCKLAB	4×30	Opal, Tinynode, IRIS, Tmote Sky	high-resolution: 28 kHz high-speed: 56 kHz	24 bit	avg/85th%: 39 μs/68 μs

Table 4: Existing testbeds supporting distributed power measurements. FLOCKLAB *is the only testbed with multiple platforms; it provides the highest resolution, and timestamps power samples with 20–200× better synchronization accuracy.*

a high-precision multimeter. FLOCKLAB clearly exceeds the capabilities of these testbeds. However, the approach of coupling targets with powerful observers is inspired by these and other systems [12]. Like FLOCKLAB, many support multiple platforms [4, 14], but, unlike FLOCKLAB, only serial I/O.

Power and energy estimation. Several sensor network simulators [1, 32] and emulators [21] provide power or energy estimation capabilities. They mainly differ in the level of detail in which they model hardware components and program execution, and hence in the accuracy of their estimates. The basic approach consists of recording the time each hardware component spends in each power state, and combining these data with a calibrated power model of the target node.

Software-based online energy estimation follows the same approach, but performs time measurements on real nodes [6]. Different from simulation or emulation, intricate effects of interrupts and timers are automatically taken into account. Changes to existing code, overhead in terms of processing, memory, and code footprint, and lack of visibility into the instantaneous power draw are the downside of this approach.

By contrast, FLOCKLAB measures power non-intrusively on several platforms, enabling detailed profiling prior to deployment. Thus, FLOCKLAB has advantages especially in the early stages of development, whereas software-based estimation allows for energy profiling on larger testbeds.

Power and energy measurement. A number of methods exist for measuring rather than estimating power or energy. Some target external profiling [24, 35], while others enable a node to measure its own consumption [7, 17]. Different from FLOCKLAB, none of them addresses the challenge of synchronizing measurements across multiple nodes.

SPOT [17] uses a voltage-to-frequency converter to feed an energy counter that is read by the node. It achieves high accuracy across a large dynamic range, assuming a constant supply voltage. Aveksha adopts a similar approach to obtain power traces [35]. The design in [36] measures also the supply voltage to accurately calculate energy as the voltage varies. iCount provides energy metering at nearly zero cost by counting the cycles of a node's switching regulator [7].

Quanto [11] builds on iCount to obtain the energy breakdown per programmer-defined activity, using regression models and causal activity tracking. Targeting high-performance sensing platforms, [33] resolves energy usage at the level of processes and hardware components using a dedicated integrated circuit. By combining GPIO tracing with power profiling, also FLOCKLAB can be used to track network-wide activities and subsequently attribute costs to each activity.

Sensor network debugging. A wealth of research has been devoted to diagnosing and debugging wireless embedded systems. Existing approaches target failures caused by interactions among multiple nodes [19, 30], network faults such as routing and node failures [22, 28], or node-local bugs including data races and stack overflows [34, 39].

Most of these systems feature a frontend that collects data about the running system and a backend that analyzes these data for possible failures. FLOCKLAB does not solve the latter, but it provides correlated power and event traces in a way that is nearly unobtrusive for the debugged application. This is in sharp contrast with many debugging techniques that perturb the timing behavior by adding debug statements, logging events into non-volatile memory, or transmitting debug messages in-band with application traffic. Because of this, FLOCKLAB can be highly effective in detecting failures due to time-critical interactions among multiple nodes, possibly by applying distributed assertions [30] or data mining techniques [19] on event traces. Moreover, power traces can be exploited for conformance testing [38] and failure diagnosis [20]. For cycle-accurate debugging of a single node, however, other solutions may be more suitable.

For instance, Aveksha uses a custom-built debug board to interface with the on-chip debug module through JTAG [35]. It provides breakpoints, watchpoints, and program counter polling for very detailed event tracing, and power measurements that can be correlated with events of interest. Aveksha is truly non-intrusive, except for breakpoints. However, the design is tied to MSP430-based platforms, and setting triggers correctly may require detailed knowledge of machine code and memory addresses. Instead, FLOCKLAB makes distributed event tracing as simple as LED and `printf` debugging, supports several platforms and MCUs, and facilitates the integration of new ones with little effort.

7. CONCLUSIONS AND FUTURE WORK

FLOCKLAB is the result of a multi-year effort to push beyond the capabilities of contemporary testbeds, providing the research community with a shared tool to study wireless embedded system in unprecedented detail. We presented the design of FLOCKLAB, benchmarked its performance, and demonstrated its utility through real-world test cases.

Looking ahead, we see the need for systematic approaches that guide developers in (or partially relieve them from) instrumenting their code with tracing statements, and for tools that visualize and aid in analyzing the possibly huge amount of test data. As a first step, we have published the sources of the test cases presented in this paper as tutorials on the FLOCKLAB website http://www.flocklab.ethz.ch/.

Acknowledgements

We thank all the people that helped us over the past years in building FLOCKLAB, most notably Matthias Woehrle for starting off the project, Mustafa Yuecel for his contribution to the design of the observer hardware, and Alexandru Caracas for adding support for IRIS. We also thank our shepherd, Prabal Dutta, and the anonymous reviewers for their valuable comments. This work was supported by nano-tera.ch and NCCR-MICS under SNSF grant number 5005-67322.

8. REFERENCES

[1] A. Barberis, L. Barboni, and M. Valle. Evaluating energy consumption in wireless sensor networks applications. In *10th Euromicro Conf. on Digital System Design Architectures, Methods and Tools (DSD)*, 2007.

[2] S. Bouckaert, W. Vandenberghe, B. Jooris, I. Moerman, and P. Demeester. The w-iLab.t testbed. In *Proc. of the 6th ICST Intl. Conf. on Testbeds and Research Infrastructures for the Development of Networks and Communities (TridentCom)*, 2010.

[3] J. Choi, M. Kazandjieva, M. Jain, and P. Levis. The case for a network protocol isolation layer. In *Proc. of the 7th ACM Conf. on Embedded Networked Sensor Systems (SenSys)*, 2009.

[4] G. Coulson, B. Porter, I. Chatzigiannakis, C. Koninis, S. Fischer, D. Pfisterer, D. Bimschas, T. Braun, P. Hurni, M. Anwander, G. Wagenknecht, S. P. Fekete, A. Kröller, and T. Baumgartner. Flexible experimentation in wireless sensor networks. *Communications of the ACM*, 55(1), 2012.

[5] M. Delvai, U. Eisenmann, and W. Elmenreich. Intelligent UART module for real-time applications. In *Proc. of the 1st Workshop on Intelligent Solutions in Embedded Systems (WISES)*, 2003.

[6] A. Dunkels, F. Österlind, N. Tsiftes, and Z. He. Software-based on-line energy estimation for sensor nodes. In *Proc. of the 4th Workshop on Embedded networked sensors (EmNets)*, 2007.

[7] P. Dutta, M. Feldmeier, J. Paradiso, and D. Culler. Energy metering for free: Augmenting switching regulators for real-time monitoring. In *Proc. of the 7th Intl. Conf. on Information Processing in Sensor Networks (IPSN)*, 2008.

[8] M. Dyer, J. Beutel, T. Kalt, P. Oehen, L. Thiele, K. Martin, and P. Blum. Deployment support network: A toolkit for the development of WSNs. In *Proc. of the 4th European Conf. on Wireless sensor networks (EWSN)*, 2007.

[9] E. Ertin, A. Arora, R. Ramnath, M. Nesterenko, V. Naik, S. Bapat, V. Kulathumani, M. Sridharan, H. Zhang, and H. Cao. Kansei: A testbed for sensing at scale. In *Proc. of the 5th Intl. Conf. on Information Processing in Sensor Networks (IPSN)*, 2006.

[10] F. Ferrari, M. Zimmerling, L. Thiele, and O. Saukh. Efficient network flooding and time synchronization with Glossy. In *Proc. of the 10th Intl. Conf. on Information Processing in Sensor Networks (IPSN)*, 2011.

[11] R. Fonseca, P. Dutta, P. Levis, and I. Stoica. Quanto: Tracking energy in networked embedded systems. In *Proc. of the 8th USENIX Conf. on Operating systems design and implementation (OSDI)*, 2008.

[12] L. Girod, J. Elson, T. Stathopoulos, M. Lukac, and D. Estrin. EmStar: A software environment for developing and deploying wireless sensor networks. In *Proc. of the USENIX Annual Technical Conf.*, 2004.

[13] O. Gnawali, R. Fonseca, K. Jamieson, D. Moss, and P. Levis. Collection tree protocol. In *Proc. of the 7th ACM Conf. on Embedded Networked Sensor Systems (SenSys)*, 2009.

[14] V. Handziski, A. Köpke, A. Willig, and A. Wolisz. TWIST: A scalable and reconfigurable testbed for wireless indoor experiments with sensor networks. In *Proc. of the 2nd Intl. Workshop on Multi-hop ad hoc networks: from theory to reality (REALMAN)*, 2006.

[15] I. Haratcherev, G. Halkes, T. Parker, O. Visser, and K. Langendoen. PowerBench: A scalable testbed infrastructure for benchmarking power consumption. In *Proc. of the Intl. Workshop on Sensor Network Engineering (IWSNE)*, 2008.

[16] A. Hergenröder, J. Wilke, and D. Meier. Distributed energy measurements in WSN testbeds with a sensor node management device (SNMD). In *Workshop Proceedings of the 23rd Intl. Conf. on Architecture of Computing Systems (ARCS)*, 2010.

[17] X. Jiang, P. Dutta, D. Culler, and I. Stoica. Micro power meter for energy monitoring of wireless sensor networks at scale. In *Proc. of the 6th Intl. Conf. on Information Processing in Sensor Networks (IPSN)*, 2007.

[18] A. Jiménez-González, J. Martínez-de Dios, and A. Ollero. An integrated testbed for heterogeneous mobile robots and other cooperating objects. In *Proc. of the 23rd IEEE/RSJ Intl. Conf. on Intelligent Robots and Systems (IROS)*, 2010.

[19] M. M. H. Khan, H. K. Le, H. Ahmadi, T. F. Abdelzaher, and J. Han. Dustminer: Troubleshooting interactive complexity bugs in sensor networks. In *Proc. of the 6th ACM Conf. on Embedded Networked Sensor Systems (SenSys)*, 2008.

[20] M. M. H. Khan, H. K. Le, M. LeMay, P. Moinzadeh, L. Wang, Y. Yang, D. K. Noh, T. Abdelzaher, C. A. Gunter, J. Han, and X. Jin. Diagnostic powertracing for sensor node failure analysis. In *Proc. of the 9th Intl. Conf. on Information Processing in Sensor Networks (IPSN)*, 2010.

[21] O. Landsiedel, K. Wehrle, and S. Götz. Accurate prediction of power consumption in sensor networks. In *Proc. of the 2nd Workshop on Embedded networked sensors (EmNets)*, 2005.

[22] K. Liu, M. Li, Y. Liu, M. Li, Z. Guo, and F. Hong. Passive diagnosis for wireless sensor networks. In *Proc. of the 6th ACM Conf. on Embedded Networked Sensor Systems (SenSys)*, 2008.

[23] M. Maroti, B. Kusy, G. Simon, and A. Ledeczi. The flooding time synchronization protocol. In *Proc. of the 2nd ACM Conf. on Embedded Networked Sensor Systems (SenSys)*, 2004.

[24] A. Milenkovic, M. Milenkovic, E. Jovanov, D. Hite, and D. Raskovic. An environment for runtime power monitoring of wireless sensor network platforms. In *Proc. of the 37th Southeastern Symp. on System Theory (SSST)*, 2005.

[25] D. Mills, J. Martin, J. Burbank, and W. Kasch. Network time protocol version 4: Protocol and algorithms specification. RFC 5905, 2010.

[26] F. Österlind, A. Dunkels, J. Eriksson, N. Finne, and T. Voigt. Cross-level sensor network simulation with COOJA. In *Proc. of the 7th IEEE Intl. Workshop on Practical Issues in Building Sensor Network Applications (SenseApp)*, 2006.

[27] J. Polastre, J. Hill, and D. Culler. Versatile low power media access for wireless sensor networks. In *Proc. of the 2nd ACM Conf. on Embedded Networked Sensor Systems (SenSys)*, 2004.

[28] N. Ramanathan, K. Chang, R. Kapur, L. Girod, E. Kohler, and D. Estrin. Sympathy for the sensor network debugger. In *Proc. of the 3rd ACM Conf. on Embedded Networked Sensor Systems (SenSys)*, 2005.

[29] O. Rensfelt, F. Hermans, L.-Å. Larzon, and P. Gunningberg. Sensei-UU: A relocatable sensor network testbed. In *Proc. of the 5th ACM Intl. Workshop on Wireless network testbeds, experimental evaluation and characterization (WiNTECH)*, 2010.

[30] K. Römer and J. Ma. Passive distributed assertions for sensor networks. In *Proc. of the 8th Intl. Conf. on Information Processing in Sensor Networks (IPSN)*, 2009.

[31] R. Shea, M. Srivastava, and Y. Cho. Scoped identifiers for efficient bit aligned logging. In *Proc. of the Conf. on Design, Automation and Test in Europe (DATE)*, 2010.

[32] V. Shnayder, M. Hempstead, B. Chen, G. Allen, and M. Welsh. Simulating the power consumption of large-scale sensor network applications. In *Proc. of the 2nd ACM Conf. on Embedded Networked Sensor Systems (SenSys)*, 2004.

[33] T. Stathopoulos, D. McIntire, and W. J. Kaiser. The energy endoscope: Real-time detailed energy accounting for wireless sensor nodes. In *Proc. of the 7th Intl. Conf. on Information Processing in Sensor Networks (IPSN)*, 2008.

[34] V. Sundaram, P. Eugster, and X. Zhang. Efficient diagnostic tracing for wireless sensor networks. In *Proc. of the 8th ACM Conf. on Embedded Networked Sensor Systems (SenSys)*, 2010.

[35] M. Tancreti, M. S. Hossain, S. Bagchi, and V. Raghunathan. Aveksha: A hardware-software approach for non-intrusive tracing and profiling of wireless embedded systems. In *Proc. of the 9th ACM Conf. on Embedded Networked Sensor Systems (SenSys)*, 2011.

[36] T. Trathnigg and R. Weiss. A runtime energy monitoring system for wireless sensor networks. In *Proc. of the 3rd Intl. Symp. on Wireless Pervasive Computing (ISWPC)*, 2008.

[37] G. Werner-Allen, P. Swieskowski, and M. Welsh. MoteLab: A wireless sensor network testbed. In *Proc. of the 4th Intl. Conf. on Information Processing in Sensor Networks (IPSN)*, 2005.

[38] M. Woehrle, K. Lampka, and L. Thiele. Exploiting timed automata for conformance testing of power measurements. In *Proc. of the 7th Intl. Conf. on Formal Modeling and Analysis of Timed Systems (FORMATS)*, 2009.

[39] J. Yang, M. Soffa, L. Selavo, and K. Whitehouse. Clairvoyant: A comprehensive source-level debugger for wireless sensor networks. In *Proc. of the 5th ACM Conf. on Embedded Networked Sensor Systems (SenSys)*, 2007.

[40] M. Zimmerling, F. Ferrari, L. Mottola, T. Voigt, and L. Thiele. pTunes: Runtime parameter adaptation for low-power MAC protocols. In *Proc. of the 11th Intl. Conf. on Information Processing in Sensor Networks (IPSN)*, 2012.

A Comprehensive Compiler-Assisted Thread Abstraction for Resource-Constrained Systems

Alexander Bernauer
Institute for Pervasive Computing
ETH Zürich
bernauer@inf.ethz.ch

Kay Römer
Institute of Computer Engineering
University of Lübeck
roemer@iti.uni-luebeck.de

ABSTRACT

While size and complexity of sensor networks software has increased significantly in recent years, the hardware capabilities of sensor nodes have been remaining very constrained. The predominant event-based programming paradigm addresses these hardware constraints, but does not scale well with the growing software complexity, often leading to software that is hard-to-manage and error-prone. Thread abstractions could remedy this situation, but existing solutions in sensor networks either provide incomplete thread semantics or introduce a significant resource overhead. This reflects the common understanding that one has to trade expressiveness for efficiency and vice versa. Our work, however, shows that this trade-off is not inherent to resource-constrained systems. We propose a comprehensive compiler-assisted cooperative threading abstraction, where full-fledged thread-based C code is translated to efficient event-based C code that runs atop an event-based operating system such as Contiki or TinyOS. Our evaluation shows that our approach outperforms thread libraries and generates code that is almost as efficient as hand-written event-based code with overheads of 1 % RAM, 2 % CPU, and 3 % ROM.

Categories and Subject Descriptors

D.1.4 [**Programming Techniques**]: Sequential Programming; D.3.4 [**Programming Languages**]: Processors—*Code generation*; D.4.1 [**Operating Systems**]: Process Management—*Threads*

Keywords

Wireless Sensor Networks, Threads, Compiler

1. INTRODUCTION

One of the main challenges in wireless sensor networks (WSNs) is to cope with the scarcity of physical resources. While in other domains Moore's law has led to hardware with ever increasing capabilities, in WSNs advances in technology are applied towards reduced size and cost [21]. Also, energy efficiency is crucial for a long system life-time, which is why today's deployments still oper-

ate with 8- or 16- bit MCUs, as a modern 32-bit MCU such as the ARM Cortex-M3 "incurs a $\sim 2\times$ overhead in power draw" [11].

Due to these resource constraints, the event-based programming paradigm is predominant in sensor networks, as it allows implementations of concurrent applications with little memory and computational overhead. While this approach is appropriate for simple sleep-sample-send applications, WSN software is recently gaining complexity with motes running IP stacks [9], HTTP/CoAP services [12], middleware [4], and business logic [18]. Such software includes complex control and data flows that do not fit well with the event-based paradigm. In fact, one has to do both, implement complex control flows via long chains of events and handlers using asynchronous functions, and manually manage data flowing across different event handlers. This often leads to confusing, hard to manage, and error-prone code (e.g., [1, 6, 10, 16, 19, 21]).

For this reason, there have been quite some efforts to enable thread-based programming on sensor nodes, as synchronous functions and sequential computation often lead to simpler and better manageable code. However, these thread libraries are either limited in their expressiveness (e.g. [25]), or they add high overheads compared to event-based programs (e.g. [16]). Compiler-assisted thread abstractions (e.g., [6, 21]) escape this trade-off by translating thread-based programs into equivalent event-based ones, thus exploiting the duality of threads and events [13]. Overall, the application is not only executed by an efficient event-based runtime system but the compiler can additionally apply application-specific optimizations, which is why this approach is promising. Unfortunately, existing compiler-assisted thread abstractions only provide incomplete thread semantics. *Protothreads*, the most popular amongst them, additionally fails to identify invalid input and generates faulty programs instead [6].

This paper presents a comprehensive compiler-assisted thread abstraction that offers a full-fledged cooperative threading model. We thereby target advanced software in the service and application layers where cooperative threads provide a good programming model, as timing issues are of lesser concern. *Ocram*, our compiler implementation, rejects invalid input and otherwise generates event-based code for any event-based runtime environment, requiring only a thin platform abstraction layer to be implemented once. The supported thread model is only marginally constricted due to limits that are inherent to the compiler-based approach.

The contributions of this paper are:

1. A platform-agnostic source-to-source transformation scheme which translates ISO/IEC 9899:1999 (C99) programs using cooperative threads and synchronous functions into equivalent C99 program using events and asynchronous functions,

2. Ocram, a GPL-licensed compiler prototype that implements the transformation,

3. platform abstraction layers to bind Ocram to Contiki and TinyOS,

4. an evaluation which a) shows the feasibility of compiler-assisted threads for three different WSN application archetypes, b) verifies the correctness of the transformation, and c) measures the resource costs of this abstraction compared to both native event-based implementations and thread libraries.

The remainder of the paper is organized as follows: Section 2 and 3 provide the context and an overview of our approach. Section 4 describes the translation scheme while Section 5 covers the interoperability between generated and existing event-based code. Section 6 documents the setup of the conducted experiments and Section 7 presents the results of our evaluation. Finally, Section 8 gives an outlook on future research directions.

2. STATE OF THE ART

Operating systems like *TinyOS* [8] and *Contiki* [5] target small WSN devices by utilizing resource-efficient event dispatching. However, a continuous demand for thread abstractions has lead to different approaches to enable threads on resource-constrained systems. Unfortunately, all of them either have high resource-demands or provide only incomplete or non-standard thread semantics.

Fibers, for instance, allow for exactly one additional thread [25], while *Y-Threads* indeed support multiple threads, but require to manually distinguish "run-to-completion threads" [19]. To implement a comprehensive thread abstractions, the most common way is to have one stack per thread and switch context either in a cooperative [16] or a preemptive fashion [2, 10]. Multiple, preallocated stacks are, however, not resource efficient for two reasons. First, each stack has to provide enough cut-off to support the worst case of occurring interrupt handlers operating on the respective current stack. And second, the size of all preallocated stacks is usually higher than the actual maximum stack consumption of an application because usually not all threads reach their maximum stack usage at the same time. As a consequence, multiple, preallocated stacks do not scale well with the number of threads.

Outside of the WSN domain, von Behren et al. have addressed this problem with *Capriccio* [24]. This system automatically augments thread-based applications with code for dynamic stack allocation, thus avoiding preallocated stacks. Although this enables high performance and scalability for Internet services on Linux, it is not a viable option for WSNs. First of all, with dynamic stack management it is hard to guarantee that out-of-memory situations do no occur, which is certainly crucial for the reliability of an embedded system. Also, dynamic memory management not only introduces a runtime overhead, but also poses the problem of memory fragmentation, as typical WSN devices are not equipped with a memory management unit (MMU).

In general, threads and events are known to be dual to each other [13]. Adya et al. even mix thread-based and event-based code in a single program by using small adaptors and a special scheduler [1]. As this is a multi-stacked, runtime-based solution, however, it is not resource-efficient. Overall, run-time based thread abstractions entail a trade-off between completeness of the thread semantics and resource overhead compared to event-based programming.

In contrast, compiler-assisted thread abstractions exploit the duality of threads and events by translating a thread-based program into an equivalent event-based program, thus escaping this trade-off. While the developer has the comfort of threads, the resulting program is both single-stacked and avoids the extra context switching overhead of a thread scheduler, as the existing event dispatcher is used instead. Additionally, while a runtime-based solution always has to support the most generic case, static analysis can exploit application-specific optimizations.

The first system that provided a compiler-assisted thread-abstraction for WSNs was Contiki's *protothreads* [6]. Technically, protothreads are a set of C preprocessor macros that enable the syntactical illusion of threads and synchronous functions. As the context of each thread (a.k.a. protothread process) comprises only two bytes, the authors claim to provide the most efficient thread implementation. At a closer look, however, this convincing performance comes at the price of incomplete thread semantics. First of all, the state of automatic variables is not preserved across yield points. Second, yield points can only be placed in the thread start function, which severely restricts the software architecture of protothreads-based applications. In addition, certain user mistakes are not detected at compile time, but have to be indirectly examined by observing unexpected runtime behavior. Such mistakes can be as subtle as using `switch` statements that interfere with those that are expanded from the protothreads macros. As the C preprocessor can only perform local substitution of language tokens, these limitations are inherent to the protothreads abstraction.

TinyVT [21] employs a dedicated compiler. This abstraction has been specifically designed for TinyOS, which provides a component-based software architecture with event-based interfaces. TinyVT enables software developers to implement single components by writing sequential code, as it is possible to inline event handlers in code blocks following a special `await` statement. Also, the runtime system preserves the state of automatic variables. Although TinyVT overcomes many of protothreads' drawbacks, the supported thread semantics is still restricted and deviates substantially from common threading models. First of all, inlined event handlers may not contain `await` statements. Additionally, it is not possible to split the implementation of a component into multiple functions, which implies that code cannot be shared between multiple threads and functions cannot be re-entrant.

The most recent compiler-assisted thread abstraction is *UnStacked C* [17], "a source-to-source transformation that can translate multi-threaded programs into stackless continuations." This is a hybrid approach, as the input application uses a thread library such as TOSThreads [10] and the generated application relies on a modified version of this library. The translation reduces the memory requirements of the application in particular by softening the timing guarantees of context switching (so-called *lazy preemption*). Overall, the generated runtime system still depends on a thread library and it remains to be seen if lazy preemption is appropriate for WSN applications.

In summary, runtime-based thread abstractions are not resource-efficient and existing compiler-assisted thread abstractions provide only incomplete or non-standard thread semantics. The core contribution of our work lies in overcoming the seemingly inherent trade-off between completeness of thread semantics and resource overheads that is prevalent in the state of the art. Specifically, our approach offers cooperative threads with only minor restrictions while achieving the efficiency of event-based programming. Our dedicated compiler performs a platform-agnostic source-to-source transformation that exploits application-specific optimizations, and the output application only relies on the existence of an event-based operating system (OS).

Up to our knowledge, similar approaches have not been taken in other embedded systems domains so far, presumably because application complexity is low enough to be manageable with events, or because availability of resources is high enough to allow for thread libraries.

3. OVERVIEW

This sections gives an overview of relevant terms and programming paradigms (Section 3.1), introduces our approach on a high level (Section 3.2), and discusses its fundamental limitations (Section 3.3).

3.1 Programming Paradigms

An application usually consists of multiple *tasks*, which are logical groups of computations that pursue a common goal. Tasks effectively perform their work by calling functions of the *application programming interface* (API) of the OS. In case of a *synchronous* function, the associated operation is guaranteed to have completed when the function returns. In contrast, calling an *asynchronous* function only triggers an operation which will complete eventually.

The reportedly most efficient way to execute multiple tasks virtually in parallel is to follow the *event-based paradigm*. In this paradigm, a task is formed by a causal chain of events and event handler functions, which is frequently initiated by recurring events. As the runtime system waits for a handler function to return before processing the next event, a single stack suffices to execute all tasks. One major source of complexity of this paradigm is that managing the control flow of a task is hard, as the code is spread out over multiple event handlers. A second major source of complexity is that the execution contexts of tasks (i.e., the values of variables) have to be manually managed and preserved between subsequent event handler invocations. Additionally, every function that calls an asynchronous function becomes asynchronous itself, which recursively applies to the whole call stack and forces all functions' implementations to be split up (cf. "stack ripping" [1]). In summary, the event-based programming paradigm is efficient, but requires a lot of cumbersome and error-prone work to be done manually.

In contrast, the *thread-based paradigm* overcomes these problems by means of synchronous OS APIs, where the control flow is sequential, and a task's context can be stored in *automatic* (i.e., function-local) variables using a scope-based automatic live-cycle management. A *thread* is one flow of control that drives the execution of a task. It starts with the invocation of a *thread start function* and sequentially executes the statements of this function.

The reason why threads are considered inefficient is that the context of a task is the complete stack of its thread. As it is generally difficult to estimate the maximum size of a stack, and as hardware interrupt handlers always operate on the current stack and can be invoked at any point in time, a common approach is to add enough cutoff to be safe from out-of-stack situations. On sensor nodes, though, the cutoffs of a reasonable amount of threads quickly sum up beyond the total amount of available memory. This is why providing comprehensive thread abstractions for WSNs is not trivial.

3.2 Our Approach

As depicted in Figure 1, in the context of our work, a dedicated compiler called Ocram translates a thread-based application (*T-code*) into an equivalent event-based application (*E-code*). The T-code application is built upon a synchronous T-code API which has been manually derived from an asynchronous OS API. Instead of implementing the T-code API — which is what runtime-based thread abstractions do — the compiler generates a corresponding E-code API which is used by the generated E-code application. The *platform abstraction layer* (PAL) (cf. Section 5) implements the E-code API by means of the OS API.

Given the call graph of a T-code application, every function that has a path leading to a T-code API function is referred to as *interruptable function* and every edge of such a path is referred to as *interruptable call*. The compiler's task is to turn interruptable

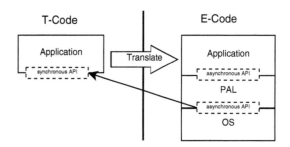

Figure 1: *System Overview*: The compiler translates the thread-based program (T-code) into an equivalent event-based program (E-code). The platform abstraction layer (PAL) mediates between the generated application and the given operating system (OS).

functions into event handlers (cf. Section 4.2) and to preserve the value of automatic variables across single invocations if needed (cf. Section 4.1). And of course, the E-code should be equivalent to the T-code (cf. Section 4.3) to ensure that it behaves as intended by the T-code programmer.

The generated E-code application contains one central event handler function per thread which contains the inlined bodies of all involved interruptable functions. Always after calling an E-code API function, the handler returns control to the PAL which invokes the handler again as soon as the requested event occurs. Resuming the task is possible, as each point of continuation is equipped with a label whose address is taken by the handler, passed to the PAL, and retrieved as a function parameter with the subsequent invocation.

Additionally, the compiler generates a static data structure for each thread which contains all variables that are read after an interruptable call. By replacing automatic variables with their static counterparts, the relevant state of the task stays available. Overall, the transformation of the control flow preserves the order of statement execution while the transformation of the data flow preserves the effect of each statement, which is why T-code and E-code are equivalent.

3.3 Limitations

A major drawback of static analysis and translation is that it is limited to decidable problems. In particular, the compiler has to be able to infer the application's call graph, which implies three things. First, it is not allowed to take the address of an interruptable function. Instead one has to use case differentiation, which causes only moderate overhead. Second, interruptable functions may not be recursive, also because this would turn the estimation of the stack consumption undecidable. For the same reason, however, recursive algorithms are uncommon in embedded systems, which makes this a minor restriction. And third, we can not support dynamic thread creation but have to statically assign threads with thread start functions. As WSN applications tend to be composed of a fixed set of tasks, we don't consider this a severe limitation either.

These limitations are all inherent to compiler-assisted approaches and our compiler reliably rejects invalid T-code. Thus, we think it is appropriate to refer to our approach as a comprehensive thread abstraction.

Besides these limitations, the scarce resources additionally call for cooperative threads as opposed to preemptive ones. In cooperative style, context switching only occurs at yield points, thus the saved context only consists of the variables that are read after the yield point. In contrast, the context in preemptive style consists of the thread's complete stack and all CPU registers.

Of course, cooperative threads can not guarantee timings, pri-

```
double c1(char* s){              typedef struct {              1
    c2(s);                           void* cont;               2
    int i = f();          ⇒         double result;            3
    c3();                            char* s;                  4
    return i;                        int i;                    5
}                                    union {                   6
                                         frame_c2_t c2;        7
                                         frame_c3_t c3;        8
                                     } frames;                 9
                                 } frame_c1_t;                 10
```

Figure 2: The *T-stack structure* of an interruptable function. c1, c2, and c3 are interruptable functions; f is not.

orities, and fairness irrespective of the concrete implementation of each thread. Thus, our approach targets application and service layers of WSN applications where real-time is less of an issue. As, in contrast to general purpose computing devices, motes are usually not deployed with untrusted and thus uncooperative code, requiring cooperative threads is feasible.

Finally, we consider cooperative threads the easier programming model, as shared state has to be checked only after yield points. In contrast, preemptive threads are non-deterministic by default [14], and practice has shown that "humans are quickly overwhelmed by concurrency and find it much more difficult to reason about concurrent than sequential code" [23].

4. TRANSLATION SCHEME

The goal of the translation is to transform valid T-code into equivalent E-code. To this end, the translation distinguishes between interruptable and non-interruptable functions. Non-interruptable functions are passed through unchanged and are not considered any further.

Regarding interruptable functions, the first step is the translation into an intermediate representation (IR). Besides some technicalities such as the uniqueness of identifiers this implies two things. First, while and for loops are replaced by if and goto statements with labels. And second, interruptable calls only appear in one of two ways. The *first normal form* is a statement consisting of a single interruptable call. In contrast, the *second normal form* contains an arbitrary assignment operator, an l-value without interruptable calls, and a single interruptable call, i.e., anything of the form expression = interruptable_call(parameters);.

To establish the normal form, we make use of the fact that interruptable calls in nested expressions can be substituted by new variables that are initialized by the same interruptable call in a directly preceding statement. Special care is needed to handle Boolean short-circuit evaluation correctly, which is achieved by splitting Boolean expressions into a sequence of if statements as needed.

4.1 Data Flow

Given the IR, we use Hoopl [20] to perform a liveness analysis on each interruptable function to find the set of *critical variables*, i.e., automatic variables that are possibly read after an interruptable call and thus have to be preserved. Because aliasing turns this into an undecidable problem, the compiler makes conservative choices such as considering a variable as critical if its address is taken somewhere.

The compiler then generates a so-called *T-stack frame* for each interruptable function (cf. Figure 2). Such a frame contains the *continuation*, i.e., information about where execution should continue when the interruptable function returns (line 2), the return value of the function if existent (line 3), its parameters (line 4), its

```
void blinky() {
    while(1) {
        wait();
        // do something
    }
}
                    ⇓
1   void thread_0(..) {
2   //...
3   start: if (!1) return;
4       stack_blinky.frames.wait.cont = &&label_blinky_1;
5       goto label_wait_0;
6   label_blinky_1:
7       // do something
8       goto start;
9   label_wait_0:
10      // E-code body of wait
11      goto *stack_blinky.frames.wait.cont;
12  }
```

Figure 3: *Interruptable call of an interruptable function*

```
void wait() {
    sleep(23);
    // do something
}
                    ⇓
1   void thread_0(void* cont) {
2       if (cont) goto *cont;
3   //... E-code body of blinky
4   label_wait_0:
5       stack_blinky.frames.wait.frames.sleep.until = 23;
6       stack_blinky.frames.wait.frames.sleep.cont = \
7           &&label_wait_1;
8       sleep(&stack_blinky.frames.wait.frames.sleep);
9       return;
10  label_wait_1:
11      // do something
12      goto *stack_blinky.frames.wait.cont;
13  }
```

Figure 4: *Interruptable call of a T-code API function*

critical variables (line 5), and a union of the T-stack frames of all callees (lines 6–9). Furthermore, one T-stack frame for each thread starting function is instantiated statically and is called the *T-stack* of the thread.

Similarly, the *E-stack frame* of a function contains all of its non-critical variables, and for each thread the union of all E-stack frames of the involved functions establish the *E-stack*, which is an automatic variable of the *thread execution function* (cf. next section). Given these stacks, the compiler is rewriting access to variables by replacing them with the corresponding variables from the stacks.

4.2 Control Flow

To translate the control flow, the bodies of all interruptable functions that are used by a thread are inlined into one common *thread execution function* for each thread. This thread execution function serves as a single event handler function for all events concerning the corresponding thread. When inlining, the compiler equips every first statement of a function body and every first statement after an interruptable call with a unique label, which serves as a continuation point. The compiler also translates all interruptable function calls and returns.

Figure 3 depicts an example of how interruptable calls to interruptable functions are replaced by the following sequence of statements: First, the callee's parameters are written to the T-stack (not shown). Second, the continuation information for the callee is written to the T-stack (line 4). Third, a `goto` jumps to the start of the callee's body (line 5). Similarly, every `return` statement in the T-code is replaced by a `goto` statement that uses the continuation information stored on the T-stack (line 11). In case of an interruptable call in second normal form, the function's return value is copied from the T-stack and assigned to the translated l-value of the normal form's assignment (not shown).

Figure 4 shows that interruptable calls to T-code API functions are replaced by a slightly different sequence of statements. First, function parameters (line 5) and continuation information (line 6–7) are also copied to the T-stack. But then, the E-code API function is called, passing it a pointer to its T-stack frame (line 8). Last, the thread execution function returns in order to pass control back to the PAL (line 9).

The PAL takes care to call the thread execution function (called `thread_0` in this example) back as soon as the operation has completed, passing it the continuation that has previously been copied to the T-stack of the API function. The first statement in each thread execution function is a `goto` (line 2) that resumes the computation at this location. Again, the return value of the API function can be copied from its T-stack frame if necessary (not shown).

4.3 Equivalence and Correctness

In order to reason about the correctness of the transformation, we define an event-based application to be *equivalent* to a thread-based application if and only if every possible *observable behavior* of the E-code corresponds to one possible observable behavior of the T-code, assuming we would actually execute the T-code. The intuition behind this definition is twofold.

First, if from an observer's point of view, the interactions with the environment performed by the E-code and T-code are indistinguishable from each other, then both variants apparently do "the same thing" and it does not matter which one is actually executed. And second, if every observed interaction of the E-code can be explained by a hypothetical execution of the T-code, then "nothing surprising" can happen.

The *observable behavior* is defined as the order of all API calls including the *values* of all input parameters. Note however, that the exact timing of the API calls is not part of the observable behavior, as cooperative threads are not viable for timing-critical tasks. The *value* of a parameter is defined as the bit representation of a variable of primitive type, recursively applied to structures and unions, and the value of a pointer is the value of the referenced object.

As void pointers cannot be dereferrenced, they have no value by this definition. Also, arrays must either be known to be null-terminated or an additional lenght parameter must be at hand in order to determine the value of all of its elements. If a given T-code API makes use of arrays of unknown length or void pointers, we can still transform the application. A programmatic comparison of the observable behaviors will, however, be incomplete.

When comparing the observable behavior, we refer to corresponding functions from the T-code API and the E-code API. As the latter is systematically generated from the former, our definition of equivalence is sound.

The transformation of the data flow leaves the observable behavior unchanged because the variables that live on the stacks can simulate the life cycle of the corresponding automatic variables. First, this is because E-stacks contain only non-critical variables and are automatic variables themselves. And second, T-stacks simulate runtime stacks of threads by design. So overall, the transla-

```
1      int dt = 500;
2    A int get_leds() { /* ... */ }
3      void set_leds(int state) { /* ... */ }
4      int time(); // included from OS header file
5
6    H __attribute__((tc_api)) void sleep(int until);
7
8      __attribute__((tc_thread)) void blinky()
9      {
10         unsigned char state;
11         state = get_leds();
12         while(1) {
13   F         wait();
14             state ^= 0xff;
15             set_leds(state);
16         }
17     }
18
19     void wait() {
20         int now;
21   G     now = time();
22         sleep(now + dt);
23     }
```

$$\Downarrow$$

```
1      int dt = 500;
2    A int get_leds() { /* ... */ }
3      void set_leds(int state) { /* ... */ }
4      int time();
5
6      typedef struct {
7          void* cont; int until;
8      } frame_sleep_t;
9      typedef struct {
10         void* cont; int now;
11         union { frame_sleep_t sleep; } frames;
12   B } frame_wait_t;
13     typedef struct {
14         unsigned char state;
15         union { frame_wait_t wait; } frames;
16     } frame_blinky_t;
17
18   C frame_blinky_t tstack_blinky;
19
20   D typedef struct { int now; } eframe_wait_t;
21
22   H void sleep(frame_sleep_t*);
23
24     void thread_0(void* cont) {
25   E     union { eframe_wait_t wait; } estack;
26
27         if (cont) goto *cont;
28
29         tstack_blinky.state = get_leds();
30     start:
31         if (!1) return;
32         tstack_blinky.frames.wait.cont = &&label_blinky_1;
33         goto label_wait_0;
34   F label_blinky_1:
35         tstack_blinky.state ^= 0xff;
36         set_leds(tstack_blinky.state);
37         goto start;
38
39         label_wait_0:
40         estack.wait.now = time();
41         tstack_blinky.frames.wait.frames.sleep.until = \
42             estack.wait.now + dt;
43   G     tstack_blinky.frames.wait.frames.sleep.cont = \
44             &&label_wait_1;
45         sleep(&tstack_blinky.frames.wait.frames.sleep);
46         return;
47         label_wait_1:
48         goto *tstack_blinky.frames.wait.cont;
49     }
```

Figure 5: *A minimal, but complete example:* Translating T-code (top) to E-code (bottom).

tion simply exchanges the memory locations of variables while all statements formed with these variables keep their effects.

Concerning the transformation of the control flow, the transformation preserves both the sequence of statement between two yield points and the continuation of each interruptable call, which maintains the equivalence of each of these steps. And as the execution of T-code is non-deterministic with regard to the order of interleaving tasks, for each possible sequence of events in the E-code there is one possible control flow in the T-code. From this we can deduce the overall equivalence.

4.4 Example

Figure 5 shows a minimal, but complete example. First, the lines labeled with A in both listings show that everything that is neither an interruptable function nor a T-code API function is passed from T-code to E-code unchanged.

Label B shows the T-stack frame structures for the interruptable functions `sleep`, `wait`, and `blinky`. For example, the integer `state` (E-code, line 14) originates from the automatic variable `state` of the function `blinky` (T-code, line 10). Label C shows the instantiation of the T-stack.

Label D shows the E-stack frame for the function `wait` which is the only function with a non-critical variable. Thus, the E-stack (Label E) contains only one member.

Label F and G show the body of the function `blinky` and `wait`, respectively, and we can see two modifications. First, access to variables and parameters is altered. For instance, access to `state` and `now` (T-code, line 11 and 21) gets translated to access to the T-stack and E-stack (E-code, line 29 and 40). And second, the control flow is translated into continuation passing style. This involves instrumenting the code with labels marking the single continuations (E-code, line 34, 39, and 47). It also involves rewriting interruptable calls to interruptable functions (E-code, line 32 and 33) and to E-code API functions (E-code, line 41–46).

Finally, label H shows how declarations of API functions get translated. The compiler knows about API functions and thread start functions because they are marked with attributes (T-code, line 6 and 8).

5. PLATFORM ABSTRACTION LAYER

As already mentioned in Section 3.2, the PAL has to implement the E-code API by means of the OS API. But it is important to note that the PAL is not a conceptual requirement of our compiler-assisted approach to cooperative threads. Instead, it is only required to use Ocram with existing operating systems. In general, however, one could very well design an OS that already provides the systematic E-code API as assumed by Ocram. In this case no PAL would be needed at all.

The complexity of the PAL directly depends on how similar the existing OS API is to the systematic E-code API. Likewise, the integration of existing native code with generated E-code is also handled by the PAL in an OS-specific manner.

To illustrate the building blocks of a Contiki PAL that we used for our evaluation (cf. Section 6), we assume a minimalistic T-code example employing only a single thread and the single API function `sleep` from Figure 5. As already depicted there, the translation generates `frame_sleep_t` and the PAL needs to implement the E-code API function `sleep(frame_sleep_t* frame)` and ensure a proper thread continuation.

Despite prothreads, Contiki builds upon an event-based approach with a single event handler function for each task. To clarify this, we avoided using any of the prothreads macros for the Contiki PAL. We are still using what is called a "process" in Contiki, as

```
typedef enum {
  APICALL_sleep,
  /* constants for other API calls */
} APICall;

typedef struct {
  union {
      struct {
          frame_sleep_t* frame;
          struct etimer et;
      } sleep;
      /* contexts of other API calls */
  } ctx;
  APICall apicall;
} ThreadContext;

ThreadContext threads[1];
ThreadContext* cur_thread;

void sleep(frame_sleep_t* fr) {
  cur_thread->ctx.sleep.frame = fr;
  cur_thread->apicall = APICALL_sleep;
  clock_time_t now = clock_time();
  etimer_set(&cur_thread->ctx.sleep.et, fr->until-now);
}
```

Figure 6: *PAL implementation of* `sleep`

this is unavoidable, but without prothreads, a process is nothing more than an event handler and some meta information.

Figure 6 shows the implementation of `sleep` and Figure 7 shows the event handler that executes the single T-code thread. We can tell that the event handler has been called for the very first time by looking at the meta information in `ptinfo`. We memorize this case and call the generated thread execution function `thread_0` with a NULL continuation, thus starting the task. Soon after that, the task calls `sleep`, which sets a timer and returns. So does the thread execution function and the PAL, leaving the system to wait for the PAL being called again with a timer event. As soon as this happens, the PAL calls the thread execution function with the registered continuation, thus resuming the task. As the PAL uses standard Contiki primitives to communicate with other modules, integrating existing native code poses no problems.

PALs for other operating systems of course look different, but in general it should always be possible to perform the necessary mapping. For example, our proof-of-concept implementation of a TinyOS PAL employs one instance of a special component per T-code thread and each of these components is wired to whatever components it needs to implement the E-code API. API functions like `sleep` are implemented similarly to Figure 6, but the occurrence of an anticipated event results in a task being posted, which then calls the thread execution function.

6. EVALUATION

In order to evaluate our approach we have written Ocram, a Haskell-based implementation of the translation scheme described in Section 4. The source code of Ocram and of the complete evaluation is published[1] under a GPL license.

We have additionally chosen a set of three case studies, each following a real WSN application archetype (cf. Section 6.2), and overall covering a representative range of application types, programming concepts and concurrency patterns. We implemented each of these case studies in three variants (cf. Section 6.1): 1) a native event-based version, 2) a thread-based version using a thread library, and 3) a T-code version using Ocram. All nine resulting pro-

---

[1]https://github.com/copton/ocram

```
static char event_handler_0(struct pt* ptinfo,
        process_event ev, process_data_t data)
{
  void* cont;
  cur_thread = &threads[0];
  if (ptinfo->lc == 0) { // first invokation
    ptinfo->lc = 1;
    cont = NULL;
  } else if (cur_thread->apicall == APICALL_sleep
          && ev == PROCESS_EVENT_TIMER
          && data == &cur_thread->ctx.sleep.et) {
    cont = cur_thread->ctx.sleep.frame->ec_cont;
  } /* else handle other API calls */
  thread_0(cont);
  return PT_YIELDED;
}
```

Figure 7: *PAL event handler running a T-code thread.*

grams are written for Contiki and executed via COOJA/MSPSim, while an extra COOJA plugin collects various logs and measurements. Section 6.3 explains how we used the logs to verify the correctness of the applications and the transformation and Section 6.4 describes which measurements we took how.

6.1 Variants

For each case study application we first implemented a *native* (NAT) variant using the event-based paradigm. To this end, we either copied existing code or wrote an implementation following common programing patterns as encountered in the Contiki community. This implies using protothreads, which disguises that the runtime system is event-based and adds an overhead of two bytes per protothread. We argue, though, that this does not significantly bias the ground truth of our evaluation, which is the performance of a native event-based application.

In Section 2 we have argued why compiler-assisted thread abstractions are more efficient than runtime-based solutions. To verify this hypothesis, we have secondly written a threaded variant of the application which is directly executed using a *thread library* (TL). For this purpose, we have ported the TinyThreads [16] thread library to Contiki, as it is the only available full-fledged thread library for cooperative threads in sensor networks. We kept the basic context switching code and the general scheduler architecture, but we had to adapt the details to Contiki's APIs. We also removed support for preemption and dynamic thread creation and termination to avoid extra overhead for features that our abstraction does not provide. Overall, a single protothread executes the scheduler and all application-level threads.

Finally, the third variant is the E-code application *generated* (GEN) from a thread-based T-code application. To enable a fair comparison, the three variants only differ from each other if the different programming models require so. We thus share most non-interruptable code via separate translation units and we also copied as many source code lines between the variants as possible.

6.2 Case Study Applications

Figure 8 shows simplified pseudo code for the three case study applications. The underlined functions are thread start functions with an endless loop executing the listed code, while the italic functions are re-entrant interruptable functions. The three applications use the API functions `sleep`, `receive`, and `wait` and all three of them can be interrupted via `notify`.

The first case study is a typical *data collection and in-network aggregation* (DCA) application consisting of three tasks. Overall, the application reads values from the local sensor, receives

```
receiving:
  receive
  add values to ring buffer

collecting:
  sleep 23 second
  read from sensor
  add value to ring buffer

sending:
  sleep 127 seconds
  empty ring buffer
  aggregate values
  send results to parent
```

(a) DCA

```
server:
  receive
  if notified:
    send response
  else:
    notify available worker

worker [1-N]:
  wait
  handle call

handle call:
  if read fast sensor:
    read sensor
  if read slow sensor:
    sleep // emulation ·
    read sensor
  if tell:
    send call to peer
    receive response
  notify server
```

(c) RPC

```
transactions:
  sleep until next timeout
  if notified:
    accept new transaction
  else:
    send transaction
    double transaction timeout

receiver:
  receive
  cancel pending transaction
  notify stop-and-wait

client:
  sleep 10 seconds
  stop-and-wait of PUT
  stop-and-wait of GET

stop-and-wait:
  for each fragment:
    create transaction
    send transaction
    wait
```

(b) CoAP

Figure 8: Pseudo code of the *case study applications*.

values from its child node(s) and sends aggregated values to its parent node. This constitutes a consumer-producer pattern with inter-thread communication via a shared ring buffer, but no explicit thread synchronization and no re-entrant code. The major architecture of this case study can be found in many deployments (e.g. [7]).

The second case study is a complete client-side implementation of the *CoAP protocol* [22] including application-level payload fragmentation via stop-and-wait [3], and a minimal application layer. The program consists of three tasks and overall the client repeatedly sends PUT and GET requests to the server. The PUT request sets the seed for a random resource on the server, while the GET request retrieves a possibly large sequence of characters from this resource. Both the value of the seed and the length of the character sequence are chosen randomly. This application involves both explicit thread synchronization via `wait` and `notify` and re-entrant code. The native implementation for this study is Contiki's CoAP implementation [12].

The third case study is motivated by a programming framework for sensor networks [18] that offers so-called *tell actions*, where a node may tell one or more other nodes to execute a (potentially synchronous) command and the tell action itself waits until all nodes have finished executing the command. In other words, a tell action basically is a synchronous one-to-many *remote procedure call* (RPC). In a network in which multiple tell actions can occur at any time, each node should be able to handle multiple RPCs at the same time. This calls for a thread pool, a common concurrency pattern that can be found in many RPC systems such as CORBA. Although there are some RPC frameworks for sensor networks [15, 26], none of them supports concurrent invocations. Thus, we implemented this framework from scratch.

In order to keep the focus on the programming model, we only support three basic remote calls that conceptually cover the whole spectrum of interest: 1) reading a value from a fast sensor such as a temperature sensor, 2) reading a value from a slow sensor, which involves some startup time and thus a synchronous function on the callee's side, and 3) a tell operation, which involves delegating any of these three remote calls to a different node and thus also requires a synchronous function on the callee's side. The application implements both the client and the server side of the RPC protocol and involves explicit thread synchronization and re-entrant functions.

6.3 Verification

The verification serves three purposes. First, we want to make sure that we measure only the effects of the different programming abstractions. Second, we want to test each variant of each application for bugs. And third, we want to verify the correctness of the transformation.

To preserve the fairness of the comparison, we used the same COOJA simulation for all variants, only exchanging the binary under test in each case. This means that spatial mote distribution, radio model, neighbor nodes, random seeds, etc. are constant. That is, the execution environment is deterministic and produces the same results repeatably. Additionally, we compared the source code of the three variants to make sure that they are not needlessly dissimilar.

In order to verify the executed applications, we wrote a COOJA plugin that collects a log of `printf` traces, which serves as an input to an application-specific verification script. And concerning the correctness of the transformation, the plugin also collects a log of the observable behavior (OB) as defined in Section 4.3. The TL variant de facto constitutes the execution of the T-code, while GEN is the execution of the E-code. Thus, comparing the OB of TL and GEN ensures the equality of T-code and E-code and thus the correctness of the transformation.

6.4 Measurements

As a first and simplest measurement, we counted the *lines of code* required to implement the application logic for each variant. Lines of code is in general not very significant, but when using identical code formatting rules, as we did in our evaluation, it provides a quick but good estimation of the expressiveness of the programming model. In order to focus on the effects of the different programming models, we did not include the shared translation units into the counting. Similarly, we neither took GEN's PAL nor TL's scheduler into account, as this code needs to be written only once and can thus be regarded as being part of the operating system, which we did not count either.

Next, we compiled each application for the Tmote Sky platform using the MSP430 port of the GNU Compiler Collection (GCC) version 3.2.3. The compilation process was performed by Contiki's build system with `SMALL=1`, which amongst other things instructs the linker to remove unused functions. To obtain static measurements from the resulting binary we used `objdump` from GCC's binutils and retrieved the size of the *text* section (i.e., the machine code itself), the size of the initialized *data* section, and the size of the uninitialized data section, also known as *bss* section.

Besides these static measurements, we were also interested in runtime properties. To obtain a precise count of *CPU cycles*, we modified the Contiki system by introducing a `volatile void*`

variable called `proc_hook`. Right before invoking a process, the scheduler writes the address of the descriptor of the particular process to `proc_hook`. And right after the process returns control, `proc_hook` is set to NULL. As `proc_hook` is declared `volatile`, its modifications are guaranteed to happen at the intended moments and in the right order. Our plugin can thus install a break point for updates to `proc_hook`, which enables it to precisely sum up CPU cycles for each process individually.

All interrupt functions and the code that logs the OB signal their invocation via `proc_hook` as well. The plugin can thus remove these CPU cycles from the current process' account, and by considering the cycles for the prologue and the epilogue of the interrupt functions and the cycles for the write operations to `proc_hook`, it measures the exact number of CPU cycles per process.

For NAT, we counted the CPU cycles of all processes that run an application task, leaving out any OS processes. For TL, we counted the CPU cycles of the single scheduler process only, as it executes all application threads. And finally, for GEN, we counted the CPU cycles of all Contiki processes that execute an application thread (cf. Section 5). Overall, the counted CPU cycles cover the same application functionality in each case.

In order to measure the *maximum stack consumption*, our plugin installs a break point for updates to the stack pointer register (SP). For NAT and GEN, tracking the maximum SP value and subtracting it from the start address of the stack is sufficient. For TL, we also need to take the stacks of the application threads into account, though. Our plugin does this accurately and thus obtains the precise amount of bytes required for each stack.

We used these values to set the size of the application stacks, thus reducing the size of the bss section as much as possible and enabling a fair comparison. As interrupts happen non-deterministically, a single simulation run might not catch the worst case of interrupt function invocations. Thus, we added a safety margin of 20 bytes to each stack and so far no stack overflows occurred during our measurements, which of course is also monitored by the plugin.

7. RESULTS

A major observation of the evaluation is that the results are deterministic. Thus we can directly interpret these values without any additional statistics methods.

Figure 9a shows that in order to implement the same application, T-code requires 8 % to 17 % less *lines of code* than a native Contiki implementation. As already mentioned in the previous section, this measurement does not cover shared translation units, which contain additional 2000 lines of code for CoAP and 300 for RPC.

As "with protothreads the number of lines of code was reduced by one third" [6], we can estimate that a T-code application requires up to 45 % less lines of code than an equivalent event-based application. Although this result is not precise, it still supports our initial motivation for this work: synchronous functions and sequential computation provide an easier programming model than asynchronous functions and event handlers. The TL variant is close to GEN but higher because it provides the same programming model as GEN, but requires extra lines to define the application stacks and to start the threads.

7.1 Memory Resources

Of course, we expect our thread abstraction to also have some costs. First of all, we are interested in the overall memory consumption because random access memory (RAM) is very limited on sensor network devices. To this end, Figure 9b shows the size of the *data* and the *bss* section along with the maximum *stack size* for each variant of each application. First, we can see that all three vari-

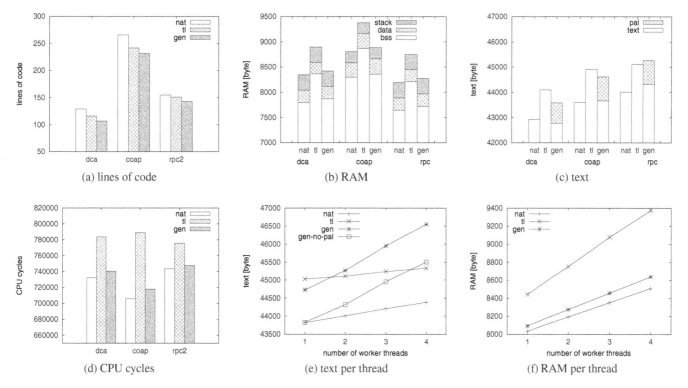

(a) lines of code   (b) RAM   (c) text

(d) CPU cycles   (e) text per thread   (f) RAM per thread

Figure 9: *Evaluation results*: (a)-(d): resource consumption of various resources per variant and application. (e)-(f): resources consumption of RPC application per variant versus number of threads.

ants have roughly the same amount of initialized data and a large common block of bss memory. This is because each variant uses the same operating system that adds its string constants, network stack buffers, etc.

Additionally, we can see that all three variants have roughly equal maximum stack sizes because none of them uses the runtime stack a lot: Protothreads use `static` variables, TL uses the stacks of the application threads for function-local automatic variables, and GEN has its T-stacks. As a consequence, we can see TL and GEN having larger bss segments.

The interesting observation is that TL's overhead is significantly higher which reflects the common wisdom that thread libraries are expensive (cf. Section 3.1). A second interesting observation is that both GEN's overhead of the bss section and its overhead of the total amount of required RAM is approx. 1 % compared to NAT.

Another limited resource of sensor network devices is ROM space, which means that we need to compare the binary size of the variants. Figure 9c thus shows the size of the *text* sections and, in case of the GEN variant, it also distinguishes between code resulting from the application layer and code added by the PAL.

First, we see the overhead of TL's scheduler as expected. Similarly, we see the overhead of GEN's PAL. But we also see that the generated code itself, i.e., the E-code not including the PAL, is almost the same size as the code of the NAT variant. And including the PAL, the overhead is below 3 %.

Overall, the results show that Ocram provides the comfort of threads for just a small amount of extra RAM and ROM.

7.2 CPU cycles

Next, we want to know if the generated code involves more computation than a native implementation because keeping the CPU busy prevents the device from going into a low-power idle state. To

this end, Figure 9d shows the *CPU cycles* count for each variant of each application. The absolute range of the values depends on the duration of the simulation of each application and thus provides little insight. But what we do see is that TL's scheduler adds up to 12 % of CPU cycles compared to the NAT variant. And we see that despite the additional PAL, GEN's number of CPU cycles is only approx. 2 % higher compared to NAT.

Although we do not know the exact division between the PAL and the application code, regarding the extra work performed by the PAL, this result suggests that the E-code actually requires less CPU cycles than the native implementation. An explanation for this is that all interruptable functions are inlined in the E-code, thus saving extra cycles for function prologue and epilogues. But of course, this comes at the cost of a larger binary size in case of re-entrant functions.

7.3 Resource consumption per thread

To analyze this trade-off, we varied the number of worker threads of the RPC application from one to four and performed the measurements for each configuration. In each case, we adapted the client mote to send the right amount of concurrent remotely waiting RPC calls to have all worker threads busy at the same time. The previous figures showed results for the RPC application with two worker threads and using more than four workers already exceeds the limited resources of the Tmote Sky.

Figure 9e shows the size of the *text* section of all three variants versus the number of worker threads. Additionally, it shows the PAL's share by plotting the GEN variant with the text section of the PAL removed.

In the case of a single worker thread, we see the overhead of TL's scheduler once again. But we also see that TL has the lowest slope of all, as increasing the number of worker threads only involves starting another application thread. The rest of TL's code is generic in that sense and can be reused. For NAT, we have a slope of 187 bytes per worker. This originates from the additional prototheads that run the extra workers. Although they share common code, the basic stub of each protothread is always required.

And finally for GEN, we see the biggest slope of 607 bytes per worker including the PAL and 559 bytes per worker without the PAL. The share added by the PAL has the same origin as in the NAT case. And the share added by the E-code reflects the trade-off that we have chosen for the translation scheme: By inlining interruptable functions, we save CPU cycles and RAM, but we pay extra for re-entrant interruptable functions. In this sense, the thread pools of the RPC application are a worst case scenario for this translation scheme.

Figure 9f shows the other side of the trade-off which is RAM. There we see that GEN has almost the same slope as NAT, i.e., 182 vs. 158 bytes per worker. In contrast, TL has a slope of 310 bytes per worker which has two major reasons. First, as already explained, each thread's stack needs an extra margin to be able to host any occurring interrupt handler functions. And second, the generic nature of a thread library indeed saves in binary size, but it pays in RAM because it has to support all possible cases. Given the limited resources, the lack of static analysis is what kept thread libraries from improving their performance [17]. With compiler-assisted thread abstractions we aim to exploit exactly this possibility.

7.4 Discussion

Overall, the evaluation results give three major insights. First, the thread-based programming paradigm yields to more compact code compared to event-based programming, which is an indication for what is generally perceived as being an easier programming model. Second, the performance overhead of generated E-code compared to hand-written event-based code is in the single digits, making the comfort of threads affordable for resource-constrained WSN devices. And third, the performance of generated E-code is better than what can currently be achieved with thread libraries.

Of course, a dedicated threads-to-events compiler is a huge initial effort, but we argue that the major advantage of compiler-assisted approaches is their capability to exploit application-specific optimizations. Although Ocram currently only applies some basic optimizations such as keeping non-critical variables on the shared runtime stack, on the medium term we expect the performance of E-code to improve with more advanced translations, while for thread libraries we do not see such opportunities of improvement.

8. FUTURE WORK

Although we believe that Ocram represents a major step towards a practical and efficient thread abstraction for sensor networks, several improvements are subject of our ongoing and future work.

Our current compiler prototype only implements some optimizations, but there are a number of further optimization opportunities. For example, if a function is only called from one location in the whole program, there is no need to save the caller's continuation in memory. Instead, it can be hard-coded into the E-code. As a second example, in case of read-only parameters, the callee can access the variables from the caller's T-stack frame instead of having them copied to its own frame. Furthermore, different translation schemes have different trade-offs. A future T-code compiler therefore could measure properties of the input application and use a heuristic to choose the most efficient translation scheme.

We have also developed an early prototype of a T-code debugger, which offers typical source-level debugging primitives such as break points and variable inspection on T-code level. To this end, the Ocram compiler saves the performed variable and code mapping in a separate debug file and the T-code debugger communicates with a common E-code debugger such as the GDB. Whenever the user wants to access a source code line or a variable, the T-code debugger consults the debug file to find the corresponding E-code source line or variable and delegates a translated request to the E-code debugger. By these means it is possible to completely hide the event-based nature of the runtime system from the programmer. Most other WSN programming abstractions fail to support fault diagnosis, forcing the developer to cope with the complexity of the underlying run-time system nevertheless and thus breaking the abstraction.

9. CONCLUSIONS

We presented the first comprehensive compiler-assisted thread abstraction to address the increasing mote software complexity at the service and application layers, where the simple event-action model of event-based programming leads to code that is hard to manage and prone to errors.

Our evaluation showed that with our approach thread-based programming is almost as efficient as event-based programming: The overhead of RAM is approx. 1 %, for ROM below 3 %, and concerning CPU cycles the overhead is below 2 %. Thus, our work shows that the trade-off between expressiveness and efficiency of thread abstractions is not inherent to resource-constrained systems.

Additional optimizations, which are part of our ongoing and future work, are expected to stress this point even further. Thus we argue that the effort of employing a dedicated threads-to-events compiler pays off. We also believe that Ocram is a practical solution, as the generated code integrates seamlessly with existing hand-written event-based code. Furthermore, Ocram can be easily ported to other event-based kernels by implementing a thin platform abstraction layer, which is a one-time overhead.

10. ACKNOWLEDGMENTS

This work has been partially supported by the National Competence Center in Research on Mobile Information and Communication Systems (NCCR-MICS), a center supported by the Swiss National Science Foundation under grant number 5005-67322, and by CONET, the Cooperating Objects Network of Excellence, funded by the European Commission under FP7 with contract number FP7-2007-2-224053.

We want to thank Matthias Kovatsch, Institute for Pervasive Computing, ETH Zurich, for helping us with his expertise in Contiki, Cooja and CoAP.

11. REFERENCES

[1] A. Adya, J. Howell, M. Theimer, W. J. Bolosky, and J. R. Douceur. Cooperative Task Management Without Manual Stack Management. In *Proceedings of the General Track of the USENIX Technical Conference*, pages 289–302, 2002.

[2] S. Bhatti, J. Carlson, H. Dai, J. Deng, J. Rose, A. Sheth, B. Shucker, C. Gruenwald, A. Torgerson, and R. Han. MANTIS OS: An Embedded Multithreaded Operating System for Wireless Micro Sensor Platforms. *Mobile Networks and Applications*, 10(4):563–579, 2005.

[3] C. Bormann and Z. Shelby. Blockwise Transfers in CoAP. http://tools.ietf.org/html/draft-ietf-core-block-10, 2011.

[4] P. Costa, L. Mottola, A. L. Murphy, and G. P. Picco. Programming Wireless Sensor Networks with the

TeenyLime Middleware. In *Proceedings of the Middleware Conference*, pages 429–449, 2007.

[5] A. Dunkels, B. Gronvall, and T. Voigt. Contiki - A Lightweight and Flexible Operating System for Tiny Networked Sensors. In *Proceedings of the Conference on Local Computer Networks*, LCN, pages 455–462, 2004.

[6] A. Dunkels, O. Schmidt, T. Voigt, and M. Ali. Protothreads: Simplifying Event-driven Programming of Memory-constrained Embedded Systems. In *Proceedings of the Conference on Embedded Networked Sensor Systems*, SenSys, pages 29–42, 2006.

[7] A. Hasler, I. Talzi, J. Beutel, C. Tschudin, and S. Gruber. Wireless Sensor Networks in Permafrost Research: Concept, Requirements, Implementation, and Challenges. In *Proceedings of the Conference on Permafrost*, pages 669–674, 2008.

[8] J. Hill, R. Szewczyk, A. Woo, S. Hollar, D. E. Culler, and K. S. J. Pister. System Architecture Directions for Networked Sensors. *ACM SIGARCH Computer Architecture News*, 28(5):93–104, 2000.

[9] J. W. Hui and D. E. Culler. IP is Dead, Long Live IP for Wireless Sensor Networks. In *Proceedings of the Conference on Embedded Networked Sensor Systems*, SenSys, pages 15–28, 2008.

[10] K. Klues, C.-J. M. Liang, J. Paek, R. Musaloiu-E, P. Levis, A. Terzis, and R. Govindan. TOSThreads: Thread-safe and Non-invasive Preemption in TinyOS. In *Proceedings of the Conference on Embedded Networked Sensor Systems*, SenSys, pages 127–140, 2009.

[11] J. Ko, K. Klues, C. Richter, W. Hofer, B. Kusy, M. Brünig, T. Schmid, Q. Wang, P. Dutta, and A. Terzis. Low Power or High Performance? A Tradeoff Whose Time Has Come (and Nearly Gone). In *Proceedings of the European Conference on Wireless Sensor Networks*, EWSN, pages 98–114, 2012.

[12] M. Kovatsch, S. Duquennoy, and A. Dunkels. A Low-Power CoAP for Contiki. In *Proceedings of the Conference on Mobile Ad-hoc and Sensor Systems*, MASS, pages 855–860, 2011.

[13] H. C. Lauer and R. M. Needham. On the Duality of Operating System Structures. *Operating Systems Review*, 13(2):3–19, 1979.

[14] E. A. Lee. The Problem with Threads. *IEEE Computer*, 39(5):33–42, 2006.

[15] T. D. May, S. H. Dunning, and G. A. Dowding. An RPC Design for Wireless Sensor Networks. *Pervasive Computing and Communications*, 2(4):384–397, 2007.

[16] W. P. McCartney and N. Sridhar. Abstractions for Safe Concurrent Programming in Networked Embedded Systems. In *Proceedings of the Conference on Embedded Networked Sensor Systems*, SenSys, pages 167–180, 2006.

[17] W. P. McCartney and N. Sridhar. Stackless Preemptive Multi-Threading for TinyOS. In *Proceedings of the Conference on Distributed Computing in Sensor Systems*, DCOSS, pages 1–8, 2011.

[18] L. Mottola, G. P. Picco, P. Valleri, F. J. Oppermann, and K. Römer. The makeSense Programming Model. Technical Report D-3.1, Swedish Institute of Computer Science, Università degli Studi di Trento, Universität zu Lübeck, 2011.

[19] C. Nitta, R. Pandey, and Y. Ramin. Y-threads: Supporting Concurrency in Wireless Sensor Networks. In *Proceedings of the Conference on Distributed Computing in Sensor Systems*, DCOSS, pages 169–184, 2006.

[20] N. Ramsey, J. Dias, and S. Peyton Jones. Hoopl: A Modular, Reusable Library for Dataflow Analysis and Transformation. In *Proceedings of the Symposium on Haskell*, pages 121–134, 2010.

[21] J. Sallai, M. Maróti, and A. Lédeczi. A Concurrency Abstraction for Reliable Sensor Network Applications. In *Proceedings of the Conference on Reliable Systems on Unreliable Networked Platforms*, pages 143–160, 2007.

[22] Z. Shelby, K. Hartke, C. Bormann, and B. Frank. Constrained Application Protocol (CoAP). http://tools.ietf.org/html/draft-ietf-core-coap-13, 2011.

[23] H. Sutter and J. Larus. Software and the Concurrency Revolution. *Queue*, 3(7):54–62, 2005.

[24] R. von Behren, J. Condit, F. Zhou, G. C. Necula, and E. Brewer. Capriccio: Scalable Threads for Internet Services. In *Proceedings of the Symposium on Operating Systems Principles*, SOSP, pages 268–281, 2003.

[25] M. Welsh and G. Mainland. Programming Sensor Networks Using Abstract Regions. In *Proceedings of the Symposium on Networked Systems Design and Implementation*, NSDI, pages 29–42, 2004.

[26] K. Whitehouse, G. Tolle, J. Taneja, C. Sharp, S. Kim, J. Jeong, J. Hui, P. Dutta, and D. E. Culler. Marionette: Using RPC for Interactive Development and Debugging of Wireless Embedded Networks. In *Proceedings of the Conference on Information Processing in Sensor Networks*, IPSN, pages 416–423, 2006.

A Real-time Auto-Adjustable Smart Pillow System for Sleep Apnea Detection and Treatment

Jin Zhang   Qian Zhang
Hong Kong University of
Science and Technology
Hong Kong, China
{jinzh,qianzh}@ust.hk

Yuanpeng Wang
Shenzhen New Element
Medical Cooperation
Shenzhen, China
wangyuanpeng@szxys.cn

Chen Qiu
Shenzhen People's Hospital
2nd Clinical Medical College
of Jinan University
szchester@163.com

ABSTRACT

Sleep apnea, which is a common sleep disorder character-ized by the repetitive cessation of breathing during sleep, can result in various diseases, including headaches, hyper-tension, stroke and cardiac arrest, as well as produce severe consequences such as impaired concentration and traffic ac-cidents. A traditional diagnosis method of sleep apnea is polysomnography, which can only be conducted in sleep cen-ter with specialized personals, thus is expensive and incon-venient. Moreover, it is only used for understanding the con-ditions, without treatment function. Some other methods or devices have been developed to alleviate sleep apnea, such as continuous positive airway pressure (CPAP) and intrao-ral mandibular advancement device and surgery. However, they only provide a treatment method without detection or monitoring function. There is no existing device which can provide both apnea detection and treatment functionality.

In this paper, we propose and implement a smart phone-based auto-adjustable pillow system, which enables both sleep apnea detection and treatment. Sleep apnea events can be detected in real-time using the blood oxygen sensor, accordingly, the height and shape of the pillow can be auto-matically adjusted to terminate the sleep apnea event. On the other hand, after the adjustment, the sensor can con-tinuously monitor the blood oxygen signal to evaluate the effectiveness of the pillow adjustment and to help in select-ing a suitable adjustment scheme. Therefore, a real-time feedback control system is formed. Besides, compared with existing diagnosis or treatment devices, our system is non-invasive, inexpensive and portable, which can be used at home or during traveling. In this paper, a real-time sleep apnea detection and classification algorithm is proposed to decide whether the pillow should be adjusted or not. We also design a real-time feedback pillow adjustment algorithm, to decide when and how to adjust the pillow and how to eval-uate the effectiveness of the adjustment. We conducted ex-periments on 40 patients, which demonstrate that using our novel smart pillow system, both the sleep apnea duration

and the number of sleep apnea events are dramatically re-duced by more than 50%.

Categories and Subject Descriptors

C.3 [**Special-Purpose and Application-Based Systems**]: Real-time and embedded systems

General Terms

Algorithm, Design, Experimentation

Keywords

Sleep Apnea Detection and Treatment, Smart Pillow, SpO_2 Detection

1. INTRODUCTION

Sleeping is an important mechanism which contributes greatly to one's physical and mental well-being as well as their overall quality of life. People with sleep disorders usu-ally suffer from various symptoms, such as difficulty concen-trating, memory lapses, loss of energy, fatigue, lethargy, and emotional instability. Among various sleep disorders, *sleep apnea* is the most common one, which is characterized by the repetitive cessation of breathing during sleep [12, 2]. Ac-cording to the world health organization, the prevalence of sleep apnea is between 2% and 4%, which means that there are 200 million sleep apnea patients all over the world. Sleep apnea is not only common but also dangerous because it leads to several severe consequences. The frequent arousals result in ineffective sleep and account for chronic sleep de-privation, thus result in sleepiness during the day, irritabil-ity, tiredness, impaired concentration, and reduced learning capabilities. These symptoms typically produce even more serious consequences, including social problems in the work place and traffic accidents. Sleep apnea also leads to morn-ing headaches, hypertension, heart attacks, heart-rhythm disorders, stroke and decreased life expectancy.

Current solutions for sleep apnea are either on detection and diagnosis, or on intervention and treatment. For sleep apnea detection and diagnosis, the most well-recognized way is polysomnography (PSG). The patient is required to sleep in a specialized sleep center for a whole night and multiple channels of physiological signals are recorded. The signals are analyzed by specialized staff and the sleep apnea can be diagnosed. However, such solution is very expensive and complicated. Due to the small number of sleep center with specialized staff, a large number of sleep apnea patients are not able to be diagnosed in time. It is reported that over 80% sleep apnea patients all over the world are unaware of their conditions. Besides, it is uncomfortable to sleep in a special sleep center wearing dozens of sensors, thus the diagnosis may not truthfully reflect the real case of the patient's sleep quality as in daily life. Recently, there are also some portable monitoring devices which use the electrocardiogram (ECG) or the pulsoximetry signal to detect apnea. However, they can only sense and detect the apnea events, without providing any intervention or alleviation solutions.

Even if the patient is diagnosed to suffer from sleep apnea, the treatment is also a challenging problem. There are several ways to cure or alleviate sleep apnea. For moderate to severe sleep apnea, the most common treatment is the use of a continuous positive airway pressure (CPAP) [10] or Automatic Positive Airway Pressure (APAP) [11] device, which is a machine that continuously or automatically blows air into patient's nose through a face mask. CPAP or APAP ensures clearer and regular breathing, thus prevents sleep apnea, however, the device is expensive and it's uncomfortable for the patients to wear a face mask and have dry air blown into their nose over night. Surgery [6] and mandibular advancement [14] are therapeutic options for sleep apnea. However, both of them are invasive and painful for the patient and there are high chances for the syndrome to relapse. There are also life style treatment, e.g. weight control or sleeping in lateral position. However, it takes a long time to be effective and one cannot control one's sleeping position during sleep. In one word, to the best of our knowledge, there is no inexpensive, comfortable and effective method for treatment of sleep apnea.

In this paper, we designed and implemented a novel real-time auto-adjustable smart pillow system. This device is able to detect sleep apnea in real time using a pulsoximeter, and to alleviate sleep apnea by adjusting the height and shape of the pillow. This is the first work to enable both sleep apnea detection and treatment in a home environment using a portable, inexpensive and non-invasive device. Our work is based on two key observations: one is that the blood oxygen saturation is a good indicator to detect sleep apnea event; by monitoring blood oxygen saturation using a pulsoximeter, the sleep apnea event can be detected in real time. The other observation is that, the height and shape of the pillow will greatly impact the level of sleep apnea, by intelligently adjusting the shape of the pillow, the sleep apnea can be alleviated.

To make sure that the device can be used at home and is easy to wear, among the multiple channels of physiological signals in the PSG, we only select arterial blood oxygen sensor (also called pulsoximeter) to detect the sleep apnea events. Blood oxygen saturation (also called SpO_2) is a good indicator to characterize the sleep apnea and hypopnea [21]. Leveraging the arterial blood oxygen sensor, the sleep apnea events can be detected in real-time in a very comfortable way. Once the sleep apnea events are detected, the pillow is automatically controlled by the smart phone-based central controller to adjust its shape and height. The patient, stimulated by the pillow, will then be able to open their airflow and regular breath is recovered. After the adjustment of pillow, the blood oxygen sensor will continuously monitor the physiological signals to make sure the correctness and effectiveness of the pillow adjustment. Leveraging such a feedback loop mechanism, the smart pillow system performs

more intelligently and personalized. Compared with other types of treatment, our system has minimal interruption to natural sleep, as it is non-invasive, not painful and takes action only when apnea events are detected.

There are several challenges during the design of the system. One is to detect sleep apnea events with limited physiological signals, the other is to adjust the pillow system to reduce the sleep apnea events. To tackle the first challenge, we design a detection and classification algorithm to detect the occurrence of sleep anomaly events and further classify the events into two categories, continuous apnea events and sporadic apnea events, using a support vector machine (SVM) - based classifier. Distinguishing between the two types of events enhances the effectiveness of the adjustment while minimizing the interruption of sleep and improving sleep quality. Since patients can recover from the sporadic events automatically, there is no need to adjust the pillow when sporadic ones are detected. Only continuous apnea events lead to a pillow adjustment. To tackle the second challenge, we design a real-time feedback pillow adjustment algorithm, to decide when and how to adjust the pillow and how to evaluate the effectiveness of the adjustment. A series of PSG-comparative experiments and pillow adjustment experiments are conducted to obtain the optimal parameters of the above two algorithms. Finally, to demonstrate the feasibility and effectiveness of our smart pillow system, comparative experiments are conducted on 40 volunteers over 80 nights. The experimental results show that our system dramatically reduces the sleep apnea duration by 55% and the number of sleep apnea events by 57%. The remaining apnea events (43%) are sporadic ones which are not as harmful for the patient and require no adjustment. The duration for each apnea event is also reduced dramatically.

The main contributions of the paper are as follows: (1) a real-time auto-adjustable smart pillow system is designed and implemented, which is the first device to enable sleep apnea detection and treatment in a comfortable and natural way in a home environment; the device is non-invasive, portable and inexpensive, which provides an intelligent, effective and personalized treatment by leveraging real-time control and feedback mechanisms; (2) an SpO_2-based sleep apnea detection and an SpO_2 desaturation classification algorithm are proposed to detect apnea events and further divide them into several types to prepare for the pillow adjustment decision making; (3) we propose a real-time pillow-adjustment algorithm which incorporates real-time SpO_2 monitoring; (4) experiments were conducted on 40 patients and the results demonstrate that our smart pillow system significantly reduces the number of sleep apnea events and the time duration of apnea episodes.

The rest of the paper is organized as follows: in Section 2, the system architecture of the smart pillow system is described. In Section 3, the sleep apnea detection and classification algorithm is proposed. In Section 4, the pillow-adjustment algorithm is proposed. In Section 5, we evaluate the overall performance of the system. The related work is discussed in Section 6 and the whole paper is concluded in Section 7.

2. SYSTEM ARCHITECTURE

In this section, we will describe the overall hardware and software architecture of the smart pillow system.

As shown in Figure 1, the system is composed of three

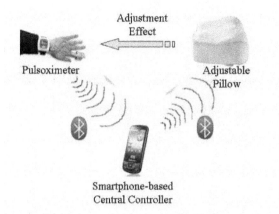

Figure 1: System components. The pulsoximeter senses the SpO$_2$ signal and transmits it to the smart phone. The smartphone detects the SpO$_2$ desaturation events and issues pillow adjustment command. The adjustable pillow adjusts its shape and height according to the command. The adjustment effect is further monitored and evaluated by the pulsoximeter.

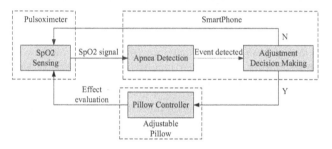

Figure 2: System architecture.

components: a pulsoximeter, a smartphone-based central controller and an adjustable pillow. The three components are physically disconnected and communicate with each other using wireless communication.

Figure 2 shows the architecture of our smart pillow system. First, the pulsoximeter performs SpO$_2$ sensing continuously and sends the signals to the apnea detection and classification module in the smartphone. The apnea detection module then detects whether this is an apnea event and sends the result to the adjustment decision making module, which is also implemented in the smart phone. Through an adjustment algorithm, the decision making module decides whether and how the pillow should be adjusted. If an adjustment decision is made, then, the adjustment command including the expected adjustment parameters is sent to pillow controller, which controls the corresponding devices to adjust the pillow, otherwise, no adjustment is required. After the pillow is adjusted, the pulsoximeter continues to sense the SpO$_2$ signals to evaluate whether the adjustment takes effect. We will describe each component in detail in the following subsections.

2.1 Pulsoximeter

The pulsoximeter measures the arterial oxygen saturation of the user, according to which, sleep apnea events are detected. There are two components in the pulsoximeter: a

blood oxygen sensor and a Bluetooth transceiver [3]. The sensor is placed in the user's fingertip and it monitors the blood oxygen saturation continuously over the night. The Bluetooth transceiver is programmed to transmit the measured signals to the cell phone in real time using Bluetooth 2.1.

There are many signals and symptoms which can help to detect sleep apnea, e.g. blood oxygen saturation, electrocardiogram (ECG), electroencephalography (EEG), airflow, etc. among which blood oxygen saturation is the most easy to monitor and whose sensor is the most comfortable to wear, compared with ECG and airflow monitor. Therefore, we select pulsoximetry as the signal to monitor. Besides, according to the analysis in Section 3, pulsoximetry alone can provide high enough detection accuracy compared with other methods.

In our system, we adopt the pulsoximeter made by New Element Medical Corp., an off-the-shelf constant monitoring oximetry sensor as shown in Figure 3(a). This sensor is small, light-weight, flexible and capable of long-term monitoring. The pulsoximeter acquires the SpO$_2$ and heart rate values, ranging from 0% to 100% and from 30 to 250 beats per minute (bpm) respectively, with a 60Hz sampling rate with an 8-bit resolution. The pulsoximeter aggregates the newly-generated SpO$_2$ and heart rate values into a 600-Byte frame every 5 second, and sends the frame to the smartphone through the Bluetooth transceiver.

2.2 Smartphone-based Central Controller

The smartphone acts as the central controller of the pillow system. We develop our pillow control software using android 2.2 SDK and the smartphone we used in our experiment is the Huawei u8800. There are four modules in the software: Bluetooth transceiver interface module, sleep apnea detection module, pillow controller module and presentation module. The Bluetooth transceiver interface receives the real-time SpO$_2$ signals from the pulsoximeter, then, it passes the signals to the sleep apnea detection module to detect whether it is an apneic episode or a normal episode and whether the pillow should be adjusted. If an apneic episode is detected and a pillow adjustment decision is made, the detection module will notify the pillow control module its detection result, then, the latter will send out the pillow adjustment command to the pillow through the Bluetooth transceiver in the smartphone. The transceiver is also programmed to transmit control signals including the configuration parameter to the blood oxygen sensor and to receive feedback from the pillow. The presentation module in the smartphone is used to display interactive information in the screen for the user or her family, including real time SpO$_2$ values, sleep apnea events and the pillow's status, etc, as shown in Figure 3(b) and 3(c).

2.3 Adjustable Pillow

The adjustable pillow is composed of a Micro Control Unit (MCU), a Bluetooth transceiver and five inflatable bladders. The transceiver receives commands from the smartphone, and passes them to the MCU, which configures the status of the bladders according to the received command. Each bladder consists of an electric pump and valve, which is controlled by the MCU to inflate or deflate the bladder inside the pillow. By maintaining different pressures on each individual bladder, the pillow will form different shape. When

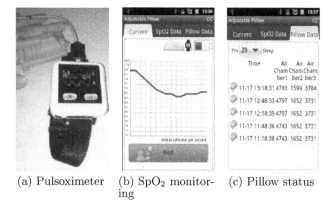

(a) Pulsoximeter   (b) SpO$_2$ monitoring   (c) Pillow status

Figure 3: Pulsoximeter and Smartphone interface.

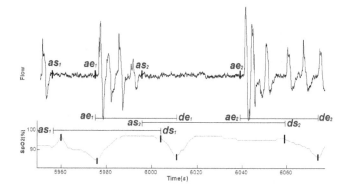

Figure 4: The upper black line is the nasal airflow signal, and the lower red line is the SpO$_2$ signal, which is collected simultaneously. as_i, ae_i are respectively the starting point and ending point of apnea episode i, which is annotated by the expert. ds_i, de_i are respectively the starting point and ending point of SpO$_2$ desaturation episode i. The apneic episode $[as_1, ae_1]$ corresponds to the desaturation episode $[ds_1, de_1]$, and the apneic episode $[as_2, ae_2]$ corresponds to the desaturation episode $[ds_2, de_2]$.

sleep apnea is detected, the smartphone can issue a command, and the pillow will change to a shape that leads to less sleep apnea events. The patient, who sleeps on the pillow will adjust their sleep gesture due to the pillow adjustment, and thus lead to apnea alleviation. If the adjustment works, the SpO$_2$ will increase and the blood oxygen detector will detect it. Otherwise, it will find that the adjustment doesn't take effect, and it will continue to adjust the shape of the pillow until it works. Therefore, a closed loop feedback is formed and the user's sleep and respiration status can be monitored in real time.

According to the system architecture described above, we face two main challenges during the design of the smart pillow system. One is to detect the sleep apnea in real time using limited signals, and the other is to appropriately adjust the pillow to alleviate the sleep apnea effectively. We will address these two challenges in the following two sections by providing a sleep apnea detection and classification algorithm as well as a pillow adjustment algorithm.

3. SLEEP APNEA DETECTION AND CLASSIFICATION ALGORITHM

As discussed in the previous section, one of the challenges is how to detect sleep apnea events with limited physiological signals. In this section, we design a detection algorithm to detect sleep apnea events based solely on the pulsoximetry signals. We test our algorithm through contrast experiment with the PSG, the result shows high accuracy on sleep apnea detection. Furthermore, we find that not every sleep apnea event requires the pillow adjustment. Some of the sleep apnea events appear sporadically while others last for a long duration, e.g. longer than dozens of minutes. For the sporadic events, even without pillow adjustment, the apnea will disappear automatically, thus, such events don't require pillow adjustment. Only for the continuous sleep apnea event, the pillow adjustment is helpful. To distinguish these two categories, we design an SVM-based event classification algorithm. We conducted a series of experiment to collect training data, and the testing result shows that our classification algorithm achieves high precision as designed.

3.1 Sleep Apnea Detection Algorithm

When sleep apnea happens, the airflow is obstructed and no fresh air goes into the lung, accordingly, the oxygen of the blood is reduced (usually called SpO_2 desaturation) due

to lack of fresh oxygen. Therefore, SpO$_2$ is a good indicator for respiratory diseases. By monitoring SpO$_2$ desaturation, sleep apnea events can be detected.

In order to eliminate artifacts in the raw signal, we first conduct data preprocessing on the collected data before sleep apnea detection. The SpO$_2$ values under 50% and samples that have a variation greater than 10% with regard to the previous one were replaced by the previous value. To reduce the complexity of the algorithm and improve the real-time performance, the SpO$_2$ signal is resampled to be 1 sample/second.

Then, the SpO$_2$ desaturation event is detected based on the preprocessed data. We use the following algorithm to define SpO$_2$ desaturation episodes:

1. Find the local minimum SpO$_2$ point de and its SpO$_2$ value V_{de}.

2. Find the nearest local maximum SpO$_2$ point before de, which is ds and its value V_{ds}.

3. If $V_{de} \leq V_a$ and $V_{ds} - V_{de} \geq V_b$, then the time period $[ds, de]$ are defined to be an SpO$_2$ desaturation event or an SpO$_2$ desaturation episode. Correspondingly, ds is called the starting point of the desaturation and de is called the ending point of the desaturation. V_a and V_b are two predefined SpO$_2$ thresholds.

The rationale behind the detection algorithm is that, an episode is defined to be an sleep apnea episode, if and only if the minimum SpO$_2$ value is lower than a given threshold V_a (usually V_a should be less than 95%) and the decline of the value is larger than a certain threshold V_b (usually V_b should be larger than 3%) [15]. For other cases, the decline of the SpO$_2$ may only refer to a regular variation of the blood oxygen saturation, without presenting any sleep apnea events.

Figure 4 shows the correlation between apnea events and SpO$_2$ events. The upper black line is the nasal airflow signal, and the lower red line is the SpO$_2$ signal, which is collected simultaneously. as_i and ae_i are respectively the starting

Table 1: Percentage Statistic of Continuous Events and Sporadic Events

Subject	Value
Percentage of Sporadic Events	35.19%
Percentage of Continuous Events	64.81%
Percentage of Sporadic Events' Duration	11.40%
Percentage of Continuous Events' Duration	88.60%

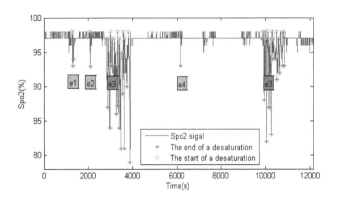

Figure 5: SpO$_2$ desaturation classification.

point and ending point of apnea episode i, which is annotated by the expert. ds_i, de_i are respectively the starting point and ending point of SpO$_2$ desaturation episode i defined by the above rule. We can see that one sleep apneic event corresponds to one SpO$_2$ desaturation event, although there is usually a several-second delay in between.

To further demonstrate the correlation between sleep apnea events and SpO$_2$ desaturation events, we conducted extensive experiment using both PSG and the pulsoximeter of our pillow system. The experiments are conducted on 40 apnea patients at a hospital in east Asia. Each subject slept in the sleeping center for one night wearing both PSG sensors and the pulsoximeter of our pillow system. Both signals are collected to do comparison. The result shows that the accuracy of our detection algorithm is higher than 90%. The detailed evaluation result is presented Section 5. Comparatively, our method obtains a little more sleep apnea epochs than the PSG, which brings no problem, we will handle it through the SpO$_2$ desaturation classification algorithm described in the next subsection.

3.2 The SpO$_2$ Desaturation Classification Algorithm

We have one more interesting observation after we analyze the physiological signals collected in the above contrast experiment. We found that SpO$_2$ desaturation events can be further divided into two categories, and not all the SpO$_2$ desaturation events require immediate pillow adjustment.

3.2.1 The Necessity of SpO$_2$ Desaturation Classification

The detected SpO$_2$ desaturation events can be divided into two categories: sporadic ones and continuous ones. Figure 5 shows the duration of one patient's SpO$_2$ signal. For the sporadic ones, e.g. E_1, E_2 and E_4, the patient can automatically recovered from the apnea and we don't need to adjust the pillow. In general, after an apnea, there is more than 20 seconds until the oxygen begins to drop, as shown in Figure 4), that is to say, when the algorithm detects an oxygen falling event, the patient may have already recovered from the apnea event and she may be back to normal breathing. So whether to adjust or not, makes no difference. Besides, in clinical terms, sporadic sleep apnea is not considered harmful as long as it happens less than 5 times per hour [2]. Further, as frequent pillow adjustment may disturb the user's sleep and worsen the sleeping experience, adjustments should be avoided when they are not necessary. On the other hand, for the continuous ones, e.g. E_3 and E_5, pillow adjustments will help the patients to recover from the apneic episode. Therefore, we need to design a classification algorithm to distinguish these two kinds of events, and make different adjustment decisions accordingly.

The statistical analysis on the experimental data further demonstrates the necessity of SpO$_2$ desaturation classification. As shown in Table 1, among all the SpO$_2$ desaturation events, 35.19% are sporadic events, with 64.81% classified to be continuous. However, the 64.81% continuous SpO$_2$ events contribute 88.60% of the time duration of apneic episodes, while sporadic events only contribute 11.4%. It means that, compared to non-distinguishable adjustment schemes, SpO$_2$ event classification can dramatically reduce the interruption to users natural sleep by 35.19%, without losing any effectiveness. No matter how the pillows are adjusted, at most, 88.60% of the apneic episode in terms of the time duration can be recovered.

3.2.2 SpO$_2$ Desaturation Classification Algorithm

For each detected SpO$_2$ desaturation event, we use $Type$ to denote its classification result.

$$Type = \begin{cases} 1 & \text{continuous event} \\ 0 & \text{sporadic event} \end{cases}$$

The event is defined to be a continuous one, if and only if there are more than 3 times of SpO$_2$ desaturation events happening in the next 5 minutes.

As the next 5-minute signal is taken into consideration, it is not applicable for real time event detection and classification. Therefore, we designed a learning-based classification algorithm, which leverages real-time signals.

For each detected SpO$_2$ event, we examine the 150 second signals from the starting point (ds) of the SpO$_2$ desaturation. A seven-feature tuple $\{N, MaxSlope, MinSpO_2, SD, MinSS, MinEE, MinES\}$ are extracted from the 150s signal block as follows.

N: The number of oxygen desaturation events in the signal block. For the block shown in Figure 6, N equals to 3.

$MaxSlope$: The maximum speed of decline in SpO$_2$, which is defined as follows:

$$MaxSlope = \max\left(\left|\frac{V_{ds_i} - V_{de_i}}{ds_i - de_i}\right|\right) i = 1, \cdots, N$$

where V_{ds_i} and V_{de_i} are the blood oxygen values of the starting point ds_i and ending point de_i of the ith SpO$_2$ desaturation event, respectively.

$MinSpO_2$: the minimum SpO$_2$ value. The more severe the sleep apnea events, the smaller the value of $MinSpO_2$

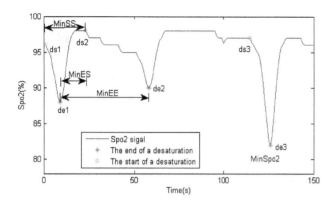

Figure 6: Feature extraction in a 150s block.

is.

$$MinSpO_2 = \min(V_{de_i}) \quad i = 1, \cdots, N$$

SD: standard deviation of the SpO_2 value. Severe apnea patients usually have higher SD values.

$MinSS$: The minimum distance of two adjacent starting points of desaturations.

$$MinSS = \begin{cases} \min(|ds_{i+1} - ds_i|) & i = 1, \cdots, N - 1 \quad N > 1 \\ 150 & otherwise \end{cases}$$

$MinEE$: the minimum distance of two adjacent ending points of desaturations.

$$MinEE = \begin{cases} \min(|de_{i+1} - de_i|) & i = 1, \cdots, N - 1 \quad N > 1 \\ 150 & otherwise \end{cases}$$

$MinES$: the minimum distance of the ending point of one desaturation event to the starting point of the next event.

$$MinES = \begin{cases} \min(|ds_{i+1} - de_i|) & i = 1, \cdots, N - 1 \quad N > 1 \\ 150 & otherwise \end{cases}$$

The rationale behind selecting 150s as the unit of signal block is as follows: with shorter duration, the classification algorithm will be less accurate. It is not easy for the classification algorithm to predict whether it is a sporadic or a continuous event with shorter duration. With longer duration, there will be longer delay from the oxygen desaturation point until the pillow is adjusted and the patient recovers. The patient will suffer for longer time from continuous apnea events. Considering the tradeoff between these two aspects, 150s is a suitable choice. Among all seven features, N, $MaxSlope$ and $MinSpO_2$ indicate the order of severity of one's sleep apnea, SD indicates the fluctuation of the SpO_2 value, while the $MinSS$, $MinEE$ and $MinES$ indicate the frequency and continuity of desaturation events. Every feature performs an important role in the classification. Comparing with a subset of the tuple, using all 7 features as the vector achieves the best classification accuracy. Here, we didn't consider the duration of the events because we find, through experiments, that most of the events are shorter than 150s, thus, the above 7 features are accurate enough.

Based on the seven-feature tuple, we use an SVM classifier to conduct training and classification. The SVM classifier is a widely-used machine learning based classifier, which requires no prior knowledge on the distribution of the data or the linear transformation characteristic. Therefore we select it as the classifier in our problem. The idea behind

the SVM classifiers is to find an optimal separating hyper plane in the multi-dimension space, which is formed by $\{N, MaxSlope, MinSpO_2, SD, MinSS, MinEE, MinES\}$ in our problem, and then use this hyper plane to find the mapping from the tuple to $Type$. In our problem, we divide all detected desaturation events in the experiment into three equally sized sets. One set is selected as the training set, and the other two as testing sets. The kernal function we used in our classifier is radial basis function (RBF) kernel, with the value of σ equal to 5 and the regularization parameter C equal to 1000. We use the LIBSVM package [5] to conduct the SVM experiment. The evaluation of the classification algorithm is shown in Section 5.

4. PILLOW ADJUSTMENT ALGORITHM

Once the SpO_2 desaturation event is detected and classified as a continuous one, the smartphone will issue the pillow adjustment command to reshape the pillow. What shape can help to recover from sleep apnea and how to control the pillow to adjust to the anticipated shape becomes a key problem. In this section, we will introduce the physiological principles of the pillow's impact on sleep apnea, describe the structure of our pillow, and then propose an effective adjustment algorithm. We also conduct extensive experiments to determine the optimal parameters in the algorithm.

4.1 Pillow's Function to Sleep Apnea Treatment

Sleep apnea is caused by the atonia of a muscle that runs from the chin to the tongue (called *genioglossus*). When the genioglossus is sloppy or relaxed during sleep, it will block the airway and result in sleep apnea.

According to the pathology of apnea, the adjustment of the pillow can help alleviating sleep apnea in two aspects. On one hand, the pillow can inflate or deflate the bladders which lie below the user's neck and head, by supporting the patient' neck to a higher level, the angle of airway can be changed and the genioglossus will not obstruct the airflow any longer. Therefore, sleep apnea is alleviated. Usually, there are several suitable pillow shapes, lying on which the airflow can keep open and sleep apnea is less likely to happen. One the other hand, when the pillow reshapes, the human's head will receive a certain external stimulus, the excitability of the genioglossus muscle as well as the sensitivity of the sleep center in brain is stimulated and recovered, which can prevent more sleep apnea in the following duration of sleep. The external stimulus can also trigger the user to change to a different sleep pose (e.g. from back to side) which will generate less apnea events.

4.2 Structure of Smart Pillow

The structure of our pillow is shown in Figure 7(a), there are five bladders inside the pillow: bladder 1 is the biggest one which lies below the pillow, bladder 2 lies on the front side right under the user's neck, bladder 3 and 4 lie on the left and right side of the pillow respectively, bladder 5 lies on the top of the pillow under the user's head. The real pillow is shown in Figure 7(b), there is an electrical air pump in the controller, which inflates or deflates the bladders in the pillow through the air pipe. We conducted extensive experiments and found that comparing with the other three bladders, bladder 2 and bladder 5 contribute to the apnea alleviation most, which is also in accordance with the pathology

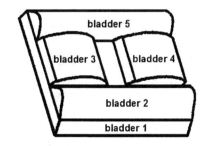

(a) Pillow Structure

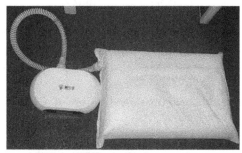

(b) Real Pillow

Figure 7: Smart Pillow.

that these two bladders lies exactly under the neck and head. Considering the limited reshaping time and other practical constraints, we will restrain our reshape decision region by focusing the adjustment on these two bladders only.

4.3 Adjustment Algorithm

We designed a feedback loop in our adjustment algorithm to adjust the pillow to suitable shapes which are less likely cause apnea. By monitoring SpO_2 signals using a pulsoximeter, sleep apnea can be detected in real time, and the smartphone will direct the pillow to adjust its shape accordingly. After the adjustment, if the new shape is a suitable shape, the patient is stimulated and the airflow is reopened, which results in the SpO_2 signal increasing, then the pulsoximeter monitors the SpO_2 signal again, it finds that the SpO_2 increases and apnea is effectively alleviated. The pillow will keep in this suitable shape which helps preventing future apnea events until the next apnea event is detected. If the new shape is not suitable and the patient is not recovered from the apnea, the SpO_2 detector will still detect an apnea, which indicates the pillow to change to another shape until the sleep apnea is alleviated and the SpO_2 desaturation is no longer detected. Usually there is a most suitable shape which is most unlikely to generate apnea, and the above mentioned feedback loop is able to automatically keep the pillow in the most suitable shape for a long duration until next sleep apnea event happens.

The adjustment algorithm executes on the smartphone. In each iteration, the smartphone monitors the SpO_2 signal from the pulsoximeter and detects SpO_2 desaturation using the detection and classification algorithm described in Section 3. If SpO_2 desaturation is detected and is classified to be a continuous one, an adjustment command, which contains the target pressure of pillow's bladders, is sent to the pillow. The pillow inflates or deflates every bladder as the command directed, until the pressure sensors in the bladders

report that the target pressure is achieved. Then, the pillow will send an acknowledgement (ACK) to the smartphone. If no ACK is received within t_1 time since the adjustment command, the smartphone will send out the command again. If an ACK is received, then, the smartphone will wait for t_2 second and start a new iteration to monitor the SpO_2 signal again. Using the detection and classification result, it can evaluate whether the previous adjustment takes effect or not and whether a new adjustment is required. Here, the introduction of the delay t_1 and t_2 is to guarantee that the pillow can be adjusted to a suitable shape which is most unlikely to cause apnea. The controller needs to wait for t_2 before a new round of SpO_2 monitoring, because there is a delay from the pillow adjustment until the airflow is reopened and the blood oxygen is recovered. To monitor the SpO_2 too frequently may cause the pillow to miss the most suitable shape and leads to frequent and endless adjustment. To wait for an ACK for at most t_1 second is because the time needed to adjust the pillow to a specific shape varies, and the controller needs to wait for the ACK instead of waiting for a constant duration, but at most, it will wait for t_1 to avoid deadlock.

One key question is that which shape is the most suitable shape the pillow should adjust to. Frankly speaking, for different persons, the shapes are different. But the most important factor is the same, which is the relative height of the back side of the head compared to that of the neck, which impacts the angle of the airflow. Therefore, bladder 2 (right under the neck) and bladder 5 (right under the back of the head) are two most helpful bladders for airflow reopen. As the controller has no knowledge about which shape and angle is the suitable one for a specific user, it need to try every potential shape before it finds the suitable one. Through extensive experiment, we find that there are several bladder pressure combinations which are more comfortable and effective for various persons, as shown in Table 2. As a result,

Table 2: Pressure Combinations of Pillow Bladder 2 and Bladder 5

No.	Bladder 2 (psi)	Bladder 5 (psi)
1	7000	2000
2	6000	3000
3	5000	4000
3	4000	5000
5	3000	6000
6	2000	7000

Table 3: Statistical Results of T_p and T_s

Parameter	Average (s)	Min. (s)	Max. (s)
T_p	55	27	98
T_s	35	29	86

Table 4: Results of the Sleep Apnea Detection Algorithm

Subject	% of A episodes (PSG)	% of A episodes (our method)	Accuracy
1	33.48%	38.5%	93.27%
2	75.48%	76.65%	97.43%
3	15.11%	17.22%	93.41%
4	48.57%	50.31%	90.11%
5	58.2%	61.27%	90.08%
6	70.68%	79.78%	95.38%
7	29.44%	32.41%	89.27%
8	86.27%	88.3%	97.38%
9	56.06%	59.17%	92.65%
10	71.16%	73.8%	94.5%

Table 5: Performance Evaluation of Classification Algorithm

Agreement	Sensitivity	Specificity	Effectiveness
93.52%	95.71%	89.47%	94.37%

these six combinations will be set in the system, and the pillow will adjust its shape to the targeting pressure according to the following sequence $1 \rightarrow 2 \rightarrow \cdots \rightarrow 6 \rightarrow 5 \rightarrow \cdots \rightarrow 1$, until the effective one is found.

Besides the target pressure of every bladder, there are also some other parameters e.g., t_1 and t_2, should be intelligently selected to guarantee the effectiveness of the pillow adjustment. The ACK timeout time t_1 depends on the pillow adjustment time T_p (the delay from the smartphone sends out an adjustment command until it receives a successful ACK from the pillow), and the duration between ACK and SpO_2 detection t_2 depends on the SpO_2 reaction time T_s (the delay from the pillow adjustment to respiration recovery until SpO_2 begins to rise). In order to configure these two parameters to be a reasonable value, we conducted experiments over 40 patients for 80 nights. The maximum, average, and minimum value of T_p and T_s are shown in Table 3. We found that T_p varies when the targeting pressures of the bladders differ, and they are independent with various persons. T_s depends on the biomedical reaction of the human body, but the average T_s of different persons are almost the same. Therefore, we don't need to select personalized t_1 and t_2. In order to make the parameters to be fit for most situations, we set t_1 to be 70 seconds and t_2 to be 65 seconds, which are both between the average value and the maximum value. We will evaluate the performance of our pillow adjustment algorithm in Section 5.

Please note that our pillow adjustment algorithm design also takes the impact of sleep quality into consideration. Excessive pillow adjustment will heavily interrupt the natural sleep and degrade sleep quality of the patient. Therefore, we divide the events to be sporadic and continuous ones and the pillow is adjusted only if continuous events happen. Also, after every adjustment, we wait for enough time t_1 and t_2 before a new round of SpO_2 monitoring. All of the above design targets at reducing number of unnecessary adjustment and achieving a balance between sleep quality and adjustment effectiveness.

5. PERFORMANCE EVALUATION

In this section, we will first evaluate the performance of the sleep apnea detection algorithm and classification algorithm, then, we will focus on the effectiveness of the pillow

adjustment, which also reflects the overall performance of the entire system.

5.1 Evaluation of Sleep Apnea Detection and Classification Algorithm

To evaluate the sleep apnea detection algorithm, we conducted extensive experiments using both PSG and the pulsoximeter of our pillow system. The experiments are conducted on 40 apnea patients in a hospital in east Asia. Each subject slept in the sleeping center for one night wearing both PSG sensors and the pulsoximeter of our pillow system. Both signals are collected to do comparison.

The signals of the entire night are divided into fragments of one minute. Each fragment is annotated by the PSG to be N (normal episode) or A (apneic episode) based on the signals from multiple channels during the whole night. In our sleep apnea detection algorithm, we define the fragment to be A if and only if any part of the fragment is defined to be an SpO_2 desaturation episode. We found that the best V_a should be 93% and the best V_b should be 4%. The evaluation result of 10 patients out of 40 patients is shown in Table 4 due to the space limit. The average accuracy of our algorithm is about 90%, which is pretty high. Besides, our algorithm performs real-time detection, whose delay is at most one minute.

The performance of the SpO_2 desaturation classification algorithm is shown in Table 5, we detected all the SpO_2 desaturation events and denoted them as sporadic (S) ones or continuous (C) ones. Totally, there are 3294 events over 40 nights. We randomly divide the data into three equally sized sets, maintaining the same S/C ratio in each set. In each round, we use one set as the training set and the other two as the testing sets. We repeated the testing for three rounds so that every set has one chance to be the training set, then calculate the agreement, sensitivity, specificity and effectiveness of each testing.

The agreement gives the percentage of correct classification of the algorithm. The sensitivity measures the ability of

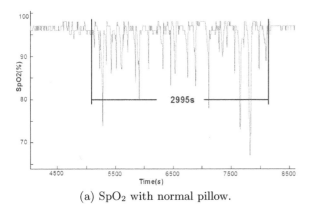

(a) SpO$_2$ with normal pillow.

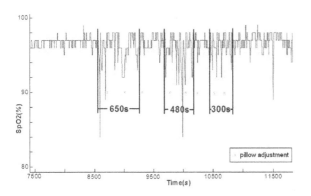

(b) SpO$_2$ with smart pillow.

Figure 8: Comparison of the SpO$_2$ value between normal pillow and developed pillow.

the classification algorithm to make a correct decision when patients suffer a continuous event. The specificity measures the ratio of the sporadic event classified by our algorithm to all real sporadic events. The effectiveness measures the percentage of correctly detected continuous events over all continuous events. The average results of the metrics are shown in Table 5. It can be seen that most of these four metrics are larger than 90%, which demonstrate the precision of our classification algorithm.

5.2 Effectiveness of the Smart Pillow System

We will demonstrate the effectiveness of our system on sleep apnea detection and treatment through extensive contrast experiments. We select 40 patients from a hospital in east Asia, to conduct experiments. Everyone of them was participated for two nights, one night with a normal pillow and the other with the developed pillow system. The same pulsoximeter is worn at both nights to monitor their blood oxygen saturation.

Figure 8(a) shows the SpO$_2$ value of one participant with a normal pillow, and Figure 8(b) shows his SpO$_2$ value with our developed pillow. The time of the pillow adjustment is also indicated in the figure. It is obvious that using our developed pillow, the duration of SpO$_2$ desaturation are dramatically decreased by more than 50%. Similar results can be found in other participants' experiments.

To demonstrate the effectiveness of our smart pillow system, we use the following metrics for evaluation: desaturation episode time, relative desaturation episode time,

number of desaturation episodes and average desaturation episode duration, as shown in Table 6. All of the metrics indicate the severity of the sleep apnea of a patient. Less desaturation episode time and less relative desaturation episode time indicate a patient suffering from apnea for shorter duration. Less number of desaturation episodes indicates a patient suffering from a reduced number of apnea events during night, while a shorter average duration of desaturation episodes indicates that, for each apnea event, the event lasts for shorter time in average. The decrease of any parameters indicates the alleviation of sleep apnea.

The average result of the metrics over all 40 participants are listed in Table 7. We can see that the average desaturation episode duration is dramatically reduced from 2701 seconds to 1215 seconds, which is about 55% decrement, which means more than 2.5 hour out of six hours of total sleep time was saved from sleep apnea with the use of our smart pillow. Correspondingly, the relative desaturation episode time is reduced from 9.34% to 4.28%. The number of desaturation episodes is reduced by 57.3% (from 75 to 32). Moreover, the average desaturation episode is also reduced from 18.02 minutes to 6.78 minutes. Most of the continuous apnea is alleviated by our algorithm, and the remaining sporadic ones are not as harmful as the continuous ones. The experimental results show that our real-time adjustable pillow system is able to effectively detect SpO$_2$ anomalies and facilitate the users to recover from that kind of desaturation.

The effectiveness of the smart pillow system can be explained from two aspects: one is that when sleep apnea is detected, by inflating or deflating the bladder of the pillow, the patient's neck can be lifted and the angle of airway can be changed and no longer be obstructed. Therefore, sleep apnea is alleviated. On the other hand, when the pillow reshapes, the human's neck will receive a certain external stimulus, and the excitability of the muscle near the tongue and pharynx as well as the sensitivity of the sleep center in the brain may be stimulated and recovered, which can prevent more sleep apnea in the following duration of sleep.

Among all 40 patients, the improvement of each metric of the most effective subject and the least effective subject is also shown in Table 7. From the experimental result, we can see that for all the patients, the adjustment algorithm is effective (the minimum reduction percentage is 42%). That is because there is a feedback loop in our adjustment algorithm, and it will automatically stop at a suitable shape for a specific person, which is most unlikely to generate apnea. Different people have different head shapes, airflow structures and different levels of sleep apnea, and the suitable shape is different, but the adjustment method required to achieve the suitable shape is similar. The key parameters of the algorithm t_1 and t_2 are independent with different persons, and the targeted shape combinations (from shape 1 to shape 6) already cover fine-enough levels of airflow angles. Therefore, it is suitable for various persons. If there is any opportunity for the development of further fine-grained personalized algorithms, we think that personalized detection and classification algorithms, personalized pillow shape initialization and reduced targeting pressure combination selection can be considered. In the detection and classification algorithm, the parameters V_a and V_b can be selected dynamically and the block window can be adjusted, which may leads to shorter detection delays and more accurate classification. In the adjustment algorithm, personalized pillow shape ini-

Table 6: Evaluation Metrics for the Effectiveness of the Smart Pillow

Metrics	Definitions
Desaturation episode time (s)	Total desaturation time during sleep
Relative desaturation episode time (‰)	Ratio of desaturation time vs. total sleep time
Number of desaturation episode	Number of desaturation events
Average desaturation episode duration (min)	Average time of SpO_2 desaturation episode

Table 7: Summary of Contrast Experiment Results

Metrics	normal pillow	developed pillow	average % of reduction	maximum % of reduction	minimum % of reduction
Desaturation episode time (s)	2701	1215	55%	69%	46%
Relative desaturation episode time (%)	9.34	4.28	54%	72%	49%
Number of SpO_2 desaturation episode	75	32	57%	65%	42%
Average SpO_2 desaturation episode (min)	18.02	6.78	62%	79%	55%

tialization and a smaller set of pressure-combinations can reduce the number of adjustment to achieve the suitable shape. However, all of the above designs require much larger training data and much more involvement of each patient. We will leave it for future work.

6. RELATED WORK

Our work is related to the research on (i) sleep apnea detection and monitoring, (ii) sleep apnea treatment and (iii) smart pillow system.

Sleep Apnea Monitoring and Detection: Many research works have proposed various strategies to automatically detect sleep apnea. Several studies [9, 17] identify apnea and hypopnea events from normal breathing events using features of ECG signal and estimate the surrogate apnea index. [13] analyzes a combination of oxygen signals and ECG signals to perform per epoch sleep apnea annotation and estimates the apnea plus hypopnea index (AHI). However, the ECG signal varies so widely that it's difficult for these methods to cover all situation, e.g. for users with arrhythmia or with pacemaker, these methods are less effective.

There are also studies that diagnose sleep apnea based on the analysis of oxygen saturation signals purely. The strategies shown in [19, 18] are the conventional algorithms to identify desaturation events from a moving baseline. The baseline is computed as a moving average after all the data lower than the ninety-five quartile are filtered off to give a more realistic baseline, and the AHI is calculated from the desaturations of the blood oxygen signal. Other studies propose nonlinear characteristics on oxygen saturation. Y. K. Lee *et al.* [15] evaluates the performance of the wavelet transform to detect sleep apnea events using only oxygen. This method has a high performance when the wavelet thresholds are individually tuned for each study. It is also shown in [7] that the approximate entropy on oxygen signals correlates strongly with the apnea plus hypopnea index (AHI), stating that positive SAHS patients have higher approximate entropy levels than native SAHS patients.

All the solutions above conduct data analysis after the whole SpO_2 signal is recorded, which are offline analysis. [4] is the only work which detects apnea episodes purely through oxygen signals in real time. It implemented a sys-

tem on a PDA which is able to acquire the oxygen signal, preprocess it, and identify the presence of sleep apnea in real time. It presented an ADTree classifier to detect the sleep apnea. However, their solution has high complexity and only targets at apnea detection. In our paper, our target is not only to detect apnea but also to classify it into continuous events or scattered events, in order to facilitate the pillow adjustment decision making. Only when the continuous (and much severe) sleep apnea events are detected, the pillow needs to be adjusted. In this case, our method improves the pillow adjustment efficiency and enhances the user experience greatly.

The Treatment of Sleep Apnea: Nasally-applied continuous positive airway pressure (CPAP) is highly effective and has become the major non-surgical, long-term form of treatment, the so-called gold standard. However, long-term compliance with CPAP has been estimated at between 60 and 70 percent [10].

Intra-oral mandibular advancement devices have also been investigated as a solution to sleep apnea [16]. Using such appliances, the size of the airway can be increased by drawing the tongue and soft palate forwards, and thus the airflow is maintained open during sleep. Limited follow-up data is available comparing the risk to benefit ratio associated with the use of mandibular advancement therapy. Furthermore, it is very uncomfortable for the patients to hold such a device in the mouth during sleep and the sleep quality of several patients are reported to be decreased.

Surgery is another choice for sleep apnea patients. Such surgery is called uvulopalatopharyngoplasty (UPPP), which is a surgical procedure used to remove excess tissue in the throat to widen the airway. This can allow air to move through the throat more easily when you breathe. However UPPP is dangerous. Accidents may occur by underestimation or blind operation, and it is also prone to serious complications [8].

In this paper, we proposed a real-time auto-adjustable smart pillow system. It is able to detect sleep apnea in real time, and restrain the sleep apnea events by adjusting the height and shape of the pillow, that can alleviate and prevent sleep apnea. Comparing with previous methods, our system is non-invasive, inexpensive, safer, and more comfortable, which also enables patients to use it on their home environment in daily life.

Smart Pillow System: There are some anti-snore pillows in the market already. Most of them are designed as a fixed shape which is claimed to be helpful for apnea alleviation. These Anti-snore pillows are made of some memory materials, which can be reshaped according to the morphology of the human neck. However, the nerve on the scruff and hindbrain is widespread, and it is difficult to find a fixed design to meet various body shapes of different users. Different from them, our smart pillow is composed of several independent bladders with different pressures. Once SpO_2 desaturation is detected, the system will intelligently choose a combination to adjust the pillow so that the angle between the neck and the body can be changed. In addition, a relatively comfortable status, which can reduce airway obstruction, can be achieved with the help of the real-time SpO_2 feedback.

There are only two existing works investigating other auto-adjustable pillow system [20, 1]. In [20], a pillow with contact microphones was developed to detect snoring sounds and restrain snoring by inflating the air bladder located inside the pillow. However, it detects the snoring by microphone, which is more sensitive to environmental noise. Compared to snoring, sleep apnea has a more severe impact to human wellness. Compared to microphone, SpO_2 is a more accurate indicator that helps characterizing sleep disorder. Besides, in [20], only the architecture of the pillow system is presented, without detailed description of detection or adjustment algorithms.

In [1], an anti-sleep apnea robot pillow called "Jukusui-kun" is developed by researchers in Waseda University. It detects sleep apnea by a pulsoximeter and a microphone. When the oxygen level decreases and the snore level increases it triggers the bear-pillow's hand to move towards the sleeper's face. Gently brushing the face causes the person to turn from lying on their back to moving onto their side, a more conducive position for a sound, snoreless night sleep. This device uses a method similar to ours to detect sleep apnea events. Both monitor the blood oxygen of the patient using a pulsoximeter. But we exploit a different method to terminate an sleep apnea episode. When the sleep apnea is detected, the Jukusui-kun simply brushes the face of the person to make him turn over his body. This may disturb the user's sleep very frequently. Instead, our pillow applies a more fine-grained adjustment method. By adjusting the shape of the pillow, the angle of the airway can be changed and the genioglossus will no longer obstruct the airflow, thus, without disrupting the user's sleep, most sleep apnea episodes can be alleviated. Only if the apnea is still severe, our pillow will continuously adjust the shape to disrupt the user to turn over, which achieves the same effect as Jukusui-kun. Until now, there are no published papers to demonstrate the effectiveness of Jukusui-kun, therefore, we cannot conduct a detailed performance comparison.

7. CONCLUSIONS

In this paper, we design and implement a real-time auto-adjustable smart pillow system for sleep apnea detection and treatment. To the best of our knowledge, this is the first pillow system which can dynamically detect the event of sleep apnea and adjust the pillow to facilitate sleep apnea patients to recover from the disorder. Compared with PSG or other sleep apnea treatment methods, our system is comfortable, portable, noninvasive, and most importantly, it can be used at home everyday requiring no professional staff, instead of going to a sleep center. We integrate the SpO_2 monitoring and pillow adjustment together and adopt a close-loop feedback mechanism to make the system more effective and intelligent. We propose a novel SpO_2-based real-time sleep apnea detection algorithm and a pillow adjustment algorithm based on sophisticated experiments. We conduct extensive experiments on 40 sleep apnea patients, and the result shows that both the duration and occurrence of apnea episodes are decreased dramatically when using our smart pillow system, therefore the sleep quality of the patients is largely improved. We believe that it will be a promising direction and a large number of users will benefit from such intelligent devices. For future work, we will investigate more personalized and fine-grained algorithms to further improve the effectiveness of the system, and conduct longer term experiments with a larger volume of patients.

8. ACKNOWLEDGEMENT

We are grateful to all the patients that participated in the experimental tests; this paper would not have been possible without them. We would like to thank our shepherd Marco Zuniga and the anonymous reviewers for helping us improve this paper. This work is partially supported in part by Hong Kong RGC grants No. 623209, 622410, Huawei-HKUST joint lab, and National Natural Science Foundation of China with grant no. as 60933012, 61173156.

9. REFERENCES

[1] Anti sleep apnea robot pillow. http://techcrunch.com/2011/12/02/video-anti-sleep-apnea-robot-pillow/.

[2] V. Abad. Obstructive sleep apnea syndromes. *Med Clin N Am*, 88:611–630, 2004.

[3] S. Bluetooth. Specification of the bluetooth system. *Core, version*, 1:2005–10, 2005.

[4] A. Burgos, A. Goñi, A. Illarramendi, and J. Bermúdez. Real-time detection of apneas on a pda. *Information Technology in Biomedicine, IEEE Transactions on*, 14(4):995–1002, 2010.

[5] C. Chang and C. Lin. Libsvm: a library for support vector machines. *ACM Transactions on Intelligent Systems and Technology (TIST)*, 2(3):27, 2001.

[6] D. Dattilo. The mandibular trapezoid osteotomy for the treatment of obstructive sleep apnea: report of a case. *Journal of oral and maxillofacial surgery*, 56(12):1442–1446, 1998.

[7] F. del Campo, R. Hornero, C. Zamarrón, D. Abasolo, and D. Álvarez. Oxygen saturation regularity analysis in the diagnosis of obstructive sleep apnea. *Artificial intelligence in medicine*, 37(2):111–118, 2006.

[8] Z. Dongdong, Y. Zhanquan, and H. Tiening. Avoidance strategies of the surgical treatment of obstructive sleep apnea hypopnea syndrome. *Chin J Otorhinolaryngol*, 37(6):422–424, 2002.

[9] R. ECG. Detection of obstructive sleep apnea in pediatric subjects using surface lead electrocardiogram features. *Sleep*, 27(4):784, 2004.

[10] H. Engleman, S. Martin, and N. Douglas. Compliance with cpap therapy in patients with the sleep

apnoea/hypopnoea syndrome. *Thorax*, 49(3):263–266, 1994.

[11] I. Fietze, M. Glos, I. Moebus, C. Witt, T. Penzel, and G. Baumann. Automatic pressure titration with apap is as effective as manual titration with cpap in patients with obstructive sleep apnea. *Respiration*, 74(3):279–286, 2007.

[12] C. Guilleminault, A. Tilkian, and W. Dement. The sleep apnea syndromes. *Annual Review of Medicine*, 27(1):465–484, 1976.

[13] C. Heneghan, C. Chua, J. Garvey, P. De Chazal, R. Shouldice, P. Boyle, and W. McNicholas. A portable automated assessment tool for sleep apnea using a combined holter-oximeter. *Sleep*, 31(10):1432, 2008.

[14] A. Johal and J. Battagel. An investigation into the changes in airway dimension and the efficacy of mandibular advancement appliances in subjects with obstructive sleep apnoea. *Journal of Orthodontics*, 26(3):205–210, 1999.

[15] Y. Lee, M. Bister, P. Blanchfield, and Y. Salleh. Automated detection of obstructive apnea and hypopnea events from oxygen saturation signal. In *Engineering in Medicine and Biology Society, 2004. IEMBS'04. 26th Annual International Conference of the IEEE*, volume 1, pages 321–324. IEEE, 2004.

[16] P. LafESTRANGE, J. Battagel, B. Harkness, M. Spratley, P. Nolan, and G. Jorgensen. A method of studying adaptive changes of the oropharynx to variation in mandibular position in patients with obstructive sleep apnoea. *Journal of oral rehabilitation*, 23(10):699–711, 1996.

[17] M. Mendez, A. Bianchi, M. Matteucci, S. Cerutti, and T. Penzel. Sleep apnea screening by autoregressive models from a single ecg lead. *Biomedical Engineering, IEEE Transactions on*, 56(12):2838–2850, 2009.

[18] S. Thoyre and J. Carlson. Occurrence of oxygen desaturation events during preterm infant bottle feeding near discharge. *Early human development*, 72(1):25–36, 2003.

[19] J. Vázquez, W. Tsai, W. Flemons, A. Masuda, R. Brant, E. Hajduk, W. Whitelaw, and J. Remmers. Automated analysis of digital oximetry in the diagnosis of obstructive sleep apnoea. *Thorax*, 55(4):302, 2000.

[20] R. Wei, H. Kim, X. Li, J. Im, and H. Kim. A development of pillow for detection and restraining of snoring. In *Biomedical Engineering and Informatics (BMEI), 2010 3rd International Conference on*, volume 4, pages 1381–1385. IEEE, 2010.

[21] A. Williams, G. Yu, S. Santiago, and M. Stein. Screening for sleep apnea using pulse oximetry and a clinical score. *CHEST Journal*, 100(3):631–635, 1991.

MARS: A Muscle Activity Recognition System Enabling Self-configuring Musculoskeletal Sensor Networks

Frank Mokaya[†], Brian Nguyen[⊕], Cynthia Kuo[⊕], Quinn Jacobson[⊕], Anthony Rowe[†] and Pei Zhang[†]
[†]Carnegie Mellon University, [⊕]Vibrado Technologies
fmokaya@andrew.cmu.edu, {Brian, Cynthia, Quinn}@vibradotech.com,
agr@ece.cmu.edu, peizhang@cmu.edu

ABSTRACT

Poor posture and incorrect muscle usage are a leading cause of many injuries in sports and fitness. For this reason, non-invasive, fine-grained sensing and monitoring of human motion and muscles is important for mitigating injury and improving fitness efficacy. Current sensing systems either depend on invasive techniques or unscalable approaches whose accuracy is highly dependent on body sensor placement. As a result these systems are not suitable for use in active sports or fitness training where sensing needs to be scalable, accurate and un-inhibitive to the activity being performed.

We present MARS, a system that detects both body motion and individual muscle group activity during physical human activity by only using unobtrusive, non-invasive inertial sensors. MARS not only accurately senses and recreates human motion down to the muscles, but also allows for fast personalized system setup by determining the individual identities of the instrumented muscles, obtained with minimal system training. In a real world human study conducted to evaluate MARS, the system achieves greater than 95% accuracy in identifying muscle groups.

Categories and Subject Descriptors

J.3 [**Life and Medical Sciences**]: Medical information systems

Keywords

Muscle activity recognition, Wearable sensing

1. INTRODUCTION

Muscle injuries are a major problem for athletes. For example, in professional soccer (football), most pre-season injuries are non-contact injuries that occur during running, jumping, or kicking. Over the course of a season, muscle injuries constituted 31% of all injuries [30].

Developing the ability to monitor body motion and skeletal muscle activity is the first step in identifying injurious patterns of body motion and muscle usage. Armed with fine-grained motion and muscle data, trainers and sports medicine doctors could help tomorrow's athletes lower their risk of injury.

Many technologies have been introduced with the aim of providing this type of sensing. Vision-based sensing techniques provide accurate motion capture in a controlled environment, assuming there is clear line-of-sight to the subject [6, 23]. However, due to clothing and skin cover, the images produced are not detailed enough to derive muscle activity. In some cases though, since muscle activity is accompanied by a change in position of relative body segments, it might be possible to infer muscle activity from the motion of body segments as captured by a camera. However, muscle activity is not always associated with motion of body segments limiting the use of vision based techniques for holistically capturing muscle activity.

On-body sensor systems provide alternative methods for gathering motion and muscle data. A network of sensors instrumenting the skeletal muscle groups can provide the necessary sensing granularity and precision. However, approaches for muscle activity monitoring, such as electromyography (EMG), use needles inserted into the muscle or large sensors with contact gels to measure real-time muscle activity [1, 10, 18]. These approaches are often painful or fail during high levels of activity. Less intrusive approaches, such as some mechanomyography (MMG) techniques need careful and frequent tagging of sensors' locations and orientations on the body. As a result, they are prone to sensor noise [21]. Setting up such sensors is time consuming and requires frequent calibration, precluding their use in daily monitoring.

In this paper, we present a Muscle Activity Recognition System (MARS). The MARS system is a wearable sensor platform that performs autonomous setup. MARS is a highly sensitive, non-invasive, and scalable multi-point inertial sensor network that detects both body motion and skeletal muscle activity. The sensed data are processed in real time to recreate human motion as well as generate individual muscle vibration signatures. Using supervised machine learning techniques, MARS infers the identity of instrumented human muscles through their vibration signatures.

After a short initial training period, the results from MARS' muscle identity inferences are used for self configuration.

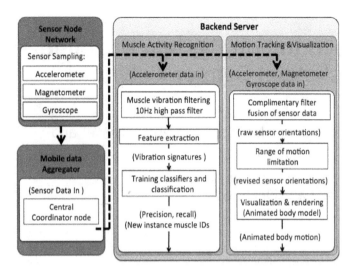

Figure 1: The overview of MARS, showing the three main components of the system and the flow taken by sensed data from sensors to the muscle identity (ID) inference and visualization stages.

MARS automatically determines the bodily location of its inertial sensors for visualization. This permits the MARS sensors to be individually removable and replaceable (for washing or maintenance) without the need for re-tagging.

The contributions of this work are threefold:

1. **Fine-grained muscle activity monitoring:** The MARS system monitors the multi-point, high frequency vibrations of individual skeletal muscles for high-fidelity identification and activity monitoring.

2. **Creation of muscle vibration signatures:** The MARS system uses superficial skeletal muscle vibrations measured on the skin to create muscle vibration signatures for identifying the muscles.

3. **Autonomous system setup independent of sensor orientation and location:** MARS leverages muscle vibration signatures to infer sensor placement on the body. Sensor orientations and placements need not be tagged. This allows our system, after an initial training phase, to configure itself for future muscle and motion monitoring.

The rest of the paper is organized as follows. In Section 2 we give an overview of our system. Section 3 discusses the physiological aspects of skeletal muscle that enables detection of muscle activity using the MARS components introduced in the previous section. Section 4 describes the components of the MARS system presented in Section 2, in detail. Next in Section 5 we discuss the implementation of the MARS system including the requirements that make it amenable to regular everyday use in the sports and fitness arena. We evaluate the system in Section 6, discuss related work in Section 7 and finally conclude in Section 8.

2. MARS SYSTEM OVERVIEW

The MARS system uses an inertial sensor node network to sense motion and muscle vibration, a mobile data aggregator

to coordinate transmission of data and a backend server to processes transmitted sensor data. We give a brief overview of these three main components, shown in Figure 1.

- **The Sensor Node Network:** This component of MARS is made up of sets of small unobtrusive inertial sensor nodes that enable fine grained activity monitoring by detecting body motion as well as the skeletal muscle vibrations. Since the sensor nodes are designed to be small and to collect data as fast as possible to capture vibrations, they are resource constrained. As a result they rely on the next component of MARS, the mobile data aggregator, to coordinate their sampling and data transmission to the backend server. We describe the sensor node network's function in detail in Section 4.1 and implementation in Section 5.1.

- **The Mobile Data Aggregator:** Since the sensor nodes are resource constrained, the MARS system uses a mobile data aggregator to coordinate the sensor sampling, error correction and data transfer to the backend server. To enable user mobility the mobile data aggregator wirelessly transmits the sensed data to the backend server. We describe the mobile data aggregator's function in detail in Section 4.2 and implementation in Section 5.2.

- **The Backend Server:** To create the muscle vibration signatures used for muscle identity inference as well as capture body motion from the transmitted sensor data, the MARS system relies on the backend server. The back end server contains the muscle activity recognition and motion tracking & visualization modules. The muscle activity recognition module performs the muscle identity inference whose results are used by the motion tracking & visualization module to facilitate easy minimal system setup and motion capture without need for sensor location and orientation tagging. We describe its function in detail in Section 4.3 and implementation in Section 5.3.

3. PHYSIOLOGY OF SKELETAL MUSCLE

MARS' muscle identity inference depends on skeletal muscle vibrations. Below, we discuss the physiology of skeletal muscle vibrations and the characteristics captured by our sensor nodes.

As shown in Figure 2, every skeletal muscle consists of three parts [1]: a muscle belly, composed of muscle fibers, and two tendon ends. Activating skeletal muscles during physical activity causes the muscle fibers to contract, resulting in mechanical vibrations due to three main processes [26]:

- Oscillations *i.e.*, tremors of the human motor system, the part of the central nervous system that is involved with movement.

- Muscle fibers sliding against each other.

- Artifacts detected when a muscle belly's circumference increases during muscle contractions and decreases during relaxation, resembling oscillations.

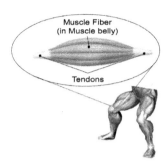

Figure 2: Skeletal muscle consists of two tendons and a muscle belly. The quadriceps, pictured here, are examples of skeletal muscle. The hamstrings and calves are also examples of skeletal muscle.

Sensor	Muscle Activity Recognition	Motion Tracking
Accelerometer	✓	✓
Gyroscope	X	✓
Magnetometer	X	✓

Table 1: A table showing the roles played by the data obtained from the accelerometer, gyroscope and magnetometer sensors, in the MARS system.

These mechanical vibrations vary depending on the muscle fatigue status, muscle group size, and location in the body, *e.g.*, muscle proximity to bones of different mass and size [26, 29]. These differences allow for differentiation of muscles.

The tremors and oscillations due to muscle belly size changes occur between 3.85 Hz and 8.8 Hz in healthy subjects [26]. The internal vibrations generated by muscle fibers sliding against each other occur between 10 Hz and 40 Hz [26]. Conveniently, these internal vibrations occur at higher frequencies than human motion and tremors. This allows MARS to target a frequency range specifically for muscle activity detection.

4. MARS SYSTEM ARCHITECTURE

Section 2 introduced the three main components of the MARS system: the sensor node network, the mobile data aggregator and the backend server. We now describe each of these system components in detail.

4.1 The Sensor Node Network

Each node in the network consists of a triple axis accelerometer, gyroscope and magnetometer. Only the accelerometer data from the sensor node network is used to perform muscle identity inference. Accelerometer, gyroscope and magnetometer data are all used for motion tracking. Table 1 shows how each sensor influences the muscle activity recognition and the motion tracking aspects of MARS.

For error detection purposes, the sensor nodes encode an extra longitudinal parity checksum word to their inertial data streams. The sensors are sampled at a nominal rate of 90 Hz. At this sampling frequency, sufficient data to perform both smooth motion tracking as well capture the inner muscle vibrations described in Section 3 could be satisfactorily obtained. The sensor nodes also apply an anti-alias filter to the accelerometer data to band-limit the constituent frequencies.

4.2 The Mobile Data Aggregator

The inertial sensors making up the MARS network are resource constrained devices with limited processing capabilities. For this reason, the MARS system uses a data aggregator to co-ordinate sensing at the MARS sensor node network level.

The mobile data aggregator is responsible for performing the low-level, time-critical scheduling of the data sampling on each of the nodes in the network. The mobile data aggregator achieved this by using a wired time division multiple access (TDMA) protocol in which all the nodes in the network transmit in rapid succession, one after the other, in their allotted time slot. In addition to scheduling the nodes, this module gathers the sampled sensor data and wirelessly transmits them to the backend server for processing. By maintaining a wireless link to the server, the data aggregator enables the mobility of the human subject using the MARS system.

Since the data transmitted from the sensor node network contains a checksum, the data aggregator decodes the checksum word in the sensor node data stream. By doing this, the mobile data aggregator ensures that only error free data is transmitted to the server since data points whose checksums are erroneous are dropped. This preserves the integrity of the data in the MARS system. We found that occasionally some errors occurred in the sensor node network data stream due to damaged sensors or clock sync errors between the nodes and the mobile data aggregator. We addressed the out of sync error by having the mobile data aggregator force any out of sync nodes whose checksums did not match, to postpone further data sampling until the beginning of a new cycle. Some data is lost this way but at a 90 Hz sample rate, there is enough data in the network to allow MARS to function adequately.

4.3 The Backend Server

In order to recreate human motion and infer muscle identity from the sensor data, the MARS system relies on a backend server. This server consists of two modules shown in Figure 1, the muscle activity recognition module and the motion tracking & visualization module.

4.3.1 Muscle Activity Recognition Module

This module is responsible for performing muscle identity inference using 'vibration signatures'. Vibration signatures are MARS's digital representation of an instrumented muscle group. They consist of a set of feature vectors extracted from the only the accelerometer data stream obtained from the sensor node network.

Only accelerometer data is used because it measures the change in acceleration, which is a direct result of the muscle vibrations that occur when skeletal muscle is active as outlined in Section 3. We describe how the vibration signatures are obtained here.

Muscle Vibration Filtering.

The first step in creating muscle vibration signatures is to pass the accelerometer data stream through a digital 10 Hz high pass filter, as shown in Figure 1. High pass filtering is necessary to isolate the high frequency component (which is limited by our sampling rate of 90 Hz) of the accelerometer data from the lower frequency components (0 Hz < 10 Hz). By doing this, the muscle vibration frequencies as described in Section 3 can be considered without the influence of gravity, the body motion or tremors.

Feature Extraction.

Once the accelerometer data stream has been filtered, the features that make up the muscle vibration signatures need to be extracted.

The feature extractor calculates a selected set of 21 feature vectors, x_m, $m \in [1, 2, \ldots, 21]$. Of these, six are time domain features, and 15 are frequency domain features.

Time Domain Features: The selected time domain features were signal root mean square and cosine correlation (between the accelerometer axes). The *root mean square* was selected as a feature because it relates to the intensity with which an action is performed [17, 10] or in our case, the intensity of the muscle vibration. The *cosine correlation* was useful in capturing the relationship between the muscle vibrations occurring along different accelerometer axes.

Each time domain feature vector instance is calculated using a fixed sliding window approach with 50% overlap, on the filtered time series accelerometer data stream [5, 16, 24]. A 50% overlap method is used so as to allow for smooth transitions from one feature instance to the next. This is important to capture the dynamics relating the vibrations occurring during the two phases of human muscle activity, the contraction and relaxation phases. This approach yields a total of six time domain feature vectors, x_m, $m \in [1, 2, 3, \ldots, 6]$, of same length, N. This length depends on the size of the incoming accelerometer data stream used for creating the muscle signatures.

Frequency Domain Features: The selected frequency domain features, included a measure of signal frequency domain entropy and signal power spectral density [5, 12]. The *signal power spectral density* measurement was useful for distinguishing muscle vibrations whose amplitude is spread out over a range of frequencies from those whose amplitude is more sharply focused at a specific frequency band. For distinguishing smoother and more uniform vibrations from discordant and jerky vibrations which may have similar power spectral densities, the *signal frequency domain entropy* was used.

To obtain the frequency domain feature vectors, the muscle activity recognition module calculates a Discrete Fourier Transform (DFT) of the filtered accelerometer data stream. Next, using the same fixed sliding window approach used to compute the time domain features, the module calculates a single instance of the signal entropy per axis for each sliding window. The signal frequency domain entropy is calculated as the normalized information entropy of the DFT component magnitudes of the signal per window [12]. This yields three, x_m, $m \in [7, 8, 9]$ of the 15 frequency domain features, one for each axis of the accelerometer data.

The signal power per window is also calculated over each axis as well as each sliding window. However, four feature instances are produced per sliding window per axis, instead of a single feature instance. Each sliding window is divided into

four contiguous parts or frequency range bands i.e., (low(L), medium(M), medium high(MH) and high(H)). The signal power spectrum measurement calculated over each part, L, M, MH and H. The power spectrum of the signal is estimated as the squared magnitude of the DFT amplitudes of each portion of the sliding window. This process yields four feature vectors per axis of the accelerometer, for a total of 12 more x_m, $m \in [10, 11, 12, \ldots, 21]$ feature vectors of equal length N.

The signal power spectrum measurement is calculated this way to allow MARS to determine a shift in vibration data frequency between sliding windows. Two sliding windows that may have the similar frequency domain entropies at different frequency bands can be distinguished.

The six time domain and 15 frequency domain feature vectors are combined into a single matrix X, shown below of dimension N by M, $M = 21$ on a per muscle basis. This matrix X is the digital representation of the vibration signal that is obtained from the sensor placed on each instrumented muscle group. It is this matrix of feature vectors that constitutes the unique vibration signal of the particular muscle group.

$$\begin{matrix} Vibration \\ Signature \end{matrix} \Rightarrow X_{n,m} = \begin{pmatrix} x_{1,1} & x_{1,2} & \cdots & x_{1,M} \\ x_{2,1} & x_{2,2} & \cdots & x_{2,M} \\ \vdots & \vdots & \ddots & \vdots \\ x_{N,1} & x_{N,2} & \cdots & x_{N,M} \end{pmatrix}$$

Training Classifiers and Classification.

With the creation of the vibration signatures, the mechanical vibrations are transformed into a digital representation that can be used to build a muscle identity classifier.

The muscle activity recognition module uses supervised machine learning techniques to build the classifier that will infer muscle identities [15, 16]. In order for the MARS system to match new future feature instances to a particular muscle group, it must first be trained using a labeled initial set of vibration signatures obtained over a specific training period. Therefore, the MARS activity recognition module is initially provided with both the muscle vibration signatures and an accompanying set of labels, stating what muscle group the signatures belong to. We accomplish this through a initial training set of isolation exercises that we describe in Section 6.

With this information, the muscle activity recognition module builds a J48 decision tree (DT) classifier which it will use to assign labels or muscle identities to future new incoming vibration feature data points. In our case, the DT algorithm learns a hypothesis $h \in H$, (where $H = \{h : h | X \rightarrow Y\}$ is the space of all functions that can approximate the target function $f : X \rightarrow Y$), to match vibration signatures to muscle groups. X in this case is the N by M vibration signature matrix corresponding to each muscle group, obtained in Section 4.3.1, comprised of the set of 21 feature vectors $X = < x_1, \ldots, x_M >$, (M =21). Y is the vector of classes intended for prediction, in our case ($Y = \{y^{quadriceps}, y^{hamstrings}, y^{calves}\}$. The function/ hypothesis (classifier) h, that MARS learns, will predict a class $y^{quadriceps}$, $y^{hamstrings}$, or y^{calves} for a new k^{th} incoming set of feature instances $< x_1^k, \ldots x_M^k >$, (M =21), calculated from specific sensor data. The learned classifier is stored locally on the backend server in form of a classifier object for future reference.

After the classifier training step, the system becomes self-tagging. MARS sensors can be shifted around, removed and even damaged sensors replaced without crippling the system. Once powered up again, new sensor readings are taken, and the data is classified using the stored classifier object.

4.3.2 Motion Tracking and Visualization Module

This module is responsible for fusing sensor data to obtain sensor/body part orientations and visualizing the orientations using an animated avatar/ human body model. We describe this process here.

Complimentary Filter Fusion of Sensor Data.

Accelerometer, gyroscope and magnetometer sensor readings exhibit drift especially as the sensors are moved. As a result, to obtain accurate orientations of the sensors, fusion of sensor data is necessary. This is so as to capture the different aspects of human motion measured by each inertial sensor while mitigating the shortcomings of either sensor with a counterpart sensor.

The motion tracking module achieves this goal through a quaternion-based complimentary filter [19, 25]. The complimentary filter effectively works as a high-pass filter for the gyroscope data stream and a low-pass filter for the accelerometer and magnetometer data streams. This allows MARS' motion tracking module to leverage the accelerometer and magnetometer data streams to provide the absolute orientation over time where they provide reliable absolute orientation information. Integrated over time, the accelerometer axis aligned with gravity and the magnetometer axis aligned with magnetic north or the dominant local magnetic field will, have dominant readings respectively. These readings are used to reduce gyroscope data drift by providing a known reference location from which rotational angles can be measured.

Over short or instantaneous periods of time, the gyroscope data stream provides accurate degrees per second ($^\circ$/s) measurements on rotational sensor orientation changes. Consequently, for instantaneous orientation information, the complimentary filter relies on the gyroscope data to correct for the results obtained from accelerometer and magnetometer data streams.

Once sensor orientations on the body have been found, the module associates them with the body part to which the sensors are attached to yield individual raw body part orientations. The sensor to body location mapping is obtained from the muscle inference information from Section 4.3.1. Since specific muscle groups are located on specific body parts, the motion recognition module can infer the sensor location on the body.

The raw orientation information of the instrumented body parts is then sent to the range of motion limiter for further refining.

Range of Motion Limitation.

The estimated raw orientations of the body parts attached to certain sensors may defy the limits of the normal human body, due to inertial sensor data drift. To correct for this, the raw sensor orientations are passed through a range of motion limiter. The limiter offsets the errors and restricts the orientations obtained from the complimentary filter to match the capabilities of the human body.

Visualization and Rendering.

In order for a human to use the revised body part orientations for analysis of body motion, they must be transformed into a visual image. This goal is achieved using an animated human-like avatar. The visualized avatar's body parts correspond to the instrumented points on a real human subject. As the revised body part orientations are received, the animated avatar moves to mimic the motion of the instrumented human subject.

5. MARS SYSTEM IMPLEMENTATION

To evaluate the feasibility of using inertial sensors to do both muscle activity recognition and motion tracking, we implemented the three-tier MARS system architecture using the following hardware setup. The setup components are shown in Figure 3.

5.1 Sensor Node Network

The sensor network is charged with sensing body motion and muscle vibrations. The network consists of inertial sensor nodes, equipped with an Atmel ATmega128RFA1 [4] microcontroller chip and three triple-axis sensors: an ADXL345 [2] accelerometer, an ITG3200 [14] strap-down gyroscope, and an HMC58833L [13] magnetometer. The sensor node network is connected to the mobile data aggregator using a wired SPI bus running at a frequency of 1Mbps. Each sensor samples at 90Hz with 18 bytes per sample from the 9-axis sensors. At this sample rate, the sensor node network and the mobile data aggregator (wearable system components) consume an average of about 0.21 amperes of current. This allows the system to operate continuously for about ten hours using the current 2200mAh lithium polymer battery technology.

5.2 Mobile Data Aggregator

The mobile data aggregator sits at the intermediate level of the MARS system. It functions as the SPI bus coordinator of the inertial sensor network. It is implemented using a Rugged Circuits Wi-Fi Yellow Jacket (YJ) board [3]. The YJ board is used as the intermediate board because it provided a SPI interface to communicate with the sensors on one end and a Wi-Fi interface to send data to the backend server.

As the SPI master, the YJ board was charged with driving the sensor network. Due to the driving limitation of the YJ, the number of sensors in each single network was limited to six, and the entire wired bus length leading all the sensors in the network limited to under 2.5 meters to reduce line capacitance. We found that using a single YJ board to drive more than six sensors with longer wires occasionally overloaded the YJ board. This caused latching issues and led to inconsistent sensor readings. To expand the number of sensors, the network is segmented into multiple groups each with a YJ coordinator board.

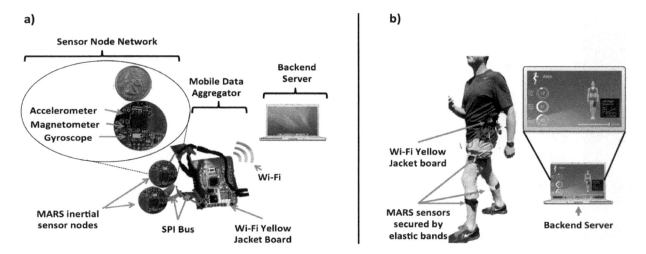

Figure 3: (a)The hardware components that make up the MARS system including a MARS sensor, the Wi-Fi Yellow Jacket (YJ) board. The locations of the accelerometer, magnetometer and gyroscope are also shown. (b) Shows a test subject wearing the MARS system and a mockup of the visualization screen on the backend server.

5.3 Backend Server

The backend server is comprised of a desktop computer in our implementation of MARS. For the muscle activity recognition feature extraction process, the length of the siding window was set to 128 samples with 64 (50%) sample points overlapping.

The muscle activity recognition module was implemented in Matlab using machine learning algorithms from the WEKA machine learning toolkit [11]. For muscle identity inference, the muscle activity recognition module uses a J48 Decision Tree (DT) algorithm described in Section 4.3.

The motion tracking and visualization module was implemented using Java and the Unity Gaming Engine [27].

5.4 Design Considerations

MARS is designed to be a real-world system for use in sports and fitness training. Thus it was designed with the following considerations.

Ease of setup: Humans sweat during exercise, and fitness gear need to be washed often. For this reason, a monitoring system should be quick and easy to wear, setup, and remove. The MARS sensors are attached to elastic belts that are quickly donned before an exercise as shown in Figure 3b. The elastic belts are easily removed so that the training gear can be washed.

The MARS system can also distinguish muscle groups from each other. This means that after a training phase, the system can automatically derive their positions during physical activity. This feature allows the sensors to be interchangeable. Moreover, this auto-labeling feature contributes to the tractability of MARS. The system remains easy to setup even as the number of sensors in the system increases. In addition, routine maintenance, such as replacing damaged sensors, is simple because individual sensors need not be tagged after replacement.

Unobtrusiveness: The MARS system relies on a user being able to wear the sensors for the duration of a workout or physical activity. For this reason, the MARS sensors are small and round, about the size of an American quarter dollar. MARS sensors can be comfortably sewn inside athletic garments to make them even less visible to the user.

The sensors are also connected using a thin, flat, wired connection, as opposed to a wireless connection. Using an entirely wireless solution would mean that each sensor would need to be powered individually by a battery. This would increase the bulk of the sensors and make the system more difficult to wear.

6. EXPERIMENTS AND EVALUATION

In this section we evaluate the effectiveness of the MARS system for both detecting and distinguishing muscle groups from each other as well as a tool for motion capture. We conduct real-world user studies to assess the accuracy of the MARS system in identifying muscle activity state, performing muscle identity inference as well as motion capture and tracking.

6.1 Vibration Signature Feature Ranking

To evaluate the extent to which each of the features determined the class of a muscle, given the vibration signatures, we calculated the correlation of each feature vector with the class predicted for each new incoming set of feature instances. Table 2 summarizes the average correlation calculated across participants of the top three features and the bottom two features.

These results imply that muscle vibrations are directional and in our case tended to be centered around the Y axis if the accelerometer rather than around the X and Z axes. This is implied by the fact that the cosine correlation between the Y and Z axes, the entropy and root mean square along the Y axis are most significant. On the other hand, the signal power in the medium range of the Z axis and the signal root mean square along the X axis are the least significant features in determining the muscle identity classes.

The results also show that the initial orientation of the sensors will determine the features which are most influen-

Feature vector	Correlation with class
Cosine Correlation YZ	0.507
Entropy Y	0.431
Root Mean Square Y	0.180
⋮	⋮
PowerZ (M)	0.055
Root Mean Square X	0.015

Table 2: A table showing the correlation between muscle vibration signature features x_m and the predicted class y. A value of 1 shows perfect correlation while a value of 0 shows no correlation.

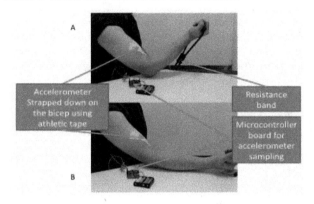

Figure 4: Setup of the proof-of-concept experiment. (A) A test subject's arm with the bicep muscle in an active position, sustaining the tension of an resistance cable. (B) A subject's arm with the biceps in a relaxed position.

tial in determining muscle identity. This does not currently limit the MARS system, since the orientation of the sensors which may be unknown, is assumed not to change once initially fixed into the garment. As part of our future work though, we are investigating extracting features using a different coordinate system such as the polar co-ordinates. We believe that these kinds of features will reduce the reliance of the system on X, Y and Z directionality.

6.2 Muscle Identity Experiments

To gather muscle vibration data to test the MARS system we conducted two user studies: a small proof-of-concept experiment and a diverse complex motion multi-user study, to evaluate our muscle inference algorithm.

6.2.1 Proof of Concept Experiment

To investigate the feasibility of using inertial sensors to detect muscle vibrations and differentiate muscle activity, we perform a small scale user study using three participants, one female and two males.

We instrument each person's biceps using accelerometers which are strapped down to the central position of the bicep muscle belly. We then collect accelerometer data from each of the participants when their muscles are relaxed, i.e. not actively engaged in any physical activity. Next we collect the accelerometer data from each of the participants when

their muscles are active, in this case, sustaining tension of an elastic exercise band in their hands as shown in Figure 4.

A plot of the power spectral densities of the accelerometer signal obtained from each participants sensor is shown in Figure 5. This plot reveals two major points. First, muscle activity can be quantified through monitoring topical vibrations. The graphs show that the vibrations produced in the relaxed state have on average about half the signal power of those produced in the active state. Second, since the body and muscle size/composition are different for different individuals, the vibration patterns their muscles produce are different. This can be seen through the variation in power spectral density patterns produced by the bicep muscles of the respective subjects as they worked their bicep muscles.

The results of this experiment also suggested that while identifying muscle activity is simple using inertial sensors, each person's skeletal muscle vibrations would be unique and would thus have to be learned individually. Therefore we performed a larger full scale user study, in which we trained and evaluated the MARS system for each individual.

6.2.2 User Study Experiment

To perform muscle identity inference during complex human motion, and validate the results obtained in Section 6.2.1, we performed a user study involving 10 diverse participants; four females and six males. The participants were drawn from varying backgrounds with disparate physical activity and exercise fitness capacities/ routines.

The study was focused on detecting and identifying the vibrations in the major muscles of the human leg, namely the quadriceps, hamstrings and calves. The goal was to use these vibrations to infer the identity of the specific muscle groups of the human leg. We selected the muscles of the lower body for two main reasons. First these muscles are larger and easier to instrument with sensors. Second, a majority of the injuries that occur in sports and fitness happen in the abdominal section of the human body [30].

With the help of trained personnel, namely, personal trainer Eddie Sumpter from Sunnyvale Fitness and Physiotherapist Roland Lucas of Lucas Physical Therapy & Fitness, both in Sunnyvale, CA, we selected a set of simple isolation and compound exercises. The personal trainer and physiotherapist were important for determining exercises which largely worked specific muscle groups, hence setting the ground truth for activated muscles. The muscle group that was largely worked/ isolated by a given exercise was marked as the ground truth muscle activated by that exercise. To ensure that the selected exercises were performed smoothly, the trained personnel set a pace or tempo with which the exercises were performed. The tempos are summarized in Table 3. The exercises include:

- **Leg extension** - This is a simple exercise which largely activates the quadriceps muscle of the human leg. The exercise is shown in Figure 6(1).

- **Leg curl** - This simple isolation exercise largely activates the hamstrings of the human leg. The exercise is shown in Figure 6(2).

- **Calf raise** - This is a simple exercise that activates the calves muscle of the human leg. The exercise is shown in Figure 6(3).

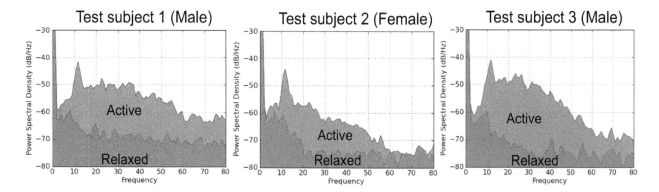

Figure 5: An example power spectrum plot of the accelerometer signal obtained during a single session from the bicep muscle of three test participants. The graphs show that muscle activity can be quantified since the signal power almost doubles as the muscle goes from a relaxed state to an active state. The observed quantified pattern is different for each participant meaning that muscle activity can be inferred as being unique from individual to individual.

- **Squat** - This is a compound exercise which activates all the muscles of the human leg including the quadriceps, hamstrings, calves as well as the gluteus. The exercise is shown in Figure 6(4).

The above exercises were performed by each participant in turn. During each exercise, we used a metronome device to standardize the tempo of each repetition of an exercise across participants as much as possible. The tempo was also selected with the help of a fitness trainer as the pace that would allow participants to exert their muscles but maintain a smooth, even motion throughout the exercise.

The isolation exercises were designed to determine the accuracy of MARS at identifying activity in individual skeletal muscle groups. The isolation exercises were performed at a tempo of 60 beats per minute (bpm), as Table 3 shows. This meant that the subjects performed each half of each repetition of each of the simple exercises within roughly $\frac{1beat*60sec}{60bpm} = 1$ second. In practice though there was still some variation among participants, so that each half of a repetition took up to 1.4 seconds, meaning that a complete repetition took up to 2.8 seconds.

The compound exercise, the squat, was designed to determine the performance of MARS in identifying muscle activity during complex motion where multiple muscles are active. As a complex exercise, the squat was performed at a slower tempo of 45 bpm to allow participants to correctly carry it out. Each half of a repetition of the squat exercise was scheduled to take about $\frac{1beat*60sec}{45bpm} = 1.33$ seconds. Again, in practice there was still some variation so that each complete repetition took about three seconds on average.

All exercises were performed until participants were completely exerted, or until failure. The exercises were performed this way so as to obtain skeletal muscle vibration data across a broad range of muscle conditions, exhaustively capturing muscle activity.

To determine the level of exertion we used the *Borg CR10* perceived exertion scale [7]. The scale was explained, handed out to participants and individual calibration exercises performed to familiarize participants with the scale. The Borg CR10 scale attempts to normalize the subjectivity in ex-

Exercise	Exercise Type	Exercise Tempo
Leg Extension	Isolation	60 bpm
Leg Curl	Isolation	60 bpm
Calf Raise	Isolation	60 bpm
Squat	Compound	45 bpm

Table 3: A table showing the isolation and compound exercises performed by the study participants and the tempo with which the exercises were performed.

ertion across participants by considering standardizing the subject's exertion ranges between a 'no effort' level and an 'all out effort', where failure occurs.

Between a state of 'no effort' and 'all out effort', the average time for each exercise was about three to five minutes. Rest periods of approximately three to five minutes were allocated in between exercises to allow participants to recover. During the exercises, the MARS sensors were sampled at a rate of 90Hz and the data transmitted wirelessly to the nearby backend server computer for processing.

To perform muscle identity inference, the accelerometer data was passed through the Muscle Activity Recognition Module. At a 90 Hz sample rate, a window size of 128 accelerometer sample points as explained in Section 5.3, corresponded to approximately 1.4 seconds worth of data per sample or roughly the time taken to perform half of a repetition of an exercise. The extracted features are used for training and testing three supervised learning classifiers whose task is to identify muscle groups based on muscle vibrations.

We report and compare the ten fold cross-validation precision and recall results of the muscle inference task across the three classifiers. Thus, using three minutes of training data, this corresponds to about 250 recognitions per user, per muscle group, per exercise, where a prediction on the activated muscle is made every 1.4 seconds.

Isolation Exercise Muscle Identity Inference Results.

The precision and recall results for the muscle identity inference for simple isolation exercises are shown in Figure 7.

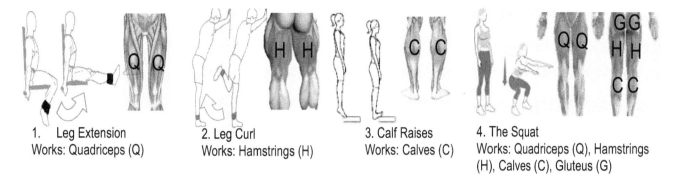

1. Leg Extension
Works: Quadriceps (Q)

2. Leg Curl
Works: Hamstrings (H)

3. Calf Raises
Works: Calves (C)

4. The Squat
Works: Quadriceps (Q), Hamstrings (H), Calves (C), Gluteus (G)

Figure 6: The set of exercises performed by the test subjects of the full scale study. The highlighted and labeled muscle groups indicate the muscles worked during the exercise.

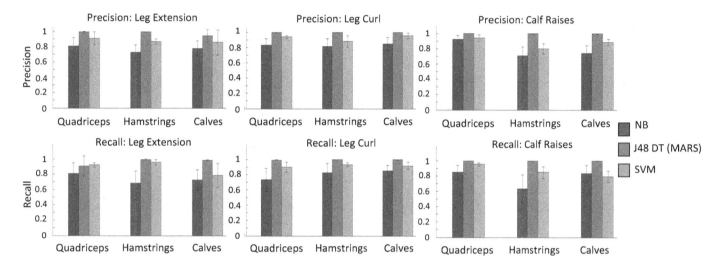

Figure 7: Averaged precision and recall results for the task of distinguishing quadriceps, hamstring and calves from each other using NB, MARS J48DT and SVM classifiers, during the isolation exercises. Error bars indicate the maximum and minimum accuracy values across participants. While other classification methods achieve accuracies greater than 60.% precision and recall, MARS achieves upwards of 90% accuracy.

The results compare the performance of the MARS system J48 decision tree classifier against a Naive Bayes and support vector machine classifier trained on the same feature set. The results includes results from all the ten participants of the study. The bars indicate the maximum and minimum values of the precision and recall values across the participants.

The results show that all of the three classifiers are capable of performing muscle identity inference with better than chance accuracies greater than 60% in terms of precision and recall. However, since the J48 decision tree achieves greater than 95% accuracy in terms of precision and recall, it is the best candidate classifier to use for muscle identity inference on a per person basis given the selected features due to the correlations of some of the features.

These results also show that using muscle vibrations it is not only possible to tell the difference between the active and relaxed/ lightly used muscle but also between the relaxed muscles. During isolation leg exercises, a single leg muscle is heavily exercised while the other muscles remain relaxed or are lightly used to coordinate the exercise. This

corroborates the fact that even in relaxed or lightly used states two different muscle groups will have different vibration patterns, a fact that would enable MARS to distinguish muscle groups even when they are only lightly active or relaxed.

Compound Exercise Muscle Identity Inference Results.

The compound exercise is used to evaluate the accuracy of MARS when multiple muscles are active at the same time. The results are shown in Figure 8. As the graphs show, the DT classifier used by mars achieves greater than 95% precision and recall values outperforming its counterparts. These results show that MARS can leverage muscle vibrations to distinguish between groups of active muscles with high accuracy (precision and recall $\geq$ 95%) even in exercises when multiple muscles are active. This is the case because during a compound exercise such as a squat, the hamstrings, quadriceps and calves muscles are all activated and heavily exercised but at different times. However, since these muscle groups have differing physical properties and are used to dif-

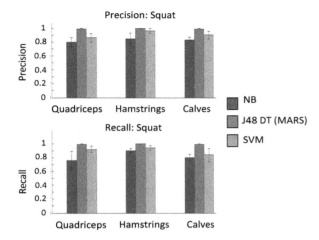

Figure 8: Averaged precision and recall results for the task of inferring the identities of the quadriceps, hamstring and calves during the squat exercise. Error bars indicate the maximum and minimum accuracy values among participants. All classifiers achieve greater than 75% precision and recall, but the MARS J48 DT achieves greater than 95% precision and recall.

ferent extents during the exercise, their vibration patterns differ. Consequently, by processing the muscular vibrations, MARS can, after a training phase, match vibration patterns to specific muscle groups.

6.3 Motion Tracking Setup And Results

To investigate how well the MARS system performs as a motion tracking tool, we instrumented a test subject with MARS sensors and performed a sequence of activities including side walking, marching in place, and standing still with out stretched arms.

For purposes of performing complete motion capture and tracking, we instrumented both the upper and lower body segments of the test subject. During the exercises, MARS sensors were sampled at the same nominal 90 Hz rate as for muscle activity recognition. Data from all the sensor streams (accelerometer, gyroscope and magnetometer) were wirelessly transmitted to the backend server and processed by the motion tracking and visualization module, as explained in Section 4.3.2.

The results of the motion tracking are shown in Figure 9. The top row of images shows a snapshot of the ground truth video captured as the test subject side walked, performed a stationary march and stood still with his arms stretched out. The bottom row indicates the rendered movements by MARS using the animated human body model. The MARS animated avatar closely mimics the ground truth video images.

6.4 Deployment Challenges

The MARS wearable system while presenting a novel approach to monitoring musculoskeletal activity, presented a few challenges during the human study deployment.

MARS inertial sensor nodes are interconnected using wires. Where as the use of wires was conscious design choice aimed at reducing the need for individual batteries for each sensor node and enabling reliable communication between nodes, they made the system slightly inconvenient to users when wearing or taking it off. In future revisions of MARS, we are sewing in and concealing the sensors and wires in athletic clothing so that it will be easier for the users to wear and remove the system.

Another challenge presented by the system during deployment was that of efficient training and calibration. Currently the MARS system cannot accommodate for per-user differences meaning that it would need to be trained individually for each user which may be inefficient and time consuming. In future revisions of MARS we are working to define a more generalized training/ learning procedure that will remove this restriction.

The sensor placement, during our experiment was consistent. The sensors were mounted at the center of the belly muscle from participant to participant as guided by the trained physiotherapist and personal trainer. However, a user interacting with the system may not be as careful in sensor placement, meaning that the accuracy of the system may vary with placement. Whereas the current system does not address the issue of sensor placement, part of our future work lies in investigating and quantifying this tradeoff between placement and system accuracy.

7. RELATED WORK

The primary goal of our work is to use inertial sensor data to achieve fine grained muscle activity and identity inference which also enables accurate minimal setup human motion capture. A number of alternative approaches have been proposed that operate in this same space.

Muscle Activity Detection: In the field of muscle activity detection current work proposes two main methods. The first is electromyography (EMG), [10, 20] which directly measures the electrical potential of active muscle fibers. EMG however, requires perfect contact with the skin, and is invasive, necessitating the use of gels or small needles inserted directly into muscles. Although accurate, this makes the use of EMG complicated and intrusive, rendering it unusable in a sports application.

Mechanomyographic (MMG) methods on the other hand use vibration transducers such as fabric stretch sensors (FSS), force sensitive resistors (FSR), or inertial sensors (accelerometers, gyroscopes and magnetometers) to detect muscle activity [1, 10, 21, 22]. Fabric stretch sensors contain conductive carbon-loaded rubber whose resistance changes as it is stretched and relaxed when the muscle is active. Their susceptibility to hysteresis however, complicates their use. Over time, their stretching ability becomes non-linear and complicating the system [1]. FSRs contain a polymer thick film device which changes its resistance according to the force applied to its active surface by the muscle belly, as it contracts and expands. One major drawback of FSRs is that they are highly susceptible to placement on the body [21]. This means that for an application where a dense network of sensors is required, system calibration and usability would be difficult since each sensor would need to be individually

Figure 9: Comparison of the motion capture capability of MARS alongside the ground truth provided by frame images obtained from a video recording of a test subject side-walking, marching in place and standing still with arms stretched out.

positioned. Such a system is not scalable and hence unsuitable for our application.

More recently, muscle activity has also been inferred through active capacitive sensing achieved by using conductive textile based electrodes [8]. While these sensors are extremely lightweight and integrable into garments, they are highly sensitive to motion, body shape and tissue changes which could easily distort their signal, complicating their use.

In the muscle activity inference arena, k nearest neighbor (k-NN) and neural network classifiers have been explored for the task of identifying posture and balance using EMG only or both EMG and inertial sensor data [10, 26]. While the results are similar, our approache is much less invasive. In addition, our approach goes beyond posture detection to exploring muscle identity inference through muscle activity detection.

Motion Capture: Current motion capture/tracking systems can generally be classified as outside-in or inside-out [28]. The former uses environmentally mounted sensors to sense and reconstruct human motion. This restricts their use to controlled laboratory-like spaces. The latter, similar to MARS, relies on body-mounted sensors such as cameras and inertial sensors to detect, and reconstruct the subject's motion accordingly. This makes the system robust, allowing for both indoor and outdoor use.

Vision based motion capture methods use wearable cameras (inside-out) or approaches that use the Microsoft Kinect sensor (outside-in) provide a richly detailed view of the environment whose images can be used to reconstruct motion very accurately [6, 23]. However, such systems can be severely derailed by blocking or shading of the cameras, which would be expected to happen often during regular human motion [23]. Moreover, they require complex vision algorithms to process the data, which makes them difficult to use. MARS function independent of lighting conditions

and are not affected by occlusion such as mud on the suit or obsticles. In addition, since inertial sensors measure gravity (accelerometer), rotation (gyroscope) and magnetic field strength (magnetometer) all of which directly change during human motion, the algorithms used by MARS are far less complex and easier to implement.

Other accelerometer based approaches such as MOCA have been proposed [9]. MOCA is a cost effective inertial motion tracking system that uses accelerometers to trackhuman body segments. While similar in nature to our motion capture system, the realized MOCA system is fairly single point, using one or two accelerometers to enable body tracking. As a result it is not capable of offering the multipoint fine-grained tracking that MARS offers.

Other wearable systems feature an exoskeleton suit with embedded lightweight rods that move with the user [23]. Using potentiometers at the joints, these systems can measure the motion information using a kinematic model. Such systems, while capable of motion estimation, are intrusive, bulky and cumbersome in addition to seseptable to drift. This makes them unsuitable for regular comfortable use in our target domains of sports, fitness training and gaming.

8. CONCLUSION

In this paper we presented MARS, a novel non-intrusive, autonomous setup capable, inertial sensor-based muscle identity recognition and motion tracking system. MARS detects muscle vibrations and create unique skeletal muscle vibration signatures. The vibration signatures are used for skeletal muscle identity recognition which enables quick body motion capture without the need for individual sensor tagging.

The evaluation results show our system can use these muscle vibration signatures to distinguish the major muscles of the human leg with accuracies greater than 95%, using a J48 DT classifier. By leveraging these muscle identity inference results, MARS can perform quick autonomous setup after an initial training phase. In addition, the MARS system can achieve accurate human motion capture and tracking, comparable to visual based camera methods.

Utilizing these MARS enables a unique wearable system that can not only capture motion but also individual muscle activity while requiring minimal setup. Such systems can provide a new tool for understanding sports, promoting correct motion and preventing injury.

9. ACKNOWLEDGMENTS

The authors would like to thank our shepherd Dr. Andreas Andreou and the anonymous reviewers for their insightful and constructive comments. This material is based upon work supported by DARPA under Grant No. 1080247-D11AP00265-DOI-ZHANG. The authors would also like to thank the Nokia Research Center for funding this research as well as Physiotherapist Roland Lucas and Personal Trainer Eddie Sumpter for their expertise in the design and execution of our studies. The views and conclusions contained here are those of the authors and should not be interpreted as necessarily representing the official policies or endorsements, either express or implied, of Nokia Research Center, Vibrado Technologies, Carnegie Mellon University, the United States Government or any of its agencies.

10. REFERENCES

[1] O. Amft, H. Junker, and P. Lukowicz. Sensing muscle activities with body-worn sensors. *Body Sensor*, pages 6–9, 2006.

[2] Analog Devices. ADXL345 Digital Accelerometer data sheet. http://www.analog.com/en/mems-sensors/mems-accelerometers/adxl345/products/product.html.

[3] AsyncLabs. Rugged Circuits Yellow Jacket description. http://ruggedcircuits.com/html/yellowjacket.html. Accessed: 1/06/2012.

[4] Atmel Corporation. ATmega128RFA1 8-bit Microcontroller with Low Power 2.4GHz Transceiver for ZigBee and IEEE 802.15.4 data sheet. http://www.atmel.com/devices/atmega128rfa1.aspx.

[5] L. Bao and S. Intille. Activity recognition from user-annotated acceleration data. *Pervasive Computing*, pages 1–17, 2004.

[6] K. Berger, K. Ruhl, and C. Brümmer. Markerless motion capture using multiple color-depth sensors. *Vision, Modeling and Visualization*, 2011.

[7] G. Borg. *Borg's Perceived Exertion and Pain Scales.* Human Kinetics, 1998.

[8] J. Cheng, O. Amft, and P. Lukowicz. Active Capacitive Sensing : Exploring a New Wearable Sensing Modality for Activity Recognition. *Pervasive Computing*, pages 319–336, 2010.

[9] E. Farella, L. Benini, B. Riccò, and A. Acquaviva. MOCA: A Low-Power, Low-Cost Motion Capture System Based on Integrated Accelerometers. *Advances in Multimedia*, 2007:1–11, 2007.

[10] H. Ghasemzadeh, R. Jafari, and B. Prabhakaran. A body sensor network with electromyogram and inertial sensors: multimodal interpretation of muscular activities. *IEEE transactions on information technology in biomedicine*, 14(2):198–206, Mar. 2010.

[11] M. Hall, H. National, E. Frank, G. Holmes, B. Pfahringer, P. Reutemann, and I. H. Witten. The WEKA Data Mining Software : An Update. *SIGKDD Explorations*, 11(1):10–18, 2009.

[12] J. Ho. Interruptions: using activity transitions to trigger proactive messages. Master's thesis, Massachusetts Institute of Technology, 2004.

[13] Honeywell International Inc. 3-Axis Digital Compass IC HMC5883L data sheet. http://honeywell.com/Pages/Search.aspx?k=hmc5883l.

[14] InvenSense Inc. ITG-3200 Product Specification data sheet. "http://www.invensense.com/mems/gyro/tripleaxis.html.

[15] S. B. Kotsiantis. Supervised Machine Learning : A Review of Classification Techniques. *Informatica*, 31:249–268, 2007.

[16] J. O. Laguna and A. Olaya. A dynamic sliding window approach for activity recognition. *User Modeling, Adaption and*, pages 1–12, 2011.

[17] X. Long, B. Yin, and R. Aarts.

[18] P. Lukowicz and F. Hanser. Detecting and interpreting muscle activity with wearable force sensors. *Pervasive*, pages 101–116, 2006.

[19] X. Meng, S. Sun, L. Ji, J. Wu, and W.-C. Wong. Displacement estimation in micro-sensor motion capture. *IEEE International Conference on Systems, Man and Cybernetics*, 2010.

[20] T. Moritani and Y. Yoshitake. The use of electromyography in applied physiology. *Journal of Electromyography and Kinesiology*, 8(6):363 – 381, 1998.

[21] G. Ogris, M. Kreil, and P. Lukowicz. Using FSR based muscle activity monitoring to recognize manipulative arm gestures. *2007 11th IEEE International Symposium on Wearable Computers*, pages 1–4, Oct. 2007.

[22] C. Orizio, M. Gobbo, B. Diemont, F. Esposito, and A. Veicsteinas. The surface mechanomyogram as a tool to describe the influence of fatigue on biceps brachii motor unit activation strategy. historical basis and novel evidence. *European Journal of Applied Physiology*, 90:326–336, 2003. 10.1007/s00421-003-0924-1.

[23] T. Shiratori, H. S. Park, L. Sigal, Y. Sheikh, and J. K. Hodgins. Motion capture from body-mounted cameras. In *ACM SIGGRAPH 2011 papers*, SIGGRAPH '11, New York, NY, USA, 2011. ACM.

[24] M. Stikic, T. Huynh, K. Van Laerhoven, and B. Schiele. Adl recognition based on the combination of rfid and accelerometer sensing. In *Proceedings of the 2nd International Conference on Pervasive Computing Technologies for Healthcare (Pervasive Health 2008)*, page 258–263, Tampere, Finland, January 2008. IEEE Xplore, IEEE Xplore.

[25] S. Sun, X. Meng, L. Ji, J. Wu, and W.-C. Wong. Adaptive sensor data fusion in motion capture. In *Information Fusion (FUSION), 2010 13th Conference on*, pages 1 –8, 2010.

[26] M. T. Tarata. Mechanomyography versus electromyography, in monitoring the muscular fatigue. *BioMedical Engineering Online*, 10:1–10, 2003.

[27] U. Technologies. Unity Gaming Engine description. http://UnityGameEngine,http://unity3d.com/. Accessed: 1/06/2012.

[28] G. Welch and E. Foxlin. Motion tracking: No silver bullet, but a respectable arsenal. *Computer Graphics and Applications, IEEE*, 22(6):24–38, 2002.

[29] J. Wood and D. Barry. Time-frequency analysis of skeletal muscle and cardiac vibrations. *Proceedings of the IEEE*, 84(9):1281–1294, 1996.

[30] C. Woods, R. Hawkins, M. Hulse, and A. Hodson. The football association medical research programme: an audit of injuries in professional football-analysis of preseason injuries. *Br J Sports Med*, 36(6):436–41; discussion 441, 2002.

Single-accelerometer-based daily physical activity classification. In *Engineering in Medicine and Biology Society, 2009. EMBC 2009. Annual International Conference of the IEEE*, volume 2009, pages 6107–6110. IEEE, Jan. 2009.

POEM: Power-efficient Occupancy-based Energy Management System

Varick L. Erickson
Elect. Eng. & Comp. Science
Univ. of California, Merced
verickson@ucmerced.edu

Stefan Achleitner
Elect. Eng. & Comp. Science
Univ. of California, Merced
sachleitner@ucmerced.edu

Alberto E. Cerpa
Elect. Eng. & Comp. Science
Univ. of California, Merced
acerpa@ucmerced.edu

ABSTRACT

Buildings account for 40% of US primary energy consumption and 72% of electricity. Of this total, 50% of the energy consumed in buildings is used for Heating Ventilation and Air-Conditioning (HVAC) systems. Current HVAC systems only condition based on static schedules; rooms are conditioned regardless of occupancy. By conditioning rooms only when necessary, greater efficiency can be achieved. This paper describes POEM, a complete closed-loop system for optimally controlling HVAC systems in buildings based on actual occupancy levels. POEM is comprised of multiple parts. A wireless network of cameras called OPTNet is developed that functions as an optical turnstile to measure area/zone occupancies. Another wireless sensor network of passive infrared (PIR) sensors called BONet functions alongside OPTNet. This sensed occupancy data from both systems are then fused with an occupancy prediction model using a particle filter in order to determine the most accurate current occupancy in each zone in the building. Finally, the information from occupancy prediction models and current occupancy is combined in order to find the optimal conditioning strategy required to reach target temperatures and minimize ventilation requirements. Based on live tests of the system, we estimate $\approx$ 30.0% energy saving can be achieved while still maintaining thermal comfort.

Categories and Subject Descriptors

J.7 [**Computers In Other Systems**]: Command & control; C.3 [**Special-Purpose and Application-Based Application Systems**]: Real-time and embedded systems

Keywords

Occupancy, HVAC, Ventilation, Energy savings

1. INTRODUCTION

Sustainable buildings represent a major paradigm shift from current practice. According to the US Department of Energy, buildings account for nearly 40% of US primary energy consumption in 2010, 72% of which is electrical energy [1].

Of this total, 50% of the energy consumed in buildings is used for heating, air-conditioning and ventilation (HVAC) systems [1]. Reducing this load is a priority if we wish to achieve energy independence. Within office buildings, one obvious source of inefficiency are the empty or partially filled rooms. Rather than assuming all rooms are used equally, rooms should be conditioned based on actual usage.

Several works have shown that approximately 25%-40% HVAC energy saving can be achieved by regulating HVAC systems based on occupancy [15, 11]. These papers discuss sensing solutions for detecting room usage. Passive infrared (PIR) sensors are commonly used for binary sensing of occupancy for lighting. These sensors, however, do not enable the adjustment of ventilation, which depends on the number of occupants. CO_2 sensors are another alternative. They can infer level of occupancy and ventilation rates but are slow to respond and suffer from calibration problems [16]. For our system, we utilize cameras deployed in public hallways along with PIR sensors within rooms to infer occupancy. Instead of deploying cameras directly in rooms to count individuals, we deploy cameras that count the number of people that pass across an area. By using cameras as optical turnstiles, it is possible to measure occupancy levels of areas connected to the turnstile area. Privacy issues are avoided by only deploying in public hallways where security cameras are already present. Moreover, by performing local video processing on the cameras, we avoid the transmission of raw video data to a central location. For our experiments we follow well-known best practices with respect to the use of privacy-critical data [5, 2]. Furthermore, our distributed data processing solution enhances scalability and significantly reduces network load, improving system lifetime of the bandwidth-limited camera sensor network. Existing optical counting systems exist, but they are difficult to retrofit to buildings and require hard wiring [8]. Wiring can be very difficult for many older buildings where drop ceilings are not available. We wish to utilize motes that can be easily deployed in even older buildings. Maintenance time can be minimized by coordinating battery replacement with routine light-bulb replacement.

Unlike lighting, the thermal ramp up or down of a room involves delay. While an optical system of occupancy monitoring can give occupancy in near real-time, reactively conditioning a room will likely leave occupants uncomfortable until target temperatures are met. In order to ensure occupant's comfort, we must be able to predict when occupants are likely to enter a room and begin conditioning beforehand. We achieve this by using a blended Markov Chain as described in [15].

This paper contributes the following:

• We developed OPTNet, an occupancy estimation system comprised of 22 node wireless camera nodes, and BONet, a 40 node PIR wireless sensor network. We show how lightweight on-board image processing algorithms along with classification techniques can be used in order to accurately detect occupants' transitions.

• We show how errors in occupancy sensing can be corrected by fusing data from an occupancy transition model together with sensor data using a particle filter.

• Our most significant contribution is the design, implementation, deployment and evaluation of the POEM system, which is a full closed-loop system that conditions rooms based on occupancy on a *real office building*. To our knowledge, our system is the first to control both temperature and ventilation based on near real-time occupancy.

• We tested our system over a period of four weeks and show that significant energy savings (26%) are possible while still maintaining conditioning effectiveness. Using a calibrated EnergyPlus simulation, we show that this system saves 30% energy annually over standard strategies.

• We perform Return On Investment (ROI) analysis, showing the sensitivity of different factors and concluding that the cost of the system could be amortized in approximately 6 to 10 months.

After examining related work in Section 2, we begin in Section 3 with an overview of POEM, a demand-driven system for optimally controlling HVAC systems. In the following sections, we describe the different components of POEM. Section 4 describes OPTNet, a 22 wireless camera deployment, which is followed by Section 5 that describes a 40 PIR wireless sensors. We then show in Section 6 how a particle filter can be used to correct errors in occupancy. Section 7 shows the programmatic interface with the building management system (BMS) and the control algorithm used to optimally condition rooms based on current and prediction occupancy. In Section 8, we evaluate the potential energy savings and the conditioning effectiveness with respect to temperature and ventilation. We then show in Section 9 that the cost of the system can be amortized in approximately 6-10 months if applied to the entire building and finally we discuss our conclusions and future work in Section 11.

2. RELATED WORK

As previously mentioned, our most significant contribution is the development of a full closed-loop occupancy based control system in a non-residential building. Since there are few such deployments, we examine work related to each of our subsystems.

In [17], the authors developed a 16 sensor node camera deployment within the hallways of an office building. While the system was shown to be accurate at counting individual components, independent tests over 24 hours showed that the system is only able to capture ≈ 80% [15] of transitions. In particular, they do not address how errors in transitions lead to cumulative errors in occupancy. Our paper examines this problem in detail and how it can be addressed using a particle filter.

In [22], the authors monitor elderly people using Imote2 motes with Enalab cameras. To track occupants, they utilize a motion histogram. The system assumes that the camera can actively monitor the entire area of interest. The problem of privacy also exists for this system; cameras must be placed directly in the room.

The authors of [11] developed and tested an occupancy-based conditioning system. For their deployment they utilize PIR and door sensors to determine if rooms are occupied and condition rooms reactively. Ventilation is not considered as part of the conditioning strategy, which impacts energy efficiency. One of the main issues of their system evaluation is the conditioning effectiveness; they do not consider the comfort of their occupants during the ramp-up period for their reactive system. Our evaluation examines in detail the thermal comfort of occupants and also considers ventilation.

Door/PIR sensors are also used in [21] for conditioning residential buildings. They utilize a Hidden Markov Model in order to determine the probability that the house is occupied, occupied with occupants asleep, or unoccupied. Ventilation is not taken into account.

In [15], the authors develop an occupancy prediction model using a blended Markov Chain. In addition, they developed a conditioning strategy utilizing the occupancy prediction model, in simulation, to estimate energy savings. While these simulations provided analysis of ventilation, the paper does not implement the model in an actual deployment. The authors also describe agent based, multivariate Gaussian, and moving window Markov Chain occupancy models in [14, 13]. The main drawback of these works is that the performance of the proposed systems is done only in simulation. In particular, it is questionable whether the unbiased error introduced into the simulated sensor data is valid; in our deployments we found that errors in particular sensor locations can be bias. We show how to correct errors and verify energy saving with an actual deployment.

The authors of [25] developed a prediction based conditioning strategy for residential buildings using k-nearest-neighbors (KNN) to predict occupancy and a deployment utilizing PIR and RFID. This prediction method was 80% to 86% accurate for a 90 minute prediction, but did not not perform well for rooms that were not consistently occupied. While the approach is appropriate for residential buildings where the usage dynamic is simple, this approach may not work as effectively for office spaces where inter-room correlations exist. They also only consider temperature for their control, and do not consider ventilation.

3. POEM OVERVIEW

The main contribution of this work is POEM, which is a complete system that controls the temperature and ventilation of a building. This system is comprised of several components. Figure 1 summarizes the system architecture and shows all components of the POEM system. OPTNet, a wireless camera sensor network, and BONet, a PIR sensor network, provide occupancy estimates. A particle filter then fuses the sensing data from OPTNet and BONet with the output of an occupancy transition model in order to better estimate the current occupancy in each room. The current occupancy estimation from the particle filter, the ramp-up time, and the predicted occupancy from the transition model 1 hour into the future are combined in a control schedule to optimally pre-condition the spaces to reach the target temperature. Thus, we can optimally schedule the HVAC system to match the likely arrival of occupants. Once the process is complete, the conditioning affects occupants completing the feedback loop. The next sections provide a detail description and evaluation of each POEM component.

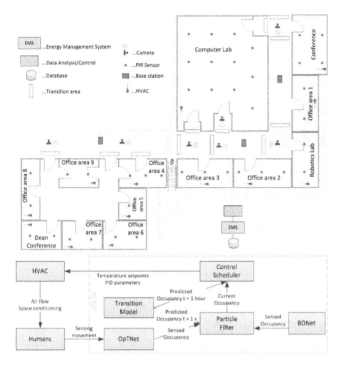

Figure 1: Architecture of the POEM system.

Figure 2: Transition areas (bigger blue boxes) and trigger areas (small red boxes).

4. OPTNET

OPtical **T**urnstile **Net**work (OPTNet) is a new low power wireless camera system that is able to accurately monitor room occupancy in near real-time. We start with a description of the hardware and deployment in Section 4.1. In Section 4.3, we describe a lightweight image processing method that can be used with a classification algorithm to detect transitions.

4.1 Overview and Design Challenges

We use the Imote2 platform developed by Intel and the IMB400 Camera [4] developed by Xbow. The mote uses an XScale processor currently set to run at 208 MHz. The mote has 64MB of memory and a CC2420 radio chip. The camera can capture 32 fps at 640x320 resolution. By utilizing a fish-eye lens fashioned from a door peephole (see Figure 2, right), we are able to roughly view 9 m^2 when the cameras are deployed at a height of 3 m. Therefore the camera has a viewing angle of about 160 degrees. We have 22 camera nodes deployed on two floors capable of measuring the occupancy of 60 areas. In our test deployment the nodes have a wired energy supply, which makes it easier for us to run different experiments. We also have the option to power a node with an 11 Ah battery pack which provides enough energy to run a node for about 45 days.

The goal of the system is accurate detection of occupants moving between areas. In order for the control system to be useful, accurate occupancy detection, particularly for empty rooms, is critical. Empty rooms provide an opportunity to let room temperatures float and thus save energy. Also important is the ventilation of the room, which is proportional to occupancy.

There are several design challenges. Motes have limited resources available. Though the IMB400 cameras are able to capture 32 fps, the Imote2 radio is only able to transmit $\approx$ 100 kbps under typical conditions, making near real-time

image streaming infeasible. This bandwidth issue can be partially solved if we only send images of interest and buffer the images until they can be sent. However, this requires heavy use of the radio, which is one of the most energy consuming components. Instead, it is more efficient to extract only useful features from the images and transmit a small amount of information. Thus, our design challenge is to design an efficient on-board image processing algorithm that can compress data to be processed at the base-station.

Occupancy tracking is still an open problem in the computer vision community. Many tracking algorithms focus on the person, typically correlating the identity of a person between frames using feature-based algorithms such as SIFT [20] and SURF [12]. While it is possible to run these algorithms on the Imote2, they are computationally expensive. Also, placing cameras directly into rooms raises serious privacy concerns. OPTnet thus only uses cameras installed along hallways. In our application, we only care about occupant transitions between areas, not the identity or precise location of specific occupants. Instead, we view this problem as a motion recognition problem, where we are attempting to recognize a sequence of images as a transition.

4.2 Camera Placement

HVAC systems are designed to condition zones within the building, where each zone is comprised of one or more rooms and is controlled to a specific temperature/ventilation. Figure 1 shows the zones for our deployment. As previously mentioned, we are attempting to capture the transitions that occur between zones in order to track the occupancy of an HVAC zone; the cameras operate as optical turnstiles. In order to capture all transitions, cameras must be deployed in such a way that all the entrances and exits are covered for a zone. Thus, the distribution and number of cameras depends on the entry/exit points of an area. More specifically, there must be one camera per entrance for a zone. For example, to track all the transitions for Offices area 1 (see Figure 1), a camera is placed in front of the Conference area and another in front of the Robotics lab. Since zones share entry/exit points, a camera can serve multiple areas; the camera deployed in front of the Conference area is used to track transitions from the Computer Lab, Conference area, and Office area 1.

4.3 Transition Detection

In this section, we describe a fast lightweight image processing algorithm that can be used for transition detection. Our strategy is to classify a sequence of images as a specific type of transition. We accomplish this by first detecting motion within a target transition area using background subtraction. We then determine the start and end of a transition from a continuous sequence of images containing motion. This sequence is then transformed into a vector that can be sent back to the base-station to be compared against

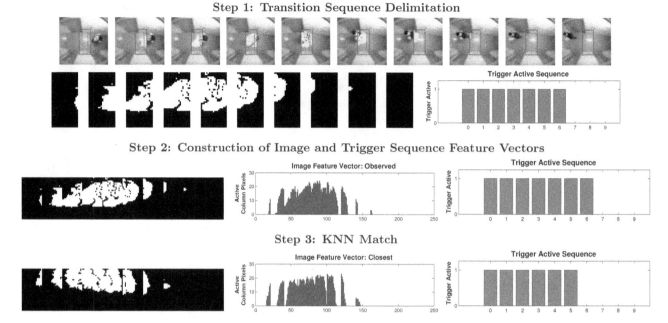

Step 1: Transition Sequence Delimitation

Step 2: Construction of Image and Trigger Sequence Feature Vectors

Step 3: KNN Match

Figure 3: Above is a summary of transition classification procedure.

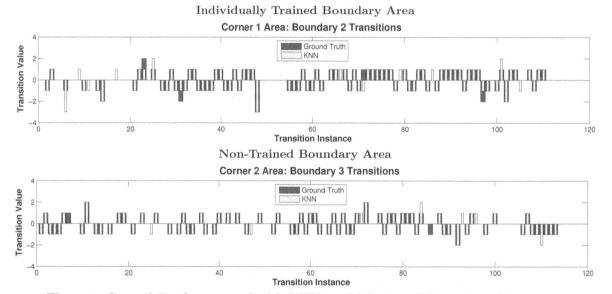

Individually Trained Boundary Area

Non-Trained Boundary Area

Figure 4: Ground Truth compared with KNN model for two different transition areas.

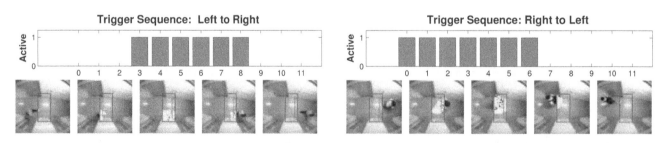

Figure 5: The sequence of the trigger state helps indicate direction. The red box indicates the trigger state is active.

known labeled data using the k-Nearest Neighbors (KNN) algorithm.

4.3.1 Motion Detection

For human motion detection we use previous frame background subtraction with a static threshold [?]. We tried several other background subtraction methods (e.g. moving average, weighted moving average), but we found previous frame subtraction to work the best for our application. In particular, it is robust against rapid lighting changes caused by opened doors as it can quickly reduce the number of pixels erroneously classified as active. This reduces the number of perceived transition sequences caused by people loitering near or within transition areas. It also quickly removes objects from images such as boxes and chairs, which occur frequently in the public hallways that our deployment is located.

4.3.2 Delimiting a Transition Sequence

The first problem we address is identifying a sequence of images that could potentially contain a transition. We start by defining a transition area, which is a small 1x2 m^2 area on the ground typically in front of a door or within a hallway. Figure 2 (left) shows an example of a transition area. In addition to a transition area, we also include a trigger area (smaller inner red boxes in Figure 2) that is placed on one side of the transition area. The trigger area helps to distinguish when someone actually crosses the area and the direction of travel (Figure 5). Figure 3 shows a transition example. If a transition area has been empty for 3 previous frames (≈ 0.6 seconds), when a person walks into the transition area, this signals the beginning of a transition sequence. Detection is achieved using previous frame background subtraction using a static threshold. A sequence is ended if there is no activity close to the trigger area (60 cm) for 3 consecutive frames. Transitions are assumed to take a minimum of 0.25 seconds. With the non-active frames buffering the front or back of the image sequence, about 0.25 seconds in duration, we assume any sequence shorter than 5 frames (≈ 1.0 seconds) is not a valid transition.

We found this method of delimiting sequences works well. The previous frame background subtraction, in particular, is useful for discarding spurious transition sequences. People loitering within the transition areas are usually relatively stationary. Movement will activate the sequence, but since they are not moving significantly, they quickly disappear as part of the background causing the sequence to end quickly. A loiterer typically generates multiple sequences less than the minimum 5 frames. Sudden flashes of light are adapted to quickly and the perceived sequences are typically shorter than the minimum 5 frame sequence.

4.3.3 Sequence Feature Vectors

Next, we define how to construct a feature vector from an image sequence, which will then be used with a KNN classifier to determine the best classification. Let $[f_0 \ldots f_n]$ denote a set of transition sequence frames, each f_i encoded as a binary matrix of size $w \times h$ where w and h are the width and height respectively. Thus, $f_0 \ldots f_n$ denotes the complete image transition sequence. Let c_i^j denote the ith column vector of f_j. We define the one dimensional image feature vector v where $v_i = \sum c_i$. By summing the columns we are removing the y axis locality of the person moving through the frame. A person transitioning at the top, middle, or bottom of a hallway will thus generate a similar image feature vector.

The number of people transitioning is also still retained. If two people walk side by side, the magnitude of the column vector will be roughly doubled.

In addition to creating a feature vector of the image sequence, we also create a feature vector of the trigger state. For each frame of the image sequence, we determine if the trigger area is active or not. The state of the trigger area is defined to be active when a certain threshold of pixels (5% for our deployment) differs from the corresponding background. For each frame of the transition sequence we determine the state of this trigger. A vector of the trigger states is incorporated into the KNN classification to determine the direction of the transition. Figure 5 shows how the sequence of the trigger state can be used to infer direction. A left to right sequence will have non-active trigger states at the beginning and end. A right to left sequence will have active trigger states only at the beginning.

While it would be possible to use the entire transition area as the feature vector, more data would be sent. If we assume a 10 image sequence, then each binary 20×40 transition area needs to be sent along with 10 bits for the trigger sequence. This would be $(20 \cdot 40) \cdot 10 + 10 = 8,010$ bits. If we were to send the feature vectors, we would only require $(20 \cdot 6) \cdot 10 + 10 = 1,210$ bits or ≈ 152 bytes for an entire sequence (6 bits per column, 10 bits for the trigger sequence). This can be roughly put in 2 packets using the node RF transceiver mentioned in Section 4.1. Further compression could be achieved by aggregating groups of columns. This along with other compression techniques are left for future work.

4.3.4 KNN Transition Classification

K-nearest neighbors is an effective classification technique when few labeled samples are available. We next define the distance metric between feature vectors.

Let $X = (x_1 \ldots x_m)$ and $Y = (y_1 \ldots y_n)$ be image feature vectors and $Xt = (xt_1 \ldots xt_m)$ and $Yt = (yt_1 \ldots yt_n)$ be the corresponding trigger feature vectors. If $m = n$, the distance between transition sequences is defined as follows,

$$d(X, Y, Xt, Yt) = \sum_i |x_i - y_i| + \alpha \sum_i |xt_i - yt_i| \quad (1)$$

where α is a weighting coefficient. This coefficient helps to favor samples with the correct direction. One issue with classification is the varying lengths of the transition sequences. Transition sequence length depends on how many people cross a transition area at walking speed. Rather than match only with transitions of equal length, we also consider sequences within $\pm 20\%$. If $m > n$ then the distance is defined as,

$$d(X, Y, Xt, Yt) = \underset{off}{\operatorname{argmin}} \sum_{i=off}^{m-off} |x_i - y_i| + \alpha \sum_{i=off}^{m-off} |xt_i - yt_i| \quad (2)$$

where off is an offset that minimizes the distance when the smaller vector subtracted from a subset of the larger vector. Next we define how we choose from the k nearest neighbors. Let $M = \{l_0 \cdots l_k\}$ be the set of k closest labeled matches and $D = \{d_0 \cdots d_k\}$ be the corresponding distances. Rather than classify based on the most frequent label of M, we weight each label l_i by $1/d_i$ and choose the label with the greatest summed weight.

4.4 OPTNet Evaluation

Next we evaluate the accuracy of the algorithm. For each boundary, we gathered 48 hours of ground truth transition sequence data. This data was gathered by manually examining the original images seen by OPTNet cameras and

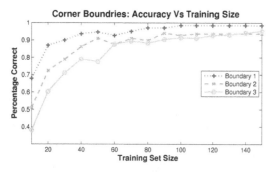

Figure 6: Overall accuracy over 24 hours as a function of training set size.

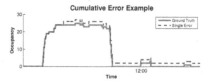

Figure 7: A single transition error continues to affect occupancy estimate.

hand labeling each transition sequence. The first 24 hours of ground truth is used for training. We trained each boundary area with 150 transition sequences taken from different periods of the day. The remaining 24 hours of ground truth is used for testing. For the weighting coefficient, we set $\alpha = 10$ after trying several weighting factors. While it would be preferable to gather data and test the system for different times of the year to examine the performance, we leave this as future work given the amount of time and effort required to gather ground truth data. We explored many different methods to help assist the gathering of ground truth data. Initially we used a state of the art technique that can count torsos and legs [24, 27, 18] to identify images that contain people but found this was only able to identify 80% of the images with people. Even the most advanced techniques are not completely accurate and need manual correction. We used a simple previous background subtraction technique to identify images that contain moving objects and manually processed these images.

In this section, we examine the directional and overall accuracy. We define directional accuracy as number of transitions where the direction is classified correctly divided by the total number of transitions. We define overall accuracy as the number of transitions where the direction <u>and</u> number of occupants are classified correctly divided by the total number of transitions. Figure 4 shows the transitions of two different boundary areas over the period of 24 hours. In both cases, we see that the classification of the KNN model is very close to the ground truth. In particular, we see that the directional error is very small. In the case of Hall 1, the directional accuracy was 98.3% and the overall accuracy was 92.4%. Corner 1 had 8 incorrect directions (5 false positive, 3 false negative) out of 110 detected transitions (92.7%) and an overall accuracy of 87.3%. For both cases, 150 training examples were used. We also found that KNN classifier had similar performance when applied to *different* transition areas using training data from *different* areas than the ones being tested. Figure 4 shows the accuracy when applying the classifier for a different transition area using 300 training examples. In this case we have a directional accuracy of 94.0% and an overall accuracy of 93.8%.

From a deployment perspective, a classifier can be substantially trained at a few transition areas and then applied to other boundaries without requiring excessive data gathering for training. Figure 6 shows the relationship between training set size and accuracy for Hall 1. We took a random subset of transitions from the training set and examined the overall accuracy over 24 hours. Only 90 samples (roughly 45 each direction) are required to achieve above 90% directional

accuracy. We found similar results for the other transition areas. Transition areas near corners or highly variable lighting tended to have lower accuracy. In these cases, additional training data would increase the accuracy as suggested by Figure 6. More generally, one wants to position transition areas where people are likely pass through and not loiter. We also found it helpful to choose areas with less changes of lighting; this cannot always be achieved since key transition points near exits must contain a transition area in order to capture the occupancy of areas. We also found that transition areas deployed in hallways performed better than transitions placed directly in front of doorways. This is because there is greater variation for the ways people transition through doorways. We also receive more and better quality training examples for transitions through hallways than for transitions directly in front of doors.

4.4.1 Occupancy Error

In order to evaluate the error of the system, we collected 15 days of ground truth occupancy data and compared it to the system estimate of occupancy. The ground truth was collected by examining all the images ($\approx 150,000$) captured by the system and manually annotating transitions between the different areas.

While the individual errors of the transitions are low, the effect of these errors is cumulative with respect to occupancy. Figure 7 shows the effect a single transition error has on occupancy. Some basic strategies can be employed to reduce the magnitude of this cumulative error such as assuming negative occupancies to be 0, imposing limits to maximum occupancy, or assuming building occupancy to be 0 early in the morning (4am). While this helps to reduce occupancy error, if a room has a positive occupancy bias, it is possible to have long stretches of time where a room is marked as occupied when it is empty, which has a significant impact on energy saving strategies. To address this issue, we use a PIR wireless network deployment to help identify empty rooms along with a particle filter.

5. BONET

Binary **O**ccupancy **Net**work (BONet) is a wireless sensor network of PIR sensors deployed in each office. Each node is comprised of a Tmote and PIR sensor (Figure 8). The sensing area of the node is approximately 11 m^2 when deployed at a hight of 3 m. For single offices, a single node provides adequate coverage. For larger areas such as the lab, multiple PIR sensors were used. The PIR sensor is sampled once per second and sends back the total number of triggers every minute. Data was collected using low power listening [7] and timestamped using Flooding Time Synchronization Protocol [23]. Out of the 34 nodes, 6 experienced false triggering due to calibration issues. However, 3 of these sensor were in the areas where redundant functional PIR sensors were available. Figure 9 shows the accuracy for one area. We found the system to have an accuracy of 94% for

Figure 8: PIR node deployed on ceiling

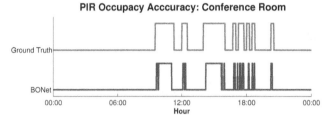

Figure 9: PIR accuracy compared with ground truth.

the 28 functional nodes when compared with ground truth data over a 48 hour period.

6. PARTICLE FILTER

We implemented a particle filter to improve the occupancy estimation. The particle filter algorithm is a nonparametric implementation of the Bayes filter [26]. The particle filter algorithm represents the posterior occupancy state of a certain number of rooms by a set of random state samples drawn from a predefined state transition model and assigns weights according to a measurement model representing the sensor accuracy. These random samples are called particles, which are used to estimate the distribution of the posterior state. Particles are defined as $X_t = x_t^1, x_t^2, \ldots x_t^M$ where, each particle x_t^m is a vector representing a set of N rooms. Each position in the vector represents a specific room occupancy; $x_t = [r_1, r_2, \ldots, r_N]$ where r_i is the room occupancy for room i.

Algorithm 1 shows the particle filter algorithm. Data from BONet is used as pre-processing step. If BONet senses a room is unoccupied and OPTNet indicates there is occupancy, then the room occupancy is assumed to be 0; BONet is more reliable than OPTNet for detecting empty rooms. We define OBNet as the combined the OPTNet and BONet system that fuses occupancy data as just described. The particle filter is initialized with the previous particle set X_{t-1} and the current processed sensor output z_t, coming from OBNet. Time t in the particle filter represents the current second of a day, starting at 1 second after midnight. M denotes the number of particles in the particle set X_t. In our experiments we tried various numbers of particles between $M = 50$ and $M = 1000$. For the results presented in this paper, we use $M = 100$ particles.

The particle filter algorithm consists of three major steps: 1. sampling from the transition model; 2. calculation of the particle weights; and 3. re-sampling.

The **sampling step** draws M samples from the transition model. The transition model is represented by a blended Markov Chain as described in [15] (see Appendix), where each state x_{t-1}^m can reach one possible successor state $\hat{x}_t^m$ with a certain probability $p(\hat{x}_t^m|x_{t-1}^m), m = 1 \ldots M$.

The **weight calculation step** assigns a specific weight $w_t^{m,n}$ to each value of each state given the estimation prob-

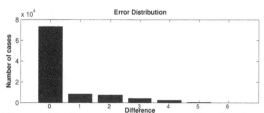

Figure 10: Sensor output error distribution.

Algorithm 1 ParticleFilter(X_{t-1}, z_t):

> **for** $m = 1$ to M **do**
> > sample $\hat{x}_t^m$ from TransitionModel(x_{t-1}^m, t)
> > add $\hat{x}_t^m$ to $\hat{X}_t$
> > **for** $n = 1$ to N **do**
> > > get $w_t^{m,n}$ from Measurement($z_t^n, \hat{x}_t^{m,n}$)
> > **end for**
> **end for**
> $\bar{w}_t^{m,n} = $ Normalize($w_t^{m,n}$), $m = 1 \ldots M, n = 1 \ldots N$
> **for** $n = 1$ to N **do**
> > draw x_t^m with probability $\bar{w}_t^{m,n}$ from $\hat{X}_t, \forall m \in M$
> > add x_t^m to X_t
> **end for**
> return X_t

---

ability $\hat{x}_t^{m,n}$ under the sensor measurement z_t^n, for a specific particle m of room n. In our case, the weight $w_t^{m,n}$ is determined by the measurement model, which is a distribution of the difference between the occupancy ground truth and the occupancy value of the processed sensor output of the training data (see Figure 10).

The weight $w_t^{m,n}$ of a specific particle is now determined by calculating the absolute difference between the model estimation $\hat{x}_t^{m,n}$ and the processed sensor output occupancy value z_t^n; $x_{tDiff}^{m,n} = \hat{x}_t^{m,n} - z_t^n$. Based on the previously created distribution, the weight $w_t^{m,n}$ of room n in particle m is now determined by dividing the number of cases of difference $x_{tDiff}^{m,n}$ by the total number of cases. For example, the observed number of cases with a difference of $x_{tDiff}^{m,n} = 1$ between ground truth and processed sensor output is 5240 out of 864k cases, which is a weight of 0.06. This is done for every room n within each state m of the transition model.

The **re-sampling step** draws with replacement M samples from the temporary particle set $\hat{X}_t$. Each estimation is drawn with probability weight $w_t^{m,n}$. This method of re-sampling transforms the temporary particle set $\hat{X}_t$ into another particle set X_t. By considering the weight of each estimated occupancy value in this step, the result is a different distribution since duplicates of values with a higher weight $w_t^{m,n}$ are more likely to be part of the new distribution than values with a lower weight. The final result is a matrix where each column represents a distribution of the occupancy of a specific room. We obtain the final occupancy state $CurrOcc$ for a number of N rooms by averaging each column over all states of the final particle filter result X_t.

$$CurrOcc = \frac{\sum_{m=1}^{M} x_t^{m,n}}{M}, \forall n \in N \quad (3)$$

6.1 Particle Filter Results

Figure 11 shows the occupancy estimation by a particle filter, the direct sensor output of the OPTNet system. The ground truth shows a meeting in the conference room starting at about 10:30 am and ending at 11:50 am. The direct

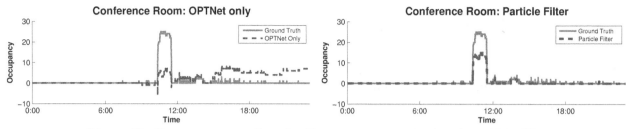

Figure 11: Occupancy over time for the raw sensor output and particle filter.

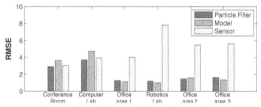

Figure 12: Occupancy error for 6 areas (2 weeks).

sensor output of the OPTNet system estimates shows negative occupancy near the beginning of the day, which persists until the meeting starts. Later in the day it overestimates the room occupancy, due to positive cumulative error. This happens between 15:00 and 00:00 when no one is in the room. This error can lead to energy waste if we were to use the direct sensor output of the OPTNet system alone.

The occupancy estimation of the particle filter, which uses the fused OBNet sensor data and transition model, correctly estimates occupancy at around 10:30 am. Further examination of these short occupancies show a janitor entering/leaving the room. The particle filter tended to show a lower prediction of occupancy than the actual ground truth for the 10:30 am to 11:50 am period. This is because the training data used for the model never experienced a large number of people and the sensor gives a lower occupancy number than the actual ground truth. This can be solved using an extended training set for the transition model.

We use root mean squared error (RMSE) to evaluate the occupancy estimation accuracy by the transition model, the OBNet sensor data and the particle filter. Figure 12 shows the RMSE for 6 different zones. For the conference room and the computer lab, the sensor is more accurate than the model; the sensor output is correcting the estimation of the transition model within the particle filter. For the office areas 1-3 and the robotics lab, the sensor output has a large error caused by transitional bias. The transition model for these rooms shows more accurate results and leads to a slightly better result than the particle filter. Here, the model estimation is correcting the sensor output within the particle filter. Since the error of the sensor is high in the case of office area 1-3 and the computer lab, it is possible that the estimation of the transition model alone is slightly better then the particle filter. The particle filter gave an average RMSE of 1.83 for our building.

7. ACTUATION SCHEDULER INTERFACE

The building being controlled utilizes both Automated Logic and Phoenix BMS systems [19, 6]. The system is maintained through a web server/interface called WebCtrl [19], which can issue BACnet commands to the various HVAC components including the variable air volume (VAV) unit. Since the sequence of operations are stored on this server, the building energy manager indicated that it would be prefer-

able to keep the logic of the system intact and change only the temperature/ventilation set-points within the server logic blocks rather than bypass the server and issue BACNet commands directly. Since the server could accept set-point changes via SOAP, we achieved control using python scripts.

7.1 Actuation Algorithm

As previously mentioned, near real-time occupancy is useful for accurate ventilation. However, occupancy prediction is necessary since time is required to reach the target temperature of a room. In order to determine the minimum time to reach a target temperature, determined the maximum amount of time it was required to reach set-point given the setbacks. Occupancy is predicted using the blended Markov Chain approach used in Section 6 (see Appendix). The main difference in application of the model is that predictions are done 1 hour in advance rather than the 1 second into the future done in for the particle filter. This is done since time is required in order for HVAC systems to react.

Algorithm 2 Actuation Algorithm
$CondTemp_{i,j} \leftarrow$ Room temp from time i to j
$CurrHour \leftarrow$ Current hour
$T_{TG} \leftarrow$ Temperature such that $PMV = 0$
$T_{ASH} \leftarrow$ Temperature such that $-0.5 < PMV < 0.5$
$pThresh \leftarrow$ Probability threshold of occupancy
$BMC(CurrOcc, predLen)$
Returns probability vector when occupancy is likely
$ThermalDelay \leftarrow$ Time to reach T_{TG} given T_{ASH}
- Program Start -
for Every n minutes **do**
$CurrOcc \leftarrow$ Current Particle Filter estimate of occupancy
$occPred \leftarrow BMC(CurrOcc, predLen)$
for Each room r and point of time t in $occPred$ **do**
$occupied \leftarrow$ Periods $occPred_{t \to t+60} > pThresh$
if $occupied > 5$ minutes of next 15 minutes **then**
$CondTemp_{t-ThermalDelay, t+15} = T_{TG}$
else if $5 \le CurrHour \le 24$ **then**
$CondTemp_{i,i} = T_{ASH}$
end if
end for
end for

Before we discuss actuation, we must first discuss American Society of Heating, Refrigerating and Air-Conditioning (ASHRAE) standards for thermal comfort. ASHRAE Standard 55 [9] uses the predicted mean vote (PMV) metric to establish levels for occupant comfort. This metric incorporates multiple parameters such as humidity and airflow to estimate occupant comfort on a continuous scale from -3 to 3, where negative values indicate slightly cool to cold (-1 to -3) and slightly warm to hot (1 to 3). The optimal temperature corresponds to PMV = 0. ASHRAE states that acceptable room conditions are temperatures such that $-0.7 \leq PMV \leq 0.7$. For our deployment we choose more conservative temperatures where $-0.5 \leq PMV \leq 0.5$.

Algorithm 2 shows how we combine the current occupancy determined by the particle filter, predicted occupancy determined by the transition model, and the estimated thermal ramping time (estimated from historical data) in order to schedule when to begin conditioning. There are two temperature set-points; T_{TG} and T_{ASHRAE}, which are the target and ASHRAE set-points respectively. The algorithm purpose is to change these set-points optimally based on room usage. Every n minutes (15 minutes for our deployment) we check the current occupancy state of the rooms. We then make a prediction $predLen$ (60 minutes) into the future using the transition model. We examine each the predicted occupancy probability for each room. If we find a window of time where the room will be occupied 5 minutes out of the next 15 minutes, we use the experimentally determined thermal delay (time required to reach the target temperature), and schedule the set-point to the target temperature. Otherwise, we condition to the ASHRAE set-point. This ensures the room will be at a reasonable temperature if a prediction is false.

8. POEM SYSTEM EVALUATION

There are two aspects of the system to be examined. The first is that rooms are conditioned appropriately given actual occupancy usage. The second is to determine how much energy could be saved when applying the strategy to the floor of a building.

We tested two versions of POEM in a live deployment. The first strategy uses only PIR for occupancy detection and the same actuation using binary occupancy data. PIR data does not have issues with cumulative error, hence a particle filter is not used. Since PIR cannot determine how many people are in an area, ventilation control is done assuming maximum occupancy; an occupied room is assumed to be fully occupied. This is equivalent to baseline ventilation strategy. This is common practice since HVAC designers and building managers tend to be over cautious with respect to ventilation. Indeed we found many areas that were over-ventilated with respect to even maximum occupancy. The second strategy uses OBNet (Camera and PIR data) along with the particle filter. Ventilation in this case is done according to ASHRAE 62.1 [10]. Each strategy was tested for two weeks for 16 zones (2 AHUs), accounting for 30% of the area that the AHUs condition. Approximately 52 people occupy these areas and occupants in the area were informed of the camera use with the experiments and the data collected during our experiments has been handled following best practices [5, 2].

Table 1 shows size of each zone and how long each zone takes to get to temperature from the setback temperature.

To evaluate the performance of the system over the course of a year, we developed a calibrated EnergyPlus [3] simulation that closely matches the performance of the actual building. This was done using 6 weeks of historical data from the building from different seasons; 2 weeks Fall, 2 weeks Winter, 2 weeks Summer. Each day was compared with a similar day from the EnergyPlus simulation with respect to weather/temperature. On average, the EnergyPlus simulation had a normalized RMSE of 6.2%. With a calibrated model, we are able to accurately determine the per-

	Area	Ramping Duration
Conference Room	40 m^2	45 min
Office Area 1-9	36 m^2	30 min
Computer Lab	111 m^2	60 min
Conference Room	40 m^2	30 min
Dean's Conference Room	52 m^2	30 min
Robotics Lab	18 m^2	30 min

Table 1: Zone information for deployment. The Ramping duration is the time required to reach the target temperature from the setback temperature.

formance of these strategies under exactly the same conditions; without a model, we would be required to run each system for potentially years for enough data for a valid comparison. Using the calibrated model, we test four different strategies. Two strategies tested are the same PIR and Camera/PIR strategies as the live deployment. In addition, we test a reactive strategy where rooms are conditioned immediately once occupied without predictive temperature ramp up. Similar to the predictive PIR approach, we assume maximum occupancy when the room is occupied for ventilation purposes. The last strategy is an "Oracle" strategy, where we condition the space assuming perfect prediction and perfect measurement of occupancy. The oracle strategy gives us an upper bound of the energy savings that is possible if the Camera/PIR system were to run with perfect information.

8.1 Energy Savings

Our building is conditioned from a centralized chilled water tower and boiler systems. The chilled water tower stores water within a tank large enough for stratification to occur; warmer water naturally rises to the top and cold water falls the bottom of the tank. Cold water is supplied by pumping water at the bottom of the tank. Additional cooling is supplied to the tank as necessary. The hot water is supplied by several hot water boilers. The chilled water tower boilers supply the hot/cold water to air handler units (AHU) and variable air volume units (VAV) for heating and cooling. The AHU is used for air cooling the air. The VAV units are used for heating and regulating cool air to individual zones. This is done by using a damper to regulate the air volume that passes over heating/cooling coils. For our deployment, we are interested in how much energy the VAV units and AHUs are consuming.

The amount of energy lost/gained by the coil is equal to the amount of energy lost/gained by the air. We can estimate the energy consumed by a VAV or AHU using the heat balance equation $Q = mC(T_{sa} - T_{da})$, where Q is energy transferred to the air, m is the total mass of the airflow over an interval of time, C is the heat capacity of air, T_{sa} is supply air temperature, T_{da} is the discharge temperature of the air after passing through the coil. By measuring the airflow and the supply and discharge temperatures, we can calculate the energy consumed.

8.2 Live Deployment Results

The baseline strategy of the building is a static schedule where the room HVAC system (temperature/ventilation) is turned on at 6 am and then shut off at 1 am the next day. From 1 am to 6 am, room temperatures "float". In order to measure the amount of energy consumed by the baseline strategy, we measure the energy consumption of the system without POEM running. Days with similar weather and temperature profile are used for the baseline comparison.

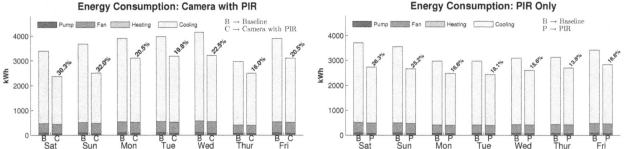

Figure 13: Energy consumption breakdown for 7 representative days. PIR and camera/PIR based POEM saves on average 21.1% to 26.0% respectively.

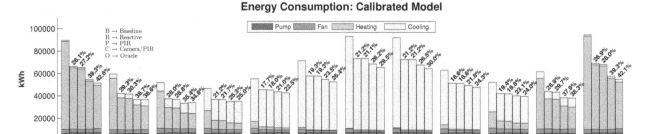

Figure 14: Energy consumption based on calibrated energy simulation. On average PIR and Camera based strategies save 24.5% and 31.0% annually respectively.

Figure 13 shows energy savings and breakdown for one particular week for both strategies. The left and right bar for each day shows the baseline and strategy breakdown respectively. Above each strategy, we show the percentage savings over the adjacent baseline bar. Since the experiments were conducted during the summer, no zone required heating. In general, the energy from the supply and return fans along with the hot/cold water pump remained fairly constant. Overall PIR and Camera/PIR saved on average 21.1% and 26.0% respectively. For both strategies, the most savings occurred on the weekend where many zones were unoccupied. For weekends, the PIR only strategy saved 25.1%-27.5% and the Camera/PIR strategy saved 30.2%-32.0%. On the weekdays, PIR saved 13.8%-18.0% and the Camera/PIR strategy saved 16.0%-22.5%. For areas that are consistently occupied with regular schedules, the savings were achieved by turning off the system earlier than the 1 am shutoff time, or delaying the ramp-up in the morning. The difference between these strategies is due to ventilation rate. Since the Camera/PIR strategy is able to reduce ventilation rates, this strategy is able to save more energy than predictive PIR strategy. For other areas not consistently occupied, such as the conference room, energy savings were possible in the morning where the temperature ramp-up could be delayed and in the evening when the room was unoccupied.

The Camera/PIR strategy saves more energy since ventilation is based on the number of people whereas the PIR only strategy ventilates based on the maximum occupancy. Ventilation has a significant impact on energy consumption since increasing ventilation increases the amount of outside air to be condition. This is similar to trying to cool a house down on a hot summer day with the front door open.

8.3 Calibrated Model Results

As previously mentioned we also test four different strategies using the calibrated model. Figure 14 show the energy savings and breakdown for each strategy. When we compare the live results to the calibrated model results, we see similar energy savings for the periods of similar weather. For the predictive conditioning, we saw 21.1% average savings for live deployment and see 19.3% for the calibrated model. We also see a similar difference between the PIR and Camera/PIR strategies for the calibrated model as compared with the live deployment. For the live deployment we saw difference of 4.9% (Camera/PIR 26.0% vs PIR 21.1%); the calibrated model showed a difference of 4.2%. These results supports our initial results (normalized RMSE of 6.2% between model and historical results) and that our calibrated model is able to accurately measure energy differences between strategies.

When comparing the predictive PIR and reactive PIR strategies, we see similar results; we only see a maximum difference of 1.1% during the coldest months (Dec, Jan). A priori one would expect the predictive strategy to use slightly more energy since it conditions spaces over longer periods of time due to the fact that is trying to anticipate expected occupancy (i.e. load). Interestingly, the predictive PIR has slightly higher energy savings. The predictive PIR indeed conditions a larger total amount of time than the reactive PIR strategy; on average the predictive PIR conditions on average 1.2 hours more per day per room compared with reactive PIR. However, the temperature differential from the initial to the final conditions for any period of occupancy is on average smaller for predictive than the reactive strategy. On average the temperature difference between the target and actual room temperature when occupants initially occupy a room is approximately 0.08 C^o (0.15 F^o) for predictive PIR and 1.7 C^o (3.0 F^o) for reactive PIR. The reactive strategy has to work harder to ramp up the room temperatures between periods of occupancy; in some cases, it is more energy efficient to maintain temperature than to ramp up temperatures from a very low level. As we'll see in the

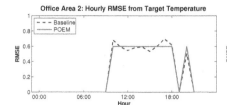 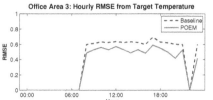 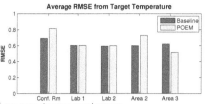

Figure 15: RMSE (F°) between the target and observed room temperatures

following section, this also dramatically impacts temperature effectiveness as perceived by the building's occupants.

The predictive PIR and the Camera/PIR strategies show 24.5% and 31.0% annually respectively, with the largest savings occurring during the coldest months. The main cause of this difference is the ventilation. We also see how ventilation plays a major role in the energy savings when comparing the Camera/PIR strategy to the Oracle strategy. In general the predicted schedules from the Camera/PIR strategies closely match the Oracle strategies (3% difference). One major difference, which is discussed in more detail in section 8.4, is that the Camera/PIR has additional ventilation added in order to account for possible errors in the occupancy count. When comparing Oracle and Camera/PIR results, we see that the Oracle saves 33.0% whereas Camera/PIR saves 31.0%. Further analysis of the energy traces shows that this difference is indeed due to over-ventilation by the later due to the small uncertainty in occupancy (i.e. a safe guard band added it by design to cope for potential undercounting). This can be seen in Figure 17 where we see that the PIR/Camera strategy is above the required ventilation rate for the majority of the time.

8.4 Conditioning Effectiveness

In this section, we examine the conditioning performance of POEM. We are interested how close operational temperatures were to the target temperature during times of occupancy and how effectively we could reduce ventilation rates using occupancy.

To evaluate the thermal effectiveness of POEM, we calculate the root mean squared error (RMSE) between the target temperature and the observed room temperature during the periods of when the room is occupied. For this analysis, we will only examine the Camera/PIR strategy as we only gathered ground truth data for the days of the Camera/PIR deployment. It is difficult and time consuming to process ground truth and was too labor intensive to process additional days. In order to have a basis of comparison, we also consider the ability of the baseline strategy to meet target temperatures. In most cases, the baseline temperature deviates approximately 0.6 C° (1 F°) from the target temperature. This is expected as the proportional-integral-derivative (PID) controller of the VAV will cause the temperature to oscillate with a small amplitude from the target temperature. Figure 15 shows the overall RMSE for each room. Of particular interest is the temperature of the conference room as this room does not have a consistent schedule and most likely to deviate from target temperatures. In this case, the RMSE of POEM is on average 0.25 C° (0.45 F°) whereas the average RMSE of the baseline strategy is 0.21 C° (0.38 F°). As this is only a difference of about 0.07 C° (0.12 F°), we can see that the conditioning effectiveness of POEM is close to baseline. This room tended to be farther from the target temperature for both baseline and POEM strategies since the conference room has two exterior

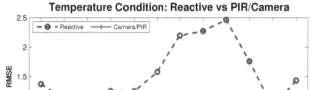

Figure 16: RMSE (F°) between the target and observed room temperatures from the calibrated model.

walls and receives solar gain. For areas with regular schedules, we found POEM's ability to condition comparable to the baseline strategy; in most cases, the difference between POEM and baseline RMSE is less than 0.06 C° (0.1 F°).

In addition to the actual results we also examined the thermal effectiveness of the reactive and Camera/PIR strategies from the calibrated model. Figure 16 shows the RMSE for each strategy for the conference room. The Camera/PIR has substantially better performance than the reactive approach; the Camera/PIR approach has an average RMSE of 0.52 C° (0.93 F°) whereas the reactive approach has an average RMSE of 0.83 C° (1.5 F°). This is expected since time is required for rooms to ramp to the target temperature. This is especially true during the warmer months where solar gain can greatly affect the ability of the HVAC system to meet load. During these months (Jun-Sept), the RMSE of the reactive system is 0.83-1.33 C° (1.5-2.4 F°), which can easily be perceived by occupants. Thus, the Camera/PIR approach is better able to meet the target temperatures.

ASHRAE standard 62.1 [10] requires the outdoor ventilation to be $V_{bz} = R_p P_z + R_a A_z$ where z denotes the zone, V_{bz} is the ventilation rate, R_p is the minimum CFM (1 CFM = 1 ft^3/min) per person, P_z is the number of people, R_a is the minimum CFM/ft^2, and A_z is the floor area. R_a and R_p changes depending on the target use of the room as specified by the ASHRAE 62.1 standard. This standard is for areas without a demand ventilation system. For our rooms, the required CFM per person is 5. Examining Figure 17, we can see that a typical baseline ventilation strategy is far more inefficient than POEM. Office 1 under-ventilated 1%. During these periods of under-ventilation, the average under-ventilation was 2.5 CFM. As 5 CFM is required per person, the magnitude of the under-ventilation is not large. The lab is theoretically under-ventilated an average of 2.98 CFM 4.8% of the time. When examining the actual CO_2 levels, we found the areas were properly ventilated. In order to evaluate proper ventilation, we examine the CO_2 levels with respect to the ASHRAE 62.1 demand response ventilation standards. This standard states 925 ppm is considered acceptable for office spaces. Figure 17 shows the CO_2 levels

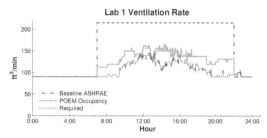

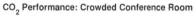

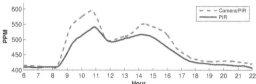

Figure 17: Ventilation and CO_2 levels

for the most densely occupied area in the deployment, which is the conference room. For the day shown, several groups meet back-to-back. From the figure we can see that the levels never exceed 925 ppm showing that adequate ventilation is being provided. We can also see that the Camera/PIR strategy has slightly higher levels since the strategy provides less ventilation, but is well under the threshold (600 ppm vs 925 ppm). This suggests the ventilation provided by the previous equation is above what is actually required.

9. RETURN ON INVESTMENT ANALYSIS

In this section, we use our results in order to estimate whether deploying POEM is economically viable. We extrapolate our results to the entire building, which contains a base area of 6,689 m^2 and is primarily used for research labs and offices. The building has an annual energy consumption for conditioning of 5,275,992 kWh electrical power and 246,000 therms of gas. The cost for electrical energy depends on the time of a day and season, it is usually between $0.13 and $0.18 per kWh, the price for gas is constant over the year at $0.7 per therm of gas. All these prices are special rates negotiated with a utility company. For reference, the same company charges $0.34 and $0.22 per kWh for residential and commercial customers. For an average price of $0.15 per kWh electrical power and $0.7 per therm gas the annual conditioning costs of the mentioned building are $963,598.80. One node of our system consists of the components listed in Table 1, which sums up to a price of $710 for camera and $215 for PIR nodes. This cost can be reduced through commercial production.

We estimate that each node costs $35 to deploy, and $8k is required for testing the system. For a 3 story 6,689 m^2 building, about 65 camera nodes and 360 PIR nodes are required to provide complete coverage. Therefore manufacturing and deploying the system would cost approximately $147k. Savings of 26% of $963k equals to $250k per year or $20.8k per month. The largest ongoing cost for our system is battery maintenance. A conservative estimation of the energy consumption of a camera node is about 80mW; with three battery packs with a capacity of 11 Ah each, the battery packs have to be exchanged and recharged every 60 days. Since the energy consumption of a PIR node is low compared to a camera node, a PIR node is able to run 175 days on one battery pack rather than 60 days. This results in a maintenance cost of about $30 per camera node per

Table 2: Prices of camera and PIR nodes

Component	Price	Component	Price
Imote2	$350	Tmote	$120
IMB 400	$250	PIR sensor	$30
Batteries	$100	Batteries	$60
Fisheye lens	$5	Assemble (10 min)	$5
Assemble (10 min)	$5		
	$710		$215

year and about $10 per PIR node per year. For the whole 65 camera and 360 PIR node system, this would cost $5,500 for maintenance each year. Depending on the market price for energy, the manufacturing and deployment costs of our system would be amortized between 6.1 and 8 months. The energy savings of a system with PIR sensors only are about 21.1%. This would result in an average amount of $203k for energy savings and an amortization time between 4.8 and 6.4 months due to the reduced system costs of $94k and maintenance costs and $3,800 per year. As shown in Figure 18, a system consisting of only PIR sensors has a shorter amortization time compared to a system with camera and PIR sensors. Since buildings are usually operated for many years (70-75 years [1]), in the long term, a combination of camera and PIR sensors always achieves higher savings.

These results also show that despite the extra work of adding cameras, the savings are significant to justify the additional effort. This is due to the magnitude of the money currently spent on energy. Though the difference of the energy savings between PIR and Camera/PIR is only 5%, this still constitutes a non-trivial amount of money. For perspective, over a 5 year period, the Camera/PIR system saves approximately $140k-$200k more than PIR alone (see Figure 18). Over the average lifetime of the building, which is approximately 70 years, the system can potentially save $15.0M to $20.0M.

10. LESSONS LEARNED

We found that deploying, testing, verifying the performance of the system to be extremely difficult. For the camera system testbed, a customized Imote2 debug board was designed and manufactured for each of the 22 cameras. For the PIR sensors, 40 nodes had to be hand "manufactured" and deployed after negotiating with facilities, staff and students. In particular, facilities required us to have CO_2 monitoring before we could proceed. In order to achieve this, we developed a wireless network of 10 CO_2 nodes using Tmotes and CO_2 sensor boards.

One of the most time consuming part was the processing of ground truth data. We tried multiple techniques to speed up the processing of the image data. Initially, we tried using state-of-the art techniques that counted torsos and legs [24, 27, 18] in order to detect the presence of humans. We found even the best techniques were only about 80% accurate and in the end found background subtraction a much more reliable method of identifying images with occupants. We also tried various types static background techniques but found that when people loitered of left static objects such as chair and boxes, this would dramatically increase the number of images needed to be manually examined. The most effective method we found for detecting transitions is similar to the one presented previously. We use previous frame background subtraction in order to identify images where objects are moving and then manually process this data. After applying this technique to the images, each camera produces 1000-3000 images per day that potentially contains transi-

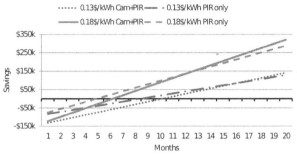
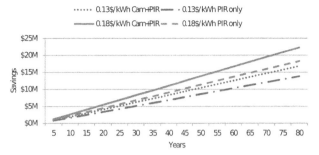

Figure 18: The left compares savings for different energy prices. The right shows savings over 80 year period.

tions. Processing the ground truth required examining approximately 150,000 images.

Despite having deployed in a new building with a BMS, we experience multiple difficulties with regards to instrumentation. For several zones, we found that during construction, temperature sensors were left out of VAV boxes. This required us to deploy commercial wireless temperature sensors so we could measure the exhaust air temperature; this was accomplished by examining the plans, locating the VAV boxes, obtaining permission from facilities to install sensors, and physically drilling duct holes and mounting the sensors. Calibration of the duct flow sensors was also an issue. While testing the system, we found the AHU flow measurements to be faulty with respect to other air flows measurements. For several months, multiple calibrations were performed and some flow sensors had to be replaced by facilities. Flow sensor measurements need to be verified prior to deployments.

11. CONCLUSIONS

In this paper, our main contribution is the design and implementation of POEM, a close loop system that conditions rooms based on occupancy on a real production building. POEM uses two wireless sensor networks; one network of cameras called OPTNet, and another network of PIR sensors called BONet. We showed that OPTNet is capable of detecting transitions with up to 94% accuracy and that the system is able to generalize to different locations. Combined with BONet and a particle filter, we can bound the error of occupancy within 1.83 people on average for our building. By opportunistically controlling the HVAC system based on occupancy, we showed savings of 26.0% are possible while maintaining conditioning effectiveness. Using a calibrated model, we estimate that $\approx$ 30% savings are possible annually. Given the cost of heating and cooling, we show that these savings would amortize the POEM system within about 6 to 10 months. This work is an initial foray into designing sensor networks for smart sustainable buildings. By providing greater value from the same physical plant, our approach can move beyond cost-to-build and cost-to-operate metrics to broader return-on-investment for new technologies.

12. ACKNOWLEDGMENTS

Special thanks to Ankur Kamthe and Tao Liu for valuable discussions on several aspects of the system, UCM Facilities for giving us access the BMS for control/experimentation with a live building, occupants for allowing us to test control strategies while they were working on their daily routines, anonymous reviewers for their insightful feedback, and Silvia Santini for shepherding this paper. This material is based upon work partially supported by the National Science Foundation under grants #0923586 and #1254192 and the Center for Information Technology Research in the Interest of Society under grants #SPF-81 and #SPF-165.

13. REFERENCES

[1] *2010 Building Energy Data Book*. U.S. Dept. of Energy.
[2] *Directive 95/46/EC of the European Parliament and of the Council of 24 October 1995 on the protection of individuals with regard to the processing of personal data and on the free movement of such data*. The European Parliament and the Council of the European Union.
[3] Energyplus - Building Energy Analysis Tool. http://apps1.eere.energy.gov/buildings/energyplus/.
[4] Intelmote2 and IMB 400 sensor board. http://www.memsic.com/.
[5] *OECD Guidelines on the Protection of Privacy and Transborder Flows of Personal Data*. Organization for Economic Cooperation and Development.
[6] Phoenix controls. www.phoenixcontrols.com/.
[7] TEP105: Low Power Listening. http://www.tinyos.net/tinyos-2.x/doc/html/tep105.html.
[8] Trueview people counter. http://www.cognimatics.com/.
[9] ASHRAE standard 55: Thermal environmental conditions for human occupancy. ASHRAE,Inc., 2004.
[10] ASHRAE standard 62.1: Ventilation for acceptable indoor air quality. ASHRAE,Inc., 2007.
[11] Y. Agarwal, B. Balaji, S. Dutta, R. Gupta, and T. Weng. Duty-cycling buildings aggressively: The next frontier in HVAC control. In *IPSN*, 2011.
[12] H. Bay, A. Ess, T. Tuytelaars, and L. V. Gool. SURF: Speeded up robust features. In *CVIU*, 2008.
[13] V. Erickson and A. Cerpa. Occupancy based demand response HVAC control strategy. In *BuildSys*, 2010.
[14] V. Erickson, Y. Lin, A. Kamthe, R. Brahme, A. Cerpa, M. Sohn, and S. Narayanan. Energy efficient building environment control strategies using real-time occupancy measurements. In *BuildSys*, 2009.
[15] V. L. Erickson, M. Á. Carreira-Perpiñán, and A. E. Cerpa. OBSERVE: Occupancy-based system for efficient reduction of HVAC energy. In *IPSN'11*.
[16] W. Fisk, D. Faulkner, and D. Sullivan. Accuracy of CO2 sensors in commercial buildings: a pilot study. Technical report, LBNL, 2006.
[17] A. Kamthe, L. Jiang, M. Dudys, and A. Cerpa. SCOPES: Smart cameras object position estimation system. In *EWSN'09*.
[18] R. Lienhart and J. Maydt. An extended set of haar-like features for rapid object detection. In *Image Processing. 2002. Proceedings. 2002 International Conference on*, volume 1, pages I–900–I–903 vol.1, 2002.
[19] A. Logic. http://www.automatedlogic.com/.
[20] D. Lowe. Object recognition from local scale-invariant features. In *ICCV*, 1999.
[21] J. Lu, T. Sookoor, V. Srinivasan, G. Gao, B. Holben, J. Stankovic, E. Field, and K. Whitehouse. The smart

Acoustic Shockwave-Based Bearing Estimation

János Sallai, Péter Völgyesi, Ákos Lédeczi, Ken Pence, Ted Bapty, Sandeep Neema,
James Davis
Institute for Software Integrated Systems
Vanderbilt University
Nashville, TN, USA
akos.ledeczi@vanderbilt.edu

ABSTRACT

The paper presents a smartphone-based shooter localization system. As muzzle blasts are difficult to detect at longer distances and consequently present higher false detection rates, the system relies on shockwaves only. Each sensor uses four microphones to detect the Angle of Arrival and the length of the shockwave. This information, along with the sensor's own GPS coordinates, are shared among nearby smartphones. Assuming a known weapon type, it then proceeds to estimate the two possible projectile trajectory candidates for each sensor that are consistent with the observations in the horizontal plane of the sensors. A simple clustering algorithm identifies the correct projectile trajectory relying on as few as two sensors. The trajectory is then used to estimate the bearing to the shooter relative to each sensor. The paper presents the overall system architecture, the design of the sensor node that interfaces with the smartphone, the trajectory and bearing estimation algorithms, and the evaluation of the system based on a field experiment.

Categories and Subject Descriptors

C.2.4 [**Computer-Communications Networks**]: Distributed Systems; J.7 [**Computers in Other Systems**]: Military

General Terms: Design, Measurement, Performance

Keywords: Sensor networks, data fusion, acoustic source localization, shooter localization

Acknowledgments: The activities described in this paper have been supported by the DARPA Transformative Apps program. We are grateful for the contributions of the Nashville Metro Police Training Academy and DataBouy, LLC. We would like to thank the anonymous reviewers and our shepherd, Andreas Andreou, for the helpful comments that greatly improved the quality of the paper.

1. INTRODUCTION

A decade after the first prototype wireless sensor network-based acoustic shooter localization system was reported in the technical literature [14], there is still no deployed or commercially available system that utilizes a network of sensors. The state-of-the-art is still a standalone unit. The reluctance of the military to embrace a wireless solution is understandable since they require any deployed networking technology to be certified and secure. The current communications infrastructure simply does not lend itself to supporting low cost wearable networked sensors. However, a recent development promises to alleviate this problem. The DARPA Transformative Apps program is built around the idea that every soldier will carry a military certified smartphone in the near future. In addition to a number of innovative military apps, a common middleware platform, called AMMO for Android Mobile Middleware Objects, is being developed that will support a variety of communication protocols [19]. The communication needs of a networked shooter localization system will be easily supported by AMMO. The caveat is that the system will have to be based on smartphones.

The typical smartphone has all the components required by acoustic shooter localization: an audio channel, processing capabilities, wireless communications, GPS, and a display. In fact, it would be possible to build a shooter localization app, but the design tradeoffs and the closed nature of the hardware platform would result in subpar performance. First, the maximum sampling rate of the audio channel (48 kHz) would be satisfactory, but the audio stream is typically preprocessed by the on-board codec chip (noise reduction, filtering, etc.), erasing and distorting important signal features, especially the sharp rising edge of the shock wave. Also, most people carry their phones in their pockets or bags making acoustic event detection nearly impossible. Second, the low-cost GPS solutions in phones contain too large of positioning errors for shooter localization where sensor positions need to be known with about a meter accuracy [8]. Third, time synchronization is typically a must for networked source localization. However, application programs running on top of smartphone OSs do not have access to precise global time in spite of the availability of GPS. Also, the exact sampling times of individual audio samples are unavailable, as well, because of the unknown delays and jitter associated with the hardware (ADC, codec, I/O bus) and the software (kernel drivers, I/O and task scheduling, etc.). The solution is to build a sensor that offloads the detection, self-localization, and time synchronization tasks from the phone. (Note that our system ended up not needing time synchronization, but this was unknown at the time of hardware design, and a precise GPS was needed in any case.) Such a sensor can have its own microphone(s), sample at a higher rate, and run the shot event detection algorithm. It only needs to notify the phone when an event detection was made. The event can be tagged with its relevant features, such as Time of Arrival (TOA), length, etc., as well as the corresponding sensor location. The sensor-phone interface can be either Bluetooth or USB. The rest of the paper presents the design, implementation and evaluation of such a system.

2. RELATED WORK

Acoustic shooter localization has a long and rich history. Here we only summarize the results that are most relevant to our work.

When the typical rifle is fired, two acoustic events are generated: the muzzle blast and shockwave. The muzzle blast is associated with the explosion that occurs in the barrel of the gun that ejects the projectile through the muzzle at a high speed. When this speed is supersonic – true for the vast majority of rifles – the projectile generates an acoustic wavefront called a shockwave. This wavefront has a conical shape. The axis of the cone is the trajectory of the bullet. The angle is determined by the ratio of the speed of the bullet to the speed of sound (also called the Mach number). Being an acoustic phenomenon, the wavefront itself propagates at the speed of sound.

Figure 1 illustrates the shockwave propagation. Shooter **S** fires a bullet along the trajectory **SA**. Microphone **M** detects the shockwave front after a certain amount of time. This is the sum of the time the projectile needed to cover the distance **SA** at its supersonic speed and the time it takes for the shockwave to cover the **AM** distance, also called slant range, at the speed of sound. The distance **BM** is called the closest point of approach (CPA) or miss distance. It is worthwhile to note that in reality, the projectile constantly decelerates, so the section of the shockwave front shown in the figure is not a straight line, but slowly curves with the angle α continuously increasing. Finally, the muzzle blast travels the SM distance at the speed of sound (not shown in the figure).

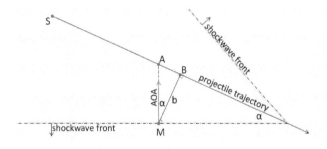

Figure 1: The geometry of a shockwave generated by a supersonic projectile originating at point S and observed at point M.

The signal shape of a shockwave is highly characteristic. It resembles the letter N with sub microsecond rise times and typical lengths of 100 to 600 microseconds. An empirical formula called the Whitham's equation [18], relates the shockwave length T to the CPA b, the Mach number M, the speed of sound c, and the projectile diameter (caliber) d and length l:

$$T = \frac{1.82Mb^{1/4}}{c(M^2-1)^{3/8}}\frac{d}{l^{1/4}} \approx \frac{1.82d}{c}\left(\frac{Mb}{l}\right)^{1/4} \qquad (1)$$

Recently, Sallai et al. rearranged Whitham's equation by grouping together most parameters into a scaling factor k [12]:

$$b \approx kT^4 \qquad (2)$$

They observed that multiple sensors detecting the same shot will necessarily have to have the same k (assuming a constant bullet speed near the sensors). They showed that measuring the shockwave length at multiple sensors is sufficient to estimate the trajectory of the projectile [12]. Interestingly, k also falls out of the solution providing accurate caliber estimation and weapon classification.

Previously, Duckworth et al. described an approach where shockwave TOAs measured by at least six sensors (either six widely distributed omnidirectional microphones or two small arrays of three microphones each) is sufficient to accurately determine the trajectory of the projectile and an approximate range to the shooter [6]. If muzzle blasts are also available, the range accuracy greatly improves. They developed a very precise ballistic model to achieve remarkable accuracy. However, the method relies on empirically derived caliber- and sensor-specific parameters for sensitivity and frequency response, making calibration necessary. Accurate measurement of the peak amplitude of the shockwave is also needed. Since nearby trajectories generate high energy shocks, microphones are often overdriven by them. Barger et al. overcomes some of these problems by introducing an accelerometer-based sensor replacing microphones altogether [2]. However, it is not clear how sensitive these methods are to sensor location and time synchronization errors.

Damarla et al. and Lindgren et al. demonstrated an innovative technique that relies on TDOA of the shockwave and muzzle blast on the same nodes only. That means that time synchronization is no longer required in the network [5, 9]. The main disadvantage of the method is that the muzzle blast needs to be detected on each node. Sensors that only detect either the shockwave or the muzzle blast cannot participate in the fusion at all. Also, the technique requires a known projectile speed along the trajectory and is computationally expensive. Recently, Ash et al. quantified what effect a constant bullet speed assumption has on the accuracy in [1].

Volgyesi et al. presented a wireless sensor network-based system in [17]. It relies on measuring both muzzle blast and shockwave AOAs on each sensor and TDOAs across the sensors. A single sensor alone can locate the shooter if it detects both events on at least three microphones each. The network fusion localizes the trajectory and shooter position, estimates the weapon caliber, and classifies the weapon at a remarkable accuracy. The main disadvantage of the system is that it cannot handle longer range shots that pass on one side of the sensor field. The problem is that if only one side of the shockwave is measured, a large number of various trajectories could explain the TDOA observations. If there are not enough muzzle blast detections in the network, the trajectory and the shooter cannot be localized with their approach.

3. DESIGN MOTIVATORS

As we have seen in the previous section, most acoustic shooter localization systems rely on both the shockwave and the muzzle blast. Unfortunately, the muzzle blast is not nearly as characteristic an acoustic event as the shockwave. Moreover, the shockwave typically originates near the sensors as they are usually placed near the protected area, since this is presumably where the shot is targeted. Muzzle blasts, on the other hand, travel much longer distances. Consequently, their energy dissipates and the signal shape gets distorted. Muzzle blast detection beyond a hundred meters quickly becomes unreliable and makes the system prone to false detections. Finally, the muzzle blasts of friendly return fire would be picked up by the sensors and would make it impossible for the sensor fusion to sort through the numerous detections. The shockwave of a soldier's shot, on the other hand, does not even reach its own sensor because of the geometry.

Hence, the most important design decision was to make the system rely on shockwaves alone. While the numerous advantages of this were described above, it comes at a steep price. Most significantly, without the muzzle blast, the range to the shooter is impossible to estimate accurately. (More precisely, it is possible to estimate by measuring the curvature of the shockwave due to the deceleration of the projectile, but it would require larger microphone spacing than is practical in a wearable sensor.) Fortunately, the bearing to the shooter is considered far more valuable information for the warfighters than the range.

The second design motivator of the system was the requirement to provide useful information relying on as few sensors as possible. The obvious consequence of this was to opt for multi-channel sensors. Having a mini microphone array provides AOA information. Having the shockwave AOA and its length makes it possible to estimate the miss distance and characterize the wavefront (see Section 5). This is almost enough to determine the trajectory of the bullet. Consider Figure 2.

Assume for a second that the speed of the projectile is known. As we have seen in Section 2, the bullet speed determines the angle of the shockwave cone and hence, the trajectory angle can be estimated from the shockwave AOA. Unfortunately, a second trajectory, called image trajectory, can generate the same shockwave observations, as shown in the figure. Therefore, a single sensor cannot determine the trajectory unambiguously. However, two sensors are enough to disambiguate the situation. See Section 5. Note that this discussion was restricted to 2D; the situation is more complicated in 3D, but the solution can be generalized. Never-

theless, the consequence of the design decisions is that the minimum number of sensors required is two.

4. SYSTEM ARCHITECTURE

The intended application and concept of operation requires a truly distributed architecture, which is a significant departure from previous shooter localization systems [13, 3, 14, 17], in which a dedicated *base station* collects low-level measurements, computes the solution, and displays the results. Due to the low-bandwidth requirements—a single message per node when a shot is fired with sporadic status updates for tracking the position of other team members—and due to a low practical bound on the number of nodes within audible range of the trajectory, we could implement a simple and robust distributed model. In this model, all detection events with time and node orientation and position information are broadcast to all other nodes. Based on these broadcasted events and the local detections, each node independently calculates its own solution. Unless messages are lost, these independent results will be identical.

The conceptual system architecture is shown in Figure 3. An Android smartphone at each mobile node (soldier) provides three high-level services: it receives and broadcasts event detection messages, executes the localization algorithm, and displays the results. The smartphone provides multiple options for message distribution. Previously, we used IP/UDP multicast with dedicated WiFi access points, UDP message broker servers where 3G services are available, and a more sophisticated middleware layer providing broadcast services over traditional and custom radio interfaces. Such a custom RF interface might be the only viable option in remote locations with no reliable cellular coverage or where the service provider cannot be trusted.

Note that these tasks require significant CPU, memory and user interface resources, thus delegating these to the smartphone seems natural. Also, the more productive and refined developer ecosystem around the Android platform significantly shortens the time and effort for refining the

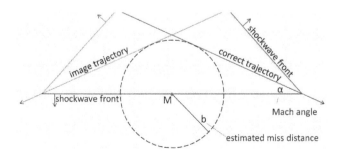

Figure 2: The trajectory ambiguity problem.

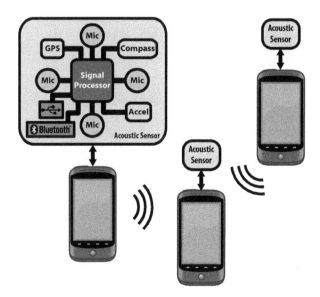

Figure 3: Conceptual system architecture.

most complex parts of our application. On the other hand, none of these tasks require real-time guarantees, an area where smartphone *apps* do not excel.

A custom sensorboard provides all real-time services of the application. First, it needs to sample and monitor multiple (four) audio channels for detecting potential shockwave signatures. Shockwave length and AOA (based on TDOA) measurements are more accurate using higher sampling rates than are typical in audio applications. This multi-channel, high-bandwidth, real-time signal processing task requires significant computational resources, which can be met with parallel architectures while staying within the limited power budget. Systems with similar requirements have used SRAM and Flash-based FPGA devices [14, 7, 15]. Alternately, the PSoC mixed-signal platform [4] is also a possible candidate for such tasks. The stream processing is easily handled by mainstream midrange FPGAs running at low (10 MHz) clock speeds, but the development time and effort is sometimes prohibitive to try out radically new ideas. The PSoC platform provides limited (re)configurable logic resources (Universal Digital Blocks) along with on-chip analog components for signal conditioning and sampling and an industry standard ARM Cortex-M3 processor core. While software development on this platform is significantly faster and more convenient, the PSoC platform does not scale well with the number of channels. Beyond two channels, the scheduling of the shockwave detection and other tasks and satisfying latency requirements becomes non-trivial.

These other tasks include communication with an onboard GPS and a 3D compass module for accurately tracking the current time, position, and orientation of the microphone array. Although our current localization algorithm does not require highly accurate timestamps of the events across nodes (only used for separating different shots), a timepulse signal provided by most GPS modules is a simple and reliable way of generating such timestamps. The position accuracy of the GPS module is more important and affects the overall accuracy of the solution. The 3D compass module uses MEMS accelerometers and magnetometers for calculating the actual heading, pitch, and roll angles of the array. Accuracy and refresh rate were the two critical parameters in selecting the compass module.

Building the connection between the sensor array and the smartphone is surprisingly challenging in this application. Although the communication channel does not have to provide real-time guarantees—all time critical information is captured and registered by the sensor node—the communication interface needs to provide a reliable yet physically flexible bridge between the endpoints. The potential technologies are limited by the built-in capabilities of the smartphone platform to USB, Bluetooth, or WiFi. The wireless interfaces provide the most flexible deployment models; however, these are also more vulnerable to eavesdropping or jamming. The USB interface requires a wired connection between the array and phone and may also enable a shared power supply solution. Unfortunately, the standard smartphone USB interface requires a host implementation on the other side, unnecessarily increasing the design complexity of the sensor node.

In typical deployment configurations, the sensor node is required to run from an independent power source for several hours during the entire length of a mission. The current architecture and detection logic offer only limited energy

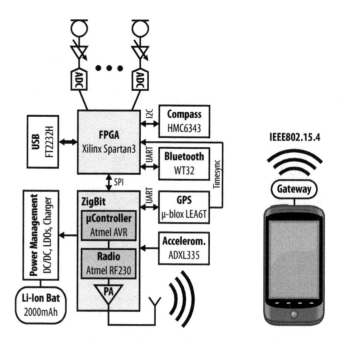

Figure 4: Current prototype system architecture.

saving opportunities via duty cycling. The channel detectors are enabled continuously—these need to find the first acoustic transient event with no advanced trigger. The GPS receiver needs to track the position and time of the node also. Here, energy saving measures can be implemented with a low-power MEMS accelerometer for detecting stationary periods when the GPS module can be powered off and falling back to internal timekeeping. Nonetheless, the sensor node requires a high energy density Li-Ion battery with a rated capacity comparable to ones in current smartphones (1000-2000 mAh).

Our current prototype implementation shown in Figure 4 follows the conceptual architecture described above. However, as it happens with most research prototypes, we had to make changes to and diverge from the ideal setup. The main factors affecting the proof-of-concept prototype were very limited time and the financial budget. To be able to build a working and deployable system, we decided to leverage an existing acoustic sensor board (Octopus) [16] and design an add-on circuit board with the components needed for the system concept. The original sensor board supports eight (8) independent channels, a high-speed USB interface, and a large PSRAM memory for instrumentation purposes, which results in a significantly higher power budget and larger physical size than is needed by the current application. Also, the two stacked circuit boards and the necessary wiring between these made the profile of the node significantly higher. Finally, to decouple the early development phases from the communication concerns of the smartphone network, we decided to use the existing IEEE 802.15.4-based RF solution readily available on the Octopus board. In this modified architecture, the smartphone still runs the sensor fusion and provides the user interface.

On the existing Octopus sensor board, we use only four (4) of the audio channels that have variable gain (44–65 dB) and 1 MSPS/12 bit sampling. The independent channels are processed by a Xilinx Spartan3 FPGA (XC3S1000) using cus-

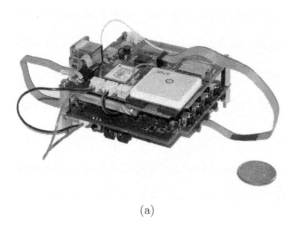 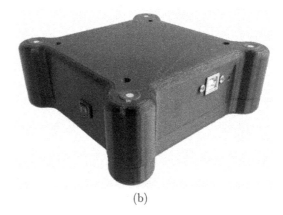

(a)   (b)

Figure 5: The prototype sensor node assembly (a) and packaging (b).

tom IP cores developed for detecting acoustic shockwave signatures. The high-speed USB interface (FTDI FT2232H) on the Octopus board provides a real-time streaming interface to the audio channels. The ZigBit OEM module provides communication, system management, and limited computational resources. It includes an Atmel AVR (ATmega1281) microcontroller, an Atmel RF230 RF transceiver chip operating in the 2.4 GHz ISM band, and an integrated power amplifier (20 dBm) for increased communication range and noise immunity. Each smartphone (Dell Streak) is connected to a TelosB [11] node using a custom USB cable to use the non-standard USB host capability built into the Streak. The TelosB acts as a wireless gateway and forwards all packets to the phone.

Mobile and autonomous operation is supported by several key components on the support board. First, we integrated a u-blox LEA-6T GPS receiver, which provides accurate position estimates in standalone mode with satellite augmentation, an extremely accurate global time reference, and access to raw measurement data. Node orientation is tracked by a Honeywell HMC6343 3D compass module at 10 Hz and 0.1° resolution. This compass module combines a 3-axis magnetometer and a 3-axis accelerometer MEMS sensor with digital/analog support circuitry and software IP for calculating heading, pitch, and roll results from raw sensor measurements. These sensitive measurements are affected by bias and noise as soon as the compass module becomes a part of a real board assembly. The module provides a self calibration process, which we used successfully for compensating the bias of the magnetometers caused by close metallic/magnetic objects (PCB traces and planes, RF shields, and antennae). We also experienced significant measurement noise, which was caused by an inductor coil of a switching-mode DC/DC converter on the board. By changing the layout of this circuitry we managed to mitigate the interference and the noise.

Acoustic shockwave detection is not the intended application of the low-cost low-power miniature electret microphones we used in our prior work. These sensors typically lack in responsiveness and dynamic range to handle such short high energy transients. The high sound pressure level (SPL>150dB) of close trajectories is especially problematic due to the long recovery time of the mic (the JFET preamplifier inside the capsule) from overload. During this re-

covery interval the microphone is practically deaf, which prevents accurate shockwave length estimation and hinders the detection of simultaneous shots. For the current system we selected a more robust, water resistant microphone assembly from Knowles Acoustics (VEK-H-30108). This is a low-sensitivity model designed for gunshot or other impulse sensing, thus can handle more extreme SPL (124dB at 1% THD, 154dB at 10%) and have a flat frequency response between 100 Hz to 10 kHz. Our field experiments show that even these special sensors are easily overloaded by AK-47 (7.62 mm) bullets if the trajectory is within 5 meters. We experimented with using rubberized paint and custom designed plastic caps on top of the capsules for protecting the microphone element from overload, but these efforts resulted in markedly distorted signal shapes even with safe (distant) trajectories.

The support board also contains a Bluetooth transceiver module (BlueGiga WT32), which provides a high-level UART based interface to the FPGA for communicating with Bluetooth enabled devices. This alternative wireless interface was not used in our experiments, but can easily replace the TelosB gateway in the architecture in future deployments.

The power source of the sensor assembly is a 2000 mAh Li-Ion battery, enabling continuous operation for approximately 6 hours. The current drain (typically 300 mA) depends significantly on the state of the GPS module (acquiring, tracking, sleeping), the state of the Bluetooth transceiver, and the communication burden on the ZigBit radio (packet transmission rate). The support board integrates a USB-based Li-Ion charger and step-up/step-down regulators for supplying the power rails needed by the Octopus board.

The twin board architecture, required interconnects, battery, antennae, and microphones (Knowles Acoustics VEK-H-30108)) needed to be packaged for supporting mobile field deployments. We used a rapid 3D printing process to design and build a custom ABS plastic enclosure. This allowed for maximum flexibility in arranging the microphones and other layout sensitive elements (connectors, antennae). The internal board assembly and the final packaged node are shown in Figure 5. Note that the existing Octopus board and the 2-board assembly drove the physical dimensions of the package. We will be able to cut each dimension in half in a future revision with a single newly designed board. This will result in a smaller microphone array, but in our estimation, it will have only a minor effect on AOA detection accuracy.

5. SENSOR FUSION

The sensor fusion computes the trajectory estimate and bearing to the shooter from the following inputs: a) a set of at least two shockwave detections, each including TDOAs and durations from four microphones; b) sensor positions and 3D orientations; c) speed of sound (assumed to be a known constant); d) microphone geometry; and e) assumed weapon parameters: a weapon specific parameter k that is used to map shockwave length to miss distance (see Equation 2), which includes the projectile muzzle speed and a deceleration parameter.

The sensor fusion algorithm consists of six steps:

1. Calculate the shockwave AOA for each sensor;

2. Compute the miss distances for each sensor;

3. Attempt to compute the speed of projectile;

4. Compute the trajectory estimates for each sensor;

5. Estimate trajectory by fusion of per-node trajectory estimates;

6. Compute bearing estimates.

Steps 1 and 2 are fairly trivial. First, the AOA of the shockwave at each sensor is computed from the TDOAs at the microphones, using the known microphone geometry and a given speed of sound. The AOA is represented as a 3-dimensional vector of unit length. Since this AOA is initially computed in the node's local coordinate system, we rotate this vector using the corresponding 3D compass readings to convert them to an absolute (East-North-Up) coordinate system. For simplicity, we convert the AOAs to 2D by discarding the z (Up) coordinates. Then, in Step 2, the miss distances are computed using Equation 2, with a predefined weapon-specific constant k.

If the projectile passes the sensors on one side, the AOAs reported by all the sensors are close to parallel. However, if there are sensors on both sides of the trajectory, the sensors on the two sides detect different AOAs. Their difference is directly related to the cone angle of the shockwave front, and, in turn, to the speed of the bullet over the sensor network. We check for this condition in Step 3, and compute the bullet speed as follows. Assuming β_1 and β_2 are the two distinct shockwave angles of arrival, such that $0 < (\beta_1 - \beta_2) < \pi$, the cone angle α is computed as $\pi - (\beta_1 - \beta_2)/2$. From here, the bullet speed estimate is computed as $v_{bullet} = c/sin(\alpha)$, where c is the speed of sound. If the bullet speed could not be computed this way—that is, for one-sided shots—we rely on the assumed weapon-specific muzzle speed, deceleration, and assumed shooter range to compute a rough bullet speed estimate.

If the trajectory passes between the sensors, the direction of the trajectory can also be computed as $2\pi - (\beta_1 + \beta_2)/2$. Note that the image trajectories for these sensors are completely different and only the real trajectory estimates align.

In Step 4, for each sensor, we compute the two trajectory estimates using the miss distance, shockwave AOA, and bullet speed values. Consider Figure 6. Notice that the trajectory is tangent to the circle whose center is the sensor

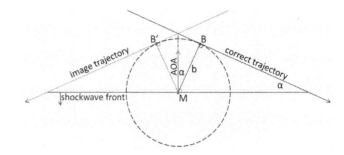

Figure 6: Computation of the two trajectory estimates.

position M and has a radius equaling the miss distance. The trajectory touches the circle at point B; therefore, the vector $\vec{MB}$ is normal to the trajectory. Also notice that the angle between the shockwave AOA vector and $\vec{MB}$ equals the cone angle α. From here, we can compute the position of point B by rotating the shockwave AOA vector clockwise by the angle α, and making its length equal to the miss distance. To get the direction of the trajectory, we need to rotate the vector by $\pi/2$ further clockwise. The trajectory solution is defined by point B and the trajectory's direction. Point B' and the second trajectory solution can be computed similarly, but with counterclockwise rotations.

If it was possible to compute the direction of the trajectory in Step 3, then the correct trajectory can be easily identified. We simply choose the one whose direction is close to the previously computed value.

If the trajectory angle is not available, we have to do some more work to eliminate the image trajectories. After completing Step 4 for all n number of sensors, we have $2n$ trajectory solutions available, of which n are incorrect.

We need to search for a consistent subset of trajectory solutions that *line up* with each other. Naturally, if a set of sensors detect the exact same shockwave direction of arrival, their respective true trajectory solutions will all be parallel. However, this is true for the image trajectory solutions, as well. This means that just by looking at the angles of the trajectory solutions it is not possible to identify the consistent subset. To further complicate things, we cannot assume that the trajectory solutions in a consistent subset are parallel: errors in the compass readings, as well as detection errors will result in slightly diverging trajectory solutions, which makes it hard to define a distance metric between them.

We observe that the even though the trajectory solutions in the correct subset may diverge far from the sensor field, they pass close to each other in the proximity of the sensors. This is not surprising, since, by construction, the the distance between a sensor M and point T on a corresponding trajectory is exactly the miss distance. Therefore, the metric we chose to score a subset of trajectories with similar angles is as follows. For all sensor-trajectory pairs in the subset, we compute the variance of the sensor-trajectory distances. The trajectory solution subset with the lowest variance is chosen as the correct one.

Once the correct subset of trajectory solutions is available, in Step 5 we compute the final trajectory solution by averaging the trajectories in the subset.

In general, two nodes are sufficient to identify the correct

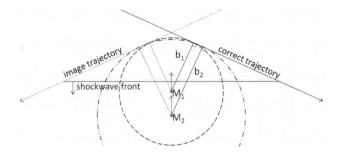

Figure 7: Degenerate geometry where it is not possible to distinguish between the true and the image trajectories.

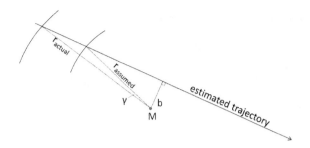

Figure 8: Bearing estimation. Although the actual range and the assumed range are quite different, the bearing estimation error γ stays low if the miss distance is much smaller than the true and the assumed ranges.

trajectory. However, there is a degenerate geometry where not just the two correct trajectory solutions line up with each other, but also the two image solutions. Consider Figure 7, where the shockwave front is perpendicular to the line defined by the two sensor locations and both sensors detect the same shockwave AOA. In this case, the miss distance estimates are not sufficient to differentiate between the correct and the image trajectory: the geometry is symmetric to the $M_1 M_2$ axis. To avoid such situations, at least three non-collinear sensors are required for unambiguous trajectory estimation.

The bearing estimates are computed in Step 6 for all sensors that reported shockwave detections. For two-sided shots, we compute the approximate range of the shooter using the previously estimated bullet speed and the weapon-specific parameters (speed at muzzle and deceleration). Using this approximate range, we find the estimated position of the shooter on the trajectory.

For one-sided shots, where the range cannot be approximated, we use a predefined value instead. Using the trajectory estimate and this *assumed* range, we find the estimated position S of the shooter on the trajectory. The angle of the $\vec{MS}$ vector is reported as the bearing estimate for sensor M.

It is important to note that, for one-sided shots, we do not have enough information to compute where exactly the shooter is on the line of trajectory. The assumed shooter-sensor distance is just an assumption that corresponds to a typical case identified by the user requirements. How can the bearing estimation still be accurate then? Clearly, if the true range is close to the assumed one, the estimated bearing will be close to the true one. More importantly, the bearing estimation error will still be low if the miss distance is much smaller than the true range and the assumed range (see Figure 8 as an example). Considering that the maximum shockwave detection range of our sensors are about 30 m (but the important shots are much closer) and the typical range that the users are interested in is 100-200 m, this assumption holds.

This leaves us with only one bad case: when the shooter is very close to the sensor, the reported bearing may have a large error. From a practical point of view, this is not a critical issue. When the shooter is that close to the sensors, the users can identify the source location without any technology and have no time to use their smartphones in any case.

6. IMPLEMENTATION

The software that enables networked trajectory and bearing estimation consists of three distinct components: a) the microcontroller code running on the ZigBit module; b) the Android code that collects detections from the network, dispatches the sensor fusion algorithm, and displays the result; and c) the sensor fusion algorithm that computes the bearing to the shooter from a set of shockwave detections.

6.1 MCU implementation

The ZigBit microcontroller is programmed in TinyOS 2.1. It handles mesh networking, location awareness and communication with the FPGA subsystem. For positioning, we rely on the u-blox GPS module, as well as on the digital compass. When the FPGA subsystem signals through an interrupt line that a shockwave detection is available, the shockwave time of arrival (TOA) and shockwave duration measurements for each microphone, as well as the compass heading, are placed in a radio packet and broadcast to the network.

For mesh networking, we rely on the Directed Flood Routing Framework (DFRF) [10], a policy-driven, configurable routing middleware, to achieve restricted network-wide broadcast. The routing framework is configured as follows. Each packet has a unique sequence number and a hop count field. The hop count field specifies how many times a particular packet can be forwarded, and is initially set to 10. On reception of a new packet, it is placed in the node's routing buffer, its hop count value is decremented and is rebroadcast. After forwarding the packet, it is kept in the routing buffer for a while. This way, the node can remember the recently forwarded packets, so that subsequent receptions of the same detection packet can be ignored. This mesh networking configuration ensures that all detections are available at every node of a fairly small mobile sensor network, and saves bandwidth by avoiding unnecessary rebroadcast of previously forwarded detections.

6.2 Android implementation

The Android code running on the Dell Streak is responsible for collecting shockwave detections from the sensor network, dispatching the sensor fusion algorithm, and displaying the result. Since Android is built on top of a Linux system and is programmed in Java, it was straightforward to port the TinyOS Java SDK to Android. This way, we can

Figure 9: Shooting range with the four sensors on tripods in the distance. The green bucket in the foreground holds a repeater, as the TelosB we used for our remote user interface had trouble picking up the messages from the distant sensors.

use the TelosB mote, connected to the Streak directly via USB, as a TinyOS base station that collects the shockwave detections coming from the sensor network.

When at least two detections of the same shot are available (and a timeout comparable to the routing delay has passed since receiving the last detection), the sensor fusion algorithm is invoked with the detection set as its input data. The computed trajectory estimate, as well as the bearing estimate to the shooter is displayed on-screen.

6.3 Sensor fusion implementation

The sensor fusion is implemented in MATLAB. We rely on MATLAB Coder to generate C code from the MATLAB source files. SWIG is used to generate JNI wrappers around the generated C code so that it can be compiled to an ARM Linux shared object file that can be loaded and used by the Dalvik virtual machine running the Android code. The sensor fusion procedure takes less than $100msec$ on the smartphone.

7. EVALUATION

We built four prototype sensor nodes and evaluated the system on a shooting range. The four sensors were placed approximately at the corners of a $6x8m$ rectangle as shown in Figure 9. Originally, the four nodes had the same orientation, but were changed randomly during the test multiple times. We took 44 shots with an AK-47. Most of the shots were approximately $35 - 40m$ from the closest sensor. 12 shots were taken from farther away at about $80m$

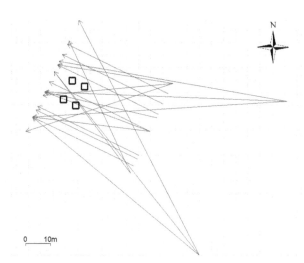

Figure 10: Map of sensor positions (squares) and shot trajectories (arrows).

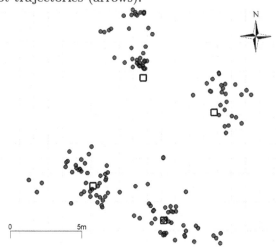

Figure 11: Map of reported GPS positions (dots) vs. the groundtruth (squares).

from the sensors. While the system is designed for longer range shots, we were constrained by the limitations of this particular shooting range.

We supplied the sensor fusion algorithm with the following parameters. We assumed that the weapon is an AK-47 and that the range is $150m$. Accordingly, the bullet speed at the muzzle was set to $720m/s$, and the projectile deceleration was assumed to be $-555m/s^2$. The weapon-specific coefficient k was set to 0.00625. The speed of sound was set to $335m/s$.

Figure 10 shows all 44 shots relative to the four sensor positions (note that we typically took 2 shots from the same position at the same target). Each arrow represents at least one shot starting at the shooter location and indicating the target with an arrowhead. As you can see, less than one third of the shots pass in-between any sensors. This is intentional; we wanted to push the limits of the technology since estimating the trajectory is much more difficult when only one side of the shockwave is detected.

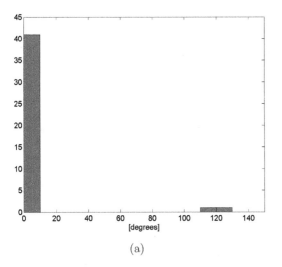

(a)

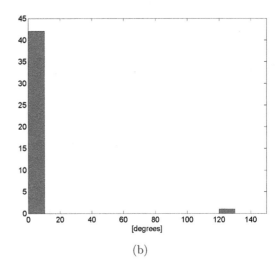

(b)

Figure 12: Histogram of trajectory angle errors in degrees derived from measurements from all sensor detections when a) the GPS-reported locations and b) the manually surveyed locations are used.

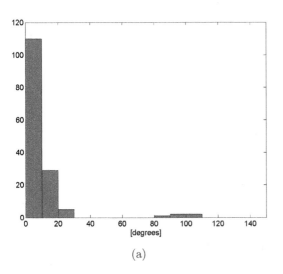

(a)

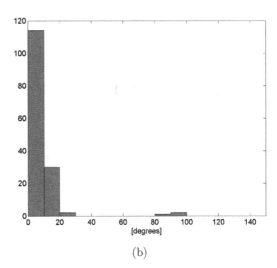

(b)

Figure 13: Histogram of bearing errors in degrees derived from measurements from all sensor detections when a) the GPS-reported locations and b) the manually surveyed locations are used.

7.1 Sensor positioning errors

Unfortunately, our sensor positioning approach displayed much larger errors than anticipated. We had used the given GPS receiver on a couple of different designs before and experienced only $1 - 2m$ errors in stationary setups under relatively benign environments. This is in line with the datasheet; however, during our field test, the GPS on this design behaved somewhat erratically showing up to $5m$ errors. Figure 11 shows the ground truth sensor positions (small squares) and the GPS reported locations (dots) corresponding to the times of the 44 shots. The average GPS error was $2.5m$ which is significantly worse than expected. We suspect that the new sensor node has some kind of noise source that proved to be too close to the GPS antenna.

Similarly, the compass was affected by the sensor node hardware as described in Section 4. We manually calibrated each compass according to the procedure described in the datasheet. This improved the accuracy significantly. Still, turning the sensor nodes 360° and comparing the reported orientation with the ground truth at multiple angles resulted in up to 8° of error. Again, this is much worse than the expected 1° error.

Previous WSN-based shooter localization systems used many sensors [14, 17]. Such systems are less sensitive to sensor location errors because the many random positioning errors have a tendency to average out. (Also, these systems were evaluated using surveyed positions.) Here we only have two or three sensors, yet sensor location errors have a small impact as we'll see.

7.2 All sensors

One of the sensors had a very low detection rate compared to the others. We suspect some kind of hardware issue with the acoustic channels on that particular node. Thus, about half of the shots were detected by three or fewer sensors. One shot was picked up by a single sensor only, so the following evaluation is based on 43 shots.

First, we use all available sensors to estimate the trajectory. The trajectory angle errors are shown in Figure 12(a). Two shots were incorrectly localized: the disambiguation algorithm picked the wrong trajectory from the possible two. All of the remaining 41 shots had trajectory angle errors of less than 10° with the average error of 3.1°. To evaluate the effect of the relatively large sensor position errors, we reran the localization algorithm for all the shots using the ground truth sensor positions. Not surprisingly, only a single trajectory was incorrectly localized in this case (see Figure 12(b)). This was caused by multiple factors. The AOA angle estimates had a larger than usual error on one node (either due to detection error or the compass). The geometry of the other two nodes were close to the degenerate case. That means that effectively, we only had the minimally required two measurements and they did not agree on the shockwave angle. Interestingly, the extra shot whose trajectory was selected correctly using the precise sensor locations increased the average trajectory angle error to 3.4°.

When you plot the trajectory using a map as the user interface, it is the trajectory accuracy that matters. However, the primary user interface for soldiers is a simple visual and/or audio indication of the bearing to the shooter. This could be as simple as a recorded audio played in the headset: "Shooter at 5 o'clock." In this case, it is the bearing to the shooter from the sensor node that matters. With this kind of feedback, the resolution of the bearing effectively becomes 30°. That is, a bearing error of ±15° is still considered perfect.

Fixing the shooter range at 150m (even though the real range varied between 35 and 85m only) and computing the individual bearing estimates from each sensor's point of view for the 41 shots that were correctly localized results in an average bearing error of 7°. The histogram of bearing estimation errors is shown in Figure 13(a). This result is much better than we anticipated considering that it includes all error sources: sensor position and orientation errors and the trajectory estimation errors (angle and displacement). If we remove just one source and use the ground truth sensor positions, the average error becomes 6.5° and the histogram of bearing estimation errors (Figure 13(b).) shows only a slight improvement. This means that the positioning errors of a consumer-grade GPS receiver does not contribute heavily to the overall bearing estimation error, which is affected predominantly by the fixed range assumption and the errors already present in the trajectory estimation. Also, this finding supports our hardware choice of the u-blox LEA-6T, a consumer-grade GPS receiver for sensor node localization.

These results indicate that the system is surprisingly insensitive to sensor position errors. Their main effect is potentially throwing off the disambiguation algorithm, but the trajectory angle and bearing errors if the correct trajectory option is picked remain very low. Why is that? The individual trajectory angle estimates do not depend on the sensor position at all. The wrong position shifts the trajectory, but it does not rotate it. If the correct trajectory option is selected by the disambiguation algorithm, it averages the two or more individual estimates. Its angle might have a few degrees of error and it may be shifted by a few meters. But the shooter is far away compared to the potential trajectory dis-

placement, so its effect is minor. This is a huge advantage of not relying on shockwave TDOAs across sensors where sensor location errors have a significant impact!

7.3 Sensor pairs

As we have shown before, the minimum number of sensors required for trajectory estimation in the general case is 2. Therefore, we took the 43 shots that were detected by at least 2 sensors and selected all possible sensor pairs for each shot and ran the trajectory and bearing estimation algorithm on the resulting 193 cases. There were 5 cases where the measurements proved inconsistent and the algorithm did not return a solution. The system picked the right trajectory for 164 cases (87% of remaining 188 shots). The average trajectory estimation error for these were 3.3°. Of the resulting 376 individual bearing estimates 307 had under 15° error. The mean error of the bearing estimates when the right trajectory was picked came to 5.8°. Figure 14 shows the histogram of bearing errors including the cases when the wrong trajectory was selected.

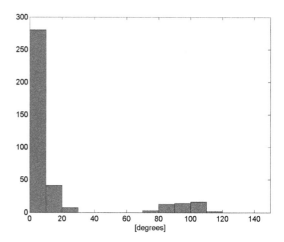

Figure 14: **Histogram of bearing errors in degrees derived from measurements from pairs of sensors. The bars above 70° correspond to cases when the wrong trajectory was selected. The figure illustrates the worst possible case for the system since it only uses the absolute minimum number of sensors, the majority of the cases are one-sided shots, it includes all cases with degenerate geometry, and suffers from relatively large sensor localization and orientation errors.**

If we use the correct sensor positions, the number of correctly selected trajectories improves significantly: while the same 188 out of 193 cases were localized, 175 (11 more) were correctly estimated. Most of the remaining 13 incorrect ones were close to the degenerate geometry. The trajectory angle and bearing accuracies were basically the same as the case using the GPS supplied locations.

7.4 Shot library

We utilized the same shot library from Aberdeen Proving Grounds as in [17]. It contains 33 AK-47 shots measured using ten sensors. The sensor field was approximately $30x30m$ and the shots were taken from ranges between 50 and 300m.

The sensor nodes were placed on surveyed locations and had known orientation. The sensor data includes the shockwave length and AOA that our system needs. Since the setup used many sensors and our objective is to use as few as possible, we first looked at all possible pairs of sensors per shot and compared it to all possible sensor triplets per shot. The former resulted in over 1300 data points, while the latter came to well over 3000 cases.

For sensor pairs, only 87% of the cases were localized. Out of these, the system identified the trajectories correctly 94% of the time. These are somewhat lower rates than we expected considering that the sensor positions and orientation were precise. There are two reasons for this. First, the shooter range and consequently, the speed of the projectile near the sensors varied significantly, hence, the fixed projectile speed assumption for one-sided shots had a more significant impact. Second, there were many cases when the bullet passed directly over the sensors. Our current 2D solution is unable to handle such cases well (however, it will not be difficult to generalize the solution to 3D).

The mean bearing error of the correctly localized shots from each individual sensor's perspective was 4.6°. As expected, using three sensors instead of two improves the situation. About 99% of the 3348 cases were detected, that is, the system reported a trajectory and bearing estimate. The correct trajectory was selected 91% of the time. In other words, 3002 cases were correctly localized. The mean trajectory angle error for these cases came to 3.3°, while the corresponding bearing error was 4.1°. Figure 15 shows the histogram of bearing errors for sensor pairs and triplets including those corresponding to image trajectories.

7.5 Summary

The evaluation of the system allows us to draw some clear conclusions. The most important lesson is that we need to improve the system's ability to resolve the trajectory ambiguity problem for one-sided shots. When the bullet passed in-between two sensors, not a single trajectory was missed. It is the easy case that most other systems have focused on. Sensor location and orientation errors have an impact, so improvement in those areas will help. But even with no measurement errors of any kind, in the case of a degenerate geometry as described in Section 5, no system can find the correct trajectory. To lessen the probability of this bad case, at least three sensors should be used.

If and when the system identifies the correct trajectory, the bearing estimation is remarkably accurate. The errors remained under 7° in all the setups we tested. This is better than what is required in most deployment scenarios. Another distinguishing characteristic of the system as opposed to TDOA-based methods is that this error is very insensitive to sensor location errors.

8. CONCLUSIONS

The presented paper has multiple novel contributions. To the best of our knowledge, it is the first shooter localization system that relies on shockwave length and shockwave AOA only. In contrast to the state-of-the-art, it does not use the TDOA of the shockwaves across multiple sensors. As such, it does not require time synchronization of the sensors. Instead, it utilizes the shockwave length and AOA at each sensor to identify the two possible trajectories in the horizontal plane of the nodes and use one or more nearby sensors to

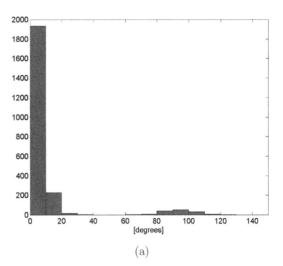

(a)

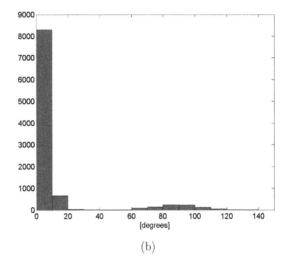

(b)

Figure 15: Histogram of bearing errors in degrees derived from measurements from all sensor pairs (a) and triplets (b) in the shot library.

disambiguate the two. Relying on shockwaves only means that the sensors do not even need to have line of sight to the shooter as the muzzle blast is not used. An additional attribute is that the system is more responsive as it does not have to wait for the muzzle blast which may arrive a full second after the shockwave for longer range shots. Moreover, it is the first reported networked system that is truly distributed. It does not require a central high-performance computer to run the sensor fusion and it still has lower latency. Each and every node calculates the solution from the information available from the network. Finally, this is the first reported implementation and field evaluation of a smartphone-based shooter localization system.

There are three tradeoffs for not utilizing muzzle blasts. First, the system assumes a known weapon type. We have focused on AK-47s, the most widely used rifle in the world. Second, the system is unable to estimate the range to the shooter for one-sided shots. However, bearing information is far more valuable than range as the latter can be usually determined by the trained eye based on the terrain given an accurate bearing estimate. In contrast, humans are not very good at determining the direction to the source of a shot especially in urban or mountainous terrain. Finally, the system becomes susceptible to the trajectory ambiguity problem for one-sided shots when only two sensors are available. However, our system is the first that we are aware of that specifically addresses one-sided shots using shockwaves only and these initial results are highly encouraging.

Our future work will include testing the system with various different weapons to try to relax the known weapon assumption. We will also generalize the trajectory estimation to 3D. Finally, we will investigate using the shockwave TDOAs for eliminating the errors in the disambiguation of the candidate trajectories.

9. REFERENCES

[1] J. Ash, G. Whipps, and R. Kozick. Performance of shockwave-based shooter localization under model misspecification. In *Acoustics Speech and Signal Processing (ICASSP), 2010 IEEE International Conference on*, pages 2694 –2697, march 2010.

[2] U.S. Patent 7,292,501 B2: Compact Shooter Localization System and Method, Nov. 2007.

[3] Raytheon BBN technologies, boomerang website. http://www.bbn.com/products_and_services/boomerang/.

[4] Cypress Semiconductor. Cypress Programmable System-on-Chip. http://www.cypress.com/?id=1353.

[5] T. Damarla, L. Kaplan, and G. Whipps. Sniper localization using acoustic asynchronous sensors. *Sensors Journal, IEEE*, 10(9):1469 –1478, Sept. 2010.

[6] U.S. Patent 6,178,141 B1: Acoustic counter-sniper system, Jan. 2001.

[7] A. Lédeczi, T. Hay, P. Völgyesi, R. Hay, A. Nádas, and S. Jayaraman. Wireless Acoustic Emission Sensor Network for Structural Monitoring. *IEEE Sensors Journal*, 2009.

[8] A. Lédeczi, A. Nádas, P. Völgyesi, G. Balogh, B. Kusý, J. Sallai, G. Pap, S. Dóra, K. Molnár, M. Maróti, and G. Simon. Countersniper system for urban warfare. *ACM Transactions on Sensor Networks*, 1(1):153–177, Nov. 2005.

[9] D. Lindgren, O. Wilsson, F. Gustafsson, and H. Habberstad. Shooter localization in wireless microphone networks. *EURASIP Journal on Advances in Signal Processing*, 2010, 2010.

[10] M. Maróti. Directed flood-routing framework for wireless sensor networks. In *In Proc. of the 5th ACM/IFIP/USENIX International Conference on Middleware*, pages 99–114, New York, NY, USA, 2004. Springer-Verlag New York, Inc.

[11] J. Polastre, R. Szewczyk, and D. Culler. Telos: enabling ultra-low power wireless research. In *Information Processing in Sensor Networks, 2005. IPSN 2005. Fourth International Symposium on*, pages 364 – 369, april 2005.

[12] J. Sallai, A. Lédeczi, and P. Völgyesi. Acoustic shooter localization with a minimal number of single-channel wireless sensor nodes. In *Proceedings of the 9th ACM Conference on Embedded Networked Sensor Systems*, SenSys '11, pages 96–107, New York, NY, USA, 2011. ACM.

[13] ShotSpotter website. http://www.shotspotter.com/products/military.html.

[14] G. Simon, M. Maróti, A. Lédeczi, G. Balogh, B. Kusý, A. Nádas, G. Pap, J. Sallai, and K. Frampton. Sensor network-based countersniper system. In *Proceedings of the 2nd International Conference on Embedded Networked Sensor Systems*, SenSys, New York, NY, USA, 2004. ACM.

[15] S. Szilvási, B. Babják, A. Lédeczi, and P. Völgyesi. Towards a versatile wireless platform for low-power applications. *International Journal of Digital Information and Wireless Communications*, 1(2), 2012.

[16] P. Volgyesi. Octopus: Wireless sensor for multichannel acoustic sensing - hardware description. *Technical Report (ISIS-10-103), http://www.isis.vanderbilt.edu*, Dec. 2010.

[17] P. Volgyesi, G. Balogh, A. Nadas, C. B. Nash, and A. Ledeczi. Shooter localization and weapon classification with soldier-wearable networked sensors. In *Proceedings of the 5th international conference on Mobile systems, applications and services*, MobiSys '07, pages 113–126, New York, NY, USA, 2007. ACM.

[18] G. Whitham. Flow pattern of a supersonic projectile. *Communications on pure and applied mathematics*, 5(3):301, 1952.

[19] J. Williams. A data distribution service for mobile devices. Master's thesis, Vanderbilt University, 2011.

Radio Tomographic Imaging and Tracking of Stationary and Moving People via Kernel Distance

Yang Zhao
Sensor and Signal Analytics
Lab, GE Global Research
One Research Circle
Niskayuna, NY, USA
yang.zhao@ge.com

Neal Patwari
Department of Electrical and
Computer Engineering,
University of Utah
Salt Lake City, Utah, USA
npatwari@ece.utah.edu

Jeff M. Phillips, Suresh
Venkatasubramanian
School of Computing,
University of Utah
Salt Lake City, Utah, USA
jeffp,suresh@cs.utah.edu

ABSTRACT

Network radio frequency (RF) environment sensing (NRES) systems pinpoint and track people in buildings using changes in the signal strength measurements made by a wireless sensor network. It has been shown that such systems can locate people who do not participate in the system by wearing any radio device, even through walls, because of the changes that moving people cause to the static wireless sensor network. However, many such systems cannot locate stationary people. We present and evaluate a system which can locate stationary or moving people, without calibration, by using kernel distance to quantify the difference between two histograms of signal strength measurements. From five experiments, we show that our kernel distance-based radio tomographic localization system performs better than the state-of-the-art NRES systems in different non line-of-sight environments.

Categories and Subject Descriptors

H.4 [**Information Systems Applications**]: Miscellaneous

General Terms

Algorithms, Design, Performance

Keywords

Localization, Tracking, Sensor networks

1. INTRODUCTION

Localization of people using wireless sensor networks has significant benefits in elder care, security, and smart facility applications [3, 19, 20]. Standard "radio localization" systems locate a transmitter tag, or allow a receiver to estimate its position [3, 16]. For these mentioned applications, it is critical to be able to locate all people, regardless of whether they carry a radio device. In this paper, we explore

"network RF environment sensing" (NRES), that is, using a static wireless sensor network to create an image map of the people and objects and thus locate them in an area of interest based on the changes they cause in the radio frequency (RF) environment. An extensive review of reported NRES research can be found in [20]. NRES is also called "device-free localization" [25], "passive localization" [28], or "sensorless sensing" [26]. Unlike infrared or thermal, RF penetrates non-metal walls, and thus NRES is useful for emergency applications. For example, in a hostage situation, police could deploy wireless devices outside of the building and learn in real time where people are located in the building, information that may save live. NRES systems can also be used in emergency situations to help rescuers like firefighters locate victims.

RF-based imaging and localization for emergency applications has been dominated by ultra-wideband (UWB) radar systems. Companies like Camero [1] have developed sophisticated phased array radar systems that are capable of penetrating walls. However, these UWB systems are expensive and are limited to military use only today. An emerging NRES technique is to monitor the received signal strength (RSS) on links in a deployed static network and to use the changes in RSS to infer the location of the people in the deployment area [28, 29, 24]. As opposed to multistatic UWB radar [4] or MIMO radar [10], RSS-based NRES requires no expensive and sophisticated hardware, and thus can be implemented with standard wireless networks and devices. We focus on such RSS-based systems in this paper.

Although different NRES systems have been reported and tested, existing methods fail in particular situations. A common method is to use the change in mean in RSS on a link to indicate the shadowing from a person obstructing the link [18]. Shadowing-based radio tomographic imaging (RTI) uses changes in link RSS mean values to estimate the shadowing loss field in the area of the wireless sensor network [13, 23, 5, 12]. Shadowing-based RTI works well in line-of-sight (LOS) environments. In cluttered and non-LOS areas, the assumption that RSS will decrease when a person is on the line between transmitter and receiver (the *link line*) fails. On a non-LOS link, the RSS may increase, decrease, or both, while a person is located on the link line [24], thus shadowing-based RTI fails in non-LOS environments. Variance-based NRES methods use the variance of RSS measurements to locate human motion [29, 24]. These methods perform well even in non-LOS environments because a moving person changes the RSS of links as she crosses through them, increasing the RSS variance, even when the change in mean of RSS is close to zero. However, a stationary person does not change the RSS variance, thus variance-based methods cannot locate her.

One contribution of this work is to use *kernel distance* to quantify the change in RSS distribution caused by a person, rather than the change in mean or variance. Using kernel distance allows us to locate a person who is stationary or moving, and who is in an LOS environment or non-LOS environment. In short, mean and variance are just two aspects of a random variable; a good metric like kernel distance quantifies the changes in mean, variance and other distribution features, in one metric. In this paper, we explore different histogram difference metrics including the Kullback-Leibler divergence (KLD) [7] and the kernel distance [21], and find that the kernel distance performs better than other metrics in NRES. A demonstration abstract has presented the idea of using a difference between two histograms as a method for RTI [32], however no algorithms, analysis, or validation was presented.

In general, kernel distance-based NRES methods require a single empty-room calibration, similar to shadowing-based RTI methods. However, a second main contribution of this work, we show that for our proposed NRES system, an empty-room calibration can be replaced with a "long-term histogram" which is calculated during operation, regardless of the presence or absence of people. By enabling online calibration, we allow the NRES system to operate without any empty-room calibration, and thus be used for emergency applications in which operators do not know *a priori* whether an area is empty or not. We show that simple filtering of online RSS measurements allows one to keep a long-term histogram in memory without significant computational complexity. This long-term histogram is close enough to the histogram which would have been measured in an empty-room calibration to perform as well as with empty-room calibration. In fact, in situations in which the environment has changed since the empty-room calibration, the long-term histogram is *closer* to a true empty-room measurement, and NRES performs *better* with it than with the offline empty-room calibration.

To summarize, the contribution of this paper is to provide a complete framework for RSS-based environmental inference, which enables localization of both moving and stationary people in both LOS and non-LOS environments, and which uses online calibration so that the system does not rely on "empty-room" offline calibration. We explore this framework using reported measurement sets and new measurement sets we collected for this purpose. We evaluate imaging, locating and tracking using our framework. The results show that some links' RSS measurements do not change significantly while a person crosses the link line, so using any single link for NRES is unreliable. However, in an N-node wireless sensor network, there is redundancy from the $\mathcal{O}\left(N^2\right)$ links in the network, and one can reliably locate people in the environment. We formulate a new NRES method that estimates a map of human presence from kernel distances in the network, which we call kernel distance-based radio tomographic imaging (KRTI). Then a person's location is estimated to be the coordinate of the pixel with the maximum image value. We then test tracking a single per-

son in the area using a Kalman filter [1]. Experimental results show that KRTI can locate a moving person more accurately than VRTI [24] and SubVRT [30]. For localization of a stationary person, KRTI also outperforms a sequential Monte Carlo method [25] both in localization accuracy and computational efficiency. Note that if a person stays still at a location for a long time such as several minutes, our online calibration would gradually "treat" the person as part of the environment, and thus the person would disappear from our KRTI images.

The rest of the paper is organized as follows. Section 2 presents related work. Section 3 first introduces two types of RSS histograms and defines two histogram difference metrics, then describes how we use these metrics to image, locate and track a person in a wireless sensor network. Section 4 describes experiments used in this paper, and Section 5 shows the imaging, localization and tracking results. We conclude in Section 6.

2. RELATED WORK

Many recent research studies have focused on RSS-based NRES method using measurements from a wireless mesh network [29, 22, 24], due to the fact that RSS measurements are inexpensive and available in almost all wireless devices. However, all reported methods so far are *ad hoc* and incomplete. For example, [23] proposes an RSS model-based method – shadowing-based RTI, to locate stationary and moving people in LOS environments. Based on a similar model, [5] proposes methods to simultaneously track people and locate sensor nodes. However, these methods do not perform well in non-LOS indoor environments due to the multipath effects. For non-LOS indoor environments, variance-based methods using different network configurations [29, 24] have been proposed to locate human motion. For example, RF sensors are placed on the ceiling of a room to track people using the RSSI dynamic, which is calculated by RSS measurements with and without people moving inside the room [29]. Variance-based RTI deploys RF sensors on top of stands outside a residential house to locate and track people walking inside the house [24]. However, these variance-based methods cannot locate stationary people, since they all use certain forms of RSS variance to locate human motion, and stationary people do not cause much RSS variance. A more recent study [25] uses a sequential Monte Carlo method to locate both stationary and moving people. This method works at both LOS and non-LOS environments, however, it requires too much computational complexity and cannot be easily implemented in real-time. Compared with all above methods, our proposed NRES method is the only real-time method that is capable of imaging and locating both stationary and moving people in both LOS and non-LOS environments.

To be able to locate both stationary and moving people, our method requires a long-term histogram from online RSS measurements. However, the measurements used here are unlabelled, which is different from the training measurements used in fingerprint-based methods [17, 27] and the offline calibration used in shadowing-based RTI methods [23, 5]. Some fingerprint-based methods use histograms of RSS

---

[1]Note that KRTI is capable of imaging the presence of multiple people, however, we focus on formulating localization and tracking of a single person in this paper.

for purposes of NRES [17, 22]. During their training period, RSS histograms are recorded on all links in a network as a person stands in a known position, which becomes a fingerprint for a person being at that location. Fingerprints are recorded as the person moves to each possible position in the environment. During operational localization period, the current RSS histogram is compared to all of the fingerprints, and the person is estimated to be at the position with the closest matching fingerprint. These methods require RSS fingerprints at each possible person location (or each combination of persons' locations in the case of multiple people), thus the training effort in fingerprint-based methods could be extensive for a large area. In contrast, shadowing-based RTI requires a single "empty-room" offline calibration. Although this offline calibration does not involve extensive training, an empty-room area may not be available in the event of an emergency. Our online calibration proposed in this paper requires neither collection of location fingerprints nor empty-room calibration.

Finally, background subtraction [9] and foreground detection [33] provide methods to classify, from unlabelled RSS data, when a link's RSS data corresponds to a period of motion near the link or a period of no motion. Such methods are an important part of future NRES systems which do not require an empty-room calibration period. The perspective of the methods proposed in this paper are complementary. The method in [9] requires a link to experience periods of motion and no motion, although unlabelled, so that the estimation algorithm can determine the distribution of RSS measurements in both cases. Both [9] and [33] model the state of the environment near the link as a binary – one of two states, obstructed by a person or not obstructed. Our kernel distance metric only measures a distance from the long-term "normal" condition, and thus might provide more "soft" information when the effect on the RSS may differ by the type or location of the obstruction, or the RSS in the "not obstructed" state does not simply stay close to one mean value.

3. METHODS

In this section, we first describe how we calculate short-term and long-term RSS histograms, and show human presence could increase the difference between these two histograms. Then we define metrics to measure histogram difference, and we formulate imaging, localization and tracking via histogram difference.

Commercial wireless devices return a discrete-valued RSS value with each received packet. We denote the RSS of the ith packet as y^i. We assume there is a finite set of possible RSS values, of size N. For example, if a device measures RSS in a range from y_{min} to y_{max} dBm and quantization is 1 dBm, then $N = y_{max} - y_{min} + 1$. Without loss of generality, we refer to the RSS integer as a number in the range $0, \ldots, N - 1$.

We assume that there is a network with L links, and packets are transmitted repeatedly and regularly on each link, so that RSS measurements can be made.

3.1 Short-Term and Long-Term Histograms

In our proposed method, a link is characterized by a histogram $\mathbf{h}$ of its recent RSS measurements. The kth element of vector $\mathbf{h}$, that is, h_k, is the proportion of time that RSS integer k is measured on the link. At time n, we denote this

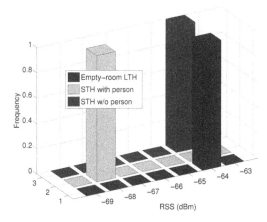

(a) Stationary person effect on STH

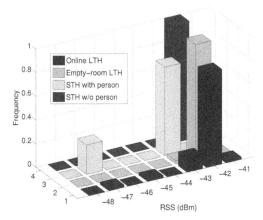

(b) Moving person effect on STH

Figure 1: Long-term histogram (LTH) from offline calibration measurements and short-term histograms (STH) with and without (a) a stationary person; (b) a moving person.

histogram as $\mathbf{h}^n$, and calculate it as a filtered version, or weighted average, of RSS measurements:

$$\mathbf{h}^n = \sum_i w_{n,i} \mathbf{I}_{y^i}, \qquad (1)$$

where y^i is the RSS at time i, $\mathbf{I}$ is an N-length indicator vector, and $w_{n,i}$ is the weight for $\mathbf{I}_{y^i}$. The indicator vector $\mathbf{I}_{y^i}$ is one in element corresponding to the RSS integer y^i and zero in all other elements. Essentially, $\mathbf{I}_{y^i}$ is an instantaneous histogram based only on the current measurement, and $\mathbf{h}^n$ is a weighted average or filtered version of past instantaneous histograms.

We test two different weighting schemes to compute $\mathbf{h}^n$, an offline uniform window, or an exponentially weighted moving average (EWMA). The EWMA scheme has weights,

$$w_{n,i} = \begin{cases} \beta(1 - \beta)^{n-i} & i \leq n \\ 0 & \text{otherwise} \end{cases}, \qquad (2)$$

where $0 < \beta < 1$ is the forgetting factor. A higher β increases the importance of the most recent measurements in the histogram estimate. The EWMA is an infinite impulse response (IIR) filter, in which $\mathbf{h}^n$ is calculated as,

$$\mathbf{h}^n = (1 - \beta)\mathbf{h}^{n-1} + \beta\mathbf{I}_{y^n}. \tag{3}$$

In this way, only the current RSS value y^n and previous histogram $\mathbf{h}^{n-1}$ are necessary to calculate the current histogram. Further, computation of (3) requires N multiplies and a single add. Thus we use the EWMA scheme for all histograms that are computed online, to minimize computational and memory complexity.

A histogram is *short-term* or *long-term* based on the chosen weights $w_{n,i}$. For the EWMA filter, the long-term histogram (LTH) would use a lower β, thus providing more weight to past measurements, than the short-term histogram (STH). In the next sections, we denote the LTH as $\mathbf{q}$ and the STH as $\mathbf{p}$.

The offline uniform window has weight $w_{n,i}$ given as,

$$w_{n,i} = \begin{cases} \frac{1}{T} & 0 \leq i \leq T-1 \\ 0 & \text{otherwise} \end{cases}. \tag{4}$$

If we substitute (4) into (1), we see that the first T RSS values are given equal weight to calculate the histogram. As is clear from the fact that $w_{n,i}$ is not a function of current time n, the histogram computed from offline empty-room calibration does not change over time. We use (4) to implement the "empty-room" calibration, that is, we compute the long-term histogram $\mathbf{q}$ from (4) when we want to test how our system would have performed if calibrated using data from an initial test period (from 0 to T) when no person was in the area. The offline uniform window is used purely to compare results when using the proposed online LTH vs. the offline empty-room LTH.

Examples shown in Figure 1 show how the STH and LTH differ for two example links. The empty-room LTH, computed from $T = 141$ and the offline uniform window, shows a consistent value of -64 dBm on the link in Figure 1(a). Two online STHs are shown, both computed with $\beta = 0.9$, when a person is present on the link line and when no person is on the link line. With no person present, the STH is nearly identical to the empty-room LTH. When a person stands still on the link line, the STH shows a consistent RSS of -68 dBm. In Figure 1(b), a similar effect is seen — the STH with no person on the link line is nearly the same as the empty-room LTH. Note also the "STH with person" in this figure is from a time when the person is moving across (rather than standing still on) the link line, and two different RSS values are present in the STH.

Finally, note that Figure 1(b) shows the similarity between the online (EWMA-based) LTH and the offline empty-room LTH. The online LTH, computed from EWMA with a forgetting factor $\beta = 0.05$ does show some non-zero probabilities of other RSS values (e.g., -41, -43, -45, ...), however, the probabilities of these values are very close to zero. It is the fact that these LTHs are very similar which allows us to replace the empty-room calibration, which requires knowing that no person is in the area for a period of time, with an LTH calculated online while people are present and moving in the area. Next, we formalize our discussion of the differences between histograms by defining two histogram difference metrics.

3.2 Histogram Difference

There are many ways to measure the difference $D(\mathbf{p}, \mathbf{q})$ between two histograms $\mathbf{p}$ and $\mathbf{q}$. The "earth mover" distance is a popular way of comparing two histograms. However, it involves solving an optimal transportation problem and thus is too computationally expensive for a real-time NRES system. Here, we choose another well known metric, the Kullback-Leibler divergence (KLD) [7]. We also propose to use the kernel distance, which has been recently applied in computational geometry [11].

3.2.1 Definitions

The Kullback-Leibler divergence between two histograms $\mathbf{p}$ and $\mathbf{q}$ can be calculated as [7]:

$$D_{KL}(\mathbf{p}, \mathbf{q}) = \sum_k p_k \log \frac{p_k}{\tilde{q}_k}, \tag{5}$$

where $\tilde{q}_k = \frac{\max(\epsilon, q_k)}{\sum_k \max(\epsilon, q_k)}$, and ϵ is a small number that we use to avoid any divide-by-zero. Note that we investigate the effect of ϵ later in Section 5.4.

The kernel distance between $\mathbf{p}$ and $\mathbf{q}$ is calculated as [21] [2]:

$$D_K(\mathbf{p}, \mathbf{q}) = \mathbf{p}^T \mathbf{K} \mathbf{p} + \mathbf{q}^T \mathbf{K} \mathbf{q} - 2\mathbf{p}^T \mathbf{K} \mathbf{q}, \tag{6}$$

where $\mathbf{K}$ is an N by N kernel matrix from a 2-D kernel function, and $()^T$ indicates transpose. One commonly used kernel is the Gaussian kernel, defined as:

$$\mathbf{K}(y_j, y_k) = \exp\left(-\frac{|y_j - y_k|^2}{\sigma_G^2}\right), \tag{7}$$

where y_j and y_k are the jth and kth elements, and σ_G^2 is the Gaussian kernel width parameter.

Another common kernel is the Epanechnikov kernel, which is optimal in the sense that it minimizes asymptotic mean integrated squared error [6],

$$\mathbf{K}(y_j, y_k) = \frac{3}{4}\left(1 - \frac{|y_j - y_k|^2}{\sigma_E^2}\right) I_{|y_j - y_k| \leq \sigma_E^2}, \tag{8}$$

where I_a is the indicator function, $I_a = 1$ where a is true and zero otherwise, and σ_E^2 is the Epanechnikov kernel width parameter. Note that the Epanechnikov kernel is not necessarily optimal for KRTI. Both Gaussian and Epanechnikov kernel functions achieve similar performance in KRTI.

3.2.2 Efficient Implementation

The computation of (6) has $\mathcal{O}(N^2)$ multiplication and add operations. We show in the following that the kernel distance can be calculated with only $\mathcal{O}(N)$ operations. First, we use the fact that $\mathbf{K}^{\frac{1}{2}}$ is a symmetric matrix $\mathbf{K}^{\frac{1}{2}} = (\mathbf{K}^{\frac{1}{2}})^T$ to change formulation (6) to the standard Euclidean distance:

$$\begin{aligned} D_K(\mathbf{p}, \mathbf{q}) &= (\mathbf{K}^{\frac{1}{2}}\mathbf{p})^T \mathbf{K}^{\frac{1}{2}}\mathbf{p} + (\mathbf{K}^{\frac{1}{2}}\mathbf{q})^T \mathbf{K}^{\frac{1}{2}}\mathbf{q} - \\ &\quad 2(\mathbf{K}^{\frac{1}{2}}\mathbf{p})^T \mathbf{K}^{\frac{1}{2}}\mathbf{q} \\ &= \|\mathbf{K}^{\frac{1}{2}}\mathbf{p} - \mathbf{K}^{\frac{1}{2}}\mathbf{q}\|^2, \end{aligned} \tag{9}$$

where $\|\cdot\|$ indicates the Euclidean distance. Letting $\mathbf{u} = K^{\frac{1}{2}}\mathbf{p}$, $\mathbf{v} = K^{\frac{1}{2}}\mathbf{q}$, we obtain,

$$D_K(\mathbf{p}, \mathbf{q}) = \|\mathbf{u} - \mathbf{v}\|^2. \tag{10}$$

Now, consider the online computation of the kernel distance at time n, that is, $D_K(\mathbf{p}^n, \mathbf{q}^n)$, where both LTH and STH are calculated using the EWMA method in (3). Instead of

---

[2] Strickly speaking, definition in (6) is the squared kernel distance. We use (6) in KRTI for computation convenience.

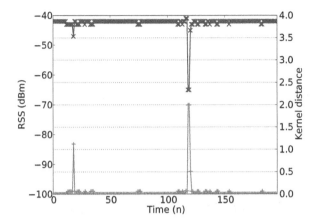

Figure 2: RSS ($\times$) and kernel distance ($+$) time series for a link which a person crosses at $n = 23$ and $n = 120$.

updating $\mathbf{p}^n$ and $\mathbf{q}^n$ each time n, we can reduce computational complexity by instead updating $\mathbf{u}^n$ and $\mathbf{v}^n$, that is, $\mathbf{u}$ and $\mathbf{v}$ at time $n > 0$, using the same EWMA method:

$$
\begin{aligned}
\mathbf{u}^n &= (1 - \beta_p)\mathbf{u}^{n-1} + \beta_p \mathbf{K}^{\frac{1}{2}} \mathbf{I}_{y^n} \\
\mathbf{v}^n &= (1 - \beta_q)\mathbf{v}^{n-1} + \beta_q \mathbf{K}^{\frac{1}{2}} \mathbf{I}_{y^n},
\end{aligned} \tag{11}
$$

where y^n is the RSS at time n, β_p is the forgetting factor for $\mathbf{u}$, and β_q is the factor for $\mathbf{v}$. The term $\mathbf{K}^{\frac{1}{2}} \mathbf{I}_{y^n}$ is simply the kth column of matrix $\mathbf{K}^{\frac{1}{2}}$, where k is the index of the RSS y^n in the histogram, and thus does not require any multiplications. Thus (11) only requires $\mathcal{O}(N)$ multiplies and adds.

Now the current kernel distance at time n is calculated as:

$$
D_K(\mathbf{u}^n, \mathbf{v}^n) = \|\mathbf{u}^n - \mathbf{v}^n\|^2. \tag{12}
$$

This formula is identical to $D_K(\mathbf{p}^n, \mathbf{q}^n)$ except that it requires $\mathcal{O}(N)$, rather than $\mathcal{O}(N^2)$, multiplies and adds. Note that initial values $\mathbf{v}_0$ and $\mathbf{u}_0$ must be given. We assume that the system has been running prior to $n = 0$ and use these initial measurements to initialize $\mathbf{v}_0$ and $\mathbf{u}_0$.

3.2.3 Examples

Consider the example histograms in Figure 1. For Figure 1(a), $D_K(\mathbf{p}, \mathbf{q}) = 0.83$ between the LTH and the STH with a person on the link line, if we use the Epanechnikov kernel with $\sigma_E^2 = 30$. Without any people on the link line, $D_K(\mathbf{p}^n, \mathbf{q}^n) = 0$, since the STH is the same as the LTH. For the moving people case in Figure 1(b), $D_K(\mathbf{p}^n, \mathbf{q}^n) = 1.2$ between the LTH and the STH with people, while $D_K(\mathbf{p}^n, \mathbf{q}^n) = 0.2$ if no people near the link. These two examples show that the presence of a stationary and moving person significantly increases the kernel distance.

As another example, we show in Figure 2 both the RSS, y^n, and kernel distance, $D_K(\mathbf{p}^n, \mathbf{q}^n)$, for a period of time in which a person crosses the link twice. Kernel distance is very close to zero except when the person crosses the link at $n = 23$ and $n = 120$, when it exceeds 1.0. Note that $0 \leq D_K(\mathbf{p}^n, \mathbf{q}^n) \leq 2$. The kernel distance indicates clearly the link crossings by its high value.

3.3 Kernel Distance-Based Radio Tomographic Imaging

Let $\mathbf{d} = [d_0, \ldots, d_{L-1}]^T$ denote a histogram difference vector with L directional link histogram distances, $d_l = D(\mathbf{p}_l, \mathbf{q}_l)$. Let $\mathbf{x} = [x_0, \ldots, x_{M-1}]^T$ denote an image vector, where x_m is a measure of the current presence of a person or object in pixel m that was not typically present in the past. In other words, x_m is the "novelty" of human presence in pixel m. We assume that $\mathbf{d}$ can be expressed as a linear combination of $\mathbf{x}$, as has been assumed for other RTI systems [18, 13, 23, 5, 12, 24]:

$$
\mathbf{d} = \mathbf{W}\mathbf{x} + \mathbf{n}, \tag{13}
$$

where $\mathbf{n}$ is a vector of measurement noise and model error. We use the elliptical weight model $\mathbf{W}$ given in [23, 24], in which the weight $W_{l,m}$ for pixel m is non-zero only if the pixel center is in an ellipse with foci at the link transmitter and receiver locations.

A radio tomographic image $\hat{\mathbf{x}}$ be estimated from histogram difference measurements $\mathbf{d}$ using:

$$
\hat{\mathbf{x}} = (W^T C_{\mathbf{n}}^{-1} W + C_{\mathbf{x}}^{-1})^{-1} W^T C_{\mathbf{n}}^{-1} \mathbf{d}, \tag{14}
$$

where $C_{\mathbf{x}}$ is the covariance matrix of $\mathbf{x}$, and $C_{\mathbf{n}}$ is the covariance matrix of the link measurement noise. Here we use a least squares formulation, which has been shown to outperform the Tikhonov regularization method [31]. The covariance matrix of the link measurement noise, $C_{\mathbf{n}}$, is not generally known here, thus we assume the noise vector has i.i.d. elements. Thus $C_{\mathbf{n}}$ becomes an identity matrix multiplied by σ_n^2. We propose to use the following modified least squares formulation:

$$
\hat{\mathbf{x}} = \Pi_K \mathbf{d} \quad \text{where} \quad \Pi_K = (W^T W + \sigma_n^2 C_{\mathbf{x}}^{-1})^{-1} W^T. \tag{15}
$$

We model the scaled image covariance the same as in [31], where the (i, j) element of $\frac{1}{\sigma_n^2} C_{\mathbf{x}}$ is given by

$$
\left[\frac{1}{\sigma_n^2} C_{\mathbf{x}}\right]_{i,j} = \frac{\sigma^2}{\delta} \exp\left(-\frac{\|\mathbf{r}_j - \mathbf{r}_i\|}{\delta}\right), \tag{16}
$$

where $\sigma^2 = \sigma_x^2 / \sigma_n^2$ is the ratio of variance of human presence σ_x^2 to the variance of noise σ_n^2, which plays the role of regularization, δ is a correlation distance parameter, $\mathbf{r}_i$ and $\mathbf{r}_j$ are the center coordinates of the ith and jth pixels, and $\|\cdot\|$ indicates Euclidian distance. From (15) we see the image estimate is the product of $\mathbf{d}$ with a projection matrix Π_K which can be calculated ahead of time. Thus, the image estimate can be easily calculated in real-time.

In Section 5.4, we compare the performance of KLD and kernel distance for calculation of $\mathbf{d}$ in (15), and show that the kernel distance consistently outperforms the KLD. Thus we generally call our method *kernel distance-based radio tomographic imaging*, or KRTI. To obtain a good image resolution of human presence, we set the pixel size of KRTI to be 0.3 m by 0.3 m in this paper. Then we choose RTI parameters as explained in [23, 24, 31]. We list new parameters and their values used in KRTI in Table 2. Note that we could tune these parameters for a particular experiment to obtain higher localization accuracy, but we use the same parameter values for all experiments to show that KRTI performs well in different environments. We investigate the effects of these parameters on KRTI in Section 5.

Name	Task	Description
Exp.1	stationary person	calm day through-wall
Exp.2	moving person	calm day through-wall
Exp.3	moving person	windy day with fans
Exp.4	moving person	environment changes
Exp.5	moving person	at a cluttered bookstore

Table 1: Experimental datasets.

3.4 Localization and Tracking

In this section, we describe how to use the image in (15) to perform localization and tracking, which is the focus of this paper. We assume, for simplifying formulation purpose, that only one person is present in the network. When multiple people are in the area, they can be seen in the KRTI image, however, multi-target localization and tracking is not the focus of this paper.

From the KRTI image estimate $\hat{x}$, the position of the person is estimated as the center coordinate of the pixel with maximum value. That is,

$$\hat{z} = r_q \quad \text{where} \quad q = \arg\max_p \hat{x}_p$$

where $\hat{x}_p$ is the pth element of vector $\hat{x}$ from (15). The localization error of this estimate is defined as: $e_{loc} = \|\hat{z} - z\|$, where z is the actual position of the person.

To increase accuracy when locating moving people, we apply a Kalman filter to the localization estimates to track people's locations over time. In the state transition model of the Kalman filter, we include both mobile people's location and velocity in the state vector, and the observation inputs of the Kalman filter are the localization estimates. Note that other NRES methods like VRTI [24] is capable of tracking a person even if she stops moving for a while by recording the last location where she was present. However, VRTI cannot image and locate a stationary person that is constantly present at a single location in the network. We evaluate both localization and tracking performance in Section 5.

4. EXPERIMENTS

In this section, we describe experiments that we use in evaluating our new framework. We use TelosB nodes running a network protocol called Spin [2]. At any particular time, only one node is broadcasting while all the other nodes are measuring pairwise RSS. The transmission interval between two nodes is set by the Spin protocol so that three link measurements are recorded each second to match the speed of human motion. For faster human motion, we can increase the transmission frequency at the cost of more power consumption. All nodes are operating on the 26th channel of IEEE 802.15.4 to avoid overlap with WiFi networks. A basestation connected to a laptop listens to the broadcast on that channel and collects RSS from these nodes.

In Experiments 1 and 2, thirty-four radio nodes are deployed outside the living room of a residential house. During the first experiment (Experiment 1), a person is asked to stand motionless at twenty different known locations inside the living room. Experiment 2 is performed with the same settings, but the task is to locate a person walking inside the living room. A person walks around a marked path at a constant speed using a metronome so that the location of the person at any particular time is known. An important

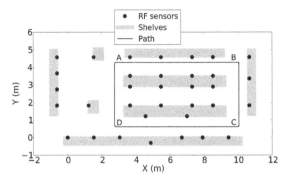

(a) Experiment layout

(b) Bookstore environment

Figure 3: Experiment layout and environment of Exp. 5.

fact about Experiment 2 is after recording offline calibration measurements, a node (node ID 32) on the PVC stand was moved to a different location. This system change affects the system performance, which we discuss later. Experiments 1 and 2 are performed and reported by [24]. The third and fourth experiments (Experiment 3 and Experiment 4) are new datasets, which are also through-wall experiments performed at the same residential house with the same hardware and software. Since a recent study [30] demonstrated the degrading effect of wind-induced motion on a variance-based localization system, we choose a windy day and we also place three rotating fans at three locations in the living room to create more motion to increase the background noise for Experiments 3 and 4. Both experiments are performed in the same condition, and both are used to locate a person walking inside the house. The difference is that we observe significant environmental difference between the offline calibration period and the online localization period in Experiment 4. During the offline calibration period, wind blows strongly causing a lot of RSS variations, but it becomes much weaker during online period. We investigate the effect of system and environment changes on the system performance in Section 5.5. The last experiment (Experiment 5) is performed by Wilson et al. [25] in the University of Utah bookstore in an area of about 12 m by 5 m with thirty-four nodes deployed on book shelves and display tables. A person walks clockwise around a known path twice from Point A to Point D as shown in the experimental layout Figure 3(a). The bookstore environment is cluttered with shelves, tables and books, as shown in Figure 3(b).

As summarized in Table 1, the first four experiments are all "through-wall" experiments with thirty-four nodes de-

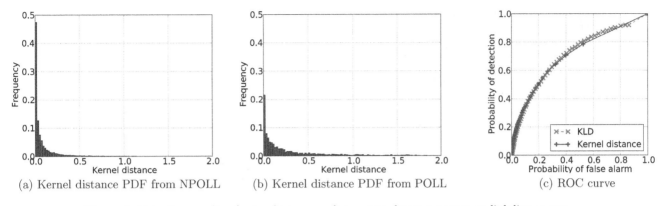

| (a) Kernel distance PDF from NPOLL | (b) Kernel distance PDF from POLL | (c) ROC curve |

Figure 4: Detection results of using histogram distance to detect a person on link line or not.

ployed outside walls. The directional radio link density for these experiments is about 15 links per m^2. For Experiment 5, the link density is about 19 links per m^2. All five experimental environments should be multipath-rich environments.

5. RESULTS

In this section, we first evaluate detection via kernel distance, then we show imaging and localization results of a stationary person. After that, we show localization and tracking results of a moving person. Finally, we discuss the performance of using KLD and kernel distance, we also discuss the effect of environment and system change on KRTI performance.

5.1 Detection of a Person on Link Line

Before showing the imaging, localization and tracking results, we first test using kernel distance from a single link to detect the presence of a person on a link line. First, we define what we mean by a person being on a link line. We denote the transmitting node and receiving node of link l as i_l and j_l, with coordinates $\mathbf{s}_{i_l}$ and $\mathbf{s}_{j_l}$, respectively. We denote the person's true location as $\mathbf{z}$. Our definition of "person on the link line" (POLL) is that the person's center coordinate $\mathbf{z}$ is in an ellipse of excess path length $\lambda > 0$ with foci at the node locations, that is,

$$\text{POLL}: \|\mathbf{s}_{i_l} - \mathbf{z}\| + \|\mathbf{s}_{j_l} - \mathbf{z}\| < \|\mathbf{s}_{i_l} - \mathbf{s}_{j_l}\| + \lambda. \quad (17)$$

Note that we use $\lambda = 0.06m$ in our results, so that the elliptical area includes only positions very close to the line between the two nodes.

We want to decide between two hypotheses, H_0 that the NPOLL condition is true, and H_1 that POLL is true. To avoid making assumptions about the distribution of histogram differences given H_0 or H_1, we simply suggest that histogram differences will be higher under H_1 than under H_0. Thus, we decide whether we believe NPOLL or POLL is true by comparing the histogram difference to a threshold:

$$D(\mathbf{p}_l, \mathbf{q}_l) \underset{H_0}{\overset{H_1}{\gtrless}} \eta, \quad (18)$$

where η is a user-defined detection threshold that is set to be the same for each link, $\mathbf{p}_l$ and $\mathbf{q}_l$ are the STH and LTH

from link l, respectively, and $D(\mathbf{p}_l, \mathbf{q}_l)$ is calculated from either KLD or kernel distance formulation.

Now, we use data from Experiment 1 and parameters as given in Table 2 to test the detection performance. First, we record all kernel distances during H_0 (NPOLL). The distribution of $D_K(\mathbf{p}^n, \mathbf{q}^n)$ given H_0 is shown in Figure 4(a). Approximately half of kernel distances are zero, and the vasty majority are below 0.5. For the data recorded on links where H_1 (POLL) is true, the kernel distance distribution is shown in Figure 4(b). Now, fewer kernel distances are zero, down to 20%, however, this means that we have no chance of detecting the person standing on the link line for 20% of links. From the distributions of $D_K(\mathbf{p}^n, \mathbf{q}^n)$ given H_0 and H_1, we calculate the receiver operating characteristic (ROC) curve in Figure 4(c). Even for a probability of false alarm (P_{FA}) of 40%, the probability of detection is below 80%. Similarly, we test the use of KLD as the difference metric, with the resulting ROC curve shown in Figure 4(c). For low P_{FA}, kernel distance has higher detection performance, while for high P_{FA}, KLD performs better. The results show the difficulties in detecting human presence using only one link's RSS data. This motivates the use of a network of many links, rather than just a single link, in order to infer the presence and location of people in an area.

5.2 Imaging and Localization of a Stationary Person

We now demonstrate that KRTI can not only locate moving people, but also stationary people, a major advantage of KRTI over variance-based methods [24, 29]. In KRTI, we use the EWMA scheme for both long-term and short-term histograms, and the kernel distance, with parameters listed in Table 2. We use measurements from Experiment 1, in which a person stands motionless inside a house, and compare imaging results from KRTI and VRTI [24]. In Figure 5(a), the KRTI image has relatively high pixel values near the true location of the person, and the pixel with maximum value is very close to the true location. Since a stationary human body does not cause much RSS variance, VRTI cannot correctly image the person's location, as shown in Figure 5(b). Note that since EWMA filter is used to update histograms using online measurements, a stationary person staying at one location for several minutes would "fade away" from the KRTI images. However, if a person is

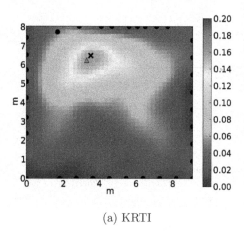

(a) KRTI

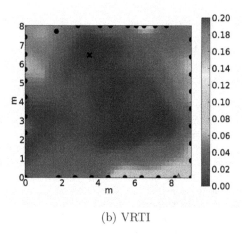

(b) VRTI

Figure 5: Imaging results of a stationary person (true location shown as ×) from (a) KRTI and (b) VRTI.

in the same location for minutes, we can always record the location where she disappears from the images, and start localization once new motion indicates that she has moved again.

A recent method able to locate a stationary person in a multipath-rich environment is the sequential Monte Carlo (SMC) approach developed by [25]. The method of [25] requires an empty-room (offline) calibration, and is substantially more computational complex than the KRTI method. Further, across experiments, we show that KRTI is more accurate in localization. We run SMC using three hundred particles using data from Experiment 1. In Experiment 1, a person sequentially stands at each of twenty known locations for a constant period τ. At each location we have about fifty KRTI estimates. For these twenty locations, we calculate the overall average error $\bar{e}_{loc} = \sum_{i=1}^{20} \|\hat{\mathbf{z}}_a - \mathbf{z}\|$, where $\hat{\mathbf{z}}_a$ is the average location estimates from KRTI and SMC during period τ. The average location estimates $\hat{\mathbf{z}}_a$ from KRTI are shown in Figure 6, in which the line between the average estimate (shown as triangle) and the true location (shown as cross) indicates the estimation error. We see the errors from KRTI are generally below 1 m, more accurate than the results from SMC shown in Figure 10 of [25]. The average error $\bar{e}_{loc}$ from SMC is 0.83 m, while $\bar{e}_{loc}$ from KRTI is 0.71 m, a 14.5% reduction. On the same 2.4 GHz

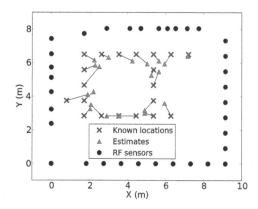

Figure 6: KRTI location estimates of a person standing at twenty locations.

Core 2 Duo processor-based laptop, it takes 0.03 seconds to produce one estimate from our KRTI Python code, while it takes three to four minutes to produce one SMC location estimate. Thus, KRTI outperforms SMC both in accuracy and computational efficiency.

5.3 Localization and Tracking of a Moving Person

Besides the improvement on imaging and locating stationary people, KRTI also provides better performance for locating moving people. Now we compare KRTI with two variance-based methods, VRTI [24] and SubVRT [30]. We run KRTI, VRTI and SubVRT on data from Experiments 2 - 5, and calculate the root mean squared error (RMSE), which is defined as the square root of the average squared localization error. As shown in Table 3, our KRTI can achieve submeter localization accuracy in all experiments. Particularly, for Experiment 3, performed on a windy day, the RMSE from VRTI is 2.1 m, while the RMSE from KRTI is 0.81 m, a 61% improvement. For Experiment 2, performed on a calm day, SubVRT has a better performance than KRTI (0.65 m vs. 0.73 m RMSE for KRTI). Since SubVRT uses offline empty-room calibration measurements to estimate the noise covariance [30], we expect it to perform particularly well during windy conditions. KRTI does not use such empty-area calibration. However, KRTI significantly outperforms Sub-VRT, by 30-35%, in all other experiments. Particularly, in Experiment 4, in which the environment changes between the offline calibration and the online measurements, Sub-VRT does not perform well. However, KRTI uses online measurements to build the long-term histogram, thus is not significantly affected by offline measurements. The RMSE of KRTI is 0.79 m in this case, a 31% improvement on Sub-VRT. We discuss the effect of environmental changes in more detail in Section 5.5. For Experiment 5, due to the strong multipath environment of the cluttered bookstore (as shown in Figure 3(b)), neither VRTI nor SubVRT perform very well. However, KRTI is particularly robust to non-LOS environments and achieves 0.74 m RMSE, a similar error as in other experiments. To summarize, KRTI does not just use RSS variance or RSS mean. Instead, it uses histogram difference to include both the effect of a stationary person and a moving person. It is particularly robust to the multi-

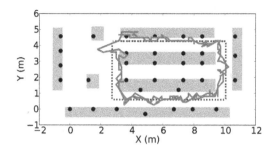

Figure 7: Kalman filter tracking results for Experiment 5 (true path shown as dash line).

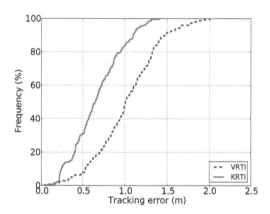

Figure 8: Kalman filter tracking CDFs from VRTI and KRTI for Experiment 5.

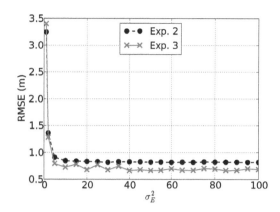

Figure 9: Kernel parameter σ_E^2 vs. RMSE from KRTI.

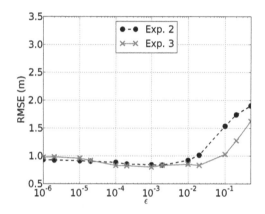

Figure 10: KLD parameter ϵ vs. RMSE from KRTI using KLD.

path environment, working just as well in strong multipath environments.

Finally, we show the Kalman filter tracking results of Experiment 5 in Figure 7. We see that tracking results have highest errors when the person is far from the closest radio node. For example, the tracking error is about 1 m when the person is located at the upper left corner of the path. However, KRTI with a Kalman filter is capable of tracking a person in a large multipath-rich environment with submeter accuracy in general. We also compare the cumulative distribution functions (CDFs) of tracking errors from KRTI and VRTI in Figure 8. For VRTI, 95% of tracking errors are below 1.7 m, while 95% of errors from KRTI are below 1.2 m, a 29% improvement. We also see the median tracking RMSE from VRTI is 1.0 m, while it is 0.6 m for KRTI, a 40% improvement.

5.4 Kernel Distance vs. KLD

In this section, we compare kernel distance and Kullback-Leibler divergence (KLD) as histogram difference metrics in localization. Using an Epanechnikv kernel defined in (8), we test different kernel width parameters σ_E^2. Figure 9 shows that KRTI performance is not sensitive to this parameter. RMSEs from Experiments 2 and 3 are both shallow functions of σ_E^2, as long as $\sigma_E^2 \geq 10$. A kernel that is too wide tends to smooth the data so much that all measurements look the same. However, a kernel that is too narrow will not smooth the data at all, and as a result is easily affected by noise. The

kernel width should be chosen so it is roughly proportional to the scale of sensing noise; then a strong signal can still be observed, modest sensing noise will not change the results much, and outliers will tend to be smoothed away.

To calculate KLD, we use parameter ϵ in (5) to avoid division by zero. As shown in Figure 10, if $\epsilon < 0.1$, the localziation RMSE is only mildly sensitive to this parameter. However, from a comparison of Experiments 2 and 3, the RMSEs when using KLD are generally above 0.8 m, while most RMSEs from kernel distance are below 0.8 m. From Figure 9 and Figure 10, we see both histogram difference metrics can achieve submeter localization accuracy, however, kernel distance is less sensitive to its parameter σ_E^2, and consistently outperforms KLD in localization accuracy.

5.5 Effects of Environment and System Changes

In the above tests, we use the EWMA filter to calculate the online LTH q. We can also use the offline empty-room calibration in order to calculate the LTH. We compare the two in this section.

Note that if the environment changes or sensors change positions after the offline empty-room calibration, the changes diminish system performance. As described in Section 4, the location of a single node is accidentally changed after the of-fline empty-room calibration period in Experiment 2, prior

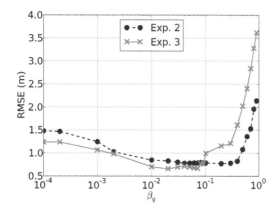

Figure 11: EWMA coefficient β_q vs. RMSE from KRTI.

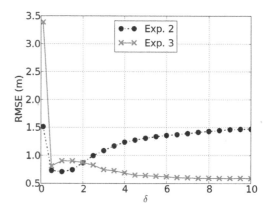

Figure 13: KRTI RMSE vs. δ.

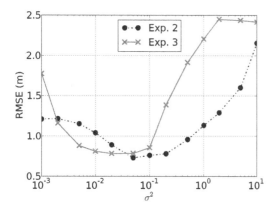

Figure 12: KRTI RMSE vs. σ.

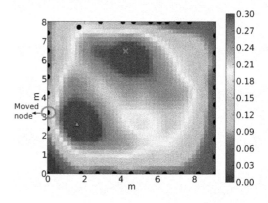

Figure 14: Effect of a moved node on KRTI when using the offline empty-room LTH.

to the online period. Even if a receiver node moves by only a fraction of its wavelength, its measured RSS values may vary by tens of dBs as a result of small-scale fading [8]. We apply the offline empty-room LTH in KRTI to generate the image in Figure 14, in which a person is walking and is at the position indicated by the cross. The figure shows two hot spot areas — besides the one close to the true location of the person, there is another one at the lower left corner of the network, close to node 32 indicated by the red circle. A similar false image, not shown, is seen during Experiment 4, in which the environment changes after the offline empty-room calibration. We avoid this false image problem by using the EWMA for online calculation of the LTH. In our KRTI, we use solely the EWMA filter for online calculation of both long-term and short-term histograms. We do, however, require initialization of the histograms at time zero. In real-time operation, we would simply run the system for a short period to collect sufficient RSS measurements [14] to allow the LTH to "settle" prior to using its results. By using the EWMA filter, our KRTI does not have such false image as shown in Figure 14. To see how EWMA overcomes the effect of position change of a node in Experiment 2, we use the offline calibration measurements as the initialization of LTH, and then use EWMA and online measurements to update LTH in our KRTI. The time series of position estimate error is shown in Figure 15. We see that KRTI estimate

error can be up to 6 m due to offline LTH affected by the node position change. However, after a few estimates, KRTI errors are all below 2 m. The false hot spot disappears from KRTI images due to the online EWMA update.

We see the relative RMSE performance of empty-room LTH (offline FIR) vs. online LTH (online EWMA) in Table 4. We see that the online LTH is as good or better than the offline LTH in every case. While the RMSEs are similar in Experiments 3 and 5, the online LTH performs significantly better for Experiments 2 and 4, for which there were either sensor position changes or environmental changes between the empty-room calibration and the online operation, as described earlier. If we control the updating speed appropriately by choosing $\beta_q = 0.05$, the "online EWMA" method can achieve submeter accuracy for all experiments. Since Experiments 3 and 5 do not have much environment and system change effect, both methods have similar performance.

For KRTI using the online LTH, we test the effect of EWMA forgetting factor β_q. The RMSEs from KRTI with different β_q values are shown in Figure 11. The RMSEs are very shallow functions of β_q and are all below 1 m in the range of 0.01 to 0.1. If β_q is below 0.01, the weight of the latest measurement becomes very small, that is, the update process of the LTH is very slow. If $\beta_q = 0$, it is equivalent to no update. At the other extreme, if β_q is too high, i.e.,

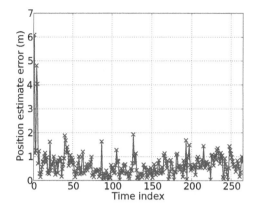

Figure 15: KRTI error time series.

Parameter	Value	Description
σ^2	0.05	Regularization parameter
δ	0.5	Space parameter (m)
σ_E^2	30	Epanechnikov kernel width
ϵ	0.001	KLD parameter
β_q	0.05	EWMA factor for $\mathbf{v}$
β_p	0.9	EWMA factor for $\mathbf{u}$

Table 2: Parameters used in KRTI.

RMSE (m)	Exp. 2	Exp. 3	Exp. 4	Exp. 5
VRTI	0.70	2.12	1.46	1.09
SubVRT	0.65	1.05	1.14	1.08
KRTI	0.73	0.81	0.79	0.74

Table 3: RMSEs of locating a moving person.

RMSE (m)	Exp. 2	Exp. 3	Exp. 4	Exp. 5
Offline FIR	1.49	0.74	5.02	0.74
Online EWMA	0.73	0.81	0.79	0.74

Table 4: RMSEs from KRTI using online IIR and offline FIR methods.

above 0.1, then the update speed becomes too fast. If β_q approaches 1, then almost all previous RSS measurements are removed from the memory. To keep sufficient history measurements in memory and also balance between these two extremes, we choose $\beta_q = 0.05$ as listed in Table 2. We also test the effect of EWMA factor β_p for updating the STH $\mathbf{p}$, we find KRTI performance is best in the range of 0.8 to 1.

Note that other methods can be used to make an NRES system more robust to the environment and system changes. For example, [30, 31] use subspace method and least squares method to reduce the noise effects due to the environment changes. Work in [15] shows that one can detect when a transmitter or receiver is mis-behaving, and future work might be able to automatically detect failed or moved nodes.

5.6 Effects of KRTI Parameters

We have examined the effects of kernel width parameter σ_E^2 and EWMA coefficient β_q on the performance of KRTI in the above two subsections. Now we investigate another two important parameters – the regularization parameter σ^2 and space parameter δ in our KRTI formulation (16).

Recall that parameter σ^2 is the ratio of human presence variance to noise variance. From (15) and (16), we see that the reciprocal of σ^2 plays the role of regularization parameter as in [24, 23]. To see its effect, we set σ^2 values in a wide range from 0.001 to 10, fix other parameter values and run KRTI to calculate the RMSEs. Figure 12 shows the RMSEs of KRTI vs. σ^2. We see that when σ^2 is in the range of 0.002 and 0.1, RMSEs from Experiments 2 and 3 are both below 1.3 m, and the RMSE vs. σ^2 curves are shallow. However, when σ^2 is above 0.2, that is, less regularization is used in the inversion, the RMSEs increase significantly for both experiments due to insufficient smoothing effect from regularization. We also notice that we need a smaller σ^2 value

for Experiment 3 compared to Experiment 2 to obtain the minimum RMSE. This is due to the fact that Experiment 3 has more noise than Experiment 2. The noise variance of Experiment 3 is greater than that of Experiment 2, thus σ^2 should be set lower for Experiment 3 to keep the variance of human presence a constant. We set $\sigma^2 = 0.05$ for all five experiments.

Another parameter listed in 2 is the correlation distance parameter δ, which controls the spatial size of the exponentially decaying regularization term in (16). While σ^2 controls the intensity of the regularization term, δ affects both the intensity and the size of the smoothing "blob" (regularization term) in the KRTI images. The RMSEs vs. δ plot is shown in Figure 13. We see when $\delta = 0.1m$, that is, the size of the smoothing blob is very small, RMSEs of both experiments are higher than 1.5 m. Even if the intensity of the regularization is high, the general smoothing effect is not sufficient due to a small sized blob. As long as the smoothing blob reaches the size of a typical human size of about 0.5 m, RMSEs are below 1 m. Increasing δ beyond 2 m causes too much smoothing effect for Experiment 2 without much noise, thus RMSE of Experiment 2 increases slowly for $\delta > 2$. For Experiment 3 with a lot of noise, a larger blob size averages out additional noise, thus RMSE continues to decrease slowly. For a single person experiment like Experiment 3, it does not hurt to increase the blob size. However, for tracking more than one person, it would be necessary to limit δ. In this paper, we choose $\delta = 0.5$ for all experiments.

5.7 Discussion

Compared with other NRES methods, KRTI demonstrates better performance in imaging, localization and tracking. Shadowing-based radio tomographic imaging [23] can locate both stationary and moving people at line-of-sight (LOS) environments, but does not work at multipath-rich environments. Compared with variance-based methods [29, 24, 30], KRTI has the ability of imaging a stationary person as well as a moving person. For tracking a moving person, KRTI also outperforms VRTI and SubVRT. In addition, KRTI

Features	RTI[23]	VRTI[24]	SMC[25]	KRTI
Through-wall?	No	Yes	Yes	Yes
Online calibration?	No	NA	No	Yes
Stationary people?	Yes	No	Yes	Yes
Real-time?	Yes	Yes	No	Yes

Table 5: Features of different NRES methods.

can use an EWMA filter to update the long-term histogram continuously during an online period, and is more robust to environmental and system changes. The advantage of KRTI over the SMC method [25] is that KRTI does not require any empty-room offline calibration, and performs better both in localization accuracy and computational efficiency. To summarize, KRTI has new properties that other methods do not. We list features of different methods in Table 5. To our knowledge, KRTI is the first NRES method that can locate both stationary and moving people in both LOS and non-LOS environments without any offline calibration.

6. CONCLUSION

In this paper, we propose a new NRES framework that uses histogram difference and online calibration to perform network RF sensing of people. Specifically, we propose a kernel distance-based RTI, which uses the kernel distance between a short-term histogram and a long-term histogram to image and locate a moving or stationary person. We explore the framework using three reported measurement sets and two new measurement sets. We evaluate detection, imaging and tracking using our framework. Our experimental results show that KRTI provides robust imaging and tracking capabilities at multipath-rich environments, even though detection from individual links is unreliable. Compared with previous methods, KRTI is the only real-time method that is capable of imaging and locating both stationary and moving people in both LOS and non-LOS environments without any training or empty-room calibration.

7. REFERENCES

[1] Camero website. http://www.camero-tech.com.
[2] Sensing and Processing Across Networks (SPAN) Lab, Spin website. http://span.ece.utah.edu/spin.
[3] P. Bahl and V. N. Padmanabhan. RADAR: an in-building RF-based user location and tracking system. In *IEEE INFOCOM 2000*, volume 2, pages 775–784, 2000.
[4] C. Chang and A. Sahai. Object tracking in a 2D UWB sensor network. In *38th Asilomar Conference on Signals, Systems and Computers*, volume 1, pages 1252–1256, Nov. 2004.
[5] X. Chen, A. Edelstein, Y. Li, M. Coates, M. Rabbat, and A. Men. Sequential monte carlo for simultaneous passive device-free tracking and sensor localization using received signal strength measurements. In *Proc. ACM/IEEE International Conference on Information Processing in Sensor Networks (IPSN)*, Chicago, U.S., April 2011.
[6] D. Comaniciu and P. Meer. Mean shift: A robust approach toward feature space analysis. *Pattern Analysis and Machine Intelligence, IEEE Transactions on*, 24(5):603–619, 2002.
[7] T. Cover and J. A. Thomas. *Elements of Information Theory.* John Wiley & Sons, 1991.
[8] G. D. Durgin. *Space-Time Wireless Channels.* Prentice Hall PTR, 2002.
[9] A. Edelstein and M. Rabbat. Background subtraction for online calibration of baseline rss in rf sensing networks. Technical Report arXiv:1207.1137v1, Arxiv.org, July 2012.
[10] A. M. Haimovich, R. S. Blum, and L. J. Cimini. MIMO radar with widely separated antennas. *IEEE Signal Processing*, 25(1):116–129, Jan. 2008.
[11] S. Joshi, R. V. Kommaraji, J. M. Phillips, and S. Venkatasubramanian. Comparing distributions and shapes using the kernel distance. In *Proceedings of the 27th annual ACM symposium on Computational geometry*, SoCG '11, pages 47–56, 2011.
[12] O. Kaltiokallio and M. Bocca. Real-time intrusion detection and tracking in indoor environment through distributed RSSI processing. In *IEEE 17th International Conference on Embedded and Real-Time Computing Systems and Applications (RTCSA)*, Toyama, Japan, August 2011.
[13] M. A. Kanso and M. G. Rabbat. Efficient detection and localization of assets in emergency situations. In *3rd Intl.*

[14] *Symposium on Medical Information & Communication Technology (ISMICT)*, Montréal, Québec, Feb. 2009.
[14] J. M. Lucas and M. S. Saccucci. Exponentially weighted moving average control schemes: Properties and enhancements. *Technometrics*, 32(1):1–12, 1990.
[15] M. Maheshwari, S. A. P.R., A. Banerjee, N. Patwari, and S. K. Kasera. Detecting malicious nodes in rss-based localization. In *Proceedings of the 2nd IEEE International Workshop on Data Security and Privacy in Wireless Networks (D-SPAN)*, pages 1–6, June 2011.
[16] G. Mao, B. Fidan, and B. D. O. Anderson. Wireless sensor network localization techniques. *Comput. Networks*, 51(10):2529–2553, 2007.
[17] M. Moussa and M. Youssef. Smart services for smart environments: Device-free passive detection in real environments. In *IEEE PerCom-09*, pages 1–6, 2009.
[18] N. Patwari and P. Agrawal. Effects of correlated shadowing: Connectivity, localization, and rf tomography. In *IEEE/ACM IPSN'08*, April 2008.
[19] N. Patwari, J. Ash, S. Kyperountas, R. M. Moses, A. O. Hero III, and N. S. Correal. Locating the nodes: Cooperative localization in wireless sensor networks. *IEEE Signal Process.*, 22(4):54–69, July 2005.
[20] N. Patwari and J. Wilson. RF sensor networks for device-free localization: Measurements, models and algorithms. *Proceedings of the IEEE*, 98(11):1961–1973, Nov. 2010.
[21] J. M. Phillips and S. Venkatasubramanian. A gentle introduction to the kernel distance. Technical Report arXiv:1103.1625, Arxiv.org, 2011.
[22] M. Seifeldin and M. Youssef. Nuzzer: A large-scale device-free passive localization system for wireless environments. Technical Report arXiv:0908.0893, Arxiv.org, Aug. 2009.
[23] J. Wilson and N. Patwari. Radio tomographic imaging with wireless networks. *IEEE Transactions on Mobile Computing*, 9(5):621–632, May 2010.
[24] J. Wilson and N. Patwari. See-through walls: Motion tracking using variance-based radio tomography networks. *IEEE Transactions on Mobile Computing*, 10(5):612–621, May 2011.
[25] J. Wilson and N. Patwari. A fade level skew-laplace signal strength model for device-free localization with wireless networks. *IEEE Transactions on Mobile Computing*, 11:947 – 958, June 2012.
[26] K. Woyach, D. Puccinelli, and M. Haenggi. Sensorless Sensing in Wireless Networks: Implementation and Measurements. In *Second International Workshop on Wireless Network Measurement (WiNMee'06)*, April 2006.
[27] C. Xu, B. Firner, Y. Zhang, R. Howard, J. Li, and X. Lin. Improving RF-based device-free passive localization in cluttered indoor environments through probabilistic classification methods. In *Proc. 11th Int. Conf. Information Processing in Sensor Networks*, pages 209–220, 2012.
[28] M. Youssef, M. Mah, and A. Agrawala. Challenges: device-free passive localization for wireless environments. In *MobiCom '07: ACM Int'l Conf. Mobile Computing and Networking*, pages 222–229, 2007.
[29] D. Zhang, J. Ma, Q. Chen, and L. M. Ni. An RF-based system for tracking transceiver-free objects. In *IEEE PerCom'07*, pages 135–144, 2007.
[30] Y. Zhao and N. Patwari. Noise reduction for variance-based device-free localization and tracking. In *Proc. of the 8th IEEE Conf. on Sensor, Mesh and Ad Hoc Communications and Networks (SECON'11)*, June 2011.
[31] Y. Zhao and N. Patwari. Robust estimators for variance-based device-free localization and tracking. Technical Report arXiv:1110.1569v1, Arxiv.org, Oct. 2011.
[32] Y. Zhao and N. Patwari. Histogram distance-based radio tomographic localization. In *Proceedings of the 11th international conference on Information Processing in Sensor Networks*, IPSN '12, pages 129–130. ACM, 2012.
[33] Y. Zheng and A. Men. Through-wall tracking with radio tomography networks using foreground detection. In *Proceedings of the Wireless Communications and Networking Conference (WCNC)*, pages 3278–3283, Paris, France, April 2012.

Using Wearable Inertial Sensors for Posture and Position Tracking in Unconstrained Environments through Learned Translation Manifolds

Aris Valtazanos
School of Informatics
University of Edinburgh
Edinburgh, EH8 9AB
a.valtazanos@sms.ed.ac.uk

D. K. Arvind
School of Informatics
University of Edinburgh
Edinburgh, EH8 9AB
dka@inf.ed.ac.uk

Subramanian Ramamoorthy
School of Informatics
University of Edinburgh
Edinburgh, EH8 9AB
s.ramamoorthy@ed.ac.uk

ABSTRACT

Despite recent advances in 3-D motion capture, the problem of simultaneously tracking human posture and position in an unconstrained environment remains open. Optical systems provide both types of information, but are confined to a restricted area of capture. Inertial sensing alleviates this restriction, but at the expense of capturing only relative (postural) and not absolute (positional) information. In this paper, we propose an algorithm combining the relative merits of these systems to track both position and posture in challenging environments. Offline, we combine an optical (Kinect) and an inertial sensing (Orient-4) platform to learn a mapping from *posture variations* to *translations*, which we encode as a *translation manifold*. Online, the optical source is removed, and the learned mapping is used to infer positions using the postures computed by the inertial sensors. We first evaluate our approach in simulation, on motion sequences with ground-truth positions for error estimation. Then, the method is deployed on physical sensing platforms to track human subjects. The proposed algorithm is shown to yield a lower average cumulative error than comparable position tracking methods, such as double integration of accelerometer data, on both simulated and real sensory data, and in a variety of motions and capture settings.

Categories and Subject Descriptors

H.4.0 [**Information Systems Applications**]: General

Keywords

Wearable inertial sensors, optical motion capture, translation models, manifold learning

1. INTRODUCTION

Many information processing applications deal with the analysis of human motion, as captured by an ensemble of sensor devices. In this context, it is often essential to determine both the absolute *position* of tracked subjects, as well as finer-grained information on their body *posture*, such as arm movements or gait patterns. Furthermore, it is often required that motion be captured in challenging, *unconstrained* areas, for example, a large office with multiple rooms and corridors, or an open outdoor environment.

The problem of simultaneous posture and position tracking is of interest to a wide range of motion capture applications. One notable domain is tracking in construction and fire-fighting missions, which requires monitoring of the deployed responders in challenging and potentially unknown environments. Position tracking systems that have been considered in this domain (e.g. indoor global positioning sensor (GPS) systems, ultra-wide bands [12], radio-frequency identification tags [11]) typically require an infrastructure that requires detailed knowledge of the environment (e.g. placing signal receivers at known positions), while also suffering from line-of-sight constraints. Addressing these needs is a challenging task when the environment is difficult to negotiate or cannot be accessed by the system designers. Furthermore, these systems cannot monitor posture, which is often important in order to determine and assess the actions performed by the deployed subjects. Similar needs arise in application areas such as physical gaming [18] and human-robot interaction in rescue missions [6], where human position and posture must also be captured in unconstrained settings. Existing techniques in these domains are similarly restricted to either providing only part of the required data, or requiring special infrastructure in order to be deployed. The above issues raise the need for tracking systems that can produce position and posture from a *single* set of sensory devices, which are not sensitive to the morphology of the capture environment, and which do not rely on synchronisation between multiple heterogeneous sources.

Despite recent advances in motion capture and sensing technologies, fulfilling the above requirements in a robust manner is a challenging task. For instance, optical motion capture systems can capture both positional and postural data, but only within contained environments limited to a small area of capture. Inertial sensing systems allow for greater flexibility in the capture environment, as they are not restricted by line-of-sight constraints between the sensing devices and the tracked subject. However, they do so at the expense of not yielding absolute positions, as their calculations are based on relative rotational estimates, e.g. gyro-

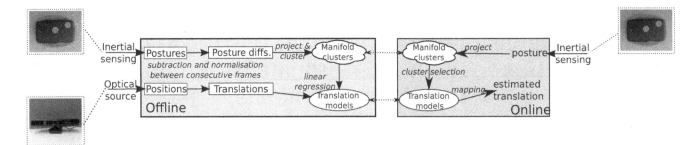

Figure 1: Overall structure of the proposed system. An inertial sensing and an optical source are synchronised and jointly used to learn generative models of whole-body translations in an offline phase. These translations are encoded as linear regression-based mappings from projected latent representations of *posture differences*, as detected from the inertial source, and *positional variations*, as detected from the optical source. Online, the optical source is removed, and the learned model is used to predict translations for the tracked subject.

scope readings. Similarly, general-purpose GPS sensors can compute absolute positions, but at a coarse level of precision and without supplying postural information, while also having limited applicability in indoor environments. Other motion capture technologies, e.g. magnetic systems, also suffer from one or multiple of the above limitations.

In order to address the challenges of simultaneous posture and position capture in unconstrained environments, one would need to combine the relative strengths of these heterogeneous systems in a principled manner. In this paper, we propose a hybrid position and posture tracking algorithm (Figure 1), which jointly uses an inertial and an optical motion capture system to learn local *models of translation* for a given human subject. The algorithm consists of an *offline* learning and *online* generation phase. In the offline phase, body posture data collected from the inertial sensors are synchronised with position data captured from the optical source and aggregated into a single dataset. Due to their high dimensionality, the posture data are projected and clustered on a low-dimensional *manifold*, which captures the salient kinematic structure of the dataset. For each cluster, the projected data are used to learn a mapping from local *posture differences* to *whole-body translations* through linear regression. In the online phase of the algorithm, the optical source is removed, and the learned models are used to generate translation vectors from estimated posture differences. By iteratively applying these translations, the proposed system can track both the position and the posture of a subject performing motions similar to those captured in the offline phase, thus overcoming the main limitation of inertial systems discussed above. Moreover, due to the removal of the optical source in the online phase, the system is not affected by the morphology of the capture environment.

In the remainder of this paper, we first review related motion capture technologies, explaining how our approach combines their relative strengths (Section 2). Then, we describe our method for posture and position tracking, distinguishing between the translation learning and generation phases (Section 3). In Section 4, our approach is evaluated in simulations and physical experiments; first, on data from the Carnegie Mellon Motion Capture Database [3], which are annotated with ground-truth positions, and then, on a human motion capture environment, where we use the Kinect and the Orient platform as sensing systems (Figure 2). Our algorithm is shown to yield a lower overall position error

than the related established tracking method of acceleration integration. Furthermore, in the physical experiments, we demonstrate examples of successful position tracking in a challenging office environment, where existing motion capture technologies cannot be applied in isolation. We review the key features of our work in Section 5.

(a) Microsoft Kinect.   (b) Orient-4 device.

Figure 2: Motion tracking platforms. (a): Optical source – Kinect device with two cameras and a depth-finding sensor. (b): Inertial measurement unit – Orient-4 device with tri-axial gyroscopes, accelerometers, and magnetometers.

2. BACKGROUND AND RELATED WORK

Traditional *optical* motion capture systems, e.g. [4], use an ensemble of high-resolution cameras to track the locations of a set of reflective markers placed on the body of a subject. The marker positions are used to compute the full pose (position and posture) of the subject. However, optical systems suffer from a number of drawbacks that impact their applicability. First, motion capture must be carried out in dedicated studios, which are often expensive to set up and maintain. Second, the total area of capture is limited to a small volume, and subjects cannot be tracked outside its boundaries. Thus, optical systems cannot be used to track subjects interacting outside the studio, e.g. moving in and out of rooms, or navigating along corridors in a building. Third, occlusion problems impact the ability of these systems to track subjects consistently and reliably.

A recent development has been the creation of devices combining stereo cameras and depth-estimating sensors, notably the Kinect [1] (Figure 2(a)). The output of these sensors is used to generate a three-dimensional point cloud, which can then be analysed to determine the pose of a tracked subject, or fit the data to a skeleton model [16]. These stereo-camera devices are significantly cheaper than traditional optical systems, and remove the need for markers on the subject's body. Furthermore, the portability of the sensors allows for anyplace motion capture. However, like traditional optical systems, these devices must remain fixed during tracking, and the volume of capture is limited to approximately 15m^3. This makes them unsuitable for tracking subjects in large or unconstrained spaces.

An alternative to optical systems are wireless *inertial* sensing platforms, such as the Orient interface [21] (Figure 2(b)). Inertial sensing systems collect data from an ensemble of sensor nodes placed on the subject's body. Each device typically consists of 3-axis inertial sensors such as gyroscopes, accelerometers, and magnetometers. These sensors jointly estimate the rotation of the body part the device is placed on, relative to a fixed point on the subject's body. Data from the different body parts are transmitted wirelessly to a base station and aggregated to determine the overall posture of the subject. Alternatively, data can also be stored on the devices and analysed offline at a later time. The latter feature makes these devices suitable for motion capture and processing in environments impacted by communication and data transmission constraints.

Due to the wireless transmission and capture of data, inertial sensing avoids the occlusion problems arising in optical systems. More importantly, as no fixed tracking source is required, subjects can be tracked in a greater variety of environments and in larger areas than with optical systems. The main drawback of inertial sensing is the relative rotational nature of estimates, which means that only postures can be determined directly. Unfortunately, this approach does not extend to absolute spatial positions, as computations are performed relative to a stationary reference point.

Position tracking using inertial measurement units has been the subject of several studies, most following a *model-based* approach, where measurements are filtered through a position model to predict the most likely translation of the tracked subject. Employed models range from Kalman [20, 8, 10] and particle filters [13], to alternative heuristic approaches based on gait event detection [15, 22, 9].

Our approach is different in being a **model-free** method with respect to the measurement units and their output data, where no assumptions are made on the placement of the sensors or the nature of the motion being performed. Instead, the aggregated sensory data is treated as a single *feature vector*, from which a mapping to whole-body translations is learned. This leads to an unsupervised method that can learn a model of translation without the incorporation of additional knowledge on the problem. However, the lack of a specific model also means that the quality of the learned mappings inevitably depends on the quality and variability of the training examples. In later sections of this paper, we provide illustrations of how the accuracy of our approach is affected by the provided data.

Motivated by the above features, in our experimental evaluation we compare against the established model-free method of double integration of accelerometer data. This method relies on the integration of data coming from a single sensor in order to track position over time, without having an internal model on the placement of that sensor. In Section 4, we show that using multiple sensors in conjunction with

a learning algorithm can lead to better tracking of whole-body positions, in both simulated and physical experiments. Furthermore, our approach can also be combined with existing models, where the generated translations can be treated as predictive estimates for a filter. Integration with model-based filtering methods is an area of future work for us.

Dimensionality reduction has been used in inertial sensor networks as a *discriminative* model for activity recognition and gait phase detection [19, 17]. In our work, we extend this notion by using low-dimensional subspaces as *generative* models for translations. In this generative context, learned manifolds have been used in robotics, in order to facilitate imitation of human gaits by humanoid robots [14, 7]. By adopting this flexible representation, our objective is to similarly approximate a wide variety of motion dynamics.

3. METHOD

3.1 Sensory device outputs

3.1.1 Kinect

Figure 3: Body contour tracking using the Kinect. The tracking software automatically detects the outline of a human body, and tracks it as a cloud of points (shown as a blue blob).

We use the OpenNI body tracking interface [2] to detect and track the position of human subjects (Figure 3). The software automatically detects the outline of a human body, and tracks it as a collection of N_I image point coordinates, $\vec{B} = \{(x_1, y_1), \ldots, (x_{N_I}, y_{N_I})\}$. The absolute position of the tracked body is approximated as the centroid of these points as computed through *image moments*.

Let W, H be the width and height (in pixels) of the camera image, and let $\mathbf{I}$ be a 2-D array, such that

$$\mathbf{I}(a,b) = \begin{cases} 1, & (x_a, y_b) \in \vec{B} \\ 0, & (x_a, y_b) \notin \vec{B} \end{cases}, \qquad (1)$$

where $1 \leq a \leq W$, $1 \leq b \leq H$. The raw image moments, M_{ij} are defined as

$$M_{ij} = \sum_{a=1}^{W} \sum_{b=1}^{H} x_a^i \cdot y_b^j \cdot \mathbf{I}(a,b). \qquad (2)$$

Based on these definitions, the image coordinates of the centroid of the tracked body, $C \doteq (\bar{x}, \bar{y})$ are given by

$$(\bar{x}, \bar{y}) = (\, \texttt{round}(M_{10}/M_{00}), \texttt{round}(M_{01}/M_{00}) \,). \qquad (3)$$

The depth of each image pixel (with respect to the device) is measured by the range-finding sensor of the Kinect. This information is used to convert the computed image centroid, $(\bar{x}, \bar{y})$, to the centroid of the body surface that is visible to the Kinect. These coordinates approximate to the absolute positional coordinates of the tracked body,

$$p = (x^B, y^B, z^B). \qquad (4)$$

3.1.2 Orient inertial measurement units

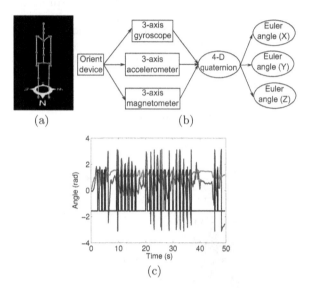

(a)   (b)

(c)

Figure 4: Posture estimation using the Orient devices. (a): 3-D model of the tracked body. Each device is mapped to a different limb. (b): Orientation estimation. Quaternions are computed from raw sensor data and converted to Euler angles. (c): Example of angles produced by an Orient device.

The posture of the tracked subject is computed by the Orient devices. Each device is placed on a limb of the subject's body (Figure 4(a)). The raw data from the device's sensors (triaxial gyroscope, accelerometer, and magnetometer) computes a quaternion representing the orientation at that limb, which is in turn converted into three-dimensional Euler angles (Figure 4(b)) based on a pre-specified rotation order. Due to this convention, an Euler angle can represent the orientation more succinctly than the corresponding quaternion, thus reducing the size of our feature set. An example of the angles output by an Orient is given in Figure 4(c). By aggregating the angles computed by all devices placed on the subject's body, we obtain the **posture vector**

$$\pi = \{(\theta_1^x, \theta_1^y, \theta_1^z), \, \ldots, (\theta_{N_D}^x, \theta_{N_D}^y, \theta_{N_D}^z)\}, \qquad (5)$$

where N_D is the number of deployed units, and $(\theta_i^x, \theta_i^y, \theta_i^z)$ are the angles computed by the i-th unit.

3.2 Learning translation manifolds

3.2.1 Offline learning phase

In the offline phase, Kinect positions are synchronised with data from the Orient devices. From this data, a mapping from **posture variations**, as computed by the Ori-

ent devices, to **translations**, as computed by the Kinect, is learned through local linear regression.

Let $\{(p_1, \pi_1, t_1), \ldots, (p_{\tau+1}, \pi_{\tau+1}, t_{\tau+1})\}$ be a set of recorded synchronised training data, comprising $(\tau+1)$ absolute position and posture pairs, along with the times t at which each pair was recorded. By taking the difference of successive instances, we obtain a training data set of τ *unnormalised* translations (i.e. position differences), posture variations[1], and time differences,

$$\widetilde{\mathbf{D}} = \{(\widetilde{dp_1}, \widetilde{d\pi_1}, dt_1), \, \ldots, (\widetilde{dp_\tau}, \widetilde{d\pi_\tau}, dt_\tau)\} = \{(p_2 - p_1,$$
$$\pi_2 - \pi_1, t_2 - t_1), \, \ldots, (p_{\tau+1} - p_\tau, \pi_{\tau+1} - \pi_\tau, t_{\tau+1} - t_\tau)\}. \qquad (6)$$

At this stage, translations $\widetilde{dp} = (\widetilde{dx}, \widetilde{dy}, \widetilde{dz})$ do not account for the absolute orientation of the subject's body. To address this problem, we assume that at least one inertial measurement unit, $\bar{u}$, is placed on a point where it can measure the subject's absolute orientation, $\bar{\theta}$, with respect to the transverse plane of motion. We focus on this single angle (instead of computing three-dimensional absolute orientations) because it is closely correlated with most turning movements that occur during walking motion sequences. Thus, by normalising with respect to $\bar{\theta}$, we can compensate for turns and changes of direction in the motion of the subject. We take $\bar{u}$ to be the device placed on the subject's waist or hips as a represantative location for this purpose. The required angle $\bar{\theta}$ is computed through $\bar{u}$'s magnetometers, which measure absolute orientations using Earth's magnetic field. Thus, the unnormalised translation components on the transverse plane, $(\widetilde{dx}, \widetilde{dy})$, can be normalised through the rotation

$$\begin{pmatrix} \widetilde{dx} \\ \widetilde{dy} \end{pmatrix} = \begin{pmatrix} \cos(-\bar{\theta}) & -\sin(-\bar{\theta}) \\ \sin(-\bar{\theta}) & \cos(-\bar{\theta}) \end{pmatrix} \cdot \begin{pmatrix} \widetilde{dx} \\ \widetilde{dy} \end{pmatrix}. \qquad (7)$$

We also normalise translations and posture differences with respect to their recorded time intervals. Thus, the *normalised* training data set is given by

$$\mathbf{D} = \{(dp_1, d\pi_1), \, \ldots, (dp_\tau, d\pi_\tau)\} =$$
$$\{(\widetilde{dp_1}/dt_1, \widetilde{d\pi_1}/dt_1), \, \ldots, (\widetilde{dp_\tau}/dt_\tau, \widetilde{d\pi_\tau}/dt_\tau)\}. \qquad (8)$$

-*Dimensionality reduction:* The size of each posture variation vector, $d\pi$, is $D = 3 \cdot N_D$, where N_D is the number of deployed devices. Even if N_D is not particularly large, it may be difficult to learn a direct mapping to associated translations, due to the different modalities of the posture data. To overcome this problem, we project posture variations to a *latent space*, from which a mapping can be learned more efficiently. We use Principal Component Analysis (PCA), which embeds data into a low-dimensional *linear manifold* by maximising their variance [5]. Thus, this method seeks to preserve the high-dimensional structure of the data in the projected space. We review the key features of PCA below.

Let $\{d\pi_i\}$, $1 \le i \le \tau$ be the set of posture variation vectors, each having dimensionality D. The mean, $\overline{d\pi}$, and covariance matrix, $\mathbf{S}$, of these vectors are given by

$$\overline{d\pi} = \frac{1}{\tau} \sum_{i=1}^{\tau} d\pi_i, \quad \mathbf{S} = \frac{1}{\tau} \sum_{i=1}^{\tau} (d\pi_i - \overline{d\pi})(d\pi_i - \overline{d\pi})^T, \qquad (9)$$

---

[1] Angle differences are constrained to lie in $[-\pi, +pi)$.

respectively. Now let d be the target dimensionality of the low-dimensional latent space, where $d < D$. We obtain the d eigenvectors (or principal components) of $\mathbf{S}$, $u_1, \ldots, u_d$, each of dimensionality D, corresponding to the d largest eigenvalues, $\lambda_1, \ldots, \lambda_d$ of this matrix. These vectors are set as the columns of a $D \times d$ matrix

$$\mathbf{M} = \begin{pmatrix} u_{1,1} & \cdots & u_{d,1} \\ \vdots & \ddots & \vdots \\ u_{1,D} & \cdots & u_{d,D} \end{pmatrix} \quad (10)$$

The latent representation of a D-dimensional posture variation vector $d\pi$ is given by

$$\phi = d\pi \cdot \mathbf{M}. \quad (11)$$

We refer to the manifold projections ϕ as the *feature vectors* of our translation learning algorithm. In both simulated and physical experiments (Section 4), we set the target subspace dimensionality to $d = 3$.

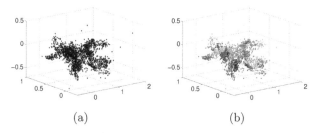

(a)   (b)

Figure 5: Feature vector clustering example. (a): Projected points. (b): Division in 100 clusters, each represented by a different colour.

-*Feature vector clustering:* In a given set of training examples, there may be groups of similar posture variations leading to related translation vectors. To exploit this similarity, we group the projected feature vectors into clusters of related data points, and learn a separate translation mapping for each cluster (instead of a single mapping for the whole dataset). We use the k-means clustering algorithm, which groups input points into a specified number of k distinct clusters [5]. As we use clustering in a learning context, we use small (with respect to the size of the dataset) values of k to avoid overfitting the training data; in our experiments, this value does not exceed 2% of the overall number of training points. Despite the need for this manually specified parameter, k-means clustering has the advantage that it does not make assumptions about cluster structure (whereas distribution methods such as expectation-maximisation [5] assume a Gaussian form), while also favouring clusters of approximately equal sizes.

Figure 5 illustrates an example of clustering on a set of three-dimensional points. When applied on a dataset of τ feature vectors, the algorithm returns the set of clusters $\mathbf{C} = \{c_1, \ldots, c_k\}$, with centres $\vec{\mu} = \{c_1.\mu_1, \ldots, c_k.\mu_k\}$, where each cluster c_i, $1 \leq i \leq k$, consists of a set of N_i feature vectors

$$c_i = \{\phi_1^i, \ldots, \phi_{N_i}^i\}. \quad (12)$$

-*Translation mapping learning:* For each data cluster $c_i = \{\phi_1^i, \ldots, \phi_{N_i}^i\}$, we learn a mapping from its constituent feature vectors to the corresponding translations, $T^c = \{dp_1^i,$

$\ldots, dp_{N_i}^i\}$. We learn a separate mapping for each direction of motion (x, y, z) through *linear regression* on the training points. In other words, we represent each translation component as a *linear function* of the projected feature vectors.

To learn these mappings, we collect all feature vectors of a cluster as a $N_i \times d$ design matrix,

$$\mathbf{X} = \begin{pmatrix} \phi_{1,1}^i & \cdots & \phi_{1,d}^i \\ \vdots & \ddots & \vdots \\ \phi_{N_i,1}^i & \cdots & \phi_{N_i,d}^i \end{pmatrix}. \quad (13)$$

Furthermore, we define three *observation vectors*, one for each of the directions of motion, such that

$$\mathbf{x} = \begin{pmatrix} dx_1^i \\ \vdots \\ dx_{N_i}^i \end{pmatrix}, \ \mathbf{y} = \begin{pmatrix} dy_1^i \\ \vdots \\ dy_{N_i}^i \end{pmatrix}, \ \mathbf{z} = \begin{pmatrix} dz_1^i \\ \vdots \\ dz_{N_i}^i \end{pmatrix}. \quad (14)$$

For each observation vector $\mathbf{v}$, we learn a linear mapping from the design matrix $\mathbf{X}$ using least squares approximation, represented by a set of d weights $\mathbf{w}$:

$$\mathbf{w} = (\mathbf{X}^T\mathbf{X})^{-1}\mathbf{X}^T\mathbf{v}. \quad (15)$$

By applying this procedure to all three observation vectors, $\mathbf{x}, \mathbf{y}, \mathbf{z}$, we obtain the linear mapping weights for cluster c_i, $\mathbf{w}_x^i, \mathbf{w}_y^i, \mathbf{w}_z^i$, respectively. These can be collectively represented as the *cluster translation mapping*

$$\mathbf{W}^i = \begin{pmatrix} \mathbf{w}_{x,1}^i & \cdots & \mathbf{w}_{x,d}^i \\ \mathbf{w}_{y,1}^i & \ddots & \mathbf{w}_{y,d}^i \\ \mathbf{w}_{z,1}^i & \cdots & \mathbf{w}_{z,d}^i \end{pmatrix}, \quad (16)$$

with a different $\mathbf{W}^i$ computed for each cluster. Thus, the latent space becomes a ***translation manifold*** that can generate translations from given feature vectors.

3.2.2 Online translation generation

Learned mappings can be applied to novel instances of posture variations and predict whole-body translations. Assuming a known initial estimate of position, (x_0, y_0, z_0) and orientation, θ_0, predicted translations can be chained together to track position over time.

Let $\breve{d\pi}_t$ be the subject's estimated posture variation at time t, and let $\bar{\theta}_t$ be the subject's absolute orientation at that time. Furthermore, let dt_t be the length of the time interval over which $\breve{d\pi}_t$ was recorded. The projection of $\breve{d\pi}_t$ on the translation manifold, $\breve{\phi}_t$, is computed as $\breve{\phi}_t = \breve{d\pi}_t \cdot \mathbf{M}$, where $\mathbf{M}$ is the learned projection mapping from the high-dimensional to the latent low-dimensional space. The cluster nearest to $\breve{\phi}_t$ is given by

$$c^* = \arg\min_{c_i \in \mathbf{C}} \ \delta(\breve{\phi}_t, c_i.\mu_i) \quad (17)$$

where $\delta(\cdot, \cdot)$ is the Euclidean distance between two points. Then, if $\mathbf{W}^*$ is the cluster translation mapping for c^*, our model predicts a normalised translation for $\breve{\phi}_t$ as

$$\widehat{dp}_t \doteq (\widehat{dx}, \widehat{dy}, \widehat{dz}) = \mathbf{W}^* \cdot \breve{\phi}_t^T \quad (18)$$

The updated predicted position at time t, $\tilde{x}_t, \tilde{y}_t, \tilde{z}_t$, is obtained by applying the orientation $\bar{\theta}_t$ to $\widehat{dp}_t$, scaling it by dt_t

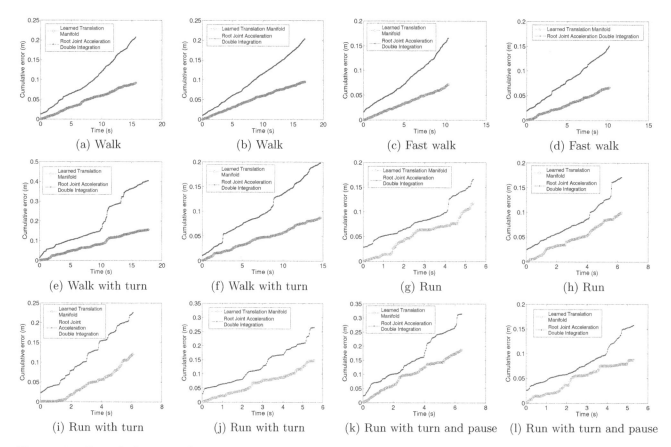

(a) Walk	(b) Walk	(c) Fast walk	(d) Fast walk
(e) Walk with turn	(f) Walk with turn	(g) Run	(h) Run
(i) Run with turn	(j) Run with turn	(k) Run with turn and pause	(l) Run with turn and pause

Figure 6: Cumulative translation errors,12 CMU database motions. *Red:* Learned translation manifold trained on given motion sequence. *Blue:* Double integration of root joint acceleration.

to reflect the length of the current time interval, and adding it to the previously estimated position, $(\tilde{x}_{t-1}, \tilde{y}_{t-1}, \tilde{z}_{t-1})$:

$$\begin{pmatrix} \tilde{x}_t \\ \tilde{y}_t \\ \tilde{z}_t \end{pmatrix} = \begin{pmatrix} \tilde{x}_{t-1} \\ \tilde{y}_{t-1} \\ \tilde{z}_{t-1} \end{pmatrix} + dt_t \begin{pmatrix} \cos(\bar{\theta}_t) & -\sin(\bar{\theta}_t) & 0 \\ \sin(\bar{\theta}_t) & \cos(\bar{\theta}_t) & 0 \\ 0 & 0 & 1 \end{pmatrix} \begin{pmatrix} \widehat{dx} \\ \widehat{dx} \\ \widehat{dz} \end{pmatrix}, \tag{19}$$

starting at the position $(\tilde{x}_{t-1}, \tilde{y}_{t-1}, \tilde{z}_{t-1}) = (x_0, y_0, z_0)$.

Our method can generate translations from novel instances of feature vectors, and track the position of a subject without an optical source. This property is important in complex unconstrained environments, where optical systems cannot be directly applied. As joint angles are inherently supplied by the inertial devices, our approach can simultaneously track both position and posture from a *single* set of sensors.

4. RESULTS

4.1 Simulation results

The learning framework was first evaluated on sequences from the Carnegie Mellon University (CMU) Database [3]. Motions in this dataset were captured using an optical system that tracks reflective body markers. Posture vectors were formed by aggregating the marker positions for the lower body joints (thighs, shins, ankles, feet). Note that this is a slightly different representation to the one given

in Section 3, where posture vectors consisted of joint angles, not joint positions. However, this differentiation does not impact the applicability of our algorithm, which has no internal model of the nature of the supplied feature vectors.

The position of the *root joint*, at the subject's hips, was taken as the absolute position of the body. This was used as a ground-truth benchmark, against which the iteratively predicted positions were checked.

We compared against a related open-loop position generation technique, the *double integration* of acceleration. This method similarly generates local translations that can be chained together to compute positions. As the CMU dataset does not explicitly provide acceleration data, we simulated this information by extracting accelerations from successive positions at the subject's root joint, and integrating them twice to generate translations.

We first assessed the ability of translation manifolds to reproduce translations on the datasets they are trained on. Towards this end, we trained the learning algorithm on several different motion sequences. We then compared the similarity of the generated translations to the ground-truth translations, as estimated by differences of consecutive root joint positions. Our metric is the *cumulative translation error*, obtained by iteratively summing the Euclidean distance of each generated vector from the corresponding ground truth.

The results for 12 distinct motion sequences, ranging from simple straight walking to running with turns, are shown in Figure 6. In all cases, the translations generated by the

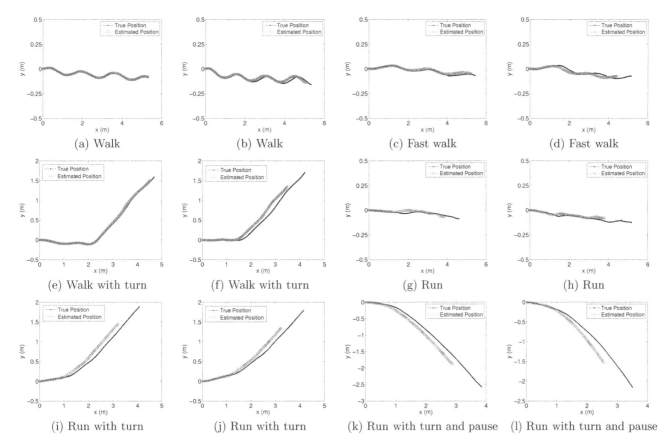

Figure 7: Overall position error estimation for 12 novel instances of unseen motion sequences. *Red:* Trajectories estimated by learned translation manifold. *Black:* Ground-truth trajectories.

learned manifold yield a lower cumulative error than the corresponding double integration ones. For the simpler walking motions, the discrepancy between the two methods is shown to increase over time, thus suggesting that the translation manifold is more effective at capturing motion dynamics.

The true potential of learned translation manifolds can be fully assessed when applied on *novel* instances of previously unseen motions. In our second simulated experiment, we trained our model on a dataset consisting of 11 different motions by the same subject: a straight walk, two straight walks followed by a 90° left/right turn, two walks with a left/right veer, a fast straight walk, a straight run, two straight runs followed by a 90° left/right turn, and two runs with a left/right veer. The total duration of these captures is 114 seconds, with walking-type and running-type motions accounting for 86 and 28 seconds, respectively. By including different types of motions, our aim was to model a wide range of posture variation-translation pairs, and improve generalisation to novel motion instances.

The learned mapping was applied on 12 new motion sequences of various types. For these motions, we measured the discrepancy between the trajectories predicted by the manifold, and the ground-truth trajectories. The resulting trajectories are demonstrated in Figure 7. As previously, our algorithm is shown to reproduce accurate positions for normal walks, with the error increasing for running-type motions. This increase is partly explained by the larger number

of walking motion data points in the training set, which biases the manifold towards translations of smaller magnitude.

4.2 Experimental results

In the physical experiments, we evaluated the translation learning algorithm on sensory data obtained from physical devices, using the Kinect as the optical and the Orient platform as the inertial sensing source. In the training phase, synchronised data from the two sources were used to learn translation manifolds. An important restriction in this case was the small capture volume of the Kinect (approximately 15m^3), which limited the variety of motions that could be performed by the subject. Thus, our framework is evaluated mainly on walking motions which require less physical space.

4.2.1 Constrained environment experiments

The learning algorithm was first compared with the acceleration integration method against ground-truth positions estimated by the Kinect. Unlike simulation experiments, accelerations were now directly supplied by the accelerometers of Orient devices, so translations were generated through double integration of this data.

We captured 18 motion sequences of variable length, ranging from 20 to 180 seconds. We used a total of 4 Orient devices, placed on the subject's waist (root joint), right thigh, left thigh, and left ankle. Motions were captured in an office environment, which impacted the quality of the sensory readings, especially magnetometers, due to metal in

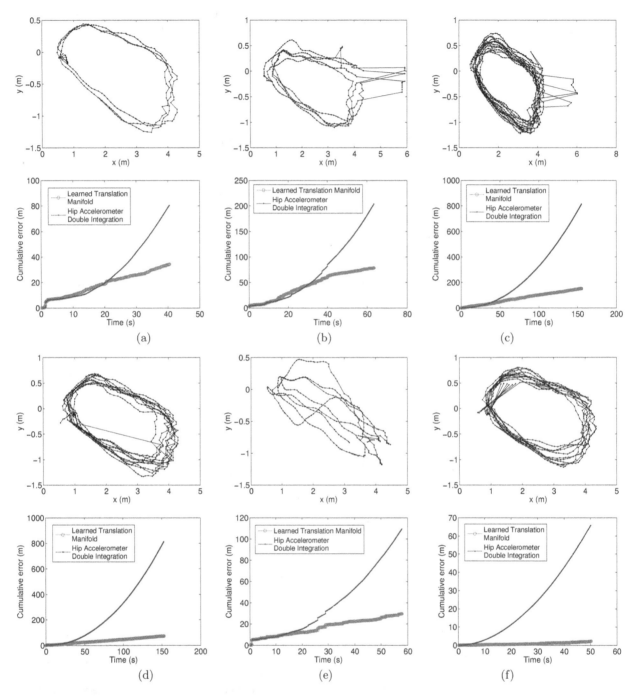

Figure 8: Cumulative generated translation errors for 6 novel motion sequences. The learning algorithm was trained on 12 sequences of varying length and motion composition. *Top of each subfigure:* Ground-truth positions computed by the body tracking interface. *Bottom:* Cumulative errors. *Red:* Learned translation manifold. *Blue:* Double integration of the acceleration of the root joint.

the building structure. For each capture, the subject was allowed to perform any sequence and combination of walking and standing, provided s/he remained within the capture area of the Kinect.

We selected 12 of the captured sequences as the training set, and we used the remaining 6 as novel instances for evaluation. As with simulation experiments, we first compared the cumulative error of translations generated by the learned

manifold, and translations from double integration of root joint accelerations.

Figure 8 illustrates this comparison, along with the corresponding ground-truth positions captured by the Kinect. In all 6 trials, the subject was observed to repeatedly move around the capture area in a loop. Although in some cases the cumulative error generated by the double integration method was initially lower, in all trials the learning method

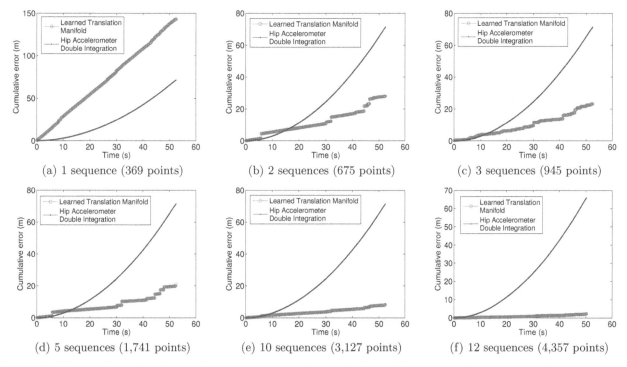

Figure 9: Effect of training data set size on generated translations. The cumulative error is shown to decrease as the number of training motion sequences (and training data points) increases.

Figure 10: Unconstrained environment illustration. (a): Office room and corridor. (b): Illustration of the approximate trajectory followed by the subject, starting and ending at the same point. (c): Approximate dimensions of the trajectory.

had a considerably lower error at the end of the sequence. This superior performance was achieved despite some irregularities in the captured positional data, as, for example, in Figures 8(b) and 8(c). This demonstrates that our approach can learn a robust translation model from noisy sensory data, which can yield more accurate translations than methods operating directly on raw data.

The error of the translation manifold algorithm inevitably depends on the size and quality of the training data set. To better understand this effect, we assessed the performance of the algorithm on the last trial of Figure 8 under varying training sets. The results are shown in Figure 9, where we start with just one training sequence, comprising only a few data points, and progressively increase this number. It can be seen that when only one short sequence is supplied, the performance is considerably worse than the double integration method. However, as more motion instances are added

to the training set, the error is shown to decrease significantly over time. This indicates that the learning model relies on a good coverage of the posture and translation space, in order to be able to generalise effectively to novel instances. Thus, when recording data, it is important to ensure that the tracked subjects perform a wide range of motions, including various combinations of different motion types (e.g. straight walks and turns).

Another related constraint on the performance of our algorithm is that motions captured during training must be similar to those executed in the online generation phase. For example, if a manifold is learned only from walking motions, it is highly unlikely to yield accurate translations on novel running motions. Thus, it is essential to capture not only a significant *quantity* of data (as shown in Figure 9), but also representative sequences that will be *qualitatively* similar to the motions the system will be tested on when deployed.

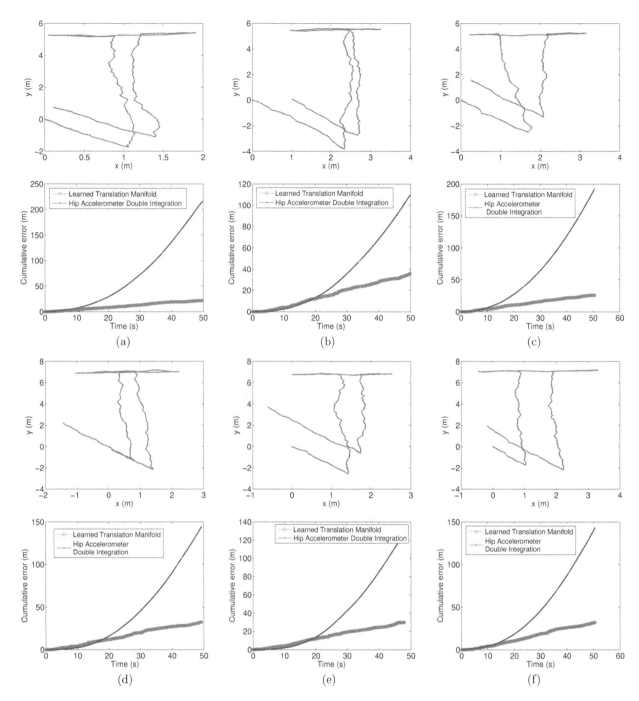

Figure 11: Generated positions for a subject following the trajectory shown in Figure 10, 6 trials. *Top subfigures:* Generated positions. *Bottom:* Cumulative errors and comparison with double integration.

4.2.2 Unonstrained environment experiments

In the second set of physical experiments, we evaluated the learning method in an unconstrained office environment (Figure 10). This represents a setting where an optical source cannot be used to track subjects, due to its larger area and morphology (doors, corridors). The subject was asked to follow a trajectory consisting of several landmark points, located inside an office room and in an adjacent corridor. There was no restriction on the time given to follow this trajectory, so the subject was allowed to pause for arbitrary periods of time.

We used the same set of training sequences as in the first set of physical experiments to learn a translation manifold. Figure 11 shows the generated trajectories for six distinct trials of the subject moving along the prescribed path, along with the corresponding error comparison with the double integration method. The true precise trajectory followed in each case was not known, however, the subject always ended his path at the same point where he started. Thus, by comparing the difference between the start and end points of each generated trajectory, we can get an estimate of the resulting error.

Despite not being aware of the duration and nature of the motions performed by the subject, the learning algorithm is observed to produce translations that closely follow the true trajectory. The computed mean error for the final position was 1.783m, with the overall sum of distances between landmark points being about 30m. Furthermore, as shown in the bottom subfigures of Figure 11, the learning algorithm maintains the superior performance level over the double integration method. A common trait of both sets of physical experiments is that they feature several alternations between straight walking and turning motions, which are characterised by repeated variations in the velocity profile of the tracked subject. In this context, the double integration method initially produces an error comparable with the learning algorithm, but in both cases the margin increases exponentially over time. The learning method is therefore successful in identifying the salient structure of the high-dimensional data, and using it to learn a mapping that can be applied to novel motions.

5. CONCLUSIONS

We have presented a method for simultaneous posture and position tracking in unconstrained environments, based on learned generative translation manifolds. In an offline learning phase, two heterogeneous tracking sources, an inertial sensing (Orient-4) and an optical (Kinect) platform, are jointly used to learn a mapping from posture variations, as estimated by the former, to whole-body translations, as estimated by the latter. This mapping is learned through linear regression on clustered latent representations of posture variations. Online, the optical source is removed, and the learned translation manifold is used to generate translations for novel motion instances. The generative method is experimentally shown to outperform the related model-free, dead-reckoning method of acceleration integration, and to correctly reproduce the structure of previously unseen trajectories in unconstrained environments.

One drawback of our approach is that a different mapping must be learned whenever the system is tested on a new user. This characteristic is due to skeletal morphology and limb dimension constraints, which vary among different subjects. Thus, motion sequences captured on a specific subject may not adequately cover the posture difference and translation space for a different subject, thus leading to incomplete mappings. Nevertheless, one interesting extension to our work would be to learn translation manifolds from datasets which contain motions from various subjects with different characteristics (e.g. short/tall). This extension would be well-suited to the feature vector clustering procedure described in Section 3.2.1. In this context, we would employ a *hierarchical* clustering approach, where the evaluated subject would first be matched to the nearest (in terms of body morphology) user in the training data set, and then a translation would be generated based on the learned mappings for the matched subject.

A major strength of our approach is that it does not make assumptions about the nature of the performed motion, the number and placement of inertial measurement units, or the morphology of the tracked subject's body. This property is advantageous for two reasons. First, our method can be ap-

plied to complex motions spanning all three dimensions (e.g. forward jumps), where traditional model-based approaches tracking gait events and foot contacts would fail. Second, for simpler, planar motion types (e.g. walking sequences), our method can be used as a predictive step for model-based filtering approaches, in order to obtain lower positional errors. Extending our work in these directions would further emphasise the benefits of using machine learning techniques to exploit the structure of high-dimensional data produced by physical sensor networks.

Acknowledgments

AV has been supported by a doctoral studentship from the Centre for Speckled Computing, funded by the Scottish Funding Council (Strategic Research Development Programme R32329) and EPSRC (Basic Technology Programme C523881).

6. REFERENCES

[1] Microsoft Kinect. http://www.xbox.com/kinect.
[2] OpenNI kinect body tracking interface. http://www.openni.org.
[3] CMU motion capture database. http://mocaps.cs.cmu.edu.
[4] Vicon motion capture systems. http://www.vicon.com.
[5] C. M. Bishop. *Pattern Recognition and Machine Learning (Information Science and Statistics)*. Springer-Verlag New York, Inc., 2006.
[6] J. Casper and R. Murphy. Human-robot interactions during the robot-assisted urban search and rescue response at the world trade center. *IEEE Transactions on Systems, Man, and Cybernetics*, 33(3):367–385, 2003.
[7] R. Chalodhorn, D. B. Grimes, K. Grochow, and R. P. N. Rao. Learning to walk through imitation. In *International Joint Conference on Artifical Intelligence (IJCCAI)*, pages 2084–2090, 2007.
[8] J. A. Corrales, F. A. Candelas, and F. Torres. Hybrid tracking of human operators using imu/uwb data fusion by a kalman filter. In *International Conference on Human-Robot Interaction (HRI)*, pages 193–200, 2008.
[9] R. Feliz, E. Zalama, and J. G. Garcia-Bermejo. Pedestrian tracking using inertial sensors. *Journal of Physical Agents*, 3(1):35–42, 2009.
[10] E. Foxlin. Pedestrian tracking with shoe-mounted inertial sensors. *Computer Graphics and Applications, IEEE*, 25(6):38 –46, 2005.
[11] J. Guerrieri, M. Francis, P. Wilson, T. Kos, L. Miller, N. Bryner, D. Stroup, and L. Klein-Berndt. Rfid-assisted indoor localization and communication for first responders. In *European Conference on Antennas and Propagation (EuCAP)*, pages 1–6, 2006.
[12] H. Khoury and V. Kamat. Evaluation of position tracking technologies for user localization in indoor construction environments. *Automation in Construction*, 18(4):444–457, 2009.
[13] Y. Kobayashi and Y. Kuno. People tracking using integrated sensors for human robot interaction. In *IEEE International Conference on Industrial Technology*, pages 1617 –1622, 2010.

[14] K. F. MacDorman, R. Chalodhorn, and M. Asada. Periodic nonlinear principal component neural networks for humanoid motion segmentation, generalization, and generation. In *International Conference on Pattern Recognition (ICPR) (4)*, pages 537–540, 2004.

[15] L. Ojeda and J. Borenstein. Personal dead-reckoning system for gps-denied environments. In *IEEE International Workshop on Safety, Security and Rescue Robotics*, pages 1 –6, 2007.

[16] J. Shotton, A. W. Fitzgibbon, M. Cook, T. Sharp, M. Finocchio, R. Moore, A. Kipman, and A. Blake. Real-time human pose recognition in parts from single depth images. In *International Conference on Computer Vision and Pattern Recognition (CVPR)*, pages 1297–1304, 2011.

[17] A. Valtazanos, D. K. Arvind, and S. Ramamoorthy. Comparative study of segmentation of periodic motion data for mobile gait analysis. In *ACM International Conference on Wireless Health*, pages 145–154, 2010.

[18] C. Wren, A. Azarbayejani, T. Darrell, and A. Pentland. Pfinder: Real-time tracking of the human body. *IEEE Transactions on Pattern Analysis and Machine Intelligence*, 19(7):780–785, 1997.

[19] A. Yang, S. Iyengar, S. Sastry, R. Bajcsy, P. Kuryloski, and R. Jafari. Distributed segmentation and classification of human actions using a wearable motion sensor network. In *Computer Vision and Pattern Recognition Workshops (CVPRW)*, pages 1 –8, 2008.

[20] A. D. Young. From posture to motion: the challenge for real time wireless inertial motion capture. In *International Conference on Body Area Networks (BodyNets)*, pages 131–137, 2010.

[21] A. D. Young, M. J. Ling, and D. K. Arvind. *Orient-2*: a realtime wireless posture tracking system using local orientation estimation. In *Workshop on Embedded Sensor Networks (EmNets)*, pages 53–57, 2007.

[22] X. Yun, E. Bachmann, H. Moore, and J. Calusdian. Self-contained position tracking of human movement using small inertial/magnetic sensor modules. In *International Conference on Robotics and Automation (ICRA)*, pages 2526 –2533, 2007.

SugarMap: Location-less Coverage for Micro-Aerial Sensing Swarms

Aveek Purohit
Carnegie Mellon University
Pittsburgh, PA, USA
apurohit@ece.cmu.edu

Zheng Sun
Carnegie Mellon University
Pittsburgh, PA, USA
zhengs@ece.cmu.edu

Pei Zhang
Carnegie Mellon University
Pittsburgh, PA, USA
peizhang@ece.cmu.edu

ABSTRACT

Micro-aerial vehicle (MAV) swarms are emerging as a new class of mobile sensor networks with many potential applications such as urban surveillance, disaster response, radiation monitoring, etc., where the swarm is tasked with collaboratively covering a hazardous unknown environment. However, efficient collaborative coverage is challenging due to limited individual sensing, computing and communication resources of MAV sensor nodes, and lack of location infrastructure in the unknown application environment.

We present SugarMap, a novel system that enables such resource-constrained MAV nodes to achieve efficient sensing coverage. The self-establishing system uses approximate motion models of mobile nodes in conjunction with radio signatures from self-deployed stationary anchor nodes to create a common coverage map. Consequently, the system coordinates node movements to reduce sensing overlap and increase the speed and efficiency of coverage. The system uses particle filters to account for uncertainty in sensors and actuation of MAV nodes, and incorporates redundancy to guarantee coverage. Through large-scale simulations and a real implementation on the SensorFly MAV sensing platform, we show that SugarMap provides better coverage than the existing coverage approaches for MAV swarms.

Categories and Subject Descriptors

C.2 [**Computer-Communication Networks**]: Distributed Systems—*Distributed applications*; I.2 [**Artificial Intelligence**]: Distributed Artificial Intelligence—*Multiagent systems*

Keywords

Mobile Sensor Networks, Micro-Aerial Vehicle, Swarm

1. INTRODUCTION

Micro-aerial vehicle (MAV) swarms are an emerging class of mobile sensor networking systems with many potential

applications such as urban surveillance, disaster response and crop pollination. These swarms comprise of miniature aerial sensor nodes capable of autonomous movement but with limited sensing, computing and communication resources on each node [25, 19]. In a majority of the proposed applications, such as surveillance or survivor search, the sensor network is tasked with moving and covering a target space. These networks must rely on collaboration to quickly and efficiently achieve their system-wide sensing objectives despite the limitations of individual nodes.

The collaborative swarm approach provides the advantage of greater resilience, adaptability and speed of sensing as compared to a monolithic robot. However, the limited individual capabilities of MAV's present many unique challenges in enabling collaboration between a swarm of nodes. A fundamental primitive for collaborative algorithms, especially for spatial sensing coverage, is a common frame of reference for location. Indeed, the knowledge of the relative locations of sensor nodes is assumed or computed in most prior work on multi-robot spatial coverage [7, 9, 11, 14, 22, 24]. However, these existing techniques are unsuitable for MAV swarms due to the following challenges:

- **Lack of Infrastructure** – Many multi-robot systems rely on existing infrastructure for inferring the relative location of nodes such as GPS, Wi-Fi access points, motion-tracking camera systems etc. This infrastructure is unavailable in many of the intended operating environments for MAV swarms such as indoor buildings (GPS denied) or disaster scenarios (infrastructure denied).

- **Limited Sensors** – Robots routinely use range sensors such as LIDARs, laser-range finders or multiple ultrasonic rangers to compute relative positions [2, 5, 6, 16]. MAV platforms have severe weight constraints and cannot accommodate most of these sensors that weigh in the hundreds of grams.

- **Limited Computing Power** – Many robotic systems employ computer vision with computation intensive feature detection algorithms to generate maps and compute their relative location. MAV swarms do not have the local processing ability to employ these algorithms.

- **Low-bandwidth Communication** – Robots have the ability to relay bandwidth intensive images and data to a base station for processing. The MAV swarms are limited in the available bandwidth and connectivity due to the their low-power and low-range radio's.

In this paper, we present SugarMap – a system that enables resource-constrained MAV sensor swarms to collaboratively cover an area. SugarMap coordinates node movements to reduce the amount of sensing overlap between swarm nodes and increase the efficiency and speed of coverage. Most importantly, the system does not rely on external location infrastructure, bulky or sophisticated sensors, computation intensive algorithms or high-bandwidth communication.

The main contribution of this paper is threefold:

- a multi-node location-less coverage algorithm that uses self-dispersed anchor nodes to obtain radio RF-signatures and provides a common spatial frame of reference for MAV swarm nodes.

- a particle filter framework to estimate coverage taking into account the uncertainties and inaccuracies introduced by semi-controlled motion in MAV systems.

- a coverage algorithm that inherently provides redundancy as per the uncertainty of node motion.

In the SugarMap system, radio RF-signatures are obtained by *explorer* sensor nodes through querying a set of *anchor* nodes. The anchor nodes are MAV nodes that SugarMap deploys (lands) in the area, through a dispersion algorithm, at initialization. The system does not require a location information for deploying anchor nodes and is thus self-establishing. Consequently, SugarMap uses the radio measurements from the anchors as a common spatial frame of reference to coordinate node motion and collaboratively cover an unknown area. The algorithm uses particle filters to account for the actuation uncertainty of low-cost MAV nodes and uses redundancy in node paths to guarantee coverage with the desired degree of confidence.

We evaluate the performance of SugarMap through large-scale simulation and validate through a real-system implementation on the SensorFly [19] MAV sensor platform. We compare the performance of SugarMap to the state-of-the-art in existing online coverage algorithms for swarms. We show that SugarMap provides faster coverage than existing approaches in absence of location information.

The rest of the paper is organized as follows. Section 2 gives an overview of the SugarMap system. Section 3 describes the different components and algorithms of SugarMap in detail. Section 4 describes our implementation, experimental setup, results and provides comparisons with other approaches. Section 6 describes the state-of-the-art in multi-agent coverage algorithms in context of MAV swarms. Finally, Section 7 summarizes our conclusions.

2. SYSTEM OVERVIEW

This section gives an overview of the different aspects of the SugarMap system, including the capabilities of nodes and the typical operating scenario.

Figure 1 gives a flow diagram of data and commands between the major components of the SugarMap system. At system initialization, nodes are sent into the environment and landed in a constrained dispersion manner. The SugarMap system has a base station *brain* running the SugarMap algorithm. The base station gives commands to the mobile nodes (explorers) to move in a coordinated

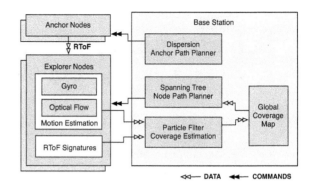

Figure 1: An overview of the SugarMap system.

fashion. The explorers collect RF-signatures from stationary nodes (anchors) and relay it to the base station. The base station uses particle filters and RF-signatures obtained from the explorer nodes to update a global coverage map for the swarm. The global coverage map in turn helps the base station recursively plan the next movement of explorer nodes.

2.1 MAV Sensor Nodes

We assume the MAV nodes to be weight-limited resource-constrained platforms. They have limited on-board computation capability and light-weight components such as MEMS-based inertial motion sensors, an altitude measurement sensor, a sensor to estimate velocity, and a radio for communication and RF-signature estimation.

For our prototype evaluation, we implement SugarMap on the SensorFly [19] MAV swarm platform. The SensorFly is a MAV platform with a 8-bit AVR AtMega128 microcontroller, inertial motion sensors – 3-axis accelerometer and 3-axis gyro, an ultrasonic ranger for altitude estimation, an optical flow sensor for velocity estimation, and a 802.15.4a compatible radio with Round-trip time-of-flight (RToF) measurement capability. The entire platform is under 30g in weight striking a careful balance between weight and sensing capability as is typical of MAV sensing platforms.

2.2 Operating Environment

The predominant application of proposed MAV swarms is in attaining sensing coverage of unknown environments that are inaccessible or hazardous for humans to enter. For example, in applications such as urban surveillance, survivor search after disasters, or nuclear radiation monitoring.

Figure 2 gives an illustration of the operating environment. The anchors are deployed by dispersion at the boundaries, explorers move and sense the area, and the base station received data from explorers and transmits commands. We make the following assumptions about the operating environment from the application scenario:

- The initial position and pose of swarm nodes is known. The swarm nodes are introduced into the operating environment manually. For example, a firefighter introduces nodes into an indoor structure damaged by an earthquake through an accessible opening.

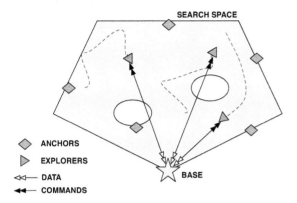

Figure 2: An illustration of the SugarMap system operating environment.

- The search space for a single group of swarm nodes is continuous. The swarm nodes do not have the capability to break through obstructing structures.

2.3 System Components

The SugarMap system has 3 major components:

- **Anchors** – Anchors are MAV nodes that the system lands at initialization in the environment. The nodes land using a simple dispersion algorithm where they seek to approximately spread out from each other but at the same time maintain radio connectivity with all other anchors. The dispersion does not use any location information but relies on the approximate proximity information provided by the radio time-of-flight measurements.

- **Explorers** – Explorers are MAV nodes that move and sense the environment. The nodes collect radio signatures from the anchor nodes, execute commanded motion with feedback from their motion sensors, sense the environment using application specific sensors and relay this data to a coordinating base station. The nodes receive high-level commands from the base station to follow a movement path.

- **Base Station** – The base station is a node at a safer location with access to higher computing power than the swarm nodes. The nodes relay information to the base station. The base station computes the probabilistic coverage from obtained data and directs the motion of all the explorer nodes as per the coverage algorithm. The base station provides a real-time coverage status to the users of the swarm.

2.4 SugarMap Coverage Algorithm

The base station runs the SugarMap online coverage algorithm. Every node in SugarMap starts with an empty grid map of the world with a known initial position. The size of a grid cell is equal to the sensing radius of each sensor. As explorer nodes move, they approximately measure their motion using sensors (optical flow and inertial), and collect RToF signatures from landed anchor nodes, and relay this data to the base station.

The SugarMap algorithm directs explorer nodes to perform a depth first search (spanning tree coverage [7]) of the environment but to avoid areas already covered by other nodes. This minimizes sensing overlap and speeds up coverage. To achieve this, the algorithm constructs a common grid map for areas covered by all nodes.

However, the motion estimation of MAV nodes is approximate and exact coverage area is hard to determine. The algorithm uses a particle filter to model the coverage uncertainty (due to motion and sensing uncertainty) of each SensorFly node. Every node is represented by n particles that track the coverage path of the SensorFly on the grid, where the weight of each particle gives the probability of each cell on its path being covered. The algorithm detects revisits in node paths by matching RToF signatures and uses this to update particle weights. The algorithm combines the probabilistic coverage map of all particles by summing and normalizing the cell coverage probabilities to arrive at a coverage map for each SensorFly.

Thus, the SugarMap algorithm constructs a probabilistic spanning tree for each node's coverage. Each node of the spanning tree corresponds to a unique RToF signature of a covered area, while the edges are defined through the relative motion estimates. Using the common initial position of all nodes, individual maps are overlaid on a common grid map by again combining the probabilities of individual cells to arrive at a global coverage map of the swarm. The algorithm uses this global coverage map to direct nodes to cells with a lower probability of having been covered.

3. SYSTEM DESCRIPTION

In this section, we describe the details of the different components and algorithms used in SugarMap. We discuss the deployment of anchors, the path planner that commands explorer nodes, and the particle filter based probabilistic coverage map estimation.

3.1 Deployment of Anchors

The SugarMap system initializes by deploying a subset of MAV nodes in the environment to act as radio anchors. The absolute position of the anchor nodes is not critical. However, it is desirable for the anchors to be dispersed over the search space to provide robust RToF signatures. Dispersion algorithms for constrained robots have been studied in prior work [17, 13, 15] and many potential approaches can be employed. In SugarMap, the anchors deploy using a *fiducial dispersion* algorithm [17] based on the nodes' ability to obtain RToF measurements from other nodes. The objective of the dispersion algorithm is for nodes to spread away from each other till they encounter obstacles or lose radio range with other anchors.

Figure 3 shows a flowchart of the algorithm used to deploy anchor nodes. The base station commands a sub-set of MAV nodes (designated as anchors) to move in randomly chosen directions. Every node periodically attempts to obtain radio RToF measurements from other anchors and relay it to the base station. If any anchor node is out of radio range and does not respond, the node attempts to retrace its path by turning 180°. Conversely, if all nodes are in range, each RToF measurement (d_i) is compared to a proximity threshold (T_p). If no other anchor is within the proximity threshold, the node lands and deploys. Otherwise, the node

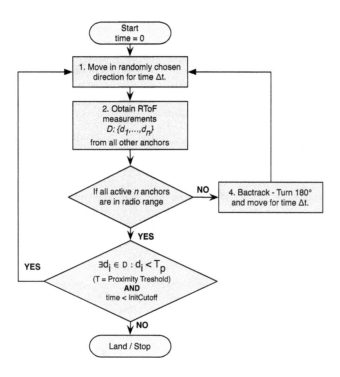

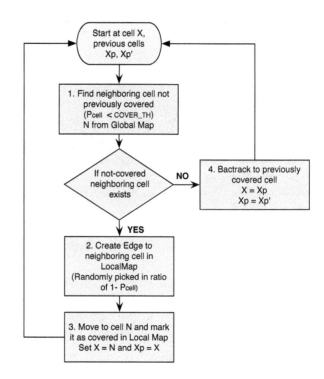

Figure 3: Figure shows a flowchart of the constrained dispersion algorithm used to deploy anchor nodes at initialization of SugarMap.

Figure 4: The figure shows a flow chart of the SugarMap coverage path planner algorithm. The distributed algorithm runs on every node and builds a spanning tree of covered nodes using a depth first exploration approach.

moves in a random direction and recursively repeats the above sequence of operations.

In addition, a maximum cutoff time for anchor deployment ($InitCutoff$) is defined. If an equilibrium is not reached within the cutoff time, the nodes still land and deploy.

It must be noted that the explorer nodes use RToF measurements from the anchor nodes as a signature and not as a measure of distance. The uniqueness of the signature is a feature of the position of the anchors and multi-path radio propagation characteristics of the physical environment. The system relies on measurements from a relatively large number of anchor nodes (at least greater than 4) to improve signature uniqueness. The system does not assume any particular anchor node topology, such as non-linear, as would be the case for computing location coordinates from deployed anchors.

3.2 Coverage Path Planner

The central idea of the SugarMap coverage algorithm is to coordinate explorer node movements so as to cover the environment with a certain measure of confidence.

In the application scenario, the explorer MAV nodes have no a priori knowledge of the search space. However, due to manual placement, the relative pose and position of the explorer nodes is known. SugarMap approximates the world with a grid with a cell size of D, where D is determined by the effective radius of the application specific sensor deployed on the MAV node.

A MAV node is commanded to move along 4 basic direction relative to itself – N, S, W and E, and must be located to within the D-size cell. For simplicity, we first describe the algorithm assuming nodes can be localized to the D-size cell

with a certain probability. In section 3.3, we explain how this is achieved by the SugarMap system in practice.

Each MAV node builds a local spanning tree of cells that it discovers, while tracking the portion of the map covered by other nodes through a global map. The global map is obtained by aggregating the local maps from all nodes in the swarm. The spanning tree is built using a depth-first approach – 1) find a neighboring cell that hasn't been covered(by itself or by any node in the swarm); 2) create a tree edge to the neighboring cell; 3) move to the cell and mark it as covered in its local map; recursively repeat steps 1,2,3 with this cell; 4) if all the neighbors are covered or blocked (obstacles), the node backtracks along its local spanning tree to the previously covered cell.

To account for the uncertainty in sensing and position of MAV's, the coverage of a cell is not designated by a binary value but a real number between 0 and 1, representing the probability that a cell is covered. The algorithm considers a cell as not covered if the coverage probability of a cell (P_{cell}) is less than a desired coverage confidence threshold ($COVER\_TH$). The algorithm chooses the next cell from neighboring non-visited cells randomly, where the probability of picking a cell is inverse of its confidence of coverage. When all neighboring cells are above the coverage confidence threshold, the algorithm increments the probability of picking the last covered cell biasing the node towards backtracking on its traversed path.

Figure 4 shows a flowchart of the coverage path planner algorithm. The algorithm is distributed and runs on every node. The nodes are coordinated using the global map that is aggregated from each node's local coverage estimates.

3.3 Probabilistic Coverage Maps

The path planner requires each node to mark coverage in a grid map of the search space. In addition, the planner requires a global coverage map that is obtained by aggregating the coverage maps of individual swarm nodes.

As the initial location of all nodes is known, the system can potentially track the cells covered by nodes keeping track of the commanded motion of the MAV nodes. However, MAV nodes have low-quality inertial sensors and imperfect actuators. This makes it impossible for MAV nodes to accurately execute the commanded path. SugarMap uses a particle filter based probabilistic approach that combines approximate motion noise models of the explorer nodes with radio round-trip time-of-flight (RToF) position signatures, to create a common probabilistic coverage map for the swarm.

3.3.1 Particle Filter (PF)

A particle filter (PF) [12] is a Bayesian estimation method used to estimate a system's state based on noisy sensor information. In a particle filter, a probability distribution $p(x)$ is represented by a number of N weighted samples or *particles* $x^{[i]}, i = 1..N$, with weights $w^{[i]}$ as:

$$p(x) = \sum_i w^{[i]} \delta(x^{[i]} - x) \tag{1}$$

With a initial probability $p(x_0)$, which is represented as equally distributed samples with equal weights, a recursive update at time t_k to estimate system state x_k is performed in 3 steps:

1. **Prediction** – Every particle $(x_{k-1}^{[i]}, w_{k-1}^{[i]})$ of the *a posteriori* distribution $p(x_{k-1}|z_0, \ldots, z_{k-1})$, where $z_0, \ldots, z_k$ are measurements about the system up to time t_k, is replaced according to a process model $p(x_k|x_{k-1})$. The process model incorporates knowledge of the evolution of the system over time. In coverage estimation, we use an empirically obtained actuation noise profile from the MAV nodes' motion sensors to construct this model. Thus a new set of particles $(\tilde{x}_k^{[i]}, \tilde{w}^{[i]})$ is obtained representing the *a priori* distribution.

2. **Correction** – The weight $w^{[i]}$ of every sample of the *a priori* distribution, is updated according to a measurement model as:

$$w^{[i]} = \tilde{w}^{[i]} \cdot p(z_k|\tilde{x}_k^{[i]}), \sum_i w^{[i]} = 1 \tag{2}$$

With the weight update, the prior particles now approximate the *a posteriori* probability. In coverage estimation, we use the radio RToF signatures obtained by the explorer nodes from the anchor nodes to compute the term $p(z_k|\tilde{x}_k^{[i]})$, which relates the coverage state of the system to its observation.

3. **Resampling** – A new set of particles is drawn with replacement from the prior set with probability of a particle being drawn given by its weight. The samples are weighted equally. The resampling step prunes the less likely state estimates.

3.3.2 Applying PF To Coverage Estimation

In this section, we describe the application of a particle filter to estimate coverage in SugarMap. We first consider a single MAV node. Each MAV node is represented by N particles. Each particle holds an array ($LocalMap$) representing the particle's coverage on a local grid map of the search space. Cells not covered are set to 0 in the array, while covered cells are set to 1. The state of a particle $x_k^{[i]}$ at time t_k is given by this $LocalMap_k^{[i]}$.

Prediction: In the prediction step, the $LocalMap_k^{[i]}$ is updated according to the commanded motion of the MAV node and a actuation noise model. The MAV node executes a motion command – turn and velocity, using feedback from its inertial sensor (gyro) and optical flow velocity sensor. Therefore, if c_x and c_y are coordinates of the last cell covered by a particle, v_k is the velocity, ϕ_k is the change in pose, the $LocalMap_k^{[i]}$ is calculated as:

$$\begin{pmatrix} c_x \\ c_y \end{pmatrix}_k^{[i]} = \begin{pmatrix} c_x \\ c_y \end{pmatrix}_{k-1}^{[i]} + (v_k^{[i]} \cdot \delta t) \begin{pmatrix} sin(\phi_k^{[i]}) \\ cos(\phi_k^{[i]}) \end{pmatrix} \tag{3}$$

$$LocalMap_k^{[i]} \left[c_{x_k}^{[i]} \right] \left[c_{y_k}^{[i]} \right] = 1 \tag{4}$$

Noise is added to the velocity and turn commands as per the empirically obtained actuation noise models $p(n_v)$ and $p(n_\phi)$. This is based on the actuation mechanism of the MAV platform used. Thus, $v_k^{[i]}$ and $\phi_k^{[i]}$ are obtained as:

$$v_k^{[i]} = v_k + n_v^{[i]} \text{ , } n_v^{[i]} \text{ is drawn from } p(n_v) \tag{5}$$

$$\phi_k^{[i]} = \phi_k + n_\phi^{[i]} \text{ , } n_\phi^{[i]} \text{ is drawn from } p(n_\phi) \tag{6}$$

Correction: In the correction step, the weight of the particles is updated using the radio RToF area signatures obtained by the MAV node. A detailed explanation of the radio RToF area signatures is given in Section 4.4.

The central idea of the correction step is to compare the radio RToF signature s^k obtained at time t_k to a set of known area signatures $S : \{s^1, \ldots, s^j\}$. The set S is empty at initialization. A list of location estimates $(c_x^{[i]}, c_y^{[i]})$ from every particle is stored for every signature in set S.

A distance function $f(s^k, s^j)$ gives the distance between the currently obtained signature and previously known signatures in set S. If distance given by $f(s^k, s^i)$ is more than a threshold (SIG_TH) for all signatures in set S i.e. the obtained signature is of an unexplored area, signature s^k is added to S. Conversely, if the distance is less than the threshold, the signatures are considered similar and the area is designated as a previously covered area.

On identifying a matching previously visited signature s^j, the corresponding distance in location estimates for the current signature s^k and known signature s^j for each particle is computed as:

$$d_{s^j, s^k}^{[i]} = EuclideanDist \left\{ (c_x, c_y)_{s^j}^{[i]}, (c_x, c_y)_{s^k}^{[i]} \right\} \tag{7}$$

Consequently, the weights of the particles are updated as a function of the distance between the two estimates as:

$$w^{[i]} = \frac{\left\{ \sum\limits_{i}^{N} d^{[i]}_{s^j, s^k} \right\} - d^{[i]}_{s^j, s^k}}{\sum\limits_{i}^{N} d^{[i]}_{s^j, s^k}} \qquad (8)$$

Resampling: In the resampling step, a new set of particles is drawn with replacement using the weights as the probability of drawing. The weights are reset to their initialization values.

Merging: Finally, the local maps of each particle are combined to compute a node coverage map at time t_k as:

$$NodeMap^j_k = \frac{\sum\limits_{i=1}^{N} LocalMap^{[i]}_k}{N} \qquad (9)$$

Similarly, the central base station combines the NodeMaps from all MAV nodes to arrive at the GlobalMap for the swarm:

$$GlobalMap_k = 1 - \prod\limits_{j=1}^{n} \left(1 - NodeMap^j_k\right) \qquad (10)$$

where n is the number of nodes in the swarm.

4. EVALUATION

In this section we evaluate the capability of SugarMap to command a swarm of MAV's collaboratively cover a search space in realistic large-scale simulations and in a real MAV testbed. We characterize the performance of our system with respect to the percentage of coverage achieved by a fixed number of nodes as a function of time. Percentage coverage as a function of time is an essential metric in applications such as disaster response, where the speed of covering an area and identifying survivors is critical to the success of the operation. Even random walk algorithms eventually attain complete coverage of an area, however we seek to minimize the time for coverage through coordinated node movement approaching that of an algorithm with accurate location measurements.

Due to the limited suitable MAV coverage algorithms available in literature, we compare SugarMap to currently available online coverage algorithms for MAV nodes namely random walk coverage [8], and Online Multi-robot Spanning Tree Coverage (OMSTC) [9] that assumes accurate node location is available.

4.1 Simulation Setup

We have developed a simulation environment for the SensorFly MAV indoor sensor swarm to evaluate our coverage algorithm at scale in a realistic scenario. The simulator incorporates a realistic physical arena, MAV node virtual sensors and sensor noise models, MAV node mobility models, wireless communication and radio path loss model, and application specific sensing models. These models are generated through data collected from MAV nodes in indoor environments. In addition, the simulator allows users to program the logic for actuation of MAV's and implement coverage algorithms such as SugarMap or Random Walk. The simulator, now ported to Python, extends previous work [20] to include additional application scenarios and

adds the ability to interface with actual hardware and run hardware-in-loop simulations.

To simulate SugarMap we configure the different aspects of the simulator as follows:

- **Arena** – We assume an indoor search and rescue scenario, where nodes are required to move and cover a continuous indoor space such as a room. The simulation arena constitutes the search space and we evaluate SugarMap in a $20m \times 20m$ square arena, but with multiple configurations of boundary walls and obstacles.

- **Node Sensors** – We model the MAV node based on the SensorFly [19] MAV platform used for our real implementation. The node is equipped with 3 virtual sensors: an inertial gyroscope sensor, an optical flow velocity sensor, an ultrasonic altitude measurement sensor, and a radio with round-trip time-of-flight measurement capability. The application sensor has a sensing footprint equal to a square cell of $0.5m \times 0.5m$. This corresponds to the cell size of the grid map used by SugarMap to compute coverage.

- **Node Mobility** – Like the SensorFly nodes, the simulated nodes can be commanded to turn by a desired angle and move forward for a designated time. The nodes execute the commands with feedback from their virtual sensors, incorporating the errors from their associated noise models. The nodes operate at speeds of $0.25m/s$ to $0.45m/s$.

- **Anchor Nodes** – We model the deployment of anchor nodes as described in Section 3.1. The simulation clock starts after initialization of the system and anchor node deployment.

- **Radio Model** – Shadowing with a path loss exponent of 3 is used as the radio link model, which is an estimate for an indoor single-floor scenario [21]. The movement algorithm ensures that nodes maintain connectivity.

- **Simulation Time-steps** – The simulation time-step is configurable and determines the resolution of node movement that can be recorded by the simulator. The nodes execute their movement based on their velocity, specified in meters per simulation-seconds. Therefore, the minimum distance that can be achieved by the node in one command is determined by the duration of the simulation time-step. For the purpose of the evaluation, we selected a time step of $1sec$ that enables nodes to cover a distance of $0.25m$ to $0.45m$ in a single simulation tick. In terms, of sensing footprint ($0.5m \times 0.5m$), a node can travel from one sensing cell to another in a single tick.

The coverage algorithm or the base-station *brain* of the swarm does not receive the real physical locations of the nodes but only their presumed locations based on movement commands. The nodes are also not aware of the map and are assumed to be at the center of an infinite space at initialization. However, nodes are aware of their relative initial positions with respect to each other in accordance with the manual deployment at the entrance to the search space.

258

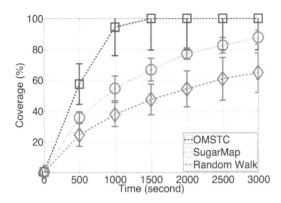

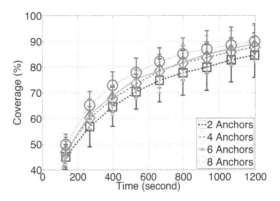

Figure 5: The figure shows the percentage coverage of two nodes as a function of time for the SugarMap algorithm, Random-Walk, and a spanning tree coverage algorithm – OMSTC that assumes locations of nodes are known. The error bars show the standard deviation over 10 runs.

Figure 6: The figure shows the evolution of coverage for a varying number of deployed anchor nodes with 4 explorer nodes. The error bars show the standard deviation over 10 runs.

4.2 Comparing Coverage

We evaluate the performance of SugarMap by comparing the percentage coverage achieved as a function of time to state-of-the-art existing online coverage approaches applicable to MAV swarms.

We implement two approaches – random walk and online multi-robot spanning tree coverage (OMSTC) (assumes locations of nodes is known with high accuracy and precision). Random walk [8] is the most popular approach used by resource-constrained nodes when no location information or prior knowledge of the environment is available. This provides us a baseline for comparison. On the other hand, OMSTC [9] is a guaranteed multi-node coverage algorithm that assumes that nodes can locate themselves in the space. Although, perfect location is unattainable, this presents us with an ideal system for comparison.

Figure 5 shows the percentage coverage as a function of time for SugarMap, Random-Walk (baseline) and OMSTC (ideal). The simulation uses 4 explorer nodes for all algorithms and runs for 3000 simulation seconds. SugarMap performs better than random walk achieving a faster rate of coverage in the simulation scenarios.

4.3 Analyzing SugarMap

In addition to comparing coverage with other approaches, we analyze the trade-offs involved in selecting parameters for a SugarMap deployment.

4.3.1 Impact of Number of Anchors

The SugarMap system uses anchor nodes to obtain a radio signature for various covered areas. Individual radio measurements (round-trip time-of-flight) are subject to variability as shown in Figure 14. However, a signature combining measurements from multiple anchors is more stable.

Figure 6 shows the coverage achieved as a function of time while the increasing number of anchors deployed by the system. The number of explorers is set at 4 and the number of particles used for each SugarMap node is 10. A stable area signature enables SugarMap to determine visited locations better and compute better trajectories for the swarm nodes.

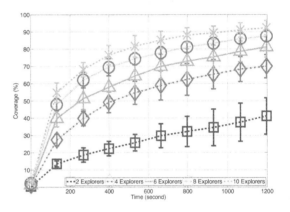

Figure 7: The figure shows the evolution of coverage for varying number of explorer nodes with 6 anchor nodes. The error bars show the standard deviation over 10 runs.

Therefore, coverage improves with an increase in the number of anchors. However, depending on the variance in individual measurements, the benefit of increasing the number of anchors diminishes after a point. The number of anchors also depends on the size of the area.

With fewer anchor nodes (2 nodes in Figure 6), the radio location signatures are not sufficiently unique and the accuracy of coverage estimation suffers. Without estimation of coverage, the path planning algorithm cannot efficiently compute motion and coverage achieved shows high variance similar to a random walk algorithm.

4.3.2 Impact of Number of Explorers

Figure 7 shows the coverage achieved as a function of time for a varying number of explorer nodes. 6 anchor nodes are used for the simulation. As nodes explore the environment in parallel, the larger the number of explorer nodes the greater is the coverage. Moreover, unlike heuristic algorithms, SugarMap coordinates node movements to reduce the overlap in area coverage. Thus, increasing the number of nodes shows

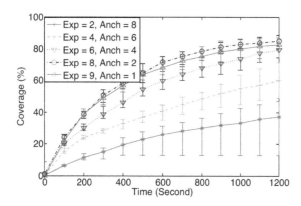

Figure 8: The figure shows the percentage coverage for fixed size 10-node deployment with varying number of anchors and explorers.

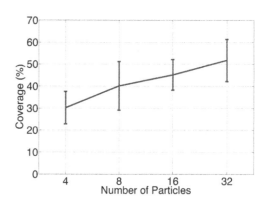

Figure 9: The figure shows the coverage achieved in 400 simulation ticks as a function of the number of particles used in the SugarMap algorithm. The number of explorer nodes is fixed at 2 and number of anchors nodes is 6. The error bars show the standard deviation over 10 runs.

an almost linear increase in speed of coverage. However, due to noise in sensor and actuation, some overlap in individual node coverage exists in SugarMap. Therefore, the benefit of increasing explorer nodes diminishes after a point.

4.3.3 Anchor-Explorer Trade-off

Figure 8 shows the rate of coverage for varying ratio of anchor nodes to explorer nodes for a fixed-size (10-node) deployment in a $20m \times 20m$ arena. The plot shows the trade-off between anchor nodes and explorer nodes. It is evident that for a given size deployment, the coverage rate is determined largely by the number of explorer nodes. The larger the number of explorer nodes the faster the coverage attained. However, the incremental performance gain of introducing additional explorer nodes diminishes when the number of anchors is reduced below 4. With a small number of anchor nodes, the radio location signatures are not sufficiently unique and the accuracy of SugarMap coverage estimation decreases with time. Consequently, the nodes cannot coordinate efficiently and performance drops.

4.3.4 Impact of Number of Particles

SugarMap uses a particle filter to model the uncertainty in actuation of MAV nodes. Each node is represented by a number of particles, each of which holds an estimate of the node's coverage map. Figure 9 shows the percentage coverage achieved by a deployment of 2 explorer nodes and 6 anchor nodes in 400 ticks of the simulation, while the number of particles used is varied. The greater the number of particles, the better is the estimation of the area covered by SensorFly's. This translates to a lower overlap in sensed area and a higher speed of coverage. As a trade-off, the larger number of particles require higher memory and computation at the base station. In addition, the choice of particles depends on the sensor and actuation noise of the MAV node. Larger sensor noise requires higher number of particles.

4.3.5 Impact of Search Space Geometry

We evaluate the performance of SugarMap in multiple space configurations. The simulation environment enables the programmer to specify walls (red cells), open navigable area (blue cells) and obstacles (green cells) by providing a

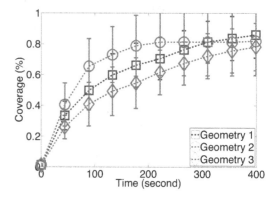

Figure 11: Figure shows the coverage as a function of time for the SugarMap algorithm in 3 different geometries (Figure 10) of the simulation arena. The error bars show the standard deviation over 10 runs.

bitmap image. Figure 10 shows 3 different geometries used to evaluate SugarMap. Geometry (a) is an almost circular open space with a few obstacles. Geometry (b) is a U-shaped region with a narrow leg similar to a room with a connecting hallway. While, geometry (c) models a narrow corridor.

Figure 11 shows the coverage as a function of time for the 3 different arena geometries. The curves for the 3 spaces follow each other closely showing that SugarMap is robust to variations in space configuration.

4.3.6 Algorithm Parameters

The SugarMap algorithm has two principal parameters – (1) a threshold to match radio signatures (SIG_TH), for determining if an observed signature is similar to a previously observed one; and (2) a threshold to select the next location for movement ($COVER\_TH$), for determining the confidence of coverage for a neighboring location as per the global coverage map.

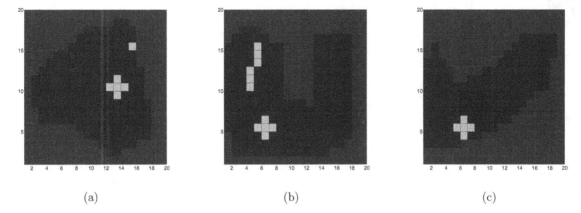

(a)   (b)   (c)

Figure 10: The figure shows 3 geometries of the simulation arena with different obstacle configurations used to evaluate the robustness of the SugarMap algorithm. The red cells are walls, the blue cells represent navigable space, and the green cells designate obstacles.

The SIG_TH is determined empirically based on the radio feature and metric used to compute the similarity of signatures. The SugarMap system implementation uses a vector of RToF (Round-trip Time-of-Flight) measurements from a set of anchor nodes as the radio signature. Purohit et. al. [19] provide a more detailed evaluation of RToF measurements and their correlation with distance. We use Euclidean distance as a metric to measure similarity between N-dimensional RToF signatures, given by,

$$d_{i,j} = \frac{\| \vec{s^i} - \vec{s^j} \|}{\text{\# of visible common anchors}} \quad (11)$$

For the purpose of our evaluation, we selected a SIG_TH of 1.2, obtained by measuring the average RToF signature distance for 20 signatures in a 2-meter radius circle, over 5 distinct locations in our lab.

The $COVER\_TH$ is defined as an exit condition for the path planning algorithm. Since, the coverage map represents confidence probabilistically it does not achieve 100% coverage confidence for a location in finite time. The parameter determines the coverage confidence that is desired by the application for the path planner to avoid revisiting a location. We chose 95% as the coverage threshold for our evaluation signifying a high degree of certainty that the area is covered.

4.3.7 Actuation Noise Model

The SugarMap algorithm uses particle filters to account for the uncertainty in the movement actually executed by MAV nodes on a given command. A model of the actuation noise is required in the prediction step of the particle filter as described in Section 3.3.2. The actuation uncertainty depends on the sensors and control algorithm for the specific MAV platform. For the purposes of the evaluation, we use the SensorFly platform to empirically determine an approximate noise model. The SensorFly platform uses PID control with feedback from an optical flow sensor (velocity) and a gyro (turn) to execute the commanded motion. We measured the standard deviation in turn executed by the platform using a vision-based ground truth measurement relative to the commanded turn value to derive a model. For the evaluation, we used a normal distribution with a standard deviation of 20% of the commanded turn value to predict turn noise. Similarly, a normal distribution with a

Figure 12: The figure shows a SensorFly node used to implement SugarMap on the prototype testbed.

standard deviation of 15% of the commanded velocity value was used as the velocity noise model.

4.4 MAV Testbed

In addition to the simulation experiments, we evaluate SugarMap in our MAV swarm testbed. We implement SugarMap on the SensorFly [19] MAV platform.

The SensorFly platform is equipped with a 8-bit 16Mhz AVR AtMega128rfa1 micro-controller, inertial motion sensors – 3-axis accelerometer and 3-axis gyro, an ultrasonic ranger for altitude estimation, an optical flow sensor for velocity estimation, and a 802.15.4a compatible radio with Round-trip time-of-flight (RToF) measurement capability. The entire platform is under $30g$ in weight and has a flight time of 6-8 minutes. The SensorFly nodes are capable of receiving high-level movement commands such as *"Turn X degrees"* and *"Move forward X seconds"*. The nodes execute the movement in accordance with on-board PID control algorithms utilizing angular and translational velocity feedback from the nodes' gyro and optical-flow sensors. Figure 12 shows a SensorFly node with the battery and basic set of sensors.

The testbed consists of a $5m \times 3m$ arena where the SensorFly nodes move. A grid is painted on the arena dividing it

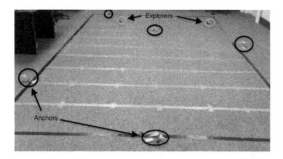

Figure 13: The figure shows the arena for the MAV swarm testbed with deployed SensorFly nodes.

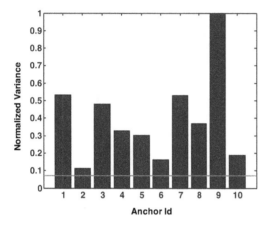

Figure 14: Figure shows the normalized variance in RToF measurements from a explorer node and 10 individual anchors (bars) over a 3 day period. The variance of the signature (combined set of 10 individual measurements) is shown by the horizontal line. The low variance of the combined vector makes it suitable as an area signature.

into cells of $0.5m \times 0.5m$. A camera is deployed on the ceiling to capture the entire arena in its field of view. A workstation running a color blob detection algorithm uses the feed from the camera to compute the *ground-truth* location of all MAV nodes on the grid. The cell size of the grid is chosen to reflect the sensing radius of the MAV node. The blades of the SensorFly nodes are affixed with red-tape so as to be easily detectable by the vision-based ground-truth tracking system. Figure 13 shows the arena of the testbed with deployed SensorFly anchors and explorers.

RToF Area Signature Stability

The explorer SensorFly nodes use a set of round-trip time-of-flight (RToF) measurements from stationary anchor nodes as a signature of area covered. The signature enables explorer nodes to determine if a covered area is being revisited. This information is used for by the coverage path planner for coordination and by the probabilistic coverage estimation algorithm for updating particle weights.

The round-trip time-of-flight method measures the elapsed time between the host node sending a data signal to the remote node, and receiving an acknowledgment from it. Our implementation, based on the SensorFly platform, uses

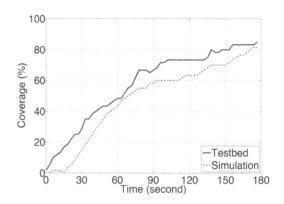

Figure 15: The figure shows the evolution of coverage for the 7-node MAV swarm testbed experiment (solid-line). The result is in agreement with our simulation (dotted-line) using similar arena-size, number of anchors, number of explorers, and the actuation noise model.

physical layer timestamps and hardware-generated acknowledgments to compute a RToF measurements [19, 18].

We perform an experiment to measure the repeatability of a set of RToF measurements and hence validate its suitability as a area signature. RToF measurements from 10 nearby anchors were collected at a mobile node location over a 3 day period, in a lab environment. The lab is subject to frequent environment changes due to movement and activity of people. Figure 14 shows the variance in RToF measurements from each anchor. We observe a large variation in individual RToF measurements over the 3-day period. However, despite these environmental variations, we observe that the overall ten-dimension signature vector of the RToF measurements remains consistent (red-line), showing very low variance over the entire test period.

Testbed Results

In our testbed experiment, we use a swarm of 7 MAV nodes running the SugarMap algorithm. 5 nodes are allowed to disperse and deploy as anchors at initialization. 2 nodes are used as explorers. The two explorer nodes start at grid locations [1,1] and [2,1], respectively, and move as per commands given by the base-station. The explorer nodes obtain RToF readings from anchor nodes and relay it to the base-station at every step. The actual coverage achieved is computed for evaluation purposes using the ground-truth vision-based tracking system of the testbed. The testbed experiment runs for 3-minutes of node flying time which enables us to execute multiple runs on a single charge.

Figure 15 shows the evolution of coverage attained by the 7-node swarm running SugarMap (solid-line). The swarm is able to cover 85% of the arena in the 3-minute experiment time. For comparison, we also plot a simulation result (dotted-line) using a similar size arena, 5 anchor nodes, 2 explorer nodes, and the actuation noise model for SensorFly nodes. The results from the simulation and real experiment closely follow each other as time progresses, validating the simulation setup and methodology.

5. DISCUSSION

Having presented the SugarMap coverage algorithm, we note that several aspects warrant further discussion and could result in possible extensions to this work.

5.1 Multi-hop Communication

The explorer nodes obtain RToF measurements from the deployed anchor nodes as a location signature. This requires explorer nodes to be in single-hop communication range with a large enough sub-set of anchor nodes to obtain a unique radio location signatures. In this paper, we limit our application and evaluation to a single-space coverage scenario where all nodes are within radio range. The explorer nodes stop exploring if they lose radio range with deployed anchor nodes. Thus explorer nodes employ a single-hop communication scheme to relay data back to the base station. We continue to explore large-space or multi-room scenarios in our ongoing work, where the network can extend its reach by progressively deploying exploring nodes as new anchors and requires support for multi-hop communication schemes.

5.2 Distributed Operation

The current SugarMap implementation has a central base station that aggregates the coverage estimates of individual nodes to arrive at a global coverage map. The global coverage map is utilized by the explorer nodes to decide their next movement. For a single-space scenario with single-hop communication range this simple mechanism reduces communication and computation on the nodes. For large-space and multi-room scenarios, it is desirable for nodes to broadcast their local coverage maps and for each node to itself aggregate neighboring nodes' maps to determine global coverage. Such distributed operation would remove the single point of failure at the base station and also provide latency advantages as nodes would not have to communicate with the base station over multiple hops. However, a distributed scheme would require consideration for lack of consensus on coverage maps due to lossy wireless links. We seek to explore this in our future work.

6. RELATED WORK

The coverage problem has been addressed in the past by research in multi-robot coverage algorithms that focus on the space swept by the robot's sensor. Choset [3] provides a survey of early coverage algorithms and classifies them into *off-line*, in which a map of the area is known beforehand, and *on-line* algorithms, in which the area is unknown. The MAV swarm applications demand an on-line multi-node coverage approach. In this section, we discuss some of the existing work in online coverage that is applicable to MAV swarms.

Gage [8] analyzes randomized robot coverage for robots without costly localization sensors or valuable computational resources for calculating their position. A random search does not guarantee coverage but may be the only approach with very low capability sensor nodes in absence of motion sensing.

Wagner et al. [24] propose a pheromone based stigmergic algorithm, where nodes coordinate by leaving markers in the environment. The algorithm is heuristic in nature and requires nodes to be capable of leaving and detecting physical markers in the environment. This is not practical for lightweight MAV nodes.

A series of simultaneous localization and mapping (SLAM) approaches [22] exist for multi-robot systems that use laser range-finders or computer vision algorithms (to extract visual features) in conjunction with noisy odometry to construct maps of the area and obtain coverage. This approach is very promising for ground-based robots or larger aerial nodes. Currently available laser rangers tend to be too bulky for deployment on MAV's, while vision-based approaches require better computation and communication capabilities.

Howard et al. [1] considers the problem of deploying a mobile sensor network in an unknown environment. The approach assumes that each node is equipped with a sensor that allows it to determine the range and bearing of both nearby nodes and obstacles, such as scanning laser range-finders or omni-cameras. Using these, the system constructs fields such that each node is repelled by both obstacles and by other nodes, thereby forcing the network to spread itself throughout the environment. The algorithm has the advantage of requiring no communication between nodes but does not guarantee completeness. In Spreading-Out [14], Batalin et al. present an algorithm for robot teams without access to maps or a Global Positioning System (location). The robots are assumed to be equipped with planar laser range-finders, color camera and vision beacons, and robots select a direction away from all their immediate sensed neighbors and move in that direction. The approach is heuristic with the premise that robots must 'spread out' over the environment in order to achieve good coverage.

Hazon et al. [9] present a guaranteed robust multi-robot coverage algorithm based on spanning tree coverage paths. Each robot works within an assigned portion of the work area, constructing a local spanning-tree covering this portion, as it moves. It coordinates movement with other robots to minimize overlap in coverage. However, the algorithm assumes the robots have access to relative location of all nodes in the area. SugarMap employs the concept of spanning trees to guarantee completeness of coverage but further extends it to remove the requirement for node location. Moreover, SugarMap introduces probabilities into the coverage map to account for and overcome the sensor and actuation uncertainty of MAV nodes.

Related work in robotics and sensor networks [4, 10, 23] uses particle filters for monitoring robot or human position in indoor environments. Their primary focus is to localize nodes using measurement from motion sensors and observed environmental landmarks. Our approach seeks to guarantee coverage of an unknown space by a swarm of nodes based on the coordinated motion commands, using particle filters to account for the uncertainty in MAV actuation.

7. CONCLUSION

This paper presents SugarMap, a location-less coverage system that allows a swarm to collaboratively and efficiently attain sensing coverage of a target area with an MAV swarm. SugarMap does not require sophisticated or bulky sensors, advanced on-device processing abilities, or a pre-existing location infrastructure as do many state-of-the-art prior approaches. We provide a comprehensive evaluation of the SugarMap system through large-scale simulations and a real implementation on the SensorFly [19] platform. Our experimental evaluations show that SugarMap performs significantly better than existing coverage approaches for resource-limited (in terms of sensors, energy, location, processing power) mobile sensing nodes such as random-walk especially in larger locations with fewer nodes. This algorithm will enable swarms of the new class of realistic resource constrained micro-aerial vehicles in new applications.

8. ACKNOWLEDGEMENTS

Special thanks to our shepherd Dr. Luca Mottola and the anonymous reviewers for their insightful and constructive comments. This research was supported by Intel, NSF under grant 1121690-CNS1135874-NSF-ZHANG and DARPA under grant 1080247-D11AP00265-DOI-ZHANG. The views and conclusions contained here are those of the authors and should not be interpreted as necessarily representing the official policies or endorsements, either expressed or implied, of NSF, DARPA, Intel, CMU, or the U.S. Government or any of its agencies.

9. REFERENCES

[1] M. J. M. Andrew Howard. Mobile Sensor Network Deployment using Potential Fields: A Distributed, Scalable Solution to the Area Coverage Problem. *Proceedings of the 6th International Symposium on Distributed Autonomous Robotics Systems (DARS02)*, 2002.

[2] J. Artieda, J. M. Sebastian, P. Campoy, J. F. Correa, I. F. Mondragón, C. Martínez, and M. Olivares. Visual 3-D SLAM from UAVs. *Journal of Intelligent and Robotic Systems*, 55(4-5):299–321, Jan. 2009.

[3] H. Choset. Coverage for robotics - A survey of recent results. *Annals of Mathematics and Artificial Intelligence*, 31(1-4):113–126, May 2001.

[4] W. B. Dieter Fox . Monte Carlo Localization: Efficient Position Estimation for Mobile Robots. In *Sixteenth National Conference on Artificial Intelligence (AAAI'99)*, 1999.

[5] L. Doitsidis, S. Weiss, A. Renzaglia, M. W. Achtelik, E. Kosmatopoulos, R. Siegwart, and D. Scaramuzza. Optimal surveillance coverage for teams of micro aerial vehicles in GPS-denied environments using onboard vision. *Autonomous Robots*, 33(1-2):173–188, Mar. 2012.

[6] S. Fu, H.-y. Liu, L.-f. Gao, and Y.-x. Gai. SLAM for mobile robots using laser range finder and monocular vision. In *2007 14th International Conference on Mechatronics and Machine Vision in Practice*, pages 91–96. IEEE, Dec. 2007.

[7] Y. Gabriely and E. Rimon. Spanning-tree based coverage of continuous areas by a mobile robot. In *Proceedings 2001 ICRA. IEEE International Conference on Robotics and Automation (Cat. No.01CH37164)*, volume 2, pages 1927–1933. IEEE, 2001.

[8] D. W. Gage. Randomized Search Strategies With Imperfect Sensors. In *SPIE Mobile Robors VIII*, pages 270–279, Boston, 1993.

[9] N. Hazon, F. Mieli, and G. Kaminka. Towards robust on-line multi-robot coverage. In *Proceedings 2006 IEEE International Conference on Robotics and Automation, 2006. ICRA 2006.*, pages 1710–1715. IEEE.

[10] L. Klingbeil and T. Wark. A wireless sensor network for real-time indoor localisation and motion monitoring. In *Proceedings of the 7th international conference on Information processing in sensor networks*, pages 39–50. IEEE Computer Society Washington, DC, USA, 2008.

[11] S. Koenig and D. Kempe. Multi-robot forest coverage. In *2005 IEEE/RSJ International Conference on Intelligent Robots and Systems*, pages 3852–3857. IEEE, 2005.

[12] J. Liu. *Monte Carlo strategies in scientific computing*. Springer Publishing Company, Jan. 2008.

[13] L. Ludwig and G. Maria. Robotic swarm dispersion using wireless intensity signals. In *International Symposium on Distributed Autonomous Robotic Systems*, 2006.

[14] G. S. S. Maxim A. Batalin. Spreading Out: A Local Approach to Multi-robot Coverage. *Proceedings of the 6th International Symposium on Distributed Autonomous Robotics System*, 2002.

[15] J. McLurkin and J. Smith. Distributed Algorithms for Dispersion in Indoor Environments using a Swarm of Autonomous Mobile Robots. *7th International Symposium on Distributed Autonomous Robotic Systems (DARS)*, 2004.

[16] M. Montemerlo, S. Thrun, D. Koller, and B. Wegbreit. FastSLAM: a factored solution to the simultaneous localization and mapping problem. In *Eighteenth national conference on Artificial intelligence*, pages 593–598, July 2002.

[17] R. Morlok and M. Gini. Dispersing robots in an unknown environment. In *7th International Symposium on Distributed Autonomous Robotic Systems (DARS)*, 2004.

[18] Nanotron Tecnologies Gmbh. Real Time Location Systems (RTLS). 2007.

[19] A. Purohit, Z. Sun, F. Mokaya, and P. Zhang. SensorFly: Controlled-mobile sensing platform for indoor emergency response applications. In *In Proceeding of the 10th International Conference on Information Processing in Sensor Networks (IPSN)*, pages 223–234, 2011.

[20] A. Purohit and P. Zhang. Controlled-mobile sensing simulator for indoor fire monitoring. In *Wireless Communications and Mobile Computing Conference (IWCMC), 2011 7th International*, pages 1124–1129, 2011.

[21] D. Rutledge. *Investigation of indoor radio channels from 2.4 GHz to 24 GHz*. IEEE.

[22] S. Thrun. An Online Mapping Algorithm for Teams of Mobile Robots. *International Journal of Robotics Research*, 2001.

[23] S. Thrun, D. Fox, W. Burgard, and F. Dellaert. Robust Monte Carlo localization for mobile robots. *Artificial Intelligence*, 128(1-2):99–141, May 2001.

[24] I. Wagner, M. Lindenbaum, and A. Bruckstein. Distributed covering by ant-robots using evaporating traces. *IEEE Transactions on Robotics and Automation*, 15(5):918–933, 1999.

[25] R. J. Wood. The First Takeoff of a Biologically Inspired At-Scale Robotic Insect. *IEEE transactions on robotics*, 24(2):341–347, 2008.

Think Globally, Act Locally: On the Reshaping of Information Landscapes

Andreas Loukas   Marco Zuniga   Matthias Woehrle   Marco Cattani   Koen Langendoen

Embedded Software Group
Delft University of Technology, The Netherlands
{a.loukas, m.a.zunigazamalloa, m.woehrle, m.cattani, k.g.langendoen}@tudelft.nl

ABSTRACT

In large-scale resource-constrained systems, such as wireless sensor networks, global objectives should be ideally achieved through inexpensive local interactions. A technique satisfying these requirements is *information potentials*, in which distributed functions disseminate information about the process monitored by the network. Information potentials are usually computed through local aggregation or gossiping. These methods however, do not consider the topological properties of the network, such as node density, which could be exploited to enhance the performance of the system.

This paper proposes a novel aggregation method with which a potential becomes sensitive to the network topology. Our method introduces the notion of *affinity spaces*, which allow us to uncover the deep connections between the aggregation scope (the radius of the extended neighborhood whose information is aggregated) and the network's Laplacian (which captures the topology of the connectivity graph). Our study provides two additional contributions: (*i*) It characterizes the convergence of information potentials for static and dynamic networks. Our analysis captures the impact of key parameters, such as node density, time-varying information, as well as of the addition (or removal) of links and nodes. (*ii*) It shows that information potentials are decomposed into wave-like eigenfunctions that depend on the aggregation scope. This result has important implications, for example it prevents greedy routing techniques from getting stuck by eliminating local-maxima. Simulations and experimental evaluation show that our main findings hold under realistic conditions, with unstable links and message loss.

Categories and Subject Descriptors

C.2.1 [**Computer-Communication Networks**]: Network Architecture and Design—*Distributed networks*

Keywords

Aggregation; Diffusion; Information Discovery; Unimodality

1. INTRODUCTION

This paper focuses on two problems pertaining to sensor networks: *information aggregation and information discovery*. These problems appear when sensor nodes need to act locally in response to a process that is monitored globally. The monitored processes may relate to the intrinsic properties of the network operation, e. g., density, channel congestion, algorithm faults, load, or to properties related to the physical environment, e. g., monitoring the climate, traffic congestion or the movement of crowds. To avoid centralized solutions where nodes report their measurements to a single point, the sensor network community has explored the concept of information potentials [15, 17, 19, 21]. Potentials are formed through the exchange of local information and provide gradients that achieve objective-specific goals, such as routing through areas with low traffic congestion.

It is known that the computation of *useful* information potentials exposes a fundamental dilemma. How much information should a node take into account? How wide should the aggregation scope be? More information leads to more informed decisions, but it comes at the cost of increased message complexity. Our work moves beyond this dilemma and proposes that *the quality of information potentials depends not only on the extent of the aggregation scope, but also on the connectivity properties of the network*. Hence, the construction of information potentials should be tailored towards the specific characteristic of the network topology.

Hitherto, two distributed approaches have been used for aggregating information in the vicinity of nodes. The first approach exploits the (possible) spatial correlation of information processes, and requires nodes to aggregate information at a decaying function of distance [10, 13, 18]. This approach requires location information and it is mainly aimed at *physical* processes with strong spatial correlations, such as temperature. The distance-based approach does not perform well for processes related to the network operation (for example, load-balanced routing), because the information of these processes depend more on the network topology than on the inter-node distances. The second approach overcomes the limitations of the first by using constrained averaging; nodes aggregate all values within their k-hop vicinity. This approach is location-independent, but it does not distinguish the relative significance of information. This means that a neighbor with degree one has the same relevance as a high-degree neighbor. Additionally, all information within k-hops is aggregated uniformly, irrespectively of whether it is one or

k hops away. Within this context, our paper provides three main contributions.

Contribution 1: an aggregation method that is sensitive to topological features (Section 3). We introduce a subtle yet important change to traditional constrained averaging algorithms. This change allows us to model information dissemination as a random walk starting at a given node, and then, moving (randomly) for k steps. The distribution of the potential destinations of these random walks captures the underlying connectivity of the graph. Similar to constrained averaging, our approach requires no location information, it is simple, and decentralized. Yet, it is also sensitive to the relative significance of information, as well as to the network topology. The latter leads to a key advantage: our algorithm can be modeled by connectivity matrices, which allows us (i) to use standard linear algebra techniques to analyze the convergence of this new way of forming information potentials, and (ii) to use spectral graph theory to demonstrate how information potentials can reshape the landscapes of information processes.

Contribution 2: an analysis of the convergence of information potentials on static and dynamic networks (Sections 4 and 5). With respect to convergence analysis, our study provides the following findings:

- The algorithm converges exponentially and the convergence is faster in dense regular networks.

- There is a critical aggregation scope under which network dynamics hardly matter. Above this threshold, higher dynamics require narrower aggregation scopes for faster convergence.

In practice, these findings provide some *dos and don'ts* for information potential deployments. Avoid concave shapes (dents), void regions and radio transceivers with high sensitivity variance because they increase degree heterogeneity (irregularity). Adding nodes to a deployment helps more if they are uniformly distributed. Prior to a deployment, analyze the dynamics of the network, which might be caused by the movement of people, the failure/addition of nodes, etc.; if the dynamics are high, it is better to avoid using very wide aggregation scopes. If the dynamics are low, the extent of the aggregation scope does not play a major role, i.e., feel free to explore the trade-off between amount-of-information and message complexity.

Contribution 3: a framework to shape the landscapes of information potentials (Section 6). Information potentials resemble landscapes with valleys and peaks; Figure 1 depicts an example of our method. By borrowing results from spectral graph theory, we reveal deep connections between these landscapes and the eigenfunctions of the normalized Laplacian:

- The eigenfunctions of the normalized Laplacian are wave-like and characterize the spatial variation of the monitored process.

- The slope of our aggregation function shapes the potential landscape. In particular, there exists a critical slope under which the potential becomes unimodal, i.e., it features a single extremum.

To understand *the practical importance* of these results, consider an information potential that needs to smoothen

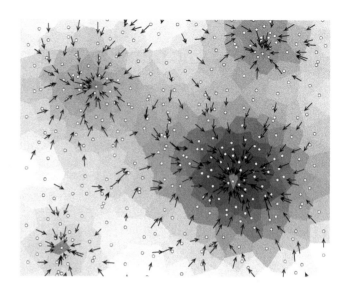

Figure 1: An information potential landscape which considers node density. Nodes within green cells have the maximum potential – highest relative density – amongst their neighbors. The arrows reveal the potential gradient.

the peaks formed by nodes with abnormally high (or low) values with respect to their neighbors. The spatial variation of information is captured by the eigenfunctions. The higher the variation, the higher the frequency; and our aggregation method filters eigenfunctions based on their frequency. In effect, this means that an information landscape can be smoothened to any desired level: the higher the slope, the smoother the landscape. Beyond a threshold, the continuous elimination of higher-frequency eigenfunctions leads to the elimination of local extrema until the point where a single maxima is present.

Section 7 validates some of our analysis by simulations and experiments on a 100+ node testbed.

Applications of information potentials. The quintessential application of information potentials in sensor networks is greedy routing [19]. Still, the advent of smart mobile embedded devices, e.g., smartphones, makes information potentials also relevant to other practical applications, such as traffic management and crowd management.

Greedy routing. In greedy routing, nodes use gradients to forward information greedily. In these scenarios, the presence of local maxima is undesirable as it prevents packets from arriving at the intended destination. Our work eliminates this issue by providing unimodality (Contribution 3). It is important to remark that the work of Lin et al. [15] also provides unimodality. However, their approach, which is based on harmonic functions, relies on a larger set of assumptions. A detailed discussion of the similarities and differences of our approach with this and other studies is presented in Section 8.

In a more general context, information potentials can be thought of as distributed primitives that (i) facilitate the discovery of areas of high (low) level of information, and (ii) provide mobile entities an efficient way of navigating towards these areas. The mobile entities can be packets, people, robots, cars, etc. In a preliminary version of this study [16], we showed through simulations how our algorithm is used for rendezvous coordination, where a swarm of mobile entities identify the nodes with the largest potentials, and the rest of the swarm moves towards their closest high-potential node in real time. Below, we describe two applications that can benefit from our work on information potentials.

Crowd management. Our interest in information potential algorithms was sparked by their ability to support the management of large crowds in open air festivals. In these type of festivals, crowds of hundreds of thousands gather in city centers within confined spaces. For safety reasons, the crowds should not exceed densities above a given margin[1]. As part of two larger projects involving several institutions (D2S2 and EWiDS), we focus on the facilitation of crowd management through self-monitoring. We aim at providing attendees with coin-size wearable devices, each equipped with sensors, actuators (light), and a wireless transceiver. In this way, information potentials will be able to monitor the density of people in real time and warn attendees if their surrounding density exceeds safe levels. The attendees will also have access to the gradients formed by the potentials to move to areas with lower densities.

Traffic management. Parking management is a highly important topic in public policy. As reported by Shou [20], on average 30% of traffic in downtown areas is due to vehicles looking for parking. Cities such as San Francisco and London are installing wireless sensors on individual parking spots that report information to a central server to help drivers in finding available parking[2]. Information potentials are a low-cost efficient distributed alternative for the current centralized methods. Neighbouring meters could exchange their occupancy information and guide cars towards free parking areas by communicating with the drivers' smartphones via bluetooth. Information potentials have the added advantage of *aggregating* the information of nearby free parking spots into "more/less crowded" regions, as opposed to tracking individual spaces.

Overall, we believe that information potentials have an important role to play in the future of SmartCities. As more and more wireless devices are embedded in our daily surroundings and more data is harvested from them, a central problem will be how to guide the various mobile entities towards the areas that they are mostly interested in. This work describes an alternative that is simple, decentralized, and generic enough such that it can be shaped to suit the needs of the application at hand.

2. MODEL AND NOTATION

Network model. We model a network as an undirected graph $\mathcal{G} = (\mathcal{V}, \mathcal{E})$, where $\mathcal{V}$ is the node set of cardinality n and $\mathcal{E}$ is the edge set. Two nodes are neighbors $i \sim j$, if $(i, j) \in \mathcal{E}$. The neighborhood of a node is captured by

the neighbor set $\mathcal{V}_i = \{j : i \sim j\}$ and the adjacent edge set $\mathcal{E}_i = \{(i, j) : i \sim j\}$, with cardinality n_i and m_i, respectively. Node density is $d_i = n_i + 1$, while the max and min densities for all $i \in \mathcal{V}$ are d_{max} and d_{min}.

Matrix notation. We describe $\mathcal{G}$ through its $n \times n$ adjacency matrix A, where $A_{ij} = 1$ if $i \sim j$ or $i = j$, and $A_{ij} = 0$ otherwise. Matrix A is symmetric. We let D be the diagonal node density matrix with $D_{ii} = d_i \ \forall i \in V$ and zero otherwise. With A and D, we define the row-stochastic transition matrix $P = D^{-1}A$, the elements of which describe the transition probability of random particle moving randomly on $\mathcal{G}$. The eigenvalues of P are denoted by μ_k. The transition matrix is similar to the well known normalized Laplacian $\mathcal{L}$ [7]. For the spectral analysis, we use a modified Laplacian matrix that considers self-loops: $\mathcal{L}_{ij} = 1 - 1/d_i$ if $i = j$, $\mathcal{L}_{ij} = 1/\sqrt{d_i d_j}$ if $i \sim j$, and $\mathcal{L}_{ij} = 0$ otherwise.

3. INFORMATION POTENTIALS

This section describes our method of computing information potentials and explains how a potential captures information with respect to the topology of the network.

3.1 Distributed computation

In a nutshell, an information potential is a function that maps local information to a value more meaningful within the global network context. For instance, the local information may be the traffic load of the node, and the potential could be a relative value that states how high (or low) this traffic is with respect to other areas in the network – to facilitate, for instance, load balanced routing. Formally, let $x, y : \mathcal{V} \to \mathbb{R}$ be functions over $\mathcal{V}$ that assign a real value to each node. We call function x the *process information*, as $x(i)$ is a value that is sensed or computed by each node $i \in \mathcal{V}$ and represents the quantity or quality of a process in the vicinity of i. Function y is the information potential derived from x.

The computation of an information potential, described in Algorithm 1, is iterative. For the duration of each round, nodes $i \in \mathcal{V}$ exchange their potential $y(i)$ with their neighbors (lines 5 and 7). Since nodes do not exchange $x(i)$, they affect their neighbors indirectly by changing the average neighborhood potential. At the end of a round, nodes update their potential to the weighted sum of their local information process $x(i)$ and of the average over the most recent potential values, including their own (line 11). Intuitively, nodes behave like anchors, each pulling the neighborhood average towards its own $x(i)$ with a force that is proportional to the difference between $x(i)$ and the average. The force also depends on a parameter which we call *inhibiting factor*, and lies in $0 < \varphi \leq 1$. In the final step (line 12), all received values are discarded and the round ends. The algorithm converges when all forces are balanced. Note that the algorithm includes no termination condition; it runs indefinitely, continuously adapting to any network or information dynamics. If no dynamics are expected, termination is locally decided by comparing the difference of the potential at consecutive rounds against some error threshold.

The reuse of the information $x(i)$ throughout the computation (line 11) differentiates our work from: (i) *average consensus*, in which y is initialized to x and, at each round t, nodes simply average their values, $y_{t+1} = Py_t$ [7], as well as from (ii) *broadcast consensus* [1], in which each node i

---

[1]In 2010, a crowd rush in a popular electronic dance festival in Germany ended up with 21 deaths and more than 500 injured people.

[2]The system for San Francisco is SFpark (`spark.org`) and for London is the Bay Sensor Technology (`www.westminster.gov.uk/services/transportandstreets/parking/bay-sensor-technology`)

Algorithm 1 Potential computation

Require: Factor $\varphi \in (0, 1]$ and i a unique node id.

```
1: initialize
2:     y(i) ← x(i)
3:     S(i) ← {y(i)}                           ▷ state set

4: event OnTransmit
5:     broadcast {i, y(i)} to all neighbors

6: event OnReceive(j, y(j))
7:     S(i) ← S(i) ∪ {y(j)}              ▷ keep only latest values

8: event OnRoundEnd
9:     update x(i)
10:    d(i) ← |S(i)|                          ▷ local density
11:    y(i) ← (1 − φ) ∑      y(j)/d(i) + φ x(i)   ▷ compute
                   j∈S(i)
12:    S(i) ← {y(i)}                          ▷ clear state
```

computes a weighted average after every received broadcast from $j \sim i$, $y_0(i) = x(i)$ and $y_{t+1}(i) = \gamma y_t(i) + (1 - \gamma)y_t(j)$. As we show in the following, this simple alteration of average consensus gives rise to very interesting properties which relate to affinity spaces (Section 3.2) and the spectrum of the graph Laplacian (Section 6), improves the convergence compared to deterministic consensus (Section 4), and increases the algorithm's resilience to message loss (Section 7).

3.2 Algorithmic analysis

We will now describe how this simple distributed algorithm captures the topology of the network. For the sake of clarity and conciseness, our analysis assumes that (i) nodes operate in synchronous rounds, (ii) at the end of which nodes have received at least one message from each of their neighbors. In Section 7 we show that, *in practice, neither assumption is necessary for the correct and timely operation of the algorithm*. We will also assume, for now, that the information x is constant, i.e., line 9 in the algorithm does not have any valid effect at this point. This assumption will be lifted in Section 4.2, which studies the convergence under time-varying x_t. Formula (1) rewrites Algorithm 1 in an iterative matrix form, where y_t is the y vector after t iterations.

$$y_{t+1} = (1 - \varphi)Py_t + \varphi x \qquad (1)$$

At round t, the potential y_t is given by

$$y_t = (\psi P)^t y_0 + \varphi \sum_{k=0}^{t-1} (\psi P)^k x, \qquad (2)$$

where, for brevity, we set $\psi = 1 - \varphi$. When t grows to infinity, the potential y has the following closed-form expression:

$$y = \lim_{t \to \infty} y_t = \varphi \sum_{k=0}^{\infty} (\psi P)^k x \qquad (3)$$

Note that Formula (2) converges under all cases. As t grows larger, $(\psi P)^t$ approaches asymptotically zero because $\psi < 1$ and P^t is a row-stochastic matrix that converges to the stationary distribution of a uniform random walk on $\mathcal{G}$. The decay of $(\psi P)^t$ removes any influence of the initial state y_0 on the potential y. In Sections 4 and 5 we analyze the

convergence rate for information processes in detail, the rest of this section provides more insights on the potential itself.

Affinity spaces. In contrast to definitions of affinity that result from other metrics of distance, such as euclidean distance [13], our method aggregates information based on a new type of affinity that is very sensitive to the topology of a network. As we will observe, this topological sensitivity is achieved because nodes aggregate information in a sort of "random-walk" manner.

Formula (3) expresses the potential as an infinite sum that, at each round k, changes information x with a weighting factor of $(\psi P)^k$. P_{ij}^k expresses the probability of a randomly moving particle starting from node i and reaching node j in k steps. The better the connectivity between i and j and the shorter the path, the higher the probability. In other words, instead of averaging the information within the k-th range of a node, our method assigns higher significance to the information residing in nearby nodes (close connectivity) and in nodes with higher centrality (better connectivity). In most graphs, centrality is an important metric that captures the "importance" of the information.

The inhibiting factor φ determines the aggregation scope: (i) When $\varphi = 1$, there is no exchange of information and hence the network topology plays no role. As Formula (1) shows, the potential has the same value as the process information ($y = x$). (ii) When $\varphi \to 0^+$, the aggregation scope is global and the network topology plays its greatest role. The iterative formulation reduces to the well studied average consensus $y_{t+1} = P y_t$ [7]. As $t \to \infty$, the potential gets closer to $\mathbb{1}\pi^\top x$, where $\mathbb{1}$ is the $n \times 1$ vector with all elements equal to one and π is the stationary distribution of the transition matrix. Within these extremes, the network has ample flexibility to shape information potentials according to the requirements of the application. In Section 6, we will analyze this characteristic in more detail and its impact on greedy search techniques. Note that, since the geometric series ψ^k converges to $1/\varphi$, the multiplication with φ serves as a normalization.

It is important to highlight that while the analysis considers the global connectivity matrix P, *the algorithm only requires communication with 1-hop neighbors*. The advantage of our simple and distributed algorithm is that it entails such global behavior inherently.

4. CONVERGENCE IN STATIC GRAPHS

In this section we bound the rate of convergence in static graphs for invariant and time-varying information processes. We limit our analysis to $\varphi \in (0, 1)$ as for $\varphi = 1$ the algorithm converges instantaneously. We will first present our theoretical analysis, and then, discuss its implications. In our study, we define the ℓ_2-distance of an information potential y_t as $\|y - y_t\|$, that is, its distance to the steady state.

4.1 Time-invariant information

We first consider the case when the information x stays constant over time and the graph $\mathcal{G}$ is static. In the next sections, we will remove these constraints.

THEOREM 1. *After t rounds, the ℓ_2-distance of an information potential on a static graph $\mathcal{G}$ with information process x is bounded by $\varepsilon_t \leq e^{-\varphi t}(c^2 + c)\|x\|$, where $c = \frac{n}{2m}d_{max} + \xi\mu_2$ and $\xi = \sqrt{d_{max}/d_{min}}$.*

PROOF. The ℓ_2-distance at the t-th round is

$$\varepsilon_t = \|y - y_t\|$$
$$= \Big\| \varphi \sum_{k=0}^{\infty}(\psi P)^k x - \varphi \sum_{k=0}^{t-1}(\psi P)^k x - (\psi P)^t y_0 \Big\|$$
$$= \Big\|(\psi P)^t \Big(\varphi \sum_{k=0}^{\infty}(\psi P)^k x - y_0 \Big)\Big\|. \tag{4}$$

Using a known bound on $P^t x$ [7], we get that for $t \geq 0$ and an arbitrary vector x,

$$\|(\psi P)^t x\| \leq \Big(\psi^t \frac{n}{2m} d_{max} + (\psi \mu_2)^t \xi \Big) \|x\|$$
$$\leq \psi^t c \|x\|. \tag{5}$$

Above, $m = |\mathcal{E}|$ is the number of edges considering self-loops, μ_2 is the second eigenvalue of the transition matrix P and $\xi = \sqrt{d_{max}/d_{min}}$ quantifies the degree irregularity of $\mathcal{G}$. In the last step, $(\psi \mu_2)^t \leq \psi^t \mu_2$ because $\mu_2 < 1$ and $0 \leq \psi < 1$. This loosens the error bound when $\mu_2 > 0$, but allows to estimate the necessary number of rounds t until the algorithm converges ε-close to the stable state. One can achieve a tighter bound if an estimate of t is not required. Substituting Inequality (5) into Formula (4) we have that

$$\varepsilon_t \leq \psi^t c \Big\| \varphi \sum_{k=0}^{\infty}(\psi P)^k x - y_0 \Big\|. \tag{6}$$

From Formula (2), we observe that the choice of the initial state y_0 is irrelevant to the stable state y. Nevertheless, a reasonable step is to set $y_0 = x$. The normed difference in Inequality (6) then is simplified to

$$\Big\| \varphi \sum_{k=0}^{\infty}(\psi P)^k x - x \Big\| \leq \varphi \sum_{k=0}^{\infty} \|(\psi P)^k x\| + \|x\|$$
$$\leq \Big(\varphi \sum_{k=0}^{\infty} \psi^k c + 1 \Big) \|x\|$$
$$= (c+1)\, \|x\|. \tag{7}$$

The substitution of (7) into (6) concludes our proof.

$$\varepsilon_t < \psi^t c\,(c+1)\,\|x\| \leq e^{-\varphi t}(c^2+c)\,\|x\|$$

$\square$

A direct consequence of Theorem 1 is that the necessary number of rounds until the algorithm converges ε-close to y is given by

$$t \geq \varphi^{-1} \log \frac{(c^2+c)\|x\|}{\varepsilon}. \tag{8}$$

4.2 Time-varying information

During the lifetime of some practical applications, the information process x may change over time. For example, a sensor network monitoring the presence of some type of animals will change its measurements when the animal moves. We proceed to examine the behavior of such time-varying information processes.

LEMMA 1. *Let an information potential be at steady state y, while its underlying information process x changes to $\hat{x}$, with $\|\hat{x} - x\| \leq \delta_x$. After $\tau > 0$ steps, the ℓ_2-distance of the potential to the new stable state $\hat{y}$ is bounded by $\varepsilon_\tau \leq e^{-\varphi \tau} c\,\delta_x$.*

PROOF. Without loss of generality, assuming that the change from x to $\hat{x}$ occurs at time t, the ℓ_2-distance to $\hat{y}$ at round τ is bounded by

$$\varepsilon_\tau = \|\hat{y} - y_{t+\tau}\|$$
$$= \Big\| \varphi \sum_{k=0}^{\infty}(\psi P)^k \hat{x} - \varphi \sum_{k=0}^{\tau-1}(\psi P)^k \hat{x} - (\psi P)^\tau y \Big\|$$
$$= \varphi \Big\| \sum_{k=\tau}^{\infty}(\psi P)^k \hat{x} - \sum_{k=\tau}^{\infty}(\psi P)^k x \Big\|$$
$$\leq \varphi \sum_{k=\tau}^{\infty} \|(\psi P)^k (\hat{x} - x)\| \leq e^{-\varphi \tau} c\,\delta_x.$$

$\square$

A direct consequence of Lemma 1 is that the minimum τ for which the algorithm manages to converge ε close to the new stable state $\hat{y}$ is given by

$$\tau \geq \varphi^{-1} \log \frac{c\,\delta_x}{\varepsilon}. \tag{9}$$

4.3 Analysis Insights

Theorem 1 and Lemma 1 provide us with four important insights: (*i*) *The convergence error decreases exponentially.* The inhibiting factor determines the rate of convergence. Smaller values of φ aggregate the values over an exponentially larger subgraphs and as a consequence exhibit slower convergence. (*ii*) *For $\varphi > 0$, the proposed algorithm converges faster than average consensus* [7]. The common ratio of the geometric series which upper bounds the convergence error decreases from μ_2 (average consensus) to $(1 - \varphi)\mu_2$ (proposed algorithm). For $\varphi = 0$, the two mechanisms are exactly the same. (*iii*) *Information dynamics proportionally increase the ℓ_2-error.* This effect should be taken into account when choosing the value of the inhibiting factor. (*iv*) *Convergence is faster in dense, degree regular graphs.* Constant c captures the influence of the network topology to the convergence. Through c we derive that convergence is faster for dense graphs (n/m is the inverse of the graph density), as well as for graphs with small node density variations (quantified by ξ).

5. CONVERGENCE IN DYNAMIC GRAPHS

In this section, we study the algorithmic behavior in the context of graphs that change over time. We model graph dynamics as a sequence of edge and node operations: *Edge operations* describe the addition or deletion of edges between pairs of nodes. *Node operations* model nodes joining or leaving the graph. Through edge and node operations we capture a wide range of network dynamics, such as node and link failures, as well as the dynamics of open networks where the network is subject to mobility and churn. Due to the complexity of the problem, we assume time-invariant information.

We will first derive a bound on the convergence error given any change in the graph. The bound, which is stated in Theorem 2, is general enough to hold for any possible graph dynamics. On the down side, the bound depends on the specifics of the graph dynamics $\delta_{\mathcal{G}}$ in question. We gain further insight by characterizing $\delta_{\mathcal{G}}$ for edge and node operations in Lemmas 2 and 3, respectively.

THEOREM 2. *For any dynamic graph $\mathcal{G}_t$ which varies with steps $\tau > 0$ and is bounded, $\|P_{t+\tau} - P_t\| \le \delta_\mathcal{G}$, the ℓ_2-distance of the potential to the stable state, just before any consecutive variation of $\mathcal{G}_t$, is bounded by*

$$\varepsilon_{t+\tau} \le e^{-\varphi(t+1)} c_{t+\tau} \left(\delta_\mathcal{G} \frac{1-\varphi}{\varphi} c_{t+\tau} c_t + \frac{\varphi}{1-\varphi} \right) \|x\|,$$

where c_t quantifies the connectivity properties of $\mathcal{G}_t$.

PROOF. Consider that the algorithm has converged to a stable state y on a graph $\mathcal{G}$. An adversary then changes the graph to $\hat{\mathcal{G}}$. In the following we annotate symbols that relate to the new graph $\hat{G}$ with a hat; as such $\hat{P}$ is the new transition matrix, $\hat{n}$ is the number of nodes in $\hat{\mathcal{V}}$, and so on. As in previous proofs, we capture convergence error through the ℓ_2-distance between the state after t iterations and the new stable state $\hat{y}$. By substituting the analytic expression of y into Formula (4) we get

$$\varepsilon_t = \|\hat{y} - y_t\| = \left\| \varphi (\psi \hat{P})^t \left(\sum_{k=1}^{\infty} \psi^k (\hat{P}^k - P^k) x - x \right) \right\|.$$

Using Inequality (5) and after some algebraic manipulation we have that

$$\varepsilon_t \le \psi^t \varphi \hat{c} \left(\Big\| \sum_{k=1}^{\infty} (\psi \hat{P})^k x - \sum_{k=1}^{\infty} (\psi P)^k x \Big\| + \|x\| \right)$$

$$= \psi^t \varphi \hat{c} \left(\Big\| (\psi \hat{P} - \psi P) \sum_{k=1}^{\infty} (\psi \hat{P})^k \sum_{l=k+1}^{\infty} (\psi P)^{l-k-1} x \Big\| + \|x\| \right)$$

$$\le \psi^{t+1} \varphi \hat{c} \left(\delta_\mathcal{G} \sum_{k=1}^{\infty} (\psi^k \hat{c}) \sum_{l=0}^{\infty} (\psi^l c) + \psi^{-1} \right) \|x\|$$

$$\le e^{-\varphi(t+1)} \hat{c} \left(\delta_\mathcal{G} \frac{1-\varphi}{\varphi} \hat{c} c + \frac{\varphi}{1-\varphi} \right) \|x\|,$$

which concludes our proof. □

Solving for t we find that the least number of rounds until $\varepsilon_t \le \varepsilon$ is at most

$$t \ge \varphi^{-1} \log \frac{\hat{c} \left(\delta_\mathcal{G} \frac{1-\varphi}{\varphi} \hat{c} c + \varphi \right) \|x\|}{\varepsilon} - 1. \quad (10)$$

Theorem 2 draws a relation between the influence of graph dynamics in convergence time and the value of φ. Depending on whether $(1-\varphi)/\varphi < \varphi/(1-\varphi)$ and thus $\varphi > 1/2$, the theorem distinguishes two regions of convergence: *(i)* $\varphi > 1/2$ and as φ grows larger, the graph dynamics ($\delta_\mathcal{G}$) become irrelevant. The convergence becomes independent of the relation between G and $\hat{G}$; convergence depends solely on the new graph $\hat{G}$. *(ii)* $\varphi < 1/2$ and as φ gets closer to 0, the rate of convergence becomes slow enough such that the graph dynamics do matter. In this region, convergence depends heavily on the nature of edge operations performed. We proceed to examine how edge and node operations influence convergence by computing δ_p for each case.

5.1 Edge operations

An adversary adds or deletes edges $\mathcal{E}_+$ and $\mathcal{E}_-$, respectively to the graph, such that either $\hat{\mathcal{E}} = \mathcal{E} \cup \mathcal{E}_+$ (edge addition), or $\hat{\mathcal{E}} = \mathcal{E} \setminus \mathcal{E}_-$ (edge deletion). We also place the constrain that the symmetric edge set difference, $\hat{\mathcal{E}} \ominus \mathcal{E} = \mathcal{E}_+ \cup \mathcal{E}_-$, contains at most one edge (i,j) for each node i in $\mathcal{V}$. The constraint demands that the adversary performs

at most one edge operation in the vicinity of each node. Multiple edge alterations on the same node are modeled as consecutive operations. As expected, self-loops cannot be deleted, that is $d_i \ge 1$ for all i in $\mathcal{V}$. We prove the following bound.

LEMMA 2. *For any graphs $\hat{\mathcal{G}}$, $\mathcal{G}$, with identical node sets, $\mathcal{V} = \hat{\mathcal{V}}$, and edge sets $\hat{\mathcal{E}} \ne \mathcal{E}$ that have at most one edge difference in the vicinity of each node, $|(i,j) \in \hat{\mathcal{E}} \ominus \mathcal{E}| \le 1$ for all $i \in \mathcal{V}$,*

$$\delta_\mathcal{G} = \frac{1}{d_{min}} + \frac{\sigma(A)+1}{\min\limits_{i \in \mathcal{V}_\pm} \{\hat{d}_i d_i\}},$$

with $\mathcal{V}_\pm = \{i \in \mathcal{V} : |(i,j) \in \hat{\mathcal{E}} \ominus \mathcal{E}| = 1 \text{ for some } j \in \mathcal{V}\}$ the set of nodes that have different neighbors in $\hat{\mathcal{G}}$ and $\mathcal{G}$, $\hat{d}_i, d_i$ their respective densities in each graph, and $\sigma(A)$ the largest singular value of A.

PROOF. The adjacency matrix of $\hat{\mathcal{G}}$ can be written as

$$\hat{A} = A + \sum_{(i,j) \in \mathcal{E}_+} (E_{ij} + E_{ji}) - \sum_{(i,j) \in \mathcal{E}_-} (E_{ij} + E_{ji}),$$

where matrix E_{ij} has only element (i,j) equal to one and the rest zero. The inverse density matrix of $\hat{G}$ can in turn be written as

$$\hat{D}^{-1} = D^{-1} + \sum_{(i,j) \in \mathcal{E}_+} (a_i E_{ii} + a_j E_{jj}) - \sum_{(i,j) \in \mathcal{E}_-} (b_i E_{ii} + b_j E_{jj}),$$

where $a_i = \frac{1}{d_i(d_i+1)}$ and $b_i = \frac{1}{d_i(d_i-1)}$. Matrix E_{ij} has the useful property of $\|E_{ij}\| = 1$ for all $i, j \in \mathcal{V}$. Due to $\hat{\mathcal{E}} \ominus \mathcal{E}$ containing at most one edge (i,j) for each node i in $\mathcal{V}$ and because $\hat{A} - A$ is a symmetric projection matrix,

$$\|\hat{A} - A\| = 1. \quad (11)$$

As in Lemma 2, $\mathcal{V}_\pm = \{i \in \mathcal{V} : |(i,j) \in \hat{\mathcal{E}} \ominus \mathcal{E}| = 1 \text{ for some } j \in \mathcal{V}\}$ is the set of nodes that were affected by an edge operation. Matrix $\hat{D}^{-1} - D^{-1}$ is diagonal and its norm is the maximum diagonal element in absolute value.

$$\|\hat{D}^{-1} - D^{-1}\| = \min_{i \in \mathcal{V}_\pm} \{\hat{d}_i d_i\}^{-1} \quad (12)$$

Observe that $\hat{d}_i d_i \ge d_{min}(d_{min} - 1) \ge 2$, for all $i \in \mathcal{V}_\pm$. The first equality is satisfied when one of the endpoints of a deleted edge was connected to the node with the minimum density, while the second equality iff $d_{min} = 2$. We re-write the ℓ_2-distance between the two random walk matrices as

$$\|\hat{P} - P\| = \|\hat{D}^{-1} \hat{A} - D^{-1} A\|$$

$$\le \left(\|D^{-1}\| + \|\hat{D}^{-1} - D^{-1}\| \right) \|\hat{A} - A\| + \dots$$

$$+ \|\hat{D}^{-1} - D^{-1}\| \|A\|.$$

The required bound is derived if we substitute Formulas (11) and (12) into $\|\hat{P} - P\|$.

$$\delta_\mathcal{G} = \|D^{-1}\| + \frac{\|A\|+1}{\min\limits_{i \in \mathcal{V}_\pm} \{\hat{d}_i d_i\}} = \frac{1}{d_{min}} + \frac{\sigma(A)+1}{\min\limits_{i \in \mathcal{V}_\pm} \{\hat{d}_i d_i\}}$$

Above, $\|A\| = \sigma(A)$ is the largest singular value of the adjacency matrix.

□

Let us reflect on the influence of edge operations on the convergence: (*i*) *Edge operations affect well connected graphs to a greater extend.* That is due to $\sigma(A) \leq n$, with the equality satisfied for fully connected networks. While in sparse networks the effects of dynamics tend to be isolated, in dense networks there is a higher likelihood that any single change affects more nodes. (*ii*) *Nevertheless, networks with few links mitigate the effects of network dynamics slower.* Our method compensates for edges added or deleted in dense areas of the network (i.e., $d_i >> d_{min}$ for $i \in \mathcal{V}_\pm$) faster than in areas where the network is sparsely connected. The effect is understood by the property of information to diffuse faster in dense than in sparse areas. (*iii*) *Convergence also depends on the density irregularity.* The algorithm exhibits faster convergence when running on regular networks, where $\xi = \hat{\xi} = 1$. (*iv*) *Last, even though edge operations affect multiple edges, the error bound is independent of the exact number of affected edges.* The error depends instead solely on the edge that connects to the least dense node.

5.2 Node operations

Node operations are operations on the set $\mathcal{V}$ of graph nodes. In node additions (deletions), an adversary adds (deletes) nodes $\mathcal{V}_+$ ($\mathcal{V}_-$), such that $\hat{\mathcal{V}} = \mathcal{V} \cup \mathcal{V}_+$ ($\hat{\mathcal{V}} = \mathcal{V} \setminus \mathcal{V}_-$). We provide an upper bound of $\delta_\mathcal{G}$ for the simultaneous addition and deletion of nodes.

LEMMA 3. *Let $\hat{\mathcal{G}}$ be the graph that results from the addition and deletion of sets $\mathcal{V}_+$ and $\mathcal{V}_-$ from $\mathcal{G}$, respectively. Given that (i) at most one edge joins each node in the graph intersection to the symmetric graph difference, $|(i,j) \in \hat{\mathcal{E}} \ominus \mathcal{E}| \leq 1$ for all $i \in \hat{\mathcal{V}} \cap \mathcal{V}$, and (ii) that no two added nodes are adjacent, $(i,j) \notin \hat{\mathcal{G}}$ for all $i,j \in \mathcal{V}_+$, then*

$$\delta_\mathcal{G} = \sum_{i \in \hat{\mathcal{V}} \ominus \mathcal{V}} \frac{\sqrt{d_i}}{d_{min}} + \max_{i \in \hat{\mathcal{V}} \ominus \mathcal{V}} \left\{ \frac{d_i - 1}{d_i} \right\} \left(\sigma(A) + \sum_{i \in \hat{\mathcal{V}} \ominus \mathcal{V}} \sqrt{d_i} \right),$$

where $\sigma(A)$ is the largest singular value of A.

PROOF. In the computation of $\delta_\mathcal{G}$ we cannot reuse our previous results. Deleting a node is equivalent to deleting all edges between the deleted node and its neighbors. The number of deleted edges can therefore be larger than one, which violates our constraint that at most one edge is deleted from each node. To avoid a loose bound, we do not model node deletion as a sequence of edge deletions. Instead, we redefine the constraint for node operations to allow multiple edge deletions if the edges are adjacent to a deleted node. More formally, at most one edge should join any node in the graph intersection to the symmetric graph difference. This constraint definition applies to both additions and deletions. An added node can simultaneously connect to multiple nodes, given that the nodes it connects to are not affected by other operations. For simplicity, we also assume that added nodes cannot be adjacent to each other. We now express $\hat{A}$ and $\hat{D}^{-1}$ as a function of A and D^{-1}, respectively.

$$\hat{A} = A + \sum_{i \in \mathcal{V}_+} \sum_{j \sim i} \left(E_{ij} + E_{ji} \right) - \sum_{i \in \mathcal{V}_-} \sum_{j \sim i} \left(E_{ij} + E_{ji} \right)$$

and

$$\hat{D}^{-1} = D^{-1} + \sum_{i \in \mathcal{V}_+} \frac{d_i - 1}{d_i} E_{ii} + \sum_{i \in \mathcal{V}_+} \sum_{j \sim i} a_j E_{jj} + \dots$$
$$+ \sum_{i \in \mathcal{V}_-} \frac{1 - d_i}{d_i} E_{ii} - \sum_{i \in \mathcal{V}_-} \sum_{j \sim i} b_j E_{jj}.$$

Naturally, a deleted node can not be simultaneously added or vice versa. Also, added nodes cannot be adjacent to deleted nodes. Last, the constraint guarantees that at most one edge changes for any of the nodes that are not added or deleted. Therefore, at most one term is added or subtracted to each diagonal element. Given that $\hat{D}^{-1} - D^{-1}$ is diagonal and because $|\frac{d_i-1}{d_i}| = |\frac{1-d_i}{d_i}| \geq \max\{a_j, b_j\}$ for all $i \in \hat{\mathcal{V}} \ominus \mathcal{V}$ and $j \sim i$,

$$\left\| \hat{D}^{-1} - D^{-1} \right\| = \max_{i \in \hat{\mathcal{V}} \ominus \mathcal{V}} \left\{ \frac{d_i - 1}{d_i} \right\}. \qquad (13)$$

For similar reasons, matrix $\hat{A} - A$ is symmetric with nonzero elements equal to one.

$$\left\| \hat{A} - A \right\| \leq \sum_{i \in \hat{\mathcal{V}} \ominus \mathcal{V}} \sqrt{d_i} \qquad (14)$$

Substituting Inequalities (13) and (14) into the definition of $\delta_\mathcal{G}$ and factoring the result we get the desired bound. □

The above bound provides three insights on how node operations affect convergence: (*i*) *Added and deleted nodes $i \in \hat{\mathcal{V}} \ominus \mathcal{V}$ introduce a convergence error that is proportional to the square root of the number of nodes they connect to.* On the left, $\sqrt{d_i}$ is normalized to the minimum network density. On the right, $\sqrt{d_i}$ is weighted by the maximum value of $(d_i - 1)/d_i$ which tends to one as $d_i \to \infty$. (*ii*) *It is the most connected node involved in a node operation which effects convergence the most.* Since the right term incurs the most significant error, we deduce that the convergence error after a node operation depends to a large extend on the density of the most connected node of the operation; *whether the node was deleted or added is of no significance.* (*iii*) *It is density irregularity that affects convergence the most, not absolute node density.* This seems to be an inherent property of information potentials as it consistently arises in all the convergence bounds we have derived so far (cf. Sections 4 and 5). In contrast to regular spaces such as continuous domains and regular graphs, the information diffusion in irregularly shaped spaces incurs a price.

6. SPECTRAL PROPERTIES

Thus far we have analyzed the impact of various network dynamics on the convergence of information potentials. In this section, we show that these potentials are not solely determined by the network's properties, but they can be shaped into different landscapes using the inhibiting factor φ. First, we employ results from spectral graph theory to showcase the connection between information potentials and the eigenfunctions of the network's Laplacian, and then, we show how the inhibiting factor can "filter" these eigenfunctions to shape the information landscape.

6.1 The spectral form

Let us start with some basic definitions. A scalar λ is an *eigenvalue* of a matrix B if there exists a non-zero vector u

such that $Bu = \lambda u$. Vector u is called a (right) *eigenfunction* and the pair (λ, u) is called an *eigenpair*. The collection of all eigenpairs is often referred to as the *spectrum* of B, where the eigenvalues are ordered with increasing magnitude. Our main result ties information potentials to the spectrum of the normalized Laplacian, which is described in Section 2.

THEOREM 3. (SPECTRAL FORM) *Let (λ, u) be eigenpairs of the normalized Laplacian $\mathcal{L}$ of a graph $\mathcal{G}$. For any information process x, the information potential y is*

$$y = D^{-1/2} \sum_{k=1}^{n} w_k \langle D^{1/2} x, u_k \rangle u_k, \qquad (15)$$

where $w_k = \frac{\varphi}{1 - \psi(1 - \lambda_k)}$.

PROOF. We exploit the spectral relations between the transition matrix P and the Laplacian $\mathcal{L}$. The reader can refer to the text by Biyikoglu et al. [3] for more details on the topic. Let (μ, v) be eigenpairs of the transition matrix P. In connected graphs, P has a unique largest eigenvalue $\mu_1 = 1$ and all other eigenvalues μ_k, with $k \in \mathbb{N}$ and $k \leq n$, have smaller magnitude. Since $\psi < 1$, matrix ψP has eigenvalues that are strictly smaller than one and we re-write Formula (3) as

$$y = \varphi (I - \psi P)^{-1} x. \qquad (16)$$

As shown next, $(I - \psi P)$ has the same eigenfunctions as P and its eigenvalues are equal to $1 - \psi \mu$,

$$Pv = \mu v$$
$$(I - \psi P)v = (1 - \psi \mu)v.$$

It is well known that invertible matrices have the same eigenfunctions as their inverse and eigenvalues that are the reciprocal of the eigenvalues of their inverse. Formula (16) can therefore be re-written through the spectral expansion of the inverse of $1 - \psi P$ as

$$y = \sum_{k=1}^{n} \frac{\varphi}{1 - \psi \mu_k} v_k v_k^{\top} x, \qquad (17)$$

where $v_k^{\top}$ is the k-th left eigenfunction of P. From [3], we know that $v_k = D^{-1/2} u_k$, $v_k^{\top} = u_k^{\top} D^{1/2}$ and $1 - \lambda_k = \mu_k$. Substituting these equalities into Formula (17) concludes our proof. $\square$

6.2 Landscape architecture

In this section we interpret the results from Theorem 3 and describe how the inhibiting factor controls the shape of the information landscape. Before describing the theoretical framework behind our method, we start with an intuitive explanation.

Intuitive explanation. In simple terms, Theorem 3 states that an information potential is a weighted sum of the eigenfunctions of the normalized Laplacian. Setting aside their discrete and irregular shape, Laplacian eigenfunctions are analogous to waves. They possess peaks and valleys, and are characterized by a spatial frequency which is determined by their rank (i.e., higher rank means more peaks). The projection of the information x on an eigenfunction captures the components of x which are characterized by that specific spatial variation; the higher the eigenfunction's rank, the higher the spatial variation of x that it captures. The weight $0 \leq w_k \leq 1$, which depends on the inhibiting factor,

decreases the significance of eigenfunctions with high spatial variation (w_1 is always equal to one and the other weights decrease monotonically). Hence, the inhibiting factor can be seen as a low-pass filter that attenuates phenomena of high spatial frequencies. By fine-tuning this parameter, our method smoothens the landscape of an information potential and, as a consequence, reduces the number of local extrema.

Formal explanation. Consider the n-dimensional biorthonormal eigenspace formed by the eigenfunctions u_k of $\mathcal{L}$. Theorem 3 rewrites the potential as a weighted projection of the density-normalized information on each of u_k. Weights $0 \leq w_k \leq 1$ decrease the significance of projections on non-principal[3] eigenfunctions.

To capture the spatial variation of eigenfunctions, we rely on the concept of nodal domains from spectral graph theory [3, 7]. Recall that an eigenfunction assigns a positive or negative value to each node in a graph. Nodal domains (also called *sign graphs*) induce a partition of the graph into maximal induced subgraphs on which a function does not change its sign. In other words, consider a graph where the real values of nodes are mapped to their positive or negative signs, then group connected nodes with the same sign into subgraphs. The number of subgraphs represent the number of nodal domains. Intuitively, the larger the number of nodal domains, the higher the variance of a function. Based on whether the subgraph also includes nodes with zero value, nodal domains are further characterized as weak or strong.

The *discrete nodal domain theorem* [8] gives an upper bound on the number of nodal domains of the eigenfunctions of a generalized Laplacian. Specifically for the normalized Laplacian of a connected graph, the theorem states that any eigenfunction u_k corresponding to the k-th eigenvalue λ_k with multiplicity r has at most k weak nodal domains and at most $k + r - 1$ strong nodal domains. Eigenfunctions with higher eigenvalues are likely to have more nodal domains. Intuitively, attenuating the projections of an information process into eigenfunctions with several nodal domains should lead to less local extrema. Below we proof Lemma 4, which provides an upper bound on the number of eigenfunction extrema. The lemma interprets positive and negative nodal domains as the peaks and valleys of eigenfunctions. It then bounds the number of extrema by showing that a positive (negative) nodal domain has at most one maximum (minimum).

LEMMA 4. *Any eigenfunction u_k corresponding to the k-th eigenvalue λ_k of the normalized Laplacian of a connected graph has at most k extrema.*

PROOF. The proof proceeds by method of contradiction. An eigenfunction of a graph Laplacian cannot have a non-negative local minimum or a non-positive local maximum [11, 12]. Without loss of generality, assume a negative nodal domain and suppose there are two local minima residing in the domain. This necessitates the existence of a negative local maximum between the two minima, which contradicts the first observation. Therefore, a single minimum (maximum) must exist at every negative (positive) nodal domain. Since the number of weak nodal domains of u_k (zeros are irrelevant) is bounded by k by the discrete nodal domain theorem, the number of extrema of u_k is at most k. $\square$

---

[3]Principal is the eigenfunction that corresponds to λ_1.

We use Lemma 4 to draw some useful observations about the shape of information potential landscapes. We saw that a potential is a composition of information projections on n eigenfunctions (Theorem 3). The rank k of an eigenfunction determines the maximum number of extrema it contains (Lemma 4). A such, projections of the information on high order eigenfunctions describe information components of progressively higher spatial frequency. As the inhibiting factor decreases so do the weights of non-principal eigenfunctions (i.e., rank > 1). By decreasing the significance of projections on non-principal eigenfunctions, the inhibiting factor removes phenomena of high spatial variation and reveals spatial patterns of lower frequency.

Potentials reshape an information landscape in more subtle ways than simply eliminating its extrema. As shown in Section 3.2, the potential of a node depends on the values of all the nodes in the node's affinity space, as well as on the underlying connectivity. Therefore, it is possible that a node that is an extremum of y, but not of x. For example, an already unimodal x will remain unimodal. The position of the extremum however will not necessarily be the same. The extremum of x is the node with the maximum value, which is not always equivalent to the node with the highest information y in its surroundings. This phenomenon is captured in our evaluation.

6.3 The unimodality property

An important outcome of our spectral analysis is that, for any graph $\mathcal{G}$ and information process x, a critical value φ exists for which the potential is *unimodal*. The unimodality property proves useful for gradient search. In unimodal search spaces, greedy search cannot get stuck in local optima. By achieving unimodality in networks of multiple information sources (i.e., each node has its own information), this part of our study in essence extends the work by Lin et al. [15].

Formally, a function defined on a graph is unimodal if it has a single extremum and, for each node, at least one path to the extremum exists on which the values of the function are monotonic. Depending on the monotonicity, the unimodality is further characterized as *weak* or *strong*. As φ becomes smaller, non-principal weights decrease the influence of information of high spatial variation and thus eliminate local extrema. Due to this trend, a value of φ exists below which a potential possesses a single, global maximum (or minimum). Since Lemma 4 does not guarantee that two neighboring nodes in the same domain do not have the same value, the unimodality of potentials is in the general case weak.

In practice, unimodal potentials are not always desirable; one has to pay in terms of convergence time for the increased search scope. In very large networks, the critical value can be too small to allow for any adaptivity and landscapes with multiple extrema incur lower computation cost. Despite its sub-optimality, greedy gradient search in multimodal potentials yields more spatially relevant results as the extrema exhibit a higher spatial correlation to node location. Nevertheless, unimodal potentials are particularly useful in specific tasks, such as robot coordination. Our previous paper demonstrated how unimodal potentials solve the problem of multi-agent rendezvous [16].

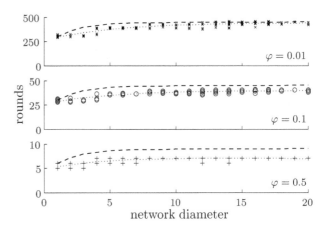

Figure 2: Number of rounds until the convergence error becomes smaller than 0.05 versus network diameter. Simulation results are depicted with markers connected by dotted lines and analytical results with dashed lines.

7. EVALUATION

Our analysis provides several insights. Due to page constraints, we can not present evaluations for all of them. Hence, we focus on the four which are the most important. We perform a controlled evaluation based on simulations (i) to evaluate the convergence of our algorithm under different settings and to validate the analytical results of Section 4.1, and (ii) to challenge our theoretical assumptions on synchronous execution and no data losses (Section 3.2). We perform a short testbed evaluation (iii) to show that the simple distributed algorithm can be implemented in resource-constrained devices, (iv) to exemplify that it is resilient to normal operating conditions such as link variability and node failures, and (v) to showcase its capability to shape the information landscapes into a unimodal potential (Section 6.3). Our evaluation is only meant to demonstrate the feasibility of our approach. A robust protocol implementation would need to consider the specific requirements of the application at hand.

7.1 Model validation

We used the COOJA simulator, a widespread tool for wireless network simulation. We chose the information values arbitrarily, by setting $x(i) = 0$ for some random $i \in \mathcal{V}$ and $x(\mathcal{V} \setminus i) = 1$, otherwise. The nodes were deployed uniformly at random and the unit-disk model was used to establish connectivity. To capture a wide range of connectivity properties, we tested four network sizes: 10, 50, 100 and 150 nodes, with four different transmission ranges. We evaluated 14 instances for each $\langle size, range \rangle$ tuple, resulting in 224 different networks. Overall, the networks had average degrees between 3.4 and 17.24, diameters between 1 and 20, and clustering coefficients between 0.27 and 1. We evaluated three representative values of the inhibiting factor, i.e., $\varphi = 0.01, 0.1,$ and 0.5, respectively.

Asynchrony. Our first set of experiments show that synchrony is not a critical assumption; the convergence bounds in Section 4.1 still hold for *asynchronous* simulations. Figure 2 summarizes our experiments. The markers represent

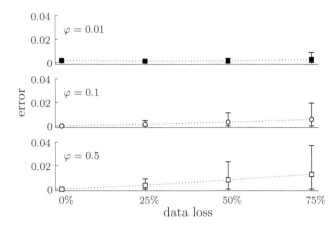

Figure 3: Error after convergence versus percentage of unknown neighboring values to the total neighbors at the end of each round. The algorithmic robustness increases for small φ.

simulation results and the dashed lines represent the convergence bounds from Section 4.1. Each marker represents a $\langle topology, \varphi \rangle$ tuple, and for each tuple, we record the round when $\|y - y_t\| \leq 0.05$, i.e., when it converges. The iterative calculation of y_t used our distributed algorithm, while the ground-truth y was calculated assuming an oracle's view of the network. To test our method under the worst possible circumstances, we intentionally bootstrap nodes to a value that is far from the stable state, $y_0 = 0 \ll x, y$. It is important to highlight the trade-offs of the inhibiting factor φ. Our method is better suited for large-scale networks. The number of rounds to reach convergence does not increase significantly with the network's diameter (for any value of φ). On the other hand, small values of φ are not suitable for small networks. Observe that, even in fully connected networks (1-hop diameter), our method incurs an overhead that is on the order of $1/\varphi$, which translates to more than 250 rounds for $\varphi = 0.01$. Setting the inhibiting factor to very small values only makes sense for large networks or in cases of high information variation. For small networks, high values of φ or simpler aggregation schemes may be preferable.

Robustness to data loss. Observe that some markers in Figure 2 are over the bounds. The observed difference suggests that message loss, i. e., our second assumption, has an effect on the algorithmic operation. Message losses require more rounds than expected to reach convergence. Figure 3 distills the results of a set of experiments which characterize the effect of imperfect knowledge. In the experiment, nodes disregarded a specific, randomly selected, percentage of their received values S_i just before recomputing their potential (line 11 of Algorithm 1). Before measuring the normalized potential error of a given topology, we waited for a sufficient number of rounds until the algorithm had converged. For each $\langle \varphi, data\ loss \rangle$ tuple, we summarize the errors across time from all 224 topologies, by the corresponding median and 68.2% confidence interval. Even under severe loss, the algorithm exhibits an error that is smaller than 0.04. The algorithm is robust because it is not based on algorithmic primitives that are sensitive to message loss, e. g., mass conservation, or to partial knowledge, e. g., count-

ing. Instead, it employs averaging as a statistical measure that, in non-skewed distributions, approximates well the central tendency, even with small sample sizes. Comparing the three subfigures we also notice that, for large percentages of data loss ($\varphi = 0.01$), the topmost subfigure reports a median error that is approximately two times smaller that the one in the bottommost subfigure ($\varphi = 0.5$). This phenomenon stems from the tendency of small φ to limit the magnitude of change between consecutive computation rounds. As such, the sensitivity of the algorithm to the high variation effects that accompany data loss decreases with φ.

7.2 Empirical results

This section evaluates our method in a wireless testbed of 105 nodes. The testbed is deployed in the ceiling of our floor in TU Delft. The devices are equipped with a MSP430 micro-controller and a CC1101 radio chip, with the transmission power set to $-30\,\mathrm{dBm}$. The algorithm was implemented on Contiki OS. For medium access control, we used NullMAC, a simple random-access MAC protocol with carrier-sense capabilities that is part of the standard Contiki OS. Each computation round lasted for 0.5 seconds, over which each node exchanged an average of 3.5 messages. An instance of the connectivity graph is shown in Figure 4(a). As also revealed by previous investigations [23], the connectivity was highly variable over time due to the well-known volatility of low-power wireless links. Figure 4(b) depicts the nodes' degree (density). The darker the Voronoi cell color (the larger the disc), the higher the density. The maxima are shown in green cells and the red arrows represent greedy searches that reach their respective local maxima. Due to the non-uniform coverage of radio transceivers, nearby nodes may not have a link, while far away nodes may – this is typical in testbeds and real-world deployments. This implies that nodes in adjacent Voronoi cells are not necessarily neighbors (in terms of distance) and the reader should refrain from interpreting Voronoi diagrams as continuous fields.

To demonstrate that our method eliminates phenomena of high variation, such as noise and false extrema, (i) we corrupted the information process by adding noise to each node's degree. The noise was uniformly distributed between $[0, d_{min}]$. Also, (ii) we introduced a false maximum at a randomly chosen "faulty" node – colored orange. Figures 4(c–d) show the computed information potentials for $\varphi = 0.50$ and 0.01, respectively. Each experiment was run for ten minutes, during which we experienced a high variability of links and some (normal) node failures between the evaluations of $\varphi = 0.50$ and 0.01. This test highlights the resilience of our method to real network phenomena. Observe how our method progressively eliminates local maxima, thus making the potential unimodal. Figure 4(c) eliminates one of the four local maxima and Figure 4(d) has a single extrema. Two of the three search queries get stuck in local maxima in Figures 4(b–c), while in Figure 4(d) all queries reach the global maximum. Observe also that the position of the global maximum is not the same across all figures, which confirms our analysis in Section 6.2. Our method uncovers the node with the largest information in its vicinity, which is not necessarily the one with the largest information (discovering paths towards a maximum value can be easily solved using a max-consensus algorithm and a distance gradient).

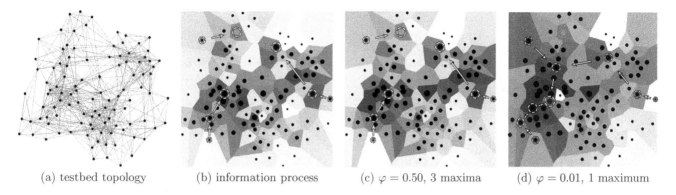

(a) testbed topology   (b) information process   (c) $\varphi = 0.50$, 3 maxima   (d) $\varphi = 0.01$, 1 maximum

Figure 4: Information potentials (c–d) and information process (b) on a testbed of 105 nodes (a). Function maxima reside in green Voronoi cells. The orange node is an artificially injected maximum. As the aggregation scope widens, our method progressively eliminates local extrema.

8. RELATED WORK

The computation of potential functions is inspired by the natural process of *chemotaxis*, in which cells respond to the concentrations of chemicals in their environment [2], and has been exploited to achieve the coordination of swarms [17]. In the following, we group related work into three subcategories. First, We discuss the connections to vicinity-based aggregation methods. Second, we focus on unimodality and thus on information discovery. Last, we classify and relate our work with respect to the family of consensus algorithms.

Vicinity-based aggregation. In sensor networks, potential functions are information specific and vicinity based; nodes consider surrounding information with a significance that decays with distance [10, 13, 18]. Gao et al. [10], use quad-trees to store data, such that each node is aware of the data in its vicinity. In their seminal paper [13], Kempe et al. propose *spatial gossiping* algorithms, in which any two nodes gossip with probabilities that decrease polynomially to their distance. Sarkar et al. [18] extend spatial gossiping to compute multi-resolution representations of information. Their algorithm computes information aggregates over exponentially enlarging areas centered at each node. All of these approaches however use physical distance to define information affinity. Our method defines affinity using the random movement of particles on the network. As a result, it is *sensitive to the network topology and independent of any knowledge of physical location or distance*.

Information discovery. A number of recent works have also employed information potentials as mediums of discovery [10, 15, 19, 21]. Skraba et al. [21] use potential gradients to sweep a sensor network. Lin et al. [15] construct smooth harmonic gradients towards node subsets, called sources, such that local forwarding guarantees their discovery. Their method achieves the absence of local extrema by keeping the information of sources constant, fixing the values of boundary nodes to zero, and averaging in between. The number of extrema however is equal to the number of sources. In comparison, our method guarantees unimodality irrespectively of the number of sources. It does not require knowledge of the network boundary. It is also more flexible as it aggregates values that stem from a real-valued monitored process, as compared to the boolean distinction between sources and non-sources. Sarkar et al. [19] design query mechanisms for

general information fields, which support the use of more advanced operations, such as iso-contour queries and value restricted routing. Their approach is complementary to ours, as it does not concern the landscape formation but advanced methods of information discovery.

Consensus algorithms. From an algorithmic point of view, this paper proposes a variant of the well known consensus algorithms [1, 9]. In a strict sense however, our algorithm does not solve the consensus problem; the stable state of a consensus algorithm is $\alpha\mathbb{1}$, where $\alpha \in \mathbb{R}$ is usually the average or the maximum of the information. In our case, each node converges to a distinct value; the collection of values form landscapes that support information discovery. However, Khan et al. recently proposed a wider family of consensus algorithms, referred to as *higher dimensional consensus algorithms*, under which our method can be classified [14]. We also have to note that, unlike most consensus and gossip algorithms that are used in sensor networks [1, 4], our method is not randomized and does not sacrifice accuracy in the presence of communication loss. Throughout the computation, information works as an anchor that steers the network towards the correct stable state. As witnessed by our evaluation, message loss mainly increases the variance of the stable state and has little effect on the mean error.

Due to its connection to the graph Laplacian, our method is also related to data clustering algorithms, such as mean shift clustering [5] and spectral clustering [22]. Choa et al. [6] independently proposed a similar approach to compute the modes of a graph. Even though their paper concerns the processing of images, it is a special case of our method as they consider only the case of $x_i = d_i$ and do not identify the property of unimodality. A preliminary version of this work was presented in [16]. The previous study focused on the analysis of the unimodality property and on its application to the multi-agent rendezvous problem. We enhanced the spectral graph analysis (Section 6) , and provide the following new contributions: the convergence bounds for static (Section 4) and dynamic (Section 5) graphs, and the algorithmic evaluation (Section 7).

9. CONCLUSIONS

Hitherto, information potentials in sensor networks have been studied without taking into consideration the topology of the network. In this study, we introduced a novel aggregation method that overcomes this limitation. By *anchoring* the information potential of each node to their *original* value – as opposed to letting the information potential *evolve "freely"* at each iteration, our method inherently considers network connectivity in the construction of information potentials. It is also simple, decentralized, robust to communication loss, and adaptive to network dynamics. We exploit linear algebra and spectral graph theory to gain deep insights into the impact of the network topology. We show that potentials are composed out of discrete waves that capture information phenomena of increasing spatial variation; our method reshapes the information landscape by attenuating information of high variation (e. g., noise). The elimination of local maxima has important implications for greedy search methods. Our analysis includes valuable guidelines for practical deployments: (*i*) dense regular networks provide faster convergence rates; (*ii*) expected information and network dynamics can be used to derive appropriate aggregation scopes.

Acknowledgements. Andreas Loukas was supported by the Dutch Technology Foundation STW and the Technology Program of the Ministry of Economic Affairs, Agriculture and Innovation (D2S2 project). Marco Cattani was supported by the Dutch national program COMMIT (project P09 EWiDS). Furthermore, we like to thank the anonymous reviewers and our shepherd Mingyan Liu for providing us detailed feedback on the draft version of this paper.

10. REFERENCES

[1] T. Aysal, A. Sarwate, and A. Dimakis. Reaching consensus in wireless networks with probabilistic broadcast. In *Annual Allerton Conference on Communication, Control, and Computing*, 2009.

[2] O. Babaoglu and et.al. Design patterns from biology for distributed computing. *Trans. Autonomous Adaptive Systems*, 2006.

[3] T. Biyikoglu, J. Leydold, and P. F. Stadler. *Laplacian eigenvectors of graphs: Perron-Frobenius and Faber-Krahn Type Theorems*. Springer, 2007.

[4] S. Boyd, A. Ghosh, B. Prabhakar, and D. Shah. Randomized gossip algorithms. *IEEE Transactions on Information Theory*, 2006.

[5] Y. Cheng. Mean shift, mode seeking, and clustering. *Trans. on Pattern Analysis and Machine Intelligence*, 1995.

[6] M. Cho and K. M. Lee. Mode-seeking on graphs via random walks. *CVPR*, 2012.

[7] F. Chung. *Spectral graph theory*. 1997.

[8] E. Davies, G. Gladwell, J. Leydold, and P. Stadler. Discrete nodal domain theorems. *Linear Algebra and its Applications*, 2001.

[9] F. Fagnani and S. Zampieri. Randomized consensus algorithms over large scale networks. *IEEE Selected Areas in Communications*, 2008.

[10] J. Gao, L. J. Guibas, J. Hershberger, and L. Zhang. Fractionally cascaded information in a sensor network. In *IPSN*, 2004.

[11] G. M. L. Gladwell and H. Zhu. Courant's nodal line theorem and its discrete counterparts. *Quarterly Journal of Mechanics and Applied Mathematics*, 2002.

[12] L. Grover. Local search and the local structure of NP-complete problems. *Operation Research Letters*, 1992.

[13] D. Kempe, J. Kleinberg, and A. Demers. Spatial gossip and resource location protocols. In *STOC*, 2001.

[14] U. Khan, S. Kar, and J. Moura. Higher dimensional consensus: Learning in large-scale networks. *Trans. on Signal Processing*, 2010.

[15] H. Lin, M. Lu, N. Milosavljevic, J. Gao, and L. J. Guibas. Composable information gradients in wireless sensor networks. In *IPSN*, 2008.

[16] A. Loukas, M. Woehrle, P. Glatz, and K. Langendoen. On distributed computation of information potentials. In *FOMC*, 2012.

[17] P. Ogren, E. Fiorelli, and N. Leonard. Cooperative control of mobile sensor networks: Adaptive gradient climbing in a distributed environment. *Trans. on Automatic Control*, 2004.

[18] R. Sarkar, X. Zhu, and J. Gao. Hierarchical spatial gossip for multiresolution representations in sensor networks. *ToSN*, 2012.

[19] R. Sarkar, X. Zhu, J. Gao, L. J. Guibas, and J. S. B. Mitchell. Iso-contour queries and gradient descent with guaranteed delivery in sensor networks. In *INFOCOM*, 2009.

[20] D. Shoup. Cruising for parking. *Transport Policy*, 13(6):479–486, 2006.

[21] P. Skraba, Q. Fang, A. Nguyen, and L. Guibas. Sweeps over wireless sensor networks. In *IPSN*, 2006.

[22] U. von Luxburg. A tutorial on spectral clustering. *Statistics and Computing*, 2007.

[23] M. Woehrle, M. Bor, and K. Langendoen. 868 MHz: a noiseless environment, but no free lunch for protocol design. In *INSS*, 2012.

Energy-Efficient Low Power Listening for Wireless Sensor Networks in Noisy Environments

Mo Sha, Gregory Hackmann, Chenyang Lu
Department of Computer Science and Engineering
Washington University in St. Louis
One Brookings Drive, Box 1045
St. Louis, Missouri 63130, USA
{msha, ghackmann, lu}@wustl.edu

ABSTRACT

Low Power Listening (LPL) is a common MAC-layer technique for reducing energy consumption in wireless sensor networks, where nodes periodically wakeup to sample the wireless channel to detect activity. However, LPL is highly susceptible to *false wakeups* caused by environmental noise being detected as activity on the channel, causing nodes to spuriously wakeup in order to receive nonexistent transmissions. In empirical studies in residential environments, we observe that the false wakeup problem can significantly increase a node's duty cycle, compromising the benefit of LPL. We also find that the energy-level threshold used by the Clear Channel Assessment (CCA) mechanism to detect channel activity has a significant impact on the false wakeup rate. We then design AEDP, an adaptive energy detection protocol for LPL, which dynamically adjusts a node's CCA threshold to improve network reliability and duty cycle based on application-specified bounds. Empirical experiments in both controlled tests and real-world environments showed AEDP can effectively mitigate the impact of noise on radio duty cycles, while maintaining satisfactory link reliability.

Categories and Subject Descriptors

C.2.2 [**Computer-Communication Networks**]: Network Protocols

General Terms

Design; Experimentation; Performance

Keywords

Wireless Sensor Networks; Low Power Listening; CCA Control

1. INTRODUCTION

Clear Channel Assessment (CCA) is a fundamental mechanism in MAC protocols for wireless networks. A CCA check [1] samples the energy level in the wireless channel and considers the channel busy if the energy level is above a threshold, or idle otherwise. CCA has been commonly used for two important (and orthogonal) purposes. First, it has been used by CSMA/CA protocols to avoid collisions on shared wireless channels, by sampling the channel for activity just before transmission. Second, CCA has been used in Low Power Listening (LPL), a popular MAC-layer approach that enables radio to operate at low duty cycles. Under LPL, every node periodically wakes up to perform CCA. It then stays awake to receive packets if the CCA check detects activity in the wireless channel, or goes back to sleep immediately otherwise. Due to its simplicity and effectiveness, LPL has been a popular approach to energy-efficient MAC protocols in Wireless Sensor Networks (WSNs). A multitude of LPL-based MAC protocols has been developed in recent years [8, 18, 19], and LPL has been implemented by many radio drivers inside sensor operating systems such as TinyOS [1] and Contiki [2].

While the effect of CCA on collision avoidance has been well studied in the literature, its impact on LPL, particularly in noisy environments such as residential and office environments, has received relatively little attention. Applications deployed in noisy wireless conditions are susceptible to frequent *false wakeups*: noise may be detected as legitimate activity on the channel, causing the node to remain awake even when no transmissions occur. False wakeups may significantly increase the duty cycle and energy consumption of the nodes, as shown by our empirical studies in residential environments (see Section 4). This limitation of LPL protocols is becoming increasingly significant as more and more WSNs are being deployed in residential environments, where co-existing wireless devices and electromagnetic equipments cause prevalent and highly variable noise.

To address this important problem, we propose a novel approach that dynamically adjusts the *CCA threshold*, i.e., the energy level threshold used to decide if a channel is active. This approach is motivated by the key observation that nodes may effectively reduce false wakeups by choosing a threshold above the background noise level, but below the

---

[1]CCA, carrier sense and energy detection are used as synonymous in this paper, as supported by [20].

level of real transmissions. Specifically, the main contributions of this work are three-fold:

- An empirical study in residential environments that demonstrates the potential benefits of adaptive CCA control based on both normal channel conditions and controlled 802.11n traffic;

- Adaptive Energy Detection Protocol (AEDP), an adaptive protocol that dynamically adjusts a node's CCA threshold to improve network reliability and duty cycle based on application-specified bounds;

- Discovery of significant shortcomings in the implementation of CCA checks in TinyOS 2.1.1 [2] caused by improper selections of key radio parameters, and a systematic methodology to tune these parameters in order to enable efficient CCA checks.

In contrast to previous studies on adjusting the CCA threshold to better avoid collisions in both 802.11 [7] and 802.15.4 [5, 6, 16, 27] networks, this paper investigates the CCA threshold's role in waking up nodes, with the goal to mitigate the false wakeup problem associated with LPL; to our knowledge, it represents the first systematic study of the CCA threshold's role in the effectiveness of LPL. The uses of CCA for collision avoidance in CSMA/CA and wakeup in LPL are orthogonal and complementary to each other, as CCA is being used at different times for different goals. Indeed, both forms of CCA adjustment could be deployed simultaneously, by simply maintaining separate thresholds for collision avoidance and LPL.

The remainder of the paper is organized as follows. Section 2 compares our approach with related works. Section 3 describes an overview of LPL. Section 4 presents an empirical study into the effect of noise on LPL behavior, and explores the use of CCA thresholds to control the associated false wakeup problem. Section 5 details the AEDP protocol for dynamically adjusting a node's CCA threshold in order to minimize false wakeups. Section 6 describes the implementation of AEDP on the TelosB mote platform and analyzes the impact of radio parameters on the effectiveness of CCA. Section 7 presents an empirical evaluation of AEDP in both controlled tests and real-world environments. Finally, we conclude the paper in Section 8.

2. RELATED WORK

Traditionally, CCA functionality has been used in CSMA/CA MAC protocols to avoid collisions on shared wireless channels. A sender performs CCA before transmission. It proceeds with the transmission if the CCA check does not detect channel activity; otherwise it backs off to avoid colliding with an on-going transmission. Numerous studies have explored the impact of the CCA thresholds used for collision avoidance on both 802.11 networks and WSNs [5–7, 16, 27]. Bertocco et al. [5] shows that the CCA threshold is critical, as false negative channel activity detections result in collisions and false positives cause increased latency. Kiryushin et al. [16] studies the real-world impact of CCA thresholds in avoiding packet collisions. Chintalapudi et al. [9] shows that a poor energy detection scheme can lead to significant

_____
[2] The shortcomings still exist in TinyOS 2.1.2 officially released on August 20, 2012.

overhead for listening to the channel and switching the radio between send and receive modes, which may take hundreds of microseconds. Boano et al. [6] shows that tuning the CCA threshold at run time can improve the robustness of existing MAC protocols under interference. Yuan et al. [27] presents that dynamically adjusting CCA threshold can substantially reduce the amount of discarded packets due to channel access failures. Brodsky et al. [7] presents an opposite conclusion based on theories of radio propagation and Shannon capacity and shows that it is possible to choose a fixed CCA threshold which performs well across a wide range of scenarios since carrier sense performance is surprisingly close to optimal for radios with adaptive bitrate. All these works focus on the impact of CCA on collision avoidance in transmissions rather than its use for wakeup in LPL-based MAC protocols.

In contrast to previous studies on CCA for channel avoidance, this paper investigates the CCA threshold's role in avoiding the false wakeup problem associated with LPL; to our knowledge, it represents the first systematic study of the CCA threshold's role in the effectiveness of LPL in achieving low duty cycles in WSNs, especially in noisy environments where traditional LPL protocols are vulnerable to false wakeup problems. Our work is therefore *orthogonal* and *complementary*.

Recently, receiver-initiated MAC protocols have been proposed to avoid the false wakeup problem. Receiver-initiated MAC protocols such as [12,23] require recipients to transmit probe packets indicating that they are ready for packet reception. As our experiments presented in Section 7.5, AEDP is more energy efficient at low data rates than the state-of-the-art receiver-initiated MAC protocol A-MAC [12], as AEDP avoids the overhead of the probe packets. On the other hand, A-MAC is more energy efficient than AEDP for high data rate applications, where the cost of sending these probe packets are offset by reduced overhead for transmissions. Our work is therefore an alternative sender-initiated approach that is complementary to receiver-initiated MACs for applications with different data rates.

ContikiMAC [11] addresses the false wakeup problem with two targeted optimizations. First, it performs *two* CCA checks spaced slightly apart, allowing it to identify phenomenon too short to be an 802.15.4 transmission. Second, it performs a "fast sleep" optimization that reduces the cost of false wakeups, by detecting patterns of activity and silence which cannot belong to ContikiMAC transmissions. In our testing, we found that our approach's CCA-threshold-adjustment can effectively avoid false wakeups without these optimizations. Since our approach requires only a *single* CCA check, it induces lower energy cost in low duty-cycle cases where nodes rarely need to wakeup to receive packets. Nevertheless, these approaches are orthogonal, and in particularly challenging environments could be combined to reduce both the likelihood and the energy overhead of false wakeups.

There has been increasing interest in studying the impact of interference on WSNs and enhancing the robustness of MAC protocols in noisy environments. Srinivasan et al. [22] examines the packet delivery behavior of two 802.15.4-based mote platforms, including the impact of interference from 802.11 and Bluetooth. Liang et al. [17] measures the impact of interference from 802.11 networks on 802.15.4 links, proposing the use of redundant headers and forward error correction to alleviate packet corruption. These studies focus on improving the reliability of transmission and do not deal with the false wakeup problem to improve energy efficiency.

3. OVERVIEW OF LPL

Low power listening (LPL) is a common MAC-layer technique for reducing energy consumption in WSNs [19]. Under LPL, nodes periodically wakeup to perform CCA, i.e., to briefly sample the wireless channel for activity. If energy is detected on the channel, the node remains awake in order to receive a packet (or until some timeout). Otherwise, the node quickly goes back to sleep. To minimize overhead when the network is idle, these periodic wakeups are not synchronized across nodes: that is, the recipient knows the recipient's wakeup interval but not its wakeup time. Accordingly, before transmitting a packet, the transmitter sends a preamble stream at least as long as the recipient's wakeup interval; this ensures that the recipient will sample the channel during the preamble. After the preamble, the sender and recipient exchange data packets.

Later LPL-based MAC layers such as X-MAC [8] modify this approach by inserting destination address information and periodic gaps in the preamble stream. When a node wakes up, it may decode the destination address and see if it is the packet's intended recipient. If so, it uses the gaps in the preamble to send an acknowledgment to the sender, which will in turn immediately transmit the payload. If not, the node may go back to sleep immediately. These enhancements significantly reduce the cost of waking up for a packet intended for another node, while also reducing the average cost of unicast packet transmissions by half. BoX-MAC-2 [18] further refines this approach by transmitting the entire data packet in place of the destination address, eliminating the need to explicitly exchange the payload after the recipient has ACKed the preamble.

Quickly and accurately assessing whether the channel is active is a critical component of a LPL-based MAC layer. Modern radios, including all 802.15.4-compliant hardware [15], provide CCA functionality that assists with this procedure. A common method for radios to implement CCA is to provide a digital readout (often a dedicated pin) indicating whether the channel's energy level currently exceeds some threshold. This particular implementation, known as *energy detection*, is commonly found in low-power radios such as the Chipcon CC2420 and has been identified as a critical feature for WSN hardware design [13]. After waking up the radio, the microcontroller may sample the CCA pin in a tight loop; the node remains awake for packet reception if some minimum number of samples are positive.

4. EMPIRICAL STUDY

This section describes a series of empirical studies that provide the motivation and insights for the design of AEDP. We first measure the false wakeup problem in office and residential environments, followed by a systematic study on the impact of CCA's energy detection threshold on wakeups in LPL.

4.1 Effects of Wireless Noise

Existing literature on LPL-based MAC layers emphasizes the ability to run applications at an extremely low duty cycle, sometimes as low as 1% [19], in exchange for moderately increasing the cost of packet transmissions. This tradeoff makes LPL well-suited for applications with low-to-moderate data rates. However, noise from other wireless devices can have a dramatic (and often unanticipated) impact on nodes' duty cycle, significantly reducing system lifetime.

Radios based on the 802.15.4 standard operate in the unlicensed 2.4 GHz band shared by many other devices. Energy detection simply looks for the presence of *some* signal on the wireless channel; it does not distinguish between the system's own traffic and noise from other devices. To illustrate how a false-negative wakeup can considerably increase the cost of a CCA check, we deployed a TelosB mote [10] running TinyOS 2.1.1 [1] in an office environment. The TelosB mote was configured to use the BoX-MAC-2 LPL-based MAC layer, TinyOS's *de facto* standard LPL implementation. BoX-MAC-2 was in turn configured with a wakeup interval of 2 seconds: i.e., the motes sleep for 2 seconds between sampling the channel for activity. In order to capture the effects of wireless noise, we configured the CC2420 radio to use channel 18, which overlaps with a campus-wide 802.11g network. All other MAC layer and radio parameters were left to their respective defaults.

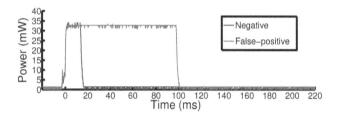

Figure 1: Oscilloscope traces comparing a TelosB node's energy consumption during a negative (idle) and false-positive (detected) energy detection check.

Figure 1 shows the energy consumption of this mote when performing a single energy detection check, as captured with an oscilloscope. When the channel is idle, the radio is powered on for 19.0 ms; in contrast, when the channel is occupied, the false wakeup causes the radio to remain powered on for 103.4 ms until it eventually times out. Similar results were observed in [12], which found that false wakeups increased the current consumption of a CCA check by 17.3×.

An equally important question is how often wireless noise will cause these false wakeups to occur in real-world environments. To measure this phenomenon, we deployed four pairs of TelosB motes on orthogonal channels (11, 16, 21, and 26, respectively) in five different apartments located in different neighborhoods in St. Louis. The motes were deployed for 24 hours in each apartment during the residents' normal activities. One mote in each pair was configured to transmit 1 packet every minute, and the BoX-MAC-2 MAC layer configured with a wakeup interval of 2 seconds. We augmented TinyOS's CC2420 radio stack to track the result of each CCA check and the radio "on time", i.e., the cumulative total time the radio was active during the entire experimental run. The latter data was in turn used to compute each mote's duty cycle. For the purposes of this experiment, the mote's onboard CC2420 was again configured with the hardware-default CCA behavior, setting its CCA pin based on an energy threshold of −77 dBm.

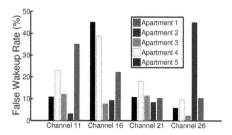

Figure 2: The false wakeup rate of each recipient mote in each apartment.

Figure 2 plots the false wakeup rate (the proportion of CCA checks resulting in wakeup but no packet reception) of each node in the experiment. From the receiver's wakeup interval and the sender's data rate, we expect a nominal duty cycle of 0.17%. However, the false wakeups caused by environmental noise result in substantially higher duty cycles, with an average duty cycle of 1.4% across all four tested channels in all five apartments. In the two worst cases — channel 16 in apartment 5 and channel 26 in apartment 2 — false wakeup rates of 45% resulted in greatly inflated duty cycles of 2.8%.

4.2 Effects of CCA Threshold

We propose to address the false wakeup problem by adjusting the CCA threshold: that is, the specific energy level used as a binary threshold to determine whether a node should remain awake. In the context of LPL, setting the CCA threshold too low will cause nodes to wakeup to receive non-existent packets. Setting the threshold too high may cause nodes not to wakeup during transmissions, forcing the sender to repeatedly retransmit. We note that adjusting the CCA threshold for LPL has *no* effect on the receiver's ability to decode packets, so long as the threshold is low enough to wakeup the receiver. Hence, link reliability will only be affected if the threshold is high enough to cause a false-negative energy detection (i.e., a node fails to stay awake to receive a legitimate packet).

As discussed earlier, the CCA threshold also plays a role in the context of collision avoidance. However, adjusting the CCA threshold has a different effect in the context of collision avoidance, where it directly affects the *sender* rather than *receivers*. Setting the threshold too low encourages spurious backoffs, while setting the threshold too high may introduce packet losses from otherwise-avoidable collisions. To distinguish the CCA threshold used by the receiver for LPL from the CCA threshold used by the sender in CSMA/CA, we henceforth refer to the former in this paper as the *wakeup threshold*. This paper focuses on reducing false wakeups by manipulating the wakeup threshold used for LPL. We do not change the CCA threshold used for transmission, an important but orthogonal problem that has been well-studied in literature.

We perform a set of controlled tests in an office environment to investigate the potential energy savings from adjusting the wakeup threshold, we deployed five groups of four TelosB motes on channel 16 at varying distances (3–15 ft) from a pair of 802.11n devices (access point+MAC pro laptop) operating on 2.4 GHz band that overlaps with 802.15.4. Each experimental run was carried out for one hour; as be-

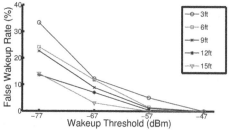

(a) False wakeup rate under office occupants' normal activities.

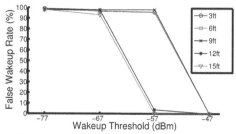

(b) False wakeup rate under controlled (5 Mbps UDP) 802.11n traffic.

Figure 3: The effects of tuning the CC2420's wakeup threshold on the motes' false wakeup rate, subject to office occupants' normal activities and controlled 802.11n traffic. The motes were located 3–15 ft away from the 802.11n router, and were configured to use a threshold ranging from −77 to −47 dBm.

fore, BoX-MAC-2 was configured with a wakeup interval of 2 seconds. In contrast to the previous experiments, which used the radio-default CCA threshold of −77 dBm, each mote in a group was configured to use one of four different thresholds (−77, −67, −57, and −47 dBm). Signal generated by motes may become part of the background noise when its strength is lower than recipients' CCA threshold. We intentionally stop motes from generating real transmissions in this set of tests, thus we can treat the total wakeup rate as the false wakeup rate.

Figure 3(a) plots the recipients' false wakeup rate under the office occupants' normal activities in real-world environment. Figure 3(b) plots the false wakeup rate when using LanTraffic V2 [3] to generate a controlled stream of 5 Mbps UDP traffic through the pair of 802.11n devices. Two important conclusions may be drawn from these figures. First, tuning the wakeup threshold provides a powerful opportunity for conserving energy. We observe that the false wakeup rate drops dramatically when increasing the threshold from the radio default of −77 dBm. Under real-world activity as shown in Figure 3(a), the default threshold incurs a false wakeup rate of 14–33%. In comparison, this rate may be reduced to 3–12% by moderately increasing the threshold by 10 dBm, or to 0% by increasing the threshold by 30 dBm. The effects of tuning the threshold are even more pronounced under the higher-bandwidth controlled experiments, as shown in Figure 3(b). At a threshold of −77 dBm, the nodes experience a false wakeup rate no lower than 97.8%, regardless of distance from the pair of 802.11n devices. This rate drops to 0–4% for two of the distances at a threshold of -57 dBm, and to 0% for all distances at a threshold of -47 dBm. Second, the "best" wakeup threshold is highly dependent on external factors such as the 802.15.4 nodes' vicinity to other devices, and the other devices' usage patterns and signal strength. Comparing Figures 3(a) and 3(b), we see that increasing the threshold from -77 dBm to -67 dBm significantly reduces the false wakeup rate under normal activities. However, under a sustained 5 Mbps UDP stream, a comparable threshold increase has virtually no impact on the false wakeup rate.

We also used motes to perform a series of measurements on signal strength of external interference generated by several real-world 802.11 applications as well as the LanTraffic V2 with various speeds. We observed that noise varies from application to application and over time for a given application depending on the distance from interference source.

Hence, picking an appropriate wakeup threshold is not simply a matter of choosing a more aggressive default setting. The minimum threshold needed to avoid noise varies from setting to setting, and even over time depending on the occupants' activities. Moreover, selecting too high of a threshold will intuitively cause the receiver to stop waking up for legitimate transmissions, decreasing network reliability.

5. PROTOCOL DESIGN

In this section, we present the design of our *Adaptive Energy Detection Protocol (AEDP)*. At a high level, AEDP tries to meet application-specified constraints on network reliability and wakeup rate. The desired network reliability is specified by the desired ETX, $ETX_{threshold}$, where ETX is the expected number of transmissions needed to successfully send a packet to its destination. The desired wakeup rate, $WR_{threshold}$ can be determined based on the application data rate (and hence the corresponding *true* wakeup rate) plus a small margin for false wakeups allowed by the application. When it is not possible to meet both constraints, network reliability takes precedence, as it is typically more critical than lifetime constraints. We set a default value of $ETX_{threshold}$ to be 5 and a default value of $WR_{threshold}$ to be 5 times of data rate according to the typical low data rate home automation systems.

AEDP maintains three variables at run time: ETX, WR, and WR_L. ETX is the average ETX value over a sliding window (default window size is 15 minutes). WR is the wakeup rate within the same sliding window. WR_L is the cumulative wakeup rate over the whole application lifetime. Note that WR_L reflects the long-term wakeup rate that affects the battery life of the node.

At runtime, AEDP periodically updates these three variables ETX, WR, and WR_L and compares their values against $ETX_{threshold}$ and $WR_{threshold}$. It then computes a new wakeup threshold T based on four different cases, described below.

- **Case 1:** ETX exceeds $ETX_{threshold}$. AEDP attempts to quickly recover by significantly reducing the wakeup threshold. This policy reflects the fact that network reliability constraints are typically more critical than lifetime constraints.

- **Case 2:** ETX meets $ETX_{threshold}$ but WR exceeds $WR_{threshold}$. This case indicates that the current

wakeup threshold is too low to achieve the desired wakeup rate. AEDP increases the wakeup threshold by a small amount ΔT to try to meet the application's bound on wakeup rate. The default value of the tuning step ΔT is set to be 2 dBm.

- **Case 3:** ETX, WR, and WR_L all meet their respective constraints. This case indicates that the current wakeup threshold is meeting the application's constraints, both in this period and over the application's lifetime. AEDP aims to find the minimum threshold that does so, as lower wakeup thresholds are potentially more robust to changes in topology and signal strength. Hence, AEDP decreases the wakeup threshold by ΔT.

- **Case 4:** ETX and WR meet their constraints but WR_L does not. Here, AEDP takes no action. Since WR is below $WR_{threshold}$, the wakeup threshold is high enough to meet the application's wakeup rate constraint in the short term. However, WR_L has still not met the application's constraint over the long term, so AEDP will not yet start to reduce the wakeup threshold.

In all cases, AEDP constrains the wakeup threshold T to a range $[T_{min}, T_{max}]$. Reducing T too much will cause the node to always be awake, while increasing T too much will cause packet loss (increased ETX). AEDP sets T_{min} to be the noise floor to avoid sustained wakeups, and sets T_{max} to be the minimum Received Signal Strength (RSS) of incoming links, since our experimental results have shown that link reliability degrades heavily when T exceeds the RSS of incoming link [21]. To accommodate topology changes, AEDP periodically resets the wakeup threshold to T_{min} for several periods (a default value of 5 wakeup intervals) enabling node to establish new incoming links with RSS lower than T.

AEDP has several key design features based on the observations in our empirical study. First, AEDP adaptively adjusts energy detection threshold based on changes in network reliability (specifically, ETX) observed at runtime. Second, AEDP performs its computations based solely on local state (WR, WR_L, and ETX), requiring no additional transmissions between sender and receiver. Third, AEDP is a lightweight protocol that only piggybacks a single byte (used to measure ETX) in each existing packet transmission, and introduces no other traffic of its own.

6. IMPLEMENTATION

In this section, we discuss our implementation of AEDP on TinyOS 2.1.1. We first describe the software architecture used by AEDP. We then discuss several key radio parameters that affected the energy efficiency of LPL, and present a methodology for picking these parameters appropriately.

6.1 AEDP Architecture

We implement the AEDP algorithm as a layer situated between the application and MAC layers. This layer consists of three important components. The *WakeupRateMonitor* component tracks the wakeup rate WR and computes the cumulative wakeup rate WR_L. The *LinkEstimator* component measures the ETX of incoming packets using sequence numbers in each packet, and computes the average ETX

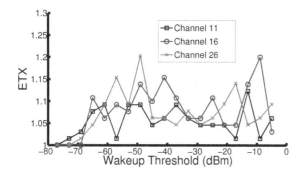

Figure 4: The relationship between wakeup threshold and ETX in the default TinyOS CC2420 stack.

value (ETX) over a sliding window. The LinkEstimator also measures the RSS of incoming packets, using the minimum average RSS value of all incoming links as the bound T_{max}. The *CCAControlEngine* component computes and sets the wakeup threshold based on the values ETX, WR and WR_L.

AEDP requires several modifications to the radio stack to support its operations, as listed below. For the purposes of this implementation, we have performed these modifications on TinyOS 2.1.1's default CC2420 + BoX-MAC-2 stack.

First, we add a *PacketInfo* interface between the MAC layer and LinkEstimator to expose the ETX and RSS values of each incoming packet. The LinkEstimator buffers the values in sliding windows, calculating the average ETX and RSS values for the variables ETX and T_{max} respectively.

Second, we augment the radio core to count wakeup events. This counter is exposed to the WakeupRateMonitor through the *WakeupCounter* interface and used to compute the values of WR and WR_L.

Finally, we add a *CCAcontrol* interface to the radio core to expose the radio's hardware CCA threshold setting. On the CC2420, this is implemented by writing the new threshold to the radio's `CCA_THR` register, plus a 45 dBm offset specified by the datasheet [24]. The CCA Control Engine uses this interface to set the newly-computed wakeup threshold T.

6.2 System Parameters

When testing our first implementation of AEDP on the TelosB mote, we were initially surprised to discover that increasing the wakeup threshold had little impact on network reliability. Figure 4 plots the relationship between the wakeup threshold and ETX that we observed in our initial testing, using three different channels and a wide range of threshold values. We initially expected that an excessively high threshold would cause significant packet loss, and a high enough threshold would prohibit the node from receiving packets at all (due to never waking up from sleep). However, in practice, we observed that an overly aggressive threshold only increased the number of retransmissions by a maximum of 20%. Indeed, the node still received packets after setting the threshold to the radio maximum of 82 dBm, or even after modifying the CC2420 stack to *always* put the radio back to sleep regardless of the energy detection result.

From these results, we hypothesized that the radio was fully receiving and decoding entire packets during the CCA check itself. TinyOS's implementation of BoX-MAC-2 on

the CC2420 detects energy by sampling the CCA pin up to 400 times in a tight loop. Modern packet-based radios like the CC2420 are designed to fully decode packets without the microcontroller's intervention, and could decode packets while the microcontroller is occupied by polling the CCA pin.

We confirmed this hypothesis using a logic analyzer to trace the sequence of events inside the radio hardware and radio stack. Figure 5 presents a sample trace that we captured with the CC2420 configured to use the maximum threshold[3]. At 0 ms, the radio stack begins sampling the wireless channel by powering on the CC2420. The CC2420 is fully powered on at T1 = 2.947 ms, and the radio stack starts energy detection. At T2 = 5.916 ms, the CC2420 signals the beginning of a packet reception; at T3 = 7.261 ms, the CC2420 signals that the packet is fully decoded. The radio stack will not finish energy detection until $T4 = 11.791$ ms. Indeed, the duration of this check (8.844 ms) is much longer than the on-air time of an 802.15.4 packet ($0.59 - 4.24$ ms in lab experiments, depending on payload size).

The apparent cause for this lengthy check is a long ACK delay built into TinyOS's CC2420 driver. After transmitting a packet, the driver waits up to 8 ms for an ACK packet. In our own measurements, this resulted in BoX-MAC-2 leaving the channel idle for 8.3 ms between retransmissions.

In principle, an ACK delay of this length is unnecessary. From the 802.15.4 specification, we can derive a tight bound of 544 μs on the ACK delay. (Specifically, the recipient must transmit an ACK exactly 192 μs after decoding the incoming packet's last bit, and transmitting the ACK packet takes 352 μs at 802.15.4's 250 kbps data rate [12, 15].) However, TinyOS disables the CC2420's hardware auto-acknowledgement feature due to concerns over its reliability [4]. Consequently, packets must pass partway through the recipient's radio stack before they are acknowledged, adding significant delay.

Nevertheless, we believe that the default ACK delay is overly conservative. In a microbenchmark experiment, we transmitted packets between a pair of TelosB motes with hardware auto-acknowledgement disabled. The transmitter requested an ACK for each transmission, and recorded the delay between finishing a transmission and receiving the corresponding ACK. Out of 2000 transmissions, the transmitter observed a mean delay of 2.2 ms and a maximum delay of 2.4 ms.

This result indicates that an 8 ms ACK delay, and the associated 8.8 ms energy detection length, is excessive. The length of this check contradicts the need for a short, inexpensive energy detection, and arguably even renders the entire check ineffective. From the 20% ETX penalty we observed in our testing, it would have been nearly as effective to simply leave the radio on for 8.8 ms, and ignore the energy detection result. Doing so would have had only a small impact on network reliability, in exchange for *never* incurring a false wakeup.

Instead, for the purposes of implementing and evaluating AEDP, we opt to retain the check but reduce the CC2420

---

[3]For illustrative purposes, we modified BoX-MAC-2 to mark the duration of the energy detection loop using a GIO pin, and to disable a code branch that short-circuits the loop when the radio starts receiving a packet. We have verified that the CC2420 will still fully decode packets during energy detection, even without these modifications.

Figure 5: A logic analyzer trace demonstrating the CC2420 fully decoding a packet during the energy detection check. The microcontroller uses the VREG_EN pin to control the CC2420's power state. The CC2420 uses the SFD and FIFOP pins to signal the beginning (T2) and end (T3) of packet reception, respectively. The GIO pin indicates the duration of the check (T4–T1).

Driver	ACK delay
CC2420(cc2420 driver)	8 ms
CC2420(cc2420x driver, most platforms)	1 ms
CC2420(cc2420x driver, micaz platforms)	0.8 ms
CC2520 (most platforms)	1 ms
CC2520(sam3s_ek platform)	0.8 ms
RF230	1 ms
IEEE 802.15.4 specification	0.544 ms
TelosB (lab measurements)	2.4 ms

Table 1: The ACK delays used by various 802.15.4 radio drivers in TinyOS, the ACK delay derived from [15], and the actual ACK delay measured on a TelosB.

driver's ACK delay to 2.8 ms (2.3 ms + 0.5 ms guard space). We accordingly modify BoX-MAC-2 to poll the CCA pin up to 115 times, reducing the energy detection duration from 8.8 ms to 2.9 ms. In general, the duration of CCA polling must be longer than the ACK delay to avoid false negatives in energy detection which can heavily worsen the performance.

As we show in Section 7, this modification alone has the effect of significantly reducing the motes' duty cycle, simply by reducing the cost of energy detection to a fraction of its default length.

Although this modification is specific to the particular radio stack used, it emphasizes the need for a general methodology — such as the analysis performed above — to tune these key radio and MAC layer parameters. Indeed, as shown in Table 1, TinyOS employs three different ACK delays on the sender side, depending on the combination of radio driver, radio stack, and underlying mote platform. None of these three different delays is consistent with the theoretical ACK turnaround time from the 802.15.4 standard, or with the actual turnaround time measured on the TelosB. Besides energy efficiency, this inconsistency raises concerns about basic interoperability.

7. EVALUATION

To validate the efficiency of our approach in reducing false wakeup rates, we performed a series of controlled experiments and real-world experiments. (1) We first evaluate the capability of AEDP to effectively converge to the desired wakeup threshold. (2) We then performed an experiment where additional transmitters were added to the network at runtime to test AEDP's resilience to network changes.

(3) We evaluate AEDP's impact on duty cycles at the link level, and compare AEDP's performance against LPL configurations in a testbed we deployed in a 3-floor apartment building. (4) We compare AEDP against A-MAC, a state-of-the-art receiver-initiated MAC protocol under different data rates. (5) Finally, we evaluate the impacts of AEDP on multi-hop data collection by running AEDP with CTP in a 55-node testbed in an academic building.

In all experiments, we deploy our benchmark applications on top of TelosB motes running the TinyOS 2.1.1 operating system. BoX-MAC-2 is configured with a wakeup interval of 2 seconds: i.e., the motes sleep for 2 seconds between sampling the channel for activity. We use a data rate of 1 packet/5 minutes [4] for all evaluations except the one in Section 7.5, where we evaluate the performance of AEDP under different data rates.

We emphasize that our experiments changed only the CCA threshold used for wakeup and did not change the threshold used for collision avoidance; hence, improvements in duty cycle are attributed to a reduction in false wakeups rather than retransmissions.

7.1 Self-tuning Wakeup Threshold

We first test the capability of AEDP to automatically adjust its wakeup threshold. For this experiment, we deployed a pair of motes with AEDP on channel 16. We also deployed an 802.11n access point and a laptop producing 1 Mbps of UDP traffic on 802.11 channel 6, which overlaps with 802.15.4 channel 16. We performed two experimental runs: to vary the impact of the interfering 802.11 network on the mote pair, the distance between the mote pair and the 802.11n devices was 10 ft during the first run, and increased to 30 ft for the second run.

Figure 6 illustrates AEDP reactively changing the wakeup threshold based on runtime conditions. During the first experimental run, the receiver mote quickly increases the wakeup threshold to −56 dBm to avoid false wakeups introduced by the nearby 802.11 interferer. At this point, the mote is still unable to meet the application-specified duty cycle, and hence the threshold remains at about −55 dBm for the remainder of the experiment. In the second experimental run, the receiver mote likewise quickly increases the wakeup threshold to −54 dBm. At this point, because the mote is located further away from the interferer, it is able to

---

[4]The data rate is chosen according to the typical sampling rate of home automation systems (for example, 1 temperature reading every 5 minutes is sufficient for an HVAC system to control ambient temperature).

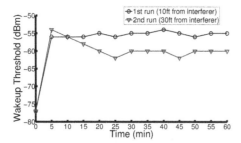

Figure 6: AEDP adapting the wakeup threshold over time.

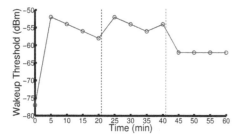

Figure 7: AEDP adapting the wakeup threshold over time when new nodes join the network. A second transmitter joined into the network at 21 minutes (vertical black line) and a third at 41 minutes (vertical red line).

meet the application-specified duty cycle; hence, it gradually decreases the wakeup threshold in increments of 2 dBm. AEDP eventually settles on a threshold between −60 and −62 dBm that closely matches the requested duty cycle, where it remains for the remainder of the experiment.

7.2 Adaptation to Network Changes

To test AEDP's resilience to network changes, we performed an experiment where additional transmitters were added to the network at runtime. We initially deployed a single transmitter mote and a single receiver mote. A second transmitter was added to the network 21 minutes into the experiment, and a third was added at 41 minutes. All three transmitters were configured to send packets to the single receiver node, where we instrumented AEDP to record its wakeup threshold over time.

Figure 7 illustrates how AEDP adapts the receiver's wakeup threshold over the course of the experiment. In order to reduce the false wakeup rate, AEDP quickly increases the wakeup threshold to −52 dBm; this closely matches the −50 dBm RSS of the first transmitter. After AEDP reaches its objective false wakeup rate, it begins steadily decreasing the threshold until the second transmitter joins at 21 minutes. The second transmitter's signal strength is slightly higher (−46 dBm) than the existing transmitter. Hence, AEDP responds to the new node by increasing the threshold to −52 dBm, slightly lower than the minimum of both transmitters, and again gradually decreases the threshold over time. At 41 minutes, the third transmitter joins with a significantly lower signal strength at the receiver (−60 dBm) than the previous two transmitters. Benefiting from the periodical wakeup threshold reset process mentioned in Section 5,

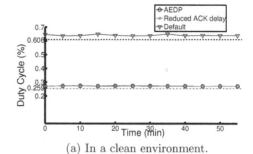

(a) In a clean environment.

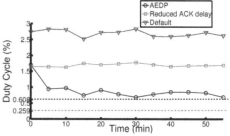

(b) In a residence with residents' normal activities.

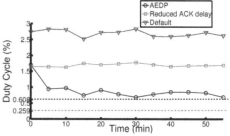

(c) In a lab stress test with generated 802.11n interference.

Figure 8: Duty cycle under minimum interference, normal residential activities, and sustained interference. Horizontal lines indicate the theoretical optimal duty cycles of 0.259% (AEDP and reduced-ACK configurations) and 0.608% (default radio configuration).

AEDP adapts by rapidly dropping the wakeup threshold to −62 dBm, again slightly below the minimum signal strength of all the transmitters. These results demonstrate AEDP dynamically adjusting the wakeup threshold to successfully accommodate network topology changes.

7.3 Impact on Duty Cycles

To explore AEDP's impact on duty cycles, we deployed a pair of motes with a modified radio stack to record the *radio on time* — i.e., the cumulative time the radio was active — on each mote. The precise duty cycle is hence derived from the radio on time and the experiment's length.

We first deployed the pair on channel 26 in an office environment, which we confirmed to be clean with a Wi-Spy spectrum analyzer [25]. We performed experimental runs, for 60 minutes each run, once with the default BoX-MAC-2 configuration and once with AEDP. To isolate the effects of the reduced ACK delay (discussed in Section 6.2) from AEDP's wakeup threshold tuning, we performed a third experimental run which reduced the ACK delay but was otherwise identical to the default BoX-MAC-2 stack.

Figure 8(a) presents the duty cycle under all three experimental runs, broken down into 5 minute windows. In each 5-minute window, the default BoX-MAC-2 configuration activates the radio with an average duty cycle of 0.64%. AEDP consistently reduces this duty cycle over the entire experimental run, by an average of 57.48%. In this clean environment, the false wakeup rate is very low; hence, AEDP achieves a duty cycle within 99.7% of the reduced-ACK configuration.

For comparison, we also plot the theoretical optimal duty cycle for both ACK delay configurations. Specifically, at a data rate of 1 packet/5 min and a wakeup interval of 2 s, the optimal duty cycle is $149 * T_{idle} + (T_p + T_i)/2 + T_p + T_d$, where T_{idle} is the time the radio is active when no energy is detected (11.5 ms under the default configuration, or 4.5 ms with the reduced ACK delay); T_p is the time needed to receive a packet (4.24 ms); T_i is the gap between packets (8.3 ms under the default configuration, or 2.8 ms with the reduced ACK delay); and T_d is the time the radio remains active after receiving a packet (100 ms). Because interference was limited, all experimental runs remained within 7% of their respective optimal duty cycles.

To evaluate AEDP's performance under a more typical deployment, we repeated this experiment in a residential setting. This experiment was carried out under normal wireless condition with residents' regular wireless activity. The mote pair is configured to use channel 16, which overlaps with the residents' 802.11g network. Figure 8(b) plots the results under this experimental setup. We observe that the adjusted ACK delay is responsible for a significant reduction in radio usage, with the average duty cycle in each 5-minute window dropping from 0.86% to 0.55%. However, in the face of typical wireless noise, AEDP's wakeup threshold adjustment has a significant impact on duty cycle. AEDP reduces the duty cycle to an average of 0.30%, resulting in a savings of 45.5% over the tweaked radio stack and 65.1% over the default radio configuration.

Because AEDP is largely able to avoid false wakeups, it comes within 15.8% of the theoretically optimal duty cycle. In contrast, the default and reduced-ACK stacks achieves a duty cycle 41.4% and 112.4% higher than their respective optimal duty cycles.

As a stress test, we repeated the experiment once more in a lab setting under controlled interference, in the form of a laptop and an access point, located 10 ft from the mote pair, generating 1 Mbps UDP traffic over an overlapping 802.11n channel 6, which overlaps with 802.15.4 channel 16.

Figure 8(c) plots the duty cycle under this controlled experiment. Due to the persistent source of interference, the default stack has an average duty cycle of 2.69% while the reduced-ACK stack has an average duty cycle of 1.69%. In contrast, AEDP achieves a duty cycle of 0.89%, a 47.3% reduction over the reduced-ACK stack and 66.9% over the default stack.

Owing to the challenging nature of the wireless environment, all three stacks perform several times worse than their theoretical optimal duty cycles. However, AEDP comes within the closest of its optimal duty cycle: 244% higher than optimal, compared to 342% for the default stack and 552% for the reduced-ACK stack.

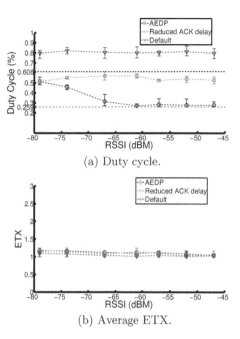

(a) Duty cycle.

(b) Average ETX.

Figure 9: AEDP's performance on links with diverse signal strengths.

7.4 Effects of Signal Strength

We explored AEDP's performance on a diverse set of links by selecting 30 links at random from the 380 links detected in a testbed we deployed in a 3-floor residential apartment building. This experiment was carried out under normal wireless condition with four residents' regular wireless activity. As with the previous experiment, we performed three runs, for 60 minutes each experimental run: one with the default LPL configuration, one with a reduced ACK delay, and one with AEDP.

For the purposes of presentation, we group the 30 links into 7 buckets based on their signal strength, using buckets 5 dBm wide. As shown in Figure 9(a), these links show highly diverse RSS at their respective receivers. For the strongest links (RSS $\in (-65, -45]$), AEDP achieves a duty cycle of 0.28%, close to the theoretical minimum of 0.259%. This represents a 40.3% reduction over the reduced-ACK configuration and 65.1% over the default LPL configuration.

AEDP shows a more moderate — but still significant — improvement in duty cycle on intermediate links (RSS $\in (-75, -65]$). For these links, AEDP achieves a 31.2% reduction in duty cycle over the reduced-ACK configuration and 52.6% over the default LPL configuration.

For the links with the lowest signal strength (RSS ≤ -75), the RSS is already close to the radio stack's default wakeup threshold of -77 dBm. AEDP cannot adjust the wakeup threshold below the signal strength, since it sets T_{max} to be the minimum RSS of incoming links to avoid sacrificing network reliability. Hence, AEDP's 35.7% reduction in duty cycle is attributable only to the reduced ACK length.

As shown in Figure 9(b), the reduced-ACK configuration and AEDP introduced a small number of false-negative energy detection checks which were not experienced under the default stack, since the number of CCA pin polling was reduced from 400 times to 115 times, as discussed in Section 6.2. The reduced-ACK configuration consequently had a 5.5% increase in average ETX (from 1.05 to 1.11) and AEDP had a 6.7% increase in average ETX (from 1.05 to 1.12). The slight increases in average ETX are in exchange for a proportionally much-larger reduction in duty cycle.

We note that links with the lowest signal strength tend to be highly bursty; while productive for routing, they must be used opportunistically. While AEDP will neither help nor hurt when such links exist, by their nature this will only happen for short bursts during the application's lifetime. During the periods where moderate-to-strong links are used for routing, AEDP will dynamically increase the wakeup threshold, resulting in significant energy savings.

7.5   Comparison with A-MAC

Receiver-initiated MAC protocols [12, 23] avoid the false wakeup problem by transmitting probe packets when nodes are ready to *receive* data, eliminating the need for recipients to actively sample the channel. Although AEDP and receiver-initiated MAC protocols approach the false wakeup problem from different directions, they share the same goal of extending network lifetime by reducing duty cycle in the face of noisy wireless channels. To understand the effectiveness of these two approaches, we performed a set of experiments comparing AEDP's performance with that of A-MAC, a state-of-the-art receiver initiated MAC protocol [12]. For this set of experiments, we choose the same set of links from the residential testbed used in Section 7.4, and configured the transmitters to transmit at data rates ranging from 1 packet/2 s to 1 packet/600 s. We performed each experimental run twice, once with AEDP and once with the A-MAC implementation provided by the authors of A-MAC [12]. A-MAC's radio stack was instrumented to record the radio on time, but was otherwise set to its default configuration. For fairness, we used the *default* parameters for both BoX-MAC-2 in TinyOS 2.1.1 [1] and A-MAC provided by the authors [12]. The only change we made for BoX-MAC-2 is reducing the ACK delay because of the implementation flaw discussed in Section 6.2.

As shown in Figure 10(a), at low data rates (Inter Packet Interval (IPI) within [300, 600] s) AEDP leads to lower duty cycles than A-MAC. For instance, AEDP achieves an average duty cycle of 0.338%, representing a 41.5% reduction over A-MAC (0.578%) when IPI is 300 s. AEDP and A-MAC achieve similar duty cycles at intermediate data rates (IPI within [100, 200] s). In contrast, at high data rates (IPI ≤ 100 s), AEDP leads to a higher duty cycle than A-MAC. For instance, with an IPI of 30 s AEDP achieves an average duty cycle of 0.803%, which is 24.1% higher than A-MAC (0.647%). As shown in Figure 10(b), AEDP introduced a small number of false-negative energy detection checks leading to an up to 16.7% increase in average ETX (from 1.000 to 1.166 when IPI is 400 s) in exchange for a proportionally much-larger reduction in duty cycle at low data rates.

The protocols' respective advantages at different date rates may be understood by analyzing their respective strategies. Under LPL, senders repeatedly transmit long preambles indicating that they are ready to send data; recipients periodically sample the channel, and turn on the radio if energy is detected. Under receiver-initiated MACs like A-MAC, recipients periodically broadcast beacons announcing that they are ready to receive data; senders keep their radios on waiting for the recipient's beacon, and then immediately ACK it. In principle, receiver-initiated MACs replace LPL's short

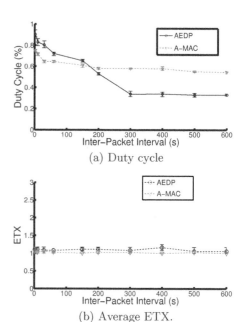

(a) Duty cycle

(b) Average ETX.

Figure 10: Comparing AEDP and A-MAC with different inter-packet intervals (IPIs)

channel sampling with an entire transmission plus a short delay waiting for a response. As discussed in Section 6.2, the default BoX-MAC-2 configuration suffers from an unnecessarily high channel sampling cost of 10.0 ms; in comparison, A-MAC pays a probing cost of 6.2 ms under our oscilloscope measurement. Consequently, previous literature has found that the overhead of receiver-initiated MAC protocols can be even lower than LPL [12]. However, after tuning the energy detection length, AEDP pays a significantly lower sampling cost of 2.9 ms. We note that receiver-initiated MACs *inherently* must pay the overhead of an entire packet transmission; hence A-MAC's overhead cannot be tuned in this fashion.

Thus, A-MAC has a higher overhead than AEDP at low data rates. However, since A-MAC saves the cost of sending a long preamble, it is able to outperform AEDP at sufficiently high data rates. This result suggests that AEDP is more suitable for low date rate applications, while A-MAC has advantages in high data rate applications. They therefore represent complementary approaches in the design space of low-power MAC protocols in noisy environments [5].

7.6   Collection Tree Protocol Performance

Finally, we study how well CTP protocol [14] performs over AEDP. Since AEDP is implemented as a layer situated on top of LPL BoX-MAC-2 MAC layers, running CTP over AEDP is largely a matter of changing configuration

---

[5]The pTunes project [28] shows that the performance of MAC protocols are sensitive to their parameters. Optimizing parameters of a MAC protocol is not the focus of this paper. The pTunes system does not support TinyOS and hence cannot be used to select the MAC parameters for our experiments. Nevertheless the experimental study presented in this subsection reveals the general trend of the complementary behavior of AEDP and a receiver-initiated MAC when facing different data rates.

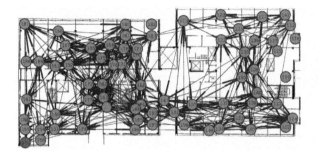

Figure 11: The Testbed topology with a transmission power of 0 dBm. Blue node is a sink node.

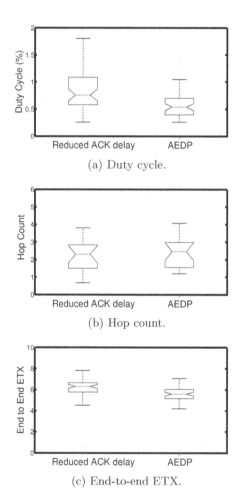

(a) Duty cycle.

(b) Hop count.

(c) End-to-end ETX.

Figure 12: Box-plot comparison between AEDP and LPL BoX-MAC-2 with reduced ACK delay. Central mark in box indicates median; bottom and top of box represent the 25th percentile (q_1) and 75th percentile (q_2); crosses indicate outliers ($x > q_2 + 1.5 \cdot (q_2 - q_1)$ or $x < q_1 - 1.5 \cdot (q_2 - q_1)$); whiskers indicate range excluding outliers.

wirings. To explore the performance on a large scale, multi-hop networks, we run the experiments on an indoor testbed consisting of 55-TelosB motes in Jolley and Bryan Hall at Washington University in St. Louis [26]. Figure 11 shows the network topology with transmission power of 0 dBm. Each node produces data at a rate of 1 packet every 5 minutes and all data packets are forwarded to a sink node. We performed two 24-hour experimental runs one with the AEDP and the other with LPL BoX-MAC-2 configuration with the reduced ACK delay. We use the default CTP setting in both two runs. To test the network's performance in a noisy environment, we set the nodes operating on channel 18 overlapping with the campus Wi-Fi channel.

Figure 12(a)- 12(c) show the box-plots of the duty cycles of all nodes in the testbed and the average hop counts and end-to-end ETX of the routes of all nodes. Since the routes of nodes may change dynamically under CTP, for each node we calculates the average values of hop count and end-to-end ETX during each 24-hour experimental run. As shown in Figure 12(a) and 12(c), AEDP reduces the median duty cycle by 35.44% (from 0.79% to 0.51%), while also reducing the median end-to-end ETX by 11.26% (from 6.30 to 5.59). This result shows that AEDA is able to mitigates the impacts of noise on LPL on node duty cycles while simultaneously reducing the multi-hop transmission cost under CTP. As shown in Figure 12(b), AEDP does result in a slight increase in the median hop count of the routes (from 2.30 hops to 2.46 hops) as a result of a higher CCA threshold used to filter out noise. The combination of a lower end-to-end ETX and higher hop counts indicate that AEDP was able to filter out weak links affected by noise while still enabling CTP to take advantage of enough good links for low-cost multi-hop communication.

8. CONCLUSION

Maintaining energy efficiency in noisy environments has become an increasingly critical problem as wireless sensor networks are gaining widely deployment in residential and office environments. While LPL has been a popular and effective approach to energy-efficient MAC protocols, false wakeups caused by wireless noise can significantly increase the duty cycle and compromise the benefit of LPL. To address this problem, we first perform an empirical study of the false wakeup problem of LPL in real-world residential environments and find that the CCA wakeup threshold is an effective knob for controlling false wakeups. We then propose AEDP, an adaptive protocol that dynamically adjusts a node's wakeup threshold to improve network reliability and duty cycle based on application-specified bounds. AEDP has been implemented on TinyOS 2.1.1 and the TelosB platform. Experimental results from both real-world residential deployments and testbed experiments show that AEDP can effectively maintain low duty cycles in noisy environments and adapt to network changes and links with varying signal strength. We also found AEDP and A-MAC more energy-efficient for applications with low data rate and high data rate, respectively, and therefore provide complementary approaches suitable for different classes of applications.

There are two limitations to AEDP. First, tuning CCA threshold is ineffective for links with low signal strength that can be close to or below the signal strength of noise. In this case AEDP will set the wakeup threshold to the minimum RSS of incoming links and as a result cannot effectively reduce false wakeups caused by noise. This makes AEDP less effective for highly sparse networks connected by mostly long links. Second, our implementation is specific to the particular CC2420 radio stack used. It is important to develop a general methodology — such as the analysis performed in Section 6.2 — to select the key radio and MAC layer parameters. For a new radio stack, developers should firstly measure the ACK delay and then tune the duration of CCA polling accordingly. In general, the duration of CCA polling must be longer than the ACK delay to avoid false negatives in energy detection which can heavily worsen the performance. On the other hand, a long energy detection contradicts the need for a short, inexpensive energy detection, and arguably even renders the entire check ineffective. Therefore, the duration of CCA polling should be slightly longer than the ACK delay.

Acknowledgment

The authors thank the anonymous reviewers, and the shepherd Matteo Ceriotti for their insightful comments. This work was supported in part by NSF under grants CNS-1035773 (CPS) and CNS-1144552 (NeTS).

9. REFERENCES

[1] http://www.tinyos.net/.

[2] http://www.contiki-os.org/.

[3] http://www.zti-telecom.com/EN/LanTrafficV2.html.

[4] http://docs.tinyos.net/index.php/CC2420_Hardware_and_Software_Acks.

[5] M. Bertocco, G. Gamba, and A. Sona. Experimental optimization of CCA thresholds in wireless sensor networks. In *EMC*, 2007.

[6] C. A. Boano, T. Voigt, N. Tsiftes, and L. Mottola. Making sensornet mac protocols robust against interference. In *EWSN*, 2010.

[7] M. Z. Brodsky and R. T. Morris. In defense of wireless carrier sense. In *SIGCOMM*, 2009.

[8] M. Buettner, G. V. Yee, E. Anderson, and R. Han. X-mac: a short preamble mac protocol for duty-cycled wireless sensor networks. In *SenSys*, 2006.

[9] K. K. Chintalapudi and L. Venkatraman. On the design of mac protocols for lowlatency hard real-time discrete control applications over 802.15.4 hardware. In *IPSN*, 2008.

[10] Crossbow Technology. TelosB mote platform. http://www.xbow.com/Products/Product_pdf_files/Wireless_pdf/TelosB_Datasheet.pdf.

[11] A. Dunkels. The contikimac radio duty cycling protocol. Technical Report 5128, Swedish Institute of Computer Science, 2011.

[12] P. Dutta, S. Dawson-Haggerty, Y. Chen, C.-J. M. Liang, and A. Terzis. Design and evaluation of a versatile and efficient receiver-initiated link layer for low-power wireless. In *SenSys*, 2010.

[13] P. Dutta, J. Taneja, J. Jeong, X. Jiang, and D. Culler. A building block approach to sensornet systems. In *SenSys*, 2008.

[14] O. Gnawali, R. Fonseca, K. Jamieson, D. Moss, and P. Levis. Collection tree protocol. In *SenSys*, 2009.

[15] IEEE. *Part 15.4: Wireless Medium Access Control (MAC) and Physical Layer (PHY) Specifications for Low-Rate Wireless Personal Area Networks (WPANs)*, 2006.

[16] A. Kiryushin, A. Sadkov, and A. Mainwaring. Real-world performance of clear channel assessment in 802.15.4 wireless sensor networks. In *SENSORCOMM*, 2008.

[17] C.-J. M. Liang, B. Priyantha, J. Liu, and A. Terzis. Surviving wi-fi interference in low power zigbee networks. In *SenSys*, 2010.

[18] D. Moss and P. Levis. BoX-MACs: Exploiting physical and link layer boundaries in low-power networking. Technical Report SING-08-00, Stanford Information Networks Group, 2008.

[19] J. Polastre, J. Hill, and D. Culler. Versatile low power media access for wireless sensor networks. In *SenSys*, 2004.

[20] I. Ramachandran and S. Roy. On the impact of clear channel assessment on mac performance. In *GLOBECOM*, 2006.

[21] M. Sha, G. Hackmann, and C. Lu. Energy-efficient low power listening for wireless sensor networks in noisy environments. Technical Report WUCSE-2011-61, Washington University in St. Louis, 2013. http://cse.wustl.edu/Research/Lists/Technical%20Reports/Attachments/957/aedp.pdf.

[22] K. Srinivasan, P. Dutta, A. Tavakoli, and P. Levis. An empirical study of low power wireless. In *ACM Transactions on Sensor Networks*, 2010.

[23] Y. Sun, O. Gurewitz, and D. B. Johnson. Ri-mac: A receiver-initiated asynchronous duty cycle mac protocol for dynamic traffic loads in wireless sensor networks. In *SenSys*, 2008.

[24] Texas Instruments. *2.4 GHz IEEE 802.15.4 / ZigBee-ready RF Transceiver*.

[25] Wi-Spy Spectrum Analyzer. http://www.metageek.net/.

[26] WUSTL Wireless Sensor Network Testbed. http://wsn.cse.wustl.edu/index.php/Testbed.

[27] W. Yuan, J.-P. M. G. Linnartz, and I. G. M. M. Niemegeers. Adaptive cca for ieee 802.15.4 wireless sensor networks to mitigate interference. In *WCNC*, 2010.

[28] M. Zimmerling, F. Ferrari, L. Mottolay, T. Voigty, and L. Thiele. ptunes: Runtime parameter adaptation for low-power mac protocols. In *IPSN*, 2012.

MediaScope: Selective On-Demand Media Retrieval from Mobile Devices[*]

Yurong Jiang[†]
University of Southern
California
yurongji@usc.edu

Xing Xu
University of Southern
California
xingx@usc.edu

Peter Terlecky
City University of New York
pterlecky@gc.cuny.edu

Tarek Abdelzaher
University of Illinois at
Urbana-Champaign
zaher@illinois.edu

Amotz Bar-Noy
City University of New York
amotz@sci.brooklyn.cuny.edu

Ramesh Govindan
University of Southern
California
ramesh@usc.edu

ABSTRACT

Motivated by an availability gap for visual media, where images and videos are uploaded from mobile devices well after they are generated, we explore the *selective, timely retrieval* of media content from a collection of mobile devices. We envision this capability being driven by *similarity-based queries* posed to a cloud search front-end, which in turn dynamically retrieves media objects from mobile devices that best match the respective queries within a given time limit. Building upon a crowd-sensing framework, we have designed and implemented a system called MediaScope that provides this capability. MediaScope is an extensible framework that supports nearest-neighbor and other geometric queries on the feature space (e.g., clusters, spanners), and contains novel retrieval algorithms that attempt to maximize the retrieval of relevant information. From experiments on a prototype, MediaScope is shown to achieve near-optimal query completeness and low to moderate overhead on mobile devices.

Categories and Subject Descriptors

H.3.3 [**Information Storage and Retrieval**]: Information Search and Retrieval; H.3.4 [**Information Storage and Retrieval**]: Systems and Software; H.4.0 [**Information Systems Applications**]: General; C.2.4 [**Computer-Communication Networks**]: Distributed Systems

---
[*]Research was sponsored by the Army Research Laboratory and was accomplished under Cooperative Agreement Number W911NF-09-2-0053. The views and conclusions contained in this document are those of the authors and should not be interpreted as representing the official policies, either expressed or implied, of the Army Research Laboratory or the U.S. Government. The U.S. Government is authorized to reproduce and distribute reprints for Government purposes notwithstanding any copyright notation here on.

[†]The first two authors contributed equally to this work and their names are listed alphabetically by last name.

General Terms

Design, Experimentation, Performance

Keywords

Crowd-sensing, Image-Retrieval, Feature-Extraction, Mobile-Device

1. INTRODUCTION

Cameras on mobile devices have given rise to significant *sharing* of media sensor data (photos and videos). Users upload visual media to online social networks like Facebook [2], as well as to dedicated sharing sites like Flickr [3] and Instagram [4]. However, these uploads are often not *immediate*. Camera sensors on mobile devices have been increasing in both image and video resolution far faster than cellular network capacity. More important, in response to growing demand and consequent contention for wireless spectrum, cellular data providers have imposed data usage limits, which disincentivize immediate photo uploading and create an *availability gap* (the time between when a photo or image is taken and when it is uploaded). This availability gap can be on the order of several days.

If media data was available immediately, it might enable scenarios where there is a need for recent (or fresh) information. Consider the following scenario: users at a mall or some other location take pictures and video of some event (e.g., an accident or altercation). An investigative team that wants visual evidence of the event could have searched or browsed images on a photo sharing service such as Flickr to retrieve evidence in a timely fashion.

To bridge this availability gap, and to enable this and other missed opportunities, we consider a novel capability for on-demand retrieval of images from mobile devices. Specifically, we develop a system called MediaScope that permits concurrent geometric queries in feature space on that may be distributed across several mobile devices.

Wireless bandwidth is limited and can vary, *concurrent queries* might compete for limited bandwidth, and query results can be large (since images are large and many images can match a query). These factors can result in unacceptably long query response times, which can impede usability. In some cases, applications might need lower query response times for correctness; in the scenario above, time may be of the essence in taking action (e.g., apprehending suspects).

MediaScope addresses this challenge using an approach that trades off query completeness[1], while meeting timeliness requirements (measured by the time between the issue of the query and when a query result is returned). It incorporates a novel credit-assignment scheme that is used to weight queries as well as differentiate query results by their "importance". A novel credit and timeliness-aware scheduling algorithm that also adapts to wireless bandwidth variability ensures that query completeness is optimized. A second important challenge is to enable accurate yet computationally-feasible feature extraction. MediaScope addresses this challenge by finding sweet spots in the trade-off between accuracy and computational cost, for extracting features from images and frames from videos.

An evaluation of MediaScope on a complete prototype (Section 4), shows that MediaScope achieves upwards of 75% query completeness even in adversarial settings. For the query mixes we have experimented with, this completeness rate is near-optimal; an omniscient scheduler that is aware of future query arrivals does not outperform MediaScope. Furthermore, MediaScope's performance is significantly different from other scheduling algorithms that lack one of its features, namely timeliness-awareness, credit-awareness, and adaptivity to varying bandwidth. Finally, we find that most overheads associated with MediaScope components are moderate, suggesting that timeliness bounds within 10s can be achievable.

2. MOTIVATION AND CHALLENGES

In this section, we first motivate the need for on-demand image retrieval, then describe our approach and illustrate the challenges facing on-demand image retrieval.

Motivation. With the increasing penetration of mobile devices with high-resolution imaging sensors, point-and-shoot cameras and camcorders are increasingly being replaced by mobile devices for taking photos and videos. This trend is being accelerated by an increase in the resolution of image sensors to the point where mobile devices have image resolutions comparable to cameras.

The availability of high resolution image sensors has prompted users to more pervasively share images and videos. In addition to giving birth to services like Instagram, it has prompted many image and video sharing sites to develop a business strategy developed on mobile devices. Beyond sharing media (photos and videos) with one's social network, this development has also been societally beneficial, e.g., in crime-fighting [1].

On the flip side, wireless bandwidth is scarce and has not been able to keep up with increases in mobile device usage. As a result, cellular operators limit data usage on mobile devices; standard data plans come with fairly restrictive data usage budgets per month (on the order of 1-2 GB). Users are increasingly becoming aware of the implications of these limits and how media transmission can cause users to exceed their monthly data usage limits.

These conflicting trends will, we posit, lead to an *availability gap* for media. The availability gap for a media item (an image or a video) is defined as the time between which the item is taken and when it is shared (uploaded to a sharing site). We believe that users will be increasingly reluctant to use cellular networks to share media, preferring instead to wait for available WiFi. Indeed, this availability gap already exists. On *Flickr* [3], we randomly selected 40 popular Flickr users and extracted about 50 recent photos from each user's gallery. We then plotted the CDF of the difference between the day when each photo was taken, and when it was uploaded (the photo's availability gap). As Figure 1 shows, more than 50% of the photos have an availability gap of greater than 10 days!

We conjecture that this availability gap will persist with mobile devices: existing data plan usage limits ensure that users treat these devices as similar to traditional cameras or camcorders from the perspective of video and photo upload (i.e., as a device with no network connectivity)[2] Furthermore, mobile device storage has been increasing to the point where multiple photos and videos can be stored; a 64GB iPad can hold 10,000 photos which can take several months to upload with a 2GB/month data plan.

This availability gap represents a missed opportunity for societal or commercial uses. For example,

1. Consider a robbery in a mall in an area uncovered by security cameras. The mall's security staff would like to be able to access and retrieve images from mobile devices of users who happen to be in the mall on that day in order to be able to establish the identity of the thief .

2. A sportswriter is writing a report on a sporting event and would like to be able to include a perfect picture of a play (e.g., a catch or a dunk). The newspaper's staff photographer happened to have been obscured when the play happened, so the sportswriter would like to be able to retrieve images from mobile devices of users who happened to be attending the event.

The focus of this paper is the exploration of a capability for bridging the availability gap by enabling media retrieval in a manner suggested by the above examples.

Approach. To bridge the availability gap, so that, in the scenarios above, the security staff or the sportswriter can obtain recent information, we explore on-demand retrieval of images from a collection of mobile devices. These devices belong to users who have chosen to *participate* and provide images on demand. In return, participating users may be incentivized by explicit micropayments; we do not discuss incentives and privacy issues in this paper, but note that our approach is an instance of crowd-sensing built on Medusa [23], which has explored these issues in the context of crowd-sensing. In what follows, we use the term *participating device* to mean a mobile device whose user has chosen to participate in image retrieval.

Our approach is inspired by *image search* techniques that support similarity searches on image feature space. There is a large body of literature that seeks to support *content-based image retrieval* by defining appropriate features that characterize images: ImgSeek[17], CEDD [9] (Color and Edge Directivity Descriptor), FCTH [10] (Fuzzy Color and Texture Histogram), Auto Color Correlogram [16], and JCD [11] (Joint Composite Descriptor). Generally, these algorithms are based on 2 features: image color and texture description. Taking CEDD as an example, for texture space, CEDD sub-divides an image into blocks and for each image block, sub-divides it into 4 sub-blocks, calculates the average gray level of each sub-block, then computes the directional area (vertical, horizontal, 45-degrees, 135-degrees and non-directional) with the sub-block parameters for this image block; thus, an image is divided to 6 regions by texture unit. For color space, it projects the color space into HSV (Hue, Saturation, Value) channels, then divides each channel into several preset areas using coordinate logic filters (CLF), so that the color space is divided to 24 sub-regions. A histogram is drawn on these parameters, so that $24 \times 6 = 144$ coefficients (ranging in value from 0 to 7) are output as the CEDD feature vector. Finally, the image processing community has experimented with a wide variety of measures of similarity. Of these,

---

[1]Completeness is intuitively defined as the proportion of desired images uploaded before the timeliness bound, see Section 4.1

[2]This may not be the only reason an availability gap exists today or is likely to persist — users may wait to process photos on a desktop or laptop computer before uploading, for example.

we pick a popular measure [9, 10, 21], the Tanimoto distance [24], which satisfies the properties for a metric space [20].

Since CEDD is popularly used and widely accepted, we have developed our system (Section 3) using this algorithm. From our perspective, this algorithm has one important property: for a single image, CEDD's feature vectors consist of 144 coefficients which require 54 bytes, a negligible fraction of the size of a compressed image, often 1-2MB. Moreover, CEDD is computationally lightweight relative to other feature extraction mechanisms, but has comparable accuracy. CEDD is defined for images; as we describe later, we are also able to derive features for video. More generally, our approach is agnostic to the specific choice of features and similarity definition; other feature extraction algorithms can be used, so long as the features are compact relative to image sizes.

On top of this image similarity search primitive, we explore a query interface that supports several queries:

Top-K Given an image, this query outputs the K most similar images among all images from all available participating devices. A special case of $K = 1$ is the typical content based image retrieval query that has been explored in the image processing literature [17, 31, 6]. Our sportswriter could use this query by presenting an image of a specific play (e.g., a dunk) taken, say, at a different game.

Spanners This query returns a collection of images whose features span the feature space of all images from all participating devices. The mall security staff in the example above can use this query to understand the range of images available in participating devices before deciding to drill down and issue more specific queries (top-k) with retrieved images.

Clusters This query returns representatives from natural clusters in the feature space and can effectively identify the most common "topics" among images from participating mobile devices. This query can also help in both scenarios to give the querier an overview of the different classes of images in participating devices, prior to drill down (as above).

Our approach can be extended to support other kinds of queries (e.g., enclosing *hulls*), as described later. While Top-K queries have been used with images, we are not aware of other work that has proposed using Spanners and Cluster queries with images. Finally, our use of these queries in conjunction with a database of images spread over mobile devices is, to our knowledge, novel.

Our queries can be *qualified* by several *attributes*. Attributes like *location* and *time* constrain the set of objects that are considered in computing the query result; the location attribute constrains media objects to those taken in the vicinity of a certain location and the time attribute specifies when the corresponding photo or video was taken. Users may also specify a *freshness* attribute, which constrains the age of media objects selected to compute the query result.

The last, but perhaps the most interesting attribute, is *timeliness*. Timeliness is a property of the query result, and specifies a time bound within which to return the result(s) of a query: if a query is issued at time T and the timeliness constraint is t, the system attempts to return query results before $T + t$. The timeliness attribute is motivated by the surveillance example discussed above; the security team might want results within a bounded time to take follow-up action. It may also be bounded by interactivity concerns: since wireless bandwidth is limited and can vary, images may be large, and multiple concurrent queries may compete for bandwidth, query response times can be large and may vary significantly.

Challenges. Our approach faces several challenges. The first of

these is *feature extraction*: it turns out that feature extraction algorithms for large images encounter memory limits even on high-end modern smartphones. Equally challenging is feature extraction for video, since the frame rate for video can overwhelm many feature extraction algorithms.

The more central challenge in our work is the design of the system that *satisfies the timeliness constraints multiple concurrent queries*. In general, this is a hard problem, primarily because of the bandwidth limitations of wireless mobile devices; the aggregate query result may need a throughput that may overwhelm the available bandwidth. There are two approaches to solve this problem. The first is admission control, whereby we restrict the number of concurrent queries such that the timeliness constraints can always be met. We did not consider this solution because of the variability and unpredictability of wireless bandwidth availability. The second approach is to *deliver maximal information within the given timeliness bound, while adapting to variability in available bandwidth*. Our work chooses the second approach, in the context of which there is an interesting challenge: what does it mean to deliver maximal information?

In the next section, we describe the design of a system called *MediaScope* that addresses these challenges.

3. MEDIASCOPE

MediaScope is a system that supports timely similarity-based queries on media objects stored on mobile devices. We begin by describing the MediaScope architecture and then discuss the design and implementation of each component.

3.1 Architecture and Overview

Mediascope is conceptually partitioned across a cloud component called MSCloud, and another component called MSMobile that runs on mobile devices. This partitioned design leverages the computation and storage in clouds to support geometric queries on the feature space; mobile devices provide sensing and storage for media objects.

These components interact as follows (Figure 2). Whenever participants take photos or videos, the *Feature Extractor* component of MSMobile continuously extracts, in the background, image and video features and uploads them to the *MSCloudDB*. Users (e.g., a security officer or a sportswriter) pose queries to MSCloud using a standard web interface, possibly on a mobile device. These queries are processed by the *MSCloudQ* query processing engine, which uses the features stored in the MSCloudDB to compute the query results. The results of the queries identify the media objects that need to be retrieved from individual mobile devices. In some cases, a media object may already have been retrieved as a result of an earlier query; query results are also *cached* in MSCloudDB in order to optimize retrieval. MSCloudQ coordinates with an *Object Uploader* component on MSMobile in order to retrieve query results. Once a query's timeliness bound expires, MSCloudQ terminates the corresponding Object Uploader and returns retrieved results.

MediaScope uses a publicly available crowd sensing platform called Medusa [23]. Medusa was originally designed to permit human users to pose crowd-sensing tasks. MediaScope's retrieval of features and media objects from mobile devices leverages Medusa's support for "sensing" stored information on these devices. To enable programmed interaction between MSCloud and Medusa, and to support MediaScope's timeliness requirements, we made several modifications to the Medusa platform (discussed later).

MediaScope thus provides a high-level abstraction (queries on media objects) that hides many of the details of object retrieval

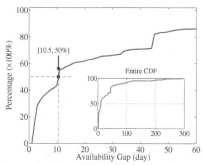

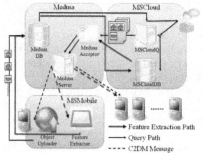

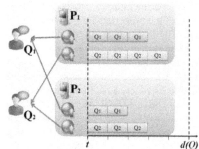

Figure 1—CDF of Flickr Photo Availablility
Gap

Figure 2—System Architecture Work Flow **Figure 3**—Illustration of Concurrent Queries

from users. In the following subsections, we describe the two most challenging aspects of MediaScope design: *support for concurrent queries*, a functionality distributed between the MSCloudQ and the Object Uploader; and *feature extraction*. We conclude with a brief description of other design and implementation issues.

3.2 Design: Concurrent Queries

The most challenging component of MediaScope is support for concurrent queries — MSCloudQ may receive one or more queries while other queries are being processed. In MediaScope, the result of a query is a list of media objects to be retrieved from a subset of the participating phones. Recall that each query has a timeliness constraint. In the presence of concurrent queries, MediaScope may need to upload all media objects before their timeliness bound expires. In general, this may be difficult to achieve because wireless bandwidth can vary significantly over time, resulting in variable upload times for images.

To illustrate this, consider the example of two concurrent queries Q_1 and Q_2 that arrive at the same time for media objects distributed across two phones P_1 and P_2 in Figure 3. Also, assume that both queries have a timeliness bound of 5 seconds, each object can upload 1 object per second, and all objects are of the same size. If Q_1 needs to retrieve 3 objects from P_1 and 2 objects from P_2, while Q_2 needs to retrieve 4 objects from P_1 and 3 from P_2. Under these circumstances, it is not possible to satisfy the timeliness requirements of one of the two queries. In practice, the problem is much harder because there may be more than two concurrent queries, many more participating devices, queries can arrive at different times, media objects may have different sizes, and wireless available bandwidth can vary dynamically. Especially because of the last reason, admission control cannot guarantee that all timeliness constraints are met, or may severely underutilize the available bandwidth.

MediaScope uses a different approach, *trading off query completeness for timeliness*. In MediaScope, not all query results may be uploaded within the timeliness bound, but the challenge is to upload the most relevant queries so as to maximize the amount of *information* retrieved. In doing this, there are two challenges: how to differentiate between queries, and how to prioritize media items for the retrieval in order to maximize the information retrieved.

MediaScope addresses these two challenges using a *credit assignment* mechanism. Each query is assigned, by MediaScope, a number of credits. The credits assigned to a query reflect the importance of that query and result in proportionally more information being uploaded for that query (and therefore the proportional completeness of the query result). The specific credit assignment mechanism for queries is beyond the scope of this paper, but MediaScope may use monetary incentives (e.g., users who pay more

get more credits for their queries) or other approaches in order to assign credits to queries.

If a query is assigned n credits, it divides up these credits among its results (media objects) in a way that reflects the importance of each object to the query. The key intuition here is that, for a given query, *the importance of a result object to the query can be determined by the feature space geometry*. For example, consider a query Q which attempts to retrieve the two nearest photos in feature space to a given photo c. If the resulting photos a and b are each 20 units and 80 units distant from c in feature space, and Q has been assigned 100 credits, a and b each receive 80 and 20 credits respectively (in inverse proportion to their distances to c).

MediaScope uses this intuition to define credit assignment to result objects. Once objects have been assigned credits, object uploading is prioritized by credit in order to maximize the total credit retrieved across all concurrent queries. In what follows, we first describe the queries that MediaScope supports and how credits are assigned for each query. We then describe MediaScope's credit-based object scheduling technique and discuss its optimality.

3.2.1 Queries and Credit Assignment

Our current instantiation of MediaScope supports three qualitatively different queries: nearest neighbor, clusters, and spanners. Below, we discuss the design of the query engine MSCloudQ and how credits are assigned to query results. Recall that for each query, users can specify time, location and freshness attributes: before performing each of the queries described below, MSCloudQ filters all the feature vectors stored in MSCloudDB to select feature vectors that match these attributes. In our description of the queries below, we assume that this filtering step has been applied.

k-Nearest Neighbors. For this query, the user supplies a *target* image and the server attempts to return the k nearest images (from photos or videos) in feature space to the target. The implementation of this query is straightforward: it is possible to build indexes to optimize the search for the K nearest neighbors, but our current implementation uses a brute force approach.

Credit assignment for this query attempts to capture the relative importance of the query results. Thus, the assignment of credits to each result is proportional to its similarity to the target image. For the i-th result, let s_i be the similarity measure to the target; we then assign credits to the i-th result proportional to $p_i = \left(1 - \frac{s_i}{\sum s_i}\right)$.

K Clustering. The second class of queries supported by MSCloudQ is based on clustering in feature space. This query takes as input the number k as well as well as a *type* parameter which describes the expected result and can have one of two values:

Cluster Representative With this parameter, the result contains k images, one from each cluster. For each cluster, our algorith-

292

m selects that image as the representative whose distance is least to the centroid of the cluster. Intuitively, this query type identifies different "topics" among images taken by participating users.

Common Interest With this parameter, the result includes images from that cluster which contains objects belonging to the most number of users. Thus, if the i-th cluster contains images from u_i users, the query returns images from that cluster for which u_i is the largest. Intuitively, this query identifies the cluster that represents the maximal common interest between participating users. Within the selected cluster, the query returns one image for each participating user, selecting that image of the user that is closest to the centroid of the cluster.

These queries can be implemented by any standard algorithm for k-means clustering.

For the *cluster representative* type of query, we assign credits proportional to the size of the cluster. Thus, if the j-th cluster's size is c_j, the credit assigned to the image selected from cluster j is proportional to $\frac{c_j}{\sum c_j}$.

For the *common interest* type of query, we assign a credit to each selected image that is inversely proportional to the image's distance from the centroid of the cluster. The credit assignment is similar to k nearest neighbors above.

Spanner. The third, and qualitatively different query that MediaScope supports is based on spanning the feature space. The intuition behind the query is to return a collection of images which *span* the feature space. In computing the spanner, we assume that each user t contributes exactly s_t images, where s_t is derived from the query's timeliness bound and a nominal estimate of the average upload rate from the corresponding mobile device[3] Our spanner maximizes the minimum dissimilarity between all pairs.

We now express this problem mathematically. Assume that K_n, the complete graph on n vertices (vertices represent images), has a vertex set V partitioned into C classes $V_1, \ldots, V_C$ (classes represent users). Let v_{i_t} denote vertex i in class V_t. Let $e_{i_t j_k}$ represent the edge connecting v_{i_t} with v_{j_k}. Assume edge $e_{i_t j_k}$ has weight $w_{i_t j_k}$ (where the weight represents the dissimilarity between objects i_t and j_k).

Assuming that exactly s_t vertices must be selected from V_t, we need to select a set of vertices so that the minimum edge weight of the selected clique is maximized. This problem can be formulated as a mixed-integer program:

$$\max z$$

$$\text{s.t. } z \leq w_{i_t j_k} y_{i_t j_k} \qquad \forall i_t, j_k \ s.t. \ i_t < j_k \quad (1)$$

$$y_{i_t j_k} \leq x_{i_t} \qquad \forall i_t, j_k \ s.t. \ i_t < j_k \quad (2)$$

$$y_{i_t j_k} \leq x_{j_k} \qquad \forall i_t, j_k \ s.t. \ i_t < j_k \quad (3)$$

$$x_{i_t} + x_{j_k} - y_{i_t j_k} \leq 1 \qquad \forall i_t, j_k \ s.t. \ i_t < j_k \quad (4)$$

$$\sum_{i_t \in V_t} x_{i_t} = s_t \qquad \forall t = 1, \ldots, C \quad (5)$$

$$x_{i_t} \in \{0, 1\} \qquad \forall i_t$$

$$y_{i_t j_k} \in \{0, 1\} \qquad \forall i_t, j_k \ s.t. \ i_t < j_k$$

In this mixed-integer program, variable x_{i_t} is used as the indicator variable for selecting vertex v_{i_t} for the clique. Similarly, variable $y_{i_t j_k}$ is used as the indicator variable for selecting edge $e_{i_t j_k}$ for the clique. Variable z is used to achieve the $\min_{i_t < j_k} w_{i_t j_k} y_{i_t j_k}$.

---

[3] As we describe later, the average upload rate is estimated dynamically by MSCloudQ.

Inequalities 2 and 3 ensure that edge $e_{i_t j_k}$ is not selected if either vertex i_t or j_k is not selected. Inequality 4 guarantees that $y_{i_t j_k}$ is selected if both vertices i_t and j_k are selected. Inequality 5 ensures that the number of vertices selected from class t is s_t.

The above problem is NP-hard so we use a $O(|V|^2)$ heuristic (Algorithm 1) for solution. The idea behind this heuristic is to select the set of vertices greedily i.e., add "qualified" vertices whose minimum weighted edge to the set selected thus far is maximum. "Qualified" vertices are vertices in the classes which have not yet met their constraint, and hence these vertices can still be selected. We deal with the issue of which vertex should be selected first by trying all possible vertices as being the first vertex in the set and taking the maximal such set.

Algorithm 1 : MAXMIN HEURISTIC

1: Define a list l for storing best vertex set and a variable max_min for minimum weighted edge
2: $l \leftarrow [\,], max\_min \leftarrow 0$
3: **for all** $i \in \{1, \ldots, V\}$ **do**
4:   $min = \infty$
5:   Define a temporary list l_t and $l_t \leftarrow i$
6:   **while** new item added to l_t **do**
7:     **for** $j \in \{1, \ldots, V\}$ and $j \notin L$ **do**
8:       $d(j) \leftarrow \min_{o \in l_t} similarity\_dist(o, j)$
9:       **if** $\exists$ qualified vertex v **then**
10:         $l_t.add(\{v|\max d(v)\})$
11:         $temp\_min \leftarrow d(\{v|\max d(v)\})$
12:     **if** $temp\_min < min$ **then**
13:       $min = temp\_min$
14:   **if** $min > max\_min$ **then**
15:     $max\_min = min$
16:     $l = l_t$

OUTPUT: l and max_min

For this query, intuitively, credit assignment should give more importance to dissimilar images. For the i-th query result, we compute d_i, the average distance from the i-th image to all other images. The credit assigned to this image is proportional to $\frac{d_i}{\sum d_i}$.

Extensibility of MSCloudQ. These are, of course, not the only kinds of geometric queries that can be supported. Developers wishing to extend MSCloudQ by adding new queries can do so quite easily by: (a) defining the query syntax and semantics, (b) implementing the query algorithm, and (c) specifying a proportional credit assignment based on the semantics of the query.

3.2.2 Credit-based Scheduling

In general, users can pose concurrent queries to MSCloudQ. Queries may arrive at different times and may overlap to different extents (we say one query overlaps with another when one arrives while the other's results are being retrieved). Furthermore, different queries may have different timeliness constraints, may retrieve different numbers of objects (e.g., for different values of k, or different sizes of spanners), and the retrieved media objects may be of different sizes (images with different resolutions). In these cases, MSCloudQ needs an algorithm that schedules the retrieval of different objects subject to some desired goal.

In MediaScope, this goal is to maximize the total completeness of queries, defined as the sum of the credits of all the uploaded images. To achieve this, recall that MSCloudQ assigns a credit budget to each query based on the importance of that query; then, using the proportions defined above, it assigns credit values to each query result.

To mathematically define the completeness goal, we first introduce some notation. Let Q_i denote the set of media objects that form the result of the i-th query, and let that query's timeliness constraint be $d(Q_i)$. Let $g(o)$ be an indicator variable that denotes whether a media object o is retrieved before $d(Q_i)$. Then, for the i-th query, the total credit for all uploaded media objects is given by:

$$g(Q_i) = \sum_{o \in Q_i} g(o) \cdot c(o)$$

Thus, given a series of concurrent queries $\mathbb{Q}$, the total number of credits retrieved is given by:

$$c(\mathbb{Q}) = \sum_{Q \in \mathbb{Q}} \sum_{o \in Q} g(o) \cdot c(o)$$

Maximizing this quantity is the objective of MediaScope's retrieval scheduling algorithm.

It turns out that it is possible to decompose this objective into a per-device *credit maximization scheduling* algorithm. To see why this is so, let $\mathbb{P}$ denote the set of participating devices, and the k-th device be denoted by p_k. Then, the above credit sum can be written, for concurrent queries $\mathbb{Q}$:

$$
\begin{aligned}
c(\mathbb{Q}) &= \sum_{Q \in \mathbb{Q}} \sum_{o \in Q} g(o) \cdot c(o) \\
&= \sum_{Q \in \mathbb{Q}} \sum_{P \in \mathbb{P}} \sum_{o \in P \cap Q} g(o) \cdot c(o) \\
&= \sum_{P \in \mathbb{P}} \sum_{o \in P} g(o) \cdot c(o)
\end{aligned}
$$

This equality shows that, in order to maximize the total credits retrieved across a set of concurrent queries $c(\mathbb{Q})$, it suffices to maximize the total credits uploaded by each participating device: $\sum_{P \in \mathbb{P}} c(P)$. This is true under the following two assumptions: (a) if two different queries retrieve the same object from P_k, then the object will need to be uploaded at most once and (b) the credit assigned to that object is the sum of the credits allocated by each query to that object.

This finding has a nice property from the systems perspective: it suffices to run a local credit-maximizing scheduler on each participating device in order to achieve the overall objective. In general, local schedulers have the attractive property that they can locally adapt to bandwidth variations without coordinating with MSCloudQ, and need only minimal coordination with MSCloudQ in order to deal with new query arrivals. In MediaScope, the Object Uploader component of MSMobile implements the scheduling algorithm.

An Optimal Scheduler. We first describe a scheduling algorithm that is *optimal* under the assumption of fixed file sizes and fixed wireless bandwidth per participating device. Under these assumptions, for each object o, it is possible to compute the exact upload time $t(o)$ which is the same for all objects. If each object's timeliness bound is $d(o)$ (different objects can have different bounds), our goal is to find an uploading sequence such that $\sum_o g(o) \cdot c(o)$ is maximized.

First, we may assume that an optimal schedule orders the objects by earliest timeliness bound first. Assume an optimal schedule does not order objects by earliest timeliness bound first. Then there exist two objects i and j for which $d(o_i) > d(o_j)$ but i is scheduled before j. By switching the order of objects i and j we can obtain another optimal schedule.

However, merely scheduling by earliest timeliness bound is not likely to maximize credit. To do this, the algorithm preprocesses the schedule to obtain a set of scheduled objects in the following

way. It orders the objects by earliest timeliness bound first. Then, it adds objects to the schedule one right after another as long as each object's finish time does not exceed the timeliness bound. If an object's end time exceeds its timeliness bound, the algorithm removes the object receiving the smallest credit of those objects scheduled thus far (including current object) and shifts objects to the right of this object to the left by $t(o)$ to cover the gap. Intuitively, this step maximizes the total credit uploaded: lower credit objects, regardless of the query they belong to, are replaced. The algorithm then selects the next object in order of timeliness.

Algorithm 2 : OPTIMAL UPLOADING SCHEDULE

1: Arrange the pending objects list $\mathbb{O}$ by earliest timeliness bound first, scheduling $\mathbb{S} \leftarrow []$
2: $l \leftarrow 0$
3: **for** $o \leftarrow \mathbb{O}.first$ **do**
4: $\quad \mathbb{S} \leftarrow o$
5: $\quad \mathbb{O}.remove(o)$
6: $\quad$ **if** $l + t(o) \leq d(o)$ **then**
7: $\quad\quad l \leftarrow l + t(o)$
8: $\quad$ **else**
9: $\quad\quad$ Remove the smallest credited object in $\mathbb{S}$
10: $\quad\quad$ Shift all objects to the right of this object to left by $t(o)$

OUTPUT: scheduling $\mathbb{S}$, uploading object $\mathbb{S}[0]$

The following example illustrates this algorithm. Suppose there are 3 queries, each with one result object. Let their respective timeliness bounds be 2, 3, and 5 and the credits they receive be 7, 8, and 6 respectively. Finally, suppose $t(o)$ is 2 time units. The algorithm would proceed in the following way. It would schedule the first object initially. Since the second object would not be delivered in a timely manner if scheduled after the first object, and since the second object receives more credits than the first, the first is removed and the second is scheduled from time 0-2. The third object is then scheduled from time 2-4 giving a maximal 14 total credits to the system.

This algorithm is a special case of an optimal pseudo-polynomial algorithm discussed below, so we omit a proof of its optimality.

Optimality under different object sizes. If object uploading times are different, the scheduling problem is NP-hard; the simple case of different object sizes with all objects having the same timeliness bound is equivalent to the NP-Hard Knapsack problem [15]. We can however give the following pseudo-polynomial time dynamic programming algorithm for this problem. Let $S[i, q]$ be the maximum credited schedule using only the first i objects, i.e., objects $o_1, \ldots, o_i$, taking up q time units. Let $s[i, q]$ be the corresponding credit for such a schedule. Then $s[i, q]$ is defined in the following way:

$$
s[i, q] = \begin{cases} \max\{s[i-1, q-t(o_i)] + c(o_i), s[i-1, q]\} & \text{if } q \leq d(o_i) \\ s[i-1, q] & \text{if } q > d(o_i), \end{cases}
$$
(6)

where the following initial conditions hold: $s[0, q] = s[i, q < t(o_1)] = 0$. If $s[i-1, q-t(o_i)] + c(o_i) > s[i-1, q]$ and $q \leq d(o_i)$, then $S[i, q] \leftarrow S[i-1, q-t(o_i)] \cup \{o_i\}$, else $S[i, q] \leftarrow S[i-1, q]$. The desired output is $S(n, d(o_n))$ for an input of n objects.

The running time of this algorithm is $O(nd(o_n))$. The optimality of Algorithm 2 follows from the optimality of this dynamic programming algorithm for the general case [7].

Practical Considerations. In a practical system, the Object Uploader estimates $t(o)$ continuously, and re-computes the schedule after each upload is completed, in order to determine the next object

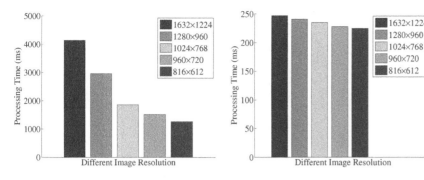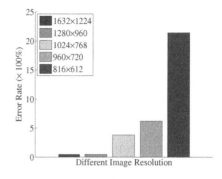

(a) Average CEDD Execution Time Per Image for Different Size

(b) Average Time of Resizing image to Different Size

(c) Average Error Rate of KMeans Clustering for Different Size

Figure 4—Image Resizing Overhead and Tradeoffs

to upload. There are two reasons for this. First, $t(o)$ can change because available wireless bandwidth can vary. Second, new queries may arrive at MSCloud; when a query arrives, MSCloud evaluates the query, assigns credits to the query results, and notifies the relevant devices (those which contain one or more result objects). Thus, at a given device, the set of objects to be uploaded can vary dynamically, so the Object Uploader needs to re-evaluate the schedule after every upload. Finally, for large objects, bandwidth variability might cause their timeliness bounds to be violated (e.g., because the available bandwidth became lower than the value that was used to compute the schedule); in this case, the Uploader can abort in-progress transmission to reduce the bandwidth consumed and and thereby trade-off query completeness for timeliness. We have left this optimization to future work.

3.2.3 Feature extraction on the phone

In MediaScope, feature extraction is performed on the mobile device by the Feature Extractor component of MSMobile[4]. This component extracts features for photos, as well as images extracted from videos. Even for high-end smartphone platforms, these are nontrivial computation tasks and some computation vs. accuracy trade-offs are required in order to achieve good performance. We now discuss these trade-offs.

Image Feature Extraction. The Samsung Galaxy S III (a high-end smartphone at the time of writing) can generate images with native resolution of 3264x2448. At this resolution, our CEDD feature extraction algorithm fails because of lack of memory on the device. One way to overcome this limitation is to resize the image to a smaller size and compute features on the smaller image.

As Figure 4(a) shows, the time to compute features (averaged over 300 images taken on the Galaxy SIII) can reduce significantly for different sizes, ranging from 4s for a resolution about 1/2 the native resolution to about 1s for 1/4 the native resolution. The cost of the resizing operation itself is about 250ms, as shown in Figure 4(b), roughly independent of the resized image size.

However, computing features on a smaller image trades off accuracy for reduced computation time. To explore this trade-off, we evaluated two queries to see how accuracy varies with resizing. Figure 4(c) shows the results for K-means clustering, whose error rate is obtained by dividing the total number mis-classified images

by the total number of images. This error rate is less than 5% for a 1280x768 resolution, but jumps to 20% for the 816x612 resolution. The error rate for K-nearest neighbor queries is defined as the ratio of incorrect images (relative to the full size) selected by feature vectors computed on a resized image and k, averaged over different values of k. In this case, the knee of the error curve occurs somewhere in between the resolution of 1280x960 and 1024x768 (figure omitted for space). Given these results, we use a resizing resolution of 1024x768 in our implementation as the best trade-off between computation time and accuracy.

Video frame extraction. The second major component of MSMobile's Feature Extractor is video frame extraction. Ideally, for videos, we would like to be able to extract every frame of the video and compute features for it. This turns out also to be computationally infeasible even on a high-end device, and one must perform a computation accuracy trade-off here as well, by subsampling the video to extract frames at a lower rate than full-motion video.

Figure 5 shows the total cost of frame extraction for videos of different durations. Clearly, for long videos, even are relatively modest sampling rate of 4 fps can incur a total processing time of 150 seconds! On the other hand, extracting a single frame takes on average 240 ms, regardless of frame rate or duration.

On the flip side, subsampling a video can introduce errors; successive frames, if they are far apart from each other, may miss important intervening content. Figure 6 shows the average distance in feature space between successive frames for videos of different durations and sampling frequencies. For context, our clustering algorithms have generally found that cluster diameters are at least about 20 units. At 0.5fps, the interframe distance is more than this number, but at 1 fps, it is less. More generally, 1 fps seems to be a good choice in the trade-off between computation time and accuracy, so our current prototype uses this value.

An alternative approach to feature extraction for videos would have been to *segment* a video on the mobile device and then select frames from within the segment. A segment roughly corresponds to a scene, so one might expect that frames within a segment might have similar feature vectors. We have left an exploration of this to future work.

3.2.4 Leveraging a Crowd-Sensing Framework

MediaScope leverages an existing, publicly available, crowd sensing programming framework called Medusa [23]. Medusa provides high-level abstractions for specifying the steps required to complete

---
[4]MSCloudQ also needs to implement the same feature extraction algorithm for a Top-K query. Since mobile devices are more constrained, we focus on feature extraction on these devices.

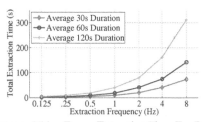

Figure 5—Average Video Frame Extraction Time For Different Duration and Frequency

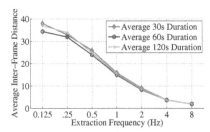

Figure 6—Average Inter-frame Feature-Space Distance

a crowd-sensing task: in our case, uploading the feature vectors can be modeled as a crowd-sensing task and so can the upload of selected media objects. Medusa employs a distributed runtime system that coordinates the execution of these tasks between mobile devices and a cloud service. In MediaScope, MSCloud uses Medusa to distribute tasks and collect the results; MSMobile consists of extensions to Medusa's runtime to implement the Feature Extractor and the Object Uploader.

However, in order to support MediaScope, we needed to extend the Medusa model, which was focused on tasks generated by human users. We also needed to make several performance modifications in Medusa. In the former category, we modified Medusa's programming language to selectively disable Medusa's recruitment feature and data privacy opt-in: these features require human interaction, and MediaScope assumes that participants have been recruited and have signed a privacy policy out-of-band. We also added a data delivery notification system that would allow Medusa's cloud runtime to deliver notification of data upload to external servers, such as MSCloudDB. In the second category, we modified Medusa's mobile device notification system, which originally used SMSs, to use Google's C2DM notification service, which greatly reduced the latency of task initiation on mobile devices. We also optimized several polling loops in Medusa to be interrupt-driven, so that we could hand-off data quickly to components within Medusa's runtime as well as to external servers.

4. EVALUATION

In this section, we evaluate the performance of MediaScope. Although MediaScope's credit assignment algorithm is optimal in a pseudo-polynomial sense, we are interested in its practical performance under bandwidth variability. Furthermore, in practice, since query arrival cannot be predicted ahead of time, the practical performance of MediaScope may deviate from the optimal. Finally, it is instructive to examine alternative scheduling mechanisms to quantify the performance benefits of MediaScope's algorithms. We are also interested in the overhead imposed by MediaScope; since timeliness is an essential attribute of many queries, system inefficiencies can impact query completeness.

All our experiments are conducted on a prototype of MediaScope. MSCloud is written mainly in Python; PHP and Python are used for MSCloudQ web interface. The implementation of MSCloud is about 4300 lines of PHP and Python code, and MSMobile requires about 1150 lines of C and Java code (measured using SLOCCount [28]).

Our experiments use commodity hardware, both for MSCloud and the mobile device. We use up to 8 Android phones, which are either the Galaxy Nexus or the Galaxy SIII. MSCloud runs on a Dell XPS 7100 (six-core AMD Phenom II X6 1055T 2.8 GHz processor and 6MB built-in cache).

Before describing our results, we give the reader some visual in-

tuition for the usefulness of MediaScope. Figures 7, 8, and 9 show the results of three different queries: a K nearest neighbor query, a Cluster Representatives query and a Spanner on a set of six groups of photos: a university campus, a garden, a view of the sky framed by trees, an athletics track, a supermarket, and a laboratory. Notice that the cluster representatives query identifies representatives from each of groups, while the Spanner extracts qualitatively different pictures, while the K nearest neighbor query extracts matching images as we might expect.

4.1 Query Completeness

In this section, we evaluate query completeness in the presence of concurrent queries.

Metrics and Methodology. Our metric for query completeness is the total credit associated with all the query results successfully uploaded before their timeliness bounds. We evaluate several *query mixes* (described below), with different concurrent queries of query types that arrive at different times and have different timeliness bounds. These queries are all posed on 320 images captured on 8 mobile devices.

Our experiments are conducted as follows. For each query mix, we first compute the results of each query and the credit assigned to each result object. This computation yields a *trace*, on each mobile device, of objects, their associated credits and the arrival time. We use this trace to replay the credit-based scheduling algorithm during repeated runs and report the average of 10 runs.

This trace-based methodology is also useful in comparing MediaScope's credit-based scheduling algorithm (henceforth, *MSC*) with several alternatives. For each alternative, we replay the trace for that particular scheduling algorithm. We consider the following alternatives: an *Omniscient* algorithm that knows about future query arrivals; a *Max Credit First (MCF)* that always selects the object with a maximum credit to upload; a *Round Robin (RR)* that allocates bandwidth fairly to each concurrent query so that, in each round, the object with the highest credit from each query is uploaded; and an *Earliest Deadline First (EDF)* scheduler that always schedules that object with the earliest timeliness bound first, breaking ties by credit. The Omniscient algorithm demonstrates the benefits of lookahead, while each of the other algorithms has at most one of MSC's features (timeliness-, credit-, and bandwidth-awareness).

In our experiments, each mobile device contains a number of images taken with its camera. These images are naturally of different sizes because they have different levels of compressibility. Furthermore, we make no attempt to control network variability; upload bandwidths in our experiments vary and MSC estimates upload bandwidth by measuring the average speed of the last upload (MSC's algorithm needs uses this estimate for $t(o)$).

Results. Our first experiment compares the performance of these alternatives for three different query mixes with different types of

Figure 7—K Nearest Neighbor Result

Figure 8—Cluster Representative

Figure 9—Spanner

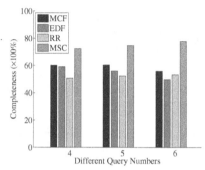
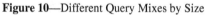

Figure 10—Different Query Mixes by Size

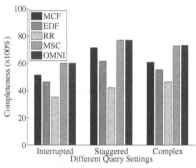

Figure 11—Different Query Mixes by Timeliness Bound

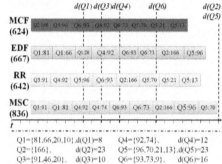

Q1={81,66,20,10},d(Q1)=8   Q4={92,74},   d(Q4)=12
Q2={166},   d(Q2)=23   Q5={96,70,21,13},d(Q5)=23
Q3={91,46,20},   d(Q3)=10   Q6={93,73,9},   d(Q6)=16

Figure 12—Sample Schedule Timeline

queries. The first mix contains 4 queries, namely, 1 Top-K, 1 Spanner, 1 Cluster Representative and 1 Common Interest. All the queries arrive at the same time but with different timeliness bounds; thus, in this experiment there are no future arrivals and we do not evaluate the Omniscient algorithm. The second mix adds one more Cluster Representative query to the first one, and the third is generated by adding one more Common Interest query. In each query mix, each query is assigned the same total credit.

Figure 10 shows the performance of various schemes. MSC achieves at least 75% completeness across all three query mixes, and its performance improves by 5% as the number of queries increases from 4 to 6. Although a 75% completeness rate seems pessimistic, we remind that reader than MSC is optimal, *so no other scheduling scheme could have done better than this*; in other words, for this query mix, this is the best result that could have been achieved.

Furthermore, MSC outperforms other schemes significantly. The superior performance of MSC comes from its timeliness-awareness, credit-awareness, and adaptivity to available bandwidth. By contrast, approaches that lack one or more of the features have much lower completeness rates. Thus, EDF does not take into account an object's credit, and thus might waste bandwidth on objects with an early deadline but small credit; on average, EDF achieves 55% completeness. RR is unaware of timeliness constraints, but uploads the result objects for each query in a round-robin fashion. It is comparable in performance to EDF, achieving 52% completeness on average. RR's poor performance arises from two factors: first, because it ignores timeliness constraints, it uses transmission opportunities by sometimes transmitting objects which could have been deferred without violating data timeliness bounds; second, RR gives equal transmission opportunities to queries, even though, on a given mobile device, one query may contain objects with far more credit than another query. MCF improves upon RR in the second

aspect, in that it always transmits the object with the highest credit first; in so doing, it achieves an average completion rate of 59% and is significantly better than EDF and RR. However, MCF is still noticeably worse than MSC, primarily because MCF ignores timeliness constraints and sometimes transmits objects that could have been deferred without violating timeliness bounds.

In order to get more insight into the relative performance of these schemes, we consider variants of the 6-query mix which have different combinations of arrival rates and deadlines. Figure 11 plots the results of these experiments.

In the first query mix, three of the six queries arrive first with the timeliness bound of 20 seconds. The remaining three queries arrive within three seconds, but have a relatively tight timeliness bound of 6 seconds. In this sense, they *interrupt* the first set of queries. This query mix is designed to demonstrate the benefits of timeliness-awareness. In this somewhat adversarial setting, MSC still outperforms other schemes but has a much lower completeness rate of about 60%. RR performs poorly, but EDF performs comparably to MCF; this is not surprising because EDF is timeliness-aware. Even so, EDF does not perform as well as MSC because it ignores credit values and uploads objects with lower credits unnecessarily.

In the second query mix, 6 queries with the same timeliness requirement arrive in a staggered fashion, with each query arriving three seconds after the previous query. This illustrates a setting where queries arrive frequently but the arrivals are not synchronized. In this setting, MSC achieves a completeness rate of nearly 80%, and, not surprisingly, MCF comes quite close with a completeness rate of 71%. Since all queries have identical timeliness bounds, it is not surprising that a credit-aware scheme like MCF performs well.

The third query mix represents a complex pattern where queries arrive at different times and have different deadlines. For this mix,

	Average Latency (ms)
MSCloud to Medusa	131
C2DM (send-to-receive)	150
Task Execution	67
Upload Scheduling	46
Medusa to MSCloud Image Transfer	67

Table 1—System Communication and App Running Overhead

	Average Latency (ms)
Query Parsing	24
Feature Vector Download	138
Medusa Server Interpretation	68
Spanner	89
K Clusters	52
K Nearest Neighbor	11
Query Result Response	54

Table 2—System Function Components Overhead

the performance advantages of MSC are clear, since this mix requires a scheduling scheme to be both credit and timeliness-aware.

Finally, for all these query mixes (Figure 11), MSC is comparable to the Omniscient scheme, which knows the arrival times of different queries. Intuitively, because MSC continuously adapts its transmission schedules when new queries arrive, it can make a different decision from Omniscient only at the times when queries arrive. To be more precise, say a new query arrives at time t: Omniscient might have scheduled an upload of an object for the new query starting at time t, but MSC has to wait until the object being uploaded at t finishes, before it updates its schedule. This difference can be fixed by adding *preemption* to the scheduler, aborting the current transmission if it does not have the highest priority; we have left this to future work.

To get some more insight into the differences between the scheduling algorithms, Figure 12 plots the timeline of decisions made by these algorithms for the 6-query mix when all queries arrive at the same time. The figure clearly shows that MSC is better able to use the available time to carefully schedule uploads so that completeness is maximized; MCF, having uploaded objects with high credits is unable to utilize the available time because the timeliness bound for the remaining objects has passed. EDF performs comparably to MCF, but, because it is credit-unaware, misses out on some transmission opportunities relative to MSC (e.g., MSC uploads Q3:91 first, but EDF does not).

In summary, our approach bridges the availability gap by extracting relevant photos and images dynamically from participating devices. The approach hinges on the observation that feature space similarity can be used to determine relevant media objects, and that image features are an extremely compact representation of the contents of an image. However, it is well-known that content based information retrieval exhibits a *semantic gap* [27]: feature-based similarity matching is oblivious to the semantic structures within an image, so the matching may not be perfect. In these cases, we rely on additional filtering by human intelligence (e.g., in our examples, the security officer, or the reporter). To put it another way, our approach may not always give the right answer, because of the semantic gap. To properly evaluate our approach, we need to conduct a user study. This is because, for example, determining whether the results of a spanner query really span a given corpus can be highly subjective. We have left this user study to future work.

4.2 System Overhead

Latency. Because MediaScope attempts to satisfy timeliness constraints, the efficiency of its implementation can impact query completeness; the less overhead incurred within the system, the greater the query completeness can be. To understand the efficiency of our system, we profiled the delays within the various components of MediaScope (Table 1). In an earlier section, we have discussed the cost of feature and frame extraction: these operations are not performed in the object retrieval path, so do not affect query timeliness.

As this table shows, the latency incurred for most components is modest; C2DM notifications take less than 1/6 second, and the

communication between MSCloud and Medusa takes about 1/8 second. Other components are under 70 ms.

Finally, latency within the MSCloudQ query engine is also moderate (Table 2). Even in our relatively un-optimized implementation, most components of query processing take less than 100ms, with the only exception being the download of feature vectors from MSCloudDB; we plan to optimize this component by caching feature vectors in memory.

These overhead numbers suggest that our current prototype may be able to sustain timeliness bounds of 10s or lower. Indeed, some of our experiments in the previous section have used 6s timeliness bounds.

Energy. The other component of overhead is energy expenditure. Frame extraction and feature extraction can take up to a second, or more, of CPU time. The energy cost, on a Motorola Droid (measured using a power meter), of frame extraction is 57 μAh, and of feature extraction (including resizing) is 331 μAh. We believe these energy costs are still reasonable: for feature extraction to consume even 10% of the Droid's battery capacity, a user would have to take more than 400 photos!

5. RELATED WORK

Perhaps the closest related piece of work to MediaScope is Crowd-Search [29], which attempts to search for the closest match image generated on a mobile device from among a set of images stored on a photo sharing service. Its focus, however, is complementary to MediaScope, and is on bridging the semantic gap inherent in feature-based image searches; most feature extraction methods do not understand the semantics of images, and CrowdSearch focuses on using human intelligence in near real-time to complete search tasks. MediaScope can use this capability to filter search results to bridge the semantic gap, but its focus is on supporting a richer query interface and enabling tighter timeliness constraints than might be possible with humans in the loop.

Also closely related is PhotoNet [25], which proposes an opportunistic image sharing and transmission capability in a delay tolerant network. PhotoNet uses similar image features to perform photo comparisons, but is otherwise very different from MediaScope in that the latter explicitly supports a query interface with timeliness constraints on queries.

MediaScope is informed and inspired by several pieces of work on techniques for content-based image retrieval, and image search on mobile devices.

In the former category are systems like Faceted Image Search [31], the Virage Image Search Engine [6] and ImgSeek [17], that support searches on a centralized database of images. MediaScope builds upon these search techniques, but unlike them, supports timely geometric queries over a distributed database of images and videos on mobile devices. Other work in content-based image retrieval has proposed clustering [8, 12], but has not explored the mobile device setting.

A second category of work has explored support for image search on a mobile device. For example, [19] discusses energy efficient feature extraction on a mobile device but supports on the local searches on the device, as does [30]. Other pieces of work have explored a client/server architecture for image search, but where the content is stored on the server [18, 14, 5]. By contrast, MediaScope supports searches on a cloud server, but where the content is stored on the mobile devices and is retrieved on demand.

Finally, tangentially related to MediaScope is work on automated or semi-automated annotation of images with context obtained from sensors [13, 26, 22]. MediaScope can use such annotations to support a broader range of queries, but we have left this to future work.

6. CONCLUSIONS

In this paper, we have discussed the MediaScope, a system that bridges the availability gap for visual media by supporting timely on-demand retrieval of images and video. MediaScope uses a credit-based timeliness-aware scheduling algorithm that optimizes query completeness, and its overheads are moderate. Much work remains, including optimizing the internals of the system to improve completeness, and supporting more geometric queries on visual media. Larger scale experiments using more mobile devices can help understand how well the system scales, and how network variability can impact query completeness. Finally, a user study focused on understanding how well MediaScope's query results bridge the semantic gap can help establish MediaScope's usefulness.

7. REFERENCES

[1] Cops using youtube to catch criminals.
    http://www.afterdawn.com/news/article.cfm/2007/03/04 /cops_using_youtube_to_catch_criminals.

[2] Facebook. http://www.facebook.com.

[3] Flickr. http://www.flickr.com.

[4] Instagram. http://www.instagram.com.

[5] I. Ahmad, S. Abdullah, S. Kiranyaz, and M. Gabbouj. Content-based image retrieval on mobile devices. In *Proc. of SPIE*, volume 5684, pages 255–264, 2005.

[6] J. Bach, C. Fuller, A. Gupta, A. Hampapur, B. Horowitz, R. Humphrey, R. Jain, and C. Shu. The virage image search engine: An open framework for image management. In *SPIE Storage and Retrieval for Image and Video Databases IV*, pages 76–87, 1996.

[7] J. Blazewicz, K. H. Ecker, E. Pesch, G. Schmidt, and J. Weglarz. *Handbook on Scheduling: From Theory to Applications*. Springer, 2007.

[8] D. Cai, X. He, Z. Li, W. Ma, and J. Wen. Hierarchical clustering of www image search results using visual, textual and link information. In *Proc. of the 12th annual ACM international conference on Multimedia*, pages 952–959. ACM, 2004.

[9] S. Chatzichristofis and Y. Boutalis. Cedd: color and edge directivity descriptor: a compact descriptor for image indexing and retrieval. *Computer Vision Systems*, pages 312–322, 2008.

[10] S. Chatzichristofis and Y. Boutalis. Fcth: Fuzzy color and texture histogram-a low level feature for accurate image retrieval. In *Ninth International Workshop on Image Analysis for Multimedia Interactive Services. WIAMIS'08.*, pages 191–196. IEEE, 2008.

[11] S. Chatzichristofis, Y. Boutalis, and M. Lux. Selection of the proper compact composite descriptor for improving content

[12] based image retrieval. In *Proc. of the 6th IASTED International Conference*, volume 134643, page 064, 2009.

[12] Y. Chen, J. Wang, and R. Krovetz. Content-based image retrieval by clustering. In *Proc. of the 5th ACM SIGMM international workshop on Multimedia information retrieval*, pages 193–200. ACM, 2003.

[13] M. Davis, N. V. House, J. Towle, S. King, S. Ahern, C. Burgener, D. Perkel, M. Finn, V. Viswanathan, and M. Rothenberg. Mmm2: mobile media metadata for media sharing. In *Proc. of CHI'05 extended abstracts on Human factors in computing systems*, pages 1335–1338. ACM, 2005.

[14] M. Gabbouj, I. Ahmad, M. Amin, and S. Kiranyaz. Content-based image retrieval for connected mobile devices. In *Proc. of Second International Symposium on Communications, Control and Signal Processing (ISCCSP)*. Citeseer, 2006.

[15] M. R. Garey and D. S. Johnson. *Computers and Intractability: A Guide to the Theory of NP-Completeness*. W.H. Freeman and Company, 1979.

[16] J. Huang, S. Kumar, M. Mitra, W. Zhu, and R. Zabih. Image indexing using color correlograms. In *Proc. of IEEE Computer Society Conference on Computer Vision and Pattern Recognition(CVPR'97)*, pages 762–768. IEEE, 1997.

[17] C. Jacobs, A. Finkelstein, and D. Salesin. Fast multiresolution image querying. In *Proc. of the 22nd annual conference on Computer graphics and interactive techniques*, pages 277–286. ACM, 1995.

[18] J.S.Hare and P. Lewis. Content-based image retrieval using a mobile device as a novel interface. In *Electronic Imaging 2005*, pages 64–75. International Society for Optics and Photonics, 2005.

[19] K. Kumar, Y. Nimmagadda, Y. Hong, and Y. Lu. Energy conservation by adaptive feature loading for mobile content-based image retrieval. In *ACM/IEEE International Symposium on Low Power Electronics and Design (ISLPED'08)*, pages 153–158. IEEE, 2008.

[20] A. Lipkus. A proof of the triangle inequality for the tanimoto distance. *Journal of Mathematical Chemistry*, 26(1):263–265, 1999.

[21] M. Lux and S. Chatzichristofis. Lire: lucene image retrieval: an extensible java cbir library. In *Proceeding of the 16th ACM international conference on Multimedia*, pages 1085–1088. ACM, 2008.

[22] C. Qin, X. Bao, R. R. Choudhury, and S. Nelakuditi. Tagsense: a smartphone-based approach to automatic image tagging. In *Proc. of the 9th international conference on Mobile systems, applications, and services(Mobisys'11)*, pages 1–14. ACM, 2011.

[23] M. Ra, B. Liu, T. L. Porta, and R. Govindan. Medusa: A programming framework for crowd-sensing applications. In *Proc. of the 10th international conference on Mobile systems, applications, and services(Mobisys'12)*, pages 337–350. ACM, 2012.

[24] T. Tanimoto. *An elementary mathematical theory of classification and prediction*. International Business Machines Corporation, 1958.

[25] M. Uddin, H. Wang, F. Saremi, G. Qi, T. Abdelzaher, and T. Huang. Photonet: a similarity-aware picture delivery service for situation awareness. In *IEEE 32nd Real-Time Systems Symposium (RTSS'11)*, pages 317–326. IEEE, 2011.

[26] W. Viana, J. B. Filho, J. Gensel, M. Villanova-Oliver, , and H. Martin. Photomap: from location and time to

Demo Abstract: Networking Algorithms on a Resource-Limited Distributed Mobile Embedded System

Mahdi Asadpour
Computer Engineering and Networks Laboratory
ETH Zurich, Switzerland
mahdi.asadpour@tik.ee.ethz.ch

Raymond Oung
Institute for Dynamic Systems and Control
ETH Zurich, Switzerland
roung@ethz.ch

ABSTRACT

This work addresses communication challenges associated with computationally limited distributed embedded systems. Methods for overcoming these challenges are implemented and tested on a robotics testbed called the Distributed Flight Array (DFA). The DFA consists of distributed computational units that can be assembled at random into a wired and/or wireless mesh network. Coordinate control of the DFA such as driving and flying, which is discussed in previous work, demonstrates successful implementation of various communication tasks in a resource constrained platform.

Categories and Subject Descriptors

C.2 [**Computer-Communication Networks**]: Distributed Systems—*Distributed applications*; I.2 [**ARTIFICIAL INTELLIGENCE**]: Robotics—*Autonomous vehicles; Sensors*

General Terms

Design, Experimentation

Keywords

Distributed Mobile Embedded Systems; Networking Algorithms; Communication Testbed

1. INTRODUCTION

This work develops and/or improves upon existing lightweight, robust, scalable communication/networking techniques for a distributed mobile embedded system. Our algorithms are implemented and validated on a robotics testbed called the Distributed Flight Array (DFA), which has been developed at ETH Zurich for investigating techniques in this area [4], see Figure 1.

The DFA consists of modular units that can drive on the ground, dock with their peers, and fly together in a coordinated fashion. Each unit is equipped with a microcontroller and a set of communication peripherals that enable it to communicate with its peers. Coordination between units over this network is essential in order to achieve coordinated tasks such as driving and flying together. Using this testbed, we are able to abstract challenging, real-world

Figure 1: The DFA is composed of interconnected units that communicate with one another in order to perform coordinated tasks such as flying.

issues that are likely to be encountered when developing the next generation of distributed embedded systems.

To be able to perform coordinated tasks, some of the most fundamental issues in networking need to be addressed, such as intercommunication between units, global topology discovery, and global time synchronization. The major contributions of our work include:

1. Design and validation of a variety of fundamental networking tasks suitable for a majority of resource-constrained distributed embedded systems, and

2. Infrastructure for real-time monitoring of the testbed.

2. HARDWARE DESCRIPTION

The testbed consists of modular units, each of which has, besides necessary sensors, six electro-mechanical interfaces enabling it to communicate with up to six neighbors. Each interface allows for full-duplex communication at 115.2 kbit/s between units over a standard universal asynchronous receiver/transmitter (UART) wired interface. The underlying communication infrastructure is therefore similar to a mesh network.

Also available on each interface is an infrared (IR) transceiver, which is used for half-duplex wireless communication at 115.2 kbit/s when units are physically separated. A multi-cast wireless system operating on a 2.4 GHz carrier band frequency is used to communicate with the units from a base station.

Handling all of the computation is a single onboard 72 MHz ARM-based 32-bit microcontroller (ST Microelectronics STM32F103x) with firmware that was developed in-house. This microcontroller resides on a custom designed printed circuit board that interfaces with all of the required peripherals.

3. COMMUNICATION

Our communication infrastructure was designed from the ground up and is implemented on board a unit's microcontroller. The resource limitation of the system demands lightweight solutions with efficient implementations.

3.1 Architecture

The communication infrastructure is implemented in three layers (for details see [1]):

1. Data link layer: In the data link layer, communication is performed in an *unreliable, but frequent* manner along with an addition-based modular checksum for error detection.

2. Network layer: derives its packet structure from the one used in IP networks, keeping only the essential fields including addresses, sequence numbers, and time-to-live (TTL). Flooding and a simplified version of the Open Shortest Path First (OSPF) [3] routing algorithms are implemented to send data from one unit to others in an effective way.

3. Application layer: handles the packet payload for accomplishing tasks such as global topology discovery and time synchronization discussed in the following subsection.

This layering is for modularity and has some resemblance to the TCP/IP protocol stack.

3.2 Applications

The previously outlined infrastructure enables various capabilities, some of which include:

- *Global Topology Discovery*:
  Units that are connected can automatically determine their local network topology by *pinging* each of their intercommunication interfaces. This local network list is then forwarded to every unit in the network. Each unit accumulates this information in order to compile the global network topology. This network topology can then be mapped to its physical configuration, which is a parameter that is needed for performing coordinated actions [4].

- *Time Synchronization*:
  We employ the *mini-sync* protocol described in [5], which provides tight, deterministic bounds on offset and clock drift, and features low complexity in processing, storage, and network bandwidth. Time synchronization is needed, for example, in data fusion and scheduling.

- *Real-Time Monitoring & Teleoperation*:
  Each unit can route packets wirelessly to a base station over a multi-cast network for logging/debugging purposes. On the base station (e.g. a desktop computer),

these packets are then sent to a front-end user interface for visualization. On the other hand, command packets can be sent from the base station to the units for feedback from external sensors and/or teleoperation.

4. DEMONSTRATION

During this demonstration, we will discuss and present the successful implementation and integration of our communication infrastructure and applications on the testbed. This will be an interactive exhibit: an audience member will teleoperate units on the ground and assemble several units together. The units will then perform some tasks including online data fusion as described in [2], which will be visualized on a base station computer.

This is only made possible through the various networking capabilities described previously. Such a successful demonstration conveys: (1) the functionality of the underlying communication infrastructure; (2) validates our global topology discovery algorithm; (3) time synchronization across the network, which is needed for distributed sensing, state estimation, and control; (4) real-time monitoring of the system and teleoperation. In addition, each unit will be individually controlled over a wireless interface (e.g. joystick).

(Demonstrative videos are available online at http://www.idsc.ethz.ch/Research_DAndrea/DFA.)

5. CONCLUSIONS

This work explores the challenges of designing and implementing networking algorithms for a real-time distributed embedded system. A variety of fundamental networking tasks were designed and/or validated on a hardware testbed.

Acknowledgements

This work is funded by the Swiss National Science Foundation (SNSF).

6. REFERENCES

[1] M. Asadpour. Distributed Flight Array: A software perspective. Technical report. http://www.tik.ee.ethz.ch/~amahdi/papers/dfa.pdf, Institute for Dynamic Systems and Control (IDSC), ETH Zurich, Jan. 2011.

[2] M. Kriegleder, R. Oung, and R. D'Andrea. Distributed altitude and attitude estimation from multiple distance measurements. In *Proceedings of the IEEE/RSJ*, pages 3626–3632, Portugal, Oct. 2012.

[3] J. Moy. Open shortest path first version 2. Technical report, STD 54, RFC 2328, April 1998.

[4] R. Oung and R. D'Andrea. The Distributed Flight Array. *Mechatronics*, 21(6):908–917, Sept. 2011.

[5] S. Yoon, C. Veerarittiphan, and M. Sichitiu. Tiny-Sync: Tight time synchronization for wireless sensor networks. *ACM Transactions on Sensor Networks (TOSN)*, 3(2), June 2007.

Demo Abstract: EnergyLab - Building Energy Testbed for Demand-Response

Madhur Behl, Neel Shah, Larry Vadakedathu, Dan Wheeler and Rahul Mangharam
Department of Electrical and Systems Engineering
University of Pennsylvania
{mbehl,shahneel,vlarry,dwheeler,rahulm}@seas.upenn.edu

ABSTRACT

A building testbed for design and evaluation of energy efficient control and demand response strategies for real buildings is presented. The testbed is a scaled down model of a centralized Heating, Ventilation and Air Conditioning (HVAC) and lighting system. Sensing and control in the tesbed is achieved using the standard Building Automation and Control Network protocol. A MATLAB based front-end can be used to run and observe experiments.

Categories and Subject Descriptors

B.1.0 [**Hardware**]: Control Structures and Microprogramming—*Algorithms, Design, Experimentation*

Keywords

Demand Response, Energy-Efficient Buildings,HVAC

1. INTRODUCTION

From peak power reduction to emergency grid response; reliable and cost effective solutions for demand response (DR) in buildings have become exceedingly important for both building operators and utility companies. Time based electricity pricing like real-time pricing, critical peak pricing and other such variants further incentivize adoption of faster, efficient and predictable DR strategies.

Successful implementation of any DR strategy in a building involves significant time and economic investment for auditing, recommissioning and retrofitting the building and enabling it to respond to electricity pricing signals and the state of the grid. Although simulation based analysis for buildings presents a viable approach for evaluating demand response strategies; the performance achieved through simulations alone are often limited and yield optimistic results due to deviations from realistic physical models and simplified assumptions.

We have built EnergyLab- a building energy testbed which can facilitate evaluation of energy efficient control and demand response strategies for real buildings. The testbed makes it easy to run controlled and realistic experiments on buildings under different scenarios and at faster time scales than real buildings. The testbed contains a scaled down model of a centralized HVAC system, sensing and control

Figure 1: EnergyLab- Building Energy Testbed shown inside its insulating enclosure

using BACnet and a MATLAB based front-end that can be used to run and observe experiments.

1.1 HVAC operation in buildings

At the heart of every HVAC system is the Air Handler Unit (AHU) which has three main functions:

1. supply conditioned air to the zones using a fan

2. pull air back from the zones using another fan &

3. allow for the ability to recycle air back into the zones.

In real buildings, chilled water supplied by condensers or chiller plants is used to cool and condition (for humidity and particulates) air inside an AHU. This is done by means of flow control valves and heat exchanging coils which control the temperature of air in the AHU. The AHU distributes the conditioned air to different zones in the building through a series of ducts and plenums with Variable Air Volume (VAV) terminal devices at the ends. A VAV device consists of dampers which help to regulate the flow of chilled

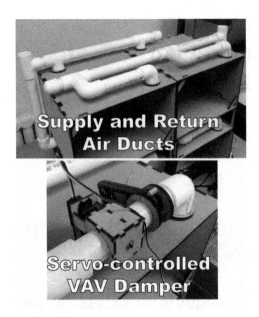

Figure 2: Custom built duct work and servo controlled VAV dampers

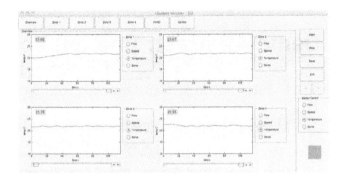

Figure 3: Testbed dashboard shows the state of the zones in real-time

air into a zone. The thermostat inside a zone controls the damper position of the VAV, and hence the flow of chilled air into the zone in order to maintain the desired temperature in the zone. Return air from each zone is collected and a fraction of it is mixed with fresh outside air before it is reconditioned and circulated back into the zones.

1.2 Testbed HVAC operation

The test bed (Fig 1) has been designed to closely mimic the operation of HVAC and lighting in a building. The following are the salient features of the testbed:

1. An AHU complete with heat exchange coils, temperature control of supply air and mixing of outside air and return air.

2. Supply and return ducts with flow sensing, flow control and mixing valves.

3. A fully functional VAV device in each zone with air flow sensors to measure air flow rate and servo controlled dampers to regulate the air flow.

4. Dimmable lights in each zone to account for zone lighting.

5. HVAC devices within the testbed communicate over BACnet, a standard buildings communication protocol.

6. The entire testbed is insulated from its surroundings by an enclosure which can also generate controlled outside environment for the building.

7. A front-end which shows real-time sensor and power consumption data for the building, allows full control of actuators in the test bed and allows easy configuration of test bed experiments through MATLAB

8. Support for remote operation and experiments which can be configured, run and observed without being physically present near the testbed.

The testbed is a scaled model of a two-floored building with four zones. A series of powerful blowers act as the AHU fan and push the air through the ducts and into the zones. Another set of blowers suck the air back from the zones and make it available for mixing and recirculating. Nearly 15 feet of elaborate PVC duct work is laid out which brings chilled/warm air into the zones as well as carries out air from each zone (Fig 2). We make use of position servo-controlled dampers for the VAV system (Fig 2). There is one VAV damper per zone placed at the supply air inlet.

It is necessary that the temperature dynamics of the zones is realistic and closely resembles the dynamics of a real buildings. This is achieved by minimizing leakages through ducts and linkages and keeping the entire testbed in a large enclosure, thereby insulated from its surroundings.

Sensing and control of supply air temperature, air flow and zone temperature occurs through the BACnet protocol. Each zone contains a temperature sensor, an airflow sensor which send data to an embedded micro-controller running a BACnet server. The micro-controller also controllers the damper position through a servo motor. The sensor data is gathered and displayed in real-time on the front-end implemented in MATLAB (Fig 3). Using the front-end the user can also control any actuator in the tesbed and can design a controller for the building within MATLAB.

Fine grained control of both HVAC and lighting makes this testbed a useful platform for evaluating demand response and energy-efficient control strategies for building operation.

2. USER EXPERIENCE

For the demo we will setup the testbed as described in the abstract and as shown in the figures. We will walk the audience through the workings of the testbed and describe how HVAC systems work.

1. The operation of the test-bed alone by itself is quite exciting to watch.

2. Using the front-end the audience can interact directly with the testbed by changing set-points and damper positions and observing the change on the dashboard.

3. Since all HVAC devices in the testbed communicate via BACnet, we will demonstrate the capability to setup, read and write device properties using BACnet.

4. Using real electricity pricing signals as an input to the building we will demonstrate different demand response strategies on the testbed.

Demo Abstract: A Radio Tomographic System for Real-Time Multiple People Tracking

Maurizio Bocca
The University of Utah
ECE department
Salt Lake City, UT, USA
maurizio.bocca@utah.edu

Ossi Kaltiokallio
Aalto University
School of Electrical Eng.
Espoo, Finland
ossi.kaltiokallio@aalto.fi

Neal Patwari
The University of Utah
ECE department
Salt Lake City, UT, USA
npatwari@ece.utah.edu

ABSTRACT

A radio tomographic (RT) system uses the received signal strength (RSS) measurements collected on the links of a wireless mesh network composed of low-power transceivers in order to form real-time images of the attenuation field of the monitored area. These images indicate the position of people, without requiring them to participate in the localization effort by wearing or carrying any electronic device. Accurate localization and tracking of multiple people in real-time is required in several real-world applications, such as ambient-assisted living, tactical operations, and pedestrian traffic analysis in stores. In these scenarios, RT systems must perform reliably also a) when the number of targets is not known a priori and varies over time, and b) when people interact, i.e., have intersecting trajectories, in the monitored area. We demonstrate a RT system which tackles all of these challenges and provides accurate tracking of a varying and unknown number of people (both stationary and mobile) in real-time.

Categories and Subject Descriptors

C.3 [**Special-Purpose and Application-Based Systems**]: Real-time and embedded systems; I.5.4 [**Pattern Recognition**]: Applications—*Computer Vision*

Keywords

Radio tomography; Device-free localization; Received signal strength; Multiple target tracking;

1. INTRODUCTION

Radio tomographic (RT) systems are RF sensor networks [7] capable of localizing and tracking people in indoor environments without requiring them to carry or wear any electronic device. These systems use the received signal strength (RSS) measurements collected on the links of a wireless mesh network composed of low-power transceivers in order to form

images of the change in the propagation field of the monitored area due to the presence of people - a process known as radio tomographic imaging (RTI) [9]. These images can be processed as *frames* of a video showing the position and movements of multiple people, as shown in Figure 1. The RT system we present in this demonstration applies machine vision methods adapted to the characteristics of RTI to track the *blobs* corresponding to real people a) when their number is not known a priori and varies over time, and b) when these have intersecting trajectories [2].

RT systems can be used in several applications, including smart buildings and perimeter surveillance, ambient-assisted living and elder care, and tactical and rescue operations. Compared to other sensing technologies applied for indoor localization, such as infrared, ultrasonic range finders, ultra-wideband (UWB) radios and video cameras, RT systems provide several advantages: they work in the dark and can penetrate smoke and walls; they are less invasive in domestic environments than video camera networks; they are significantly less expensive than UWB transceivers; their installation and maintenance time is minimal.

Previous works in this area [3, 5, 10] have mostly focused on localizing a single person, while the few existing methods for multiple people tracking are either non-real time, assume that the number of targets is fixed and known a priori, or do not attempt to track people having intersecting trajectories [8, 6]. However, the real-world scenarios in which RT systems can be used require them a) to correctly estimate the number of people to be tracked as they enter and exit the monitored area, b) to be able to track people even when they have intersecting trajectories, and c) to do this in real-time. The RT system we demonstrate tackles all of these challenges.

A RT system is composed of several radio transceivers, placed at known positions, which form a wireless mesh network. These RF *sensors* collect RSS measurements which are then processed in order to estimate a discretized image of the change in the propagation field of the monitored area caused by the presence of people. People moving in a space where wireless transceivers are communicating affect the propagation of the radio signals by shadowing, reflecting, diffracting or scattering a subset of their multipath components. In uncluttered environments, where line-of-sight (LoS) communication among the transceivers is predominant, a person obstructing a link line generally decreases the measured RSS. However, in cluttered environments, where multipath propagation is predominant, the change in RSS due to the presence of a person on the link line is more un-

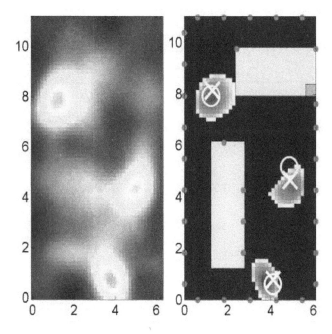

Figure 1: On the left, the original RT image formed by the system when three people are located in the monitored area. On the right, the RT image after being processed by the machine vision methods used to track multiple people. The dots represent the radio transceivers, the white circles the true position of people, the white crosses their estimated position, and the grey rectangles furniture present in the area.

predictable, as the RSS can also remain constant or increase. In addition, due to the multipath propagation, people can affect the RSS also when located far away from the link line. To mitigate the undesired effects of multipath propagation, our system exploits frequency diversity in order to reduce the noise of the formed RT images and facilitate multiple people tracking [4].

The radio transceivers composing our RT system continuously collect RSS measurements on all the links of the network on different frequency channels through a multi-channel TDMA token-passing protocol. The measurements are then weighted differently based on the fade level [8, 1] of the frequency channel on which they were collected. The system forms a new RT image at the completion of each round of communication. Machine vision methods adapted to the characteristics of RTI process the RT images in real-time to detect and track the blobs (see Figure 1) corresponding to people located in the monitored area. Due to measurement noise and the simultaneous presence of multiple people, objects and obstructions, spurious blobs (not corresponding to real people) can appear in the image. For the same reasons, blobs corresponding to real people can also temporarily disappear from the image. These factors increase the difficulty of multiple people tracking, especially when these have intersecting trajectories. In our system, we apply computationally light-weight, yet effective methods providing real-time execution and accurate tracking also in the case of intersecting trajectories.

2. DEMONSTRATION

In our demonstration, battery-powered radio transceivers are deployed on all four sides of an area in which people are free to move individually or interact with other people. The sensors are placed on podiums at a height of one meter. A laptop is used to collect the RSS measurements of all the links of the wireless network and execute in real-time the image estimation and tracking algorithms. The display of this laptop shows in real-time the RT images formed by the system and the position estimates of the people located in the deployment space. The system indicates also at all times the number of people that are located in the monitored area, detecting in real-time their entry and exit.

3. REFERENCES

[1] M. Bocca, O. Kaltiokallio, and N. Patwari. *Radio Tomographic Imaging for Ambient Assisted Living.* Springer - Communications in Computer and Information Science 362, 2013.

[2] M. Bocca, O. Kaltiokallio, N. Patwari, and S. Venkatasubramanian. Multiple target tracking with RF sensor networks. *IEEE Trans. Mobile Computing.* submitted (Nov. 2012).

[3] X. Chen, A. Edelstein, Y. Li, M. Coates, M. Rabbat, and M. Aidong. Sequential monte carlo for simultaneous passive device-free tracking and sensor localization using received signal strength measurements. In *ACM/IEEE Information Processing in Sensor Networks (IPSN)*, April 2011.

[4] O. Kaltiokallio, M. Bocca, and N. Patwari. Enhancing the accuracy of radio tomographic imaging using channel diversity. IEEE, 2012. 9th IEEE International Conference on Mobile Ad hoc and Sensor Systems (IEEE MASS 2012), October 2012.

[5] O. Kaltiokallio, M. Bocca, and N. Patwari. Follow @grandma: Long-term device-free localization for residential monitoring. In *Local Computer Networks Workshops (LCN Workshops), 2012 IEEE 37th Conference on*, pages 991 –998, oct. 2012.

[6] S. Nannuru, Y. Li, Y. Zeng, M. Coates, and B. Yang. Radio frequency tomography for passive indoor multi-target tracking. *IEEE Transactions on Mobile Computing*, PP(99):1, 2012.

[7] N. Patwari and J. Wilson. RF sensor networks for device-free localization and tracking. *Proceedings of the IEEE*, 98(11):1961–1973, Nov. 2010.

[8] J. Wilson and N. Patwari. A fade level skew-Laplace signal strength model for device-free localization with wireless networks. *IEEE Trans. Mobile Computing.* appeared online 12 May 2011.

[9] J. Wilson and N. Patwari. Radio tomographic imaging with wireless networks. *Mobile Computing, IEEE Transactions on*, 9(5):621 –632, may 2010.

[10] Y. Zheng and A. Men. Through-wall tracking with radio tomography networks using foreground detection. In *WCNC*, pages 3278–3283, 2012.

Demo Abstract: A Magnetic Field-based Appliance Metering System

Niranjini Rajagopal †   Suman Giri ‡   Mario Berges ‡   Anthony Rowe †

† Electrical and Computer Engineering Department
‡ Civil and Environmental Engineering Department
Carnegie Mellon University
Pittsburgh, PA 15213

{niranjir,sgiri,agr,mberges}@andrew.cmu.edu

ABSTRACT

In this demonstration, we show an energy measurement system that estimates the energy consumption of individual appliances using a wireless sensor network consisting of contactless electromagnetic field (EMF) sensors deployed near each appliance, and a whole-house power meter [1]. The EMF sensor can detect appliance state transitions within close proximity based on magnetic field fluctuations. Data from these sensors are then relayed back to the main meter using a low-latency wireless sensor networking protocol, where changes in the total power consumption of the house are used to determine the power usage of individual appliances. The sensors are low-cost, easy to deploy and are able to detect current changes associated with the appliance from a few inches away making it possible to externally monitor in-wall wiring to devices like overhead lights or heavy machinery that might operate on multiple phases of the AC distribution system of the building. Appliance-level energy data provide continuous feedback to end users about their consumption patterns and provide building managers accurate information that can be used to target the most effective update and retrofit strategies.

Categories and Subject Descriptors

J.2 [**Physical Sciences and Engineering**]: Miscellaneous

Keywords

CPS, Energy Metering, Sensor Networks

1. SYSTEM DESCRIPTION

Figure 1 shows an overview of the general system architecture which consists of a three-phase meter used for overall mains power metering, plug-meter devices used for ground-truth data collection and the EMF event detectors. These components are connected to a networked backend and the real-time results are displayed on an application running on a personal computer (PC). The hardware components and the appliance metering algorithm are described in the following sections.

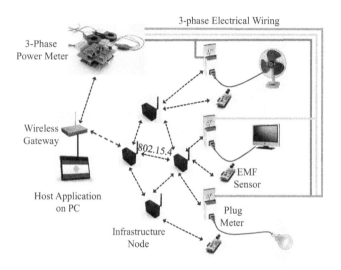

Figure 1: Network Architecture

1.1 Three-Phase Meter

We designed a custom three-phase power meter, shown in Figure 2, which employs the cutting edge ADE7878 energy metering chip from Analog Devices, specifically to collect high resolution data which can be correlated with events from our EMF detectors. Off-the-shelf energy meters often make it difficult to capture high-speed raw waveforms. In contrast, our meter samples both the current and the voltage on each phase at 1KHz, and uses an on-chip DSP to compute true, apparent and reactive power, as well as several other energy metrics. The main board is powered from either 120 or 240 VAC and can sense voltages as large as 600VAC. Current sensing uses split-core current transformers and both voltage and current values are read at 24-bit resolution. The overall range and accuracy values depend on the particular configuration of the current transformer used, but this configuration typically meets the 0.2% accuracy requirements for most utility billing standards.

1.2 Plug Meter

We use the FireFly plug meter [2] for ground-truth validation and for devices that can benefit from remote actuation. Each plug meter, shown in Figure 3 contains the ability to monitor and control two electrical outlets using wireless communication. The meter uses an efficient switching power supply that draws less than 0.1 watts ensuring that it does

Figure 2: Wireless Three-Phase Circuit-Panel Meter

Figure 3: Plug-Level Meter

not unnecessarily increase the building power consumption. The meter measures power and energy consumed by an appliance. We use plug meters solely for ground-truth measurements and hence they would not be required in a real deployment.

1.3 EMF Sensor

The core principle behind the EMF event detector is that an alternating current (AC) flowing through a conductor generates a corresponding magnetic field. The EMF event detector senses an appliance state change (transition between *on* and *off*), by monitoring changes in nearby electromagnetic fields. Typically AC wires run as parallel pairs and hence most of the magnetic fields cancel out. However, imbalances in wires and stray currents flowing on ground lines as well as through appliances produce a significant magnetic field. The amplitude of this field is generally small (millivolts), but if sufficiently amplified, one can reconstruct the original source to a reasonable degree of approximation.

In [3], the authors present ViridiScope which uses indirect sensing of appliances to estimate per-appliance energy consumption. This work suggests using magnetic field sensors to estimate the power consumption of a device. Due to the difficulty in estimating power consumption without device and installation-specific calibration, our EMF event detector shown in Figure 4 focuses on detecting appliance state changes rather than trying to directly measure power. The magnetic field is detected using an instrumentation amplifier (INA) and an inductor. In order to increase robustness on the magnetic field sensing front-end, an MSP430 controller performs continuous automatic-gain adjustment to keep the

Figure 4: EMF event detector stacked on FireFly3 sensor node.

peak-to-peak range of the signal at approximately $\frac{V_{dd}}{2}$ to avoid clipping while still capturing events of interest. Each EMF sensor transmits its auto-gain value every 640ms. Significant changes in this value would indicate that a nearby appliance has changed its power consumption.

1.4 Appliance Metering

When the EMF sensor detects an event, it sends a time-stamped message to the gateway. Our algorithm then determines the change in power of the three-phase meter across a time window before and after the event. We assume that the power consumption for this appliance remains constant when the appliance is *on*. This constant value is found by averaging the absolute value of the power change during the *off-on* and *on-off* transitions, and the energy is found by integrating the power for the *on* period.

2. DEMONSTRATION

Our demonstration consists of a setup similar to Figure 1. It consists of multiple portable appliances (Example - light bulb, fan, laptop and iron) connected to an electrical outlet, which is monitored by a three-phase energy meter. Each appliance is connected to the outlet through an individual plug-meter. An EMF sensor is placed in the proximity of the electrical cable connected to each appliance. The users can turn *on* and *off* the different appliances. Our real-time results are displayed on a Graphical User Interface on a PC. The results show the dis-aggregation of total energy from the three-phase meter into the energy consumed by the various appliances. The ground-truth, which is provided by the plug meter is shown for validation.

3. REFERENCES

[1] Rajagopal N., Giri S., Rowe A., Berges M. A Magnetic Field-based Appliance Metering System. *ICCPS*, April 2013.

[2] Rowe A., Berges M., Bhatia G., Goldman E., Rajkumar R., Soibelman L., Garrett J., Moura J. . Demonstrating Sensor Andrew: Large-Scale Campus-Wide Sensing and Actuation. *Demo Abstract, IPSN*, 2009.

[3] Kim Y., Schmid T., Charbiwala Z. M., and Srivastava M. B. Viridiscope: Design and implementation of a fine grained power monitoring system for homes. *UbiComp*, September 2009.

Demo Abstract - Netamorph: Field-Programmable Analog Arrays for Energy-Efficient Sensor Networks

Brandon Rumberg   Brandon M. Kelly   David W. Graham   Vinod Kulathumani

Lane Department of Computer Science and Electrical Engineering
West Virginia University
{brumberg, bkelly6}@mix.wvu.edu,
{david.graham, vinod.kulathumani}@mail.wvu.edu

ABSTRACT

The limited power budgets of sensor networks necessitate some level of in-network pre-processing to reduce communication overhead. The low power consumption of analog signal processing (ASP) is well-suited for this task. However, the quick adoption of this technology has been restrained by the fact that ASP implementation requires *a priori* knowledge of the application space. Our solution to this challenge is to enable run-time reconfiguration through the use of a field-programmable analog array (FPAA). In the same way that reconfigurable digital systems allow system designers to change the infrastructure of digital blocks, an FPAA allows an application developer to change the infrastructure of, and even tune, ASP blocks without circuit-level expertise. We will demonstrate that an FPAA can be used to (1) facilitate the use of ASP to reduce power consumption, and to (2) allow run-time reconfigurability to maximize ASP impact.

Categories and Subject Descriptors

B.7 [**Integrated Circuits**]: Miscellaneous; C.3 [**Special-purpose and Application-Based Systems**]: Real-time and embedded systems, Signal processing systems; B.8 [**Performance and Reliability**]: Miscellaneous

General Terms

Design, Performance, Measurement

Keywords

Analog Signal Processing; Field-Programmable Analog Array; Energy-Efficient; In-Network Processing; Sensor Networks

1. INTRODUCTION

Wireless sensor networks are capable of a myriad of tasks, from monitoring the integrity of critical infrastructure such as bridges, to biomedical applications capable of monitoring a person's vital signs. However, their deployment is impractical for many applications due to their limited power budget, which is mostly spent on communication [3, 4]. In-network pre-processing can help reduce this communication overhead. As we demonstrated in [5], analog signal processing (ASP) is one form of in-network pre-processing that can

be used to process a signal locally, provide event detection for wake-up scenarios, and more, all while consuming very little power. An ASP's implementation could be further improved by making the design reconfigurable, which would allow a single ASP to be used for a variety of applications and to be updated in the field as its application is redefined. To that end, we will expand upon our previous work by (1) including a field-programmable analog array (FPAA), similar to [1, 2], for added reconfigurability and by (2) utilizing an architecture that allows for more complex processing, and thus more discriminating detection.

2. NETAMORPH DESIGN

By utilizing an FPAA locally at individual nodes (Figure 1), an application developer can easily respond to the dynamic needs of the network. The FPAA can be configured to perform various processing tasks, thus reducing the information required to be transmitted. This reduction of transmitted information is significant from a power budget standpoint, because transmission is usually characterized as one of the most power-intensive tasks of a node. Also, an FPAA can be used to characterize and detect certain events, thus creating the frame-work for a wake-up circuit. This wake-up circuit can be used to keep the power-intensive digital portion of the mote in a low-power sleep state until a predefined event is detected.

Figure 2 illustrates the use of the FPAA for a detection task. In this example, the objective is to detect when the frequency of the input signal rises from 2kHz to 4kHz. Specifically, a detection pulse should be generated when signal content is present in the 4kHz band shortly after content was present in the 2kHz band. To perform this task, the FPAA was configured such that the spectral analysis stage decomposes the signal into 2kHz and 4kHz subbands. The subband processing stages were configured to delay the output of the 2kHz band and to trigger when content was simultaneously present in the 4kHz band and the delayed version of the 2kHz band, but not present in the non-delayed version of the 2kHz band. Successful detection is shown in the bottom pane of Figure 2.

Our FPAA architecture was constructed in a standard $0.5\mu m$ CMOS process available through MOSIS and is approximately $2.25mm^2$ in area. The FPAA can be reconfigured in 100ms through a TelosB mote. The device consists of two stages: a spectral-analysis stage and a subband processing stage. The spectral analysis stage is capable of filtering and/or finding the envelope of the signal. The signal is then passed to the subband processing stage which is capable of

IPSN'13, April 8–11, 2013, Philadelphia, Pennsylvania, USA.
ACM 978-1-4503-1959-1/13/04.

Field Programmable Analog Array

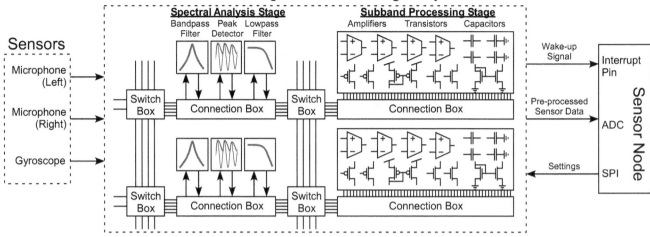

Figure 1: A sensor node equipped with a field-programmable analog array (FPAA). The FPAA can be reconfigured in run-time to perform event detection and pre-processing at a power consumption that is significantly lower than the mote's built in capabilities.

being reprogrammed to perform a myriad of tasks. In total, our FPAA has 1436 switches that can be configured to synthesize circuits with up to 40 distinct nets.

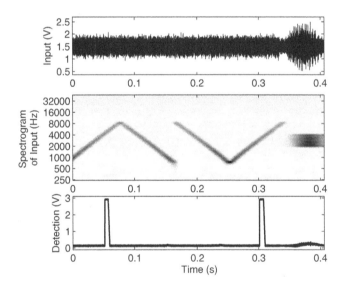

Figure 2: Example spectral analysis system implemented on the FPAA in which it is configured to detect a rising frequency in the 2-4kHz range. (Top, Middle) The input sinusoidal signal, which includes Gaussian noise, varies from 1kHz to 8kHz and concludes with an input of ten simultaneous sine waves with frequencies ranging from 2kHz to 4kHz. (Bottom) The output of the FPAA showing successful detection of the portions of the input signal where the frequency content was rising in the 2-4kHz range.

3. DEMONSTRATION

We will demonstrate the use of the FPAA for event detection and sensor pre-processing. To demonstrate these uses, we will show how a base station can send reconfiguration commands to a TelosB mote equipped with the Netamorph device. In addition to demonstrating the ability of the FPAA to implement complex signal processing tasks, we will allow conference attendees to interact with the FPAA themselves. We will demonstrate a simple user interface through which they can implement various processing tasks on the FPAA.

4. ACKNOWLEDGMENTS

This material is based upon work supported by the National Science Foundation under Award No. 1148815.

5. REFERENCES

[1] A. Basu, S. Brink, C. Schlottmann, S. Ramakrishnan, C. Petre, S. Koziol, F. Baskaya, C. M. Twigg, and P. Hasler. A floating-gate-based field-programmable analog array. *IEEE Journal of Solid-State Circuits*, 45(9):1781 –1794, Sept. 2010.

[2] E. K. F. Lee and P. G. Gulak. A CMOS field-programmable analog array. *IEEE Journal of Solid-State Circuits*, 26(12):1860 –1867, Dec. 1991.

[3] S. N. Pakzad, G. L. Fenves, S. Kim, and D. E. Culler. Design and implementation of scalable wireless sensor network for structural monitoring. *Journal of Infrastructure Systems*, 14(1):89–101, 2008.

[4] V. Raghunathan, C. Schurgers, and M. B. Srivatsava. Energy-aware wireless microsensor networks. *IEEE Signal Processing Magazine*, 19(2):40–50, Mar. 2002.

[5] B. Rumberg, D. W. Graham, and V. Kulathumani. Hibernets: Energy-efficient sensor networks using analog signal processing. In *Proceedings of IPSN*, 2010.

Demo Abstract: Distributed Debugging Architecture for Wireless Sensor Networks

Philipp Sommer
Autonomous Systems Laboratory
CSIRO ICT Centre, Brisbane, QLD, Australia
philipp.sommer@csiro.au

Branislav Kusy
Autonomous Systems Laboratory
CSIRO ICT Centre, Brisbane, QLD, Australia
brano.kusy@csiro.au

ABSTRACT

Limited visibility into the global network state renders testing and debugging sensor network applications a challenging task. Existing debugging methods are often non-intrusive and require modifications of the binary image. Hardware based debugging instrumentation such as JTAG has not been widely used beyond a single node, mainly due to its relatively high cost and lack of software support for distributed debugging. This demonstration presents a novel architecture for distributed debugging of wireless sensor networks using a low-cost extension board to access the on-chip debug module of the node's processor. Connecting several of those debug boards using a backbone network provides distributed control and monitoring of the sensor network in test.

Categories and Subject Descriptors

D.2.5 [**Software Engineering**]: Testing and Debugging—
distributed debugging, tracing

General Terms

Design, Experimentation

Keywords

Wireless Sensor Network, Tracing, Debugging, JTAG

1. INTRODUCTION

Debugging sensor networks is most challenging when deployed nodes are out of reach for debugging tools (*e.g.*, serial cable, JTAG adapter). Existing approaches provide debug instrumentation using additional software components and in-band control packets. Marionette [3] embeds remote procedure calls within TinyOS binaries to allow developers to call methods and read/write variables from a PC. Clairvoyant [4] is a source-level debugger for sensor networks that enables debugging operations such as memory inspection, watchpoints, and breakpoints. However, both tools create additional in-band control traffic and require to bundle the test application with additional debugging components, thus increasing both RAM and ROM size.

Most microcontrollers used on common sensor node platforms provide an integrated debugging port that can be ac-

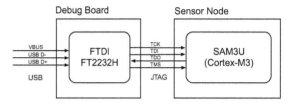

Figure 1: Hardware architecture of the debug board: The FT2232H chip converts I/O instructions sent over USB into physical JTAG signals.

cessed through a *JTAG* hardware adapter. JTAG provides versatile debugging support such as setting breakpoints, halting the microcontroller, and stepping through the program code. Due to the relatively high cost of JTAG adapter hardware and proprietary software that JTAG-enabled debuggers require, sensor network testbeds have not leveraged the powerful capabilities of debug modules so far. Recently, Tancreti et al. presented Aveksha [2], a debug extension board for the TelosB platform. Aveksha uses the on-board debugging chip to capture and log execution traces of an application for offline analysis.

This demonstration will showcase a novel debugging architecture for wireless sensor networks, which is completely distributed and operates in real-time. The key idea is to access the debugging port of sensor nodes from an *Observer* node co-located with each sensor node. The JTAG debug port provides non-intrusive methods for debugging and is independent of the operating system running on the sensor node. By monitoring and controlling observers from a central *Testbed Controller* instance, it becomes possible to halt, inspect, and resume nodes within a sensor network simultaneously.

2. DEBUG EXTENSION BOARD

We are using the Opal sensor node platform [1] to demonstrate the feasibility of our approach. The Opal node features an Atmel SAM3U microcontroller, which implements the ARM Cortex-M3 architecture. We developed a *Debug Board* to connect to the debug port of the Cortex-M3, as shown in Figure 1. At the core of the debug board is the FTDI FT2232H chip, which is a high-speed USB 2.0 (480Mb/s) to serial device supporting two separate channels. In addition to the UART protocol used by the Opal's serial port, the FTDI chip also provides a hardware engine to facilitate the implementation of synchronous serial protocols such as JTAG, SPI, or I2C. This allows the host controller

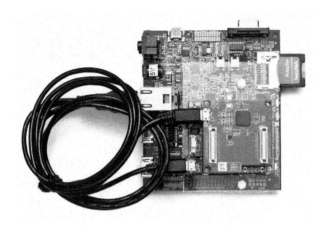

Figure 2: Testbed Observer node: The PandaBoard is connected through USB to the Opal sensor node and the Debug Board stacked on top of the Opal.

to communicate using the JTAG protocol by sending USB commands to the FT2232H chip. The Opal's Cortex-M3 core implements the ARMv7 debug architecture specification, which enables a debug adapter to determine and modify the state of the Cortex-M3 processor from the outside. To this end, the FT2232H chip connects to the JTAG port of the Cortex-M3. The USB host controlling the FT2232H chip can send JTAG instructions to halt, single step, or resume the processor. Furthermore, the processor state can be polled to determine if the core has been halted (*e.g.*, due to a breakpoint or exception). Furthermore, access to the internal system bus allows to read and write the memory and peripherals of the microcontroller. We employ the Open On-Chip Debugger (OpenOCD) [5] to generate the corresponding JTAG sequences to control and monitor the Opal node.

3. DISTRIBUTED DEBUGGING

We based our *Testbed Observer* node on the PandaBoard, a low-cost embedded Linux platform, which acts as a USB host for the debug board, as shown in Figure 2. To enable monitoring and control of several distributed observers, we use a Wi-Fi or Ethernet backbone network.

A central unit, the *Testbed Controller*, communicates with the observers using UDP packets, as shown in Figure 3. Each observer is listening for control packets from the controller, *e.g.*, to halt or resume the Opal node by sending the corresponding JTAG commands via OpenOCD. Furthermore, the observer can poll the status of memory blocks on the Opal and notify the controller upon detecting a change.

Our distributed debugging approach complements the existing set of debugging modalities for testbeds (*e.g.*, logging serial output, packet sniffing, GPIO pin monitoring, and power profiling) with the following additional debugging capabilities:

- **Control:** Ability to synchronously halt and resume the sensor network under test.

- **Inspection:** Read/write access to the system memory and peripherals for state inspection.

- **Tracing:** Non-intrusive tracing of internal node state (*e.g.*, global variables).

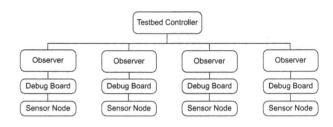

Figure 3: The Testbed Controller monitors several Observer nodes and can synchronously halt/resume all Sensor Nodes in the network.

Aggregating distributed monitoring and control capabilities at a single controller instance further provides the basic building blocks to provide novel high-level debugging modalities for wireless sensor networks. Non-intrusive tracing can be used to implement mechanisms for distributed assertion checking without the need for any additional in-band network traffic, while control and inspection capabilities allow implementation of network-wide snapshots of node state.

4. DEMONSTRATION HIGHLIGHTS

We will showcase our debugging architecture with an example network on the basis of three PandaBoard observers with corresponding Opal nodes and debug boards. The PandaBoards will be connected to the Testbed Controller (*i.e.*, a laptop) over Ethernet.

The interactive demo application will run on the Opal nodes. It will continuously read the light sensor at each node and disseminate sensor readings within the network. Nodes will aggregate those values and indicate the global state (*e.g.*, whether a user covers an individual light sensor with his hand) using their LEDs. The Testbed Controller will visualize the network state (sensor values, dissemination state, number of packets received) on the laptop's screen. Furthermore, users are encouraged to interact with the system by setting network-wide breakpoints (*e.g.*, when the sensor readings falls below a certain threshold) to inspect the node state.

5. REFERENCES

[1] R. Jurdak, K. Klues, B. Kusy, C. Richter, K. Langendoen, and M. Brunig. Opal: A Multiradio Platform for High Throughput Wireless Sensor Networks. *IEEE Embedded Systems Letters*, 3(4):121–124, Dec. 2011.

[2] M. Tancreti, M. S. Hossain, S. Bagchi, and V. Raghunathan. Aveksha: A Hardware-Software Approach for Non-intrusive Tracing and Profiling of Wireless Embedded Systems. In *Proceedings of the 9th ACM Conference on Embedded Networked Sensor Systems (SenSys)*, pages 288–301, 2011.

[3] K. Whitehouse, G. Tolle, J. Taneja, C. Sharp, S. Kim, J. Jeong, J. Hui, P. Dutta, and D. Culler. Marionette: Using RPC for Interactive Development and Debugging of Wireless Embedded Networks. In *Proceedings of the 5th International Conference on Information Processing in Sensor Networks (IPSN)*, pages 416–423, 2006.

[4] J. Yang, M. L. Soffa, L. Selavo, and K. Whitehouse. Clairvoyant: A Comprehensive Source-Level Debugger for Wireless Sensor Networks. In *Proceedings of the 5th International Conference on Embedded Networked Sensor Systems (SenSys)*, pages 189–204, 2007.

[5] OpenOCD - Open On-Chip Debugger
http://openocd.sourceforge.net

Demo Abstract - MediaScope: Selective On-Demand Media Retrieval from Mobile Devices*

Xing Xu[†]
University of Southern
California
xingx@usc.edu

Yurong Jiang
University of Southern
California
yurongji@usc.edu

Peter Terlecky
City University of New York
pterlecky@gc.cuny.edu

Tarek Abdelzaher
University of Illinois at
Urbana-Champaign
zaher@illinois.edu

Amotz Bar-Noy
City University of New York
amotz@sci.brooklyn.cuny.edu

Ramesh Govindan
University of Southern
California
ramesh@usc.edu

ABSTRACT

Motivated by an availability gap for visual media, where images and videos are uploaded from mobile devices well after they are generated, we explore the *selective, timely retrieval* of media content from a collection of mobile devices. We envision this capability being driven by *similarity-based queries* posed to a cloud search front-end, which in turn dynamically retrieves media objects from mobile devices that best match the respective queries within a given time limit. Building upon a crowd-sensing framework, we have designed and implemented a system called MediaScope that provides this capability. MediaScope is an extensible framework that supports nearest-neighbor and other geometric queries on the feature space (e.g., clusters, spanners), and contains novel retrieval algorithms that attempt to maximize the retrieval of relevant information. From experiments on a prototype, MediaScope is shown to achieve near-optimal query completeness and low to moderate overhead on mobile devices.

Categories and Subject Descriptors

H.3.3 [**Information Storage and Retrieval**]: Information Search and Retrieval; H.3.4 [**Information Storage and Retrieval**]: Systems and Software; H.4.0 [**Information Systems Applications**]: General; C.2.4 [**Computer-Communication Networks**]: Distributed Systems

General Terms

Design, Experimentation, Performance

Keywords

Crowd-sensing, Image-Retrieval, Feature-Extraction, Mobile-Device

---

*Research was sponsored by the Army Research Laboratory and was accomplished under Cooperative Agreement Number W911NF-09-2-0053. The views and conclusions contained in this document are those of the authors and should not be interpreted as representing the official policies, either expressed or implied, of the Army Research Laboratory or the U.S. Government. The U.S. Government is authorized to reproduce and distribute reprints for Government purposes notwithstanding any copyright notation here on.

[†]The first two authors contributed equally to this work and their names are listed alphabetically by first name.

1. INTRODUCTION

Cameras on mobile devices have given rise to significant *sharing* of media data (photos and videos). Users upload visual media to online social networks like Facebook [1], as well as to dedicated sharing sites like Flickr [2] and Instagram [3]. However, these uploads are often not *immediate*. Camera sensors on mobile devices have been increasing in both image and video resolution far faster than cellular network capacity. Moreover, in response to growing demand and consequent contention for wireless spectrum, cellular data providers have imposed data usage limits, which disincentivize immediate photo uploading and create an *availability gap* (the time between a photo or image is taken and it is uploaded). This availability gap can be on the order of several days.

If media data was available immediately, it might enable scenarios where there is a need for recent (or fresh) information. Consider the following scenario: users at a mall or some other location take pictures and video of some event (e.g. an accident or altercation). An investigative team that wants visual evidence of the event could have searched or browsed images on a photo sharing service such as Flickr to retrieve evidence in a timely fashion.

To bridge this availability gap, and to enable this and other missed opportunities, we consider a novel capability for on-demand retrieval of images from mobile devices. Specifically, we develop a system called MediaScope that permits concurrent geometric queries in feature space on that may be distributed across several mobile devices.

Wireless bandwidth is limited and can vary, *concurrent queries* might compete for limited bandwidth, and query results can be large (since images are large and many images can match a query). These factors can result in unacceptably long query response times, which can impede usability. In some cases, applications might need lower query response times for correctness; in the scenario above, time may be of the essence in taking action (e.g., apprehending suspects).

MediaScope addresses this challenge using an approach that trades off query completeness[1], while meeting timeliness requirements (measured by the time between the issue of the query and when a query result is returned). It incorporates a novel credit-assignment scheme that is used to weight queries as well as differentiate query results by their "importance". A novel credit and timeliness-aware scheduling algorithm that also adapts to wireless bandwidth variability ensures that query completeness is optimized. A second im-

---

[1]Completeness is intuitively defined as the proportion of desired images uploaded before the timeliness bound.

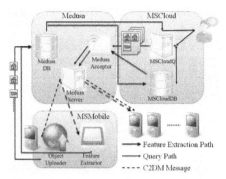

Figure 1—System Architecture Work Flow

Figure 2—Query Interface

portant challenge is to enable accurate yet computationally-feasible feature extraction. MediaScope addresses this challenge by finding sweet spots in the trade-off between accuracy and computational cost, for extracting features from images and frames from videos.

2. MEDIASCOPE DESIGN

MediaScope is a system that supports timely similarity-based queries on media objects stored on mobile devices. Mediascope is conceptually partitioned across a cloud component called MSCloud, and another component called MSMobile that runs on mobile devices. This partitioned design leverages the computation and storage power of clouds to support geometric queries on the feature space; mobile devices provide sensing and storage for media objects.

These components interact as follows (Figure 1). In the background, whenever participants take photos or videos, the *Feature Extractor* component of MSMobile continuously extracts image and video features and uploads them to the *MSCloudDB*. Users (e.g., a security officer or a reporter) pose queries to MSCloud using a standard web interface, possibly on a mobile device. These queries are processed by the *MSCloudQ* query processing engine, which uses the features stored in the MSCloudDB to compute the query results. The results of the queries identify the media objects that need to be retrieved from individual mobile devices. In some cases, a media object may already have been retrieved as a result of an earlier query; query results are also *cached* in MSCloudDB in order to optimize retrieval. MSCloudQ coordinates with an *Object Uploader* component on MSMobile in order to retrieve query results.

MediaScope uses a publicly available crowd sensing platform called Medusa [8], to enable programmed interaction between MSCloud and Medusa, and to support MediaScope's timeliness requirement, we made several modifications to Medusa Platform. The most challenging component of MediaScope is support for concurrent queries, we designed a *credit assignment mechanism*, the main idea is as follows, each query is awarded a certain amount of credit, and the query itself is responsible for assigned these amount of credit to the qualified objects given by the query optimizer, so each object of uploading request in MSMobile is associated with a credit, MSMobile is going to upload in a way that maximizing the total credit of uploadable objects. Our current instantiation of MediaScope supports three qualitatively different queries: nearest neighbor, clusters, and spanners. Detailed implementation is discussed in the full paper.

3. DEMO DETAILS

We have built MediaScope prototype system using a commodity server machine and Android smartphones. The query interface of MSCloudQ is shown in Figure 2. This demonstration will show the crucial steps of MediaScope: 1) the mobile device once capture an image, the corresponding feature will be extracted and uploaded to MSCloudDB automatically; 2) when MSCloud received query, it will select best media files and ask for uploading; 3) MSMobile will upload media files selected by MSCloud, and then MSCloud return results. For step 2), it is possible that MSCloud get concurrent queries (in the demo, we will issue multiple queries from different tabs of the browser); consequently, MSMobile will receive concurrent uploading tasks, sometimes this means that not all the uploading tasks can be completely uploaded before its timeliness bound and in this situation, the scheduling is critical for the sake of maximizing information (credit) collected.

4. RELATED WORK

There are some other works focus on search over resources, [4] deal with people-centric sensor data; however MediaScope focuses on image search. MediaScope is inspired by leveraging semantics of features [10, 9], techniques for content-based image retrieval from a centralized database of images [11, 6] and image retrieval from mobile devices [7, 5]. Compared to existing works, MediaScope uniquely supports searches on a cloud server, but where the content is stored on the mobile devices and is retrieved on demand.

5. REFERENCES

[1] Facebook. http://www.facebook.com.

[2] Flickr. http://www.flickr.com.

[3] Instagram. http://www.instagram.com.

[4] B. M. Elahi, K. Romer, B. Ostermaie, M. Fahrmair, and W. Kellerer. Sensor ranking: A primitive for efficient content-based sensor search. In *Proc. of ACM Information Processing in Sensor Networks (IPSN)*, pages 217–228. ACM, 2009.

[5] M. Gabbouj, I. Ahmad, M. Amin, and S. Kiranyaz. Content-based image retrieval for connected mobile devices. In *Proc. of Second International Symposium on Communications, Control and Signal Processing (ISCCSP)*. Citeseer, 2006.

[6] C. Jacobs, A. Finkelstein, and D. Salesin. Fast multiresolution image querying. In *Proc. of the 22nd annual conference on Computer graphics and interactive techniques*, pages 277–286. ACM, 1995.

[7] J.S.Hare and P. Lewis. Content-based image retrieval using a mobile device as a novel interface. In *Electronic Imaging 2005*, pages 64–75. International Society for Optics and Photonics, 2005.

[8] M. Ra, B. Liu, T. L. Porta, and R. Govindan. Medusa: A programming framework for crowd-sensing applications. In *Proc. of the 10th international conference on Mobile systems, applications, and services(Mobisys'12)*, pages 337–350. ACM, 2012.

[9] M. Uddin, H. Wang, F. Saremi, G. Qi, T. Abdelzaher, and T. Huang. Photonet: a similarity-aware picture delivery service for situation awareness. In *IEEE 32nd Real-Time Systems Symposium (RTSS'11)*, pages 317–326. IEEE, 2011.

[10] T. Yan, V. Kumar, and D. Ganesan. Crowdsearch: exploiting crowds for accurate real-time image search on mobile phones. In *Proc. of the 8th international conference on Mobile systems, applications, and services(Mobisys'10)*, pages 77–90. ACM, 2010.

[11] K. Yee, K. Swearingen, K. Li, and M. Hearst. Faceted metadata for image search and browsing. In *Proc. of the SIGCHI conference on Human factors in computing systems*, pages 401–408. ACM, 2003.

Demo Abstract: Low Capacity Devices with Semantic Interfaces

Arto Ylisaukko-oja
Jussi Kiljander

Esa Viljamaa
Janne Takalo-Mattila

Pasi Hyttinen
Juha-Pekka Soininen

VTT Technical Research Centre of Finland
Kaitoväylä 1
90570 Oulu
+358 20 722 111

firstname.lastname@vtt.fi

ABSTRACT

In this paper, we describe a demonstration of a semantic data interface implemented into a low capacity, battery operated wireless sensor. The demonstration scenario is a home greenhouse application where plant jars are equipped with plant sticks that contain moisture sensors. The gardener is provided with alarms that help caring for the plants properly. The alarm is given both as a visual LED blinking at the plant stick as well as shown at the UI of a smart phone. The overall solution is based on M3 Smart Space architecture. In addition, ucode technology in combination with NFC and optical tag technologies is utilized for configuring the smart space.

Categories and Subject Descriptors

I.2.4 [**ARTIFICIAL INTELLIGENCE**]: Knowledge Representation Formalisms and Methods – *Semantic networks*

Keywords

Semantic data, internet of things, ubiquitous computing, ambient intelligence, semantic web

1. INTRODUCTION

Semantic interfaces are still rarely used for communications with low capacity devices since such devices typically have limited resources in terms of energy, processing, memory, communication and cost. Typical examples are battery operated sensors that utilize technologies such as ZigBee or Bluetooth Low Energy for their wireless communications and are based on low cost, power optimized, often 8-bit microcontrollers. Low capacity devices typically use data formats that are defined separately for each application.

The objective of a semantic interface is to achieve inter-operability by enabling meaningful sharing of information between devices that can be very heterogeneous and were not even originally designed to utilize each other's data. This potentially enables new applications and use of the same device for multiple applications.

Standardized short-range radio technologies such as IEEE 802.15.4 or Bluetooth Low Energy define relatively short message payloads. These technologies are optimized for sending short messages, preferably infrequently. This is the best method for achieving long operating times before battery replacement. It is a challenge to apply semantic interfaces to resource constrained devices, since memory, processing time and message length overheads easily increase, potentially leading to more expensive and power-hungry devices. The challenge is mainly related to the resulting larger amount of data, due to overhead caused by semantic messages.

2. SYSTEM MODEL

M3 Smart Space architecture utilizes the idea and technologies of Semantic Web for interoperability of devices in physical environments. The M3 based software agents can more autonomously interpret the meaning of information, since they use ontology based information model. Therefore, they can obtain a greater degree of smartness and flexibility than could be achieved with traditional, use case specific data models. [1].

M3 utilizes RDF, RDFS and OWL for presenting the semantics of information in a computer-interpretable manner [2]. The M3 architecture consists of Knowledge Processors (KP) and Semantic Information Brokers (SIB). For SIB, we used a specific implementation called RIBS (RDF Information Base Solution). SIB is a shared RDF databases that provide publish/subscribe based interface for KPs. The KPs provide applications for end-users by inter-acting with each other via the SIB.

Smart Space Access Protocol (SSAP) defines the message format for KP–SIB interaction. In our case, we used WAX encoding of SSAP messages. WAX stands for Word Aligned XML and it provides a much more compact message format than conventional XML based SSAP messages. WAX is a key technology in reducing message length, memory and processing requirements [3]. For example, XML parser is not needed. This alone saves even 200 kB of code size.

M3 utilizes existing solutions for the communication and service levels – various different technologies can be applied.

3. THE DEMONSTRATION

The home gardening demonstration consists of the following basic components:

1. Moisture sensing plant sticks (refer to Figure 1). These are KPs that insert moisture values to SIB and read gardener presence data from SIB. Implementation is based on Freescale MC13224V ARM7 processor based, commercially available platform by Redwire LLC, called Econotag. Contiki OS is used. IEEE 802.15.4 radio is applied for SIB connection.

2. Google Nexus S smart phone, including a gardening application (refer to Figure 1). The application includes a KP that reads moisture values from SIB and inserts gardener presence data to SIB. The application is also used to pair the sensors with jars – this information is inserted to SIB.

3. M3Box (refer to Figure 2). This is the heart of the local M3 system, including the SIB database. It is based mainly on Seco Qseven Quadmo747-E660 computer.

The basic idea of the moisture sensors is to indicate if the moisture of the soil in the plant jar is correct. The indication is given to user by two different ways:

1. The gardening application gives indication of moisture.

2. A bright LED blinks in each of the sensors in jars, giving visual location indication for the gardener about the plants in need of water. This only happens if the gardener is present.

When the gardener touches an NFC *location tag* with his phone, his presence is inserted to the SIB. The plant sticks regularly query the presence information and use this to avoid blinking the LEDs in vain, therefore reducing power consumption. Refer to [4] for video of the demonstration.

The moisture sensors also include an NFC tag that includes a unique identifier, *ucode* [5]. The jars have optical tags (QR codes) that also include a ucode. By using the pairing function at the phone, the user can configure the smart space and pair a sensor to a specific jar (containing a specific plant). This way, the moisture sensor gets correct moisture threshold values from SIB.

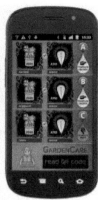

Figure 1. Moisture sensing plant stick prototype (left) and the gardening application in a smart phone (right).

Figure 2. M3Box (contains RIBS implementation of SIB).

4. PERFORMANCE

Despite some imperfection in implementation, we got an average current consumption of 241 µA from 3 volts @ 60 second wake-up interval for the sensors. For two 1.5V, 2700 mAh alkaline batteries in series this yields a theoretical battery duration of 1.3 years. With 10 s interval we would get 2.7 months duration.

The program code size was 39.7 kB (26% increase compared to a reference software without semantic interface). Increase in RAM memory use was more dramatic: from 14.3 kB of a reference software to 25.3 KB of our plant stick software (77%).

5. REFERENCES

[1] M3 smart space architecture: http://www.open-m3.org/

[2] RDF Vocabulary Description Language 1.0: RDF Schema, W3C Recommendation 10 February 2004. URL: http://www.w3.org/TR/rdf-schema/

[3] Ylisaukko-oja, A., Hyttinen, P., Kiljander, J., Soininen, J-P., Viljamaa, E. Semantic interface for resource constrained wireless sensors, Proceedings of the International Conference on Knowledge Engineering and Ontology Development, KEOD 2011, 26 – 29.

[4] Demonstration video: youtu.be/QBxqGpDYmw8

[5] Koshizuka, N., Sakamura, K.: Ubiquitous ID:Standards for Ubiquitous Computing and the Internet of Things. Pervasive Computing, IEEE, 2010, pp. 98-101.

Demo Abstract - Nemo: A High-fidelity Noninvasive Power Meter System for Wireless Sensor Networks

Ruogu Zhou, Guoliang Xing
Department of Computer Science and Engineering, Michigan State University, USA
{zhouruog,glxing}@cse.msu.edu

ABSTRACT

This demo abstract presents the design and the demonstration plan of *Nemo* – a practical *in situ* power metering system for wireless sensor networks. Nemo features a new circuit design called *shunt resistor switch* that can dynamically adjust the resistance of shunt resistors based on the current load. This allows Nemo to achieve a wide dynamic current range and high measurement accuracy. Nemo transmits real-time power measurement to the host node solely through the power line, by modulating the current load and the supply voltage. This feature leads to a noninvasive, plug & play design that allows Nemo to be easily installed on existing mote platforms without physical wiring or soldering. We describe the set-up of demonstration and outline our demonstration plan.

Categories and Subject Descriptors

C.2.3 [**Computer-communication Networks**]: Network Operations—*Network monitoring, Network management*; C.4 [**Performance of Systems**]: Measurement techniques

Keywords

Wireless Sensor Networks, Power Monitoring, Power-line Communication

1. INTRODUCTION

Energy-efficiency is one of the most important design objectives of wireless sensor networks because of limited energy resource. Despite the significant research efforts in energy-aware approaches at various network layers (MAC/routing/application), it remains challenging to actually validate the energy-efficiency claims of existing solutions, largely due to the lack of ability to track the real-time power consumption of a sensor network at runtime. In addition, real-time power usage data is also vital for senor nodes to modify their behavior and adapt to variable network conditions and dynamic physical environments.

The aforementioned requirements have motivated the development of *in-situ* power metering systems [1] [2] that can measure the power consumption of sensor nodes in real-time. A practical power meter system must meet several key requirements due to the unique characteristics of wireless sensor networks. First, it must achieve high measurement

fidelity, including wide dynamic range, high sampling rate, high measurement resolution and accuracy. Second, a power meter should be minimally *invasive* to the host node in terms of both installation and operation. To be practically useful, a power meter should be easy to install on existing sensor hardware, with little or no physical wiring/soldering. Moreover, it should operate in a stand alone manner, without relying on host resources like memory and CPU. Third, a power meter must be able to communicate with the host node in real-time. This will not only allow the host node to dynamically configure the meter, but also enable real-time feedback of power measurement to the host node for run-time adaptation.

We have developed *Nemo* – a Noninvasive high-fidElity power-Meter for sensOrnets [4]. As a key advantage, Nemo connects to the host node via merely the power/ground lines, requiring no dedicated data communication wires. This leads to a noninvasive, plug & play design, allowing Nemo to be easily installed on almost any existing mote platforms without physical wiring or soldering. At the same time, Nemo implements real-time, high-speed bi-directional communication with the host node based on current/voltage modulation, in which the current load and the supply voltage of power line are modulated to carry information. Nemo also employs a circuit design called *shunt resistor switch* that can dynamically adjust the resistance of shunt resistors based on the current load. This allows Nemo to achieve a wide dynamic current range without resorting to expensive and power-hungry components like high-resolution analog-to-digital converters (ADCs).

2. DESIGN OF NEMO

Fig. 1 illustrates the system architecture of Nemo, which consists of a MCU, a current measurement circuit, and a voltage modulator. The measurement circuit measures the current draw of the host node, and sends the measurement to the MCU. The voltage modulator, which is directly connected to an I/O pin of the MCU, modulates the voltage on the power line to transmit data to the host node. The power and ground wires are the only physical connection between the meter and the host node. Fig.2 shows a possible Nemo packaging that allows a wire-free, easy installation on existing sensor platforms.

2.1 High Fidelity Current Measurement

The current that passes the the measurement circuit creates a small voltage over the shunt resistor, which is proportional to the current intensity. The voltage is amplified

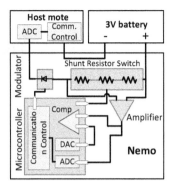

Figure 1: Nemo system architecture.

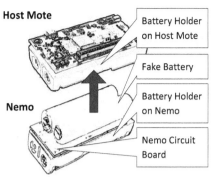

Figure 2: A possible Nemo packaging for easy installation.

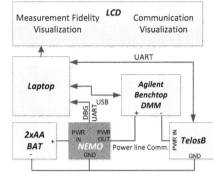

Figure 3: Demonstration set-up.

by a differential amplifier, and then digitalized by the on-chip low power 12-bit ADC in the MCU. The key difference between Nemo's current measurement circuit and traditional designs [3] is the shunt resistor. Typical current sensing design uses a single shunt resistor and a low resolution ADC, which cannot achieve wide dynamic current range and high sampling rate at the same time. In contrast, Nemo adopts a series of shunt resistors called *shunt resistor switch* whose resistance can be dynamically adjusted according to the required dynamic range. This design provides wide dynamic range without requiring expensive and power-hungry high-resolution ADCs.

During sleep state, the current draw of the sensor node is small and does not change drastically. In our design, Nemo can automatically enter sleep state when the host node falls asleep. A comparator on Nemo acts as a host wake-up detector which notifies the MCU of Nemo when the host wakes up. This design offers good energy saving without compromising measurement fidelity.

2.2 Host-Meter Communication

A key feature of Nemo is that the meter can communicate with the host node without dedicated data wires. This is achieved by a novel technique called current/voltage modulation, in which the current load and the supply voltage are modulated to carry information. Specifically, when the host node transmits data to Nemo, it modulates its own current draw to encode data bits. On the reversed link where the data is transmitted from Nemo to the host node, the supply voltage of the host is modulated by Nemo to encode data bits. Our design achieves high link throughput while incurring low computational overhead. Although this technique introduces minor supply voltage fluctuation, it has no impact on the performance of host nodes [4]. The power line modulation techniques remove the need of any data wires between Nemo and the host node. The details of the host-meter comm. protocol are presented in [4].

3. DEMONSTRATION OF NEMO

Fig. 3 illustrates the setup of the demonstration, which comprises a Nemo node, a TelosB mote, an Agilent 34410A Benchtop Digital Multimeter (DMM), and a laptop. 2 AA batteries are connected to Nemo to power Nemo and the TelosB mote. While measuring mote current consumption, Nemo also communicates with the TelosB mote through power rails using power-line communication scheme. The DMM, configured as an Ampere meter, is placed between

Nemo and TelosB to provide ground-truth current measurement data. Nemo, DMM, and TelosB are connected to the laptop via UART port, USB, and UART port, respectively, which enables data transferring and visualization. An LCD monitor is used to display all the data. To showcase the merits of power monitoring with Nemo, we run a variety of representative sensing applications on the TelosB mote, whose current draw patterns differ significantly from each other. Our demonstration requires a table of at least 70 inch X 30 inch and about 60 minutes to set up.

We plot the measurement results of Nemo and DMM on the LCD monitor along with the computed measurement error of Nemo in realtime. Measurement range, sampling rate, and measurement resolution of Nemo are also displayed. To show the performance of Nemo under different scenarios, different applications will be downloaded into the TelosB mote from laptop. This also illustrates the significant difference among current consumption patterns of different applications.

Nemo communicates with the host mote via power-line current/voltage modulation. The modulated waveform of mote current draw observed by DMM is shown on the LCD monitor in realtime. Bit error rate (BER), packet reception ratio (PRR) and throughput are computed by the laptop and displayed on the LCD monitor. We show the performance of communication under 3 modulation rates, 16kpbs, 8kbps and 4kbps, in the demonstration.

4. REFERENCES

[1] P. Dutta, M. Feldmeier, J. Paradiso, and D. Culler. Energy metering for free: Augmenting switching regulators for real-time monitoring. IPSN '08, pages 283–294, Washington, DC, USA. IEEE Computer Society.

[2] X. Jiang, P. Dutta, D. Culler, and I. Stoica. Micro power meter for energy monitoring of wireless sensor networks at scale. IPSN '07, pages 186–195, New York, NY, USA. ACM.

[3] A. Rice and S. Hay. Decomposing power measurements for mobile devices. In *PerCom'10*, pages 70 –78, 29 2010-april 2.

[4] R. Zhou and G. Xing. Nemo: A high-fidelity noninvasive power meter system for wireless sensor networks. In *IPSN*, 2013.

Demo Abstract - Skitracker: Measuring Skiing Performance using a Body-Area Network

Thomas Homewood
Swedish Institute of Computer
Science
Isafjordsgatan 22
Kista, Sweden
thomash@sics.se

Christer Norström
Swedish Institute of Computer
Science
Isafjordsgatan 22
Kista, Sweden
cn@sics.se

Per Gunningberg
Department of Information
Technology
Uppsala University
Uppsala, Sweden
per.gunningberg@it.uu.se

ABSTRACT

We have developed a framework for capturing various performance related sensor data from elite-level cross-country skiers and feeding this information to a set of bespoke analysis tools.

The core of the system involve tri-axle accelerometers for skier's upper body movement and an analysis tool which allow us to classify which technique they are using, and how well it is being performed. Other sensor data, such as physiological and positioning information, is used to provide context to the classification. The project is run in conjunction with our national cross-country skiing team, who are currently providing us with sample data from their international-level skiers.

Categories and Subject Descriptors

C.2.1 [**Network Architecture and Design**]: Wireless Communication.

Keywords

Body Sensor Networks, Cross country skiing, Data fusion

1. INTRODUCTION

Initial measurements on international-level cross country skiers show that there are significant differences in their technique and body movement, and that some skiers are more efficient in using their body's energy than others. Most of the research in this field has been conducted in controlled indoor lab environments with specialist wired equipment attached to the skiers to record parameters such as breathing rate, heart rate and so on [2].

In this project we instead instrument skiers on real race tracks with wireless sensors measuring their energy consumption as well as when, where and how their muscle power is used with respect to their speed and endurance. The results can be used in real time by coaches and skiers or at a post analysis of a training session. GPS data is collected to give the position of the skiers so that we can compare performance at different parts of the track. From tri-axle accelerometer data processing it is possible to see systematic differences between skiers and to communicate the differences to the coaches. For example, some skiers have ef-

IPSN'13, April 8–11, 2013, Philadelphia, Pennsylvania, USA.
ACM 978-1-4503-1959-1/13/04.

ficient movement of the upper body in the skiing direction while others have good timing when poling. We can also see how fatigue leads to less efficient movement and technique. Other sensor metrics we capture of importance for the skier are the pose, breathing frequency, heart rate and skin temperature.

The main challenges we were facing were how to handle the noise induced into sensors and smartphones when skiing bumpy tracks and how to present information from many (un)synchronized sensors in such a way that it is useful to coaches and skiers in real time. Another, more technical challenge we faced was where to put a strain sensor gauge on a pole to ensure that it captures the poling force through the whole strike.

Our research and demo contribution are: (1) We are the first to demonstrate that it is possible to capture the skier's movement in such a detail that has not been available to coaches and elite skiers before. (2) A strain gauge sensor placed on the wrist strap of a pole.

Sensor Body Area Networks is an active research area, see for example the survey paper [1] but there are very few papers on skiing [3].

2. THE DESIGN AND SENSORS

Initially we started with movement measurements using the built-in accelerometer in a smartphone. It was put in a belt carried by the skier. It was sufficient enough to see differences between skiers and their different skiing techniques but lacked in precision due to movement noise. Now we also use a Sensor Body Area Network (SBAN), with a chest-mounted sensor belt from Zephyr to record the athletes' temperature, heart rate and breathing rate as well as body posture. The belt has a tri-axial accelerometer with enough precision to classify different skiing techniques. The pole force is measured using a strain gauge sensor (LSB200 by Futek) that we mounted on on the wrist strap with a Shimmer node to drive the sensor. The SBAN uses a smartphone, running Android 2.1, as a gateway. It reads all sensor data, and sends it to the "cloud", where the coaches are able to see it presented in real time with a general web interface.

3. ANALYSIS AND VISUALISATION

Using our analysis tool, we are able to identify which technique, or "gear" the skier is using at a certain location. Looking deeper at the data, we can see how consistent the skier's motions are in three planes, and also see how symmetrical their technique is. Comparing the amplitude of their move-

Figure 1: An elite-level skier using our system. Shown highlighted is a small smartphone attached to the subject, which is recording accelerometer and GPS data.

Figure 2: A strain gauge sensor attached to the wrist strap of a pole to measure the force at poling.

ments with the forward speed achieved gives us an estimate of the skier's efficiency.

One very effective visualisation of the movement is a pair plots of smoothed, gravity - compensated accelerometer data, see figure 3. These plots differ radically based on the technique used by the skiers, their consistency, and some other not so significant factors. When studying the plots we see clear differences between various elite skiers that have not been exposed before, and hence they suggest areas for improvements.

In addition, we determine the efficiency of a skier's motions when using the ski poles for propulsion. By overlaying their vertical and sagittal acceleration, the relation between the force exerted through the poles and the forwards acceleration achieved can be understood.

All the data generated can be viewed in our web interface, where sets of data can be shown on maps, in graphs, or broken down into tabulated data. One skiers data can be compared with another one.

4. DEMO EXPERIENCE

- We will give visitors a concise introduction to the underlying principles of cross-country skiing, including the various techniques and to physiological of importance.

- We will show the full system running live, with data being transmitted from our various sensors to a smartphone gateway, and from there on to our web interface. Visitors are invited to wear our sensor belt and test the system first-hand.

- We will also demonstrate the various analysis tools that we have developed as part of our web interface. This will include a demonstration of our technique

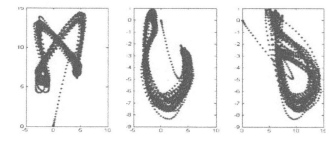

Figure 3: Pair plots of a skier's movements (from left to right: front, side and above) in gear 2. The tight grouping of the data shows this skier is able to reproduce this technique very consistently. From the leftmost plot, it can also be seen that this skier tends to lean to the left.

classification tool using data collected from our national team skiers.

5. ACKNOWLEDGEMENTS

This work has been partly funded by the VINNOVA through the Uppsala VINN Excellence Center for Wireless Sensor Networks (WISENET).

6. REFERENCES

[1] M. Chen, S. Gonzalez, A. Vasilakos, H. Cao, and V. C. Leung. Body area networks: A survey. *Mobile Networks and Applications*, 16(2):171–193, 2011.

[2] L. J. Holmberg, M. L. Ohlsson, M. Supej, and H.-C. Holmberg. Skiing efficiency versus performance in double-poling ergometry. *Computer Methods in Biomechanics and Biomedical Engineering*, 2012.

[3] F. Marsland, K. Lyons, J. Anson, G. Waddington, C. Macintosh, and D. Chapman. Identification of cross-country skiing movement patterns using micro-sensors. *Sensors*, 12(4):5047–5066, 2012.

Poster Abstract: Connected Wireless Camera Network Deployment with Visibility Coverage

Hua Huang
Department of Computer and
Information Science
Temple University
hua.huang@temple.edu

Chien-Chun Ni,
Xiaomeng Ban, Jie Gao
Department of Computer
Science
Stony Brook University
{chni, jgao}@cs.sunnysb.edu

Shan Lin
Department of Computer and
Information Science
Temple University
shan.lin@temple.edu

ABSTRACT

First responder applications often require safety surveillance using wireless camera networks [1]. To ensure visual sensing coverage, it is crucial to place optical sensor nodes at proper locations. Under the scenario of energy constrained wireless camera deployment, the issue of communication cost should also be considered. Previous camera deployment research (e.g Art Gallery Problem) mainly concerned sensing coverage. One well-known solution for the art gallery problem is to triangulate the objective polygon and then select vertices to ensure full coverage. However, deploying cameras only in the vertices of polygon may induce inefficiency both in number of necessary cameras and overall communication cost. To reduce the cost, we propose two deployment algorithms: 1) connected visibility region planning algorithm for static deployment given the floor plan is known, and 2) connected visibility region tracking algorithm for the dynamic deployment during the run time. In extensive simulations with real floor plans, our algorithms outperform previous solutions significantly.

Categories and Subject Descriptors

C.2.2 [**Computer-Communication Networks**]: Network Protocols

Keywords:

Sensor Networks; Sensing Coverage; Camera networks; Connectivity

1. INTRODUCTION

We model each camera as a node whose sensing range is only restricted by line of sight. That is, each point with a direct line of sight path to a camera is within its range. This is a generalization of the "cone "model[3] of a camera. As can be seen later, we would like to focus on the non-trivial problem caused by using visibility as the sensing range. The cameras are equipped with wireless radio transceivers for easy deployment. We will model the indoor domain as a polygon P and we consider the problem of deploying cameras to ensure (1) full coverage of P by their sensing ranges, defined by visibility; (2) the cameras form a connected network through their radio links. Formally, Our research problem can be stated as the **Minimum Connected Guarding Network Problem:** Given a polygon P with n vertices of possibly k holes, place a minimum number of cameras with communication range of r such that (i) the cameras form a connected network through wireless links; (ii) every point of P has direct line of sight to at least one camera.

The solution of the minimum connected guarding network problem clearly depends on the scale of the communication link connecting these nodes. Take one extreme, say the communication range of the sensor nodes is so big such that any two nodes inside the domain P can directly communicate with each other. The minimum connected guarding network problem boils down to the classical art gallery problem âĂŞ finding a minimum number of point guards such that any point of P is within direct line of sight of at least one guard. The art gallery problem is a well known NP-hard problem and it has been extensively studied for approximation solutions [2]. Take the other extreme, say that the communication range r is very small compared to the scale of the domain P. When r goes to zero, we basically need to place the sensors along a path to keep them connected. Thus the problem converges to one of finding a connected geometric network such that any point is visible to at least one point of the network. It is not hard to show that such a network of minimum length must be a tree. The problem of finding a minimum guarding tree for a polygon has not been studied before. A problem similar to our problem is the watchman tour problem [4], i.e., finding a tour of minimum length that guardâĂŹs the entire polygon P. It is known that the watchman tour problem is NP-hard for the general polygon with holes. But nothing is known about the problem if we replace the tour by a tree.

Researchers have proposed many camera deployment algorithms to to maximize the visual coverage of the camera network, but little attention is given to provide a connected network while minimizing the wireless communication cost. To fill this missing gap, our design goal is to achieve full visibility coverage with the minimal number of necessary cameras and also optimize the overall communication costs. Two algorithms have been proposed in this work: Connected Visibility region Planning algorithm (CVP) and Connected Visibility region Tracking algorithm (CVT). Given the floor plan abstraction in terms of a polygon, CVP identifies a set of visibility regions for concave angles of a polygon, and then

IPSN'13, April 8–11, 2013, Philadelphia, Pennsylvania, USA.
ACM 978-1-4503-1959-1/13/04.

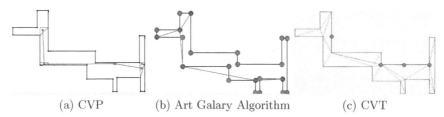

(a) CVP   (b) Art Galary Algorithm   (c) CVT

Figure 1. Simulation with a Real Floor Plan

compute the a minimal connected set of regions with the wireless communication range constraint. CVT is designed for the run-time deployment on a tour inside the building. A related problem is the shortest watchman path. Instead of finding a minimum single path, we search the shortest route for the minimum connected guarding network problem.

2. ALGORITHM DESIGN

Connected Visibility Region Planning Algorithm. Let $P=\{p_1, p_2,...,p_n\}$ denote the input polygon. We can define the Visibility Region of a reflex point p_i. The Visibility Region of reflex point p_i has the following property: for each point in this region, it is visible to the two adjacent points of p_i in the polygon P. For a given list of reflex points of the polygon, we generate the Visibility Region for each of them. For each reflex angle $\angle\, p^r$, we compute its opposite angle $\angle\, p_o^r$. Then we compute the two intersection points between $\angle\, p_o^r$ and P, denoted by p_1^{angle} and p_2^{angle}. After this, all vertexes of polygon P that lies within the angle $\angle\, p_o^r$ can be found, denoted by $\{p^{in}\}$. Combining p^r, p_1^{angle}, p_2^{angle} and $\{p^{in}\}$ and sort them, we get the polygon $R = \{p^r\ p_1^{angle},\ p_1^{in},..., p_k^{in}\ , p_2^{angle}\}$. To ensure the property of the region to be visible to both adjacent points of p^r, we compute if lines $p_1^{angle}p_1^{in}$ and $p_k^{in}\ p_2^{angle}$ divide R into two parts, respectively. If so, we remove the part that does not contain p^r.

After obtaining the Visibility Regions $\{R_i\}$ for all the reflex points, we further reduce the redundancy by selecting only the intersections between visibility regions. After obtaining the intersections between Visibility Regions, we select a subset from these regions to ensure full coverage. The regions are selected according to their sizes of unoverlapped visibility areas. We denote these regions by $\{R_i^f\}$. For each region in $\{R_i^f\}$, we deploy a camera in its centroid. Then we generate an Euclidean minimum spanning tree to interconnect all these cameras. After getting the minimum spanning tree among the cameras, we examine if there are any connections within the spanning tree that have geometric distance that are larger than the maximum communication range of wireless cameras. If so, we would deploy wireless relays between those pairs of cameras for connectivity.

Connected Visibility Region Tracking Algorithm. Tan proposed an $O(n^5)$ algorithm to find a simple watchman route for simple polygon in [4]. For input polygon P, suppose x is a reflex vertex in P and its adjacent vertex is v. Let a ray from v to x, hitting the polygon at y, then $C = \overline{xy}$ is a cut of P and separated P into two parts. We call the part of P that not containing v the cut, denoted as $P(C)$, and the watchman should pass this cut to see through the other part. A cut C_j is dominated by the other cut C_i if $P(C_j)$ contains $P(C_i)$, and a cut is essential if it is not dominated by any other cuts.

With the essential cut, the origin problem is reduced to find the shortest route that touch every essential cut. To solve this problem, we triangulate the given polygon and

"unrolled" the polygon using the essential cut as mirrors, and pick the route on that unrolled polygon. We first list the essential cuts in clockwise order. Starting from point s, we want to find a path to visit this cut list. Once the path touch the other essential cut, it mirrors the essential cut's belonging triangle next to the cut, hence the path go through the cut as reflected by the cut. The path finding process will stop until it reach the mirroring s, we can get the watchman route by mapping this path back to the original polygon. We can prove that given a polygon, let the shortest watchman route be R, the minimum connected guarding path be P, then $|R| \leq 2 \cdot |P|$.

3. EVALUATION

We have implemented a completed camera deployment algorithm simulation framework, which can plug in deployment algorithms such as CVP and CVT. We use one of the well-known solution to art gallery problem, the 3-coloring algorithm as a baseline. In our experiments, we take the floor plan of a realistic building as inputs. From these experiment results, we can see our algorithms can achieve significant improvement against the classic 3-coloring algorithm, both in reducing the number of necessary cameras and in reducing the communication costs.

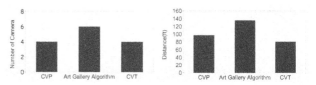

(a) Camera Number   (b) Communication Distance

Figure 2. Deployment Cost

A case study with three algorithms is shown in Figure 1. The red lines represent communication links that connect wireless camera nodes. In Figure 1 (c), the dotted lines represent essential cuts. The deployment cost is shown in Figure 2. From Figure 2 (a), we can see that CVP requires only 4 cameras, the same number as CVT. The 3-coloring art galary algorithm requires 6 cameras to ensure full coverage. In Figure 2 (b), the total communication distances for CVP, art gallery algorithm, and CVT are 97.44 feet, 135.56 feet, and 80.85 feet respectively.

4. REFERENCES

[1] H. Liu, and J. Li and Z. Xie and S. Lin and K. Whitehouse and J. A. Stankovic and D. Siu, *Automatic and robust breadcrumb system deployment for indoor firefighter applications*, in MobiSys '10.

[2] J. O'Rourke, *Art gallery theorems and algorithms*, Oxford: Oxford University Press, 1987.

[3] U. Erdem and S. Sclaroff, *Optimal placement of cameras in floorplans to satisfy task requirements and cost constraints*, in OMNIVIS Workshop '04.

[4] X. Tan, *Fast computation of shortest watchman routes in simple polygon* Information Processing Letters, 2001.

Poster Abstract: ASFECs – Using Approximately Synchronized Fetch-and-Execute Cycles as Basic Operation Cycles for Wireless Sensor Networks

Gerhard Fuchs
science@g-fuchs.de

SUMMARY

I present preliminary results of my work on an architecture for Wireless Sensor Networks (**net**s) that realizes the novel concept of **ASFECs** (approximately synchronized fetch-and-execute cycles). This architecture extends the classical fetch-and-execute cycles of computers by syncing phases. It guarantees a consistent value of the instruction pointer for all (sensor) **nodes** and a maximum skew between the starting times of the corresponding instructions on the nodes. In addition, I present my current work. I show how ASFECs can process net-assemblies. So far, I have studied centralized nets, only. I expect that ASFECs can be a important step towards fully deterministic, hard real time measurements fulfilled by nets.

Categories and Subject Descriptors

C.1.4 [**Processor Architectures**]: Parallel Architectures—*Distributed Architectures*; C.2.4 [**Computer-Communic. Networks**]: Distributed Systems—*Distributed Applications*

General Terms

Theory, Algorithms

Keywords

Wireless Sensor Network, Architecture, Assembly-Language

1. INTRODUCTION AND RELATED WORK

Flury and Wattenhofer introduced the concept of slotted programming for sensor networks [1]. Their approach assures that at any time at most one task (e.g. clock synchronization, routing, ...) is active. The developer has to decouple the task, temporally. So, it is possible to assign their execution to a time slot.

I use the concept of slots, too. In contrast to their approach, I want to bring the programming closer to domain experts. I am developing a domain specific, declarative high-level language to describe a measurement process that is fulfilled by a net. In addition, I am working on a compiler that transfers this high level description into net-assemblies. Those net-assemblies are a novel, slot based low level assembly language for nets. Net-assemblies are executed by the means of ASFECs.

ASFEC is a centralized mechanism that joins the concept of the traditional fetch-and-execute cycle of computers and the concept of the 802.15.4 superframe structure [2]: A fix number of fetch-and-execute cycles are embedded between synchronization slots. So, an important aspect of ASFECs is the continuous synchronization of the nodes' clocks. Römer et al. summarize other existing synchronization mechanisms for nets [3] and explain the common model of ρ-bounded clocks, which I use for my work, too: $\delta(t) := -1 + dh(t)/dt$; $-\rho \leq \delta(t) \leq \rho \ \forall t$ where $h(t)$ is the reading of a node's local clock at real time t; $\delta(t)$ is the drift at t and ρ bounds $\delta(t)$.

2. APPROXIMATELY SYNCHRONIZED FETCH-AND-EXECUTE CYCLES

The considered **system** consists of a **client** and a net. The net consists of at least two nodes. One of them – the **sink** – is connected to the client. The others – the **spots** – are deployed in the field. The connectivity of the net is at least centralized. This means, the sink must be able to communicate with all spots via radio and vice versa. To hide the complexity of the net from the client, the client solely interacts with the sink. The basic memory areas of the nodes are an instruction list register **INL**, an instruction pointer register **IP**, an instruction register **I**, and a instruction count register **IC**.

A node continuously processes the extended instruction cycle (Fig. 1). It alternates between a **syncing**- and an **operating**-phase. **IBS** (number of instructions between syncing) instruction cycles are embedded between two syncing phases. An instruction cycle consists of a **fetching**- and an **executing**-phase. A node fetches an instruction **I** from **INL** according to **IP** and executes it, afterwards. When **syncing**, the sink transmits a sync-message (**TS**) that contains its IP-value. The spots receive the sync-message (**RS**) and adapt their IP. Further, the spots synchronize the start of the next operating phase. $\mathbf{d_s}$ is the syncing-, $\mathbf{d_f}$ is the fetching-, and $\mathbf{d_e}$ is the executing-duration. The activities of the states must be finished before the transition fires. α, $\phi^{\mathbf{IC}+1}$, and $\chi^{\mathbf{IC}}$ identify the events that occur when a node switches its state.

3. PRELIMINARY RESULTS

Consider a set of nodes $N \equiv \{ N_0, N_1, \ldots N_{|N|-1} \}$, where N_0 is the sink and the others are spots. Let t be a real time; $\dot{\alpha}_j$, $\dot{\alpha}'_j$, $\dot{\phi}^z_j$, $\dot{\chi}^z_j$ be the real times when the corresponding events occur at N_j and ip(t, j) be N_j's value of IP at t. Consider the nodes' clocks as ρ-bounded and a $\mu < d_s$. Let

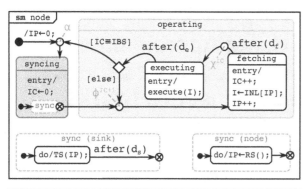

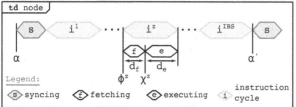

Figure 1: Extended fetch-and-execute cycle of a node. Within the sm, α, ϕ^{IC+1} and χ^{IC} are annotations, only. The nodes do not need to consider them during execution. α' is the end of the shown cycle and the beginning of the next cycle (see td).

$E \geq d_s \cdot 2\rho / (1 - \rho)$ be the maximum error after syncing and $\epsilon_j(t) \in [-E/2, E/2]$ $\forall t$ be the initial sync error of N_j. Further consider a synchronization mechanism that guarantees:

$$\forall (N_j \in N]) \, (\dot{\alpha}_j \leq \dot{\alpha}_0 + \mu) \rightarrow \dot{\phi}_j^1 \equiv \dot{\alpha}_0 + d_s + \epsilon_j(\dot{\alpha}_0)$$

Let $d_i := d_f + d_e$, $d_o := IBS \cdot d_i$, $\Delta(t) := [t - \Delta^l, t + \Delta^u]$ where $\Delta^l := \frac{E}{2} + \frac{\rho}{1+\rho} \cdot d_o$, and $\Delta^u := \frac{E}{2} + \frac{\rho}{1-\rho} \cdot d_o$. Then the concept of ASFECs allows to specify $\dot{\phi}^z := \dot{\alpha}_0 + d_s + (z - 1) \cdot d_i$, $\dot{\chi}^z := \dot{\alpha}_0 + d_s - d_e + z \cdot d_i$, $\dot{\alpha}' := \dot{\alpha}_0 + d_s + d_o$. Then and ensures that

- the nodes' clocks are approxymately synchronized;
  $\forall (N_j \in N) \, (\dot{\alpha}_j \leq \dot{\alpha}_0 + \mu) \rightarrow \{ (\dot{\alpha}'_j \in \Delta(\dot{\alpha}')) \wedge \forall (z \in [1, IBS]) \, ((\dot{\phi}_j^z \in \Delta(\dot{\phi}^z)) \wedge (\dot{\chi}_j^z \in \Delta(\dot{\chi}^z))) \}$

- the nodes' IP-values are approxymately synchronized;
  $\forall (N_j \in N) \, (\dot{\alpha}_j \leq \dot{\alpha}_0 + \mu) \rightarrow \{ (\mathrm{ip}(\dot{\alpha}'_j, j) \equiv \mathrm{ip}(\dot{\alpha}'_0, 0)) \wedge \forall (z \in [1, IBS]) \, ((\mathrm{ip}(\dot{\chi}_j^z, j) \equiv \mathrm{ip}(\dot{\chi}_0^z, 0)) \wedge (\mathrm{ip}(\dot{\phi}_j^z, j) \equiv \mathrm{ip}(\dot{\phi}_0^z, 0))) \}$

- the nodes keep synchronized if $\mu \geq \Delta^l + \Delta^u$.
  $\forall (N_j \in N) \, (\dot{\alpha}_j \leq \dot{\alpha}_0 + \mu) \rightarrow (\dot{\alpha}'_j \leq \dot{\alpha}'_0 + \mu)$

Fig. 2 shows the simulation results of an example experiment. It is a worst case scenario: N_1's IP-value is too low, it starts the first fetching too early ($\epsilon_1 = -E/2$), and its clock is too fast ($\delta_1(t) = \rho$). N_2's IP-value is too high, it starts the first fetching too late ($\epsilon_2 = E/2$) and its clock is too slow ($\delta_2(t) = -\rho$). The parameters of N_0 are in between those of N_1 and N_2. $\Delta(t)$ is calculated as presented and plotted as reference below the simulated values. All observed values fit to their intervals. In addition, all $\dot{\alpha}'_j$ are before $\dot{\alpha}'_0 + \mu$, so the next cycle will be synchronized, too.

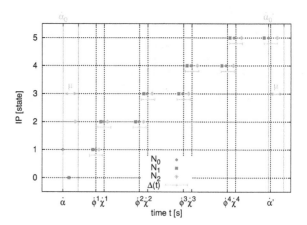

Figure 2: Result of an *AnyLogic*-simulation.

4. CONCLUSIONS AND CURRENT WORK

A net that executes ASFECs, generates super cycles (Fig. 3). The length and the starting time of the slots (S^z) can be calculated, as depicted. Within a slot, all nodes execute the instruction $I = INL[\mathrm{ip}(S^z)]$ where $\mathrm{ip}(S^z) \equiv \mathrm{ip}(\phi_0^z, 0)$. This allows to specify the behavior of the net with net-assemblies (Fig. 4). The net executes one step per slot. E.g. if $\mathrm{ip}(S^z) \equiv z$, node **A** transmits 8 bits $\langle td, 8 \rangle$ and node **B** receives them $\langle rd, 8 \rangle$. So, the net transfers data.

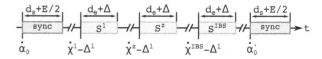

Figure 3: Resulting super cycle.

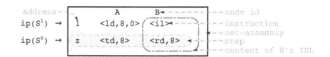

Figure 4: Example of a net-assembly.

5. REFERENCES

[1] R. Flury and R. Wattenhofer. Slotted Programming for Sensor Networks. In *Proc. of the 9th ACM/IEEE Int. Conf. on Information Processing in Sensor Networks*, pages 24–34. ACM, 2010. (IPSN: Stockholm, SE-AB; Apr. 2010).

[2] LAN/MAN Standards Committee. IEEE Standard for Local and metropolitan area networks - Part 15.4: Low-Rate Wireless Personal Area Networks (LR-WPANs). IEEE Std 802.15.4™-2011, IEEE Computer Society, June 2011.

[3] K. Römer, P. Blum, and L. Meier. Time Synchronization and Calibration in Wireless Sensor Networks. In I. Stojmenovic, editor, *Handbook of Sensor Networks: Algorithms and Architectures*, pages 199–238. John Wiley & Sons, Hoboken, US-NJ, 2005.

Poster Abstract: Managing Road Lighting with a Hitchhiking Sensor System

Huang-Bin Huang, Yen-Shuo Huang, Pei-Che Huang, Hsiao-Hsien Lin, Huang-Chen Lee[*]

Department of Communications Engineering and the

Advanced Institute for Manufacturing with High-tech Innovations (AIM-HI),

National Chung-Cheng University, Taiwan

[*] huclee@ccu.edu.tw

ABSTRACT

Road lighting management, i.e., finding a faulty street lamp or street lamps blocked by overgrown trees for example, can improve road illumination and reduce traffic accidents. Based on previous work [1], which explores the use of **illumination maps** to detect faulty lamps, we present a road lighting management system for detecting significant changes in road lighting automatically. This system is characterized by eliminating any need to modify conventional street lamps. Therefore, the cost is extremely low compared to other approaches, e.g., Wireless sensor network for street lamp monitoring. We design a special embedded system, the **Hitchhiker**, for installation on fixed-route vehicles, such as shuttle buses, to collect illumination readings along the vehicle's route. All data from the Hitchhiker is uploaded to the Google App Engine (GAE) server for data storage, analysis, and user query; this allows identification of possible locations of faulty street lamps on the web-based management interface. We designed and implemented a prototype of the Hitchhiker and GAE server to demonstrate the practicability of this system; we are working toward enabling this design for automatic faulty street lamp detection in the near future.

Categories and Subject Descriptors

C. 3 [Special-Purpose and Application-Based Systems]: Real-time and Embedded Systems

General Terms

Design, Experimentation, Measurement, Performance

Keywords: street lamps, wireless sensor, fault, management, intelligent

1. INTRODUCTION

Realizing intelligent street lamps has been quite difficult; wireless sensor networks are a promising technology to enable this goal. However, the cost of modifying conventional street lamps is so high as to be prohibitive in the short-term. The concept of the illumination map proposed in [1] opens a new direction toward managing street lamps automatically without the need to install additional devices on every individual conventional lamp. The key is to take advantage of existing fixed-route vehicles, e.g., shuttle buses, to carry our specially designed embedded system, the Hitchhiker, to collect illumination data over the bus route. As shown in Figure 1, the Hitchhiker is installed on the roof of the shuttle bus, and collects road lighting readings, and the location

IPSN'13, April 8–11, 2013, Philadelphia, Pennsylvania, USA.
ACM 978-1-4503-1959-1/13/04.

and acceleration of the bus. The huge amount of data generated by the Hitchhiker is saved on its SD card. Once the bus is back to the depot, the Hitchhiker detects the wireless signal from the Hitchhiker Access Point (hereafter denoted HAP), and actively uploads the SD card data to our cloud server built on GAE. Since the amount of data collected by several Hitchhikers is quite large, all the jobs of data processing, faulty lamp detection, and the web-based management interface, are executed on GAE to minimize the loading of the Hitchhiker.

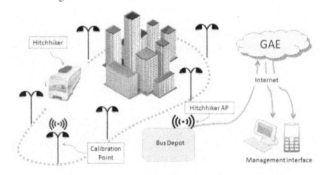

Fig. 1. The architecture of the proposed road lighting management system.

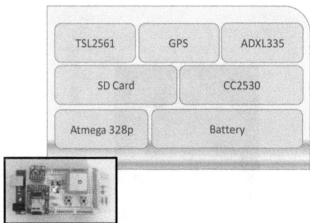

Fig. 2. The system components and a photo of the prototype Hitchhiker

2. PRELIMINARY DESIGN AND RESULTS

To increase acceptance toward deploying Hitchhikers on shuttle buses (as they are owned by a bus company), we kept the following principles in mind in designing the Hitchhiker: (1) It must be a non-intrusive device for shuttle buses. No modification of the vehicle is allowed. (2) The Hitchhiker must be able to run autonomously without human intervention or manual control, thereby not adding to the workload of the bus driver. (3) Errors or damage to the Hitchhiker must not hinder the shuttle bus service. All maintenance work must be done by us, not the bus driver or bus company. (4) The operation and hardware cost of the Hitchhiker must be low to allow installation of as many as possible without exceeding budgets and limited labor resources.

According to these criteria, we designed the Hitchhiker as a self-contained device powered by a rechargeable battery and encapsulate in a weatherproof box. The system components of the Hitchhiker and its photo are shown in Fig. 2. To prolong operating time, as it runs by battery, the Hitchhiker turns on the power-hungry GPS module only while the bus is moving. This is done by using the ADXL335 accelerometer to save valuable energy as well as collecting acceleration data for the moving shuttle bus. The illumination readings of the road lights from the light sensor TSL2561 and the GPS location are collected at 10 Hz. All data are stored on the SD card and wait to be uploaded by the CC2530 low-power RF transceiver while communicating with the HAP at the bus depot.

Since different weather conditions, such as rain, fog, or dirt on the illumination sensor can affect the road lighting readings, the calibration point (hereafter denoted CP, as indicated in Fig. 1) is designed to provide the ground-truth of the illumination reading at a specific location. The CP is a special device equipped with a TSL2561 illumination sensor and a CC2530 low-power RF transceiver that broadcasts its sensed reading of illumination periodically. The CP is installed on a street lamp. As long as the shuttle bus moves into the range of wireless communication of the CP (about 30 meters), the Hitchhiker can receive the wireless signals from the CP and saves this data onto its SD card for later verification and calibration of its illumination reading. This is important since the illumination readings from several Hitchhikers at the same location may be inconsistent, requiring the CP to verify the readings. If one of the Hitchhiker's illumination readings is significantly different from the CP and the other Hitchhiker readings, its data may be discarded, and hardware service may be needed.

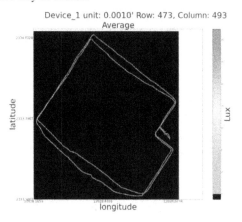

Fig. 3. Moving trajectory generated by a GPS module drifting from the road.

Choosing a good GPS module also helps to generate accurate moving trajectories, and enables us to compare the illumination maps in high-resolution. Fig. 3 shows the moving trajectories of the first version of Hitchhiker. Although we drove the vehicle

carrying the Hitchhiker on the same road loop several times, the trajectories did not overlap perfectly. We unwittingly changed to use another model of GPS module with a *Sirf4* chipset and found that the moving trajectories became nearly perfectly overlapped, as shows in Fig. 4

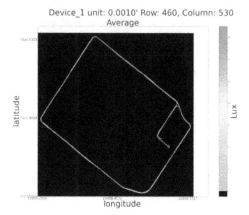

Fig. 4. Moving trajectory generated by a *Sirf4* chipset GPS module.

As all data on the Hitchhikers will upload to the cloud server on GAE eventually, the illumination maps are generated to indicate locations with significant changes in road lighting on the web-based management interface, as shown in Fig. 5. The numbers inside the red and black marks indicate illumination readings at their locations..

Fig. 5. Web-based management interface of the cloud server on GAE showing the possible locations of faulty lamps in black marks.

3. ACKNOWLEDGMENTS

The authors acknowledge support from the National Science Council, Taiwan, under grant 100-2218-E-194-006-MY3. The authors thank Research Assistant Mr. Pei-Jyi Kuo, and Mrs. Pin-Chen Kuo for their excellent technical assistance.

4. REFERENCES

[1] Huang-Bin Huang, Huang-Chen Lee, Detecting Faulty Street Lamps with Illumination Maps, The 11th ACM/IEEE Conference on Information Processing in Sensor Networks (IPSN 2012), Poster Session, Beijing, China, April 2012.

Poster Abstract: A Mobile-Cloud Service for Physiological Anomaly Detection on Smartphones

Dezhi Hong[1], Shahriar Nirjon[1], John A. Stankovic[1], David J. Stone[2], Guobin Shen[3]

[1]Department of Computer Science, University of Virginia, USA
[2]School of Medicine, University of Virginia, USA
[3]Microsoft Research Asia, Beijing, China

{dh5gm, smn8z, stankovic, djs4v}@virginia.edu, jackysh@microsoft.com

ABSTRACT

There is a growing number of examples that use the microphones in phone for various acoustic processing tasks as mobile phones become increasingly computationally powerful. However, there is no general physiological acoustic anomaly detection service on smartphones. To this end, we propose a physiological acoustic anomaly detection service which contains classifiers that can be used to detect irregularity and anomalies in lung sounds and notifies the user. We also present and discuss on some preliminary results.

Categories and Subject Descriptors

C.3 [**Special-Purpose And Application-Based Systems**]: Real-time and embedded systems

General Terms

Performance, Experimentation

Keywords

Physiological Sound Classifier, Anomaly Detection, Mobile Service

1. MOTIVATION

As mobile phones become increasingly computationally capable and powerful, m-Health has been in rapid development in the past years. Mobile health platforms could free users from frequenting doctors as well as enable remote diagnosis. A daily acoustic footprint of a user's heart and lung can be referred to in later medical consultations. Smartphones have begun to use their microphones for various acoustic processing tasks, some state-of-the-art examples include: emotion and stress detection [2, 5], cough detector [1], heart beats counter [4]. However, these are generally limited to voice and environmental sounds detection, and specifically, MusicalHeart [4] only delves into heart beats. Currently, there is no general physiological acoustic anomaly detection service on smartphones. To this end, we propose a physiological acoustic anomaly detection service based on the mobile-cloud platform [3]. Our service contains classifiers that can be used to detect irregularity and anomalies in lung sounds and notifies the user. Such a service could provide promising opportunities for early pulmonary problems

detection. There are multiple parts in our work. First, is to perform an analysis of lung sounds as sounds acquired on different parts of body will vary case-by-case in their intensity, pitch and inspiration-expiration temporal ratio (detailed in Section 2.1). Second, to explore what features in lung sounds can be used to build a classifier for recognizing or matching any irregular patterns in respiratory cycles and differentiating between various adventitious lung sounds. Third, such a cloud-based service could get more users involved thus contributing to a larger repository of sound samples.

2. LUNG SOUNDS BACKGROUND

In this section, we give a brief introduction to a few typical normal and abnormal lung sounds.

2.1 Normal Lung Sounds

Normal lung sounds can be heard from different positions on body and the sounds vary a lot in terms of intensity, pitch and inspiration-expiration temporal ratio.

- **Tracheal**: Heard over the trachea as harsh, high-pitched and discrete sounds. This originates from turbulent air flow in the upper airways of the body and cover a wide range of frequency from 100 Hz to 1500Hz. In general, the expiration phase is slightly longer than inspiration.

- **Bronchial**: Mostly heard from over the manu-brium or upper part of the sternum and usually consist of high-pitched and large amplitude sounds similar to the sound of air blowing through a tube. There is a brief pause between expiration and inspiration, where expiration is longer than inspiration.

- **Bronchovesicular**: Heard near the main stem bronchi, i.e., the median upper chest. They contain pitch and intensity characteristics between vesicular and bronchial sounds. They can be heard during the inspiratory and expiratory pass, which each last for approximately the same period and do not have a pause in between them.

- **Vesicular**: Heard over majority of the lung during the shallow breathing of normal respiration. They possess low-pitched and soft sounds which are generated as a result of changing airflow patterns in the lungs. There is no pause in between the two phases and the inspiration is longer than expiration.

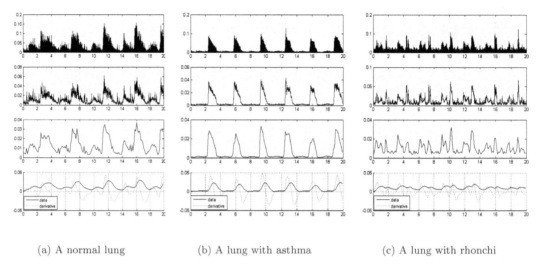

(a) A normal lung   (b) A lung with asthma   (c) A lung with rhonchi

Figure 1: Sound recording samples of lungs

2.2 Adventitious Lung Sounds

Adventitious sounds usually signify a pulmonary disorder or disease in patients. Here are several adventitious lung sounds commonly encountered in clinical auscultation:

- **Crackles**: Are discrete and explosive popping sounds and generally heard during inspiration. They are caused by air passing through moist airways and alveoli. Short duration (5-10 ms duration) crackles are called fine crackles and long duration (20-30 ms) ones are called coarse crackles. They are associated with lung disease such as pneumonia as well as with heart disease.

- **Wheezes**: They are high-pitched sounds that are more prominent in expiration with a duration longer than 100 ms. They are caused by air flowing across obstructed passages and create a few sharp spectral peaks around 400 Hz. These sounds indicate diseases such as pneumonia, asthma and emphysema.

- **Rhonchi**: They are continuous and low-pitched sounds with causes similar to those for wheezes. They occur at frequencies lower than 300 Hz and usually come with bronchitis and chronic obstructive pulmonary disease (COPD).

3. PRELIMINARY RESULTS

We perform preliminary processing on some lung sound recording samples [6] to identify the respiratory cycle which is a basic feature of lung sounds. The samples range from normal lungs to lungs with wheezes, crackles and bronchi. Several steps of processing (from top to bottom in the figure) includes: 1) down sample to extract the envelope, 2) denoise and further down sample, 3) apply a low pass filter, 4) take the derivative of the signal in 3). The zero-crossing points in the derivative help locate the peaks on the original signal and the interval between two adjacent peaks is used to calculate the respiratory cycles per minute, i.e., cpm. Clear differences are seen in Figure 1: the cpm increases from normal lung (a) to diseased (b) and (c); the amplitude ratio of inspiration to expiration (I/E) also varies from (a) to (c).

Parameters such as cpm and amplitude ratio of I/E can act as indicators of how well a user's lung functions on a daily basis and these fingerprints can be referred to in our service.

We will next compare the power spectral density (PSD) of the signals to see if it helps better distinguish between abnormal lung sounds. We will also examine the likelihood of simply using the microphones built in phone to reliably collect physiological sound clips and determine if a new accessory is needed.

4. REFERENCES

[1] E. C. Larson, T. Lee, S. Liu, M. Rosenfeld, and S. N. Patel. Accurate and privacy preserving cough sensing using a low-cost microphone. UbiComp '11, New York, NY, USA, 2011.

[2] H. Lu, D. Frauendorfer, M. Rabbi, M. S. Mast, G. T. Chittaranjan, A. T. Campbell, D. Gatica-Perez, and T. Choudhury. Stresssense: detecting stress in unconstrained acoustic environments using smartphones. UbiComp '12, New York, NY, USA, 2012.

[3] S. Nirjon, R. F. Dickerson, P. Asare, Q. Li, D. Hong, J. A. Stankovic, P. Hu, X. Jiang, and G. Shen. Auditeur: A mobile-cloud service platform for acoustic event detection on smartphones. In Submission, 2012.

[4] S. Nirjon, R. F. Dickerson, Q. Li, P. Asare, J. A. Stankovic, D. Hong, B. Zhang, X. Jiang, G. Shen, and F. Zhao. Musicalheart: a hearty way of listening to music. SenSys '12, New York, NY, USA, 2012.

[5] K. K. Rachuri, M. Musolesi, C. Mascolo, P. J. Rentfrow, C. Longworth, and A. Aucinas. Emotionsense: a mobile phones based adaptive platform for experimental social psychology research. Ubicomp '10, New York, NY, USA, 2010.

[6] StethoGraphics. http://www.stethographics.com/.

Poster Abstract: Range-Based Localization in Sensor Networks: Localizability and Accuracy

Liang Heng and Grace Xingxin Gao
University of Illinois at Urbana-Champaign
104 S Wright St, Urbana, IL 61801, USA
{heng, gracegao}@illinois.edu

ABSTRACT

Localizability and accuracy are two fundamental problems in many range-based localization schemes for sensor networks. This poster addresses the two problems theoretically by introducing two new concepts: the effective degree and the lower bound of geometric dilution of precision (GDOP). We prove that the network is not localizable unless the average effective degree is greater than or equal to the dimension of the location space. We further show that the average localization accuracy is approximately inversely proportional to the average degree.

Categories and Subject Descriptors

C.2.1 [**Network Architecture and Design**]: Sensor networks—*localization*

Keywords

Sensor networks, localization, positioning, localizability, accuracy, dilution of precision

1. Introduction

Sensor networks hold the promise of many exciting applications including assisted navigation and surveillance, wildlife habitat monitoring, climate control, disaster management, fraud detection, and automated billing [1]. Many of these applications require accurate information of sensor node locations. Localization schemes that have been widely explored thus far can be classified into three categories: range-based [2,3], range-free [4,5], and event-driven [6]. In general, range-based schemes can achieve high localization accuracy more easily then other schemes [7].

This poster addresses two fundamental problems theoretically in range-based localization schemes: localizability and accuracy. We propose a new metric, effective degree, which directly characterizes localizability. Furthermore, for the first time (to the best of our knowledge), we introduce a lower bound of geometric dilution of precision (GDOP), and use it to assess the localization accuracy for random sensor networks.

2. Problem Formulation

In this poster, a sensor network is modeled as a *simple graph*[1] $G = (V, E)$, where $V = [1, 2, \ldots, N]$ is a set of N nodes or vertices in a d-dimensional real space $\mathbb{R}^d$ ($d \geq 1$), and $E = \{e_1, e_2, \ldots, e_K\}$ is a set of K links or edges that connect the nodes [8]. The first N_S nodes, labeled 1 through N_S, are ordinary *sensor* (or mobile) nodes, whose locations are unknown; the rest $N_A = N - N_S$ nodes, labeled $N_S + 1$ through N, are special *anchor* (or beacon) nodes, whose exact locations are known.

An unordered pair $e_k = (i, j) \in E$ if and only if there exists a direct communication link between nodes i and j. The link provides the distance information $\rho_k = r_k + \epsilon_k$, where r_k is the actual distance between nodes i and j, and ϵ_k is the error of range measurement. ρ_k can be obtained by a variety of methods, such as one-way ranging, two-way ranging, and received signal strength indication (RSSI) [9]. The dimension d depends on not only the physical space containing the nodes but also the ranging method used. For two-way ranging and RSSI, the vector space $\mathbb{R}^d$ is simply the coordinate space: $d = 1$ for sensors in a straight line, $d = 2$ for a plane or a curved surface, or $d = 3$ for a 3-dimensional space. Since one-way ranging is usually affected by clock synchronization errors, the corresponding vector space $\mathbb{R}^d$ is the coordinate space plus a 1-dimensional space that models the clock bias of each node.

The sensor network localization problem is to determine generalized locations (coordinates and, if applicable, clock biases) of sensors $p_n \in \mathbb{R}^d$, $n = 1, \ldots, N_S$, given a fixed network graph G, known locations of anchors $p_n \in \mathbb{R}^d$, $n = N_S + 1, \ldots, N$, and distance information ρ_k, $k = 1, \ldots, K$.

3. Localizability and Effective Degree

In this poster, a node is *uniquely localizable* if its location can be uniquely determined. When a node is not uniquely localizable but it is possible to determine several candidate locations, this nodes is *nitely localizable* [3]. A network is uniquely localizable if *all* nodes are uniquely localizable, and a network is finitely localizable if *all* nodes are finitely localizable.

With the previously defined graph $G = (V, E)$, we assume no anchor-to-anchor links and define the following degrees for an arbitrary node n:

- Anchor degree: $\deg_A(n)$, the number of anchor-to-sensor links incident to node n;

---

[1]A simple graph is an undirected graph containing no loops or multiple edges.

- Sensor degree: $\deg_S(n)$, the number of sensor-to-sensor links incident to node n;

- Degree: $\deg(n) = \deg_A(n) + \deg_S(n)$, the number of links incident to node n;

- Effective degree: $\deg_E(n) = \deg_A(n) + \frac{1}{2}\deg_S(n)$.

In addition, the average degree for all the sensor nodes is defined as

$$\delta_* = \frac{1}{N_S}\sum_{n=1}^{N_S}\deg_*(n). \qquad (1)$$

This poster proves the following necessary conditions:

- The average effective degree $\delta_E \geq d$ is necessary for the network to be finitely localizable;

- The average effective degree $\delta_E > d$ is necessary for the network to be uniquely localizable.

4. Localization Accuracy and Its Lower Bound

Let $\boldsymbol{\varepsilon} = \hat{\boldsymbol{p}} - \boldsymbol{p}$ denote the localization errors. Assume the range errors $\boldsymbol{\epsilon} = (\epsilon_1, \ldots, \epsilon_K)^{\mathrm{T}}$ is a zero-mean Gaussian random vector with the covariance matrix Σ. When the network is at least finitely localizable, the covariance of localization errors under the principle of maximum likelihood estimation is given by [10]

$$\mathrm{cov}(\boldsymbol{\varepsilon}, \boldsymbol{\varepsilon}) = (G^{\mathrm{T}}\Sigma^{-1}G)^{-1}, \qquad (2)$$

where the *geometry matrix*

$$G = \frac{\partial \boldsymbol{r}}{\partial \boldsymbol{p}} = \begin{bmatrix} \dfrac{\partial r_1}{\partial p_{1,1}} & \dfrac{\partial r_1}{\partial p_{1,2}} & \cdots & \dfrac{\partial r_1}{\partial p_{N_S,d}} \\ \vdots & \vdots & \vdots & \\ \dfrac{\partial r_K}{\partial p_{1,1}} & \dfrac{\partial r_K}{\partial p_{1,2}} & \cdots & \dfrac{\partial r_K}{\partial p_{N_S,d}} \end{bmatrix}. \qquad (3)$$

If all the range measurement errors are independent and identically distributed, i.e., $\Sigma = \sigma^2 I$, the covariance of localization errors can be simplified to

$$\mathrm{cov}(\boldsymbol{\varepsilon}, \boldsymbol{\varepsilon}) = (G^{\mathrm{T}}\Sigma^{-1}G)^{-1} = \sigma^2(G^{\mathrm{T}}G)^{-1}. \qquad (4)$$

The sum of the diagonal elements of the matrix $H = (G^{\mathrm{T}}G)^{-1}$, $\mathrm{trace}[(G^{\mathrm{T}}G)^{-1}]$, is an important factor in localization accuracy, and usually referred as to GDOP.

Given a network with fixed connectivity and random node locations, it is very difficult to obtain a closed-form expression of the expected GDOP, $\mathrm{E}[\mathrm{trace}(H)]$. This poster proves that the lower bound of expected GDOP is given by

$$\begin{aligned} \mathrm{E}[\mathrm{trace}(H)] &= \mathrm{E}\left[\mathrm{trace}[(G^{\mathrm{T}}G)^{-1}]\right] \\ &\geq \left(\mathrm{E}[\mathrm{trace}(G^{\mathrm{T}}G)]\right)^{-1}. \end{aligned} \qquad (5)$$

Furthermore, this poster proves that the lower bound of expected GDOP for each sensor node is approximately inversely proportional to the average degree:

$$\begin{aligned} \frac{\left(\mathrm{E}[\mathrm{trace}(G^{\mathrm{T}}G)]\right)^{-1}}{N_S} &\approx \frac{d^2}{\delta}\left(1 + \frac{2}{N_S(\delta^2 - 1)}\right)^{\frac{1}{2}N_S\delta_S} \\ &\to \frac{d^2}{\delta}\exp\left(\frac{\delta_S}{\delta^2 - 1}\right) \end{aligned} \qquad (6)$$

when $N_S \to \infty$. This equation also shows that localization accuracy deteriorates if $\delta_S \to \delta$, i.e., the network contains mostly mobile-to-mobile links.

5. Summary

This poster addresses two fundamental problems in range-based localization schemes for sensor networks: localizability and accuracy. The major contributions include

- Effect degree of a node and average effective degree of all sensor nodes, a new metric that directly characterizes localizability;

- Lower bound of expected GDOP, based on which the location accuracy is proven to be approximately inversely proportional to the average degree.

6. References

[1] I. Akyildiz, W. Su, Y. Sankarasubramaniam, and E. Cayirci, "Wireless sensor networks: a survey," *Computer Networks*, vol. 38, no. 4, pp. 393–422, 2002.

[2] D. Moore, J. Leonard, D. Rus, and S. Teller, "Robust distributed network localization with noisy range measurements," in *Proceedings of the 2nd international conference on Embedded networked sensor systems*, SenSys '04, (New York, NY, USA), pp. 50–61, ACM, 2004.

[3] A. Y. Teymorian, W. Cheng, L. Ma, X. Cheng, X. Lu, and Z. Lu, "3d underwater sensor network localization," *IEEE Transactions on Mobile Computing*, vol. 8, pp. 1610–1621, Dec. 2009.

[4] Y. Shang, W. Ruml, Y. Zhang, and M. P. J. Fromherz, "Localization from mere connectivity," in *Proceedings of the 4th ACM international symposium on Mobile ad hoc networking & computing*, MobiHoc '03, (New York, NY, USA), pp. 201–212, ACM, 2003.

[5] Y. Wang, X. Wang, D. Wang, and D. Agrawal, "Range-free localization using expected hop progress in wireless sensor networks," *IEEE Transactions on Parallel and Distributed Systems*, vol. 20, pp. 1540–1552, Oct. 2009.

[6] Z. Zhong and T. He, "Sensor node localization with uncontrolled events," *ACM Trans. Embed. Comput. Syst.*, vol. 11, pp. 65:1–65:25, Sept. 2012.

[7] V. Chandrasekhar, W. K. Seah, Y. S. Choo, and H. V. Ee, "Localization in underwater sensor networks: survey and challenges," in *Proceedings of the 1st ACM international workshop on Underwater networks*, WUWNet '06, (New York, NY, USA), pp. 33–40, ACM, 2006.

[8] J. Aspnes, T. Eren, D. K. Goldenberg, A. S. Morse, W. Whiteley, Y. R. Yang, B. D. O. Anderson, and P. N. Belhumeur, "A theory of network localization," *IEEE Transactions on Mobile Computing*, vol. 5, pp. 1663–1678, Dec. 2006.

[9] M. F. i Azam and M. N. Ayyaz, *Wireless Sensor Networks: Current Status and Future Trends*, ch. Location and Position Estimation in Wireless Sensor Networks, pp. 179–214. CRC Press, Nov. 2012.

[10] F. Penna, M. A. Caceres, and H. Wymeersch, "Cramér-rao bound for hybrid gnss-terrestrial cooperative positioning," *IEEE Communications Letters*, vol. 14, pp. 1005–1007, Nov. 2010.

Poster Abstract:
SmartRoad: A Crowd-Sourced Traffic Regulator Detection and Identification System

Shaohan Hu, Lu Su, Hengchang Liu, Hongyan Wang, and Tarek F. Abdelzaher
Department of Computer Science
University of Illinois at Urbana-Champaign
Urbana, IL, 61801, USA
{shu17, lusu2, hl4d, wang44, zaher}@@illinois.edu

ABSTRACT

In this paper we present SmartRoad, a crowd-sourced sensing system that detects and identifies traffic regulators, traffic lights and stop signs in particular. As an alternative to expensive road surveys, SmartRoad works on participatory sensing data collected from GPS sensors from in-vehicle smartphones. The resulting traffic regulator information can be used for many assisted-driving or navigation systems. We implement SmartRoad on a vehicular smartphone testbed, and deploy on 35 external volunteer users' vehicles for two months. Experiment results show that SmartRoad can robustly, effectively and efficiently carry out its detection and identification tasks without consuming excessive communication energy/bandwidth or requiring too much ground truth information.

Categories and Subject Descriptors

C.5.3 [**Computer System Implementation**]: Microcomputers—*Portable devices*

General Terms

Algorithms, Design, Performance

Keywords

Crowd Source, Road Sensing, Traffic Regulator

1. INTRODUCTION

Traffic regulators, such as stop signs and traffic lights, are designed to regulate competing flows of traffic at intersections. They are among the most commonly used traffic control signals, and play significant roles in people's daily driving behaviors. Despite the safety and convenience benefits they bring, the stop signs and traffic lights do charge their toll. The stop-and-go movement pattern of vehicles caused have resulted in substantial increase of gas consumption and CO_2 emissions. Driven by this problem, some recent efforts are taken to reduce the negative effects, such as GreenGPS [3]. Navigation services like this need to take into account the actual locations of traffic lights and stop signs. Yet, unlike the case with road-maps, no nationwide database exists

today that documents traffic light and stop sign locations. Instead, this information is quite fragmented, buried in physical archives of different counties and municipalities.

To address the above challenge, in this paper, we develop a novel crowd-sourced traffic regulator detection and identification system, called SmartRoad, that can automatically detect and identify stop signs and traffic lights from participatory sensing data shared by individuals from their vehicles.

The general design of SmartRoad follows a client-server framework. We place the client component on a vehicular smartphone testbed, and the server component on a workstation. Compared with dedicated sensing, computing, or communication devices, smartphones are more suitable for large deployment due to their popularity. Users can easily download and install SmartRoad just like any other normal mobile applications. We implement SmartRoad on a vehicular smartphone testbed, and deploy it on 35 external volunteer users' vehicles. Through an experiment of two months collecting around 4000 miles of driving data containing hundreds of regulator-controlled and uncontrolled locations, we demonstrate that SmartRoad can deliver outstanding detection and identification performance without consuming excessive communication energy/bandwidth or requiring too much ground truth information.

2. SYSTEM ARCHITECTURE

In this section, we provide an overview of our SmartRoad participatory sensing system that carries out the traffic regulator detection and identification tasks. SmartRoad contains three modules: a data acquisition module, a detection and identification module, and a feedback module. They are deployed on two different platforms: distributed in-vehicle deployed smartphones, and a central server. Figure 1 illustrates the architecture overview of the SmartRoad system. We next discuss each of these three modules in more detail.

2.1 Data Acquisition Module

The data acquisition module is implemented on Google's Galaxy Nexus Android phones, equipped with 1.2GHz dual core CPU, 1GB memory, and 16GB flash storage, running on Android 4.0 operating system. We collect readings from the following phone sensors: i) *GPS Sensor*, the main source of the data to be used for our detection and identification tasks. Every single GPS reading includes the instantaneous latitude-longitude location, speed, and bearing of the vehi-

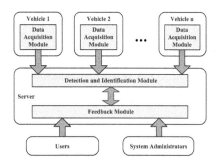

Figure 1: Architecture of the SmartRoad system

cle; and ii) *Power Sensor*, which reflects the car's engine on/off status, is used to start or stop data collection and communication.

Given the GPS data, we extract 5 features that can characterize the different driving patterns generally displayed and observed for the differently regulator-typed intersections:

Final Stop Duration: This feature captures the time duration of the last stop that a car makes in front of an intersection before crossing.

Minimum Crossing Speed: This feature represents the lowest speed at which a car crosses an intersection.

Number of Decelerations: This feature captures the number of times that a car decelerates as it approaches an intersection.

Number of Stops: This feature captures the number of stopping actions in the road segment between two intersections.

Distance from Intersection: This feature measures the distance between the intersection coordinate location and the point where a car makes its last stop, if any, before crossing the intersection.

2.2 Detection and Identification Module

The detection and identification module resides on the central server. It takes as input the extracted features together with a training set of intersections whose ground truth traffic regulator information are known, and outputs the label indicating the type of traffic regulator for each intersection. We use random forest [1] as our base classifier. Random forest is a decision tree based classification algorithm that trains multiple decision trees simultaneously and has them vote for the final classification decision. In practice, ground truth label information is limited and expensive to acquire, thus we consider a realistic scenario where initially only a tiny amount of training data is available, with further label information being acquired incrementally either on demand or opportunistically. To leverage this, we design and implement two adaptive mechanisms as follows:

Active Learning Adapter: In realistic participatory sensing applications, it is feasible that budget allows to manually acquire ground truth information, but only up to some small amount compared to the size of the entire sensing task. Thus, an important question to ask here would be, for which intersections should we pay to get their ground truth information in order to maximize our final system detection and identification performance? To answer this question, we propose an *Active Learning Adapter*, which looks at the past classification results, identify the intersections for which the

classification algorithms are the least confident about, and then hire people to manually acquire the ground truth information for these particular intersections. Here we borrow the active learning philosophy [2].

Self Training Adapter: The *Self Training Adapter*, which adopts the idea of self training [4], looks at its own past classification results and try to take advantage of them to improve system performance. More specifically, the classified intersections that have the highest confidence scores from the classifiers are progressively collected and added to the training set. The intuition behind is that classification results with high classification confidences are most likely to be correct, and thus including these data points into the training set will likely help expedite the overall classification tasks.

2.3 Feedback Module

The feedback module also resides on the central server. It visually presents detection and identification results via a web service interface. The web service interface can also be used by system administrators and users to correct detection errors or provide ground truth information, which is then sent back to the detection and identification module for dynamic and adaptive performance improvement.

3. PERFORMANCE EVALUATION

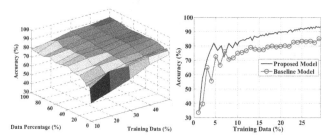

Figure 2: Classification with Active Learning and Self Training Deactivated **Figure 3: Classification with Active Learning and Self Training Activated**

Figure 2 shows the classification performance when the active learning and self training adapters are deactivated. As can be seen, as the amount of data, or labeled training data, or both, increases, classification performance also improves.

The classification results with two adapters activated are shown in Figure 3. For comparison, we design a baseline classification model trained from the same amount of training data, which are selected at random. As one can see, the proposed method outperforms the baseline scheme at all the iterations.

4. REFERENCES

[1] L. Breiman. Random forests. *Machine learning*, 45(1):5–32, 2001.
[2] S. Dasgupta and J. Langford. A tutorial on active learning.
[3] R. Ganti, N. Pham, H. Ahmadi, S. Nangia, and T. Abdelzaher. GreenGPS: A participatory sensing fuel-efficient maps application. In *MobiSys*, 2010.
[4] X. Zhu. Semi-supervised learning literature survey, 2006.

Poster Abstract: A Machine Learning Approach for Vehicle Classification using Passive Infrared and Ultrasonic Sensors

Ehsan Ullah Warriach
Department of Mathematics and Computer
Science
University of Groningen
Groningen, The Netherlands
e.u.warriach@rug.nl

Christian Claudel
Department of Electrical Engineering
King Abdullah University of Science and
Technology
Thuwal, Kingdom of Saudi Arabia
christian.claudel@kaust.edu.sa

ABSTRACT

This article describes the implementation of four different machine learning techniques for vehicle classification in a dual ultrasonic/ passive infrared traffic flow sensors. Using k-NN, Naive Bayes, SVM and KNN-SVM algorithms, we show that KNN-SVM significantly outperforms other algorithms in terms of classification accuracy. We also show that some of these algorithms could run in real time on the prototype system.

Categories and Subject Descriptors

I.5.3 [**Computing Methodologies**]: Metrics—*Pattern Recognition - Clustering, Algorithms and Similarity measures*

General Terms

Algorithm, Experimentation, Measurement, Performance

Keywords

Vehicle Classification, K-NN, SVM, Naive Bayes, Clustering

1. INTRODUCTION

Wireless Sensor Networks (WSN) are widely used for monitoring and control applications such as environmental surveillance, industrial sensing, or traffic monitoring [2]. While sensors usually forward all measurement data to a gateway, the system investigated in this article requires some estimation to be performed at the node level because of bandwidth and energy constraints.

In this article, we investigate the vehicle classification problem for a newly developed passive infrared/ultrasonic urban traffic flow and flood sensor. Vehicle classification (VC) is very important data, which is used to improve traffic speed estimates, or as a measure of road usage for transportation agencies. We propose a VC scheme adapted to the developed traffic flow sensor. It follows a architecture that consists of pre-processing, segmentation, feature extraction, modeling and validation. The proposed approach uses an online statistical clustering algorithm (k-means) and then used k-nearest neighbor (k-NN), naive bayes, support vector machine (SVM) and KNN-SVM machine learning (ML) algorithms to classify vehicle types. The aim of this work is to classify vehicles from

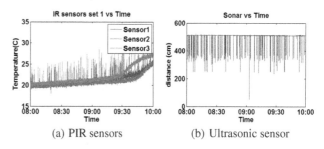

(a) PIR sensors   (b) Ultrasonic sensor

Figure 1: Sample time series and Classification features

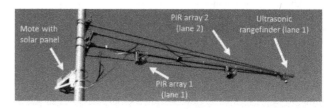

Figure 2: Traffic sensor node installed on a public lamp post

the temperature anomalies caused by vehicles on roads and the distance measurements between the sensor node and the vehicle, under severe memory and computational efficiency constraints.

2. SYSTEM

The traffic sensor node consists in six passive infrared (PIR) sensors and one ultrasonic (US) rangefinder connected to a microcontroller platform. The six PIR sensors are Melexis MLX90614 mounted with different orientations and monitoring two lanes of traffic (3 PIR sensors per lane), transmitting the temperature of objects in their narrow field of view via SMBus at 10Hz. The ultrasonic rangefinder is a MaxBotix MB7066 transmitting its distance to objects below it (or to the ground when no objects are present) via serial at an identical 10Hz rate. All sensors are connected to a Libelium Waspmote, which stores the data into packets and send them to a gateway connected to a database via IEEE 802.15.4, at a rate of 7 data packets per second. The dataset that is being discussed throughout this article was collected at the KAUST campus in December 2012. In this experiment, the sensor node was deployed on a lamp post as illustrated in Figure 2. The individual sensor time series illustrated in Figure 1 show various spikes that can have a diversity of lengths, magnitudes, and patterns. These spikes correspond to vehicle presence: a shorter distance measured

		Accuracy(%)	Computing time (sec)	Classification error (%)	Absolute error	Relative error (%)	RMSE	Correlation	Recall (%)	Precision (%)
	k-NN	90.61	2.7	0.39	0.004	0.39	0.061	0.891	69.04	66.78
Sonic	Naive Bayes	88.73	0.9	0.6	0.006	0.6	0.075	0.879	68.77	61.07
	SVM	87.38	1.7	0.5	.005	0.5	0.069	0.818	66.18	65.35
	KNN-SVM	95.89	3.1	0.44	0.004	0.47	0.066	0.886	67.13	62.25
	KNN	89.11	2.9	0.40	.003	0.41	0.060	0.895	64.84	63.77
PIR	Naive Bayes	86.69	0.87	0.62	0.005	0.58	0.074	0.883	67.17	65.67
	SVM	84.55	1.8	0.49	.006	0.56	0.063	0.838	68.38	67.35
	KNN-SVM	94.90	3.3	0.40	0.007	0.46	0.064	0.896	68.19	66.39

Table 1: VC machine learning algorithms performance metrics

		Bus			Pickup Truck			Sedan			SUV			Dune/golf buggy			Motorcycle		
		CC	DP(%)	FN	CC	DP(%)	FN	CC	DP(%)	FN	CC	DP(%)	FN	CC	DP(%)	FN	CC	DP(%)	FN
K-NN	Sonic	10	83.33	2	4	100	0	21	75	7	18	69.23	8	7	100	0	7	53	6
	PIR	9	75	3	3	75	1	20	71.42	8	23	88.47	3	6	85.72	1	11	84.62	2

Table 2: Vehicle Classification with K-NN (CC = Correctly Classified, DP = Detection Probability, FN = False Negative)

by the US corresponds to the presence of a vehicle below it, while a temperature increase or decrease (depending on the environmental conditions) can be associated with a vehicle in the sensor field-of-view.

3. VEHICLE CLASSIFICATION

We defined six classes of vehicles for classification purposes: Bus, Pickup Truck, Sedan, SUV, Dune/golf buggy and Motorcycle. The time-series samples are used to extract multidimensional features for classification purposes, such as the distance between the vehicle and the node and emitted temperature. We assume that each sensor periodically sends a message (t,x) to a sink, where t is the time of reading of the value x from a sensor i such that $x_i = Q(t)$. Suppose that a sensor sample $V = \{(t,x)\}$ is measured at a base station and split the given sample into intervals of period T to have an array of measured samples $\{V_i\}$ such that $V_i = \{x|(t,x) \in V \wedge T.(i-1) \leq t \geq T.i\}$. The constraint T have to be large enough so that V_i are non-empty sets. We used an on-line statistical clustering algorithm (k-means) at given samples to recognize the likely states $S = \{s_1, s_2..., s_N\}$ of the environment. The ultimate goal of this method is to provide an updated set of states V_i that is obtained from given dataset. While there are numerous ML algorithms exist for clustering and classification problems. We consider following methods for VC and their combinations to achieve better performance (trade-off between accuracy and computing time).

K-Nearest Neighbor algorithm is relatively precise, but the time required to classify a vehicle is high, because the distance of new instance is compared to all the instances in the training set. Consequently, the classification time in k-NN algorithm is proportional to the number of features and the number of training instances. Naive Bayes is one of the most efficient and effective inductive learning algorithms [4]. SVM provides a robust, accurate, and effective method for classification and pattern recognition [1]. The SVM method generates a model based on the training data that predicts the target values from the test data given only the test data attributes. Given a training labeled dataset pairs (x_i, y_i), $i = 1, ...l$ where $x_i \in R^n$ and $y \in \{1, -1\}^l$, the SVM needs the solution of the optimization problem $min_{w,b,\xi} 1/2w^T w + C\sum_{i=1}^{l} \xi_i$ subject to $y_i(w^T \phi(x_i) + b) \geq 1 - \xi_i$. We also propose a hybrid method of KNN and SVM methods that has realistic computational complexity both in training and at run time, and promising results [3]. KNN-SVM algorithm first computes distances of the new instance to all training examples and choose the nearest K neighbors. If the K neighbors have all the same labels, the new instance is labeled and exit, otherwise, compute the pair wise distances between the K neighbors and convert the distance matrix to a kernel matrix and apply multi-class SVM to the given dataset and use the resulting classifier to label the new instance.

4. COMPUTATIONAL CONSIDERATIONS

The VC algorithms described above are to be implemented on a new ARM-based computational platform developed at KAUST. The computational platform is built around an ARM Cortex M4 with configurable clock speeds up to 8-168 MHz, 1 MB of flash ROM and 192 kilobytes of RAM.

5. PRELIMINARY EVALUATION

Our preliminary evaluation of VC approach on given dataset is promising. We collected vehicles' data patterns during the experiment at KAUST campus, which resulted in over 100 vehicles detected in two hours. We applied the K-NN, naive bayes, SVM and KNN-SVM to identify vehicle types from US and PIR sensors data. It is significant to mention that we experienced numerous challenges while analyzing our dataset, such as high inconsistency in vehicle speed (including vehicles stopping below our sensor node), vehicles straddling multiple lanes and noise. We first compared different methods based on performance metrics, such as accuracy, computation time, classification error, absolute error, relative error, root mean squared error, correlation, recall and precision (Table 1). Our preliminary results conclude that K-NN performs better accuracy but computation time increases, on the other hand, we decrease the computation time for a bit low accuracy by having a combination of KNN-SVM. We then presented results as a confusion matrix (Table 2) that classifies the vehicles by their real classification, and the experimental classification result.

Our future work is to investigate the stability of these algorithms across a broader variety of vehicles, sensors, and environments. One significant research direction is also to automate a selection of ML classification algorithms' parameters, so that our developed system can be deployed with as little effort and training as possible.

ACKNOWLEDGMENTS

We would like to thank Guodong Li, Jiming Jiang, Edward Canepa and Sergio Favela for their help developing the sensor and writing the embedded code.

6. REFERENCES

[1] C. Cortes and V. Vapnik. Support-vector networks. In *Machine Learning*, pages 273–297, 1995.

[2] C. yee Chong, Ieee, S. P. Kumar, and S. Member. Sensor networks: evolution, opportunities, and challenges. *Proc. of the IEEE*, 2003.

[3] H. Zhang, A. Berg, M. Maire, and J. Malik. Svm-knn: Discriminative nearest neighbor classification for visual category recognition. In *IEEE CVPR, 2006*.

[4] H. Zhang and J. Su. Naive bayesian classifiers for ranking. In *15th ECML*. Springer, 2004.

Poster Abstract: Extensible Sensor Network Solutions for Visitor Identification and Tracking

Richard M. Abbot, Jacquilene Jacob, Hock M. Ng

Alcatel-Lucent Bell Laboratories, 600 Mountain Avenue, Murray Hill, NJ 07974, USA

{Rich.Abbot, Jacquilene.Jacob, Hock.Ng}@alcatel-lucent.com

ABSTRACT

We present the rationale, architecture, and implementation of an intelligent room, built upon a dense radio-based network of diverse electronic sensors, and interfaced with a cluster of dedicated computers. This room (an "iRoom") is capable of high-order tasks in event detection, analysis, processing, deduction, and inference. Initial focus has been to provide answers to the "Five W's" regarding a human visitor: Who, What, When, Where, and Why. The foundation technique that underpins this research is Sensor Fusion: the mathematical combination of disparate sensor reports and analyses into a rational result which is more accurate and more useful than its constituent parts.

Categories and Subject Descriptors

H.5.1 [**Multimedia Information Systems**]

General Terms

Design, Experimentation.

Keywords

Sensor fusion; Environmental discovery; Context-aware computing.

1. INTRODUCTION

Our team has used the technology in the Twentieth Century Fox motion picture "Minority Report" (2002) as a source of inspiration, with additional emphasis on finding potential commercial applications. Continual increases in computing power and advancements in sensor and perceptive technologies have promoted the ideas of ubiquitous computing [1] and context-awareness [2] in the community.

We have chosen to do this work in an indoor space of limited size, roughly 150 ft^2. The use case for this chamber is that of a casual lounge or meeting place, where small numbers of guests arrive, freely walk around or sit if they prefer, stay for a short time, and then leave. Repeat visitors are identified upon entry, and any records from their prior visits are fetched from a database by application software. Unknown visitors are cataloged for later comparison and identification. The room is populated with approximately 30 sensors of various types, creating 100-150 data reports each second. These reports are aggregated and analyzed by a progressive "winnowing" process that combines algebraic and rule-based logic, whose aim is to remove false indications and data noise and arrive at useful facts

with a high confidence value. Intermediate data and final results are made available through public interfaces, to enable the creation of specialized applications.

2. ARCHITECTURE

The solution architecture was designed with the following considerations in mind: 1) extensibility to allow adding new types of sensors/actuators, 2) real-time messaging, 3) several levels of data abstraction with varying reporting frequency, and 4) multimodal sensor fusion for increasing the reliability of context information. An overview of the system architecture is shown in Figure 1.

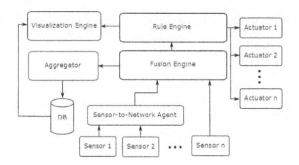

Figure 1: System architecture.

The main components are the sensor/actuator endpoints, sensor-to-network agent, fusion engine, aggregator, rule engine and visualization engine. The sensor-to-network agent serves as a concentration point for all wireless sensor nodes. Imaging sensor nodes are attached to PCs for graphical analysis and processing.

The fusion engine consumes raw sensor data and low-level context information from the sensor network and generates a fusion message (Fig. 2) which can be fed to a rule engine. The rule engine (with an associated rule base) determines the final context. The asserted facts are derived from lower level contexts using probabilistic inference to account for the uncertainty of different sensor measurements. Context reasoning through fusion of inputs from multi-modal sensors is shared between the fusion engine and the rule engine.

The aggregator receives fusion messages and performs two roles: database communication and report generation. Room Status Reports (RSRs) are XML documents which contain static information about the room configuration, and dynamic information based on sensor reports and visitors detected in the room. The visualization engine displays the sensor and context information in real-time, which can be used for algorithm testing and development.

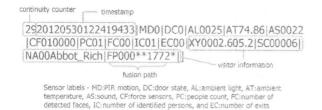

Figure 2: Sample fusion message.

Sensor labels - MD:PIR motion, DC:door state, AL:ambient light, AT:ambient temperature, AS:sound, CF:force sensors, PC:people count, FC:number of detected faces, IC:number of identified persons, and EC:number of exits detected.

We utilize UDP messaging for sending sensor data, actuation commands, and fusion messages between the distributed processing nodes (Fig. 2). The message uses a lightweight syntax containing a continuity counter and a timestamp, followed by a two-character label and a fixed length data field. Multiple data fields can be appended to compose a longer message string with separating characters. Sensor data messages contain an identifier for the sensor type, model and ID. We infer high-level context from low-level context using levels of data abstraction as shown in Fig 3.

Raw Sensor Readings->Sensor Data Messages->Fusion Data Messages->
Relational Database Entries->Room Status Reports

Figure 3: Data abstraction hierarchy.

3. IMPLEMENTATION

Our implementation is cross-platform (Linux, BSD, Windows) and cross-language (C, C#, Python, Java, XML, .NET). We use open-source components for processing of raw data and a relational database to serialize and control runtime data. The architectural components are based on a network of cooperating computers with processing tasks mapped to maximize real-time performance. The rule engine is based on CLIPS. We implement multi-modal sensing via wireless and wired sensor nodes. Sensors such as ambient light, temperature, sound, ultrasound, thermopile and gravitational force are connected wirelessly via a ZigBee network in a star configuration. Several cameras are used for face detection and recognition, while an overhead panoramic camera is used for tracking visitor paths.

Fusion messages combine sensor data and visitor information (Fig. 2). In this example, a visitor is identified as sitting in the "second chair" along with an (x,y) location and shirt color. Our implementation can answer questions such as who visited the room, how long the visit lasted, and which furniture and equipment were used. We also record the motion-track for visitors inside the room.

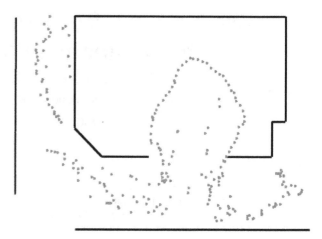

Figure 4: Visualization of a visitor's path.

Data for additional visitors to the room can be appended to the fusion message, with five simultaneous visitors possible. The fusion path (FP) contains three different sources of identification – face recognition, active RFID tag, and mobile device Wi-Fi MAC ID if sensed (e.g. laptop, smartphone, tablet). The first two parameters return a confidence percentage, while the last parameter is a Boolean value. Multiple sources of evidence can be fused into a final confidence value using $C = 1 - (1-S_1)(1-S_2)...(1-S_n)$ where S_n are the individual confidence values. Using sensor fusion, we are able to identify visitors within approximately two seconds of entry to the room.

To detect entry/exit events or for path tracking, we use location data of a moving person abstracted from the overhead panoramic camera (Fig. 4) and fuse it with lower-level contextual data such as opened door state, activated motion sensor states, and changes in the ping-distance detected by the ultrasonic sensors in the room.

Accurate visitor identification allows a public space to self-configure to the profile of a known individual (personalization). Our architecture can be extended to other types of spaces for various purposes, including health monitoring and alerting for elder care, access control systems for sensitive public or private areas, diagnosis systems for mobile medical facilities, remote collaboration for enterprise workgroups, and advisory systems for retail or scholastic environments.

4. REFERENCES

[1] Weiser, M. The Computer for the 21st Century. *Scientific American,* vol. 265, no. 3, 1991, pp. 94-104.

[2] Salber, D., Dey, A.K. and Abowd, G.D. The Context Toolkit: Aiding the Development of Context-Enabled Applications. *Proc. SIGCHI Conf. Human Factors in Computing Systems: The CHI is the Limit.* ACM Press, 1999, pp. 434-441.

Poster Abstract: Human Localization and Activity Detection Using Thermopile Sensors

Hock M. Ng

Alcatel-Lucent Bell Laboratories, 600 Mountain Avenue, Murray Hill, NJ 07974, USA

hock.ng@alcatel-lucent.com

ABSTRACT

We describe a method of using a network of thermopile sensors distributed along the walls of a room to locate a person within the room. At any given time, a person would be in the view of at least one of the sensor nodes. An algorithm is used to calculate the distance of a person from each sensor node based on its temperature reading and locate the person based on a combination of the sensor readings from the distributed nodes. This method is immune to lighting changes and works even in total darkness. Furthermore, this method of sensing can also detect events such as a person walking past the doorway to a room, lingering outside, and entering or leaving the room.

Categories and Subject Descriptors

C.3 [**Special-Purpose and Application-Based Systems**]: Real-time and embedded systems

General Terms

Algorithms, Measurement, Experimentation.

Keywords

Thermopile sensor; indoor spatial localization; event detection.

1. INTRODUCTION

Indoor spatial localization is a topic of interest for ubiquitous computing because it enables the design of intelligent environments that can respond to the user's location. There are several localization methods [1] that have been proposed by the research community and commercial systems are beginning to emerge. Broadly speaking, different localization techniques can be classified into two categories depending on whether or not the user has to carry a sensing device/tag. Requiring a tag can be problematic as they tend to be forgotten or misplaced. The tags can also be damaged or require frequent battery changes. On the other hand, camera-based techniques are sensitive to ambient lighting conditions whereas audio-based processing can only locate the user when he/she is speaking. A more practical concern is user privacy. Many people are not comfortable with cameras installed in their homes or work areas even if assured that privacy filters are in place.

In this work, we explore a method of detecting the presence and proximity of a human being via a network of thermopile sensors. There are only a few reports in the literature [2,3] utilizing thermopile sensing for people detection. This approach does not require the user to wear a sensing device. Moreover, since only the heat signature from a human body is being detected, there is no privacy concern as identifying information is not collected. We furthermore demonstrate that even with

these relatively simple and inexpensive sensors, certain human activities such as walking past a doorway, lingering outside or entering a room can be reliably detected. Such information may be useful in retail analytics, advertising and building management.

2. THERMOPILE SENSING

Human bodies emit heat in the form of infrared radiation that can be detected by a thermopile which converts thermal energy into electrical energy. According to the Stefan-Boltzmann law, the total radiation power of an object with area A is given by

$$P_{obj} = A \cdot \sigma \cdot \varepsilon \cdot T_{obj}^4 \qquad (1)$$

where σ is the Stefan-Boltzmann constant, ε is the emissivity of the object, and T_{obj} is the object temperature. For a thermopile sensor, the output voltage is related to the amount of thermal radiation impinging upon the sensing element. Assuming the temperature and area of the sensed object are constants, the distance of the object from the sensor can be derived from the detected temperature.

Figure 1: (a) Thermopile sensor node with a wireless transceiver, battery and microcontroller board. A size comparison of the thermopile sensor (b) and (c) the sensor node enclosure.

For calibration measurements, sensor nodes (Fig. 1) were mounted on a wall at a height of about 1.2m from the floor. A person stood facing one of the sensors and several temperature readings were recorded for each distance increment. The experiment was repeated with the person facing perpendicular to the sensor to measure the differences in the sensor readings due to pose.

Figure 2 shows the temperature-distance measurements from a single sensor node corresponding to the two poses. Each set of data points was fitted to an equation of the form

$$T_{sens} = c_0 + \frac{c_1}{c_2 + d^2} \qquad (2)$$

where c_0, c_1, and c_2 are the fitting parameters. The maximum detection range is ~3 m.

IPSN'13, April 8–11, 2013, Philadelphia, Pennsylvania, USA.
ACM 978-1-4503-1959-1/13/04.

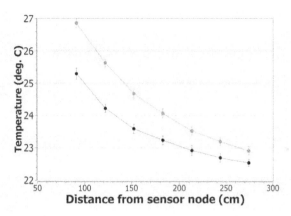

Figure 2: Data fitting to obtain a temperature-distance relationship. The top and bottom curves represent the front- and side-facing poses, respectively.

3. EXPERIMENTAL EVALUATION

Five thermopile sensors were located along the room walls as shown in Fig. 3 along with the sensor fields of view. For testing human localization, a person walked along the paths *1-2* and *3-4* denoted by the thick vertical and horizontal lines, respectively as shown in Fig. 4. The sensor data were collected, processed and plotted as a two-dimensional spatial representation.

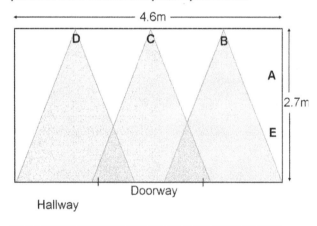

Figure 3: Schematic layout of the room and sensor locations. The fields of view of nodes A and E are not shown for simplicity.

To calculate the horizontal distance, the highest temperature between nodes A and E was selected. Eq. (2) was then solved for *d* in terms of the temperature. Similarly, for the vertical distance, the highest temperature among nodes B, C, and D was used. It should be noted that the sensitivity of the thermopile is highest along its main axis and falls off gradually away from it. To compensate for this effect, a percentage of the signal value detected by the nearest neighbor node was added when a person is standing in the region where sensing fields overlap. The detection accuracy was estimated to be ± 0.5m.

Fig. 5 shows data captured from node C. The ground truth was based on video captured from a camera facing the doorway. The dip occurring at ~170 s is due to a person walking in from the cold and going past the doorway. Since these experiments were carried out during the winter, the outside temperature was considerably colder than the indoor ambient temperature.

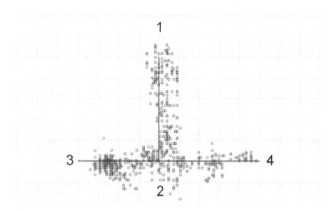

Figure 4: Comparison of the calculated positions and two different paths taken within the room. The spacing for each grid cell is 30 cm.

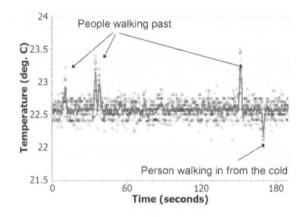

Figure 5: Raw and smoothed data highlighting the differences between warm and cold body detections.

In addition, by analyzing the temperature data we were able to detect when someone was entering, leaving or lingering outside the room. Extending this work to multi-person localization and tracking will be the next step.

4. REFERENCES

[1] J. Hightower and G. Borriello, Location systems for ubiquitous computing, *IEEE Computer*, 34(8):57-66, August 2001.

[2] Hauschildt, D. and Kirchhof, N. (2010). Advances in thermal infrared localization: Challenges and Solutions. *International Conference on Indoor Positioning and Indoor Navigation* (IPIN 2010), 1-8.

[3] Honorato, J. L., Spiniak, I. and Torres-Torriti, M. (2008). Human detection using thermopiles. *IEEE Latin American Robotic Symposium* (LARS 2008), 151-157.

Poster Abstract: Studied Wind Sensor Nodes Deployment Towards Accurate Data Fusion for Ship Movement Controlling

Lei Shu
Guangdong Petrochemical
Equipment Fault Diagnosis
Key Laboratory, Guangdong
University of Petrochemical
Technology, China
lei.shu@lab.gdupt.edu.cn

Jianbin Xiong[*]
Guangdong Petrochemical
Equipment Fault Diagnosis
Key Laboratory, Guangdong
University of Petrochemical
Technology, China
jianbin.xiong@lab.gdupt.edu.cn

Lei Wang
School of Software, Dalian
University of Technology,
China
lei.wang@dlut.edu.cn

Jianwei Niu
State Key Laboratory of
Software Development
Environment, Beihang
University, China
niujianwei@buaa.edu.cn

Qinruo Wang
School of Automation,
Guangdong University of
Technology, Guangzhou,
Guangdong, China
wangqr2006@gdut.edu.cn

ABSTRACT

This paper focuses on studying the sensor nodes deployment towards accurate data fusion for ship movement controlling. Furthermore, this study provides a node deployment layout with better measurement accuracy, which is surprisedly different from the layout that we originally predicted.

Categories and Subject Descriptors

H.4 [**Information Systems Applications**]: Miscellaneous; D.2.8 [**Software Engineering**]: Metrics—*complexity measures, performance measures*

General Terms

Measurement

Keywords

Sensor nodes deployment, Data fusion, Ship movement controlling

1. THE RESEARCH PROBLEM

As shown in Fig.1, an experimental ship model (length 2.80m, width 0.76m, height 1.00m) has been built. The ship is put in an indoor pool (length 11m, width 6m, height 1m) in Marine Hydrodynamics Laboratory at the Guangdong University of Technology, China. This test bed can simulate the ship moving environment by providing wind, water wave and water current.

The movement of ship can be highly affected by the environment, e.g., wind, water wave and water current. The

---

[*]Jianbin Xiong is the corresponding author.

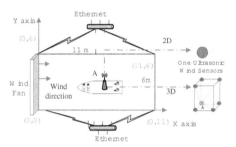

Figure 1: When the ship moves, the wind sensor can swing around, which will results in measurement error of the sensory data.

purpose for building up this test bed is to accurately and dynamically control the movement of ship to make it be more stable, based on the measured wind sensory data [1]. However, to achieve this goal, it is necessary to gather accurate sensory data. In this research work, we are interested in dynamically controlling the movement of ship based on only wind sensor's reading. Particularly, we want to study the following problem in this short paper: **How to deploy multiple wind sensor nodes in the ship to increase the measurement accuracy?**

2. MULTIPLE SENSOR NODES

Considering the influence of working environment, e.g., wind, wave, current and other uncertainties, it is hard to accurately measure the wind direction and speed by using only one sensor node in this ship. Multiple sensor nodes are required to be deployed in this ship to improve the accuracy of the measured sensory data based on intelligent data fusion method. Taking the realistic cost of sensor nodes hardware into consideration, in this research work, we deployed 7 wind sensors on the ship. After conducting a large number of

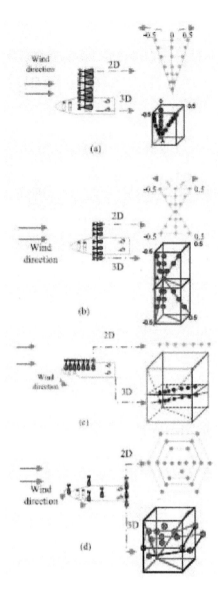

Figure 2: 4 different layouts.

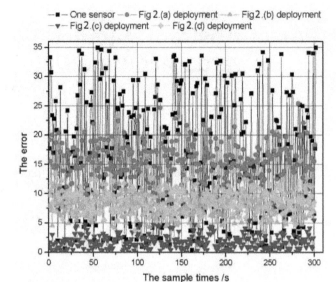

Figure 3: The measurement errors of 5 deployment layouts.

experiments, it confirmed that using multiple wind sensors can effectively improve the sensory data accuracy.

3. NODES DEPLOYMENT STRATEGY

However, different node deployment strategy also results in significantly different measurement accuracy. As shown in Fig.2, we used 4 different layouts for wind sensor nodes deployment: In Fig.2(a) all 7 nodes are deployed along with a vertical stick on the surface of the ship; In Fig.2(b) all 7 nodes are deployed along with a vertical stick, but 3 of them are above the surface of the ship, and 3 others are under the surface of the ship (inside the body); In Fig.2(c) all 7 nodes are deployed along with a horizontal stick on the surface of the ship; In Fig.2(d) all 7 nodes are deployed on the surface of the ship, but one sensor node is deployed in the center, and others are deployed along the boundary of the ship.

After processing the gathered sensory data by using intelligent data fusing method, the experiment results are shown in Fig.3. For the deployment in Fig.2(a), the maximum error

of wind direction is around 35 degree. For the deployment in Fig.2(b), the maximum error of wind direction is around 26 degree. For the deployment in Fig.2(c), the maximum error of wind direction is around 5 degree. For the deployment in Fig.2(d), the maximum error of wind direction is around 16 degree.

The experiment results surprisedly discover that the node deployment in Fig.2(c) has the best working performance, which is better than the one that we originally predicted from the node deployment in Fig.2(d).

4. SCIENTIFIC IMPACTS

Research work in this paper reveals two important insights as: 1) the measured wind sensory data is not accurate when the ship is moving since the wind sensory data is affected by the moving speed and direction of the sensor node; 2) different node deployment strategy also results in significantly different measurement accuracy. The discovered research results in this work are very meaningful since it can be applied on the offshore oil drilling platform to make it be more stable [2].

5. ACKNOWLEDGMENTS

This work is supported by the National Natural Science Foundation of China under Grant No. 50905063, No. 61070181, No. 61272524, and by the Guangdong University of Petrochemical Technology's Internal Project No. 2012RC0106.

6. REFERENCES

[1] T. Fossen and T. Perez. Kalman filtering for positioning and heading control of ships and offshore rigs. *IEEE Control Systems Magazine*, 29(6):32–46, 2009.
[2] B. Ye, Q. Wang, J. Xiong, and J. Wan. Parallel distributed compensation fuzzy controller design for dynamic positioning. *Journal of Convergence Information Technology*, 7(15):409–418, 2012.

Poster Abstract: Enabling a Cloud-Based Logging Service for Ball Screw with an Autonomous Networked Sensor System

Huang-Chen Lee[*1,] Yu-Chang Chang[*], Yen-Shuo Huang[*], Wei-Kuan Wang[+], and Yuan-Sun Chu[+]

Department of Communications Engineering[*], Department of Electrical Engineering[+],
and the Advanced Institute for Manufacturing with High-tech Innovations (AIM-HI)
National Chung-Cheng University, Taiwan
[*1] huclee@ccu.edu.tw

ABSTRACT

Precision ball screw assembly (hereafter called "ball screw"), as shown in Fig. **1**, is a mechanical wear out part that widely used in CNC (computer numerical control) machine tools to control the movement of processing targets and spindles. Up until now, there has been no simple way to directly measure ball screw for knowing the state of wear quantitatively. An indirect approach is logging all the signals (vibration, temperature, and preload change) during the operation of ball screw, and to use them to construct the wear model for estimating its remaining lifetime. To achieve this goal, we proposed a cloud-based logging system in this study that emphasizes (1) logging all the signals during operation in a ball screw's whole lifetime, and transferring to the data server without data loss; and (2) saving all the data into the cloud data storage of the ball screw's manufacturer. The data collected from many ball screws can be used to analyze and construct the wear model of ball screw, allowing the manufacturer to understand the state of wear and send a warning to the tool machine's owner before excessive wear.

Categories and Subject Descriptors

C. 3 [Special-Purpose and Application-Based Systems]: Real-time and Embedded Systems

Keywords: ball screw, wireless sensor, factory

1. INTRODUCTION

A ball screw is a mechanical device composed of steel balls, a shaft, and a nut body that is used to convert rotary motions to linear motions. The rotation of a ball screw's shaft causes the metal balls rolling in the threads of the ball screw and nut body with little friction. The cumulative friction of balls, regardless of whether it is due to long-time use or improper installation, may cause the ball screw to wear out, thus controlling the linear movement inaccurately. In addition, unnoticed wear of ball screws could cause excessive backlashes, skids, or lock-ups, as well as deteriorating the quality of processing object, which could result in loss of time and money. Because the amount being worn is invisible to the naked eye, we often rely on the judgments of experienced engineers, who make their judgments based on unusual sounds and vibrations produced during the movement of the ball screw, or significant quality changes of processing object.

Recently, several sensor systems [1] were proposed to estimate the wear of a ball screw. These studies focused on two points: (1) how to collect signals like vibration, temperature, and the change of preload force between nut, balls, and shaft during operation by using a wire or wireless sensor system; and (2) how to interpret the collected data to estimate the wear condition.

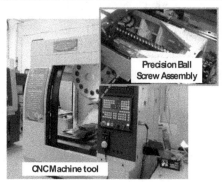

Fig. 1 A precision ball screw assembly installed in a CNC machine tool.

In previous studies, the proposed systems have collected the signals of the operating ball screw to estimate the state of wear. The sensing components were attached on the surface of the nut or shaft of the ball screw and connected by wires to transfer data to the data server for further analysis. Later studies [2] added wireless communication capability to the sensor system to transfer data. Although wireless communication provides the freedom to install locations, the reliability of data transmission becomes one of the major challenges in making this system commercially viable.

Wireless communication in factory environments is generally degraded and unstable for the following reasons: (1) the metal-made tool machines and buildings reflect RF signal considerably, and (2) running motors in machine tools generates significant radio interferences. In addition, the quality of wireless communication in factory environments is worsening since the type of wireless transceiver used in this application (built-in to the ball screw assembly) must be in low-power and small form-factor. This limits the antenna design and degrades its communication performance.

While data cannot be reliably transmitted to the data server over wireless communication, an expedient solution is that buffers the unsent data into temporary local storage, and retransmits it once the wireless channel becomes available. However, the microprocessor used in this type of application (due to the hardware cost and size limitation) has very constrained internal

RAM (typically 2~16 Kbytes), so it is not practical for buffering a large amount of collected raw data (i.e., sampling 3-axis vibration at 2 kHz in 16 bits ADC can generate 3×2000×2 bytes=12 Kbytes per second) into RAM for a long time before it could be sent out. To our knowledge, in previous studies, some data may have been discarded before being sent out, or the data transferred over wireless communication may have been lost and not recovered. In their designs, data transmission without data loss is not possible.

Moreover, in order to build an accurate wear model, we need to log as many real signals from numerous ball screws in machine tools as possible. However, this raises a substantial problem: How could we collect a large amount of real signals from ball screws that were sold by their manufacturer and installed in many machine tools—which could be located anywhere in the world—and aggregate data for wearing model analysis and construction?

2. PRELIMINARY SYSTEM DESIGN

In response to the previous issues, the **autonomous networked sensing system** (hereafter called ANSS), a promising system for logging ball screws, was proposed and implemented in this study. Referring to Figure 2, ANSS is an embedded system that is used to log signals of ball screws during operation. The long-term vision is integrate ANSS into the ball screw (i.e., the circuit system is embedded into the shaft or nut of the ball screw) as it is shipped from its manufacturer. The current prototype version of ANSS consists of an Atmel ATmega328p microprocessor and several sensing components to measure vibration, temperature, and preload of the ball screw assembly. All the collected data will be transferred wirelessly to the ANSS server by Nordic NRF24L01+ RF transceivers, and be forwarded to the manufacturer's cloud storage via the internet for data aggregation and analysis afterwards.

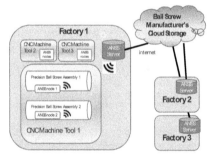

Fig. 2 The system architecture of the proposed cloud-based ball screw monitoring system.

As shown in Figure 2, in this system, a machine tool may have several ANSS-enabled ball screw assemblies, and an ANSS data server (at least one ANSS server in each factory) may control and collect data from many ANSS nodes in several machine tools.

In contrast to previous studies, our system ensures that all the data collected by an ANSS node will eventually be sent to the factory's ANSS data server without data loss. Referring to Figure 3, the ANSS node saves all the logged data to its local storage (i.e., an SD card), and sends out the buffered data while the wireless channel is clear. As the running electric motors of CNC machine tools often generate considerable radio interferences, the expedient solution is to transfer data to the ANSS server only if the motor has been stopped. Also, the network protocol of the ANSS node and server ensures the data's integrity by adapting transmission acknowledgement and checksum techniques. Therefore, all the data in the ANSS node can be reliably

transferred wirelessly to the ANSS server and eventually uploaded to the manufacturer's cloud storage. So, the manufacturer can use this huge amount of data to (1) know the usage and correctness of installation of the ball screw by the tool machine owner; (2) build the wear model of a ball screw and estimate the state of wear; and (3) send notifications to remind the owner of the machine tool to execute maintenance services in time, i.e., adjust, repair, or replace with the new ball screw assembly.

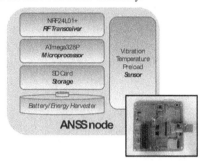

Fig. 3 The prototype of an ANSS node.

3. DISCUSSION AND CONCLUSION

As presented in Figure 3, we implemented an ANSS node prototype and executed a preliminary test to measure the signals of an operating ball screw in a machine tool and shown that this idea is feasible. The foreseeable issues are (1) the current version of ANSS node is powered by batteries. An additional energy harvester, such as an electromagnetic generator, may help to supply energy to ANSS; (2) the circuit of ANSS node may be embedded and enclosed inside the steel-made ball screw shaft or nut, which may cause RF signals to degrade when going through metals. A good antenna design is critical for good wireless communication; and (3) as some ANSS nodes may not be able to communicate to the local data server directly in factory (i.e., in single-hop, due to low RF power or obstacles), a multi-hop networking protocol may be needed. However, this would complicate the issue of wireless communication regarding bulk data transmission.

We hope to design a miniature ANSS node in the near future and integrate it into ball screw assembly. This will make it possible for machine tool owners to know the state of wear and the time to execute maintenance, therefore reducing the loss of time and money due to over-wear ball screw assembly.

4. ACKNOWLEDGMENTS

The authors acknowledge support from the National Science Council, Taiwan, under the grant 100-2218-E-194-006-MY3. The authors would like to thank Professor Shyh-Leh Chen, Professor Chin-Chun Cheng, Research Assistant Mr. Pei-Jyi Kuo, and Mrs. Pin-Chen Kuo for their excellent technical assistance.

5. REFERENCES

[1] Guo-Hua Feng; Yi-Lu Pan; , "Embedded temperature and vibration sensing system for monitoring ball screw preload," *Control Conference (ASCC), 2011 8th Asian* , vol., no., pp.171-174, 15-18 May 2011

[2] Liqun Hou; Bergmann, N.W.; , "Novel Industrial Wireless Sensor Networks for Machine Condition Monitoring and Fault Diagnosis," *Instrumentation and Measurement, IEEE Transactions on* , vol.61, no.10, pp.2787-2798, Oct. 2012

Poster Abstract: High Throughput Data Collection with Topology Adaptability in Wireless Sensor Network

Jinzhi Liu, Makoto Suzuki, Doohwan Lee, Shigemi Ishida, and Hiroyuki Morikawa
Research Center for Advanced Science and TechnologyАCThe University of Tokyo
4-6-1, Komaba, Meguro-ku, Tokyo 153-8904, Japan
liujinzhi,makoto,leedh,ishida,mori@mlab.t.u-tokyo.ac.jp

ABSTRACT

To reduce the complexity of scheduling while exploiting the advantages of TDMA-based data collection, we propose TKN-TWN, a token-scheduled multi-channel data collection protocol. The TKN-TWN uses two tokens to arbitrate data-packet transmissions and associates the ownership of tokens with transmission slot assignment. For the reduction of scheduling burden, the TKN-TWN provides topology adaptability while maintaining high throughput in burst data transfer. In this paper, we present the system design of TKN-TWN with enhancement toward topology adaptability based on a previous work. We evaluate TKN-TWN on a local test bed using 31 TelosB sensor nodes. Evaluation results show that the TKN-TWN achieves throughput of 6.4 KByte/s with more than 99 % delivery ratio even with occasional node failures.

Categories and Subject Descriptors

C.2.1 [**Network Architecture and Design**]: Wireless communication

Keywords

Wireless Sensor Network; Token; TDMA; Topology

1. INTRODUCTION

Node failures in resource limited wireless sensor network might cause network changes. Toward robust data collection, it is important to develop a collection protocol capable of topology adaptability. Several studies have investigated high throughput data collection [1, 2]. However, topology adaptability has not been well discussed since these studies assume fixed networks. There are some typical collection protocols such as [3] that have topology adaptability. Since such protocols are tailored for light traffic, they are not suitable for high throughput collection.

TDMA is more suitable for high throughput data collection than CSMA. However, TDMA-based protocols require complex rescheduling of the transmission time slot when topology changes because each sensor node is scheduled with a fixed time slot.

We have been developing a TDMA-based multi-channel high throughput data collection protocol named TKN-TWN.

We break the myth that TDMA does not adapt well to network changes [4] by utilizing a connection recovery scheme to the TKN-TWN. The TKN-TWN uses two tokens and associates the token ownership with time slot assignment toward throughput optimization. In the TKN-TWN the connection recovery scheme achieves high topology adaptability since the sensor nodes can perform slot reassignment based on routing information by themselves after connection recovery.

We have presented design of the TKN-TWN in [5]. In this paper we show the protocol enhancement toward topology adaptability and evaluate the TKN-TWN on a local test bed that consists of 31 TelosB sensor nodes.

2. DESIGN

2.1 Token-scheduled multi-channel TDMA

Data transmission of TKN-TWN is arbitrated through a centralized token passing mechanism. The sink node generates two different tokens and passes them to two top-subtrees respectively. A top-subtree is defined as a subtree whose root node is the child of a sink node. When a sensor node is the token owner, it transmits packets generated by the sensor node itself in a burst. Other nodes relay the packets to their parent nodes when necessary. A round of collection finishes when tokens finish visiting all of the sensor nodes.

Transmission time slot is determined on each sensor node by $TXSlot = (token + hopCnt) \mod 2$, where $token$ is the token type 0 or 1, and $hopCnt$ is the hop count. To eliminate interference different channels are allocated to two different top-subtrees. Within each top-subtree channel assignment is based on the hop count. To maintain synchronization sensor nodes periodically broadcast synchronization message in common channel slot. In order to guarantee reliable synchronization, we schedule broadcasting of synchronization messages as the order of node ID. The detailed protocol design is presented in [5].

2.2 Topology adaptability

In TDMA-based protocols, topology adaptability can be realized by node failure detection, connection recovery, and time-slot rescheduling. The TKN-TWN requires only the node failure detection and the connection recovery since the time-slot rescheduling is automatically performed at each sensor node by token passing. To reduce the token loss or duplication, robust token management is also elaborated.

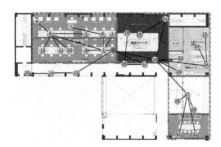 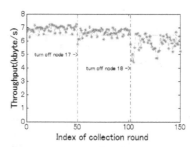 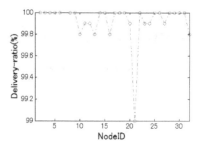

Figure 1: Indoor deployed testbed including the data gathering tree. **Figure 2: Throughput on indoor deployed testbed.** **Figure 3: Delivery ratio of the data transfer process.**

2.2.1 Node failure detection

Node failure detection is based on the communication loss as is a commonly used method. Sensor nodes monitor the drop of data packets and the loss of synchronization messages. Certain number of either continuous packet drops or consecutive reception failures of synchronization messages indicates node failure.

2.2.2 Connection recovery

When sensor nodes detect the failure of parent node, the sensor nodes recover connection by selecting a new parent from a neighborhood table that maintains link status as well as routing information. The sensor nodes select a parent node of which link is robust by a simple EWMA (Exponentially Weighted Moving Average) link estimation based on LQI (Link Quality Indicator). The LQI is exclusively calculated from synchronization messages. In order to maintain throughput, the sensor nodes choose parent nodes that belongs to the same top-subtree with a higher priority, which considers the load balancing between two tokens. Parent selection algorithm avoids routing loops by such as using hop count. The sensor node transmits a synchronization message including hand-shake commands to the new parent node in order to ensure that connection recovery is succeeded.

Since new parent selection indicates topology change, all related child nodes update their routing information. The TKN-TWN piggybacks updated routing information on synchronization message to reduce communication overhead. As soon as routing information is updated, sensor nodes automatically reconfigure channel and transmission time slot in self-determined way.

2.2.3 Token management

The topology-adaptive TKN-TWN realizes robust token management using the same method presented in [5]. Sink node monitors the existence of the tokens based on the reception of the associated packets. The sink node generates a new token when tokens are lost. The TKN-TWN also eliminates duplicated tokens by recording the track of tokens in neighborhood tables. Sensor nodes regard the token from the non-owner as duplicated token and drop it. Therefore TKN-TWN is stable with occasional token loss and duplicated token generation by network changes.

3. EVALUATION AND CONCLUSION

We evaluate the TKN-TWN on a testbed that consist of 31 TelosB sensor nodes deployed in laboratory environment (36 x 25 meters) as shown in Fig. 1. Network topology is con-

structed using ETX- (Expected Transmission Count-) based link estimator. Node 0 is the sink node. The maximum size packet (128 bytes) of CC2420 radio component is used.

Figure 2 shows the throughput of 150 rounds of continuous data collection with burst size of 20 packets. To test the topology adaptability, the node 17 and node 18 were manually turned off at the time as marked in Fig. 2. We confirmed that the child nodes of both node 17 and 18 selected new parent nodes afterwards by using a network snooper. Although throughput tends to drop to a certain degree right after the node failure, it gradually recovers to be steady. The failure of node 18 affects more number of sensor nodes than that of the node 17. The failure of node 18 therefore tends to affect the throughput more than the node 17, as depicted in Fig. 2. The throughput has been roughly maintained in the same level on the whole. The average throughput of the whole collection process is about 6.4 KByte/s.

The delivery ratio in the experiment is nearly 100 %, as shown in Fig. 3. In case of node failure, the related token owner is prone to packet loss. For example, as the token owner node 21 drops more packets when node 18 fails. In spite of this, delivery ratio of 99 % has been achieved for node 21 in the whole.

In this paper, we elaborate a token-scheduled collection protocol. It feasibly solves the issue of topology adaptability. Experimental results show that the throughput of 6.4 KByte/s have been achieved with high delivery ratio even with occasional node failure.

4. ACKNOWLEDGMENTS

This work is in part supported by the research and development of network conversion of communication processing functions in large-scale communication congestion of the Ministry of Internal Affairs and Communications, Japan.

5. REFERENCES

[1] B. Raman et al. PIP: A connection-oriented, multi-hop, multi-channel TDMA-based MAC for high throughput bulk transfer. *ACM SenSys*, Nov. 2010.

[2] S. Duquennoy et al. Lossy links, low power, high throughput. *ACM SenSys*, Nov. 2011.

[3] O. Gnawali et al. Collection tree protocol, *ACM SenSys*, Nov. 2009.

[4] V. Cionca et al. TDMA protocol requirements for wireless sensor networks. *IARIA SENSORCOMM*, Aug. 2008.

[5] J. Liu et al. A token scheduled high throughput multi-channel data collection protocol for wireless sensor network. *IEEE VTC-Spring*, Jun. 2013. (will appear)

Poster Abstract - Exploiting Nonlinear Data Similarities: A Multi-Scale Nearest-Neighbor Approach for Adaptive Sampling in Wireless Pollution Sensor Networks

Manik Gupta
Eliane Bodanese
Queen Mary University of London
United Kingdom

{manik.gupta, eliane.bodanese}
@eecs.qmul.ac.uk

Lamling Venus Shum
Stephen Hailes
University College London
United Kingdom

{v.shum, s.hailes}@ucl.ac.uk

ABSTRACT

Air pollution data exhibit characteristics like long range correlations and multi-fractal scaling that can be exploited to implement an energy efficient, adaptive spatial sampling technique for pollution sensor nodes. In this work, we present a) results from de-trended fluctuation analysis to prove the presence of non-linear dynamics in real pollution datasets gathered from trials carried out in Cyprus, b) a novel Multi-scale Nearest Neighbors based Adaptive Spatial Sampling (MNNASS) technique that determines the predictability and in turn the directional influences between data from different sensor nodes, and c) performance analysis of the algorithm in terms of energy savings and measurement accuracy.

Categories and Subject Descriptors: E.0 General

Keywords

Adaptive algorithm; Fractals; Nearest neighbor searches; Nonlinear dynamical systems; Time series analysis.

1. INTRODUCTION

The impact of air pollution caused by traffic is of significant scientific, social and economic interest to countries across the globe. In recent years, the advances in pervasive sensing have provided an opportunity for researchers to deploy larger number of wireless sensor nodes to investigate air pollution in fine-grain temporal and spatial details, opening new research arena in micro-environmental studies and pollution modeling techniques that can be used for urban planning, street and building designs. For real time fine grained air pollution monitoring, the sensor nodes should be able to sense/sample the environment, only when, an important event happens and collect "sensible" statistics relevant to the environmental scientist. But owing to the presence of non-linear dynamics in pollution datasets, existing adaptive sampling strategies might not be efficient for these datasets. Hence, the aim of the current work is to propose a design for a data centric adaptive spatial sampling that takes peculiar air pollution data characteristics into consideration.

2. DATA ANALYSIS OF REAL AIR POLLUTION DATASETS

2.1 Trial Details

Pollution datasets have been collected as a part of the trials carried out in Cyprus. The details of hardware equipment, sensor calibration and software used can be found in [1]. The trial comprises of 14 Bracelet nodes deployed along a narrow urban street. The nodes have been sampled at 1Hz for consecutive 5 hours. The spatial interpolation of the data as measured by the sensor nodes is shown in Figure 1.

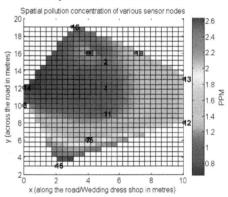

Figure 1 Spatial distribution of the pollutants as measured by the sensor nodes

2.2 Pollution Data Analysis

There are several investigations carried out by researchers in environmental sciences [2] that confirm that the air pollution concentration time series exhibit right skewed frequency distribution that can be well represented by a log normal model. Furthermore, auto-correlations do not decay to zero exponentially, but in a slower manner indicating the presence of long range correlations. In the current work, data analysis has been further extended to explore the statistical properties of pollution time series. The data

IPSN'13, April 8–11, 2013, Philadelphia, Pennsylvania, USA.
ACM 978-1-4503-1959-1/13/04.

analysis presented here is different from a perspective that typically such fine grained data is not available to environmental scientists. One of the data analysis methods called de-trended fluctuation analysis *(DFA)* [3] has been applied for pollution datasets. DFA is a technique used for determination of multi-fractal scaling (self-similarity at different observation scales) properties and detection of long-range correlations in noisy, non-stationary time series. DFA is an offline data analysis technique, but an online method that can capture non-linear dynamics of self-similarity in a surrounding area is required for the sampling algorithm design.

3. TECHNICAL DETAILS

3.1 Description of the NN based Directionality Measure

NN based directionality measure that uses a phase space representation called an embedding can be used to derive interdependence relationship between the measurements obtained from different nodes. Owing to the self-similarity exhibited by the pollution datasets, these embedded vectors or pieces of time series in the past might have a resemblance to pieces in the future. The similar patterns of behaviour can be located in terms of NN and can be used to generate predictions. This kind of application of nonlinear dynamical methods to time series analysis can be used to characterize the amount of predictability in a time series. *Predictability* [4] indicates to what extent the past can be used to determine the future. In the NN method, cross predictions are used for finding out directional influences between two time series X and Y. The method evaluates how well the embedded vectors of X can anticipate the prediction values of Y and vice-versa and is depicted in Figure 2. Details of the NN algorithm are omitted due to space constraints.

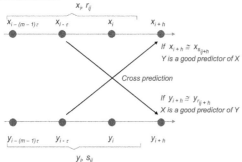

Figure 2 Illustration of the directionality measure based on cross-prediction using the nearest neighbors

3.2 MNNASS Algorithm

MNNASS is run in clustered network architecture and each node's sensing schedule consists of few $full_{sense}$ time cycles of duration equal to time scale, s, during which data is collected at pre-determined sampling intervals. The NN based directionality measure algorithm is run using the collected data at one of the cluster members to generate the

directionality matrix. This matrix specifies directional influences amongst all the pair of nodes in the cluster and is used to assign sampling intervals to different cluster nodes in proportion to their directional influences to be used during $adapt_{sense}$ time cycle. Each of the nodes collects data at reduced sampling frequencies during $adapt_{sense}$ time cycle and reinitiates a $full_{sense}$ time cycle whenever the required statistical confidence intervals are not met.

The metrics that have been considered to evaluate the MNNASS performance are a) Energy savings, b) Deviations between true and sampled mean. In atmospheric sciences field, environmental scientists are concerned about true averages and that's why deviations from the true mean has been used as a metric for evaluating measurement accuracy. It has been found out during the trials that the lifetime of pollution sensor nodes is approx. 34 hours at a sampling frequency of 1Hz. The aim in environmental monitoring using WSN is to stretch it to longer time spans, say a year or six months. Hence keeping the required sampling budget in mind, performance of MNNASS has been analyzed. It was found that parameter values that provide least mean deviations, while satisfying the fixed sampling budget of 30 samples every hour (i.e. sensor node lifetime of approx. 6 months) are time scale s=2700s, embedding dimension m=5, embedding lag τ=150s and number of nearest neighbors K=12 for a threshold δ=1.5ppm.

4. FUTURE WORK

We further wish to investigate the use of an information theoretic directional measure called transfer entropy for analyzing the information flow and see how it compares with the NN approach. Though, this work presents a specific spatial scenario, the results look promising. We wish to investigate this technique further and generalize the results shown in this work over a larger spatial domain using a geo-statistical model.

5. REFERENCES

[1] L. V. Shum, P. Rajalakshmi, A. Afonja, G. McPhillips, R. Binions, L. Cheng, et al., "On the Development of a Sensor Module for Real-Time Pollution Monitoring," in Information Science and Applications (ICISA), 2011 International Conference on, 2011, pp. 1-9.

[2] C.-K. Lee, "Multifractal Characteristics in Air Pollutant Concentration Time Series," Water, Air, and Soil Pollution, vol. 135, pp. 389-409, 2002/03/01 2002.

[3] J. W. Kantelhardt, S. A. Zschiegner, E. Koscielny-Bunde, S. Havlin, A. Bunde, and H. E. Stanley, "Multifractal detrended fluctuation analysis of nonstationary time series," Physica A: Statistical Mechanics and its Applications, vol. 316, pp. 87-114, 12/15/ 2002.

[4] U. Feldmann, and J. Bhattacharya, "Predictability Improvement as an Asymmetrical Measure of Interdependence in bivariate Time Series," I. J. Bifurcation and Chaos 14 (2), 505-514.

Poster Abstract: Occupancy Estimation Using Real and Virtual Sensors

Seshan Srirangarajan and Dirk Pesch
Nimbus Center for Embedded Systems Research
Cork Institute of Technology
Cork, Ireland
{seshan.srirangarajan, dirk.pesch}@cit.ie

ABSTRACT

In this paper we present occupancy estimation techniques using real (motion, door closure) and virtual (PC activity detector) sensors. The techniques considered here are based on the decision tree and artificial neural network models. Results from an experimental test-bed in a four person office room are also presented.

Categories and Subject Descriptors

I.5.4 [**Computing Methodologies**]: Pattern Recognition—*Applications*; J.2 [**Computer Applications**]: Physical Sciences and Engineering—*electronics*

General Terms

Algorithms, Design, Experimentation

Keywords

Occupancy, decision tree, neural networks

1. INTRODUCTION

Buildings are one of the largest end users of energy representing over 40% of primary energy use globally [1]. This has led to research and development in the design of smart buildings which can facilitate a comfortable, healthy and productive environment for the occupants while minimizing the energy consumption.

Detection of occupant presence is extremely useful in many applications such as demand controlled HVAC and lighting, security as well as human-centered environmental control. Occupancy detection is primarily achieved through direct sensing or tracking of occupants. Passive infrared (PIR) sensors are commonly used in these cases. However, they are unreliable for detecting immobile occupants resulting in frequent false negatives. Other sensing technologies that have been used include ultrasonic, video, ambient sensors such as carbon dioxide (CO_2) and relative humidity.

The proliferation of information technology (IT) infrastructure is seen as an opportunity to use the existing IT devices to infer presence. Together with the different sensing modalities, the use of statistical or probabilistic models have been shown to offer improved capability of estimating occupancy [2]. However, obtaining occupancy information which is highly accurate and reliable, using low-cost and non-intrusive sensors, remains a challenge in most situations.

IPSN'13, April 8–11, 2013, Philadelphia, Pennsylvania, USA.
ACM 978-1-4503-1959-1/13/04.

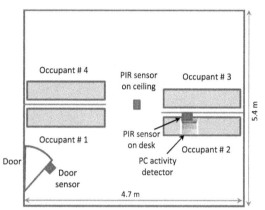

Figure 1: Experimental test bed layout.

The proposed occupancy estimation methodology aims to use multiple sensing modalities and infers the occupant presence by combining these observations. We apply two commonly used machine learning approaches for pattern recognition and classification, namely decision trees and artificial neural networks.

2. EXPERIMENT DESIGN

In many office environments, the occupant desks are equipped with task lights, and in colder climates with personal heaters to supplement the centrally controlled lighting and heating which might be operating at a lower setting to reduce energy wastage. Thus, to provide a comfortable and personal environment to each occupant, it is necessary to detect occupant presence.

The occupant presence will be inferred by combining observations from PIR sensors, door sensor and computer activity detector tool. The PC activity detector software tool senses keyboard and mouse activity. The experimental test bed is deployed in a four person office room and the layout is shown in Figure 1. Occupant # 2 has the PC activity detector software installed in addition to a PIR sensor on the desk. A webcam is used to establish true occupancy to be used as ground truth information for training the models.

With this layout, we investigate if it is possible to distinguish between the presence of occupant # 2 and the other occupants. We thus define three occupancy states as below:

- *State 1*: room is unoccupied,
- *State 2*: occupant 2 is in the room (with or without other occupants),
- *State 3*: room is occupied but occupant 2 is not present.

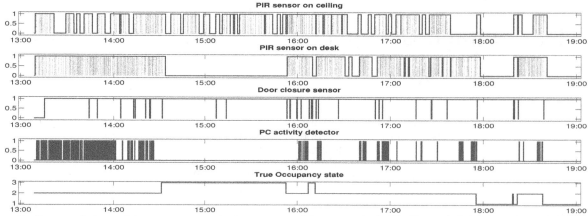

Figure 2: Sensor data and true occupancy state over a 6-hour period. Unfiltered PIR data is in lighter shade.

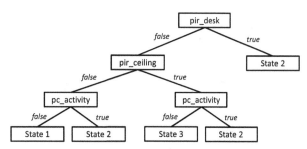

Figure 3: Decision tree model.

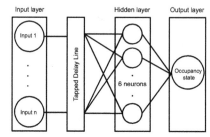

Figure 4: Focussed time delay neural network.

3. RESULTS AND DISCUSSION

Experimental data was collected for a continuous period of about 2.5 days (Wednesday through Friday), refer to Figure 2 for a representative data set. The PIR sensors were found to report very high percentage of false negatives (ceiling PIR: 80%, desk PIR: 59%). Thus, the PIR sensor data is preprocessed using a causal window (W) filter which replaces the current data sample with a logical OR of the current sample and past (W − 1) samples. Using a window size of $W = 120$ sec, the false negatives were significantly reduced (ceiling PIR: 24%, desk PIR: 4%) without any significant increase in the false positives. The two filtered PIR data streams together with the PC activity and door sensor data are provided as input features to the learning models.

The decision tree model generated automatically from the training data is shown in Figure 3. Decision trees are informative and provide insights into combinations of input features which distinguish the different states. Static and dynamic neural network (NN) models were also tested on the experimental data. The static model consisted of a fully connected, feed-forward network with one hidden layer of six neurons. The dynamic model was based on the focussed time delay (FTDNN) model, shown in Figure 4, which has a tapped delay line at the input.

The occupancy state estimation results are shown in Figure 5[1]. All three models provide good overall estimation accuracies: decision tree (95.2%), static NN (95.2%) and dynamic FTDNN (95.4%). However, the occupancy state estimations are somewhat noisy with frequent state transitions. In this case, the computationally powerful neural

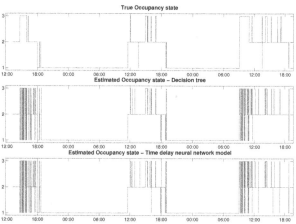

Figure 5: Occupancy state estimation results.

network models do not provide improved performance compared to the decision tree. Specifically, the FTDNN does not seem to fully exploit the temporal correlations across the sensor data streams (such as the door sensor and the other sensors), which needs further exploration.

Acknowledgments

This research is supported through a fellowship from the Irish Research Council and co-funded by Intel Ireland.

4. REFERENCES

[1] Energy efficiency in buildings facts and trends - full report. Technical report, World Business Council for Sustainable Development, 2008.
[2] B. Dong et al. An information technology enabled sustainability test-bed (ITEST) for occupancy detection through an environmental sensing network. *Energy and Buildings*, 42(7):1038–1046, 2010.

---

[1]Results for static NN model are not shown due to space constraints.

Poster Abstract: Human Tracking Based on LRF and Wearable IMU Data Fusion

Lin Wu[1,2], ZhuLin An[1], YongJun Xu[1] and Li Cui[1]

[1]Institute of Computing Technology, Chinese Academy of Sciences, Beijing 100190, China
[2]University of Chinese Academy of Sciences, Beijing 100049, China
{wulin, anzhulin, xyj, lcui}@ict.ac.cn

ABSTRACT

Human tracking is one of the most important requirements for service mobile robots. Cameras and Laser Ranger Finders (LRFs) are usually used together for human tracking. But these kinds of solutions are too computationally expensive for most embedded processors on these robots as complex computer vision algorithms are needed to process large number of pixels. In this paper, we describe a method combining kinematic measurements from LRF mounted on the robot and Inertial Measurement Unit (IMU) carried by the target. These two types of sensors can calculate human's velocity and position independently, which are used as information for both indentifying and tracking the target. As pixels observed by LRF and IMU are 1D rather than 2D, our method requires much less computation and memory resources and can be implemented with low-performance embedded processors.

Categories and Subject Descriptors

I.2.9 [Robotics]: Autonomous vehicles; C.3 [Special-Purpose and Application-Based Systems]: Microprocessor/Microcomputer Applications; Real-time and embedded systems; Signal Processing Systems

Keywords

Tracking; LRF; IMU; Pedestrian Dead Reckoning

1. INTRODUCTION

Assistive companion robots need to track and follow a target human to offer convenient and timely service, such as tour guide, accompanying children, carrying luggage   and so on. LRF has been widely adopted for this purpose as it has high accuracy in distance measurement. Laser scans are divided into segments, from which candidates are selected according to shape and size. The results of successive laser scans compose the track of target person. But LRF is unable to identify the target, it can only measure the distance to the nearest obstacle. As a result, LRF can't handle occlusions or crossing alone. In the work of [1] and [2], multiple lasers and Kalman Filter (KF) were used to alleviate the impact of occlusions. A particle filter algorithm was adopted by [3] for laser-based human tracking in a simple scenario where a robot followed behind a person. However, these above methods are still sensitive to occlusion, which was considered as the greatest challenge for LRF-based human tracking by [1].

As cameras do well in target identification, it's common to combine them with LRFs to track people as [4][5][6] did. In this kind of methods, target's orientation is detected by a camera, and then a LRF measures the distance. But the use of cameras has some significant disadvantages. First of all, vision-based methods are typically so computationally expensive that a powerful PC is needed to process data. The PC used by [5] is 1.5GHz with 2GB RAM and the one used by [4] is Core 2 Duo 2.5GHz with 4GB RAM. In comparison, the solely LRF-based method proposed by [1] worked on a laptop with 64MB RAM and a 300MHz P-II Processor tracking up to 10 objects. Secondly, vision-based methods need extra training processes. Thirdly, these methods are sensitive to ambient light. They are not valid in darkness, fog, etc.

Wearable IMU-based especially mobile phone-based Pedestrian Dead Reckoning (PDR) has been studied by many researchers like [7][8][9][10], which studied how to calculate the velocity and position of a pedestrian with an IMU carried by him. In this paper, we propose a novel tracking method combining LRF mounted on the robot and IMU (e.g., sensor-enriched mobile phone) carried by the target. The features we extract about target person are his velocity and location, which can be measured by the IMU as well as the LRF. Thus, the LRF is able to identify the target from candidates according to kinematic features. In this way, our method can achieve the tracking accuracy similar with LRF and vision-based ones at the computation cost of solely LRF-based ones, because we reduce the observed data from 2D to 1D while remaining the ability to identify target.

2. TRACKING METHOD FRAMEWORK

The flow chart of our proposed tracking method is shown in Figure 1. For convenience, we take mobile phone as an example of IMU in this figure.

First of all, the mobile phone and the robot calculate the velocity and location of the target independently. Mobile phone-based PDR calculate the target's velocity and integrate it over time to get current location. LRF mounted on the robot can detect locations of candidates at successive scans, thus velocity of each candidate can be calculated. The newly calculated velocity and location compose the current state, which will be enqueued into queues of history states. After that, the possibility of each candidate's belonging to the target is calculated according to the similarity between their history states and the target's. Afterwards, the candidate with the largest possibility is identified as the target. Then the velocity and location of the target is updated by fusing the data from the mobile phone and robot. The updated result will be sent back to the mobile phone to calibrate parameters used in PDR and reset accumulated errors. Finally, the robot tracks the target according to the result.

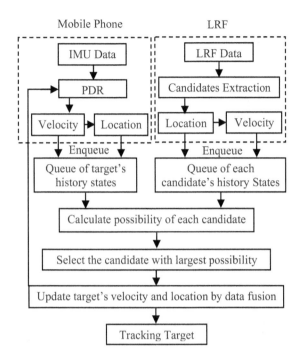

Mobile Phone   LRF

IMU Data

PDR

Velocity   Location

LRF Data

Candidates Extraction

Location   Velocity

Enqueue   Enqueue

Queue of target's history states

Queue of each candidate's history States

Calculate possibility of each candidate

Select the candidate with largest possibility

Update target's velocity and location by data fusion

Tracking Target

Figure 1: Tracking Method Framework

In comparison with tracking method based on camera and LRF, our method extracts kinematic features instead of image features to identify the target. It requires much less computing power and is applicable for embedded processors. Besides, our method can handle occlusion well which those methods based solely on LRF can't.

3. ACKNOWLEDGMENTS

This paper is supported in part by Important National Science & Technology Specific Projects under grant No.(2010ZX03006-002 , 2010ZX03006-007), the National Basic Research Program of China (973 Program) (No. 2011CB302803), and National Natural Science Foundation of China (NSFC) under grant No.(61173132,61003307). The authors alone are responsible for the content of the paper.

4. REFERENCES

[1] A. Fod, A. Howard and M.J. Mataric. A laser-based people tracker. In Proceedings of IEEE International Conference on Robotics and Automation (ICRA '02), Washington D.C., USA, May 11-15, 2002, 3024-3029.

[2] M. Hashimoto, Y. Matsui and K. Takahashi. People tracking with in-vehicle multi-laser range sensors. In Proceedings of SICE Annual Conference, Kagawa University, Japan, Sept. 17-20, 2007, 1851-1855.

[3] R. Gockley, J. Forlizzi and R. Simmons. Natural person-following behavior for social robots. In Proceedings of the ACM/IEEE international conference on Human-robot interaction (HRI'07), Arlington, Virginia, USA, March 8-11, 2007, 17-24.

[4] M. Kristou, A. Ohya and S. Yuta. Target person identification and following based on omnidirectional camera and LRF data fusion. In Proceedings of 20th IEEE International Symposium on Robot and Human Interactive Communication (2011 RO-MAN), Atlanta, GA, USA, July 31-August 3, 2011, 419-424.

[5] R.C. Luo, N.W. Chang, S.C. Lin, and S. C.Wu. Human tracking and following using sensor fusion approach for mobile assistive companion robot. In Proceedings of 35th Annual Conference of the IEEE Industrial Electronics Society (IECON'09), Porto, Portugal, November 3-5 2009, 2235–2240.

[6] K. Morioka, S. Kuroiwa, F. Hashikawa and T. Takigawa. Human tracking based on integration of laser range scanners and cameras in intelligent space. In Proceedings of 2011 8th Asian Control Conference (ASCC), Kaohsiung, Taiwan, May 15-18, 2011, 719-724.

[7] U. Steinhoff and B. Schiele. Dead reckoning from the pocket - An experimental study. In proceedings of IEEE International Conference on Pervasive Computing and Communications (PerCom), Mannheim, Germany, March 29-April 2 2010, 162-170.

[8] D. Pai, M. Malpani, et al. Padati: A Robust Pedestrian Dead Reckoning System on Smartphones. In Proceedings of IEEE 11th International Conference on Trust, Security and Privacy in Computing and Communications (TrustCom). Liverpool, England, UK, Jun 25-Jun 27 2012, 2000-2007.

[9] I. Constandache, R.R. Choudhury and I. Rhee. Towards Mobile Phone Localization without War-Driving. In Proceedings of INFOCOM, San Diego, CA, USA, 14-19 March 2010, 1-9.

[10] M. Alzantot and M. Youssef. UPTIME: Ubiquitous pedestrian tracking using mobile phones. In Proceedings of Wireless Communications and Networking Conference (WCNC), Paris, France, 1-4 April 2012, 3204-3209.

Poster Abstract - ASWP: A Long-Term WSN Deployment for Environmental Monitoring

Miguel Navarro   Tyler W. Davis   Yao Liang   Xu Liang

Department of Computer and Information Science, Indiana University – Purdue University Indianapolis
Department of Civil and Environmental Engineering, University of Pittsburgh
{mignavar, yliang}@cs.iupui.edu   {twd2, xuliang}@pitt.edu

ABSTRACT
ASWP testbed, a long-term wireless sensor network (WSN) deployment for environmental monitoring, is presented. This testbed integrates 42 MICAz nodes that implement a periodic sampling application for external sensors exposed to a forested nature reserve at the Audubon Society of Western Pennsylvania (ASWP), USA. It has been running for the past two years using TinyOS-based platforms and the commercially available routing software XMesh. Network performance analysis indicates that the critical impact due to the outdoor environment and node physical failures significantly reduced the network yield when long-term periods were considered. In particular, it is found that an over-used routing path across the network was responsible for most of the packet retransmitted and dropped in ASWP. This preliminary work intends to provide a useful reference point for WSN research and development targeted towards outdoor WSNs for long-term deployments.

Categories and Subject Descriptors
C.2.1 [**Computer-Communication Networks**]: Network Architecture and Design – *Wireless communication.*

Keywords
WSN deployment, outdoor testbed, data quality, XMesh.

1. INTRODUCTION
The adoption of WSNs represents new challenges for scientists and engineers who require reliable data collection for various applications and optimal network behavior for cost-effective deployment. WSNs are deployed in multiple scenarios where outdoor locations represent a critical challenge. Indeed, simulation and laboratory methods are unable to represent the complexity of outdoor environments (e.g., forests, oceans, or glaciers), which affect the WSN functionality. Consequently, experimental deployments are required to study and analyze these harsh conditions.

Related experiments have shown unexpected behaviors and observations in outdoor deployments compared to indoor conditions [1-2]. To better understand these situations,

previous studies have tested larger networks; however, as networks scale (+50 nodes) it is more difficult to conduct experiments for longer terms, especially in power-constrained scenarios. ASWP testbed represents a long-term WSN deployment in outdoor environmental conditions. This study presents the first comprehensive evaluation of a commercially available WSN platform for environmental monitoring research, providing a valuable reference point for future investigation on real-world sustainable WSN deployments and evaluations.

Figure 1. ASWP node locations. Base station located at the upper-right corner. Colors indicate different sensor types

2. NETWORK ANALYSIS
XMesh's multi-hop routing protocol [3] offers three basic types of application packets, which are transmitted along the network and stored at the gateway: sensor data packets contain the readings from the MDA 300 acquisition board [4] used, node health packets contain node level accumulated statistics (i.e., node health packets generated, total packets generated, forwarded packets, retransmissions, path cost, link quality), and neighbor health packets are used to report the cost and link information from up to five neighbor nodes.

The initial processing of the data considered more than 900,000 packets collected between August 2011 and August 2012. It was found that between 3% and 4% of the packets received were duplicates, independent of the packet type. In addition, there were up to 7 duplicates for the same packet, which corresponds to the maximum number of retransmissions configured. Analyzing the nodes generating those duplicate packets provided an initial overview on the

IPSN'13, April 8–11, 2013, Philadelphia, Pennsylvania, USA.
ACM 978-1-4503-1959-1/13/04.

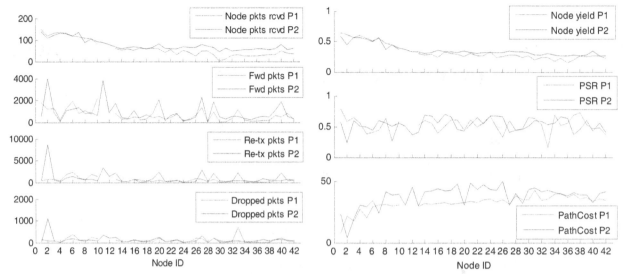

Figure 2. (Left) Received pkts, forwarded pkts, retransmissions, and dropped pkts in average values per day per node. (Right) Node yield, PSRs, and XMesh path cost in average values per day per node. P1: Aug'11-Feb'12 and P2: Mar'12-Aug'12

network performance, showing that only a few nodes were responsible for this network behavior.

Table 1. Network level performance

Period	Network Yield	Packet Success Ratio (PSR)	Node Packets Received (Avg. per day)	Node Packets Generated (Avg. per day)
Aug2011 - Feb2012	35.17%	49.09%	2,391	6,798
(35 days)	61.04%	53.92%	3,861	6,250
Mar2012 – Aug2012	36.01%	46.08%	3,194	8,869
(35 days)	42.16%	45.33%	3,577	8,484

Once duplicates were removed, different indicators were evaluated based on the statistics provided by the node health packets. Results at the network level, presented in Table 1, are divided into two main periods that differentiate the first stage when the network operated with 40 nodes and then, two additional nodes were deployed. In contrast, 35 days from each period were also analyzed separately, indicating the significant performance drops of a long-term operation. Similarly, detailed node-level results are illustrated in Figure 2 and include the average values per node per day for each statistic provided. The node IDs increase for nodes located farther from the base station.

3. CONCLUSIONS AND FUTURE WORK
In the context of environmental monitoring applications, accurate results can be produced with sub-daily samples, in addition to the benefit from a higher special resolution provided by WSNs. However, from the network perspective, the overall performance is lower to what was initially expected as seen from the network-level results. From node-level results it is possible to identify highly used nodes by their number of forwarded packets and

retransmissions. An unexpected result was obtained when several of these highly used nodes presented a lower PSR and path cost compared to their neighbors, indicating that the routing protocol was not able to identify and correct this problem, which created bottlenecks in the network. Future work includes: (1) implementing this network analysis into the INDAMS online management system [5] to generate updated and accurate indicators of the network performance in near real time, which helps optimize the network operations and maintenance; and (2) improving the protocol stack to address the main challenges identified.

4. ACKNOWLEDGMENTS
This work was supported by NSF under CNS-0758372 and CNS-0721474 to IUPUI and the University of Pittsburgh, respectively.

5. REFERENCES
[1] I. F. Akyildiz, W. Su, Y. Sankarasubramaniam, and E. Cayirci. Wireless sensor networks: a survey. Computer Networks, 38, 393–422, 2002.

[2] P. Dutta, J. Hui, J. Jeong, S. Kim, C. Sharp, J. Taneja, G. Tolle, K. Whitehouse, and D. Culler. Trio: Enabling Sustainable and Scalable Outdoor Wireless Sensor Network Deployments. In ACM IPSN 2006.

[3] MEMSIC, Inc. XMesh User Manual. Revision A, 2010

[4] MEMSIC, Inc. MDA 300 Data Acquisition Board Datasheet. Revision A.

[5] M. Navarro., D. Bhatnagar, and Y. Liang. An integrated network and data management system for heterogeneous WSNs. In IEEE MASS 2011.

Poster Abstract: Virtualizing External Wireless Sensors for Designing Personalized Smartphone Services

JeongGil Ko
Electronics and Telecommunications
Research Institute
218 GajeongRo, YuseongGu
Daejeon, Republic of Korea
jeonggil.ko@etri.re.kr

Byung-Bog Lee
Electronics and Telecommunications
Research Institute
218 GajeongRo, YuseongGu
Daejeon, Republic of Korea
bblee40@etri.re.kr

Sang Gi Hong
Electronics and Telecommunications
Research Institute
218 GajeongRo, YuseongGu
Daejeon, Republic of Korea
sghong@etri.re.kr

Naesoo Kim
Electronics and Telecommunications
Research Institute
218 GajeongRo, YuseongGu
Daejeon, Republic of Korea
nskim@etri.re.kr

ABSTRACT

By interacting with external sensors, smartphones can gather high-fidelity data on the surrounding environment to develop various environment-aware, personalized applications. In this work we introduce the *sensor virtualization module (SVM)* which virtualizes external sensors so that smartphone applications can easily utilize a large number of sensing resources. Implemented on the Android platform, our SVM simplifies the management of external sensors by abstracting them as virtual sensors to provide the capability of resolving conflicting data requests from multiple applications and also mashing-up sensing data from different sensors to create new customized sensors. We envision our SVM to open the possibilities of designing novel personalized smartphone applications.

Categories and Subject Descriptors

D.2.10 [**Software Engineering**]: Design

General Terms

Design; Management.

Keywords

Sensor virtualization; wireless sensor interfacing;

1. OVERVIEW AND MOTIVATION

Smartphones possess a number of on-board sensors (e.g., GPS, accelerometer, light sensor, etc.) for various applications to utilize and enrich their quality. Nevertheless, the capability to add *additional* sensors to a smartphone can further enable new applications and provide useful services for its users. While extending a smartphone's sensing capability (internally) is difficult, fortunately, by using Bluetooth, WiFi, NFC, or Zigbee (with a IEEE 802.15.4 radio attached

to a smartphone via USB), external sensors with wireless connectivity can provide high-resolution data regarding the surrounding environment and its inhabitants. Such data can enable various novel smartphone applications that take the accurate local environmental factors in consideration. Examples of these applications include personal healthcare, private living environment control, and more generally, social IoT systems [1]. Such a system architecture where external sensors communicate *directly* with smartphones (e.g., without Internet connectivity) can allow privacy sensitive sensor resources to associate on a per-smartphone basis and securely report their data.

Considering that the same set of external sensing modules can be utilized in multiple smartphone applications simultaneously, these applications can benefit heavily from a software module that manages the usage of the shared resources (e.g., sensors, module parameters, etc.) [2]. We would expect this "sensor controlling module" to be implemented benieth the applications and expose interfaces for applications to easily discover, access and configure locally present external sensors. In this work we introduce the design and architecture of a sensor virtualization module (SVM), a software component that manages the profiles and data from external wireless sensors. The proposed SVM provides a set of APIs for applications to access external sensors, resolves conflicts among differnet sensor data requests, and allows the design a new virtual sensors by "mashing-up" existing sensors.

2. SENSOR VIRTUALIZATION MODULE

Our implementation of the sensor virtualization module (SVM) on the Android platform, illustrated in Figure 1, performs two major tasks. First, the SVM virtualizes external physical sensors so that applications can easily access the sensing information that they offer. For this purpose, our SVM exposes a set of interfaces that applications can use to discover external sensors, control parameters such as reporting and radio duty cycling intervals (**Physical Sensor Handler** in Figure 1), and store/retrieve sensor data to/from an internally managed repository so that data can be shared

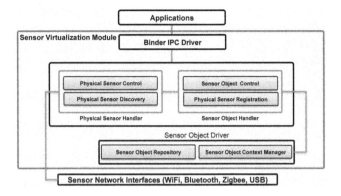

Figure 1: Our proposed sensor virtualization module (SVM) architecture. The SVM provides applications with interfaces and interacts with various network interfaces to control external sensors.

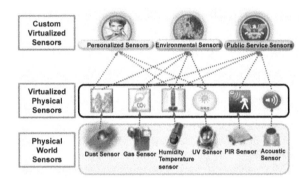

Figure 2: Diagram of the custom virtualized sensor generation process using data from physical sensors. The SVM exposes data from physical sensors in a virtualized format and also allows the combination (e.g., mashup) of multiple sensors.

among different applications (`Sensor Object Handler` and `Sensor Object Driver` in Figure 1).

The second major role of the SVM is to resolve conflicts caused by sensor data requests from different applications (`Binder IPC` in Figure 1). When multiple applications request for data from the same sensor with conflicting characteristics (e.g., different reporting intervals requested from two applications), the SVM can computes the best option to satisfy (all of) the incoming requests. Without this conflict resolution feature at the SVM, external sensor devices would be expected to perform this functionality. Nevertheless, such application-level algorithms are not enforced by any standards; thus, smartphone applications cannot assure that conflict resolution from different requests would be possible at external sensor devices themselves.

Note that the SVM operates as a background process on Android platforms. While managing both on-board and external sensors, most components in the SVM are not executed until receiving a request from the application in order to minimize the added current draw that an additional hardware controlling module may introduce.

3. BENEFITS OF THE SVM

Managing external sensors using our proposed SVM pro-

vides three distinct benefits. First, since the SVM restricts all data to/from external sensors to pass through a single data path, it helps simplify the development process of applications by providing a common API to access any available sensor in the field. With the standards designed for sensor networks [3], new sensors can be quickly discovered and their data can be reported to requesting applications through the virtualization process. Second, the sensor profiles and data that our SVM exposes can be a way of sharing data among different applications. When multiple applications request for data from the same sensor, the SVM, by utilizing the sensor repository, can reduce the number of interactions between the sensors and the smartphone to conserve power at both ends. Finally, as Figure 2 shows, the SVM allows users to "build" custom virtual sensors. Specifically, using existing data in the data repository, users can "mash-up" multiple sensors to form a *new* virtual sensor which is updated along with the original sensor readings. For example, an application can form and register a discomfort-index sensor using the combination of local humidity and temperature readings. This new custom virtual sensor, registered in the repository, can be used by other applications as well.

4. FUTURE RESEARCH DIRECTIONS

The sensor virtualization module introduced in this work provides a set of APIs for smartphone applications to use when accessing external sensing modules. An important next step that we foresee is well-defining a protocol for data exchange between the smartphone and external sensors. While various standards allow the devices to communicate, depending on the physical sensors' initial configurations (e.g., offering push or pull-based services, or a predefined wireless channel configuration) the quality and stability of data gathering can fluctuate. We argue that an application level standard should address this issue (e.g., defining the format of sensor profiles). Furthermore, by providing an modular environment for designing new virtual sensors, we believe that applications can maximize the usage of external sensors for designing various personalized services.

Acknowledgments

This work was supported by project #10041725, "Development of application service and software to support sensor terminals for providing personalized service based on smart devices", from the Korean Ministry of Knowledge Economy.

5. REFERENCES

[1] Luigi Atzori, Antonio Iera, Giacomo Morabito, and Michele Nitti. The social internet of things: When social networks meet the internet of things: Concept, architecture and network characterization. *Computer Networks*, 56(16):3594 – 3608, 2012.

[2] Rohit Chaudhri, Waylon Brunette, Mayank Goel, Rita Sodt, Jaylen VanOrden, Michael Falcone, and Gaetano Borriello. Open data kit sensors: mobile data collection with wired and wireless sensors. In *ACM Symposium on Computing for Development*, 2012.

[3] JeongGil Ko, Stephen Dawson-Haggerty, David E. Culler, Jonthan W. Hui, Philip Levis, and Andreas Terzis. Connecting Low-power and Lossy Networks to the Internet. *Communications Magazine, IEEE*, 49(4):96 –101, April 2011.

Poster Abstract: Voxnet Acoustic Array for Multiple Bird Source Separation by Beamforming using Measured Data

Shengsheng Cai[*], Travis Collier[^], Lewis Girod[+], Ralph E.Hudson[^],
Kung Yao[^], Charles E.Taylor[^], Ming Bao[#], Zhi Wang[*]

[*] Zhejiang University, Hangzhou 310027, China
[^] University of California, Los Angeles, CA 90095
[+] Massachusetts Institute of Technology, Cambridge, MA 02142
[#] Institute of Acoustics, Chinese Academy of Sciences, Beijing 100190, China

ABSTRACT

In this paper, we present simulation and experimental studies of multiple bird source separation based on the Voxnet acoustic array node. The Approximate Maximum Likelihood (AML) method is used to estimate blindly the direction-of-arrivals (DOAs) of the sources to generate the steering vectors in order to separate the sources via beamforming. Simulation and measured data confirmed the proper operations of the AML beamforming algorithm and the Voxnet hardware node.

Categories and Subject Descriptors

C.2.4 [Computer-Communication Networks]: Distributed Systems---Distributed applications

Keywords

Source separation, Voxnet, AML, beamforming.

1. Introduction

Animal vocalizations are important ways for biologists to discover the presence of animals and to study their behavior. In practice, more than one animal/species will emit sounds simultaneously. Biologists want to separate the mixed acoustic signals for further research purposes. However, even experienced biologists may have difficulty accurately identifying the animals/species from the mixed signals. Thus, use of an embedded acoustic array can aid biologists in the difficult and time-consuming tasks of detection and separation, in order to focus on their detailed bio-complexity research.

The Voxnet acoustic array node is a newly developed self-contained system that can be easily used in the field for collecting, detecting, and separating acoustic signals. This paper describes an application on multiple source DOA estimation and source separation for bird songs using a Voxnet acoustic array node. Utilizing the AML method [1] to estimate the DOAs of multiple bird sources and generate the steering vectors of the DOAs, then the AML beamforming method is used to separate the sources from the mixed acoustic signals. We evaluated the performance of the AML beamforming based method first by simulation then from measured data collected by a Voxnet acoustic array node.

2. Beamforming algorithm

2.1. Approximate maximum likelihood

For an arbitrarily distributed array of J microphones, the data collected by the j-th microphone at time t can be given by

$$x_j(t) = \sum_{m=1}^{M} s^{(m)}(t - t_j^{(m)}) + n_j(t), \qquad (1)$$

where M is the number of sources, $s^{(m)}$ is the m-th source signal, $t_j^{(m)}$ is the fractional time-delay and n_j is the noise.

In the frequency domain, the model is given by

$$X(k) = D(k)S(k) + N(k), \qquad (2)$$

$D(k)$ is the steering matrix. The AML source locations estimate can be obtained by solving the following maximization problem:

$$\max_{\tilde{r}_s} J(\tilde{r}_s) = \max_{\tilde{r}_s} \sum_{k=1}^{L/2} \left\| P(k, \tilde{r}_s) X(k) \right\|^2, \qquad (3)$$

where the orthogonal projection is given by

$$P(k, \tilde{r}_s) = D(k)D^{\dagger}(k), \; D^{\dagger}(k) = (D^H(k)D(k))^{-1}D^H(k), \quad (4)$$

$J(\tilde{r}_s)$ is the AML matrix and $\tilde{r}_s$ is the source locations [2].

2.2. Beamformer

Data from M sources collected by *the* J microphones of (1) are used to form the beamformer in the frequency domain given by

$$Y(k) = D^{\dagger}(k)S(k). \qquad (5)$$

Information on the DOAs of the sources is contained in $D^{\dagger}(k)$ which is computed by the AML algorithm.

3. Voxnet acoustic array node

The Voxnet node is a compact, self-contained package, as shown in Figure 1. Each node is a wireless recording and processing device which has a tetrahedral microphone array (63.5 mm between microphones) with four-channel 16 bits ADC and 48 kHz sampling rate per channel. The node has a 433 MHz packet radio module and a GPS module. Both of them can offer a precise time-synchronization for the whole system. Two 50mm*50mm, 5W speakers which can be used for self-localization of the node are mounted at two sides of a laser-cut plastic box. The node is powered by a 14.4 V and 2.9 Ah lithium-ion battery working up to 20hours. More details are given in https://grassi2.ucdavis.edu/~travc/voxnet.

4. Simulation

In the simulation, we assumed a four-channel array with the same geometric position of microphone sensors as the Voxnet node. We used recordings of songs from Bewick's Wren (*Thryomanes bewickii*) (BW) and Black-headed Grosbeak (*Pheucticus melanocephalus)* (BHG) as the sources to arrive at the four-channel array from directions 0° and 120°. The estimated AML DOA is shown in Figure 2. This simulation estimated the DOAs to be the same as the true DOAs. From the estimated DOAs, we generated steering vectors and were able to separate the sources by beamforming. The source separation results are shown in Figure 3. The 4th and 5th sub-pictures are the separated signals from the mix signal (3rd sub-picture) by beamforming, and are similar to the original signals (1st and 2nd sub-pictures).

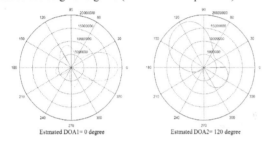

Figure 2. DOA estimation results by AML in simulation

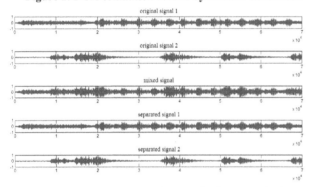

Figure 3. Sources separation results from simulation

5. Field Measurements

In the field measurement experiment, a Voxnet node was used to record the acoustic signals. Two speakers played the songs of BW and BHG simultaneously. The relative positions of the node and the speakers (5 m from the node) are shown in Figure 4. The estimated DOAs of the two bird sources collected using the Voxnet node were quite close to the true 0° and 120° as shown in Figure 5. Figure 6 shows the sources separation results by beamforming. The separated signals (4th and 5th sub-pictures) are quite close to the original signals (1st and 2nd sub-pictures), and thus the two bird sources were separated from the mixed signal recorded by the Voxnet node. Degradation of the separated signals is inevitable due to noises and estimation errors in the field experiment.

Fig. 1. Voxnet node. Fig. 4. Field measurement loc.

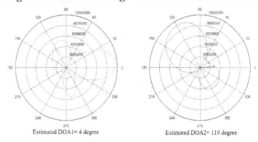

Figure 5. DOA estimation results by AML in experiment

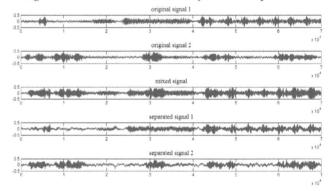

Figure 6. Sources separation results in experiment

6. Conclusions

In this paper, we present both simulation and experimental collected data to perform multiple bird source separation by AML beamforming method using the Voxnet node.

7. Acknowledgments

This work was supported by the NSF grant IIS-1125423, NSFC grant No.61273079 and No.61104208, and the "Strategic Priority Research Program" of the Chinese Academy of Sciences, Grant No. XDA06020201.

8. REFERENCES

[1] J. C. Chen, R. E. Hudson, and K. Yao, "Maximum-Likelihood Source Loc. and Unknown Sensor Loc. Est. for Wideband Signals in the Near-Field". *IEEE Trans. Signal Proessing*, pp. 1843-1854, Aug. 2002.

[2] P. Bergamo, S. Asgari, H. Wang, D. Maniezzo, L. Yip, R.E. Hudson, K. Yao, and D. Estrin, "Collaborative. Sensor Networking Toward Real-Time Acoustical Beamforming in Free-Space and Limited Reverberance," *IEEE Trans. on Mobile Computing*, pp. 211- 224, July 2004.

Author Index

IPSN 2013: ACM/IEEE International Conference on Information Processing in Sensor Networks List of Reviewers

Reviewers: Andreas Andreou *(Johns Hopkins University)*
Matteo Ceriotti *(RWTH Aachen University)*
Wan Chieh-yih *(Intel Labs)*
Lenzen Christoph *(Massachusetts Institute of Technology)*
Marco Duarte *(University of Massachusetts, Amherst)*
Prabal Dutta *(University of Michigan)*
Jakob Eriksson *(University of Illinois, Chicago)*
Deepak Ganesan *(University of Massachusetts, Amherst)*
Jie Gao *(Stony Brook University)*
Michael Gastpar *(EPFL and University of California, Berkeley)*
Raffa Giuseppe *(Intel Labs)*
Omprakash Gnawali *(University of Houston)*
Marco Gruteser *(Rutgers University)*
Lu Hong *(Intel Labs)*
Wen Hu *(Commonwealth Scientific and Industrial Research Organization)*
Polly Huang *(National Taiwan University)*
Karl Henrik Johansson *(KTH Royal Institute of Technology)*
Vana Kalogeraki *(Athens University of Economics and Business)*
Minyoung Kim *(SRI)*
Andreas Krause *(ETH Zurich and Caltech)*
Chieh-Jan Mike Liang *(Microsoft Research Asia)*
Mingyan Liu *(University of Michigan)*
Chenyang Lu *(Washington University, St. Louis)*
Thomas Moscibroda *(Microsoft Research Asia)*
Luca Mottola *(Politecnico di Milano and Swedish Institute of Computer Science)*
Lama Nachman *(Intel Labs)*
Suman Nath *(Microsoft Research)*
Neal Patwari *(University of Utah)*
Jamie Payton *(University of North Carolina)*
Gian Pietro Picco *(University of Trento)*
Wouhaybi Rita *(Intel Labs)*
Anthony Rowe *(Carnegie Mellon University)*
Silvia Santini *(TU Darmstadt)*
Olga Saukh *(ETH Zurich)*
Sahay Saurav *(Intel Labs)*
Andreas Savvides *(Yale University)*
John Stankovic *(University of Virginia)*
Andreas Terzis *(Johns Hopkins University)*

Lothar Thiele *(ETH Zurich)*
Kamin Whitehouse *(University of Virginia)*
Adam Wolisz *(Technical University of Berlin)*
Pei Zhang *(Carnegie Mellon University)*
Marco Zuniga *(Delft University of Technology)*